Information Systems: A Manager's Guide to Harnessing Technology Version 4.0

By
John Gallaugher

Information Systems: A Manager's Guide to Harnessing Technology
Version 4.0

John Gallaugher

Published by:

Flat World Knowledge, Inc.
1111 19th St NW, Suite 1180
Washington, DC 20036

Brief Contents

Contents

About the Author

John Gallaugher is an associate professor of information systems (IS) at Boston College's Carroll School of Management.

As founding faculty for the Boston College TechTrek programs, and the former colead of the school's graduate field studies in Europe and Asia, Professor Gallaugher has had remarkable access studying technology growth and impact worldwide. Professor Gallaugher and his students spend several weeks each year visiting with technology executives, entrepreneurs, and venture capitalists in San Francisco, Silicon Valley, Seattle, Boston, New York, and Ghana. Gallaugher and his students were present at the launch of the iPhone, were at Sequoia Capital the day LinkedIn went public, and are regularly hosted in master-class sessions at firms from Amazon to Zynga. This unique opportunity helps provide his teaching and writing with a broad, deep, and continually refreshed perspective on key industry trends and developments. Gallaugher also works closely with collegiate entrepreneurs and is coadvisor to the Boston College Venture Competition, an organization whose affiliated businesses have gone on to gain admittance to elite accelerator programs (Y-Combinator, TechStars, MassChallenge, Summer@Highland), launch multiple products, and raise millions in capital.

© 2014 Cate Jones Photography

A dedicated teacher and active researcher, Professor Gallaugher has been recognized for excellence and innovation in teaching by several organizations, including Boston College, *BusinessWeek*, *Entrepreneur Magazine*, and the Decision Sciences Institute. Professor Gallaugher's research has been published in the *Harvard Business Review*, *MIS Quarterly*, and other leading IS journals. Professor Gallaugher has been a featured speaker at Apple Inc's AcademiX educator conference, and was the international keynote speaker at AIBUMA (the African International Business and Management Conference) in Nairobi Kenya. He has consulted for and taught executive seminars for several organizations, including Accenture, Alcoa, Duke Corporate Education, ING, Partners Healthcare, Staples, State Street, the University of Ulster, and the U.S. Information Agency. His comments on business and technology have appeared in the *New York Times*, National Public Radio, *BusinessWeek*, the *Boston Globe*, *Wired*, the Associated Press, Chronicle (WCVB-TV), *The Daily Yomiuri* (Japan), and the *Nation* (Thailand), among others.

Professor Gallaugher publishes additional content related to his teaching and research at http://gallaugher.com. He is also active on Twitter at @gallaugher.

Acknowledgments

First and foremost, my enduring thanks to my current and former students, who continue to inspire, impress, and teach me more than I thought possible. It's deeply rewarding to see so many former students return to campus as executive speakers and to host visiting students at their own start-ups. Serving as your professor has been my greatest professional privilege, and I am grateful for such an extraordinary opportunity. Keep at it and continue to make us all proud!

Thanks also to the many alumni, parents, and friends of Boston College who have so generously invited me to bring my students to visit with and learn from them. The experiences that you've provided to us have been nothing short of astonishing. We were present at the launch of the iPhone. We've not only made pilgrimages to Sand Hill Road, but many of our former students were funded and mentored by the VCs we've visited with. Name a tech firm making waves and we've almost certainly got an alumnus there, and when asked, they've uniformly opened their offices to share insight with our students. The East and West Coast leadership of the Boston College Technology Council have played a particularly important role in making this happen. From Bangalore to Boston, Guangzhou to Ghana, Seoul to Silicon Valley, you've provided my students with world-class opportunities, enabling us to meet with scores of CEOs, senior executives, partners, and entrepreneurs. You've positively impacted lives, shaped careers, and helped make our university stronger. My students and I remain deeply grateful for your commitment and support.

A tremendous thanks to my student research team at Boston College. In particular, the work of Rootul Patel, Kelly Pedersen, Michael Lapointe, Abhinav Arora, Mujtaba Syed, Phil Gill, Xin (Steven) Liu, and Kathie Chang sped things along and helped me fill this project with rich, interesting examples. You have all been so kind to tolerate my constant and unreasonable requests.

I am also deeply grateful to my colleagues at Boston College. My former department chair, Jim Gips, is not only the consummate mentor and educator, as creator of the EagleEyes and CameraMouse project (cameramouse.org) he has given voice to countless people with disabilities worldwide and is the single most impactful researcher that I know. Tremendous thanks, as well, to my current department chair, Rob Fichman, for his unwavering support of this project; to my BC IS Department colleagues Jerry Kane for helping shape the social media section, and Sam Ransbotham for guiding me through the minefield of information security (Jerry and Sam both hold NSF CAREER grants and are MIT Sloan Management Review's editors for Social Media and Big Data, respectively); to BC's Mary Cronin, Burcu Bulgurcu, Peter Olivieri, and Jack Spang for suggestions and encouragement; and to the many administrators who have been so supportive of this effort. Allen Li and Marios Kokkodis, welcome to the team! A special thanks to BC Prof. George Wyner, who has provided extraordinary guidance, encouragement, ideas, and friendship, which have kept me motivated on such a high-demand project. I'm so lucky to work with such brilliant and caring faculty. Do know how very much I appreciate you all.

Sincerest thanks, also, to the cofounders of Flat World Knowledge, Jeff Shelstad and Eric Frank, for their leadership and passion in restructuring the textbook industry and for approaching me to be involved with their efforts. Thanks also to Flat World CEO Chris Etesse and the firm's dynamite team of editorial, marketing, and sales professionals—in particular to Vicki Brentnall, Melissa Yu, Shawn Cook and Micah Chi.

I would also like to thank the following colleagues who so kindly offered their time and comments while reviewing this work:

- Donald Army, Dominican University of California
- David Bloomquist, Georgia State University
- Teuta Cata, Northern Kentucky University
- Chuck Downing, Northern Illinois University
- John Durand, Pepperdine University
- Marvin Golland, Polytechnic Institute of New York University
- Brandi Guidry, University of Louisiana
- Kiku Jones, The University of Tulsa
- Fred Kellinger, Pennsylvania State University–Beaver Campus
- Ram Kumar, University of North Carolina–Charlotte
- Eric Kyper, Lynchburg College
- Alireza Lari, Fayetteville State University
- Mark Lewis, Missouri Western State University
- Eric Malm, Cabrini College
- Roberto Mejias, University of Arizona
- Esmail Mohebbi, University of West Florida
- John Preston, Eastern Michigan University
- Shu Schiller, Wright State University
- Tod Sedbrook, University of Northern Colorado

- Richard Segall, Arkansas State University
- Ahmad Syamil, Arkansas State University
- Sascha Vitzthum, Illinois Wesleyan University

I'm also grateful to the kindness and insight provided by early adopters of this text. Your comments, encouragement, suggestions, and student feedback were extremely helpful in keeping me focused and motivated on advancing the current edition:

- Animesh Animesh, McGill University
- Elizabeth Bagnani, Boston College
- Geneviève Bassellier, McGill University
- Michel Benaroch, Syracuse University
- Hanyin Cheng, Morgan Stanley
- Barney Corwin, University of Maryland—College Park
- Brad Crisp, Abilene Christian University
- Lauren B. Eder, Rider University
- Rob Fichman, Boston College
- James Gips, Boston College
- Wolfgang Gatterbauer, Carnegie Mellon University
- Roy Jones, University of Rochester
- Jakob Iverson, University of Wisconsin—Oshkosh
- Jerry Kane, Boston College
- Fred Kellinger, Penn State University—Beaver Campus
- Eric Kyper, Lynchburg College
- Ann Majchrzak, University of Southern California
- Eric Malm, Cabrini College
- Michael Martel, Ohio University
- Ido Millet, Pennsylvania State University—Erie Campus
- Ellen Monk, University of Delaware
- Marius (Florin) Niculescu, Georgia Tech
- Sam Ransbotham, Boston College
- Nachiketa Sahoo, Carnegie Mellon University
- Shu Schiller, Wright State University
- Tom Schambach, Illinois State University
- Avi Seidman, University of Rochester
- J. P. Shim, Georgia State University
- Jack Spang, Boston College
- Veda Storey, Georgia State University
- Sascha Vitzthum, Illinois Wesleyan University

Boston College students Courtney Scrib and Nate Dyer also pointed me to examples I've used in this edition, as did ACU student Aaron Andrew. Thanks for thinking of me and for sharing your very useful ideas!

I'll continue to share what I hope are useful insights via my blog, The Week In Geek (http://www.gallaugher.com), Twitter (@gallaugher), and Google+ (https://plus.google.com/+JohnGallaugher). Do feel free to offer comments, encouragement, ideas, and examples for future versions. I am hugely appreciative of all who continue to share the word about this project with others. Your continued advocacy helps make this model work!

And finally, a thanks to my family, to whom I've dedicated this book. That really doesn't do a shred of justice to my great fortune in being Kim's husband and father to Ian, Maya, and Lily. You've been epically tolerant of the time commitment associated with this project. You are my world.

Dedication

For Ian, Maya, Lily, and Kim—zettabytes of love!

Preface

WHAT'S NEW IN VERSION 4.0

FRESHLY UPDATED:

Every chapter has received an update to ensure that it covers the latest topics and material. Today's cutting edge firms and headline grabbing topics presented through durable frameworks and concepts.

PROFILING WOMEN IN TECH ENTREPRENEURSHIP:

New chapter on Rent the Runway highlights Jenn Hyman and Jenny Fleiss as they've built a user base of over 5 million for their **sharing economy standout**, a "Fashion Company with a Technology Soul." The entrepreneur's path in building value for a two-sided market, leveraging social media, scouring big data, and building a multi-channel operations marvel is covered in depth.

MICKEY'S WEARABLE:

A mini-case in the "Moore's Law and More" chapter discusses the launch of Disney's billion dollar MagicBand and MyMagic+ systems. Low cost consumer tech is leveraged for better customer experience and operational efficiency gains, but not before tackling challenging systems integration and team coordination issues.

BIG DATA STANDOUTS:

New examples show how Spotify's The Echo Nest is creating a machine-learning tastemaker, while L.L. Bean dives deep into NoSQL to wrangle a business that now spans some 30 customer engagement channels.

EMBEDDED VIDEO FOR KEY UPDATES

Students using the online version will find embedded video for several new topics, including Amazon's use of robotics to automate fulfillment centers, Zara's new RFID initiative, the Cognitoy/Watson-using child learning aid, and Disney's MagicBand, among others.

CUTTING EDGE COVERAGE:

From Facebook's move to make Messenger a platform to Google's evolution to Alphabet, students will feel their text and classroom are alive with the most current content available.

LETTER FROM THE AUTHOR

Thanks for using this book. I very much hope that you enjoy it!

I find the space where business and technology meet to be tremendously exciting, but it's been painful to see the anemic national enrollment trends in tech disciplines. The information systems (IS) course should be the most exciting class within any university. No discipline is having a greater impact on restructuring work, disrupting industries, and creating opportunity. And none more prominently features young people as leaders and visionaries. But far too often students resist rather than embrace the study of tech.

My university has had great success restructuring the way we teach our IS core courses, and much of the material used in this approach has made it into this book. The results we've seen include a fourfold increase in IS enrollments in four years, stellar student ratings for the IS core course, a jump in student placement, an increase in the number of employers recruiting on campus for tech-focused jobs, and the launch of several student-initiated start-ups.

Material in this book is used at both the graduate and undergraduate levels. I think it's a mistake to classify books as focused on just grad or undergrad students. After all, we'd expect our students at all levels to be able to leverage articles in the *Wall Street Journal* or *BusinessWeek*. Why can't our textbooks be equally useful?

You'll also find this work to be written in an unconventional style for a textbook, but hey, why be boring? Let's face it, *Fortune* and *Wired* wouldn't sell a single issue if forced to write with the dry-encyclopedic prose used by most textbooks. Many students and faculty have written with kind words for the tone and writing style used in this book, and it's been incredibly rewarding to hear from students who claim they have actually looked forward to assigned readings and have even read ahead or explored unassigned chapters. I hope you find it to be equally engaging.

The mix of chapter and cases is also meant to provide a holistic view of how technology and business interrelate. Don't look for an "international" chapter, an "ethics" chapter, a "mobile" chapter, or a "systems development and deployment" chapter. Instead, you'll see these topics woven throughout many of our cases and within chapter examples. This is how professionals encounter these topics "in the wild," so we ought to study them not in isolation but as integrated parts of real-world examples. Examples are consumer-focused and Internet-heavy for approachability, but the topics themselves are applicable far beyond the context presented.

Also note that many chapters are meant to be covered across multiple classes. For example, the chapter about Google is in three parts, the one about Netflix is in two, and the one on strategy and technology likely covers more than one lecture as well. Faculty should feel free to pick and choose topics most relevant to their classes, but many will also benefit from the breadth of coverage provided throughout the book. I'd prefer our students to be armed with a comprehensive understanding of topics rather than merely a cursory overview of one siloed area.

There's a lot that's different about this approach, but a lot that's worked exceptionally well, too. I hope that you find the material to be as useful as we have. I also look forward to continually improving this work, and I encourage you to share your ideas with me via Twitter (@gallaugher), Google+ (https://plus.google.com/+JohnGallaugher), or the Web (http://www.gallaugher.com). And if you find the material useful, do let others know, as well. I remain extremely grateful for your interest and support!

Best wishes!

Professor John Gallaugher

Carroll School of Management

Boston College

CHAPTER 1
Setting the Stage: Technology and the Modern Enterprise

1. TECH'S TECTONIC SHIFT: RADICALLY CHANGING BUSINESS LANDSCAPES

LEARNING OBJECTIVES

1. Appreciate how, in recent years, technology has helped bring about radical changes across industries and throughout societies.

This book is written for a world that has changed radically in the most recent years of your lifetime. Consider just a few examples: Uber, the world's largest "taxi service," owns no vehicles for hire. Airbnb, the world's largest accommodations provider, doesn't own a single hotel or rental property. Facebook, the world's most visited media destination, creates no content. And the world's most valuable retailer, China's Alibaba, owns no product inventory of its own.[1] Change is clearly afoot, and it's wearing silicon sneakers, carrying a smartphone, and is being blown forward by cloud-fueled hurricane tailwinds.

Here are some more examples: At the start of the prior decade, Google barely existed and well-known strategists dismissed Internet advertising models.[2] By decade's end, Google brought in more advertising revenue than any firm, online or off, and had risen to become the most profitable media company on the planet. Today, billions in advertising dollars flee old media and are pouring into digital efforts, and this shift is reshaping industries and redefining skills needed to reach today's consumers. The firm's ambitions have grown so large that Google has rechristened itself Alphabet (http://abc.xyz), a holding company with divisions focused on markets as diverse as driverless cars and life extension.

At roughly the same time Google was being hatched, Apple was widely considered a tech industry has-been, but within ten years and powered by a succession of handheld consumer electronics hits (iPod, iPhone, iPad) Apple had grown to be the most valuable firm in the United States. The firm has since posted several of the most profitable quarters of any firm in any industry, ever.[3] If app sales through iTunes, alone, were considered a separate business, they would constitute a firm larger than *more than half* of the companies ranked in the Fortune 500.[4]

The smartphone and app store are the modern accelerant of business growth. It took telephones seventy-five years to get to 50 million users, but it took Angry Birds just thirty-five days to do the same. WhatsApp gained 700 million adherents in its six years of existence, a figure Christianity took nineteen centuries to achieve.[5]

Social media barely warranted a mention a decade ago. Today, Facebook's user base is larger than any nation in the world. Mobile is its lynchpin, with more than 1.25 billion users visiting on handheld devices each month, and roughly two-thirds visiting each day.[6] Firms are harnessing social media for new product ideas, for millions in sales, and to vet and build trust. But with promise comes peril. When mobile phones are cameras just a short hop from YouTube, Facebook, Instagram, and Twitter, every ethical lapse can be captured, every customer service flaw graffiti-tagged on the permanent record that is the Internet. The service and ethics bar for today's manager has never been higher. Social media has also emerged as a catalyst for global change, with Facebook and Twitter playing key organizing roles in uprisings worldwide. While a status update alone won't depose a dictator or expunge racism, technology can capture injustice, broadcast it to the world, disseminate ideas, and rally the far-reaching.

Moore's Law and other factors that make technology faster and cheaper have thrust computing and telecommunications into the hands of billions in ways that are both empowering the poor and poisoning the planet.

IPO

Initial public stock offering, the first time a firm makes shares available via a public stock exchange, also known as 'going public.'

China started the century as a nation largely unplugged and offline. But today, China has more Internet users than any other country. China now tops the United States as the worldwide leader in iPhone sales.[7] Watch your back, Apple; Chinese handset maker Xiaomi ended 2014 as the world's most valuable startup.[8] And China has spectacularly launched several publicly traded Internet firms including Baidu, Tencent, and Alibaba the largest **IPO** of all time.[9]

The world's second most populous nation, India, has ridden technology to become a global IT powerhouse. In two decades, India's tech sector has grown from almost nothing to a $73 billion industry, expanding even during the recent global recession. Technology has enabled the once almost-exclusively-agrarian nation to become a go-to destination for R&D and engineering across sectors as far-flung as aircraft engine design, medical devices, telecom equipment, and microprocessors.[10]

Think the United States holds the top ranking in home broadband access? Not even close; the United States is ranked thirty-first in download speeds[11] and twenty-sixth in mobile broadband.[12]

Today smartphones are used by 2 billion people worldwide. By the end of this decade that number will be 4 billion, with 80 percent of adults being smartphone equipped. The most popular brand in India, Micromax, sells entry-level smartphones priced below $40.[13]

Even in the far reaches of nations in sub-Saharan Africa, fast/cheap tech is becoming an economic lubricant. Seventy percent of the region's population lives within range of mobile phone coverage, a percentage of the population greater than those who have access to reliable and safe water or electricity. Forty percent of sub-Saharan Africans already have mobile phones.[14] Tech giants including Google, IBM, and Microsoft now run R&D centers and significant operations in several African nations, tapping into world-class tech talent that's finally gaining infrastructure for growth.[15] Many nations in sub-Saharan Africa now rank among the world's fastest growing economies.[16] And entrepreneurs with local expertise are increasingly serving local needs and building impactful businesses. Ghanaian firm Esoko leverages mobile phones to empower the agrarian poor with farming info and commodity pricing, raising incomes and lowering the chance of exploitation by unscrupulous middlemen. The firm Sproxil uses text message verification to save lives by fighting drug counterfeiting in developing nations around the world. Kenya's M-PESA and Somaliland's Zaad use text messages to replace cash, bringing the safety and speed of electronic payment and funds transfer to the unbanked and leveraging mobile money at rates that far outstrip any nation in the West.[17] Mobile money can cut corruption, too, an effort with broad implications as this tech spreads worldwide. When Afghan police officers adopted M-PESA and began receiving pay using mobile money, many reportedly thought they had received a big raise because the officers handing out their pay were no longer able to cheat workers by skimming cash for themselves.[18]

FIGURE 1.1

Many nations in sub-Saharan Africa are seeing significant tech-fueled growth. Throughout the continent, technologies substitute for cash, deliver insights to farmers, and help uncover counterfeit pharmaceuticals. This plant in Accra owned by Ghanaian firm Rlg is the first sub-Saharan PC, tablet, and cell phone assembly facility.

Source: Photograph taken with permission of the Rlg plant.

Fast/cheap computing is also helping create the multi-billion dollar **Internet of Things** (IoT), putting smarts in all sorts of products: lamps, watches, thermostats, door locks. Disney has embedded smarts in a wristband it uses to replace ticketing at DisneyWorld. GE thinks sensors and computing will save the planet trillions of dollars through a hyper-efficient, data-driven, collectively orchestrated set of devices,[19] and has embedded smarts in everything from home air conditioners to high-end aircraft parts.[20] Think the smartphone market is big? Research firm Gartner says there are already some 5 billion connected IoT devices in use today, with 25 billion on the way by the end of the decade.[21]

The way we conceive of software and the software industry is also changing radically. Apple, Facebook, Google, IBM, Netflix, and Oracle are among the firms that collectively pay thousands of programmers to write code that is then given away for free. Today, open source software powers most of the websites that you visit. And the rise of open source has rewritten the revenue models for the computing industry and lowered computing costs for start-ups to blue chips worldwide.

Cloud computing and software as a service are turning sophisticated, high-powered computing into a utility available to even the smallest businesses and nonprofits. Amazon Web Services, by far the world's biggest provider of cloud computing services, has been adding about as much server capacity each day as its entire e-commerce parent required ten years earlier.[22]

Three-dimensional printers, which allow designs for fabrication to be shared as easily as an e-mail, are poised to reshape manufacturing and transportation. Crafts marketplace Etsy is full of artist-created and custom-printed products, from jewelry to cookie cutters,[23] and this technology has also been used to print tools on-demand for the international space station.[24]

An astronaut shows a tool produced on-demand using a 3D printer on the International Space Station.

Source: NASA

Many organizations today collect and seek insights from massive datasets, which are often referred to as "Big Data." Data analytics and business intelligence are driving discovery and innovation, redefining modern marketing, and creating a shifting knife-edge of privacy concerns that can shred corporate reputations if mishandled.

And the pervasiveness of computing has created a set of security and espionage threats unimaginable to the prior generation.

As recent years have shown, tech creates both treasure and tumult. These disruptions aren't going away and will almost certainly accelerate, impacting organizations, careers, and job functions throughout your lifetime. It's time to place tech at the center of the managerial playbook.

Internet of Things

A vision where low-cost sensors, processors, and communication are embedded into a wide array of products and our environment, allowing a vast network to collect data, analyze input, and automatically coordinate collective action.

KEY TAKEAWAYS

- In the previous decade, tech firms have created profound shifts in the way firms advertise and individuals and organizations communicate.
- New technologies have fueled globalization, redefined our concepts of software and computing, crushed costs, fueled data-driven decision making, and raised privacy and security concerns.

QUESTIONS AND EXERCISES

1. Search online and compare profits from Google, Apple, and other leading tech firms with those of major media firms and other nontech industry leaders. How have profits at firms such as Google and Apple changed over the past few years? What do you think is behind such trends? How do these compare with changes in the nontech firms that you chose?
2. How do recent changes in computing impact consumers? Are these changes good or bad? Explain. How do they impact businesses?
3. Serial entrepreneur and venture capitalist Marc Andreessen has written that "software is eating the world," suggesting that software and computing are transforming entire industries and creating disruptive new upstarts. Come to class with examples of firms and industries that have been completely transformed through the use of software.
4. Venture capitalist Ben Evans, who works with Andreessen, has said "mobile is eating the world." Give examples of how mobile has built billion dollar industries that wouldn't exist without handheld computing power. How should today's managers be thinking about mobile as an opportunity and threat?
5. How is social media impacting firms, individuals, and society?
6. What kinds of skills do today's managers need that weren't required a decade ago?
7. Investigate the role of technology in emerging markets. Come to class with examples to share on how technology is helping fuel economic growth and provide economic opportunity and public good to consumers outside of North America, Europe, and Asia's wealthier nations.
8. Work with your instructor to identify and implement ways in which your class can leverage social media. For example, you might create a Facebook group where you can share ideas with your classmates, join Twitter and create a hash tag for your class, leverage Google Hangouts and other tools on Google+, or create a course wiki. (See Chapter 9 for more on these and other services.)

2. IT'S YOUR REVOLUTION

LEARNING OBJECTIVES

1. **Name firms across hardware, software, and Internet businesses that were founded by people in their twenties (or younger).**

The intersection where technology and business meet is both terrifying and exhilarating. But if you're under the age of thirty, realize that this is *your* space. While the fortunes of any individual or firm rise and fall over time, it's abundantly clear that many of the world's most successful technology firms—organizations that have had tremendous impact on consumers and businesses across industries—were created by young people. Consider just a few:

Bill Gates was an undergraduate when he left college to found Microsoft—a firm that would eventually become the world's largest software firm and catapult Gates to the top of the *Forbes* list of world's wealthiest people (enabling him to also become the most generous philanthropist of our time).

Michael Dell was just a sophomore when he began building computers in his dorm room at the University of Texas. His firm would one day claim the top spot among PC manufacturers worldwide.

Mark Zuckerberg founded Facebook as a nineteen-year-old college sophomore.

Steve Jobs was just twenty-one when he founded Apple.

Sergey Brin and Larry Page were both twenty-something doctoral students at Stanford University when they founded Google. So were Jerry Yang and David Filo of Yahoo! All would become billionaires.

Kevin Systrom was twenty-six when he founded the photo-sharing service Instagram. In just eighteen months, his thirteen-person start-up garnered 35 million users worldwide, including 5 million Android users in just a single week, and sold to Facebook for a cool $1 billion. Systrom's take was $400 million.[25] Snapchat founder Evan Spiegel dropped out of undergrad to focus on his new firm. By age twenty-four he was running a firm valued at over $15 billion[26] with a personal net worth of over $1.5 billion.[27] Tony Hsieh proved his entrepreneurial chops when, at twenty-four, he sold LinkExchange to Microsoft for over a quarter of a billion dollars.[28] He'd later serve as CEO of Zappos, eventually selling that firm to Amazon for $900 million.[29]

Steve Chen and Chad Hurley of YouTube were in their late twenties when they launched their firms. Jeff Bezos hadn't yet reached thirty when he began working on what would eventually become Amazon. The founders of Dropbox, Box, and Spotify were all under thirty when they founded businesses that would go on to be worth billions.[30] The founders of Rent the Runway, Jenn Hyman and Jenny Fleiss, were in their twenties and still in grad school when they launched the firm that is recasting how millions of consumers engage with high-end designer apparel and accessories. And just a few years out of undergrad, dancer and fitness enthusiast Payal Kadakia launched ClassPass, a service allowing customers to take fitness classes from multiple providers. Today the firm is valued at over $200 million, more than the firm behind the New York, Boston, Washington DC, and Philadelphia sports clubs.[31]

David Karp was another early bloomer. Karp wasn't just another college dropout; he actually quit high school for self-paced, tech-focused home schooling. It was a good move: He was taking meetings with venture capitalists at twenty, went on to found what would become one of the world's most visited websites, and sold that website, Tumblr, to Yahoo! for $1.1 billion at an age when he was younger than most MBA students.[32] Another young home-schooler, Palmer Luckey, started "modding" video game controllers at age fifteen, founded Oculus as a teenager, and sold it to Facebook for $2 billion (that's two Instagrams) by age twenty-one, and all before his company had even shipped its first consumer product.[33] In another brilliant sign of the times, Luckey jump started his effort not by gaining investment from angel investors or venture capitalists, who would demand an ownership stake in his business, but from a Kickstarter campaign. Hoping to raise $250,000, Luckey's Oculus Rift campaign actually raised over $2.4 million without giving up a single share of equity.[34]

FIGURE 1.2

Payal Kadakia, founder of ClassPass

Source: Image courtesy of ClassPass.

FIGURE 1.3

Wealth accumulation wasn't the only fast-paced activity for young Bill Gates. The Microsoft founder appears in a mug shot for a New Mexico traffic violation. Microsoft, now headquartered in Washington State, had its roots in New Mexico when Gates and partner Paul Allen moved there to be near early PC maker Altair.

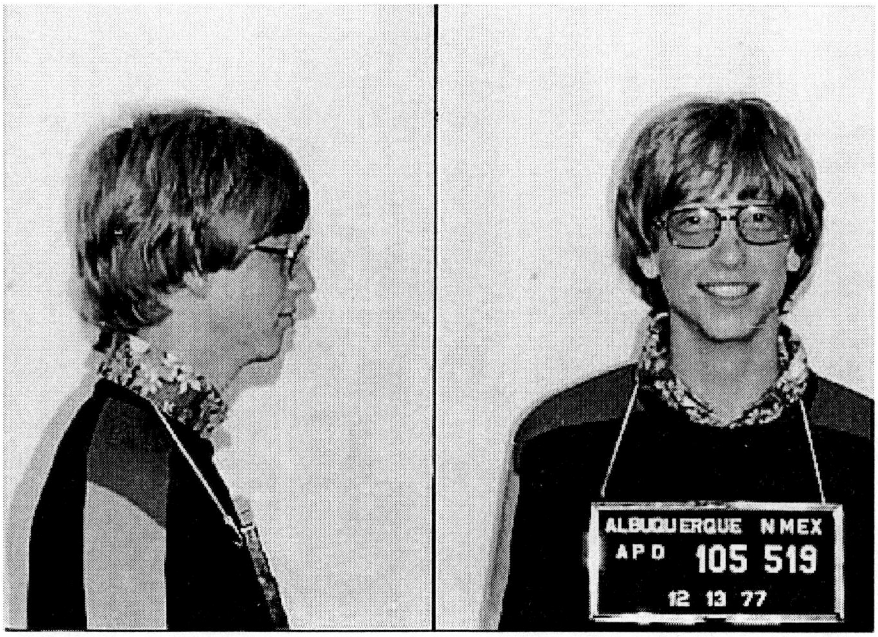

Source: Wikimedia Commons.

This trend will almost certainly accelerate. We're in a golden age of tech entrepreneurship where ideas can be vetted and tested online, and funding crowdsourced, Kickstarter-style; "the cloud" means a start-up can rent the computing resources one previously had to buy at great expense; app stores give code jockeys immediate, nearly zero-cost distribution to a potential market of hundreds of millions of people worldwide; and social media done right can virally spread awareness of a firm with nary a dime of conventional ad spending. Crafting a breakout hit is tough, but the jackpot can be immense.

But you don't have to build a successful firm to have an impact as a tech revolutionary. Shawn Fanning's Napster, widely criticized as a piracy playground, was written when he was just nineteen. Fanning's code was the first significant salvo in the tech-fueled revolution that brought about an upending of the entire music industry. Finland's Linus Torvalds wrote the first version of the Linux operating system when he was just twenty-one. Today Linux has grown to be the most influential component of the open source arsenal, powering everything from cell phones to supercomputers.

TechCrunch crows that Internet entrepreneurs are like pro athletes — "they peak around [age] 25."[35] *BusinessWeek* regularly runs a list of America's Best Young Entrepreneurs — the top twenty-five aged twenty-five and under. *Inc.* magazine's list of the Coolest Young Entrepreneurs is subtitled the "30 under 30." While not exclusively filled with the ranks of tech start-ups, both of these lists are nonetheless dominated with technology entrepreneurs. Whenever you see young people on the cover of a business magazine, it's almost certainly because they've done something groundbreaking with technology. The generals and foot soldiers of the technology revolution are filled with the ranks of the young, some not even old enough to legally have a beer. For the old-timers reading this, all is not lost, but you'd best get cracking with technology, quick. Junior might be on the way to either eat your lunch or be your next boss.

KEY TAKEAWAYS

- Recognize that anyone reading this book has the potential to build an impactful business. Entrepreneurship has no minimum age requirement.
- The ranks of technology revolutionaries are filled with young people, with several leading firms and innovations launched by entrepreneurs who started while roughly the age of the average university student.
- Several forces are accelerating and lowering the cost of entrepreneurship. These include crowdfunding, cloud computing, app stores, 3D printing, and social media, among others.

QUESTIONS AND EXERCISES

1. Look online for lists of young entrepreneurs. How many of these firms are tech firms or heavily rely on technology? Are there any sectors more heavily represented than tech?
2. Have you ever thought of starting your own tech-enabled business? Brainstorm with some friends. What kinds of ideas do you think might make a good business?
3. How have the costs of entrepreneurship changed over the past decade? What forces are behind these changes? What does this mean for the future of entrepreneurship?
4. Many universities and regions have competitions for entrepreneurs (e.g., business plan competitions, elevator pitch competitions). Does your school have such a program? What are the criteria for participation? If your school doesn't have one, consider forming such a program.
5. Research business accelerator programs such as Y-Combinator, TechStars, and DreamIt. Do you have a program like this in your area? What do entrepreneurs get from participating in these programs? What do they give up? Do you think these programs are worth it? Why or why not? Have you ever used a product or service from a firm that has participated in one of these programs?
6. Explore online for lists of resources for entrepreneurship. Use social media to share these resources with your class.
7. Why are we in the 'golden age' of technology entrepreneurship? What factors are helping entrepreneurs more rapidly achieve their vision, and with a lower cost?
8. Have any alumni from your institution founded technology firms or risen to positions of prominence in tech-focused careers? If so, work with your professor to invite them to come speak to your class or to student groups on campus. Your career services, university advancement (alumni giving and fundraising), alumni association, and LinkedIn searches may be able to help uncover potential speakers.

3.   GEEK UP—TECH IS EVERYWHERE AND YOU'LL NEED IT TO THRIVE

LEARNING OBJECTIVES

1. Appreciate the degree to which technology has permeated every management discipline.
2. See that tech careers are varied, richly rewarding, and poised for continued growth.

Shortly after the start of the prior decade, there was a lot of concern that tech jobs would be outsourced, leading many to conclude that tech skills carried less value and that workers with tech backgrounds had little to offer. Turns out this thinking was stunningly wrong. Tech jobs boomed, and as technology pervades all other management disciplines, tech skills are becoming more important, not less. Today, tech knowledge can be a key differentiator for the job seeker. It's the worker without tech skills that needs to be concerned.

As we'll present in depth in a future chapter, there's a principle called Moore's Law that's behind fast, cheap computing. And as computing gets both faster and cheaper, it gets "baked into" all sorts of products and shows up everywhere: in your pocket, in your vacuum, and on the radio frequency identification (RFID) tags that track your luggage at the airport.

Well, there's also a sort of Moore's Law corollary that's taking place with people, too. As technology becomes faster and cheaper and developments like open source software, cloud computing, software as a service (SaaS), and outsourcing push technology costs even lower, tech skills are being embedded inside more and more job functions. And ubiquitous tech fuels our current era of "Big Data" where bits-based insights move decision making from hunch to science. What this means is that even if you're not expecting to become the next Tech Titan, your career will doubtless be shaped by the forces of technology. Make no mistake about it—there isn't a single modern managerial discipline that isn't being deeply and profoundly impacted by tech.

3.1   Finance

Many business school students who study finance aspire to careers in investment banking. Many i-bankers will work on IPOs (initial public stock offerings), in effect helping value companies the first time these firms wish to sell their stock on the public markets. IPO markets need new firms, and the tech industry is a fertile ground that continually sprouts new businesses like no other. Other i-bankers will be involved in valuing merger and acquisition (M&A) deals, and tech firms are active in this space, too. Leading tech firms are flush with cash and constantly on the hunt for new firms to acquire. In just five years, Google has bought a whopping 103 firms, IBM has bought sixty-four, Microsoft has bought sixty-three, Cisco has bought fifty-seven, and Intel has bought forty-eight![36] Yahoo! bought thirty-seven companies in a year and a half.[37] Apple bought twenty-seven firms in roughly the same period, spending over $14 billion, including $3 billion just for Beats (note to rappers: Want to be a billionaire? Then form a tech firm like Beats co-founder Andre Young, a.k.a. Dr. Dre.).[38] And even in nontech industries, technology impacts nearly every endeavor as an opportunity catalyst or a disruptive wealth destroyer. The aspiring investment banker who doesn't understand the role of technology in firms and industries can't possibly provide an accurate guess at how much a company is worth.

TABLE 1.1   Tech Deals by Sector in 2014

Sector	Deals	Value (millions)
Software	84	$42,322
IT Services	76	$49,746
Internet	52	$36,259
Hardware	37	$15,655
Semiconductor	28	$17,380

Source: PwC, US Technology Deal Insights, Feb. 2015.

Those in other finance careers will be lending to tech firms and evaluating the role of technology in firms in an investment portfolio. Most of you will want to consider tech's role as part of your personal investments. And modern finance simply wouldn't exist without tech. When someone arranges for a bridge to be built in Shanghai, those funds aren't carried over in a suitcase—they're digitally transferred from bank to bank. And forces of technology blasted open the 200-year-old floor trading mechanism of the New York Stock Exchange, in effect forcing the NYSE to sell shares in itself to finance the acquisition of technology-based trading platforms that were threatening to replace it. Computer-automated trading, where a human doesn't touch the deal at all, is responsible for some 60 percent of US equity trading volume.[39] As another example of the importance of tech in finance, consider that Boston-based Fidelity Investments, one of the nation's largest mutual fund firms, spends roughly $2.8 billion a year on technology. Tech isn't a commodity for finance—it's the discipline's lifeblood.

3.2 Accounting

Sarbanes-Oxley Act

Also known as Sarbox or SOX; U.S. legislation enacted in the wake of the accounting scandals of the early 2000s. The act raises executive and board responsibility and ties criminal penalties to certain accounting and financial violations. Although often criticized, SOX is also seen as raising stakes for mismanagement and misdeeds related to a firm's accounting practices.

If you're an accountant, your career is built on a foundation of technology. The numbers used by accountants are all recorded, stored, and reported by information systems, and the reliability of any audit is inherently tied to the reliability of the underlying technology. Increased regulation, such as the heavy executive penalties tied to the **Sarbanes-Oxley Act** in the United States, have ratcheted up the importance of making sure accountants (and executives) get their numbers right. Negligence could mean jail time. This means the link between accounting and tech have never been tighter, and the stakes for ensuring systems accuracy have never been higher.

Business students might also consider that while accounting firms regularly rank near the top of *BusinessWeek*'s "Best Places to Start Your Career" list, many of the careers at these firms are highly tech-centric. Every major accounting firm has spawned a tech-focused consulting practice, and in many cases, these firms have grown to be larger than the accounting services functions from which they sprang. Today, Deloitte's tech-centric consulting division is larger than the firm's audit, tax, and risk practices. At the time of its spin-off, Accenture was larger than the accounting practice at former parent Arthur Andersen (Accenture executives are also grateful they split before Andersen's collapse in the wake of the prior decade's accounting scandals). Now, many accounting firms that had previously spun off technology practices are once again building up these functions, finding strong similarities between the skills of an auditor and skills needed in emerging disciplines such as information security and privacy.

3.3 Marketing

Technology has thrown a grenade onto the marketing landscape, and as a result, the skill set needed by today's marketers is radically different from what was leveraged by the prior generation. Online channels have provided a way to track and monitor consumer activities, and firms are leveraging this insight to understand how to get the right product to the right customer, through the right channel, with the right message, at the right price, at the right time. The success or failure of a campaign can often be immediately assessed based on online activity such as website visit patterns and whether a campaign results in an online purchase.

The ability to track customers, analyze campaign results, and modify tactics has amped up the return on investment of marketing dollars, with firms increasingly shifting spending from tough-to-track media such as print, radio, and television to the Web.[40] And new channels continue to emerge: smartphone, tablet, smart TV, smart watch and other wearables, smart auto, and more. Look to Apple to show how fast things grow: in roughly four years, iOS devices were in the hands, backpacks, purses, and pockets of over two hundred million people worldwide, delivering location-based messages and services and even allowing for cashless payment.[41] Roughly one-third of mobile phones used worldwide are smartphones, with the number expected to exceed 50 percent in four years. Billions will have a computer in their pockets, and this will become the primary channel for all sorts of customer engagement.[42]

The rise of social media is also part of this blown-apart marketing landscape. Now all customers can leverage an enduring and permanent voice, capable of broadcasting word-of-mouth influence in ways that can benefit and harm a firm. Savvy firms are using social media to generate sales, improve their reputations, better serve customers, and innovate. Those who don't understand this landscape risk being embarrassed, blindsided, and out of touch with their customers.

Search engine marketing (SEM), search engine optimization (SEO), customer relationship management (CRM), personalization systems, and a sensitivity to managing the delicate balance between gathering and leveraging data and respecting consumer privacy are all central components of the new marketing toolkit. And there's no looking back—tech's role in marketing will only grow in prominence. Analyst firm Gartner predicts that chief marketing officers are on a path to spend more on technology than any other function within the firm.[43]

3.4 Operations

A firm's operations management function is focused on producing goods and services, and operations students usually get the point that tech is the key to their future. Quality programs, process redesign, supply chain management, factory automation, and service operations are all tech-centric. These points are underscored in this book as we introduce several examples of how firms have designed fundamentally different ways of conducting business (and even entirely different industries), where value and competitive advantage are created through technology-enabled operations.

3.5 Human Resources

Technology helps firms harness the untapped power of employees. Knowledge management systems are morphing into social media technologies—social networks, wikis, and Twitter-style messaging systems that can accelerate the ability of a firm to quickly organize and leverage teams of experts. And crowdsourcing tools and question-and-answer sites like Quora and StackOverflow allow firms to reach out for expertise beyond their organizations. Human resources (HR) directors are using technology for employee training, screening, and evaluation. The accessibility of end-user technology means that every employee can reach the public, creating an imperative for firms to set policy on issues such as firm representation and disclosure and to continually monitor and enforce policies as well as capture and push out best practices. The successful HR manager recognizes that technology continually changes an organization's required skill sets as well as employee expectations.

The hiring and retention practices of the prior generation are also in flux. Recruiting hasn't just moved online; it's now grounded in information systems that scour databases for specific skill sets, allowing recruiters to cast a wider talent net than ever before. Job seekers are writing résumés with keywords in mind, aware that the first cut is likely made by a database search program, not a human being. The rise of professional social networks also puts added pressure on employee satisfaction and retention. Prior HR managers fiercely guarded employee directories for fear that a headhunter or competitive firm might raid top talent. Now the equivalent of a corporate directory can be easily pulled up via LinkedIn, a service complete with discrete messaging capabilities that can allow competitors to rifle-scope target your firm's best and brightest. Thanks to technology, the firm that can't keep employees happy, engaged, and feeling valued has never been more vulnerable.

And while many students have been wisely warned that inappropriate social posts can ruin their job candidacy, also know that the inverse is also true. In many ways social media is "the new résumé."[44] Thoughtful blog posts, a compelling LinkedIn presence, Twitter activity reflecting an enthusiastic and engaged mind, and, for tech students, participation in collaborative coding communities like GitHub all work to set apart a candidate from the herd. If you can't be found online, some employers may wonder if you have current skills, or if you have something to hide.

3.6 The Law

And for those looking for careers in corporate law, many of the hottest areas involve technology. Intellectual property, patents, piracy, and privacy are all areas where activity has escalated dramatically in recent years. The number of US patent applications waiting approval has tripled in the past decade, while China saw a threefold increase in patent applications in just five years.[45] Firms planning to leverage new inventions and business methods need legal teams with the skills to sleuth out whether a firm can legally do what it plans to. Others will need legal expertise to help them protect proprietary methods and content, as well as to help enforce claims in the home country and abroad.

3.7 Information Systems Careers

While the job market goes through ebbs and flows, recent surveys have shown there to be no end in sight for the demand for technical skills. *Money* magazine ranked tech jobs as three of the top ten "Best Jobs in America."[46] Around 1 in every 20 open job postings in the United States relates to information systems or computer science, and tech specializations are among the top three most-demanded college majors.[47] By some estimates, there will be three times the number of new US programming jobs created than newly minted programmers graduating from US colleges.[48] In some regions demand is even more pressing. In Massachusetts, for example, there is only one qualified graduate for every seventeen tech firm job openings requiring a bachelor's degree.[49] Tech jobs make up two of the top three "Best Jobs" on the *US News* list.[50] *BusinessWeek* ranks consulting (which heavily hires tech grads) and technology as the second and third highest paying industries for recent college graduates.[51] Technology careers have actually ranked among the safest careers to have during the most recent downturn.[52] The *Harvard Business Review* has declared "Data Scientist" the "Sexiest Job of the twenty-first century."[53] And *Fortune's* ranks of the "Best Companies to Work For" is full of technology firms and has been topped by a tech business for eight years straight.[54] Want to work for a particular company? Chances are they're looking for tech talent. The demand for technology skills stretches across industries. Employers with the greatest number of recent technical job openings included JP Morgan Chase (finance), UnitedHealth (healthcare/insurance), Northrup Gruman (defense), and General Motors (automotive). And everyone wants to hire more coders from underrepresented groups. Apple[55], Etsy,[56] Square,[57] Facebook,[58] and Google[59] are among the firms with programs to prep and encourage more women and minorities to pursue tech careers (details in endnotes).[60]

Students studying technology can leverage skills in ways that range from the highly technical to those that emphasize a tech-centric use of other skills. And why be restricted to just the classes taught on campus? Resources like Coursera, iTunes U., CodeAcademy, Udemy, edX, YouTube, and others provide a smorgasbord of learning where the smart and motivated can geek up. Carve out some time to give programming a shot—remember, the founders of Tumblr and Instagram were largely self-taught. The high demand for scarce technical talent has also led many tech firms to offer six-figure starting salaries to graduating seniors from top universities.[61] Opportunities for programmers abound, particularly for those versed in new technologies. But there are also nonprogramming roles for experts in areas such as user-interface design (who work to make sure systems are easy to use), process design (who leverage technology to make firms more efficient), and strategy (who specialize in technology for competitive advantage). Nearly every large organization has its own information systems department. That group not only ensures that systems get built and keep running but also increasingly takes on strategic roles targeted at proposing solutions for how technology can give the firm a competitive edge. Career paths allow for developing expertise in a particular technology (e.g., business intelligence analyst, database administrator, social media manager), while project management careers leverage skills in taking projects from idea through deployment.

Even in consulting firms, careers range from hard-core programmers who "build stuff" to analysts who do no programming but might work identifying problems and developing a solutions blueprint that is then turned over to another team to code. Careers at tech giants like Apple, Google, and Microsoft don't all involve coding end-user programs either. Each of these firms has their own client-facing staff that works with customers and partners to implement solutions. Field engineers at these firms may work as part of (often very lucratively compensated) sales teams to show how a given company's software and services can be used. These engineers often put together prototypes that are then turned over to a client's in-house staff for further development. An Apple field engineer might show how a firm can leverage iPads in its organization, while a Google field engineer can help a firm incorporate search, banner, and video ads into its online efforts. Careers that involve consulting and field engineering are often particularly attractive for those who are effective communicators who enjoy working with an ever-changing list of clients and problems across various industries and in many different geographies.

Upper-level career opportunities are also increasingly diverse. Consultants can become partners who work with the most senior executives of client firms, helping identify opportunities for those organizations to become more effective. Within a firm, technology specialists can rise to be chief information officer or chief technology officer—positions focused on overseeing a firm's information systems development and deployment. And many firms are developing so-called *C-level* specialties in emerging areas with a technology focus, such as chief information security officer (CISO), and chief privacy officer (CPO). Senior technology positions may also be a ticket to the chief executive's suite. A recent *Fortune* article pointed out how the prominence of technology provides a training ground for executives to learn the breadth and depth of a firm's operations and an understanding of the ways in which firms are vulnerable to attack and where it can leverage opportunities for growth.[62]

3.8 Your Future

With tech at the center of so much change, realize that you may very well be preparing for careers that don't yet exist. But by studying the intersection of business and technology today, you develop a base to build upon and critical thinking skills that will help you evaluate new, emerging technologies. Think you can afford to wait on tech study, and then quickly get up to speed at a later date? Whom do you expect to have an easier time adapting and leveraging a technology like social media—today's college students who are immersed in technology or their parents who are embarrassingly dipping their toes into the waters of Facebook? Those who put off an understanding of technology risk being left in the dust.

Consider the nontechnologists who have tried to enter the technology space these past few years. News Corp. head Rupert Murdoch piloted his firm to the purchase of MySpace only to see this one-time leader lose share to rivals.[63] Former Warner executive Terry Semel presided over Yahoo!'s[64] malaise as Google blasted past it. Barry Diller, the man widely credited with creating the Fox Network, led InterActive Corp. (IAC) in the acquisition of a slew of tech firms ranging from Expedia to Ask.com, only to break the empire up as it foundered.[65] And Time Warner head Jerry Levin presided over the acquisition of AOL, executing what many consider to be one of the most disastrous mergers in US business history.[66] Contrast these guys against the technology-centric successes of Mark Zuckerberg (Facebook), Steve Jobs (Apple), and Sergey Brin and Larry Page (Google).

While we'll make it abundantly clear that a focus solely on technology is a recipe for disaster, a business perspective that lacks an appreciation for tech's role is also likely to be doomed. At this point in history, technology and business are inexorably linked, and those not trained to evaluate and make decisions in this ever-shifting space risk irrelevance, marginalization, and failure.

KEY TAKEAWAYS

- As technology becomes cheaper and more powerful, it pervades more industries and is becoming increasingly baked into what were once nontech functional areas.
- Technology is impacting every major business discipline, including finance, accounting, marketing, operations, human resources, and the law.
- Tech jobs rank among the best and highest-growth positions, and tech firms rank among the best and highest-paying firms to work for.
- Information systems (IS) jobs are profoundly diverse, ranging from those that require heavy programming skills to those that are focused on design, process, project management, privacy, and strategy.

QUESTIONS AND EXERCISES

1. Look at *Fortune*'s "Best Companies to Work For" list. How many of these firms are technology firms? Which firm would you like to work for? Are they represented on this list?

2. Look at *BusinessWeek*'s "Best Places to Start Your Career" list. Is the firm you mentioned above also on this list?

3. What are you considering studying? What are your short-term and long-term job goals? What role will technology play in that career path? What should you be doing to ensure that you have the skills needed to compete?

4. Which jobs that exist today likely won't exist at the start of the next decade? Based on your best guess on how technology will develop, can you think of jobs and skill sets that will likely emerge as critical five and ten years from now?

5. Explore online resources to learn technology on your own and search for programs that encourage college students. If you are from an underrepresented group in technology (i.e., a woman or minority), search for programs that provide learning and opportunity for those seeking tech careers. Share your resources with your professor via a class wiki or other mechanism to create a common resource everyone can use to #geekup. Then tweet what you create using that hashtag!

4. THE PAGES AHEAD

LEARNING OBJECTIVE

1. **Understand the structure of this text, the issues and examples that will be introduced, and why they are important.**

Hopefully this first chapter has helped get you excited for what's to come. The text is written in a style similar to business magazines and newspapers (i.e., the stuff you'll be reading and learning from for the rest of your career). The introduction of concepts in this text are also example rich, and every concept introduced or technology discussed is grounded in a real-world scenario to show why it's important. But also know that while we celebrate successes and expose failures in that space where business and technology come together, we also recognize that firms and circumstances change. Today's winners have no guarantee of sustained dominance. What you should acquire in the pages that follow are a fourfold set of benefits that (1) provide a description of what's happening in industry today, (2) offer an introduction to key business and technology concepts, (3) offer a durable set of concepts and frameworks that can be applied even as technologies and industries change, and (4) develop critical thinking that will serve you well throughout your career as a manager.

Chapters don't have to be read in order, so feel free to bounce around, if you'd like; and your professor may ask you to skip or skim over certain sections. But many students write that they've enjoyed reading even those areas not assigned (the ultimate compliment for a textbook author). I hope you find the text as enjoyable, as well. Here's what you can expect:

Chapter 2 focuses on building big-picture skills to think about how to leverage technology for competitive advantage. Technology alone is rarely the answer, but through a rich set of examples, we'll show how firms can weave technology into their operations in ways that create and reinforce resources that can garner profits while repelling competitors. A mini-case examines tech's role at FreshDirect, a firm that has defied the many failures in the online grocery space and devastated traditional rivals. Amazon, BlueNile, Cisco, Dell, Google, OpenTable, Uber, TiVo, and Yahoo! are among the many firms providing a set of examples illustrating both successes and failures in leveraging technology. The chapter will show how firms use technology to create and leverage brand, scale economies, switching costs, data assets, network effects, and distribution channels. We'll introduce how technology relates to two popular management frameworks—the value chain and the five forces model. And we'll provide a solid decision framework for considering the controversial and often misunderstood role that technology plays among firms that seek an early-mover advantage.

In Chapter 3 we see how a tech-fed value chain helped Spanish clothing giant Zara craft a counterintuitive model that seems to defy all conventional wisdom in the fashion industry. We'll show how Zara's model differs radically from that of the firm it displaced to become the world's top clothing retailer: Gap. We'll show how technology ranging from handheld mobile devices to communications and scheduling systems to RFID tags work together to impact product design, product development, marketing, cycle time, inventory management, and customer loyalty; and how technology decisions influence broad profitability that goes way beyond the cost-of-goods thinking common among many retailers. We'll also offer a mini-case on Fair Factories Clearinghouse, an effort highlighting the positive role of technology in improving ethical business practices. Another mini-case shows the difference between thinking about technology versus broad thinking about systems, all through an examination of how high-end fashion house Prada failed in its roll out of technology that on the surface seemed very similar to Zara's.

Chapter 4 studies Netflix in two parts. The first half of the chapter tramples the notion that dotcom start-up firms can't compete against large, established rivals. We'll show how information systems at Netflix created a set of assets that grew in strength and remains difficult for rivals to match. The economics of pure-play versus brick-and-mortar firms is examined, and we'll introduce managerial thinking on various concepts such as the data asset, personalization systems (recommendation engines and collaborative filtering), the long tail and the implications of technology on selection and inventory, crowdsourcing, using technology for novel revenue models (subscription and revenue-sharing with suppliers), forecasting, and inventory management. The second part of the chapter covers Netflix's challenges as it tries what many firms have failed at—maintaining leadership even as industry-related shifts fundamentally alter a firm's business. We present how the shift from atoms (physical discs) to bits (streaming and downloads) creates additional challenges and opportunities. Issues of digital products, licensing and partnerships, bargaining power of unique-good suppliers, content creation, revenue models, brand building and customer satisfaction, disparate competitors, global expansion challenges, and delivery platforms are all discussed. The section also covers how the streaming business has additional advantages in data collection and leverage, distinctly different but still significant scale assets, compelling benefits for consumers and content providers, and more. The chapter also provides an overview of the cloud-based Netflix technical infrastructure, the firm's open-source contributions and use of crowdsourcing, and the uniqueness and influence of the firm's culture.

Chapter 5 focuses on understanding the rate of technology change from a computing power and cost perspective, and the implications for firms, markets, and society. The chapter offers accessible definitions for technologies impacted by Moore's Law but goes beyond semiconductors and silicon to show how the rate of magnetic storage (e.g., hard drives) and networking price and performance improvement create markets filled with uncertainty and opportunity. The chapter will show how tech has enabled the rise of Apple and Amazon, created mobile phone markets that empower the poor worldwide, and created six waves of disruptive innovation over six decades. We'll also show how Moore's Law, perhaps the greatest economic gravy train in history, will inevitably run out of steam as the three demons of heat, energy demands, and limits on shrinking transistors halt the advancement of current technology. Studying technologies that "extend" Moore's Law, such as multicore semiconductors, helps illustrate both the benefit and limitation of technology options, and in doing so, helps develop skills around recognizing the pros and cons of a given innovation. Supercomputing, grid, and cloud computing are introduced through examples that show how these advances are changing the economics of computing and creating new opportunities. Extended examples of IBM's Watson technology are offered, including the firm's efforts to turn Watson into a platform to serve other firms and to be baked into new products and services, such as the Cognitoy dinosaur—a children's learning helper. A mini-case on the development of Disney's Magic Band shows how fast-cheap technology is being used to replace paper ticketing in DisneyWorld in ways that improve the customer experience, streamline operations, and cut costs. The case also raises issues on the challenges of developing complex new technology initiatives that impact many areas of the firm and its customers. Issues of e-waste are explored in a way that shows that firms need to consider not only the ethics of product sourcing but also the ethics of disposal.

In Chapter 6 we'll also introduce the concept of disruptive innovation to help managers understand why so many large incumbents are beat by new entrants, and we'll offer methods for becoming the disruptor rather than the disrupted. Concepts of disruptive technologies and disruptive innovation are introduced in a way that will help managers recognize potentially firm-destroying and career-crushing tech-driven challenges and get new possibilities on a firm's early radar. Mini-cases show disruption in action—for example, competition between Intel and ARM and Intuit's migration from packaged software to cloud. The chapter also includes a section examining the potentially disruptive innovation of bitcoin. The section describes how bitcoin works, its appeal and advantages, its disruptive opportunity, and the challenges and limitations it needs to overcome to hit the mainstream.

Chapter 7 explores one of the most disruptive firms of the post-Internet era. The chapter is broken into three parts. The first discusses the firm's physical goods e-commerce business and provides an opportunity to examine how it seeks tech-driven efficiencies in warehouse operations, fuels strategic goals, creates advantages through the accounting and finance concept of the cash conversion cycle, reinforces brand strength, enables scale and network effects, creates a powerful data asset, and is fundamentally redefining shopping habits. New device experimentation, such as Amazon Dash, the Dash Button, and Amazon Echo, are also introduced. The second section looks at the rise of Amazon's Kindle business and its evolution, which has moved from e-book reader to include tablet, TV, and smartphone. The chapter also covers the importance of platform creation, challenges in "going mobile," issues of channel conflict, and how the firm is disrupting the entire publishing and media creation value chain. The final chapter examines Amazon's personal and corporate cloud computing initiatives, the infrastructure that underpins these efforts, and the business opportunities that these efforts create.

In Chapter 8 we'll see how technologies, services, and platforms can create nearly insurmountable advantages. Tech firms from Facebook to Intel to Microsoft are dominant because of network effects—the idea that some products and services get more valuable as more people use them. Studying network effects creates better decision makers. The concept is at the heart of technology standards and platform competition, and understanding network effects can help managers choose technologies that are likely to win, hopefully avoiding getting caught with a failed, poorly supported system. Students learn how network effects work and why they're difficult to unseat. The chapter ends with an example-rich discussion of various techniques that one can use to compete in markets where network effects are present.

Peer production and social media have created some of the Internet's most popular destinations and most rapidly growing firms, and they are empowering the voice of the customer as never before. In Chapter 9 students learn about various technologies used in social media and peer production, including blogs, wikis, social networking, Twitter, and more. Prediction markets and crowdsourcing are introduced, along with examples of how firms are leveraging these concepts for insight and innovation. Finally, students are offered guidance on how firms can think SMART by creating a social media awareness and response team. Issues of training, policy, and response are introduced, and technologies for monitoring and managing online reputations are discussed.

Chapter 10 expands on peer production concepts introduced in the earlier chapter to explore the so-called "Sharing Economy" and "Collaborative Consumption." Examples are offered of citizens coming together to create or share resources across markets, and of the creation of electronic markets to facilitate these services. Drivers that help bring about the sharing economy, the advantages enjoyed by sharing economy firms, and the challenges these firms face are also introduced. The chapter also discusses how mainstream firms are leveraging Sharing Economy concepts, and the future outlook for these firms is explored. Extended mini-cases on Airbnb and Uber discuss the impact, success, competitive advantage, platform creation, the use of APIs, and major issues facing two of the sector's most successful firms. Success strategies and challenges for firms involved in the sector are illustrated, and the future outlook for the space is explored.

Chapter 11 will allow us to study success and failure in IS design and deployment by examining one of the Internet's hottest firms. Facebook is one of the most accessible and relevant Internet firms to so many, but it's also a wonderful laboratory to discuss critical managerial concepts. The founding story of Facebook introduces concepts of venture capital, the board of directors, and the role of network effects in entrepreneurial control. Feeds show how information, content, and applications can spread virally but also introduce privacy concerns. Facebook's strength in switching costs demonstrates how it has been able to envelop additional markets from photos to chat to video and more. The challenges Facebook has faced as it transitions from a primarily desktop service to one where most users access it via mobile phone are also addressed, exposing how resources do and don't transfer from desktop to mobile and why mobile is "different" for many firms. Also included is managerial insight on how mobile is, in some ways, a richer platform with a high potential for innovation. Facebook's struggles in mobile are illustrated alongside its major acquisitions, including Instagram, WhatsApp, and Oculus VR. Lessons from Facebook as an apps platform are also discussed in a way that provides insight to managers thinking beyond services, and toward successful platform creation. The discussion includes information on the desktop platform's early success, stagnancy, the firm's mobile platform struggles, attempts to build Messenger into a platform (and contrast with WeChat and other international efforts), and continued challenges. The failure of the Beacon system shows how even bright technologists can fail if they ignore the broader procedural and user implications of an information systems rollout. Social networking advertising is contrasted with search, and the perils of advertising alongside social media content are introduced. Issues of privacy, global growth, and the firm's Internet.org effort to bring more data services to the developing world are also discussed.

Chapter 12 provides a fascinating look at how two young women entrepreneurs have crafted a business that has attracted millions of customers and recast how women relate to designer fashion. A discussion of the firm's early stage allows for the introduction of key concepts in entrepreneurship, such as product-market fit and minimum viable product. The case illustrates how a new firm developed strong network effects through crafting a win-win for customers and fashion brands. Social and mobile are detailed as being key enablers for the firm's unique sharing economy model. A section on how the firm leverages analytics to inform everything from pricing to product sourcing to customer service shows the advantages of the tech-centric firm over conventional retailers. Technology, as well as human capital, are described in a firm that is at its heart a highly-complex reverse logistics business where everything that goes out must come in and often heads right out again after cleaning and treatment. The firm's expansion into traditional storefronts provides an opportunity to discuss when physical retail may make sense for a tech firm.

Chapter 13 offers a primer to help managers better understand what software is all about. The chapter offers a brief introduction to software technologies. Students learn about operating systems, application software, and how these relate to each other. Enterprise applications are introduced, and the alphabet soup of these systems (e.g., ERP, CRM, and SCM) is accessibly explained. Various forms of distributed systems (client-server, Web services, APIs, messaging) are also covered. The chapter provides a managerial overview of how software is developed, offers insight into the importance of Java and scripting languages, and explains the differences between compiled and interpreted systems. System failures (including an analysis of the failure and resurrection of systems associated with the US Affordable Care Act), total cost of ownership, and project risk mitigation are also introduced. The array of concepts covered helps a manager understand the bigger picture and should provide an underlying appreciation for how systems work that will serve even as technologies change and new technologies are introduced.

The software industry is changing radically, and that's the focus of Chapter 14 The issues covered in this chapter are front and center for any firm making technology decisions. We'll cover open source software, software as a service, hardware clouds, app software, and virtualization. Each topic is introduced by discussing advantages, risks, business models, and examples of their effective use. The chapter ends by introducing issues that a manager must consider when making decisions as to whether to purchase technology, contract or outsource an effort, or develop an effort in-house.

In Chapter 15 we'll study data, which is often an organization's most critical asset. Data lies at the heart of every major discipline, including marketing, accounting, finance, operations, forecasting, and planning. We'll help managers understand how data is created, organized, and effectively used. We'll cover limitations in data sourcing, issues in privacy and regulation, and tools for access, including various business intelligence and so-called "Big Data" technologies. A mini-case on Walmart shows data's use in empowering a firm's entire value chain, while examples from Spotify to L.L. Bean underscore Big Data's impact on the modern enterprise.

Chapter 16 unmasks the mystery of the Internet—it shows how the Internet works and why a manager should care about IP addresses, IP networking, the DNS, peering, and packet versus circuit switching. We'll also cover last-mile technologies and the various strengths and weaknesses of getting a faster Internet to a larger population. The revolution in mobile technologies and the impact on business will also be presented.

Chapter 17 helps managers understand attacks and vulnerabilities and how to keep end users and organizations more secure. The ever-increasing number of megabreaches at firms that now include Target, TJX, Heartland, Epsilon, Sony, and even security firm RSA, plus the increasing vulnerability of end-user systems, have highlighted how information security is now the concern of the entire organization, from senior executives to frontline staff. This chapter explains what's happening with respect to information security—what kinds of attacks are occurring, who is doing them, and what their motivation is. We'll uncover the source of vulnerabilities in systems: human, procedural, and technical. Hacking concepts such as botnets, malware, phishing, and SQL injection are explained using plain, accessible language. Also presented are techniques to improve information security both as an end user and within an organization. The combination of current issues and their relation to a broader framework for security should help you think about vulnerabilities even as technologies and exploits change over time.

Chapter 18 discusses one of the most influential and far-reaching firms in today's business environment. As pointed out earlier, a decade ago Google barely existed, but it now earns more ad revenue and is a more profitable media company than any other media firm, online or off. Google is a major force in modern marketing, research, and entertainment. In this chapter you'll learn how Google (and Web search in general) works. Issues of search engine ranking, optimization, and search infrastructure are introduced. Students gain an understanding of search advertising and other advertising techniques, ad revenue models such as CPM and CPC, online advertising networks, various methods of customer profiling (e.g., IP addresses, geotargeting, cookies), click fraud, fraud prevention, and issues related to privacy and regulation. The chapter concludes with a broad discussion of how Google is evolving (e.g., Android, Chrome, Apps, YouTube) and how this evolution is bringing it into conflict with several well-funded rivals, including Amazon, Apple, and Microsoft.

Nearly every industry and every functional area is increasing its investment in and reliance on information technology. With opportunity comes trade-offs: research has shown that a high level of IT investment is associated with a more frenzied competitive environment.[67] But while the future is uncertain, we don't have the luxury to put on the brakes or dial back the clock—tech's impact is here to stay. Those firms that emerge as winners will treat IT efforts "as opportunities to define and deploy new ways of working, rather than just projects to install, configure, or integrate."[68] The examples, concepts, and frameworks in the pages that follow will help you build the tools and decision-making prowess needed for victory.

KEY TAKEAWAYS

- This text contains a series of chapters and cases that expose durable concepts, technologies, and frameworks, and does so using cutting-edge examples of what's happening in industry today.
- While firms and technologies will change, and success at any given point in time is no guarantee of future victory, the issues illustrated and concepts acquired should help shape a manager's decision making in a way that will endure.

QUESTIONS AND EXERCISES

1. Which firms do you most admire today? How do these firms use technology? Do you think technology gives them an advantage over rivals? Why or why not?
2. What areas covered in this book are most exciting? Most intimidating? Which do you think will be most useful?

ENDNOTES

1. T. Goodwin, "The Battle Is For The Customer Interface," *TechCrunch*, March 3, 2015.

2. M. Porter, "Strategy and the Internet," *Harvard Business Review* 79, no. 3 (March 2001): 62–78.

3. G. Kumparak, "Apple Just Had The Most Profitable Quarter Of Any Company Ever," *TechCrunch*, Jan. 27, 2015.

4. Reported App stores sales in 2014 = $14 billion (source: Ulloa, "The App Store Brought in More than $14 Billion in 2014," *Digital Music News*, Jan. 8, 2015. The 250th ranked firm in the 2015 Fortune 500 was JCPenny, with revenues of just $12.2 billion (source: 2015 Fortune 500). Reported App stores sales in 2014 = $14 billion (source: Ulloa, "The App Store Brought in More than $14 Billion in 2014," *Digital Music News*, Jan. 8, 2015. The 250th ranked firm in the 2015 Fortune 500 was JCPenny, with revenues of just $12.2 billion (source: 2015 Fortune 500).

5. C. Frey and M. Osborne, Technology at Work: The Future of Innovation and Employment, published by Citibank, New York, NY, February 2015.

6. E. Protalinski, "Facebook passes 1.44B monthly active users and 1.25B mobile users; 65% are now daily users," *VentureBeat*, April 22, 2015.

7. S. Tibkin, "China passes US to become Apple's biggest iPhone market," *CNet*, April 27, 2015.

8. D. Alba, "Chinese Smartphone Maker Xiaomi is Now the World's Most Valauble Startup," *Wired*, Dec. 29, 2014.

9. R. Mac, "Alibaba Claims Title For Largest Global IPO Ever With Extra Share Sales," *Forbes*, Sept. 22, 2014.

10. V. Wadhwa, "Indian Technology's Fourth Wave," *BusinessWeek*, December 8, 2010.

11. D. Kerr, "US Download Speeds Sluggish Compared with Other Countries," *CNET*, November 26, 2013.

12. H. Waxman, "Competition and choice in wireless broadband," *The Hill*, June 24, 2015.

13. Unattributed, "The truly personal computer," *The Economist*, Feb. 28, 2015.

14. M. Maneker, "Benedict Evans wants you to know that Google is a tiny company," *Quartz*, Feb. 23, 2015.

15. *Economist*, "The Next Frontier," February 16, 2013.

16. J. O., "Growth and Other Good Things," *Economist*, May 1, 2013.

17. G. York, "How Mobile Phones Are Making Cash Obsolete in Africa," *The Globe and Mail*, June 21, 2013.

18. Unattributed, "A phoneful of dollars," *The Economist*, Nov. 15, 2014.

19. S. Higginbotham, "GE's Industrial Internet Focus Means It's a Big Data Company Now," *GigaOM*, June 18, 2013

20. T. Team, "GE Is Beginning To See Strong Returns On Its Industrial Internet Investments," *Forbes*, Nov. 12, 2014.

21. B. Cha, "A Beginner's Guide to Understanding the Internet of Things," *Re/code*, Jan. 15, 201

22. Unattributed, "The truly personal computer," *The Economist*, Feb. 28, 2015.

23. E. Palermo, "How 3D Printing Is Changing Etsy," *TomsGuide*, Aug. 7, 2013.

24. J. Buck, T. McMahan, and D. Huot, "Space Station 3-D Printer Builds Ratchet Wrench To Complete First Phase Of Operations," *Nasa*, Dec. 22, 2014.

25. J. Guynn, "Insta-Rich: How Instagram Became a $1 Billion Company in 18 Months," *Los Angeles Times*, April 20, 2012.

26. B. Stone and S. Friar, "Evan Spiegel Reveals Plan to Turn Snapchat Into a Real Business," *BusinessWeek*, May 26, 2015.

27. M. Stone, "The fabulous life of Snapchat CEO Evan Spiegel, the youngest billionaire in the world," *Business Insider*, March 12, 2015.

28. M. Chafkin, "The Zappos Way of Managing," *Inc.*, May 1, 2009.

29. S. Lacy, "Amazon Buys Zappos; The Price Is $928m., Not $847m.," *TechCrunch*, July 22, 2009.

30. J. Bort, "Oculus Founder Palmer Luckey Dropped Out of College—And So Did All These Other Tech Superstars," *Business Insider*, March 25, 2014.

31. Y. Chernova, "ClassPass, Valued at More Than $200M, Taps Into Gym Craze," *The Wall Street Journal*, March 12, 2015.

32. J. Wortham and N. Bolton, "Before Tumblr, Founder Made Mom Proud. He Quit School," *New York Times*, May 20, 2013.

33. T. Clark, "How Palmer Luckey Created Oculus Rift," *Smithsonian Magazine*, Nov. 2014.

34. D. Ewalt, "Palmer Luckey: Defying Reality," *Forbes*, January 5, 2015.

35. M. Arrington, "Internet Entrepreneurs Are Like Professional Athletes, They Peak Around 25," *TechCrunch*, April 30, 2011.

36. S. Miller, "The Trouble with Tech M&A," *The Deal*, May 7, 2012.

37. V. Ravisankar, "How to Hack Hiring," *TechCrunch*, April 26, 2014.

38. D. Dilger, "Apple's Voracious Appetite for Acquisitions Outspent Google in 2013," *AppleInsider*, March 3, 2014; P. Kafka, "Tim Cook Explains Why Apple Is Buying Beats (Q&A)," *Re/code*, May 28, 2014; and P. Kafka, "Apple Will Buy Beats for $3 Billion," *Re/code*, May 28, 2014.

39. M. Philips, "How the Robots Lost: High-Frequency Trading's Rise and Fall," *BusinessWeek*, June 6, 2013.

40. J. Pontin, "But Who's Counting?" *Technology Review*, March/April 2009.

41. D. Coldewey, "iOS Passes 200 Million Devices, 25 Million of Which Are iPads," *TechCrunch*, June 6, 2011.

42. eMarketer, "Smartphone Adoption Tips Past 50 Percent in Major Markets Worldwide," May 29, 2013.

43. L. Arthur, "Five Years from Now, CMOs Will Spend More on IT than CIOs Do," *Forbes*, February 8, 2012.

44. R. Silverman and L Weber, "The New Résumé: It's 140 Characters," *Wall Street Journal*, April 9, 2013.

45. J. Schmid and B. Poston, "Patent Backlog Clogs Recovery," *Milwaukee Journal Sentinel*, August 15, 2009.

46. "Best Jobs in America 2013," *CNNMoney*.

47. S. Gallagher, "Software Is Eating The Job Market," *TechCrunch*, June 9, 2015.

48. K. McDonald, "Sorry, College Grads, I Probably Won't Hire You," *Wall Street Journal*, May 9, 2013.

49. D. Adams, "Mass. tech sector flourishing with challenges ahead," *The Boston Globe*, March 13, 2015.

50. "The 100 Best Jobs," U.S. News & World Report, accessed July 1, 2014.

51. L. Gerdes, "The Best Places to Launch a Career," *BusinessWeek*, September 15, 2008.

52. T. Kaneshige, "Surprise! Tech Is a Safe Career Choice Today," *InfoWorld*, February 4, 2009.

53. T. Davenport and D. Patil, "Data Scientist: The Sexiest Job of the 21st Century," *Harvard Business Review*, October 2012.

54. See "Best Companies to Work For," *Fortune*, 2007–2014.

55. M. Lev-Ram, "Apple commits more than $50 million to diversity efforts," *Fortune*, March 10, 2015.

56. A. Kamanetz, "How Etsy Attracted 500 Percent More Female Engineers," *Fast Company*, March 5, 2013.

57. L. Rao, "For Aspiring Female Engineers, a Square Meal of Code," *TechCrunch*, May 17, 2014.

58. Careers at Facebook, https://www.facebook.com/careers/university/fbu.

59. J. Jackson, "Google Boldly Did the Right Thing," June 2, 2014. J

60. A. Kuchment, "Encouraging More Minority Girls to Code," *Scientific America*, July 9, 2013.

61. E. Goode, "For Newcomers in Silicon Valley, the Dream of Entrepreneurship Still Lives," *New York Times*, January 24, 2012.

62. J. Fortt, "Tech Execs Get Sexy," *Fortune*, February 12, 2009.

63. O. Malik, "MySpace, R.I.P.," *GigaOM*, February 10, 2010.

64. J. Thaw, "Yahoo's Semel Resigns as Chief amid Google's Gains," *Bloomberg*, June 18, 2007.

65. G. Fabrikant and M. Helft, "Barry Diller Conquered. Now He Tries to Divide," *New York Times*, March 16, 2008.

66. J. Quinn, "Final Farewell to Worst Deal in History—AOL-Time Warner," *Telegraph* (UK), November 21, 2009.

67. E. Brynjolfsson, A. McAfee, M. Sorell, and F. Zhu, "Scale without Mass: Business Process Replication and Industry Dynamics," *SSRN*, September 30, 2008.

68. A. McAfee and E. Brynjolfsson, "Dog Eat Dog," *Sloan Management Review*, April 27, 2007.

CHAPTER 2

Strategy and Technology: Concepts and Frameworks for Understanding What Separates Winners from Losers

1. INTRODUCTION

LEARNING OBJECTIVES

1. Define operational effectiveness and understand the limitations of technology-based competition leveraging this principle.
2. Define strategic positioning and the importance of grounding competitive advantage in this concept.
3. Understand the resource-based view of competitive advantage.
4. List the four characteristics of a resource that might possibly yield sustainable competitive advantage.

Managers are confused, and for good reason. Management theorists, consultants, and practitioners often vehemently disagree on how firms should craft tech-enabled strategy, and many widely read articles contradict one another. Headlines such as "Move First or Die" compete with "The First-Mover Disadvantage." A leading former CEO advises, "destroy your business," while others suggest firms focus on their "core competency" and "return to basics." The pages of the *Harvard Business Review* have declared, "IT Doesn't Matter," while a *New York Times* bestseller hails technology as the "steroids" of modern business.

Theorists claiming to have mastered the secrets of strategic management are contentious and confusing. But as a manager, the ability to size up a firm's strategic position and understand its likelihood of sustainability is one of the most valuable and yet most difficult skills to master. Layer on thinking about technology—a key enabler to nearly every modern business strategy, but also a function often thought of as easily "outsourced"—and it's no wonder that so many firms struggle at the intersection where strategy and technology meet. The business landscape is littered with the corpses of firms killed by managers who guessed wrong.

Developing strong strategic thinking skills is a career-long pursuit—a subject that can occupy tomes of text, a roster of courses, and a lifetime of seminars. While this chapter can't address the breadth of strategic thought, it is meant as a primer on developing the skills for strategic thinking about technology. A manager that understands issues presented in this chapter should be able to see through seemingly conflicting assertions about best practices more clearly; be better prepared to recognize opportunities and risks; and be more adept at successfully brainstorming new, tech-centric approaches to markets.

1.1   The Danger of Relying on Technology

sustainable competitive advantage

Financial performance that consistently outperforms industry averages.

Firms strive for **sustainable competitive advantage**, financial performance that consistently outperforms their industry peers. The goal is easy to state, but hard to achieve. The world is so dynamic, with new products and new competitors rising seemingly overnight, that truly sustainable advantage might seem like an impossibility. New competitors and copycat products create a race to cut costs, cut prices, and increase features that may benefit consumers but erode profits industry-wide. Nowhere is this balance more difficult than when competition involves technology. The fundamental strategic question in the Internet era is, "*How can I possibly compete when everyone can copy my technology and the competition is just a click away?*" Put that way, the pursuit of sustainable competitive advantage seems like a lost cause.

But there are winners—big, consistent winners—empowered through their use of technology. How do they do it? In order to think about how to achieve sustainable advantage, it's useful to start with two concepts defined by Michael Porter. A professor at the Harvard Business School and father of the *value chain* and the *five forces* concepts (see the sections later in this chapter), Porter is justifiably considered one of the leading strategic thinkers of our time.

Operational effectiveness

Performing the same tasks better than rivals perform them.

commodity

A basic good that can be interchanged with nearly identical offerings by others--think milk, coal, orange juice, or to a lesser extent, Windows PCs and Android phones. The more commoditized an offering, the greater the likelihood that competition will be based on price.

fast follower problem

Exists when savvy rivals watch a pioneer's efforts, learn from their successes and missteps, then enter the market quickly with a comparable or superior product at a lower cost before the first mover can dominate.

According to Porter, the reason so many firms suffer aggressive, margin-eroding competition is because they've defined themselves according to operational effectiveness rather than strategic positioning. **Operational effectiveness** refers to performing the same tasks better than rivals perform them. Everyone wants to be better, but the danger in operational effectiveness is "sameness." When offerings are roughly the same, they are more **commodity** than differentiated. That often means that competition will focus on offering the lowest price, and this can pull down profits for all players that consumers see as basically equivalent in features. This risk is particularly acute in firms that rely on technology for competitiveness. After all, technology can be easily acquired. Buy the same stuff as your rivals, hire students from the same schools, copy the look and feel of competitor websites, reverse engineer their products, and you can match them. The **fast follower problem** exists when savvy rivals watch a pioneer's efforts, learn from their successes and missteps, then enter the market quickly with a comparable or superior product at a lower cost.

Since tech can be copied so quickly, followers can be fast, indeed. Groupon founder Andrew Mason claimed the daily deal service had spawned 500 imitators within two years of launch,[1] and venture capitalist Ben Evans notes that at the time of Facebook's WhatsApp purchase, there were over fifty social apps in the Google Play store with over 1 million downloads each.[2] When technology can be matched so quickly, it is rarely a source of competitive advantage. And this phenomenon isn't limited to the Web.

Consider TiVo. At first blush, it looks like this first mover should be a winner since it seems to have established a leading brand; TiVo is now a verb for digitally recording TV broadcasts. But despite this, TiVo has largely been a money loser for most of its life, going years without posting an annual profit. By the time 1.5 million TiVos had been sold, there were over thirty million digital video recorders (DVRs) in use.[3] Rival devices offered by cable and satellite companies appear the same to consumers and are offered along with pay television subscriptions—a critical distribution channel for reaching customers that TiVo doesn't control.

The Flip video camera is another example of technology alone offering little durable advantage. The pocket-sized video recorders used flash memory instead of magnetic storage. Flip cameras grew so popular that Cisco bought Flip parent Pure Digital, for $590 million. The problem was digital video features were easy to copy, and constantly falling technology costs (see Chapter 5) allowed rivals to embed video into their products. Later that same year Apple (and other firms) began including video capture as a feature in their music players and phones. Why carry a Flip when one pocket device can do everything? The Flip business barely lasted two years. Cisco killed the division, taking a more than half-billion-dollar spanking in the process.[4]

strategic positioning

Performing different tasks than rivals, or the same tasks in a different way.

Operational effectiveness is critical. Firms must invest in techniques to improve quality, lower cost, and design efficient customer experiences. But for the most part, these efforts can be matched. Because of this, operational effectiveness is usually not sufficient enough to yield sustainable dominance over the competition. In contrast to operational effectiveness, **strategic positioning** refers to performing different activities from those of rivals, or the same activities in a different way. Technology itself is often very easy to replicate, and those assuming advantage lies in technology alone may find themselves in a profit-eroding arms race with rivals able to match their moves step by step. But while technology can be copied, technology can also play a critical role in creating and strengthening strategic *differences*—advantages that rivals will struggle to match.

1.2   Different Is Good: FreshDirect Redefines the Grocery Landscape in New York City and Beyond

For an example of the relationship between technology and strategic positioning, consider FreshDirect. The New York City-based grocery firm focused on the two most pressing problems for Big Apple shoppers: selection is limited and prices are high. Both of these problems are a function of the high cost of real estate in New York. The solution? Use technology to craft an ultraefficient model that makes an end-run around stores.

The firm's "storefront" is a website offering a product mix heavy on fresh produce, as well as one-click menus and semiprepared specials like "meals in four minutes." The ability to pull up prior grocery orders fuels fast reorders, and a mobile app eliminates the need for a grocery list. Enter order items as you think of them, then click a button to schedule next-day delivery. All these features appeal to the time-strapped Manhattanites who were the firm's first customers. Area shoppers—many of whom don't have cars or are keen to avoid the traffic-snarled streets of the city—were quick to embrace the model. The service is now so popular that apartment buildings in New York have begun to redesign common areas to include secure freezers that can accept FreshDirect deliveries, even when customers aren't there.[5]

Deliveries set out from a vast warehouse the size of five football fields located in a lower-rent industrial area of Queens. A new facility planned for the Bronx will double the firm's capacity. This kind of size allows FreshDirect to offer a fresh goods selection that's over five times larger than local supermarkets. And a bigger facility allows FreshDirect to service more customers, too. The firm has expanded service to ninety zip codes in New York, New Jersey, and Pennsylvania.[6]

FIGURE 2.1   The FreshDirect Website and the Firm's Tech-Enabled Warehouse Operation

Source: Used with permission from FreshDirect. See the photographic tour at the FreshDirect website, http://www.freshdirect.com/about/index.jsp?siteAccessPage=c_aboutus.

The FreshDirect model crushes costs that plague traditional grocers. Worker shifts are highly efficient, avoiding the downtime lulls and busy rush hour spikes of storefronts. The result? Labor costs that are 60 percent lower than at traditional grocers. FreshDirect buys and prepares what it sells, leading to less waste. Waste is otherwise a big risk among grocers, which often throw out one in seven truckloads of food delivered to stores.[7] At FreshDirect, food waste is only about 1 percent, an advantage that the firm claims is "worth 5 percentage points of total revenue in terms of savings."[8] Overall perishable inventory at FreshDirect turns 197 times a year versus 40 times a year at traditional grocers.[9] Higher **inventory turns** mean the firm is selling product faster, so it collects money quicker than its rivals do. And those goods are fresher since they've been in stock for less time, too. Consider that while the average grocer may have seven to nine days of seafood inventory, FreshDirect's seafood stock turns each day. Stock is typically purchased direct from the docks in order to fulfill orders placed less than twenty-four hours earlier.[10] Cofounder David McInerney maintains that FreshDirect's super-fast "farm-to-fork" supply chain also allows food to be harvested for optimal freshness, yielding taste that far outpaces the competition.[11] The firm goes a step beyond conventional grocery stores by regularly evaluating product taste and sharing these results with customers. Every day, teams inspect and sample between 400 and 500 items. The ratings (from one to five) that accompany produce on the website help consumers make more informed shopping decisions than by a trip to the local market.[12]

Artificial intelligence software, coupled with some seven miles of fiber-optic cables linking systems and sensors, supports everything from baking the perfect baguette to verifying orders with 99.9 percent accuracy.[13] Since it doesn't need the money-sucking open-air refrigerators of the retail store competition, the firm even saves big on energy (instead, staff bundle up for shifts in climate-controlled cold rooms tailored to the specific needs of dairy, deli, and produce). The firm also uses recycled biodiesel fuel to cut down on delivery costs. Customers who would otherwise drive to the grocery store can also

inventory turns

Sometimes referred to as inventory turnover, stock turns, or stock turnover. It is the number of times inventory is sold or used during a given period. A higher figure means that a firm is selling products quickly.

feel green about their decision to order online. One study suggests delivery trucks produce 20 to 70 percent less emissions than trips made in personal vehicles.[14]

FreshDirect buys directly from suppliers, eliminating middlemen wherever possible. The firm also offers suppliers several benefits beyond traditional grocers, all in exchange for more favorable terms. These include offering to carry a greater selection of supplier products while eliminating the "slotting fees" (payments by suppliers for prime shelf space) common in traditional retail, cobranding products to help establish and strengthen supplier brand, paying partners in days rather than weeks, and sharing data to help improve supplier sales and operations. Add all these advantages together and the firm's big, fresh selection is offered at prices that can undercut the competition by as much as 35 percent.[15] And FreshDirect does it all with margins in the range of 20 percent (to as high as 45 percent on many semiprepared meals), easily dwarfing the razor-thin 1 percent margins earned by traditional grocers.[16]

FreshDirect's customer base has ballooned to over 600,000 paying customers. That's a population roughly the size of metro-Boston, serviced by a single grocer with no physical store. The privately held firm has been solidly profitable for several years. Even during the recent recession, the firm's CEO described earnings as "pretty spectacular."[17] Annual are estimated at roughly $500 million.[18]

Technology is critical to the FreshDirect model, but it's the collective impact of the firm's differences when compared to rivals, this tech-enabled strategic positioning, that delivers success. Over time, the firm has also built up a set of strategic assets that not only address specific needs of a market but are now extremely difficult for any upstart to compete against. Traditional grocers can't fully copy the firm's delivery business because this would leave them **straddling** two markets (low-margin storefront and high-margin delivery), unable to gain optimal benefits from either. Entry costs for would-be competitors are also high (the firm spent over $75 million building infrastructure before it could serve a single customer), and the firm's complex and highly customized software, which handles everything from delivery scheduling to orchestrating the preparation of thousands of recipes, continues to be refined and improved each year.[19] On top of all this comes years of relationship building with suppliers, as well as customer data used to further refine processes, speed reorders, and make helpful recommendations. Competing against a firm with such a strong and tough-to-match strategic position can be brutal. Just five years after launch there were one-third fewer supermarkets in New York City than when FreshDirect first opened for business.[20]

straddling

Attempts to occupy more than one position, while failing to match the benefits of a more efficient, singularly focused rival.

Better than Grocers, but Other Rivals?

The FreshDirect model is superior to conventional grocery stores in just about every way, and the firm has devastated the competition while delivering on quality, selection, and value. However, one threat successful firms face is the potential entry of even better-funded, growth-seeking rivals to try to squeeze them out of the current market. For years, the king of e-commerce, Amazon, has had its eye on tapping the $700 billion market for grocery retail. The firm has been refining its AmazonFresh service in its hometown in Seattle, and has been slowly expanding it to other cities. Amazon has recently shown up in FreshDirect's backyard, buying a massive Northern New Jersey distribution center formerly owned by grocer PathMark. Estimates suggest the facility may be able to move ten times the dollar volume of FreshDirect's new Bronx distribution center.[21] Amazon also offers same-day delivery free to AmazonPrime subscribers. Even more troubling: many delivery items are cheaper from AmazonFresh than from FreshDirect (a firm once known for its low prices, but now seen as a premium price for premium quality supplier). And AmazonFresh can also deliver many of the non-grocery items you can order on Amazon's main website, too.[22] There are other players in the market, too, including Instacart, which leverages a network of Uber-style contract delivery workers to pick groceries from popular retailers that include Whole Foods and Costco. Google offers a similar service, known as Google Express.

Early reviews of AmazonFresh in New York City have criticized the firm for a poor online shopping experience and an uneven selection,[23] these are problems a well-funded and patient giant may be able to iron out over time. It's unclear if FreshDirect's initial advantages will hold up over time, but executives seem confident. Says FreshDirect's CEO: "In a $700 billion industry, there's plenty of space for a lot of different people to play. [The firm] is doing spectacularly, and we continue to see strong growth in this environment."[24]

1.3 But What Kinds of Differences?

The principles of operational effectiveness and strategic positioning are deceptively simple. But while Porter claims strategy is "fundamentally about being different,"[25] how can you recognize whether your firm's differences are special enough to yield sustainable competitive advantage?

An approach known as the **resource-based view of competitive advantage** can help. The idea here is that if a firm is to maintain sustainable competitive advantage, it must control a set of exploitable resources that have four critical characteristics. These resources must be (1) *valuable*, (2) *rare*, (3) *imperfectly imitable* (tough to imitate), and (4) *nonsubstitutable*. Having all four characteristics is key. Miss value and no one cares what you've got. Without rareness, you don't have something unique. If others can copy what you have, or others can replace it with a substitute, then any seemingly advantageous differences will be undercut.

Strategy isn't just about recognizing opportunity and meeting demand. Resource-based thinking can help you avoid the trap of carelessly entering markets simply because growth is spotted. The telecommunications industry learned this lesson in a very hard and painful way. With the explosion of the Internet it was easy to see that demand to transport Web pages, e-mails, MP3s, video, and everything else you can turn into ones and zeros, was skyrocketing.

Most of what travels over the Internet is transferred over long-haul fiber-optic cables, so telecom firms began digging up the ground and laying webs of fiberglass to meet the growing demand. Problems resulted because firms laying long-haul fiber didn't fully appreciate that their rivals and new upstart firms were doing the exact same thing. By one estimate there was enough fiber laid to stretch from the Earth to the moon some 280 times![26] On top of that, a technology called **dense wave division multiplexing (DWDM)** enabled existing fiber to carry more transmissions than ever before. The end result: these new assets weren't rare and each day they seemed to be less valuable.

For some firms, the transmission prices they charged on newly laid cable collapsed by over 90 percent. Established firms struggled, upstarts went under, and WorldCom became the biggest bankruptcy in US history. The impact was also felt throughout all industries that supplied the telecom industry. Firms like Sun, Lucent, and Nortel, whose sales growth relied on big sales to telecom carriers, saw their value tumble as orders dried up. Estimates suggest that the telecommunications industry lost nearly $4 trillion in value in just three years,[27] much of it due to executives that placed big bets on resources that weren't strategic.

resource-based view of competitive advantage

The strategic thinking approach suggesting that if a firm is to maintain sustainable competitive advantage, it must control an exploitable resource, or set of resources, that have four critical characteristics. These resources must be (1) valuable, (2) rare, (3) imperfectly imitable, and (4) nonsubstitutable.

dense wave division multiplexing (DWDM)

A technology that increases the transmission capacity (and hence speed) of fiber-optic cable. Transmissions using fiber are accomplished by transmitting light inside "glass" cables. In DWDM, the light inside fiber is split into different wavelengths in a way similar to how a prism splits light into different colors.

KEY TAKEAWAYS

- Technology can be easy to copy, and technology alone rarely offers sustainable advantage.
- Firms that leverage technology for strategic positioning use technology to create competitive assets or ways of doing business that are difficult for others to copy.
- True sustainable advantage comes from assets and business models that are simultaneously valuable, rare, difficult to imitate, and for which there are no substitutes.

QUESTIONS AND EXERCISES

1. What is operational effectiveness?
2. What is strategic positioning?
3. Is a firm that competes based on the features of technology engaged in operational effectiveness or strategic positioning? Give an example to back up your claim.
4. What are the dangers of competing on operational effectiveness? Are firms more likely to be considered commodities or differentiated offerings? How would you describe the basis for consumer decision-making when evaluating products that are highly similar?
5. What is the "resource-based" view of competitive advantage? What are the characteristics of resources that may yield sustainable competitive advantage?
6. TiVo has a great brand. Why hasn't it profitably dominated the market for digital video recorders?
7. Examine the FreshDirect business model and list reasons for its competitive advantage. Would a similar business work in your neighborhood? Why or why not?
8. What effect did FreshDirect have on traditional grocers operating in New York City? Why?
9. Choose a technology-based company. Discuss its competitive advantage based on the resources it controls.
10. Use the resource-based view of competitive advantage to explain the collapse of many telecommunications firms in the period following the burst of the dot-com bubble.
11. Consider the examples of Barnes & Noble competing with Amazon, and Apple offering iTunes. Are either (or both) of these efforts straddling? Why or why not?

2. POWERFUL RESOURCES

LEARNING OBJECTIVES

1. Understand that technology is often critical to enabling competitive advantage, and provide examples of firms that have used technology to organize for sustained competitive advantage.
2. Understand the value chain concept and be able to examine and compare how various firms organize to bring products and services to market.
3. Recognize the role technology can play in crafting an imitation-resistant value chain, as well as when technology choice may render potentially strategic assets less effective.
4. Define the following concepts: brand, scale, data and switching cost assets, differentiation, network effects, and distribution channels.
5. Understand and provide examples of how technology can be used to create or strengthen the resources mentioned above.

Management has no magic bullets. There is no exhaustive list of key resources that firms can look to in order to build a sustainable business. And recognizing a resource doesn't mean a firm will be able to acquire it or exploit it forever. But being aware of major sources of competitive advantage can help managers recognize an organization's opportunities and vulnerabilities, and can help them brainstorm winning strategies. And these assets rarely exist in isolation. Oftentimes, a firm with an effective strategic position can create an arsenal of assets that reinforce one another, creating advantages that are particularly difficult for rivals to successfully challenge.

2.1 Imitation-Resistant Value Chains

imitation-resistant value chain

A way of doing business that competitors struggle to replicate and that frequently involves technology in a key enabling role.

value chain

The set of activities through which a product or service is created and delivered to customers.

While many of the resources below are considered in isolation, the strength of any advantage can be far more significant if firms are able to leverage several of these resources in a way that makes each stronger and makes the firm's way of doing business more difficult for rivals to match. Firms that craft an **imitation-resistant value chain** have developed a way of doing business that others will struggle to replicate, and in nearly every successful effort of this kind, technology plays a key enabling role. The **value chain** is the set of interrelated activities that bring products or services to market (see below). When we compare FreshDirect's value chain to traditional rivals, there are differences across every element. But most importantly, the elements in FreshDirect's value chain work together to create and reinforce competitive advantages that others cannot easily copy. Incumbents trying to copy the firm would be *straddled* across two business models, unable to reap the full advantages of either. And late-moving pure-play rivals will struggle, as FreshDirect's lead time allows the firm to develop brand, scale, data, and other advantages that newcomers lack (see below for more on these resources).

Key Framework: The Value Chain

The *value chain* is the "set of activities through which a product or service is created and delivered to customers."[28] There are five primary components of the value chain and four supporting components. The primary components are:

- *Inbound logistics*—getting needed materials and other inputs into the firm from suppliers
- *Operations*—turning inputs into products or services
- *Outbound logistics*—delivering products or services to consumers, distribution centers, retailers, or other partners
- *Marketing and sales*—customer engagement, pricing, promotion, and transaction
- *Support*—service, maintenance, and customer support

The secondary components are:

- *Firm infrastructure*—functions that support the whole firm, including general management, planning, IS, and finance
- *Human resource management*—recruiting, hiring, training, and development
- *Technology / research and development*—new product and process design
- *Procurement*—sourcing and purchasing functions

While the value chain is typically depicted as it's displayed in the figure below, goods and information don't necessarily flow in a line from one function to another. For example, an order taken by the marketing function can trigger an inbound logistics function to get components from a supplier, operations functions (to build a product if it's not available), or outbound logistics functions (to ship a product when it's available). Similarly, information from service support can be fed back to advise research and development (R&D) in the design of future products.

FIGURE 2.2 The Value Chain

When a firm has an imitation-resistant value chain—one that's tough for rivals to copy in a way that yields similar benefits—then a firm may have a critical competitive asset. From a strategic perspective, managers can use the value chain framework to consider a firm's differences and distinctiveness compared to rivals. If a firm's value chain can't be copied by competitors without engaging in painful trade-offs, or if the firm's value chain helps to create and strengthen other strategic assets over time, it can be a key source for competitive advantage. Many of the examples used in this book, including FreshDirect, Amazon, and Zara, illustrate this point.

An analysis of a firm's value chain can also reveal operational weaknesses, and technology is often of great benefit to improving the speed and quality of execution. Firms can often buy software to improve things, and tools such as *supply chain management* (SCM; linking inbound and outbound logistics with operations), *customer relationship management* (CRM; supporting sales, marketing, and in some cases R&D), and *enterprise resource planning* software (ERP; software implemented in modules to automate the entire value chain), can have a big impact on more efficiently integrating the activities within the firm, as well as with its suppliers and customers. But remember, these software tools can be purchased by competitors, too. While valuable, such software may not yield lasting competitive advantage if it can be easily matched by competitors as well.

There's potential danger here. If a firm adopts software that changes a unique process into a generic one, it may have co-opted a key source of competitive advantage particularly if other firms can buy the same stuff. This isn't a problem with something like accounting software. Accounting processes are standardized and accounting isn't a source of competitive advantage, so most firms buy rather than build their own accounting software. But using packaged, third-party SCM, CRM, and ERP software typically requires adopting a very specific way of doing things, using software and methods that can be purchased and adopted by others. Many of the firms covered in this text, including Netflix and Amazon, have elected to develop their own proprietary software solutions in large part because they see their uniqueness in certain operations as key to creating difficult-to-imitate competitive advantages.

Dell's Struggles: Nothing Lasts Forever

Michael Dell enjoyed an extended run that took him from assembling PCs in his dorm room as an undergraduate at the University of Texas at Austin to heading the largest PC firm on the planet. For years Dell's supereffcient, vertically integrated manufacturing (where it built its own PCs rather than outsourcing manufacturing like nearly all other competitors) and direct-to-consumer sales combined to help the firm earn seven times more profit on its own systems when compared with comparably configured rival PCs.[29] And since Dell PCs were usually cheaper, too, the firm could often start a price war and still have better overall margins than rivals.

It was a brilliant model that for years proved resistant to imitation. While Dell sold direct to consumers, rivals had to share a cut of sales with the less efficient retail chains responsible for the majority of their sales. Dell's rivals struggled in moving toward direct sales because any retailer sensing its suppliers were competing with it through a direct-sales effort could easily choose another supplier that sold a nearly identical product. It wasn't that HP, IBM, Sony, and so many others didn't see the advantage of Dell's model—these firms were wedded to models that made it difficult for them to copy Dell.

private

As in "to go private" or "take a firm private." Buying up a publicly traded firm's shares. Usually done when a firm has suffered financially and when a turn-around strategy will first yield losses that would further erode share price. Firms (often called *private equity*, *buyout*, *LBO*, or *leveraged buyout firms*) that take another company private hope to improve results so that the company can be sold to another firm or they can reissue shares on public markets.

But then Dell's killer model, one that had become a staple case study in business schools worldwide, began to lose steam. Nearly two decades of observing Dell had allowed the contract manufacturers serving Dell's rivals to improve manufacturing efficiency.[30] Component suppliers located near contract manufacturers, and assembly times fell dramatically. And as the cost of computing fell, the price advantage Dell enjoyed over rivals also shrank in absolute terms. That meant savings from buying a Dell weren't as big as they once were. On top of that, the direct-to-consumer model also suffered when sales of notebook PCs outpaced the more commoditized desktop market. Notebooks can be considered to be more differentiated than desktops, and customers often want to compare products in person—lift them, type on keyboards, and view screens—before making a purchase decision.

In time, these shifts knocked Dell from its ranking as the world's number one PC manufacturer. Dell has even abandoned its direct-only business model and now also sells products through third-party brick-and-mortar retailers. The firm has fallen on such hard times that management has "taken the firm **private**," working with investors (that include Michael Dell himself) to buy up all of Dell's publicly-traded stock. Going private removes the relentless stock market punishment of Dell shares from continued bad quarterly results as executives try to find a path to recovery.[31] Dell's struggles as computers, customers, and the product mix changed all underscore the importance of continually assessing a firm's strategic position among changing market conditions. There is no guarantee that today's winning strategy will dominate forever.

2.2 Brand

A firm's **brand** is the symbolic embodiment of all the information connected with a product or service, and a strong brand can also be an exceptionally powerful resource for competitive advantage. Consumers use brands to *lower search costs*, so having a strong brand is particularly vital for firms hoping to be the first online stop for consumers. Want to buy a book online? Auction a product? Search for information? Which firm would you visit first? Almost certainly Amazon, eBay, or Google. But how do you build a strong brand? It's *not* just about advertising and promotion. First and foremost, customer experience counts. A strong brand *proxies quality* and *inspires trust*, so if consumers can't rely on a firm to deliver as promised, they'll go elsewhere. As an upside, tech can play a critical role in rapidly and cost-effectively strengthening a brand. If a firm performs well, consumers can often be enlisted to promote a product or service (so-called **viral marketing**). Firms that grew to gargantuan size before committing any substantial investment on advertising include Google, Hotmail, Skype, eBay, Facebook, LinkedIn, Twitter, and YouTube. Social services like Facebook and Twitter are viral marketing machines. Instagram, Pinterest, and Spotify are just some of the firms that have built thriving businesses with millions of followers by increasing its public awareness through social sharing. Early customer accolades for a novel service often mean that positive press (a kind of free advertising) will also likely follow.

But show up late and you may end up paying much more to counter an incumbent's place in the consumer psyche. Google's brand is so strong that it has become a verb, and the cost to challenge it is astonishingly high. Yahoo! and Microsoft's Bing each spent $100 million on Google-challenging branding campaigns, but the early results of these efforts seemed to do little to grow share at Google's expense.[32] Branding is difficult, but if done well, even complex tech products can establish themselves as killer brands. Consider that Intel has taken an ingredient product that most people don't understand, the microprocessor, and built a quality-conveying name recognized by computer users worldwide.

2.3 Scale

Many firms gain advantages as they grow in size. Advantages related to a firm's size are referred to as **scale advantages**. Businesses benefit from **economies of scale** when the cost of an investment can be spread across increasing units of production or in serving a growing customer base. Firms that benefit from scale economies as they grow are sometimes referred to as being *scalable*. Many Internet and tech-leveraging businesses are highly scalable since, as firms grow to serve more customers with their existing infrastructure investment, profit margins improve dramatically.

Consider that in just one year, the Internet firm BlueNile sold as many diamond rings with just 115 employees and one Web site as a traditional jewelry retailer would sell through 116 stores.[33] And with lower operating costs, BlueNile can sell at prices that brick-and-mortar stores can't match, thereby attracting more customers and further fueling its scale advantages. Profit margins improve as the cost to run the firm's single Web site and operate its one warehouse is spread across increasing jewelry sales.

A growing firm may also gain *bargaining power with its suppliers or buyers*. Apple's dominance of smartphone and tablet markets has allowed the firm to lock up 60 percent of the world's supply of advanced touch-screen displays, and to do so with better pricing than would be available to smaller rivals.[34] Similarly, for years eBay could raise auction fees because of the firm's market dominance. Auction sellers who left eBay lost pricing power since fewer bidders on smaller, rival services meant lower prices.

The scale of technology investment required to run a business can also act as a barrier to entry, discouraging new, smaller competitors. Intel's size allows the firm to pioneer cutting-edge manufacturing techniques and invest $7 billion on next-generation plants.[35] And although Google was started by two Stanford students with borrowed computer equipment running in a dorm room, the firm today runs on an estimated 1.4 million servers.[36] The investments being made by Intel and Google would be cost-prohibitive for almost any newcomer to justify.

2.4 Switching Costs and Data

Switching costs exist when consumers incur an expense to move from one product or service to another. Tech firms often benefit from strong switching costs that cement customers to their firms. Users invest their time learning a product, entering data into a system, creating files, and buying supporting programs or manuals. These investments may make them reluctant to switch to a rival's effort.

Similarly, firms that seem dominant but that don't have high switching costs can be rapidly trumped by strong rivals. Netscape once controlled more than 80 percent of the market share in Web browsers, but when Microsoft began bundling Internet Explorer with the Windows operating system and (through an alliance) with America Online (AOL), Netscape's market share plummeted. Customers migrated with a mouse click as part of an upgrade or installation. Learning a new browser was a breeze, and with the Web's open standards, most customers noticed no difference when visiting their favorite Web sites with their new browser.

> **switching costs**
>
> The cost a consumer incurs when moving from one product to another. It can involve actual money spent (e.g., buying a new product) as well as investments in time, any data loss, and so forth.

Sources of Switching Costs

- Learning costs: Switching technologies may require an investment in learning a new interface and commands.
- Information and data: Users may have to reenter data, convert files or databases, or may even lose earlier contributions on incompatible systems.
- Financial commitment: Can include investments in new equipment, the cost to acquire any new software, consulting, or expertise, and the devaluation of any investment in prior technologies no longer used.
- Contractual commitments: Breaking contracts can lead to compensatory damages and harm an organization's reputation as a reliable partner.
- Search costs: Finding and evaluating a new alternative costs time and money.
- Loyalty programs: Switching can cause customers to lose out on program benefits. Think frequent purchaser programs that offer "miles" or "points" (all enabled and driven by software).[37]

It is critical for challengers to realize that in order to win customers away from a rival, a new entrant must not only demonstrate to consumers that an offering provides more value than the incumbent, they have to ensure that their value added exceeds the incumbent's value *plus* any perceived customer switching costs (see Figure 2.3). If it's going to cost you and be inconvenient, there's no way you're going to leave unless the benefits are overwhelming.

Data can be a particularly strong switching cost for firms leveraging technology. A customer who enters her profile into Facebook, movie preferences into Netflix, or grocery list into FreshDirect may be unwilling to try rivals—even if these firms are cheaper or offer more features—if moving to the new firm means she'll lose information feeds, recommendations, and time savings provided by the firms that already know her well. Fueled by scale over time, firms that have more customers and have been in business longer can gather more data, and many can use this data to improve their value chain by offering more accurate demand forecasting or product recommendations.

FIGURE 2.3

In order to win customers from an established incumbent, a late-entering rival must offer a product or service that not only exceeds the value offered by the incumbent but also exceeds the incumbent's value and any customer switching costs.

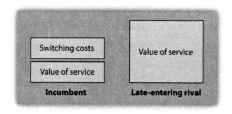

2.5 Differentiation

Commodities are products or services that are nearly identically offered from multiple vendors. Consumers buying commodities are highly price-focused since they have so many similar choices. In order to break the commodity trap, many firms leverage technology to *differentiate* their goods and services. Data is not only a switching cost, it also plays a critical role in differentiation. Each time a visitor returns to Amazon, the firm uses browsing records, purchase patterns, and product ratings to present a custom home page featuring products that the firm hopes the visitor will like. Customers value the experience they receive at Amazon so much that the firm received the highest score ever recorded on the University of Michigan's American Customer Satisfaction Index (ACSI). The score was not just the highest performance of any online firm; it was the highest ranking that any service firm in any industry had ever received.

Apple is another firm that has distinguished itself through differentiation. Unlike rival offerings from Microsoft and Google, Apple mobile and computer operating systems only run on Apple hardware. This allows the firm to tightly integrate the experience across Apple products. Apple systems consistently receive high customer satisfaction ratings,[38] are considered easier to use, are more secure, and have fewer privacy issues.[39] While Apple's market share in computer operating systems is less than Microsoft Windows, and Apple's worldwide smartphone market share is less than Google's Android, Apple's differentiation (and the ability to avoid price-eroding, commodity-based competition of other hardware rivals) has helped make Tim Cook's firm the most profitable company in the United States.[40] Consider that in recent years, nine out of ten premium priced PCs sold in the United States are Macs[41] ; and with the iPhone, Apple takes in an astonishing 92 percent of smartphone industry profits.[42]

2.6 Network Effects

network effects

Also known as Metcalfe's Law, or network externalities. When the value of a product or service increases as its number of users expands.

Facebook is by far the most dominant social network worldwide. Microsoft Windows has a 90 percent market share in operating systems. EBay has an 80 percent share of online auctions. Why are these firms so dominant? Largely due to the concept of **network effects** (see Chapter 8). Network effects (sometimes called *network externalities* or *Metcalfe's Law*) exist when a product or service becomes more valuable as more people use it. If you're the first person with a Facebook account, then Facebook isn't very valuable. But with each additional user, there's one more person to communicate with. A firm with a big network of users might also see value added by third parties. Apple's iOS devices (the iPhone, iPod touch, and iPad) and Google's Android dominate rivals from Microsoft and Blackberry in part because Apple and Google have tens of thousands more apps that run on and enhance these devices, and most of these apps are provided by firms other than Apple and Google. Third-party add-on products, books, magazines, or even skilled labor are all attracted to networks of the largest number of users, making dominant products even more valuable.

Switching costs also play a role in determining the strength of network effects. Tech user investments often go far beyond simply the cost of acquiring a technology. Users spend time learning a product; they buy add-ons, create files, and enter preferences. Because no one wants to be stranded with an abandoned product and lose this additional investment, users may choose a technically inferior product simply because the product has a larger user base and is perceived as having a greater chance of being offered in the future. The virtuous cycle of network effects[43] doesn't apply to all tech products, and it can be a particularly strong asset for firms that can control and leverage a leading standard (think Apple's iPhone and iPad with their closed systems versus the once-dominant but now rarely used Netscape browser, which was almost entirely based on open standards), but in some cases where network effects are significant, they can create winners so dominant that firms with these advantages enjoy a near-monopoly hold on a market.

Open Table: Network Effects That Fill Restaurants Seats

Network effects earned through making a market more efficient, are at the center of OpenTable's dominance in restaurant reservations. By getting in between restaurants and their customers, and adding lots of value along the way, OpenTable has built the world's largest online restaurant reservation system, one so dominant it is effectively a monopoly. OpenTable can get you a reservation at over 32,000 restaurants worldwide[44] (as recently as 2013, its largest US rival had only 1,000), and the firm handles roughly ninety nine percent of all online reservations in North America.[45]

The system delivers high value to the industry by exposing inventory and lowering search costs, thereby reducing frustration. Customers are attracted to the service that has the most restaurants, and restaurants are attracted to the service with the most customers. Strategists call this a *two-sided market*, and the strong network effects that result often crown one clear winner ahead of all other competitors. OpenTable's captive audience of restaurants and diners effectively creates a new *distribution channel* for introducing all sorts of additional value-added services, including loyalty programs to encourage repeat use and payments to lower customer wait times and free up more table inventory. The firm's industry dominance is so complete that Priceline Group (a firm that also includes over half a dozen brands, including Booking.com, RentalCars.com, and Kayak.com in addition to Priceline.com) offered $2.6 billion to acquire the firm.[46]

FIGURE 2.4

Roughly half of all reservations are made from the firm's mobile apps. Network Effects make OpenTable the first place diners go to for reservations. It is also the first choice for restaurants seeking diners. This dynamic helped the firm build a business valued at over $2.6 billion.

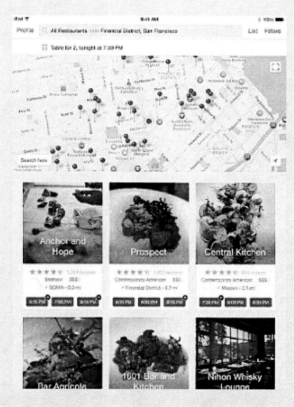

Source: Open Table

2.7 Distribution Channels

If no one sees your product, then it won't even get considered by consumers. So **distribution channels**—the path through which products or services get to customers—can be critical to a firm's success.

Apple Stores show firm-crafted retail distribution channels at their most effective. As mentioned earlier, one of Apple's key competitive strengths lies in the firm's differentiation vs. rival products, however firms offering highly differentiated offerings may face difficulty convincing potential customers of a product's unfamiliar benefits. Apple gear at a Best Buy might face price or simple feature checklist comparisons. However, Apple products offered at the Apple store give firm-trained employees an opportunity to present advantages of the company's unique products, how they work together, and offer free on-site customer support. While many in the business press thought the Apple store would be a dismal failure (it was introduced at a time when PC maker Gateway was shuttering its own failed retail experiment),[47] for Apple this formula has resulted in the single most successful retail chain in the United States on a sales-per-square-foot basis. Apple Store sales dwarf not just consumer electronics categories, but also clothing retailers, high-end jewelers, and every other store regardless of category.[48]

distribution channels

The path through which products or services get to customers.

TABLE 2.1 Top Retailers: Sales per Square Foot[49]

Rank	Firm	Sales / Sq. Ft.
1	Apple Stores	$4,798.82
2	Tiffany & Co.	$3,132.20
3	Michael Kors	$1,895.65
4	Lululemon Athletica	$1,675.16
5	Kate Spade	$1,558.00
6	Coach	$1,416.52
7	Kay Jewelers	$1,035.42
8	Tumi (travel goods)	$1,030.00
9	Costco	$1,032.00
10	Select Comfort (beds)	$1,023.07

Source: Fortune US retailers ranked by sales per square foot

Being dependent on distribution channels provided by other firms can present challenges if distribution partners suddenly decide to cut you off. When the iPhone was introduced, Google was Apple's exclusive map provider. However, Apple eventually launched its own map service, kicking out Google as a default option and relegating it to an iOS also-ran. Two years after the change, fewer than one in six iOS users had installed the Google Maps app on their devices, even though Apple's mapping product was initially considered inferior.[50] The ability to distribute products by bundling them with existing offerings can be a key advantage. But beware: sometimes these distribution channels can provide firms with such an edge that international regulators have stepped in to try to provide a more level playing field. European regulators have forced Microsoft to unbundle the firm's own Web browser and media player from Windows, and Google is also being fined for allegedly favoring its own products in search over those provided by rivals.[51]

Technology also opens up opportunities for new ways to reach customers.

Users can be recruited to create new distribution channels for your products and services (usually for a cut of the take). You may have visited Web sites that promote books sold on Amazon. Web site operators do this because Amazon gives them a percentage of all purchases that come in through these links. Amazon now has over one million of these "associates" (the term the firm uses for its **affiliates**), yet it only pays them if a promotion gains a sale. Google similarly receives some 30 percent of its ad revenue not from search ads, but from advertisements distributed within third-party sites ranging from lowly blogs to the *New York Times*.[52]

affiliates

Third parties that promote a product or service, typically in exchange for a cut of any sales.

2.8 What about Patents?

Intellectual property protection can be granted in the form of a patent for those innovations deemed to be useful, novel, and nonobvious. In the United States, technology and (more controversially with certain restrictions) even business models can be patented,[53] typically for periods of twenty years from the date of patent application. Firms that receive patents have some degree of protection from copycats that try to identically mimic their products and methods.

The patent system is often considered to be unfairly stacked against start-ups. US litigation costs in a single patent case average about $5 million,[54] and a few months of patent litigation can be enough to sink an early stage firm. Large firms can also be victims. So-called patent trolls hold intellectual property not with the goal of bringing novel innovations to market but instead in hopes that they can sue or extort large settlements from others. A $612 million settlement paid by Blackberry (at the time known as Research in Motion) to the little-known holding company NTP is often highlighted as an example of the pain trolls can inflict.[55] Litigation threats are pushing rivals to cooperate in patent portfolio acquisition. Apple, EMC, Ericsson, Microsoft, RIM, and Sony pooled resources for a $4.5 billion purchase of some 6,000 patents formally held by the bankrupt telecom equipment firm Nortel.[56]

Even if an innovation is patentable, that doesn't mean that a firm has bulletproof protection. Some patents have been nullified by the courts upon later review (usually because of a successful challenge to the uniqueness of the innovation). Software patents are also widely granted, but notoriously difficult to defend. A unanimous ruling of the US Supreme Court recently ruled that simply taking an existing, well-known business method and simply applying technology to the process is no longer patent eligible.[57] Also, in many cases, coders at competing firms can write substitute algorithms that aren't the same, but accomplish similar tasks. For example, although Google's PageRank search algorithms are fast and efficient, Microsoft, Yahoo! and others now offer their own noninfringing search that presents results with an accuracy that many would consider on par with PageRank. Patents do protect tech-enabled operations innovations at firms like Netflix and Caesars Entertainment Corporation (formerly known as Harrah's), and design innovations like the iPod click wheel. And Microsoft actually earns several times more money from Google's Android (more than a dozen Android manufacturers license technology owned by Microsoft) than it makes off of the Windows Phone.[58] But in a study of the factors that were critical in enabling firms to profit from their innovations, Carnegie Mellon professor Wes Cohen found that patents were only the fifth most important factor. Secrecy, lead time, sales skills, and manufacturing all ranked higher.[59]

KEY TAKEAWAYS

- Technology can play a key role in creating and reinforcing assets for sustainable advantage by enabling an imitation-resistant value chain; strengthening a firm's brand; collecting useful data and establishing switching costs; creating a network effect; creating or enhancing a firm's scale advantage; enabling product or service differentiation; and offering an opportunity to leverage unique distribution channels.
- The value chain can be used to map a firm's efficiency and to benchmark it against rivals, revealing opportunities to use technology to improve processes and procedures. When a firm is resistant to imitation, a superior value chain may yield sustainable competitive advantage.
- Firms may consider adopting packaged software or outsourcing value chain tasks that are not critical to a firm's competitive advantage. A firm should be wary of adopting software packages or outsourcing portions of its value chain that are proprietary and a source of competitive advantage.
- Patents are not necessarily a sure-fire path to exploiting an innovation. Many technologies and business methods can be copied, so managers should think about creating assets like the ones previously discussed if they wish to create truly sustainable advantage.
- Nothing lasts forever, and shifting technologies and market conditions can render once strong assets as obsolete.

QUESTIONS AND EXERCISES

1. Define and diagram the value chain.
2. Discuss the elements of FreshDirect's value chain and the technologies that FreshDirect uses to give the firm a competitive advantage. Why is FreshDirect resistant to imitation from incumbent firms? What advantages does FreshDirect have that insulate the firm from serious competition from start-ups copying its model?
3. Identify two firms in the same industry that have different value chains. Why do you think these firms have different value chains? What role do you think technology plays in the way that each firm competes? Do these differences enable strategic positioning? Why or why not?
4. How can information technology help a firm build a brand inexpensively?
5. Describe BlueNile's advantages over a traditional jewelry chain. Can conventional jewelers successfully copy BlueNile? Why or why not?
6. What are switching costs? What role does technology play in strengthening a firm's switching costs?
7. What are network effects? Name a product or service that has been able to leverage network effects to its advantage.
8. What role did network effects play in your choice of an operating system, a social network, a word processor, or a mobile phone?
9. How can technology be a distribution channel? Name a firm that has tried to leverage its technology as a distribution channel.
10. How does Apple compete with rivals? What competitive assets does the firm leverage when competing against Google, Microsoft, and others?
11. Do you think it is possible to use information technology to achieve competitive advantage? If so, how? If not, why not?
12. What are the potential sources of switching costs if you decide to switch cell phone service providers? Cell phones? Operating systems? PayTV service?
13. Why is an innovation based on technology alone often subjected to intense competition?
14. Can you think of firms that have successfully created competitive advantage even though other firms provide essentially the same thing? What factors enable this success?
15. What can a firm do to prepare for the inevitable expiration of a patent (patents typically expire after twenty years)? Think in terms of the utilization of other assets and the development of advantages through employment of technology.

3. BARRIERS TO ENTRY, TECHNOLOGY, AND TIMING

LEARNING OBJECTIVES

1. **Understand the relationship between timing, technology, and the creation of resources for competitive advantage.**
2. **Argue effectively when faced with broad generalizations about the importance (or lack of importance) of technology and timing to competitive advantage.**
3. **Recognize the difference between low barriers to entry and the prospects for the sustainability of new entrant's efforts.**

Some have correctly argued that the barriers to entry for many tech-centric businesses are low. This argument is particularly true for the Internet where rivals can put up a competing Web site or deploy a rival app seemingly overnight. But it's absolutely critical to understand that market entry is *not* the same as building a sustainable business and just showing up doesn't guarantee survival.

Platitudes like "follow, don't lead"[60] can put firms dangerously at risk, and statements about low entry barriers ignore the difficulty many firms will have in matching the competitive advantages of successful tech pioneers. Should Blockbuster have waited while Netflix pioneered? In a year where Netflix profits were up sevenfold, Blockbuster lost more than $1 billion, and today Blockbuster is bankrupt.[61] Should Sotheby's have dismissed seemingly inferior eBay? Sotheby's made $130 million in 2013, but eBay earned over $2.8 billion. Barnes & Noble waited seventeen months to respond to Amazon. In 2013 Amazon earned $274 million in profits, while Barnes & Noble lost nearly $158 million. Amazon's market cap is over *120 times* greater than Barnes & Noble.[62] Today's Internet giants are winners because in most cases, they were the first to move with a profitable model and they were able to quickly establish resources for competitive advantage. With few exceptions, established offline firms have failed to catch up to today's Internet leaders.

Timing and technology alone will not yield sustainable competitive advantage. Yet both of these can be *enablers* for competitive advantage. Put simply, it's not the time lead or the technology; it's what a firm *does* with its time lead and technology. True strategic positioning means that a firm has created differences that cannot be easily matched by rivals. Moving first pays off when the time lead is used to create critical resources that are valuable, rare, tough to imitate, and lack substitutes. Anything less risks the arms race of operational effectiveness. Build resources like brand, scale, network effects, switching costs, or other key assets and your firm may have a shot. But guess wrong about the market or screw up execution and failure or direct competition awaits. It is true that most tech can be copied—there's little magic in eBay's servers, Intel's processors, Oracle's database software, or Microsoft's operating systems that past rivals have not at one point improved upon. But the lead that each of these tech-enabled firms had was leveraged to create network effects, switching costs, data assets, and helped build solid and well-respected brands.

But Google Arrived Late! Why Incumbents Must Constantly Consider Rivals

Gmail is the dominant e-mail provider today, but it took Google eight years to finally top early leaders Yahoo! Mail and Hotmail. Yahoo! and Hotmail were able to hold onto their lead in e-mail market share for several years after Gmail's introduction, likely because these firms quickly matched and nullified Gmail's most significant tech-based innovation (more free storage) before Google could inflict real damage.[63] Perhaps Yahoo! had learned from prior errors. The firm's earlier failure to respond to Google's emergence as a credible threat in search advertising gave Sergey Brin and Larry Page the time they needed to build the planet's most profitable Internet firm.

By some accounts, Google was actually the twenty first notable firm to enter the Internet search market.[64] Yahoo! (and many Wall Street analysts) saw search as a commodity—a service the firm had subcontracted out to other firms including Alta Vista and Inktomi. Yahoo! saw no conflict in taking an early investment stake in Google or in using the firm for its search results. But Yahoo! failed to pay attention to Google's advance. As Google's innovations in technology, interface, and advertising remained unmatched over time, this allowed the firm to build its brand, scale, and advertising network (distribution channel) that grew from network effects because content providers and advertisers attract one another. These are all competitive resources that rivals have never been able to match.

Now Google (and Apple, too) are once again running from this playbook—turning the smartphone software market into what increasingly looks like a two-horse race. Many rivals, including Microsoft, had been trying to create a mobile standard for years, but their technical innovations offered little durable strategic value. It wasn't until app stores flourished, offered with a high-quality user experience, that dominant smartphone platforms emerged. Yes, Google and Apple arrived late, but nothing before them had created defensible strategic assets, and that left an opening.

Google's ability to succeed after being late to the search and mobile party isn't a sign of the power of the late mover; it's a story about the failure of incumbents to monitor their competitive landscape, recognize new rivals, and react to challenging offerings. That doesn't mean that incumbents need to respond to every potential threat. Indeed, figuring out which threats are worthy of response is the real skill here. Video rental chain Hollywood Video wasted over $300 million in an Internet streaming business years before high-speed broadband was available to make the effort work.[65] But while Blockbuster avoided the balance sheet–cratering gaffes of Hollywood Video, the firm also failed to respond to Netflix—a new threat that had timed market entry perfectly (see Chapter 4).

Firms that quickly get to market with the "right" model can dominate, but it's equally critical for leading firms to pay close attention to competition and innovate in ways that customers value. Take your eye off the ball and rivals may use time and technology to create strategic resources. Friendster was once known as the largest social network in the United States but has become virtually irrelevant today. And even the heir to social, Facebook, has been tripped up. Zuckerberg's slow-to-execute mobile strategy led to the rise of SnapChat, Instagram, and WhatsApp. Facebook eventually bought the latter two for $1 billion and $19 billion, respectively. Taking your eye off the competition can have a high price, indeed.[66]

KEY TAKEAWAYS

- It doesn't matter if it's easy for new firms to enter a market if these newcomers can't create and leverage the assets needed to challenge incumbents.
- Beware of those who say, "IT doesn't matter" or refer to the "myth" of the first mover. This thinking is overly simplistic. It's not a time or technology lead that provides sustainable competitive advantage; it's what a firm does with its time and technology lead. If a firm can use a time and technology lead to create valuable assets that others cannot match, it may be able to sustain its advantage. But if the work done in this time and technology lead can be easily matched, then no advantage can be achieved, and a firm may be threatened by new entrants.

QUESTIONS AND EXERCISES

1. Does technology lower barriers to entry or raise them? Do low entry barriers necessarily mean that a firm is threatened?
2. Is there such a thing as the first-mover advantage? Why or why not?
3. Why did Google beat Yahoo! in search?
4. A former editor of the *Harvard Business Review*, Nick Carr, once published an article in that same magazine with the title "IT Doesn't Matter." In the article he also offered firms the advice: "Follow, Don't Lead." What would you tell Carr to help him improve the way he thinks about the relationship between time, technology, and competitive advantage?
5. Name an early mover that has successfully defended its position. Name another that had been superseded by the competition. What factors contributed to its success or failure?
6. You have just written a word processing package far superior in features to Microsoft Word. You now wish to form a company to market it. List and discuss the barriers your start-up faces.
7. What kinds of strategic assets are Google's Android and Apple's iOS seeking to create and exploit? Do you think these firms will be more successful than rivals? Why or why not?

4.   KEY FRAMEWORK: THE FIVE FORCES OF INDUSTRY COMPETITIVE ADVANTAGE

LEARNING OBJECTIVES

1. Diagram the five forces of competitive advantage.
2. Apply the framework to an industry, assessing the competitive landscape and the role of technology in influencing the relative power of buyers, suppliers, competitors, and alternatives.

Professor and strategy consultant Gary Hamel once wrote in a *Fortune* cover story that "the dirty little secret of the strategy industry is that it doesn't have any theory of strategy creation."[67] While there is no silver bullet for strategy creation, strategic frameworks help managers describe the competitive environment a firm is facing. Frameworks can also be used as brainstorming tools to generate new ideas for responding to industry competition. If you have a model for thinking about competition, it's easier to understand what's happening and to think creatively about possible solutions.

One of the most popular frameworks for examining a firm's competitive environment is **Porter's five forces**, also known as the *Industry and Competitive Analysis*. As Porter puts it, "analyzing [these] forces illuminates an industry's fundamental attractiveness, exposes the underlying drivers of average industry profitability, and provides insight into how profitability will evolve in the future." The five forces this framework considers are (1) the intensity of rivalry among existing competitors, (2) the threat of new entrants, (3) the threat of substitute goods or services, (4) the bargaining power of buyers, and (5) the bargaining power of suppliers (see Figure 2.5).

Porter's five forces

Also known as Industry and Competitive Analysis. A framework considering the interplay between (1) the intensity of rivalry among existing competitors, (2) the threat of new entrants, (3) the threat of substitute goods or services, (4) the bargaining power of buyers, and (5) the bargaining power of suppliers.

FIGURE 2.5 The Five Forces of Industry and Competitive Analysis

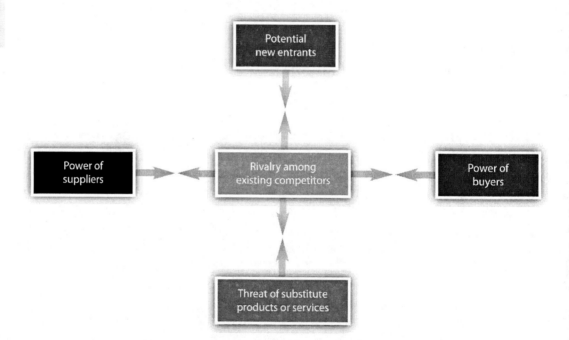

New technologies can create jarring shocks in an industry. Consider how the rise of the Internet has impacted the five forces for music retailers. Traditional music retailers like Tower and Virgin found that customers were seeking music online. These firms scrambled to invest in the new channel out of what is perceived to be a necessity. Their *intensity of rivalry* increases because they not only compete based on the geography of where brick-and-mortar stores are physically located, they now compete online as well. Investments online are expensive and uncertain, prompting some firms to partner with *new entrants* such as Amazon. Free from brick-and-mortar stores, Amazon, the dominant new entrant, has a highly scalable cost structure. And in many ways the online buying experience is superior to what customers saw in stores. Customers can hear samples of almost all tracks, selection is seemingly limitless (the *long tail* phenomenon—see this concept illuminated in Chapter 4), and data is leveraged using *collaborative filtering* software to make product recommendations and assist in music discovery.[68]

Tough competition, but it gets worse because CD sales aren't the only way to consume music. The process of buying a plastic disc now faces *substitutes* as digital music files become available on commercial music sites. Who needs the physical atoms of a CD filled with ones and zeros when you can buy the bits one song at a time? Or don't buy anything and subscribe to a limitless library instead.

From a sound quality perspective, the *substitute good* of digital tracks purchased online is almost always inferior to their CD counterparts. To transfer songs quickly and hold more songs on a digital music player, tracks are encoded in a smaller file size than what you'd get on a CD, and this smaller file contains lower playback fidelity. But the additional tech-based market shock brought on by digital music players (particularly the iPod) has changed listening habits. The convenience of carrying thousands of songs trumps what most consider just a slight quality degradation. ITunes is now responsible for selling more music than any other firm, online or off. Apple can't rest on its laurels, either. The constant disruption of tech-enabled substitute goods has created rivals like Spotify and Pandora that don't sell music at all, yet have garnered tens of millions of users across desktop and mobile platforms. The need for a strong streaming service was widely given as the reason Apple purchased Beats for $3 billion. As a sign of the change, Warner Music recently became the first major label to earn more from streaming than from online sales.[69] Most alarming to the industry is the other widely adopted substitute for CD purchases—theft. Illegal music "sharing" services abound, even after years of record industry crackdowns. And while exact figures on real losses from online piracy are in dispute, the music industry has seen album sales drop by 45 percent in less than a decade.[70] All this choice gives consumers (buyers) *bargaining power*. They demand cheaper prices and greater convenience.

The Internet can also create models that strengthen the *bargaining power of suppliers*. Consider the rise of taxi services such as Uber. In the old model, cab firms own the right to run a taxi through the purchase of expensive medallions. Drivers work as independent contractors and pay a "shift fee" to lease the cab from the medallion-owning cab firms. Drivers pay gas and insurance, too, and all this expense can cost drivers $150 upward per twelve-hour shift. Because of this, it's not uncommon for traditional cab drivers to run a shift where they can't even cover their costs.[71] By contrast, ride-sharing services cut out the medallion-owning middleman for anyone who could use their own car for transport, and they often deliver enough fares to triple wages[72] all while offering fares that can (depending on the city and cab supply) undercut cab rates by 30 percent.[73] According to the San Francisco Cab Drivers Association, one-third of its drivers ditched their registered cabs in a twelve-month span to drive for ride-sharing companies such as Uber, Lyft, and Sidecar.[74] In some cities where Uber operates, business for traditional cabs is down 35 to 40 percent.[75] (For more about ride-sharing services, see Chapter 10 "Sharing Economy")

While it can be useful to look at changes in one industry as a model for potential change in another, it's important to realize that the changes that impact one industry do not necessarily impact other industries in the same way. For example, it is often suggested that the Internet increases bargaining power of buyers and lowers the bargaining power of suppliers. This suggestion is true for some industries like auto sales and jewelry where the products are commodities and the **price transparency** of the Internet counteracts a previous **information asymmetry** where customers often didn't know enough information about a product to bargain effectively. But it's not true across the board.

In cases where network effects are strong or a seller's goods are highly differentiated, the Internet can strengthen supplier bargaining power. The customer base of an antique dealer used to be limited by how many likely purchasers lived within driving distance of a store. Now with eBay, the dealer can take a rare good to a global audience and have a much larger customer base bid up the price. Switching costs also weaken buyer bargaining power. Wells Fargo has found that customers who use online bill pay (where switching costs are high) are 70 percent less likely to leave the bank than those who don't, suggesting that these switching costs help cement customers to the company even when rivals offer more compelling rates or services.

Tech plays a significant role in shaping and reshaping these five forces, but it's not the only significant force that can create an industry shock. Government deregulation or intervention, political shock, and social and demographic changes can all play a role in altering the competitive landscape. Because we live in an age of constant and relentless change, managers need to continually visit strategic frameworks to consider any market-impacting shifts. Predicting the future is difficult, but ignoring change can be catastrophic.

price transparency

The degree to which complete information is available.

information asymmetry

A decision situation where one party has more or better information than its counterparty.

KEY TAKEAWAYS

- Industry competition and attractiveness can be described by considering the following five forces: (1) the intensity of rivalry among existing competitors, (2) the potential for new entrants to challenge incumbents, (3) the threat posed by substitute products or services, (4) the power of buyers, and (5) the power of suppliers.
- In markets where commodity products are sold, the Internet can increase buyer power by increasing price transparency.
- The more differentiated and valuable an offering, the more the Internet shifts bargaining power to sellers. Highly differentiated sellers that can advertise their products to a wider customer base can demand higher prices.
- A strategist must constantly refer to models that describe events impacting their industry, particularly as new technologies emerge.

QUESTIONS AND EXERCISES

1. What are Porter's "five forces"?
2. Use the five forces model to illustrate competition in the newspaper industry. Are some competitors better positioned to withstand this environment than others? Why or why not? What role do technology and resources for competitive advantage play in shaping industry competition?
3. What is price transparency? What is information asymmetry? How does the Internet relate to these two concepts? How does the Internet shift bargaining power among the five forces?
4. How has the rise of the Internet impacted each of the five forces for music retailers?
5. In what ways is the online music buying experience superior to that of buying in stores?
6. What is the *substitute* for music CDs? What is the comparative sound quality of the substitute? Why would a listener accept an inferior product?
7. Based on Porter's five forces, is this a good time to enter the retail music industry? Why or why not?
8. What is the cost to the music industry of music theft? Cite your source.
9. Discuss the concepts of price transparency and information asymmetry as they apply to the diamond industry as a result of the entry of BlueNile. Name another industry where the Internet has had a similar impact.
10. Under what conditions can the Internet strengthen supplier bargaining power? Give an example.
11. What is the effect of switching costs on buyer bargaining power? Give an example.
12. How does the Internet impact bargaining power for providers of rare or highly differentiated goods? Why?

ENDNOTES

1. B. Weiss, "Groupon's $6 Billion Gambler," *The Wall Street Journal*, December 20, 2010.

2. B. Evans, "Whatsapp and $19B," *Ben-Evans.com*, Feb. 19, 2014.

3. N. DiMeo, "TiVo's Goal with New DVR: Become the Google of TV," *Morning Edition*, National Public Radio, April 7, 2010.

4. E. Rusli, "Cisco Shutters Flip, Two Years after Acquisition," *New York Times*, April 12, 2011.

5. L. Croghan, "Food Latest Luxury Lure," *New York Daily News*, March 12, 2006.

6. C. Makin, "FreshDirect Delivers Locally Sourced Food to Homes in 14 Counties," *MyCentralJersey.com*, May 8, 2013.

7. E. Main, "You're Throwing Away $2,275 Every Year," *Rodale's Organic Life*, July 29, 2013.

8. P. Fox, "Interview with FreshDirect Co-Founder Jason Ackerman," Bloomberg Television, June 17, 2009.

9. E. Schonfeld, "The Big Cheese of Online Grocers Joe Fedele's Inventory-Turning Ideas May Make FreshDirect the First Big Web Supermarket to Find Profits," *Business 2.0*, January 1, 2004.

10. T. Laseter, B. Berg, and M. Turner, "What FreshDirect Learned from Dell," *Strategy+Business*, February 12, 2003.

11. D. McInerney, "Good Foods Taste Great," *TEDxManhattan*, March 4, 2013.

12. C. Makin, "FreshDirect Delivers Locally Sourced Food to Homes in 14 Counties," *MyCentralJersey.com*, May 8, 2013.

13. J. Black, "Can FreshDirect Bring Home the Bacon?" *BusinessWeek*, September 24, 2002; S. Sieber and J. Mitchell, "FreshDirect: Online Grocery That Actually Delivers!" *IESE Insight*, 2007.

14. B. Walsh, "Why the Lazy Way to Shop for Groceries—Online—Is the Green Way," *Time*, April 29, 2013.

15. H. Green, "FreshDirect," *BusinessWeek*, November 24, 2003.

16. S. Sieber and J. Mitchell, "FreshDirect: Online Grocery That Actually Delivers!" *IESE Insight*, 2007; D. Kirkpatrick, "The Online Grocer Version 2.0," *Fortune*, November 25, 2002; P. Fox, "Interview with FreshDirect Co-Founder Jason Ackerman," Bloomberg Television, June 17, 2009.

17. P. Fox, "Interview with FreshDirect Co-Founder Jason Ackerman," *Bloomberg Television*, June 17, 2009.

18. T. McEnry, "Amazon Squeezes FreshDirect," *Crain's New York Business*, Oct. 26, 2014.

19. C. Valerio, "Interview with FreshDirect Co-Founder Jason Ackerman," *Venture*, September 18, 2009.

20. R. Shulman, "Groceries Grow Elusive for Many in New York City," *Washington Post*, February 19, 2008.

21. T. McEnry, "Amazon Squeezes FreshDirect," *Crain's New York Business*, Oct. 26, 2014.

22. A. Kadet, "New York City's Grocery Delivery Wars: Who's the Winner?" *The Wall Street Journal*, Feb. 6, 2015.

23. A. Kadet, "New York City's Grocery Delivery Wars: Who's the Winner?" *The Wall Street Journal*, Feb. 6, 2015. Also S. Hoxie, "Online Grocer FreshDirect Beats AmazonFresh and Google," *And Now You Know*, April 14, 2014.

24. T. McEnry, "Amazon Squeezes FreshDirect," *Crain's New York Business*, Oct. 26, 2014.

25. M. Porter, "What Is Strategy?" *Harvard Business Review* 74, no. 6 (November–December 1996): 61–78.

26. L. Kahney, "Net Speed Ain't Seen Nothin' Yet," *Wired News*, March 21, 2000.

27. L. Endlich, *Optical Illusions: Lucent and the Crash of Telecom* (New York: Simon & Schuster, 2004).

28. M. Porter, "Strategy and the Internet," *Harvard Business Review* 79, no. 3 (March 2001): 62–78.

29. B. Breen, "Living in Dell Time," *Fast Company*, December 19, 2007, http://www.fastcompany.com/magazine/88/dell.html.

30. T. Friscia, K. O'Marah, D. Hofman, and J. Souza, "The AMR Research Supply Chain Top 25 for 2009," *AMR Research*, May 28, 2009, http://www.amrresearch.com/Content/View.aspx?compURI=tcm:7-43469.

31. A. Hesseldahl, "Dell's Special Committee Asks Carl Icahn to Get Specific on Buyout Plans," *AllThingsD*, May 13, 2013.

32. J. Edwards, "JWT's $100 Million Campaign for Microsoft's Bing Is Failing," *BNET*, July 16, 2009.

33. T. Mullaney, "Jewelry Heist," *BusinessWeek*, May 10, 2004.

34. S. Yin, "Report: Apple Controls 60% of Touchscreen Supply," *PCMag.com*, February 17, 2011.

35. J. Flatley, "Intel Invests $7 Billion in Stateside 32nm Manufacturing," *Engadget*, February 10, 2009.

36. R. Katz, "Tech Titans Building Boom," *IEEE Spectrum* 46, no. 2 (February 1, 2009): 40–43.

37. Adapted from C. Shapiro and H. Varian, "Locked In, Not Locked Out," *Industry Standard*, November 2–9, 1998.

38. M. Andronico, "Apple Tops Customer Satisfaction Rankings, Again," *Laptop Magazine*, Sept. 17, 2013. J. Khan, "Apple tops J.D. Power's 2014 survey in smartphone satisfaction across all U.S. carriers," *9 to 5 Mac*, April 24, 2014. AppleInsider Staff, "Apple's iPad ranks highest in overall consumer satisfaction for tablets, says JD Power," *AppleInsider*, May 7, 2014.

39. D. Morganstern, "Sorry to say that Apple platforms are still more secure," *ZDNet*, Feb. 28, 2014.

40. D. Goldman, "Apple just posted the best quarter in corporate history," *CNNMoney*, Jan. 28, 2015.

41. J. Wilcox, "Nine out of 10 premium-priced PCs sold at US retail is a Mac," *BetaNews*, Feb. 1, 2010.

42. S. Ovide and D. Wakabayashi, "Apple's Share of Smartphone Industry's Profits Soars to 92%," *The Wall Street Journal*, July 12, 2015.

43. A virtuous adoption cycle occurs when network effects exist that make a product or service more attractive (increases benefits, reduces costs) as the adopter base grows.

44. S. Caldicott, "A Tasty Innovation Mashup: Why Priceline Bought Open Table," *Forbes*, August 2014.

45. J. Colao, "Despite A Near Monopoly In Online Reservations, OpenTable Is Finally Innovating," *Forbes*, Nov. 6, 2013. And OpenTable.com

46. M. Merced, "Priceline to Buy OpenTable for $2.6 Billion," *New York Times*, June 13, 2014.

47. C. Gallo, "Why The 'Experts' Failed To Predict The Apple Store's Success," *Forbes*, April 8, 2015.

48. B. Thau, "Apple And The Other Most Successful Retailers By Sales Per Square Foot," *Forbes*, May 20, 2014.

49. P. Wahba, "Apple extends lead in U.S. top 10 retailers by sales per square foot," *Fortune*, March 13, 2015.

50. A. Efrati, "The Hole in Google's Mobile Strategy," *The Information*, Dec. 9, 2014.

51. T. Fairless and R. Winkler, "EU Files Formal Antitrust Charges Against Google," *The Wall Street Journal*, April 15, 2015.

52. Google Fourth Quarter 2008 Earnings Summary, http://investor.google.com/earnings.html.

53. A. Liptak, "Justices Deny Patent to Business Methods," *The New York Times*, June 19, 2014.

54. B. Feld, "Why the Decks Are Stacked against Software Startups in Patent Litigation," *Technology Review*, April 12, 2009.

55. T. Wu, "Weapons of Business Destruction," *Slate*, February 6, 2006; R. Kelley, "BlackBerry Maker, NTP Ink $612 Million Settlement," *CNNMoney*, March 3, 2006.

56. E. Mills, "DOJ Clears Apple-Microsoft-RIM Deal to Buy Nortel Patents," *CNET*, February 13, 2012.

57. R. Preston, "Supreme Court Toughens Business Process Patent Test," June 20, 2014.

58. M. Asay, "Microsoft's Mobile Patent Strategy: Threaten, Don't Sue," *Read Write*, May 8, 2013.

59. T. Mullaney and S. Ante, "InfoWars," *BusinessWeek*, June 5, 2000.

60. N. Carr, "IT Doesn't Matter," *Harvard Business Review* 81, no. 5 (May 2003): 41–49.

61. "Movies to Go," *Economist*, July 9, 2005.

62. June 18, 2014, figures for both firms: BKS = $1.25B, AMZN = $153.87B.

63. S. Ludwig, "Gmail finally blows past Hotmail to become the world's largest email service," *VentureBeat*, June 28, 2012.

64. M. O'Neill, "From 21st to 1st: How Google Won in a Saturated Market," *The Huffington Post*, November 16, 2014.

65. N. Wingfield, "Netflix vs. the Naysayers," *Wall Street Journal*, March 21, 2007.

66. J. Hemple, "Why Facebook Has Entrusted Its Future to the CEO of PayPal," *Wired*, Nov. 10, 2014.

67. G. Hamel, "Killer Strategies That Make Shareholders Rich," *Fortune*, June 23, 1997.

68. For more on the long tail and collaborative filtering, see Chapter 4.

69. P. Kafka, "Warner Music Says Streaming Revenue Has Passed Downloads, and It Wants More," *Re/code*, May 11, 2015.

70. K. Barnes, "Music Sales Boom, but Album Sales Fizzle for '08," *USA Today*, January 4, 2009.

71. I. Smith, "Another Lawsuit Filed on Wage Issues of Cab Drivers," *Dorchester Reporter*, November 8, 2012.

72. M. McFarland, "Uber's Remarkable Growth Could End the Era of Poorly Paid Cab Drivers," *Washington Post*, May 27, 2014.

73. Annika, "New Uber X Prices, Now 30% Cheaper than a Taxi!," *Uber Blog*, October 15, 2013.

74. M. McFarland, "Uber's Remarkable Growth Could End the Era of Poorly Paid Cab Drivers," *Washington Post*, May 27, 2014.

75. T. Keane, "In Taxis' Battle with Uber, Ugly Endgame Looms," *Boston Globe*, June 1, 2014.

CHAPTER 3
Zara: Fast Fashion from Savvy Systems

1. INTRODUCTION

LEARNING OBJECTIVE

1. Understand how Zara's parent company Inditex leveraged a technology-enabled strategy to become the world's largest fashion retailer.

It wasn't supposed to be called Zara. Spanish entrepreneur Amancio Ortega was brainstorming names for his new clothing shop and had settled on Zorba, after the classic movie *Zorba the Greek*. Unfortunately, there was already a bar in town with the same name, and the bar's owner was worried that patrons would be confused by a new, unaffiliated, non-boozy Zorba. By this time, the molds for the letters for Ortega's shop sign had already been cast, so they played around with what they could spell and came up with Zara, instead.[1] Zara is probably the more fashionable name, anyway, but the magic isn't in the moniker. For Zara, it's technology that has made all the difference in its rise to dominate the decidedly ungeeky fashion industry. That little shop with the second-choice name was the start of a world-spanning empire—an enterprise that is now the largest pure-play fashion retailer on the planet.

Today, Zara is the game-changing crown jewel in the multibrand empire of Inditex Corporation (Industrias de Diseño Textil), a firm that's bigger than Gap, H&M, Topshop, and anyone else in the space. The firm's supremacy is plotted and executed from "The Cube," the gleaming, futuristic headquarters located in the northern Spanish coastal city of La Coruña (or A Coruña in the local Galician language). The blend of technology-enabled strategy that Zara has unleashed deviates widely from the standard fashion retail playbook. Unlike rivals, Zara shuns advertising, rarely runs sales, and while nearly every other major player outsources manufacturing to low-cost countries, Inditex is highly vertically integrated, keeping huge swaths of its production process in-house. These counterintuitive moves are part of a recipe for success that's beating the pants off the competition and has catapulted Ortega to become the world's third richest man, ahead of Warren Buffet.

The firm tripled in size between 1996 and 2000, and then its revenue skyrocketed from $2.43 billion in 2001 to more than $20 billion in 2015. In August 2008, sales edged ahead of Gap, making Inditex the world's largest fashion retailer.[2] Table 3.1 compares the two fashion retailers. While Inditex supports eight brands, Zara is unquestionably the firm's crown jewel and growth engine, accounting for roughly two-thirds of sales.[3]

FIGURE 3.1

Zara's operations are concentrated in Spain, but they have stores around the world, like these in Manhattan and Shanghai.

Source: Used with permission from Inditex.

TABLE 3.1   Gap versus Inditex at a Glance

	Gap	**Inditex**
Revenue	$16.4 billion	$20.5 billion
Net Income	$1.26 billion	$2.83 billion
Number of Stores	3,709	6,683
Number of Countries	31	88
Biggest Brand	Gap	Zara
Number of Other Brands	4	8
Based in	San Francisco, USA	Arteixo (near La Coruña), Spain
First Store Opened	1969	1975

Sources: Year-end 2013 figures from http://www.gapinc.com, http://www.inditex.com, and http://www.bloomberg.com.

1.1   Why Study Zara?

While competitors falter, Zara is undergoing one of the fastest global expansions the fashion world has ever seen, opening one store per day and entering new markets worldwide—eighty-eight countries so far. The chain's profitability is among the highest in the industry.[4] The fashion director for luxury goods maker LVMH calls Zara "the most innovative and devastating retailer in the world."[5]

Zara's duds look like high fashion but are comparatively inexpensive (average item price is $27, although prices vary by country).[6] A Goldman analyst has described the chain as "Armani at moderate prices," while another industry observer suggests that while fashions are more "Banana Republic," prices are more "Old Navy."[7] Legions of fans eagerly await "Z-day," the twice-weekly inventory delivery to each Zara location that brings in the latest clothing lines for women, men, and children. One well-known fan of the brand is the Duchess of Cambridge. The day after the wedding of Prince William, the former Kate Middleton made an appearance in a cornflower blue, pleated polyester dress from Zara. The price was £49.99[8] for high-quality, inexpensive fashion that's good enough for a future queen.

In order to understand and appreciate just how counterintuitive and successful Zara's strategy is, and how technology makes all of this possible, it's important to first examine the conventional wisdom in apparel retail. To do that we'll look at former industry leader—Gap.

1.2   Gap: An Icon in Crisis

Most fashion retailers place orders for a seasonal collection months before these lines make an appearance in stores. While overseas contract manufacturers may require hefty lead times, trying to guess what customers want months in advance is a tricky business. In retail in general and fashion in particular, there's a saying: inventory equals death. Have too much unwanted product on hand and you'll be forced to mark down or write off items, killing profits. For years, Gap sold most of what it carried in stores. Micky Drexler, a man with a radar-accurate sense of style and the iconic CEO who helped turn Gap's button-down shirts and khakis into America's business casual uniform, led the way. Drexler's team had spot-on tastes throughout the 1990s, but when sales declined in the early part of the following decade, Drexler was left guessing on ways to revitalize the brand, and he guessed wrong—disastrously wrong. Chasing the youth market, Drexler filled Gap stores with miniskirts, low-rise jeans, and even a much-ridiculed line of purple leather pants.[9] The throngs of teenagers he sought to attract never showed up, and the shift in offerings sent Gap's mainstay customers to retailers that easily copied the styles that Gap had made classic.

The inventory hot potato Drexler was left with crushed the firm. Gap's same-store sales declined for twenty-nine months straight. Profits vanished. Gap founder and chairman Dan Fisher lamented, "It took us thirty years to get to $1 billion in profits and two years to get to nothing."[10] The firm's debt was downgraded to junk status.

Drexler was out and for its new head the board chose Paul Pressler, a Disney executive who ran theme parks and helped rescue the firm's once ailing retail effort. Under Pressler, Gap's struggles continued, largely due to bad bets on colors and styles.[11] Pressler's tenure saw same-store sales decline in eighteen of twenty-four months.[12] The marketing model used by Gap to draw customers in via big-budget television promotion had collapsed. A *Fortune* article on Pressler's leadership was titled "Fashion Victim." *BusinessWeek* described his time as CEO as a "Total System Failure."[13] Under the firm's third CEO in a decade and after years of restructuring that resulted in the closure of hundreds of stores, Gap profits have finally returned, but the firm's admiration of Inditex, and its inability to act on this envy, remains clear. Says one Gap exec, "I would love to organize our business like Inditex, but I would have to knock the company down and rebuild it from scratch."[14]

Contract Manufacturing: Lower Costs at What Cost?

Conventional wisdom suggests that leveraging cheap **contract manufacturing** in developing countries can keep the cost of goods low. Firms can lower prices and sell more product or maintain higher profit margins—all good for the bottom line. But many firms have also experienced the ugly downside to this practice. Global competition among contract firms has led to race-to-the-bottom cost-cutting measures. Too often, this means that in order to have the low-cost bid, contract firms skimp on safety, ignore environmental concerns, employ child labor, and engage in other ghastly practices.

The apparel industry in particular has been plagued by accusations of sweatshop labor and unsafe working conditions. Incidents such as the Spring 2013 Bangladesh Rana Plaza disaster, which killed more than 1,100 people in the collapse of an illegally constructed eight-story building housing multiple contract garment factories, underscore the human toll of unacceptable contract manufacturing practices. Walmart, The Children's Place, and Benetton were among the firms said to have purchased clothing from firms operating in Rana Plaza.[15] The track record of Bangladeshi garment factories has been notably grim. In the dozen years prior to the Rana Plaza incident, over 700 workers in Bangladesh were killed in garment factory fires.[16] While Gap was not implicated in the Rana Plaza incident, the firm was singled out as a protest target because it is one of the largest importers of clothing from Bangladesh,[17] and it refused to sign a safety accord backed by H&M and Zara, among others.[18]

Big firms are big targets, and those that fail to adequately ensure their products are made under acceptable labor conditions risk a brand-damaging backlash that may turn off customers, repel new hires, and leave current staff feeling betrayed. Today's manager needs to think deeply not only about their own firm's ethical practices, but also those of all of their suppliers and partners.

Source: Wikimedia, http://en.wikipedia.org/wiki/File:Dhaka_Savar_Building_Collapse.jpg.

Tech for Good: The Fair Factories Clearinghouse

The problem of sweatshop labor and dismal industry practices has plagued the clothing industry for years. Managers often feel the pressure to seek ever-lower costs and all too often end up choosing suppliers with unacceptably poor practices. Even well-meaning firms can find themselves stung by corner-cutting partners that hide practices from auditors or truck products in from unmonitored off-site locations. The results can be tragic for those exploited, and can carry lasting negative effects for the firm. The sweatshop moniker continues to dog Nike years after allegations were uncovered and the firm moved aggressively to deal with its problems.[19]

Nike rival Reebok (now part of Adidas) has always taken working conditions seriously. The firm even has a Vice President of Human Rights and has made human dignity a key platform for its philanthropic efforts. Reebok invested millions in developing an in-house information system to track audits of its hundreds of suppliers along dimensions such as labor, safety, and environmental practices. The goal in part was to identify any bad apples, so that one division, sporting goods, for example, wouldn't use a contractor identified as unacceptable by the sneaker line.

The data was valuable to Reebok, particularly given that the firm has hundreds of contract suppliers. But senior management realized the system would do even more good if the whole industry could share and contribute information. Reebok went on to donate this system and provided critical backing to help create the nonprofit organization Fair Factories Clearinghouse. With management that included former lawyers for Amnesty International, Fair Factories (FairFactories.org) provides systems where apparel and other industries can share audit information on contract manufacturers. Launching the effort wasn't as easy as sharing the technology. The U.S. Department of Justice needed to provide a special exemption and had to be convinced the effort wouldn't be used by buyers to collude and further squeeze prices from competitors (the system is free of pricing data).

Suppliers across industries now recognize that if they behave irresponsibly the Fair Factories system will carry a record of their misdeeds, notifying all members to avoid the firm. As more firms use the system, its database becomes broader and more valuable. To its credit, Nike has since joined the Fair Factories Clearinghouse.

KEY TAKEAWAYS

- Zara has used technology to dominate the retail fashion industry as measured by sales, profitability, and growth.
- Excess inventory in the retail apparel industry is the kiss of death. Long manufacturing lead times require executives to guess far in advance what customers will want. Guessing wrong can be disastrous, lowering margins through markdowns and write-offs.
- Contract manufacturing can offer firms several advantages, including lower costs and increased profits. But firms have also struggled with the downside of cost-centric contract manufacturing when partners have engaged in sweatshop labor, poor working conditions, and environmental abuse.
- Firms with products manufactured under acceptable labor conditions face multiple risks, including legal action, brand damage, reduced sales, lower employee morale, and decreased appeal among prospective employees.

QUESTIONS AND EXERCISES

1. Has anyone shopped at Zara? If so, be prepared to share your experiences and observations with your class. What did you like about the store? What didn't you like? How does Zara differ from other clothing retailers in roughly the same price range? If you've visited Zara locations in different countries, what differences did you notice in terms of offerings, price, or other factors?
2. What is the "conventional wisdom" of the fashion industry with respect to design, manufacturing, and advertising?
3. What do you suppose are the factors that helped Gap to at one point rise to be first in sales in the fashion industry? Why do you suppose Gap profits collapsed?
4. Where do Gap clothes come from? Who makes them? Why? Are there risks in this approach?
5. Describe the downside of working with a supplier exposed as having used unethical practices. How does this potentially damage a firm? How can technology play a role in helping a firm become more socially responsible with its supply sourcing?
6. Describe the Fair Factories Clearinghouse. Which firm thought of this effort? Why did they give the effort away? Think in terms of strategic resources: what happens as more firms join this effort and share their data?

2. DON'T GUESS, GATHER DATA

LEARNING OBJECTIVE

1. Contrast Zara's approach with the conventional wisdom in fashion retail, examining how the firm's strategic use of information technology influences design and product offerings, manufacturing, inventory, logistics, marketing, and ultimately profitability.

Having the wrong items in its stores hobbled Gap for roughly a decade. But how do you make sure stores carry the kinds of things customers want to buy? Try asking them. Zara's store managers lead an intelligence-gathering effort that heavily influences the products that the firm produces. Armed with custom apps on mobile devices (initially Windows **PDAs**, now touch-screen iPods) staff regularly chat up customers to gain insight on what patrons would like to see on store racks and shelves. A Zara manager might casually ask, "What if this skirt were in a longer length?" "Would you like it in a different color?" "What if this V-neck blouse were available in a round neck?" Staff enter responses on their mobile devices and send these insights back to headquarters. Managers are motivated to use these systems and accurately record data because they have skin in the game. As much as 70 percent of salaries can come from store sale performance,[20] with an additional 10 percent of the firm's overall profit increase shared across all firm employees.[21]

PDAs

Personal Digital Assistants, an early name for handheld mobile computing devices.

Another level of data gathering starts as soon as the doors close. Then the staff turns into a sort of investigation unit in the forensics of trendspotting, looking for evidence in the piles of unsold items that customers tried on but didn't buy. Are there any preferences in cloth, color, or styles offered among the products in stock? Record these insights, as well.[22]

Information on what's selling is also tallied via the stores' **point-of-sale (POS) system**—the cash registers that ring up sales and deduct sold items from inventory. Nearly every retailer in every industry has a POS system, and the sales data gathered from these systems is very important. But Zara goes beyond most firms by also leveraging staff to gather more data via PDA and other means. This helps point to new products that customers want to see Zara produce, while also helping to uncover reasons why some products are being rejected.[23] In essence, the POS tells the firm what's selling, while PDA and related data tell the firm what customers at a given location want to see on shelves. All this valuable data allows the firm to plan new styles and issue rebuy orders based on *feedback* rather than hunches and guesswork. The goal is to improve the frequency and quality of decisions made by the design and planning teams.

point-of-sale (POS) system

Transaction processing systems that capture customer purchases. Cash registers and store checkout systems are examples of point-of-sale systems. These systems are critical for capturing sales data and are usually linked to inventory systems to subtract out any sold items.

2.1 Design

Rather than create trends by pushing new lines via catwalk fashion shows, Zara designs follow evidence of customer demand. The firm's chairman and CEO notes, "Our business model is the opposite of the traditional model. Instead of designing a collection long before the season, and then working out whether clients like it or not, we try to understand what our customers like, and then we design it and produce it."[24] Data on what sells and what customers want to see goes directly to "The Cube," where teams of some three hundred designers crank out an astonishing thirty thousand items a year[25] versus two thousand to four thousand items offered up at big chains like H&M (the world's third largest fashion retailer) and Gap.[26] While H&M has offered lines by star designers like Stella McCartney and Karl Lagerfeld, as well as celebrity collaborations with Madonna and Kylie Minogue, the Zara design staff relies heavily on young, hungry *Project Runway* types fresh from design school. There are no prima donnas in "The Cube." Team members must be humble enough to accept feedback from colleagues and share credit for winning ideas. Individual bonuses are tied to the success of the team, and teams are regularly rotated to cross-pollinate experience and encourage innovation.

2.2 Manufacturing and Logistics

In the fickle world of fashion, even seemingly well-targeted designs could go out of favor in the months it takes to get plans to contract manufacturers, tool up production, then ship items to warehouses and eventually to retail locations. But getting locally targeted designs quickly onto store shelves is where Zara really excels. In one telling example, when one pop star played a set of concerts in Spain, teenage girls arrived to the final show sporting a Zara knockoff of the outfit she wore during her first performance.[27] The average time for a Zara concept to go from idea to appearance in store is fifteen days versus their rivals who receive new styles once or twice a season. Smaller tweaks arrive even faster. If enough customers come in and ask for a round neck instead of a V neck, a new version can be in stores within just ten days.[28] To put that in perspective, Zara is *twelve times* faster than Gap despite offering roughly *ten times* more unique products![29] At H&M, it takes three to five months to go from creation to delivery—and they're considered one of the best. Other retailers need an average of six months to design a new collection and then another three months to manufacture it. VF Corp (Lee, Wrangler) can take nine months just to design a pair of jeans, while J. Jill needs a year to go from concept to store shelves.[30] At Zara, most of the products you see in stores didn't exist three weeks earlier, not even as sketches.[31]

The firm is able to be so responsive through a competitor-crushing combination of **vertical integration** and technology-orchestrated coordination of suppliers, just-in-time manufacturing, and finely tuned logistics. Vertical integration is when a single firm owns several layers in its **value chain**.[32] While H&M has nine hundred suppliers and no factories, nearly 60 percent of Zara's merchandise is produced in-house, with an eye on leveraging technology in those areas that speed up complex tasks, lower cycle time, and reduce error. Profits at Zara come in part from blending math with a data-driven fashion sense. Inventory optimization models help the firm determine how many of which items in which sizes should be delivered to each specific store during twice-weekly shipments, ensuring that each store is stocked with just what it needs.[33] Outside the distribution center in La Coruña, fabric is cut and dyed by robots in twenty-three highly automated factories. Zara is so vertically integrated, the firm makes 40 percent of its own fabric and purchases most of its dyes from its own subsidiary. Roughly half of the cloth arrives undyed so the firm can respond as any midseason shifts in taste and trends. When cotton prices rose to record levels, Zara was able to shift offerings away from more costly fabrics, preserving margins. By contrast, during that same period rival H&M saw profits drop 10 percent largely due to margin pressure.[34] After cutting and dying, many items are stitched together through a network of local cooperatives that have worked with Inditex so long they don't even operate with written contracts. The firm does leverage some contract manufacturers, but most of those used for trendy clothes are fairly close (Portugal, Morocco, and Turkey). There are far cheaper places to seek partners, but for Zara, speed beats manufacturing costs and drives profits.[35] Any contractors employed in farther regions (the firm has used partners in Asia and Latin America) produce staple items with longer shelf lives, such as t-shirts and jeans, but such goods account for only about one-eighth of dollar volume (also lessening exposure to events, which have occurred, associated with poor partner labor practices). [36]

All of the items the firm sells end up in a 5-million-square-foot distribution center in La Coruña, or a similar facility in Zaragoza in the northeast of Spain. When it debuted, the La Coruña facility was some nine times the size of Amazon's warehouse in Fernley, Nevada, or about the size of ninety football fields.[37] The facilities move over 17 million items every week,[38] with no item staying in-house for more than seventy-two hours. Ceiling-mounted racks and customized sorting machines patterned on equipment used by overnight parcel services, and leveraging Toyota-designed logistics, whisk items from factories to staging areas for each store. Clothes are ironed in advance and packed on hangers, with security and price tags affixed. This system means that instead of wrestling with inventory during busy periods, employees in Zara stores simply move items from shipping box to store racks, spending most of their time on value-added, sales-focused functions like helping customers find what they want.[39]

Zara inventory is smart. Security tags are custom made to also include **RFID**-technology. RFID (Radio Frequency Identification) tags wirelessly emit a unique identifying code for the individual item that they are attached to. As an item moves around the Zara distribution center, or into Zara stores, wall mounted or hand-held scanners can listen in, track product, and take inventory. RFID lets Zara know where products are, so if a customer asks for an item in a store (perhaps in a different size or color), staff using custom apps on an iPod Touch can immediately tell if a product is in store, in a nearby store, or if it can be ordered from the distribution center or Zara.com. Firms from Walmart to JCPenny have struggled to effectively implement RFID, but Zara's vertical integration is an advantage here, as well. Since the entire supply chain is under Zara control and all items flow through one of two warehouses, Zara can affix tags to all products before sending them out to stores (a challenge for other retailers that have third-party suppliers ship to multiple warehouses or directly to stores). Stores remove tags when customers buy items (avoiding any privacy concern that customer goods may be electronically tracked post-purchase).[40] Stores then send tags back to Zara warehouses for reuse (reassigning a tag's unique item to a new clothing item). Although tags only cost ten cents, with hundreds of millions of items sold each year, these costs would easily add up, so the reusable tag system makes solid financial sense (Zara bought so many tags at launch that it actually consumed one in every six tags produced for the entire apparel industry that year).[41] RFID tags also allow Zara staff to take in-store inventory four times as often as the pre-RFID rate, with greater accuracy, and using one forth the staff.[42]

Watch RFID tags announce inventory items from warehouse to store, increasing efficiency and customer service.

View the video online at: http://www.youtube.com/embed/XQAQ1Gvd9yY?rel=0

To get products into stores quickly, trucks serve destinations that can be reached overnight, while chartered cargo flights serve farther destinations within forty-eight hours.[43] The firm recently tweaked its shipping models through Air France–KLM Cargo and Emirates Air so flights can coordinate outbound shipment of all Inditex brands with return legs loaded with raw materials and half-finished clothes items from locations outside of Spain. Zara is also a pioneer in going green, with an environmental strategy that includes the use of renewable energy systems at **logistics** centers and biodiesel for the firm's trucking fleet.

> **logistics**
>
> Coordinating and enabling the flow of goods, people, information, and other resources among locations.

2.3 Stores

Most products are manufactured for a limited production run. While running out of bestsellers might be seen as a disaster at most retailers, at Zara the practice delivers several benefits.

First, limited runs allow the firm to cultivate the exclusivity of its offerings. While a Gap in Los Angeles carries nearly the same product line as one in Milwaukee, each Zara store is stocked with items tailored to the tastes of its local clientele. A Fifth Avenue shopper quips, "At Gap, everything is the same," while a Zara shopper in Madrid says, "You'll never end up looking like someone else."[44] Upon visiting a Zara, the CEO of the National Retail Federation marveled, "It's like you walk into a new store every two weeks."[45]

Second, limited runs encourage customers to buy right away and at full price. Savvy Zara shoppers know the newest items arrive on black plastic hangers, with store staff transferring items to wooden ones later on. Don't bother asking when something will go on sale; if you wait three weeks the item you wanted has almost certainly been sold or moved out to make room for something new. Says one twenty-three-year-old Barcelona shopper, "If you see something and don't buy it, you can forget about coming back for it because it will be gone."[46] A study by consulting firm Bain & Company estimated that the industry average markdown ratio is approximately 50 percent, and less than 1 percent of JCPenney revenue came from items bought at full price.[47] Contrast this with Zara, where 85 percent of products are sold without a discount.[48]

The constant parade of new, limited-run items also encourages customers to visit often. The average Zara customer visits the store seventeen times per year, compared with only three annual visits made to competitors.[49] Even more impressive—Zara puts up these numbers with almost no advertising. The firm's founder has referred to advertising as a "pointless distraction." The assertion carries particular weight when you consider that during Gap's collapse, the firm increased advertising spending but sales dropped.[50] Fashion retailers such as H&M spend as much as 4 percent of revenue promoting their products, while ad spending at Inditex ranges from 0.3 to 0.05 percent.[51]

Finally, limited production runs allow the firm to, as Zara's CEO once put it, "reduce to a minimum the risk of making a mistake, and we do make mistakes with our collections."[52] Failed product introductions are reported to be just 1 percent, compared with the industry average of 10 percent.[53] So even though Zara has higher manufacturing costs than rivals, Inditex gross margins are nearly 60 percent compared to 39 percent at Gap.[54]

While stores provide valuable frontline data, headquarters plays a major role in directing in-store operations. Software is used to schedule staff based on each store's forecasted sales volume, with locations staffing up at peak times such as lunch or early evening. The firm claims these more flexible schedules have shaved staff work hours by 2 percent. This constant refinement of operations throughout the firm's value chain has helped reverse a prior trend of costs rising faster than sales.[55]

Even the store displays are directed from "The Cube," where a basement staging area known as "Fashion Street" houses a Potemkin village of bogus storefronts meant to mimic some of the chain's most exclusive locations throughout the world. It's here that workers test and fine-tune the chain's award-winning window displays, merchandise layout, and even determine the in-store soundtrack. Every two weeks, new store layout marching orders are forwarded to managers at each location.[56]

information system (IS)

An integrated solution that combines five components: hardware, software, data, procedures, and the people who interact with and are impacted by the system.

return on investment (ROI)

The amount earned from an expenditure.

Technology ≠ Systems. Just Ask Prada

Here's another interesting thing about Zara. Given the sophistication and level of technology integration within the firm's business processes, you'd think that Inditex would far outspend rivals on tech. But as researchers Donald Sull and Stefano Turconi discovered, "Whether measured by IT workers as a percentage of total employees or total spending as a percentage of sales, Zara's IT expenditure is less than one-fourth the fashion industry average."[57] Zara excels by targeting technology investment at the points in its value chain where it will have the most significant impact, making sure that every dollar spent on tech has a payoff.

Contrast this with high-end fashion house Prada's efforts at its flagship Manhattan location. The firm hired the Pritzker Prize—winning hipster architect Rem Koolhaas to design a location Prada would fill with jaw-dropping technology. All items for sale in the store would sport radio frequency identification (RFID) tags. Walk into a glass dressing room and customers could turn the walls opaque, then into a kind of combination mirror and heads-up display. By wirelessly reading the tags on each garment, dressing rooms would recognize what was brought in and make recommendations of matching accessories as well as similar products that patrons might consider. Customers could check inventory, and staff wielding PDAs could do the same. A dressing room camera would allow clients to see their front and back view side-by-side as they tried on clothes.

It all sounded slick, but execution of the vision was disastrous. Customers didn't understand the foot pedals that controlled the dressing room doors and displays. Reports surfaced of fashionistas disrobing in full view, thinking the walls went opaque when they didn't. Others got stuck in dressing rooms when pedals failed to work, or doors broke, unable to withstand the demands of the high-traffic tourist location. The inventory database was often inaccurate, regularly reporting items as out of stock even though they weren't. As for the PDAs, staff reported that they "don't really use them anymore" and that "we put them away so tourists don't play with them." The investment in Prada's in-store technology was also simply too high, with estimates suggesting the location took in just one-third the sales needed to justify expenses.[58]

The Prada example offers critical lessons for managers. While it's easy to get seduced by technology, an **information system (IS)** is actually made up of more than *hardware* and *software*. An IS also includes *data* used or created by the system, as well as the *procedures* and the *people* who interact with the system.[59] Getting the right mix of these five components is critical to executing a flawless information system rollout. Financial considerations should forecast the **return on investment (ROI)**—the amount earned from an expenditure—of any such effort (i.e., what will we get for our money and how long will it take to receive payback?). And designers need to thoroughly test the system before deployment. At Prada's Manhattan flagship store, the effort looked like tech chosen because it seemed fashionable rather than functional.

KEY TAKEAWAY

- Zara store management and staff use mobile devices and POS systems to gather and analyze customer preference data to plan future designs based on feedback, rather than on hunches and guesswork.
- Zara's combination of vertical integration and technology-orchestrated supplier coordination, just-in-time manufacturing, and logistics allows it to go from design to shelf in days instead of months.
- RFID tags help Zara keep better track of inventory – improving warehouse-to-store distribution, and making it easier to locate items that customers want to purchase.
- Advantages accruing to Inditex include fashion exclusivity, fewer markdowns and sales, lower marketing expenses, and more frequent customer visits.
- Zara's IT expenditures are low by fashion industry standards. The spectacular benefits reaped by Zara from the deployment of technology have resulted from targeting technology investment at the points in the value chain where it has the greatest impact, and not from the sheer magnitude of the investment. This is in stark contrast to Prada's experience with in-store technology deployment.
- While information technology is just hardware and software, information systems also include data, people, and procedures. It's critical for managers to think about systems, rather than just technologies, when planning for and deploying technology-enabled solutions.

QUESTIONS AND EXERCISES

1. In what ways is the Zara model counterintuitive? In what ways has Zara's model made the firm a better performer than Gap and other competitors?
2. What factors account for a firm's profit margin? What does Gap focus on? What factors does Zara focus on to ensure a strong profit margin?
3. How is data captured in Zara stores? Using what types or classifications of information systems? How does the firm use this data?
4. What role does technology play in enabling the other elements of Zara's counterintuitive strategy? Could the firm execute its strategy without technology? Why or why not?
5. Why has Zara's RFID rollout been less problematic than those at Walmart and JC Penny? How does Zara's use of RFID reduce concerns that customer products will be tracked post-purchase? How does Zara reduce the expense associated with tagging each item? How does RFID improve efficiency and customer service?
6. How does technology spending at Zara compare to that of rivals? Advertising spending? Failed product percentages? Markdowns?
7. What risks are inherent in the conventional practices in the fashion industry? Is Zara susceptible to these risks? Is Zara susceptible to different risks? If so, what are these?
8. Consider the Prada case mentioned in the sidebar "Technology ≠ Systems." What did Prada fail to consider when it rolled out the technology in its flagship location? Could this effort have been improved for better results? If you were put in charge of this kind of effort, what would determine whether you'd go forward with the effort or not? If you did go forward, what factors would you consider and how might you avoid some of the mistakes made by Prada?

3. MOVING FORWARD

LEARNING OBJECTIVES

1. **Detail how Zara's approach counteracts several profit-eroding challenges that many fashion retailers struggle with.**
2. **Identify the environmental threats that Zara is likely to face, and consider options available to the firm for addressing these threats.**

The holy grail for the strategist is to craft a sustainable competitive advantage that is difficult for competitors to replicate. And for nearly two decades Zara has delivered the goods. But that's not to say the firm is done facing challenges.

Consider the limitations of Zara's Spain-centric, just-in-time manufacturing model. By moving all of the firm's deliveries through just two locations, both in Spain, the firm remains hostage to anything that could create a disruption in the region. Firms often hedge risks that could shut down operations—think weather, natural disaster, terrorism, labor strife, or political unrest—by spreading facilities throughout the globe. If problems occur in northern Spain, Zara has no such fallback.

In addition to the **operations** vulnerabilities above, the model also leaves the firm potentially more susceptible to financial vulnerabilities during periods when the euro strengthens relative to foreign currencies, especially the dollar (which many developing nations peg their currency to). A stronger euro means Zara's Spain-centric costs would rise at higher rates compared to competitors. Rising transportation costs are another concern. If fuel costs rise, the model of twice-weekly deliveries that has been key to defining the Zara experience becomes more expensive to maintain.

Still, Zara is able to make up for some cost increases by raising prices overseas (in the United States, Zara items can cost 40 percent or more than they do in Spain). Zara reports that all North American stores are profitable, and that it can continue to grow its presence, serving forty to fifty stores with just two US jet flights a week.[60] Management has considered a logistics center in Asia, but expects current capacity will suffice for now.[61]

Another possibility might be a regional center. China has surpassed France to become Zara's second largest market after Spain,[62] meaning some of the clothing that Zara sells travels from Asia to Spain, only to be routed back to stores in China.[63] If Zara could replicate what it does in Spain with a facility in China, Vietnam, or other nation in the region, this could give the firm more global sourcing flexibility and likely decrease cost. Still, experts remain skeptical of Zara's ability to replicate the firm's high-tech, flexible capacity half a world away.[64] One advisor to the firm voices concerns in having

operations

The organizational activities that are required to produce goods or services. Operations activities can involve the development, execution, control, maintenance, and improvement of an organization's service and manufacturing procedures.

"two brains, one in Spain and one in China."[65] A similar facility in the Maquiladora region of northern Mexico could serve the US markets via trucking capacity similar to the firm's Spain-based access to Europe, while also providing a regional center to serve expansion throughout the Western Hemisphere. Rising incomes and a cultural link to Spain make Latin America look like an increasingly attractive market, but United States may not be as ripe for growth. While Zara now has over forty-five stores in the United States and is running a profitable stateside business, one industry watcher calls the United States a "graveyard of European retailers."[66] Among US expansion challenges cited are American fashionistas tend to be concentrated on the coasts and American sizes are often a significantly different in cut than the rest of the world.[67]

Rivals have studied the Zara recipe, and while none have attained the efficiency of Amancio Ortega's firm, many are trying to learn from the master. There is precedent for contract firms closing the cycle time gap with vertically integrated competitors that own their own factories. Dell (a firm that once built its own PCs while nearly all its competitors use contract labor) has seen its manufacturing advantage from vertical integration fall as the partners that supply rivals have mimicked its techniques and have become far more efficient.[68] In terms of the number of new models offered, clothing is actually more complex than computing, suggesting that Zara's value chain may be more difficult to copy. Still, H&M has increased the frequency of new items in stores, Forever 21 and Uniqlo get new looks within six weeks, and Renner, a Brazilian fast fashion rival, rolls out mini collections every two months.[69] Rivals have a keen eye on Inditex, with the CFO of luxury goods firm Burberry claiming the firm is a "fantastic case study" and "we're mindful of their techniques."[70]

Finally, firm financial performance can also be impacted by broader economic conditions. When the economy falters, consumers simply buy less and may move a greater share of their wallet to less-stylish and lower-cost offerings from deep discounters like Walmart. Zara is also particularly susceptible to conditions in Europe since that market accounts for roughly two-thirds of firm sales.[71] Global expansion will provide the firm with a mix of locations that may be better able to endure downturns in any single region. Recent Spanish and European financial difficulties have made clear the need to decrease dependence on sales within one region, underscoring the importance of the firm's continued, aggressive pace of opening stores in new markets worldwide.

Zara's winning formula can only exist through management's savvy understanding of how information systems can enable winning strategies (many tech initiatives were led by José Maria Castellano, a "technophile" business professor who became Ortega's right-hand man in the 1980s).[72] It is technology that helps Zara identify and manufacture the clothes customers want, get those products to market quickly, and eliminate costs related to advertising, inventory missteps, and markdowns. A strategist must always scan the state of the market as well as the state of the art in technology, looking for new opportunities and remaining aware of impending threats. With systems so highly tuned for success, it may be unwise to bet against "The Cube."

KEY TAKEAWAY

- Zara's value chain is difficult to copy; but it is not invulnerable, nor is future dominance guaranteed. Zara management must be aware of the limitations in its business model, and must continually scan its environment and be prepared to react to new threats and opportunities.

QUESTIONS AND EXERCISES

1. The Zara case shows how information systems can impact every single management discipline. Which management disciplines were mentioned in this case? How does technology impact each?

2. Would a traditional Internet storefront work well with Zara's business model? Why or why not?

3. Zara's just-in-time, vertically integrated model has served the firm well, but an excellent business is not a perfect business. Describe the limitations of Zara's model and list steps that management might consider to minimize these vulnerabilities.

4. What challenges might Zara face in expanding to China or to the United States? Do you think Zara should increase capacity in Spain or open a regional distribution center in another part of the world? What are the pros and cons of each approach?

5. Search online to find examples of firms that suffered production problems because they employed just-in-time manufacturing or kept limited inventory on hand. What caused the production problems? List any steps you can think of that the firms might consider to minimize the potential of such problems from occurring in the future. What role might technology play in your solution?

ENDNOTES

1. B. White, "How Zara Got Its Name," *Telegraph*, November 12, 2012.

2. J. Hall, "Zara Is Now Bigger than Gap," *Telegraph*, August 18, 2008.

3. R. Murphy, "Expansion Boosts Inditex Net," *Women's Wear Daily*, April 1, 2008.

4. T. Buck, "Fashion: A Better Business Model," *Financial Times*, June 18, 2014.

5. J. Surowiecki, "The Most Devastating Retailer in the World," *New Yorker*, September 18, 2000.

6. C. Rohwedder, "Zara Grows as Retail Rivals Struggle," *Wall Street Journal*, March 26, 2009.

7. J. Folpe, "Zara Has a Made-to-Order Plan for Success," *Fortune*, September 4, 2000.

8. R. Parekh, "How Zara Ballooned into a Multi-Billion Dollar Brand without Advertising," *Advertising Age*, August 19, 2013.

9. J. Boorstein, "Fashion Victim," *Fortune*, April 13, 2006.

10. P. Sellers, "Gap's New Guy Upstairs," *Fortune*, April 14, 2003.

11. L. Lee, "Paul Pressler's Fall from the Gap," *BusinessWeek*, February 26, 2007.

12. J. Boorstein, "Fashion Victim," *Fortune*, April 13, 2006.

13. L. Lee, "Paul Pressler's Fall from the Gap," *BusinessWeek*, February 26, 2007.

14. *The Economist*, "Inditex: Fashion Forward," March 24, 2012.

15. S. Greenhouse, "Retailers Split on Contrition after Collapse of Factories," *New York Times*, April 30, 2013; and S. Greenhouse, "As Firms Line Up on Factories, Walmart Plans Solo Effort," *New York Times*, May 14, 2013.

16. S. Zain Al-Mahmood and J. Burke, "Bangladesh Factory Fire Puts Renewed Pressure on Clothing Firms," *Guardian*, May 9, 2013.

17. E. Fox, "Why I'm Protesting against Gap over Bangladesh," *CNNMoney*, May 21, 2013.

18. *BBC News*, "H&M and Zara Sign Bangladesh Safety Accord," May 14, 2013.

19. M. Nisen, "Why the Bangladesh Factory Collapse Would Never Have Happened to Nike," *Business Insider*, May 10, 2013.

20. K. Capell, "Zara Thrives by Breaking All the Rules," *BusinessWeek*, October 9, 2008.

21. C. Bjork, "Booming Inditex to Share Profits with Employees," *The Wall Street Journal*, March 18, 2015.

22. D. Sull and S. Turconi, "Fast Fashion Lessons," *Business Strategy Review*, Summer 2008.

23. C. Rohwedder and K. Johnson, "Pace-Setting Zara Seeks More Speed to Fight Its Rising Cheap-Chic Rivals," *Wall Street Journal*, February 20, 2008.

24. T. Buck, "Fashion: A Better Business Model," *Financial Times*, June 18, 2014.

25. T. Buck, "Fashion: A Better Business Model," *Financial Times*, June 18, 2014.

26. M. Pfeifer, "Fast and Furious," *Latin Trade*, September 2007; and "The Future of Fast Fashion," *Economist*, June 18, 2005.

27. "The Future of Fast Fashion," *Economist*, June 18, 2005.

28. J. Tagliabue, "A Rival to Gap That Operates Like Dell," *New York Times*, May 30, 2003.

29. M. Helft, "Fashion Fast Forward," *Business 2.0*, May 2002.

30. L. Sullivan, "Designed to Cut Time," *InformationWeek*, February 28, 2005.

31. J. Surowiecki, "The Most Devastating Retailer in the World," *New Yorker*, September 18, 2000.

32. Definition from the "father" of the value chain, Michael Porter. See M. Porter, "Strategy and the Internet," *Harvard Business Review* 79, no. 3 (March 2001): 62–78, among others.

33. C. Gentry, "European Fashion Stores Edge Past U.S. Counterparts," *Chain Store Age*, December 2007.

34. M. Johnson, "Investors Relieved as Inditex Profit Soars," *Financial Times*, March 21, 2011.

35. S. Hansen, "How Zara Grew into the World's Largest Fashion Retailer," *New York Times*, November 9, 2012.

36. N. Tokatli, "Global Sourcing: Insights from the Global Clothing Industry—The Case of Zara, a Fast Fashion Retailer," *Journal of Economic Geography* 8, no. 1 (2008): 21–38.

37. M. Helft, "Fashion Fast Forward," *Business 2.0*, May 2002.

38. T. Buck, "Fashion: A Better Business Model," *Financial Times*, June 18, 2014.

39. C. Rohwedder and K. Johnson, "Pace-Setting Zara Seeks More Speed to Fight Its Rising Cheap-Chic Rivals," *Wall Street Journal*, February 20, 2008; and K. Capell, "Zara Thrives by Breaking All the Rules," *BusinessWeek*, October 9, 2008.

40. C. Bjork, "Zara Builds Its Business Around RFID," *The Wall Street Journal*, Sept. 16, 2014.

41. SCDigest Editorial Staff, "RFID and AIDC News: Zara's Aggressive Move to Item-Level Tagging Features Plan to Re-Use Tags," *Supply Chain Digest*, Sept. 30, 2014.

42. L. Dejarlais, "Fashion-Forward Retailer Zara Leverages RFID Item Intelligence, Improves Key Metrics," *Impinj*, Nov. 5, 2014.

43. K. Capell, "Zara Thrives by Breaking All the Rules," *BusinessWeek*, October 9, 2008.

44. K. Capell, "Fashion Conquistador," *BusinessWeek*, September 4, 2006.

45. M. Helft, "Fashion Fast Forward," *Business 2.0*, May 2002.

46. K. Capell, "Fashion Conquistador," *BusinessWeek*, September 4, 2006.

47. B. Tuttle, "In Major Shakeup, JCPenney Promises No More 'Fake Prices,'" *Fortune*, January 26, 2012.

48. D. Sull and S. Turconi, "Fast Fashion Lessons," *Business Strategy Review*, Summer 2008; and K. Capell, "Fashion Conquistador," *BusinessWeek*, September 4, 2006.

49. N. Kumar and S. Linguri, "Fashion Sense," *Business Strategy Review*, Summer 2006.

50. P. Bhatnagar, "How Do You Ad(dress) the Gap?" *Fortune*, October 11, 2004.

51. E. O'Leary, A. Ringstrom, and E. Thomasson, "Zara-owner Inditex has the edge in online battle with H&M," *Reuters*, March 16, 2015. And unattributed author "Zara, A Spanish Success Story," *CNN.com*, June 15, 2001.

52. C. Vitzthum, "Zara's Success Lies in Low-Cost Lines and a Rapid Turnover of Collections," *Wall Street Journal*, May 18, 2001.

53. N. Kumar and S. Linguri, "Fashion Sense," *Business Strategy Review*, Summer 2006.

54. Inditex Press Release, "Inditex's 2012 Net Sales Rose 16%," March 3, 2013; and Gap Press Release, "Gap Inc. Reports Fourth Quarter Earnings per Share Increase of 66 Percent," February 28, 2013.

55. C. Rohwedder and K. Johnson, "Pace-Setting Zara Seeks More Speed to Fight Its Rising Cheap-Chic Rivals," *Wall Street Journal*, February 20, 2008.

56. C. Rohwedder and K. Johnson, "Pace-Setting Zara Seeks More Speed to Fight Its Rising Cheap-Chic Rivals," *Wall Street Journal*, February 20, 2008.

57. D. Sull and S. Turconi, "Fast Fashion Lessons," *Business Strategy Review*, Summer 2008.

58. G. Lindsay, "Prada's High-Tech Misstep," *Business 2.0*, March 1, 2004.

59. A. Sanchenko, "Foundations of Information Systems in Business" (lecture, October 13, 2007), http://www.scribd.com/doc/396076/Foundations-of-Information-Systems-in-Business.

60. J. Tagliabue, "A Rival to Gap That Operates Like Dell," *New York Times*, May 30, 2003.

61. C. Rohwedder and K. Johnson, "Pace-Setting Zara Seeks More Speed to Fight Its Rising Cheap-Chic Rivals," *Wall Street Journal*, February 20, 2008.

62. C. Robertson, "Inditex's Zara Faces Rising Competition," *eft*, April 22, 2014.

63. T. Buck, "Fashion: A Better Business Model," *Financial Times*, June 18, 2014.

64. S. Berfield and M. Baigorri, "Zara's Fast Fashion Edge," *BusinessWeek*, November 14, 2013.

65. S. Berfield and M. Baigorri, "Zara's Fast Fashion Edge," *BusinessWeek*, November 14, 2013.

66. S. Hansen, "How Zara Grew into the World's Largest Fashion Retailer," *New York Times*, November 9, 2012.

67. S. Hansen, "How Zara Grew into the World's Largest Fashion Retailer," *New York Times*, November 9, 2012.

68. T. Friscia, K. O'Marah, D. Hofman, and J. Souza, "The AMR Research Supply Chain Top 25 for 2009," *AMR Research*, May 28, 2009, http://www.amrresearch.com/Content/View.aspx?compURI=tcm:7-43469.

69. M. Pfeifer, "Fast and Furious," *Latin Trade*, September 2007; and C. Rohwedder and K. Johnson, "Pace-Setting Zara Seeks More Speed to Fight Its Rising Cheap-Chic Rivals," *Wall Street Journal*, February 20, 2008.

70. C. Rohwedder and K. Johnson, "Pace-Setting Zara Seeks More Speed to Fight Its Rising Cheap-Chic Rivals," *Wall Street Journal*, February 20, 2008.

71. M. Baigorri, "Inditex 2011 Profits Rise 12% on Asian, Online Expansion," *Bloomberg*, March 21, 2012.

72. C. Rohwedder and K. Johnson, "Pace-Setting Zara Seeks More Speed to Fight Its Rising Cheap-Chic Rivals," *Wall Street Journal*, February 20, 2008.

CHAPTER 4

Netflix in Two Acts: The Making of an E-Commerce Giant and the Uncertain Future of Atoms to Bits

1. INTRODUCTION

LEARNING OBJECTIVES

1. Understand the basics of the two subscription services that Netflix has operated, DVD-by-mail and video streaming. Also appreciate that the dynamics at work in these two services are fundamentally different in many key ways that influence product offerings, operating cost, competitors, and more.
2. Recognize that the firm has experienced wild swings in market perception and stock performance as it attempts the difficult transition from relying on a model that may soon be obsolete (DVD-by-mail subscriptions) to one that holds promise for the firm's long-term viability (video streaming).

Perhaps no CEO in recent memory has experienced more significant whipsaw swings than Netflix cofounder Reed Hastings. In less than three years, Hastings has gone from tech industry pinnacle to business press punching bag, to bounce back and again be considered (as *BusinessWeek* headlined) one of "Silicon Valley's Elite."[1]

For years, Netflix was known for best-in-class service, regularly and repeatedly ranking atop multiple customer satisfaction surveys. Hastings had been appointed to the board of directors of two of the tech industry's most influential firms—Microsoft and Facebook.[2] *Fortune* featured Hastings on its cover as "Businessperson of the Year," and Netflix's profits, customer base, and stock had each hit an all-time high.

But concerns over transitioning the firm to a future where Internet streaming dominates and DVDs go away resulted in a painful series of self-inflicted wounds that left the firm reeling. A poorly communicated repricing scheme was followed by a botched attempt to split the firm into two separate services. This caused an exodus of nearly 1 million customers in three months, a collapse of the firm's share price, and calls for Hastings's resignation (see the sidebar in section 3, "The Qwikster Debacle").[3] Since then, Hastings has aggressively expanded the firm's customer base at home and abroad; he's sponsored the creation of critically acclaimed, original content; and a series of Street-beating earnings reports has fueled the firm's previously beaten-down stock to record highs.

While the DVD business built Netflix into a sector-dominating powerhouse, Hastings is correct in understanding that digital streaming is where consumers, technology, and the industry are headed. The need to transition was clear to Netflix execs, but the business of streaming video is radically different from DVD-by-mail in several key ways, including content costs, content availability, revenue opportunities, rivals and their motivation, and more. Whether Netflix can maintain long-term dominance as it makes the transition from the certain-to-wither DVD-by-mail business to a profitable and dominant future in streaming remains to be seen.

1.1 Why Study Netflix?

Studying Netflix gives us a chance to examine how technology helps firms craft and reinforce a competitive advantage. While the DVD-by-mail business is dying, many will still want to read this section for key learning. Topics covered in this section include how technology played a starring role in developing assets such as scale, brand, and switching costs that combined to repel well-known rivals and place Netflix atop its industry. This section also introduces important business and technology concepts such as the long tail, collaborative filtering, and the value of the data asset. In the second part of this case, we examine Netflix, the sequel, and the firm's transition to video streaming. This section looks at the very significant challenges the firm faces as its primary business shifts from shipping the atoms of DVDs to sending bits over the Internet. We'll see that a highly successful firm can still be challenged by technical shifts, and we'll learn from Netflix's struggles as well as its triumphs. This section gives us an opportunity to examine issues that include digital goods, licensing, content creation, international growth, supplier power, crowdsourcing, platform competition, legal and regulatory issues, and technology infrastructure. We'll also look at the kinds of competitive advantages that Netflix is crafting now that it's fully committed to a video streaming future.

How Netflix Works: A Model in Transition

Netflix got its start offering a DVD-by-mail service for a monthly, flat-rate subscription fee. Under this model, customers don't pay a cent in mailing expenses, and there are no late fees. Videos arrive in red Mylar envelopes that are addressed and postage-paid for reuse in disc returns. When done watching videos, consumers just slip the DVD back into the envelope, reseal it with a peel-back sticky strip, and drop the disc in the mail. Users make their video choices in their "request queue" at Netflix.com. If a title isn't available, Netflix simply moves to the next title in the queue. Consumers use the Web site to rate videos they've seen, specify their viewing preferences, get video recommendations, check out title details, and even share their viewing habits and reviews.

This model helped Netflix grow into a giant, but Hastings knew that if his firm was to remain successful, it would have to transition from mailed DVDs to streamed video. Says Hastings, "We named the company Netflix for a reason; we didn't name it DVDs-by-mail."[4] Today the firm is so focused on digital distribution that it offers its streaming-only subscription as the default option for consumers. The default page at Netflix.com doesn't even mention DVDs; the disc subscription service that Netflix built its user base with has become an optional add-on that the firm is actively discouraging new consumers from joining. For less than $9 a month, customers gain unlimited access to the entire Netflix streaming library (which is smaller than the number of DVDs available for mailing). Netflix streaming is available on PCs, as well as all major tablets, smartphones, and Internet-connected televisions, DVD players, video game consoles, and a wide variety of specialty TV streaming hardware.

KEY TAKEAWAYS

- Netflix operates via a DVD subscription and video-streaming model. These started as a single subscription, but are now viewed as two separate services. Although sometimes referred to as "rental," the model is really a substitute good for conventional use-based media rental.
- Many firms are forced to deal with technology-fueled disruption that can challenge the current way they do business. However, successfully transitioning to a new business model is often extremely difficult, even for firms that were dominant under a prior operating model.

QUESTIONS AND EXERCISES

1. Describe the two separate Netflix offerings.
2. During his time as CEO of Netflix, Hastings has also served roles for other firms. What additional managerial roles outside of Netflix has Reed Hastings accepted? Why might these roles potentially be important for Netflix?
3. Can you think of once-successful firms that were forced to radically redesign their businesses based on technology change? How did the firms in your list fair with the new model—better or worse than their prior success? Why do you suppose they experienced the outcomes you've identified?

2.   ACT I: DAVID BECOMES GOLIATH: CRAFTING KILLER ASSETS FOR DVD-BY-MAIL DOMINANCE

LEARNING OBJECTIVES

1. Recognize the downside the firm may have experienced from an early IPO.
2. Appreciate why other firms found Netflix's market attractive, and why many analysts incorrectly suspected Netflix was doomed.
3. Understand how many firms have confused brand and advertising, why branding is particularly important for online firms, and the factors behind Netflix's exceptional brand strength.
4. Understand the *long tail* concept, and how it relates to Netflix's ability to offer the customer a huge (the industry's largest) selection of movies.
5. Know what *collaborative filtering* is, how Netflix uses collaborative filtering software to match movie titles with the customer's taste, and in what ways this software helps Netflix garner sustainable competitive advantage.
6. Describe the sources of Netflix's size advantage in the DVD-by-mail business, and how this large scale is a difficult-to-create asset for any start-ups trying to compete in DVD-by-mail. Understand the role that scale economies play in Netflix's strategies, and how these scale economies pose an entry barrier to potential competitors.
7. Recognize how Netflix built a data asset and why this asset was so valuable in the firm's original business model.
8. Understand the role that market entry timing has played in the firm's success.

Reed Hastings once said his biggest strategic regret was taking his firm public too early. Once public, the firm was required to disclose its financial position, and the whole world soon learned that Netflix was on a profit march with a remarkable growth trajectory.[5] The news was like blood in the water, attracting two very big sharks. First came Blockbuster, a firm with forty million card-carrying customers and a name synonymous with home video rental. Following Blockbuster was Walmart, not just a Fortune 500 firm, but Fortune One—the *biggest* firm in the United States as ranked by revenues. One analyst referred to the firm's impending competition as "The Last Picture Show" for Netflix,[6] and another called the firm a "worthless piece of crap," setting a $3 target on a stock that was then trading at $11 a share.[7] How did Netflix respond? With constant customer and revenue growth, record profits, and a stock price that skyrocketed past $400. Like the triumphant final scene in a feel-good movie, the dot-com did it. David knocked off not one but two Goliaths.

Understanding how this dot-com won the DVD-by-mail business provides a useful lesson in the execution of successful strategy. Netflix was able to create critical and mutually reinforcing resources—*brand*, *scale*, and a *data asset*—that rivals simply could not match. The Netflix example also underscores lessons, from Chapter 2 that timing and technology can be critical in nurturing assets for competitive advantage.

2.1   Brand Strength from Best-in-Class Customer Experience

First let's look at the Netflix brand. Don't confuse brand with advertising. During the dot-com era, firms thought brands could be built through Super Bowl ads and expensive television promotion. Advertising can build awareness, but *brands are built through customer experience*. This is especially critical online, where opinion spreads virally and competition is just a click away. During the firm's ascendency in the DVD-by-mail business, Netflix wasn't simply a provider of good customer experience; it was often ranked the best. The firm was top in the American Customer Satisfaction Index (ACSI) and Nielsen rankings, while ratings agency ForeSee named Netflix the number one e-commerce site in eleven out of twelve surveys conducted (placing it ahead of Apple and Amazon).

Blockbuster and Walmart, however, discovered that their strong consumer awareness didn't translate into any advantage when competing with Netflix. While both firms were well known, neither name was synonymous with a DVD-by-mail subscription service. Reed Hastings's early market entry and effective execution made Netflix the first firm consumers thought of. Everyone else in the space had to spend big to try to create awareness alongside the mindshare leader.

2.2   Scale from the Distribution Network

The high degree of customer satisfaction that Netflix enjoyed is tightly linked with the firm's size-based advantages. Yes, even though Netflix was the upstart, it managed to gain relevant scale greater than Blockbuster (even though that firm had 7,800 stores) and Walmart (with its nation-leading sales might). It did so by building and leveraging an asset that neither competitor had: a nationwide network of fifty-eight highly automated distribution centers that collectively could deliver DVDs overnight to some 97 percent of the US population. Drop a disc in the mail, and in most cases you'd get a new one the next day. No one else had a comparable network at launch, so the lack of scale among rivals harmed their customer experience, weakening their brand.

2.3   Scale from Selection: The Long Tail

long tail

In this context, it refers to an extremely large selection of content or products. The long tail is a phenomenon whereby firms can make money by offering a near-limitless selection.

Netflix appeal also came from the scale of the firm's entertainment selection. A traditional video store would stock a selection of roughly 3,000 DVD titles on its shelves. Netflix, however, offered its customers over 125,000 unique DVD titles. The battle over who had the better selection wasn't even close. This nearly limitless selection allows Internet retailers to leverage what is often called the **long tail** (the tail refers to the large number of products unavailable through conventional retail stores, see Figure 4.1). Customers saw advantage in having vast choice. Roughly 75 percent of DVDs Netflix shipped were from back-catalog titles, versus the 70 percent of Blockbuster rentals that came from new releases.[8] While some debate the size of the profitable tail, two facts are critical to keep above this debate: (1) selection attracts customers, and (2) the Internet allows large-selection inventory efficiencies that offline firms can't match.

FIGURE 4.1   The Long Tail

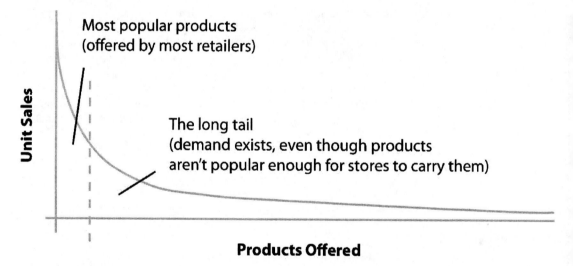

2.4   The Big Customer Base—Delivering True Economies of Scale

While Netflix's warehouse network and product selection were greater than those of rivals, these assets could be bought by a competitor with a big wallet. Says Netflix's Vice President of Operations, "Anyone can replicate [our] operations if they wish. It's not going to be easy. It's going to take a lot of time and a lot of money."[9] The yearly cost to run a Netflix-comparable nationwide delivery infrastructure is about $300 million.[10] This is where another critical component of scale comes in—the size of the firm's customer base.

In Chapter 2 we learned that *scale economies* are achieved by firms that leverage the cost of an investment across increasing units of production. If the entry price for getting into the national DVD-by-mail game is $300 million, but one firm has far more customers than the other (see Figure 4.2 for estimates in the one-time Netflix versus Blockbuster competition), then the bigger firm has a better cost structure and better profit prospects and should be able to offer better pricing. Walmart had the cash to compete with Netflix but decided doing so would require a massive investment and extended periods of loss to unseat the early-moving leader, so Walmart pulled the plug on their DVD-by-mail effort. Blockbuster decided to fight to the death—and lost. The firm never had the necessary threefold scale advantages (distribution centers, selection, and customers) needed to create a competitive DVD-by-mail business.

FIGURE 4.2

Running a nationwide sales network cost an estimated $300 million a year. But Netflix had several times more subscribers than Blockbuster did. Which firm had economies of scale?[11]

2.5   Leveraging the Data Asset: Collaborative Filtering and Beyond

Netflix also keeps customers happy in brand-building ways by leveraging its massive and growing arsenal of user data. Data is collected when customers rate movies they've seen, and this data on customer likes and dislikes is fed into a proprietary Netflix recommendation system called Cinematch. Cinematch is a software technology known as **collaborative filtering**. These systems monitor trends among customers and use this data to personalize an individual customer's experience. Firms use collaborative filtering systems to customize webpages and make all sorts of recommendations, including products, music, and news stories.

Recommended titles made up over 60 percent of the content that Netflix users placed in their DVD request queues—an astonishing penetration rate. This data is also a switching cost. Drop Netflix for a rival, and the average user abandons the two hundred or more films they've rated. The year after Blockbuster and Walmart launched copycat efforts, the Netflix **churn rate** actually fell.[12] It seems that even though big-name rivals had arrived with shiny new offerings, the Netflix value proposition was actually growing stronger over time.

Cinematch data also offers Netflix operational advantages. The firm examines inventory availability in the warehouse closest to a given customer and tailors recommendations to favor movies that are in stock so that users aren't frustrated by a wait.

Netflix also learned to make studios happy by leveraging Cinematch to help them find an audience for their back catalog of movies and television shows. The firm developed a revenue-sharing system where studios could offer Netflix their DVD catalog at a wholesale price in exchange for a cut of Netflix subscriber revenues each time someone requests a given DVD. This was huge for studios; suddenly they had a way to extend the profit-earning life of their movie and TV catalogs, and all without requiring a dime extra in additional marketing. As an example of this power, consider that Netflix delivered more revenue to Fox from the critically acclaimed but box-office-weakling film *The Last King of Scotland* than it did from the blockbuster film *X-Men: The Last Stand*.[13]

2.6   Winning Act I

Blockbuster tried to combat Netflix on the playing field that Reed Hastings had defined, but the results were disastrous. During the three-year period that included the launch of DVD-by-mail by Blockbuster's rival Total Access, the firm lost over $4 billion and closed hundreds of stores.[14] Blockbuster never recovered and was eventually purchased by Dish Network at a bankruptcy auction.[15]

As for Netflix, what delivered the firm's triple scale advantage of the largest selection, the largest network of distribution centers, and the largest customer base, along with the firm's industry-leading strength in brand and data assets? Moving first. Timing and technology don't always yield sustainable competitive advantage, but in this case, Netflix leveraged both to craft an extraordinarily valuable and mutually reinforcing pool of assets.

But as we'll see in Section 3 while technology shifts helped Netflix attack Blockbuster's once-dominant position, even newer technology shifts may threaten Netflix. As they like to say in the mutual fund industry, "Past results aren't a guarantee of future returns."

collaborative filtering

A classification of software that monitors trends among customers and uses this data to personalize an individual customer's experience.

churn rate

The rate at which customers leave a product or service.

KEY TAKEAWAYS

- Analysts and managers have struggled to realize that dot-com start-up Netflix could actually create sustainable competitive advantage, beating back challenges in its initial and highly successful DVD-by-mail business, from Walmart and Blockbuster, among others.
- Data disclosure required by public companies may have attracted these larger rivals to the firm's market.
- In understanding the initially successful DVD-by-mail business, technology leveraged across the firm's extensive distribution network offers an operational advantage that allows the firm to reach nearly all of its customers with one-day turnaround.
- Durable brands are built through customer experience, and technology lies at the center of the Netflix top satisfaction ratings and hence the firm's best-in-class brand strength.
- Physical retailers are limited by shelf space and geography. This limitation means that expansion requires building, stocking, and staffing operations in a new location.
- Internet retailers serve a larger geographic area with comparably smaller infrastructure and staff. This fact suggests that Internet businesses are more scalable. Firms providing digital products and services are potentially far more scalable, since physical inventory costs go away.
- The ability to serve large geographic areas through lower-cost inventory means Internet firms can provide access to the long tail of products, potentially earning profits from less popular titles that are unprofitable for physical retailers to offer.
- Netflix technology revitalizes latent studio assets. Revenue sharing allows Netflix to provide studios with a costless opportunity to earn money from back catalog titles: content that would otherwise not justify further marketing expense or retailer shelf space.
- The strategically aligned use of technology by this early mover has allowed Netflix to gain competitive advantage through the powerful resources of brand, data and switching costs, and scale.
- Collaborative filtering technology has been continually refined, but even if this technology is copied, the true exploitable resource created and leveraged through this technology is the data asset.

QUESTIONS AND EXERCISES

1. What were Netflix's sources of competitive advantage in the DVD-by-mail business?
2. Does Netflix have a strong brand? Offer evidence demonstrating why the firm's brand is or isn't strong. How is a strong brand built?
3. Scale advantages are advantages related to size. In what key ways is Netflix "bigger" than the two major competitors who tried to enter the DVD-by-mail market?
4. What is the long tail? How "long" is the Netflix tail in the DVD-by-mail business compared to traditional video stores?
5. What "class" of software does Netflix use to make movie recommendations? Think about Chapter 2: Which key competitive resource does this software "create"? What kinds of benefits does this provide to the firm? What benefits does it provide to Netflix's suppliers?
6. Could a new competitor match Netflix's recommendation software? If it did, would this create a threat to Netflix? Why or why not?
7. What is the Netflix churn rate and what are the reasons behind this rate?

3.   ACT II: NETFLIX AND THE SHIFT FROM MAILING ATOMS TO STREAMING BITS

LEARNING OBJECTIVES

1. Understand the shift from atoms to bits, and how this is impacting a wide range of industries.
2. Identify how digital products differ from physical products and specify how the streaming business is substantially different from the DVD-by-mail business.
3. Know the methods that Netflix is using to attempt to address these differences.
4. Understand how the "First Sale Doctrine" applies to physical versus virtual products.
5. Understand key terms such as windowing, fixed versus marginal costs, and bandwidth caps.
6. Discuss how Netflix is attempting to create competitive advantage through catalog offerings despite not being able to secure a "longest tail."
7. Identify opportunities for Netflix to further strengthen and leverage its data asset, and detail how the asset can offer the firm competitive advantage.
8. Understand that while scale in DVD-by-mail differs from scale in streaming, some scale advantages may be achievable.
9. Understand opportunities and challenges as Netflix seeks to expand its subscription streaming offerings to international markets.
10. Recognize how Netflix made streaming widely available on products offered by many different consumer electronics firms and why the Netflix approach offers advantages over offerings from Apple or other consumer-electronics firms.
11. Identify the major issues driving what is widely considered to be a disastrous rollout and recall of the Qwikster service, and intelligently discuss options that may have limited the fallout in transitioning the firm's business.
12. Describe crowdsourcing and discuss the positive benefits from code contests that Netflix has conducted.

Nicholas Negroponte, the former head of MIT's Media Lab and founder of the One Laptop per Child effort, wrote a now-classic essay on the shift from **atoms to bits**. Negroponte pointed out that most media products are created as bits—digital files of ones and zeros that begin their life on a computer. Music, movies, books, and newspapers are all created using digital technology. When we buy a CD, DVD, or even a "dead tree" book or newspaper, we're buying physical atoms that are simply a container for the bits that were created in software—a sound mixer, a video editor, or a word processor.

The shift from atoms to bits is realigning nearly every media industry. Newspapers struggle as readership migrates online and once-lucrative classified ads and job listings shift to the bits-based businesses of Craigslist, Monster.com, and LinkedIn. Apple and Spotify rule the new world of music without selling a single CD, while most of the atom-selling "record store" chains of the past are bankrupt. Amazon jumped into the atoms-to-bits shift when it developed the Kindle digital reader. Who needs to kill a tree, spill ink, fill a warehouse, and roll a gas-guzzling truck to get you a book? Kindle can slurp your purchases through the air and display them on a device lighter than a paperback. When the Kindle was released, many thought it to be an expensive, niche product for gadget lovers, but in less than four years, the firm was selling more electronic books than print titles.[16] With video games shifting to digital downloads, any firm relying on sale of physical game discs and cartridges is also in a world of hurt. GameStop, the largest gaming retail chain, saw a 23 percent decline in new product sales during Holiday 2013,[17] and a further 11 percent decline in 2014,[18] prompting the closure of roughly 400 stores in two years.[19] The new plan: shift to new, non-gaming stores focused on mobile phones and computing accessories.

The DVD-by-mail business, as important as it was for Netflix's rise to category-defining growth and much-envied profitability, is now going away. In 2010, Netflix had 19.5 million DVD subscribers,[20] but the number had fallen to roughly 5.5 million by early 2015.[21] Fortunately the firm was able to retain most of these customers with its streaming-only offering, but ultra-efficient, scale-driven DVD delivery infrastructure will increasingly look like a scale-sized liability, delivering weakening margins as subscribers move on to other offerings. The decline has prompted the firm to close roughly twenty distribution centers nationwide,[22] as well as a call center supporting the DVD business.[23] The DVD business is still a money maker, earning Netflix $88 million in quarterly profits in Q4 2014, but that's down from roughly $200 million the same quarter just three years earlier.[24] There is some potential upside to the Netflix model as it shifts from mailing atoms to streaming bits, including the ability to eliminate a huge chunk of costs associated with shipping and handling. But just about

atoms to bits

The idea that many media products are sold in containers (physical products, or atoms) for bits (the ones and zeros that make up a video file, song, or layout of a book). As the Internet offers fast wireless delivery to TVs, music players, book readers, and other devices, the "atoms" of the container aren't necessary. Physical inventory is eliminated, offering great cost savings.

everything in the streaming business is different: content availability, content acquisition costs, the legal and regulatory environments, potential opportunities for revenue and expansion, potential partners, competitors, and their motivation.

The Qwikster Debacle

We can learn a lot from Reed Hastings's deft management of Netflix in the firm's ascendency to industry-leading dominance in the DVD-by-mail and video streaming businesses, but Hastings has also presided over what some have called one of the worst product launches of all time,[25] the announcement and repeal of the Qwikster service, and there are lessons to be learned from examining the firm's painful stumbles as well.

The damage started when the $10 base Netflix service was unbundled into two separate $8 plans: one for DVD-by-mail and one for streaming over the Internet. For customers who still expected both discs and streaming, the move effectively constituted a 60 percent price hike. Following the plan change, the firm's Facebook page quickly amassed over 44,000 negative comments, "Dear Netflix" complaints became a trending topic on Twitter, and customers began referring to the firm's CEO as "Greed Hastings."[26] Two months later the firm announced it would split into two distinct services with two separate Web sites. The switch reads as a primer on what not to do when transitioning a business. The unpopular price hikes were followed by changes that would have actually made the firm's products *harder* to use by forcing customers to access two different Web sites, each with a separate database of offerings. Adding to the pain was the embarrassment of a botched rebranding of the DVD-by-mail service under the new name Qwikster. At the time of the rebranding announcement, Netflix had secured the domain Qwikster.com, but not the Twitter handle @Qwikster. The latter was owned by a guy whose drug-referencing, foul-mouthed tweets were accompanied by a profile picture of a pot-smoking Elmo from *Sesame Street*. Hastings, who stood at the peak of the industry just a few weeks earlier, had become both a target of customer vitriol and an industry laughing stock, the subject of *Saturday Night Live* skits and comedian punch lines. Netflix quickly dropped plans for the Qwikster split, but it chose to hold firm with the price increase that started the slide. Over the course of ninety nightmarish days, Netflix lost over 800,000 customers, its stock tumbled from $304 a share to below $75 (eventually falling to near $50), and its market value shed over $12 billion, including $2.3 billion in a single day.

When announcing Qwikster, Hastings wrote in a blog post, "My greatest fear at Netflix has been that we wouldn't make the leap from success in DVDs to success in streaming. Most companies that are great at something—like AOL dialup or Borders bookstores—do not become great at new things people want (streaming for us) because they are afraid to hurt their initial business…Companies rarely die from moving too fast, and they frequently die from moving too slowly." But in this case the poorly handled transition, served up with little user dialog or warning, was too much, too soon. Hastings has since admitted, "We moved too quickly for our customers."[27] In 2014, Netflix streaming price increase was handled with far more customer sensitivity. The firm announced that while it was raising rates by $1 a subscriber, it would only apply to new customers; existing customers would be grandfathered in with a two-year grace period before seeing their bills go up.[28] The result? There was no notable customer outrage or protest.

Digital Products and Marginal Costs

fixed costs

Costs that do not vary according to production volume.

marginal costs

The costs associated with each additional unit produced.

Imagine you're an auto manufacturer. Before you can begin producing any vehicles you'll need to make some investments to get started. These **fixed costs** might include buying land and building a manufacturing plant. There are also costs associated with each individual unit produced. These are the **marginal costs** and would include things like the parts, materials, labor, and energy used to produce each additional car.

It's often argued that the marginal cost of digital goods is effectively zero. That's because computers can make limitless duplicates of digital content—no material required—and the Internet can be used to almost instantly distribute content to customers. In practice there are some costs associated with digital distribution. These might include the costs that a firm must pay to telecommunications providers that connect them to the Internet (the more a firm transmits, the more it typically has to pay), or the cost of running programs on the servers of other companies (see the cloud computing discussion in Chapter 14). For example, to deliver streaming video, Netflix actually uses computers provided by the cloud computing services of Amazon (making Amazon and Netflix both partners and competitors, a phenomenon often referred to as coopetition, or *frenemies*[29]). License fees can also add to the marginal costs of Netflix streaming. While computing costs might total just a nickel for each video streamed, if content providers charge Netflix a per-unit basis for streamed content, then this also gets added to marginal costs.

3.1   Content Acquisition: Escalating Costs, Limited Availability, and the "Long-Enough Tail"

The old DVD-by-mail business allowed Netflix to offer up the longest tail of video content that money could buy. An over-100-year-old US Supreme Court ruling known as the "First Sale Doctrine" made this possible. This ruling states that a firm can distribute physical copies of legally acquired copyright-protected products. For Netflix this means that if studios sell their DVDs retail, they can't prevent Netflix or anyone else from buying DVDs at full price and distributing the discs to others. (The ruling makes possible all sorts of efforts, including library lending and video rental.) But the "First Sale Doctrine" applies only to the atoms of the physical disc, not to the bits needed in streaming, so Netflix can't offer Internet streaming without separate streaming licenses.[30] That's a big problem for Netflix. Licensing costs are skyrocketing, and some firms are outright refusing to make their content available for streaming on Netflix.

While studios offer new films and television shows each year, the number of firms offering high-demand content remains more or less fixed, essentially operating as an oligopoly with concentrated supplier power. In fact, just six firms control over 90 percent of US media consumed.[31] Also realize that video content is perfectly differentiated, and as we learned in the Strategy and Technology chapter, providers of differentiated goods also have stronger bargaining power. Want to license the new Star Wars movie? There's only one owner that can provide that content: Disney. By contrast, in the DVD days, content acquisition was more like buying a commodity since, even if studios wouldn't directly sell Netflix their discounted discs, Netflix could always buy discs from any retailer selling to the public. And while the number of influential studios remains roughly the same, over the past several years the ranks of bidders jostling elbows at the streaming media negotiating table has increased. Amazon, Hulu, Walmart's Vudu, the Dish Network's revived Blockbuster On Demand, Sony-backed Crackle, Comcast Xfinity Streampix, and a host of overseas rivals are all in a mix that can push content prices higher. Also consider that when you buy a DVD you own it for life, but streaming costs are usually licensed for a limited time period, and renewal costs have been increasing over time. Consider that the Starz network initially licensed its content to Netflix for $30 million but the network turned down *ten times* that amount to renew the deal just three years later.[32] The trends are troubling. Netflix's recent cost of acquiring streaming content rose to forty-three times the amount it spent just five years earlier! [33]

Streaming licensing deals also complicate a firm's long-term planning and cost estimates because rates can vary widely. Studios might offer titles via a flat rate for unlimited streams, a rate according to a service's overall subscribers, a per-stream rate, a rate for a given number of streams, a premium for exclusive content, and various permutations in between. Some vendors have been asking as much as $4 per stream for more valuable content—a fee that would quickly erase profits in Netflix's fixed-price subscription fee. And some deals may require separate licenses to stream to international markets.

Title availability is also complicated by a distribution practice known as windowing. Content is available to a given distribution channel (in theaters, through hospitality channels like hotels and airlines, on DVD, via pay-per-view, via pay cable, and later broadcast on commercial TV) for a specified time window, usually under a different revenue model (ticket sales, disc sales, and license fees for broadcast). Even those studios that embrace the audience-finding and revenue-enhancing advantages of Netflix don't want to undercut higher-revenue early windows. Adding to this complexity are exclusivity contracts negotiated by many key channels—in particular, the so-called *premium* television networks (think pay channels like HBO, Showtime, and Cinemax). Windows controlled by pay television channels can be particularly challenging, since many have negotiated exclusive access to content as they strive to differentiate themselves from one another. This exclusivity means that if HBO or Showtime has exclusive rights to broadcast a film, it's pulled from the Netflix streaming service until any exclusive pay-television time window closes. Netflix's partnerships with the cable networks Starz and Epix initially helped provide access to some content locked up inside these networks' windows.[34] However, even these sorts of deals can get caught up in licensing details. For example, Sony titles were available on Netflix via a deal with Starz, but they were pulled from Netflix when the firm's subscriber base grew so big that a contract cap specifying the maximum number of subscribers that can stream Sony content was exceeded.[35] Want to be a player in the streaming media business? You'd better lawyer up.

Another problem: some firms steadfastly refuse to offer Netflix streaming rights. Time Warner's HBO offers the HBO Go app that serves up current shows and back catalog original programming free to anyone already subscribed to the pay channel, and it offers the HBO Now on-demand streaming service for those who don't want a channel subscription, but it won't license to Netflix. Exclusives are also perfectly differentiated goods available from no-one else, and exclusives are critical for HBO. Who would pay $15 for HBO's service if Netflix could offer the same content and more for just $9? HBO did agree to take $300 million of Amazon's money to offer up a limited selection of HBO-back-catalog series, but the three-year deal leaves out current programming as well as ultra-hot titles like *Game of Thrones*.[36]

Taken together, all these content acquisition factors make it clear that attempts to profitably shift the long tail from atoms to bits will be significantly more difficult than buying DVDs and stacking them in a remote warehouse. The difference in content acquisition between the atoms (DVDs) and bits (streaming) businesses has forced Netflix to shift from offering the *longest tail* to a *long-enough tail*, a service that might not have all of what you want but that consistently has something for everyone. In a statement to investors, Netflix makes this clear: "We are actively curating our service rather than carrying as many titles as we can."[37]

FIGURE 4.3 Film Release Windows

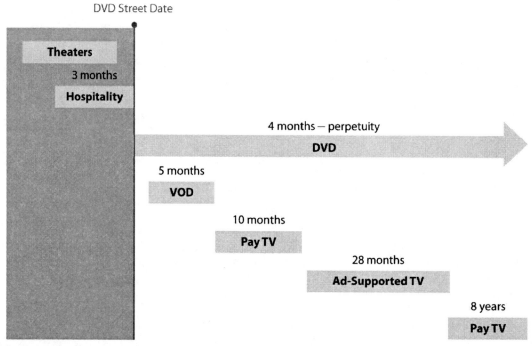

Supplier Power and Atoms to Bits

The winner-take-all and winner-take-most dynamics of digital distribution can put suppliers at a disadvantage. Studios may be wary of granting Netflix increasing power over product distribution, and as such, they may be motivated to keep rivals around. If firms rely on one channel partner for a large portion of deals, that partner has an upper hand in negotiations. For years, record labels and movie studios complained that Apple's dominance of iTunes allowed them little negotiating room in price setting. A boycott where NBC temporarily lifted television shows from iTunes is credited with loosening Apple's pricing policies. Similarly, when Amazon's Kindle dominated the e-reader market, Amazon enforced a $9.99 price on electronic editions, even as publishers lobbied for higher rates. It wasn't until Apple arrived with a creditable e-reader rival in the iPad that Amazon's leverage was weakened to the point where publishers were allowed to set their own e-book prices.[38] Streaming licensing fees have become an important part of studio profitability, and an increase in Netflix streaming scale offers the firm even more leverage. However, Hastings is wary of zero-sum negotiations and the bad blood this can create between his firm and suppliers, stating publicly that the firm's goal is to develop the kinds of partnerships where both sides benefit.[39]

3.2 Exclusives and Original Content

One way Netflix can counter rivals with exclusive content is to offer exclusive content of its own. The firm has secured sole streaming rights for several popular shows, including the AMC series *Mad Men*, *Breaking Bad*, and *The Walking Dead*; and NBC's The Blacklist. In 2012, Netflix inked a $300-million-a-year deal with Disney will give the firm first-run exclusive streaming access to Disney shows (including Pixar, Marvel, and Lucasfilm), but not until 2016. Why the wait? Starz had an exclusive deal with Disney prior to 2016.[40]

In an even bolder move, Netflix has aggressively backed the development of multiple original offerings for debut on its service, broadly experimenting with programming genres. Early efforts include the critically acclaimed *House of Cards*, featuring Oscar-winner Kevin Spacey and produced by

David Fincher (director of *The Social Network*), *Orange Is the New Black* by the creator of *Weeds*, and new episodes of the cult comedy *Arrested Development*, which once aired on Fox. *Sense8*, a sci-fi series created by the Wachowski Brothers of *The Matrix* fame. The network is also producing several series based on superheroes from Disney-owned Marvel entertainment (Daredevil was released, first), a talk show featuring comic Chelsea Handler, and several original movies, including a sequel to the martial arts flick Crouching Tiger, Hidden Dragon (which the firm will also release in theaters), and a four-film deal with Adam Sandler. Netflix is investing in new shows for kids, too. These include new shows based on DreamWorks characters *All Hail King Julian* (from *Madagascar*), and *The Adventures of Puss and Boots* (from *Shrek*), and rebooting series for *How to Train Your Dragon*, and the classic *Magic School-bus* show.

Being the sugar daddy to original content doesn't come cheap. The first two seasons of *House of Cards* reportedly cost $100 million, and Netflix outbid both HBO and AMC for rights to the project. The new *Arrested Development* episodes reportedly cost $45 million.[41] And not all original content has been a success—the firm's $90 million *Marco Polo* series was widely panned.[42] Despite this, the firm tripled its annual original programming commitment from 2014 to 2015.[43] Netflix credits original content with subscriber growth and increased customer engagement,[44] and analysts also suspect the content helps reduce customer churn.[45] By Spring 2015 Netflix was already accounting for some 6 percent of *all* TV viewing in North America.[46] The firm's subscribers watch, on average, about two hours of Netflix streaming each day (also up two-fold in about two years).[47] A great trajectory for Netflix and evidence of customer-experience-created brand strengthening, but bad for the networks. Netflix is said to have accounted to a 43 percent decline in quarterly network TV viewership during Q1 2015.[48]

The first batch of Netflix-backed originals (including *House of Cards*, *Orange Is the New Black*, and *Arrested Development*) gave the firm exclusive first-window US streaming rights, but even though these titles lead with the claim of being "A Netflix Original Series," they are actually licensed from other studios. Since Netflix doesn't outright own these properties, early seasons of *House of Cards* are available from competitors—including Comcast, Vudu, and Amazon (for *House of Cards* are actually owned by Sony)—and Lionsgate, which controls licensing of *Orange Is the New Black*, has made that series available to others as well.[49] Streaming *House of Cards* internationally will require Netflix to pay up again. Licencing costs only about half of what Netflix would pay for full ownership; however, with the value of original content now proven, Netflix has begun to do deals for complete ownership of some new projects, a level of control that HBO has with many of its series. Ownership could keep titles worldwide-exclusive to Netflix (an option that becomes even more valuable as the firm aggressively expands abroad), and it could allow Netflix to pursue additional revenue streams, such as DVD sales or licensing to other channels and services.[50]

The new Netflix looks less like an Amazon shipping center and more like a must-watch network, offering the kind of critically and culturally resonant content one would find on HBO or AMC. Says Netflix Chief Content Officer Ted Sarandos, "The goal is to become HBO faster than HBO can become us."[51] How have they done? By early 2013, the Netflix streaming audience had grown larger than HBO's subscriber base, while viewing hours surpassed those of cable's most-watched network, The Disney Channel.[52]

Disintermediation and Digital Distribution

The purchase of NBC/Universal by Comcast, the largest cable television provider in the United States, has consolidated content and distribution in a single firm. The move can be described as both vertical integration (when an organization owns more than one layer of its value chain) and **disintermediation** (removing an organization from a firm's distribution channel).[53] Some also consider Netflix's move into the content creation business a form of vertical integration as it moves backward in the value chain.[54] Disintermediation in the video industry offers two potentially big benefits. First, studios don't need to share revenue with third parties; they can keep all the money generated through new windows. Also critically important, if a studio goes directly to consumers, then studios get to collect and keep a potentially valuable data asset. If another firm sits between a supplier and its customers, the supplier loses out on a key resource for competitive advantage. For more on the value of the data asset in maintaining and strengthening customer relationships, see Chapter 15

3.3 Streaming and the Data Asset

Netflix has one very critical asset that is far stronger than what rivals, especially cable television networks, can assemble: a growing and exquisitely detailed treasure trove of data. This data asset is used to make more accurate recommendations, improve user interface design, and help the firm determine the appropriate cost for acquiring content, and it can even shape creative decisions in original program offerings.

The data gathered via streaming can be more revealing than ratings received via DVD-by-mail. Even if someone doesn't rate a given title, if they binge-watch multiple episodes, Netflix has a pretty good indicator that the user likes the show. The reverse is usually true for the unrated property that a user streamed for the first fifteen minutes and never came back to.[55] In the DVD-by-mail days, the firm had no idea if you'd actually watched unrated shows you'd received, watched them multiple times, finished watching titles you started, and so forth. Once captured, this data can be fed into the firm's Cinematch collaborative filtering software to further group user tastes and help subscribers discover the content most likely to delight them. Netflix possesses not only several hundred genres, or even several thousand, but also over seventy-six thousand (and climbing) unique ways to describe different types of movies. While Netflix does employ a team of "entertainment classification experts" to initially tag and rate movie characteristics, the real magic happens during data analysis.[56] Each user's Netflix screen is the result of analyzing terabytes of data. Every recent click, view, review, early abandon, and guide page view, as well as other data, is considered in order to identify the content the firm believes users will most likely want to see. Some 75 to 80 percent of what people watch on the service comes from Netflix recommendations, not search.[57]

A/B test

A randomized group of experiments used to collect data and compare performance among two options studied (A and B). A/B testing is often used in refining the design of technology products, and A/B tests are particularly easy to run over the Internet on a firm's Web site. Amazon, Google, and Facebook are among the firms that aggressively leverage hundreds of A/B tests a year in order to improve their product offerings.

Data analysis doesn't just drive the collaborative filtering software for user recommendations; it's also used to tailor and improve the experience over time. Like Google, Amazon, and many other firms, Netflix will roll out new features to a subset of users, running an **A/B test** to determine how the new stacked up against the old. If feature A is better than feature B, then A will be rolled out to everyone. Metrics used to evaluate the slew of constant tests include sign-up, viewing, and retention rates.[58] (For more about A/B testing, see Chapter 7).

The data also help Netflix make better content investments. When licensing new work, Netflix examines a variety of inputs, including things like actors' names and title genre, to determine the likely size of an audience and that property's value to the firm.[59] When content comes up for renewal, Netflix crunches the data, including how often a given title has been viewed, its user rating score, and key viewing trends. All this helps the firm determine just how much a given asset is worth, and it directly informs decisions on choosing projects and setting budgets.[60] Says Content Chief Sarandos, "I can justify the spend with our data and do so with a far greater degree of confidence than the television networks."[61] While many observers gasped when Netflix chose to pass at Viacom's hefty price tag on a big bundle of popular kids' shows that included *Dora the Explorer* and *SpongeBob SquarePants*, the decision making of Hastings and Sarandos was informed by data. And even though rival Amazon swooped in to grab the Nickelodeon titles for Amazon Prime, Netflix opted to choose replacement Disney titles, such as the SpongeBob-beating tween ratings champ, *Phineas and Ferb*.[62] Data-driven decision making isn't perfect, but it should be a lot more reliable than the gut instinct of studio heads that still drives many media industry deals.

Data also informs the original content investments that Netflix is making. For example, Netflix made the decision to revive *Arrested Development* in part based on its ability to monitor customer attitudes toward the original series over time. The series was a cult hit—it was one of the most popular programs on DVD and streaming—and data clearly showed that interest had steadily grown since cancellation.[63] Content Chief Sarandos says, "We can bring to the table really factual and data-based information."

Netflix also uses data to create ultratailored audience promotions. When advertising *House of Cards* to Netflix users, Director David Fincher cut seven different trailers for the series. Some of these focused on female characters, some played up that the series was a political thriller, others highlighted actor Kevin Spacey, and one focused on Fincher himself. Netflix would only show you a *House of Cards* suggestion if its math thought you'd like it,[64] and any trailers that a given user saw on Netflix were chosen and targeted based on their viewing history.[65] While Reed Hastings has clearly said he won't let data interfere with the creative process or dictate terms to showrunners,[66] Netflix's data-driven insights can offer value if artists request a look. For example, firm data is said to have been used by showrunners on *Orange Is the New Black* to influence casting.[67]

3.4 Streaming Changes Viewing Habits and Frees Creative Constraints

Conventional, schedule-driven television viewing is being replaced by the new "WWW"—the ability to view *what* you want, *when* you want it, on *whatever* screen is available.[68] As apps replace channels and content is available at all times across all screens, the streaming experience is liberating both consumers and content creators from constraints of channel-driven "linear TV." Consider the phenomenon of *binge-watching*, or viewing several episodes of a program in a single sitting. As Sarandos puts it, "In the world of weekly serialized television you get fifty minutes of joy watching a show and then 10,000 minutes of waiting for the next one."[69] Over that time, users can lose track of characters and complex plot lines, and they may be distracted, miss an episode, and stop viewing all together. With streaming, users are likely to watch multiple episodes at once. Shortly after *Arrested Development* debuted, 10 percent of viewers watched a string of fifteen episodes.[70]

For producers, writers, and directors, the creative side feels less constrained, too. Netflix execs state, "If you give people a more creative format, then they can tell their stories better."[71] With streaming, there's no need to plan cliff-hangers at the end of a program or even write for the standard time lengths, like the 22-minute standard for commercial sitcom television. The revived *Arrested Development* has one episode that's just fifteen minutes long. Binge-watching also works well for programming with dense and complicated storytelling, such as the Netflix-backed sci-fi series *Sense8*. A blog post from Netflix underscores the appeal of working for the streaming service rather than a traditional network: "Because we are not allocating scarce prime-time slots like linear TV does, a show that is taking a long time to find its audience is one we can keep nurturing. This allows us to prudently commit to a whole season, rather than just a pilot episode."[72] The kind of artistic creativity offered by streaming makes Netflix, as stated by the *Hollywood Reporter*, "one of the most attractive buyers of original programming in town."[73]

Breaking Bad to Netflix, "Thanks!"

"I don't think you'd be sitting here interviewing me if it weren't for Netflix. In its third season, 'Breaking Bad' got this amazing nitrous-oxide boost of energy and general public awareness because of Netflix. Before binge-watching, someone who identified him- or herself as a fan of a show probably only saw 25 percent of the episodes."[74]

Breaking Bad creator Vince Gilligan in a *New York Magazine* interview

3.5   Customer Experience, Complexity, Pricing, and Brand Strength

While the world of bits offers firms the ability to take advantage of different pricing models for digital entertainment, Netflix had been steadfast in insisting that all of its content will be available anywhere for a single monthly subscription fee. This is in contrast to firms like Apple, Google, Amazon, Hulu, and cable operators, who all offer a mix of pricing schemes that might include buying content, pay-per-view, commercially supported content, and subscription for additional premium offerings.

In the Netflix view, you shouldn't have to choose between commercial content, pay-per-view, buying a title, or waiting for a viewing window. While the service is defined simply, competition is defined broadly—the firm is really in a battle to be a first-choice entertainment destination across all possible offerings. As the firm stated in a letter to shareholders, "Our North Star is to win more of our members' 'moments of truth'…when our member wants to relax, enjoy a shared experience with friends and family, or is just bored. They could play a video game, surf the Web, read a magazine, channel surf, buy a pay-per-view movie, put on a DVD, turn on Hulu or Amazon Prime, or they could tap on Netflix. We want our members to choose Netflix in these moments."[75] Simplicity seems to be working. While Netflix's customer satisfaction tanked following the firm's pricing split and Qwikster debacle, less than two years later consumers had rated Netflix more positively than any of its peers, including offerings from Amazon, Apple, and Google—all of which offer more complex media pricing.[76]

3.6   Streaming and Scale Advantages

Despite rising costs, a difficult-to-control cost structure, and increased competition, there are still key advantages that can be created by a leading player in the streaming business, and Netflix hopes that its advantages will be large enough to sustain it as the dominant firm for years to come. First, regarding scale, while studios may charge more for deals involving more users, the firm with more users is likely to be able to pay far more than smaller rivals. A studio would rather accept a $200 million check from Netflix than three $50 million checks from smaller players. Start talking exclusives, and advantage once again goes to the biggest player.

FIGURE 4.4 US Penetration of Subscription Video Streaming Services and N. American Home Bandwidth Usage

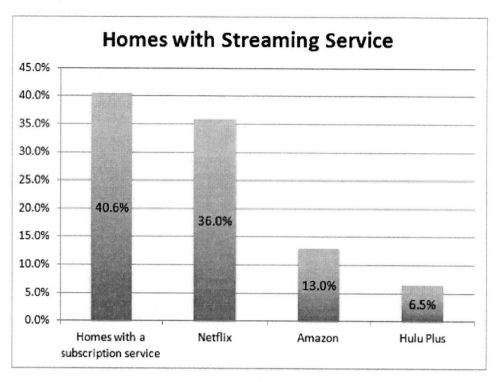

Nearly three times as many US homes have a Netflix subscription than have access to Amazon Prime's Instant Video. Usage statistics weigh even more heavily in Netflix favor, with Netflix streaming accounting for over one-third of home broadband traffic, while Amazon and Hulu Plus are in the low single digits.

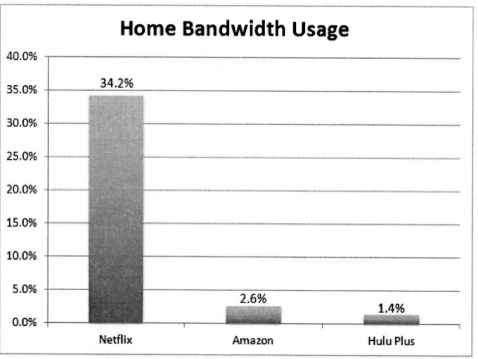

Source: Based on data from P. Kafka, "Netflix Still Dominates Streaming, but Amazon Is Picking Up Steam," Re/code, Nov. 20, 2014. And E. Steel, "Nielsen Charts Reach of Streaming Services," The New York Times, March 11, 2015.

Size-based advantages come from both the scale of a firm's streaming library (a longer tail) and the scale of the customer base (the ability to pay for that tail). Once a firm gets big, there's a virtuous cycle where more titles attract more customers, and more customers increase a firm's ability to bid on attractive content. Netflix doesn't just see growth as a way to advance profitability; it sees it as a vital competitive asset to keep competitors at bay. Netflix is expected to spend an estimated $5 billion on content in 2016. For comparison, content expenses in 2014 for HBO, Amazon, and Showtime combined were only $4.6 billion. The only network that spends more on content than Netflix is ESPN. Netflix can spend so much because it has more subscribers than rivals. And while Amazon's content spend has been about half of the Netflix bill, Netflix is seeing 1,250 percent greater usage,[77] scale economies in action.

Just how much bigger is Netflix's streaming selection than that of rivals? Information Hastings shared in 2013 a shareholders letter[78] can be seen in Figure 4.5 While all services have aggressively moved to acquire more content of all types, Netflix continues to dominate in key measures of subscriber base, estimated titles available, title quality, and viewer hours.[79] It's also worth noting that the smallest firm in this chart, Redbox Instant, has since shut down, unable to compete with larger rivals despite backing from Verizon.[80]

In that letter, Hastings also details why he believes Netflix will outdo pay television: "From a high-level, HBO-linear [meaning the premium cable channel] is our closest comparison, and they have about 30 million domestic members. We have more content, more viewing, a broader brand proposition, are on-demand, on all devices, and are less expensive, so we estimate that we can be two to three times larger than current linear-HBO, or 60 to 90 million domestic members. This factors in that as we grow, our content and service can continue to get better."[81] Since new customers often gravitate toward the best-known firms and favor products recommended by friends, dominant firms should also see customer acquisition costs, as a percentage of sales, go down.

3.7   The March to Global Dominance

Global expansion plays a key role in the Netflix drive for scale-driven dominance. Netflix sees the magic number for long-term profitable scale in any given market as 20 to 30 percent of households,[82] and getting there will be a land-grab. Global expansion is complicated by powerful regional players such as Clarovideo, Sky NOW TV, LOVEFiLM (the Amazon-owned "Netflix of Europe"), and HBO Nordics, but Netflix is the biggest global player—by far.[83] By 2015, Netflix was in over 50 countries, including Cuba,[84] with Hastings stating his intention to have Netflix in two hundred nations by 2017.[85] Expanding internationally is not without cost. Entering new markets usually involves heavy up-front expenses including ramping up marketing campaigns to create awareness and securing licenses for both American and local content. Some Netflix content is already locked up by foreign rivals (France's Canal Plus already has the rights to *House of Cards*). As an international player, Netflix may one day allow the firm to strike worldwide licensing deals rather than having to negotiate on a country-by-country basis, but the ability to do this on any significant scale is described by one Netflix executive as being "years" away.[86] Legal issues can present a country-by-country challenge as well. For example, French law requires a wait time of three years after a film is released in theaters before it can be streamed online; it also require distributors to invest in local production[87] (on tap is the original series *Marseille*, billed as a French *House of Cards*[88]). French legal issues and taxation policies proved so onerous that they prompted Netflix to move its European headquarters from France to Amsterdam.[89] Nations with heavy censorship laws (like China) will also pose challenges. But the overall outlook for global growth is good, with international customers increasing by over 2.25 million users a quarter and outpacing US subscribers growth.[90] Hastings has set a long-term target of generating 80 percent of Netflix revenue outside the United States, which will require a lot of growth. But there's plenty of room. Currently, the firm's 20 million plus global customers represent less than one-third of all subscribers, but analysts expect international subs to balloon past 87 million by 2020.

3.8   It's a Multiscreen World: Getting to Netflix Everywhere

Another major challenge in the migration from DVD to streaming involved getting content to the television. While Apple had its own low-cost television add-on and Amazon had partnered with TiVo, Netflix was still streaming only on PCs. An internal team at Netflix developed a prototype set-top box that Hastings himself supported offering. But most customers aren't enthusiastic about purchasing yet another box for their set top, the consumer electronics business is brutally competitive, and selling hardware would introduce an entirely new set of inventory, engineering, marketing, distribution, and competitive complexities.

Netflix eventually decided to think beyond one hardware alternative and instead recruit others to provide a wealth of choice. The firm developed a software platform and makes this available to manufacturers seeking to include Netflix access in their devices. It was an especially smart move given the explosion in content watching that occurs on screens that are not televisions, and Netflix tools made it

FIGURE 4.5   Top 100 Most Popular Movies and Television Shows on Netflix and Their Availability on Major Streaming Competitors

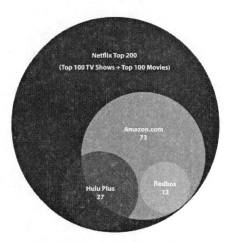

Source: R. Hastings and D. Wells, "Letter to Shareholders," Netflix Investor Relations Document, January 23, 2013.

easier to build apps. Today, Netflix streaming is available either as an app or baked directly into over a thousand consumer electronics products, including televisions, DVD players, video game consoles, phones, and tablets.[91] And that internally developed Netflix set-top box? The group was spun out to form Roku, an independent firm that launched their own low-cost Netflix streamer.

By working with consumer electronics firms, offering Netflix streaming as a feature or an app, Hastings's firm has ended up with more television access than either Amazon or Apple, despite the fact that both of these firms got their streaming content to the television first. Today, Netflix access is considered a must-have component for any Internet-connected media device. Partnerships have helped create distribution breadth, giving Hastings an enviable base through which to grow the video streaming business.

While you can get Netflix from your TV, game system, phone, DVD player, or streaming-specific hardware like Chromecast, FireTV, or Roku, Netflix has been slow to show up as an icon offered through the cable provider settop box. Cable providers are leery of streaming services that don't require their networks, fearing that rich product offerings accessible without channel subscriptions could prompt existing subscribers to become cord cutters (eliminating cable all together) or cord shavers (who drop premium cable channels). By comparison, the HBO Now streaming service is less of a threat to cable firms, since a channel subscription (where cable firms get their monthly cut) also includes unlimited streaming, and is usually the same price or less than if you bought just streaming a la carte direct from HBO.

So What's It Take to Run This Thing?

It might surprise many to hear that the bulk of the Netflix computing infrastructure runs on Amazon's servers. But using Amazon Web Services (AWS—see Chapter 7 for more details) has enabled Netflix to grow its services by millions of customers without adding any data center capacity since 2008. Lots of firms offer cloud services, and Microsoft may have seemed a more logical partner than Amazon. Hastings was a Microsoft board member at the time Netflix was shopping for cloud providers, and Redmond was seen as less of a competitor than Amazon. But Netflix engineers determined that Amazon was the "biggest and baddest" cloud house around, with unmatched expertise in providing computing scale and power. Netflix doesn't see owning its own data centers as a way to create a substantial, defensible advantage.[92] Instead, it lets Amazon handle the hardware while the Netflix engineering staff of over 700 focus on creating the second-to-none software needed by the video-streaming giant.

Netflix is the biggest AWS customer, drawing on upwards of 20,000 servers at a time to handle tasks that include streaming video, collaborative filtering, video encoding, digital rights management, and additional number crunching. Netflix cloud architect Adrian Cockcroft (who you can follow on Twitter and SlideShare to learn more about the geekier details of Netflix) is considered one of cloud computing's biggest rock stars. Says Cockcroft, "We're using Amazon more efficiently than the retail arm of Amazon is... We're pretty sure about that."[93]

Netflix's storage appetite is voracious. The master copies of all the shows and movies that the firm streams requires a 3.14-petabyte-and-growing chunk of Amazon cloud storage.[94] Each time a studio uploads a file to Netflix, the firm leverages the Amazon cloud to rapidly configure more than a hundred specially sized copies (for example, large HD files for big screens and files that are much smaller for streaming to phones over a 3G network).

In order to keep high-demand content streaming as speedily as possible, Netflix runs a nightly analysis to figure out which titles are going to be popular the next day. Titles in high demand (say, the new installment of recently released popular television series) are queued up on flash storage, which is more expensive but faster than conventional hard drives. In an effort to further speed content to consumers, Netflix places its own storage appliances in or near the networks of key Internet Service Providers worldwide and then uses predictive models to make sure content is close to most-likely requesters before they even ask for it.[95] Regularly distributing the firm's highest-demand titles and caching it in these "islands of access" around the world reduces the number of overall customer requests that come into Amazon's cloud. There are firms that Netflix could hire to distribute its content at caching locations close to users—this is the business of so-called Contend Distribution Network (CDN) companies like Akamai, CDNNetworks, and Limelight. But Netflix has such a high volume of traffic that scattering its own special-purpose servers around the globe helps keep costs low.[96]

As the pioneer in the field, Netflix has been forced to build most of the software it needs from scratch. In-house user interface specialists focus on designing easy-to-use software for a variety of devices. The television interface designer is known as the "ten-foot guy," since that's about the distance between the user and the big screen. The designer for laptops is the "two-foot guy," and the tablet designer is the "eighteen-inch guy."[97] So-called *localization specialists* work on making sure each of the available interfaces is customized to the appropriate language for each of the over forty-five countries where Netflix is offered.

Also surprising—Netflix gives away a huge portion of software that its team has developed. Source code relating to competitive advantage in the media streaming industry remain under wraps (think collaborative filtering systems and the firm's decision-driving analytics), but Netflix has been especially generous in sharing tools that it feels will also be useful to a wide variety of cloud users across industries. Among the firm's better-known open-source contributions is code that tests the robustness of systems running in the cloud. Examples include the playfully named "chaos monkey," which simulates random system failure, and the "security monkey," which probes for hacking holes.[98] Intel and eBay are among the multibillion-dollar firms leveraging Netflix software, and the Obama campaign directly attributed Netflix code with helping shift computing needs to the West Coast when East Coast operations were taken out by Hurricane Sandy.[99] With more geeks worldwide using this open-source code, there's a greater chance the tools will be improved by others, which would eventually benefit Netflix as well.

Crowdsourcing and Code Contests: The Netflix Prize and Beyond

While Netflix is widely considered to have a best-in-class collaborative filtering engine in Cinematch, the firm also realizes that it has no monopoly on math. So the firm previously ran a competition, known as the Netflix Prize, ponying up $1 million to the first team that could improve Cinematch scores by 10 percent. For contest purposes, Netflix released a subset of ratings data, stripped of customer identity,[100] and over 30,000 teams from over 170 countries eventually entered the contest. The winning team consisted of engineers that entered the competition on separate teams. It included a pair of coders from Montreal; two US researchers from AT&T Labs; a scientist from Yahoo! Research, Israel; and a couple of Austrian college students turned consultants.[101] It's safe to say that without the Netflix Prize, these folks would likely never have met, let alone collaborated.

The Netflix Prize is an example of crowdsourcing, a technique in which a firm states a problem it would like solved, the reward it will provide, and then makes this available to a broader community in the form of an open call. While Netflix did not implement the final winning algorithm as introduced, it had already begun incorporating changes based on learning from submissions even before the contest was complete.[102] The effort was also a public relations bonanza, with articles on the effort (and Netflix superior Cinematch software) appearing in major news and business publications worldwide.

The positive crowdsourcing experience has led Netflix to run several other contests, including one rewarding hackers for improving the firm's open-source cloud tools. Not only does the firm benefit from code submissions; the contest also has a recruiting payoff. Says one manager about these efforts, "We can see people who already know our code base and are doing interesting things."[103]

3.9   A Crowded Field of Rivals and Other Challenges

While Netflix has a strong global lead, picking a winner in the race for delivering bits to a multiscreen world is still very much an uncertain bet. The market remains highly fragmented, with a long list of potential competitors and a varied list of models for reaching consumers. While new start-ups seem unlikely to threaten Netflix given the firm's scale advantages, the more significant threat is from firms that have thriving businesses in other areas. These firms can come to market with cash that lets them credibly crash the Netflix party, and they may be more willing to endure short- and midterm losses as they try to steal share from the leader. Amazon is integrating its own streaming service into televisions and consumer devices, making Amazon instant video into its successful Kindle Fire products, launching the sub-$100 Fire TV streaming and gaming set-top box, a sub-$40 Fire TV streaming stick, and aggressively expanding its content library. Amazon may be losing a billion dollars a year in streaming,[104] but Jeff Bezos has motivation beyond subscription: viewing video as a free add-on that encourages adoption of the firm's Amazon Prime shipping service and as a way to ensure that Kindle can serve up an iPad-rivaling depth of content. Apple's iTunes offers video purchases and "rentals" across PCs and Macs, as well as the iPod, iPhone, iPad, and an aggressively redesigned, Siri-powered Apple TV . Microsoft offers an online rental and purchase service via Xbox. Google offers thousands of television shows and movies over YouTube via both ad-supported and rental models, and it continues to refine Google TV as well as the Google Play online store. Comcast's Universal Studios is among the major film studios that has experimented with direct streaming to consumers over Facebook. With Netflix offering apps on so many of these competing platforms, the firm's frenemies list is a long one. Networks and content providers also have their own offerings: many stream content on their own websites; Comcast and Verizon have apps that stream content to phones, PCs, and tablets; and Hulu is a joint venture backed by NBC, Fox, and other networks. Netflix also faces me-too subscription efforts from its previously vanquished DVD-by-mail rivals, Blockbuster (now part of Dish network) and Wal-mart (which owns VUDU).

A bits-based business can also be risky if the infrastructure is unreliable. If a store or warehouse has a problem, a firm can try to service customers from another location. But if the technology that supports your services breaks and redundancy fails, then your entire business is brought to its knees. Netflix and its cloud provider, Amazon, have suffered a series of such outages in the past, and any repeated reliability concerns risks prompting customers to seek alternatives.[105] But since everyone in streaming has a service that lives in the cloud (either private, like Apple's, or rented from a provider like Amazon AWS), nearly everyone is vulnerable to issues with online reliability.

Then there's the issue of unhappy consumer Internet service providers. Netflix streaming uses up more North American broadband traffic than any other service, and more than YouTube, Hulu, Amazon, HBO Go, iTunes, and BitTorrent *combined*![106] Many Internet service providers (ISPs) aren't pleased by the firm's growth, viewing Netflix as a rapidly expanding, network-clogging traffic hog. Netflix pays its own ISPs to connect the firm to the Internet and to support its heavy volume of outbound traffic, but cable companies that control the so-called last mile to your home (usually with little to no competition) want Netflix to pay more. Netflix has cut deals with Comcast and Verizon to connect directly to their networks to improve streaming performance. This runs contrary to principles of *net neutrality*—that is, the principle that all Internet traffic should be treated equally and that ISPs should not discriminate, slow down access, or charge differentially by user, content, site, platform, application, type of attached equipment, or modes of communication[107] (for more, see Chapter 16). 2015 FCC rule change "address threats to the open Internet by, among other things, prohibiting [broadband] providers from interfering with an individual's ability to access Netflix's video service," but the ultimate fate of these rulings remains in flux.[108] Internet access and usage rules in global markets also continue to develop, and Hastings has also called for stronger net neutrality protections in Europe.[109]

Another threat is that several ISPs, including Comcast, AT&T, and Charter, have experimented with **bandwidth caps** that place a ceiling on a customer's total monthly consumption (users can usually bump up the ceiling, but they have to pay for it). Today, few US users are running into the ceiling, but that may change as more family members sport tablets, smartphones, and other streaming devices and as new, traffic-heavy technologies like FaceTime and Skype become more widely used. In Canada, Netflix has already lowered stream quality to deal with that nation's more restrictive traffic consumption limits.

If bandwidth is capped, then consumers might pay a penalty (or pay more) just for being Netflix customers. And if Netflix has to pay to cut special deals with ISPs, then it'll have less money for content and innovation and may pass on some costs to consumers in the form of higher subscription prices. Others worry that a loss of net neutrality will hurt entrepreneurship and innovation since only the largest players will be able to pay for the best access. Cable outfits see it differently, stating that their profits allow them to make investments in faster, more reliable networks, which actually empowers the next-gen Zuckerbergs. Netflix has been fiercely critical of the cable industry and continues to push for net neutrality reforms, but if fast-lane access or bandwidth caps become commonplace, the firm could suffer.

bandwidth caps

A limit, imposed by the ISP (e.g., a cable or telephone company) on the total amount of traffic that a given subscriber can consume (usually per each billing period).

Hacking Corporate Culture

A few years back, Reed Hastings wrote what is now considered to be one of the most highly influential documents on corporate culture. Hastings started this as a sort of letter to himself, where he wrote down what he wished he'd known when he started his journey in entrepreneurship twenty years earlier.[110] As the founder of two successful software firms (before Netflix, Hastings founded and led Pure Software, a firm that he eventually sold for three-quarters of a billion dollars), Hastings has learned a lot along the way. Facebook COO (chief operating officer) Sheryl Sandberg calls the slide deck of Hastings's notes, titled *Netflix Culture: Freedom & Responsibility*, "the most important document ever to come out of the Valley." That's high praise from one of the most powerful women in business—and likely an influencing factor on why Hastings was chosen as a Facebook board member.

Hastings outlined the central tenet: "We want responsible people who are self-motivating and self-disciplined, and we reward them with freedom."[111] Included in the document are some suggestions that run counter to widespread industry practices. For example, while many firms delay compensation, shelling out stock options over time in vesting periods that act as "golden handcuffs" to aid in employee retention, all Netflix employee compensation vests immediately. Netflix wants employees motivated by the challenge and excitement of the firm's operating environment, eliminating any clock punchers waiting for a calendar date to arrive. "During the trying time for Netflix [when stock dropped to one-sixth its value following the Qwikster debacle], our culture helped us hold everything together…there was a lot of strength and resilience on the management team."[112]

Also unusual is the firm's vacation policy: there is none at Netflix. Employees are encouraged to do what they need to in order to get the job done and to take the time off that they need and feel they deserve. Hastings himself takes plenty of vacation to set an example to other employees, claiming, "I do some of my creative thinking on vacation." The policy requires honesty and maturity, but that's precisely the kind of employee Netflix is after.

Employees at Netflix are among the highest paid in Silicon Valley. The firm regularly monitors top pay at peer firms—and then adds 10 to 20 percent on top of that number. As a result it can hire just about anyone it wants. Get fired from Netflix? Severance is described as ultragenerous as well. The policy is meant to "remove guilt as an obstacle to management parting ways with subpar performers."[113] Managers are directed to only keep those employees they'd be "willing to fight for."[114]

Rather than view the firm as a family (as many firms claim to be), Hastings's analogy for his company is a sports team. The goal is to have star performers in every position. But unlike a sports team, a growing firm doesn't have a finite set of slots on its roster, so there's more room for talent growth. The team analogy also translates into other directives—don't hire "brilliant jerks," and "cutthroat" behavior toward fellow employees is not tolerated. Frankness is encouraged, however. The firm regularly uses so-called "stop, start, continue" feedback, where anyone can give any other employee their thoughts on what they should stop doing, start doing, and continue doing. The technique is also used in group employee reviews sessions.[115]

Want more insight on life at Netflix? See the slide deck at http://www.slideshare.net/reed2001/culture-1798664.

3.10 No Turning Back

While the firm is seeing a decreased payout from its investment in its warehouse infrastructure, nearly all assets have a limited lifespan. That's why corporations depreciate assets, writing their value down over time. The reality is that the shift from atoms to bits isn't flicking on like a light switch; it is a hybrid transition taking place over several years. Try to make the transition to streaming-only too quickly, and as the Qwikster debacle showed, customers may leave. But move too slowly and rivals can gain ground. If Netflix can grab compelling content at manageable costs, broaden distribution options, grow its customer base, and lock them in with the switching costs created by Cinematch (all big "ifs"), it just might cement its position as a key player in a bits-only world.

Is the hybrid atoms and bits strategy a dangerous straddling gambit or a clever expansion that will keep the firm dominant? Netflix really doesn't have a choice but to try. Hastings already has a long history as one of the savviest strategic thinkers in tech. And while analysts have underestimated Hastings in the past, the firm's sky high stock price and pundit expectations seem to have swung the other way. Positive recent statements about the globally ambitious firm include: "[Netflix] is quickly becoming one of the most powerful media companies in the world" and "the streaming video giant could soon become the next $100 billion tech company."[116] Does the firm deserve the hype? As the networks say, stay tuned!

TABLE 4.1   Netflix DVD-by-Mail versus Streaming

	Netflix DVD-by-Mail	Netflix Streaming	Notes
Content Acquisition Costs	Fixed.	Variable and increasing. No consistency in licensing parameters (variants include per subscriber, per use, per stream, duration of deal, exclusivity). Has pushed Netflix to back exclusive content in hopes of drawing customers with high-quality, unique, first-run offerings.	Starz turned down a Netflix 10x offer to renew licensing just three years after first pact. US "first sale doctrine" means Netflix can buy and send out DVDs, but this ruling doesn't apply to streaming/broadcast.
Competitors	Mostly vanquished (bankrupt, inefficient Blockbuster bought by Dish). Indirect competition from Redbox kiosks but rival selection is small without delivery convenience.	Numerous with different models.	Digital video content available from Amazon, Apple, Dish/Blockbuster, Google/YouTube, Hulu, Walmart/Vudu, Cable providers (OnDemand), Pay channels (e.g., HBO Go).
Competitor Motivation	Market has little appeal for new entrants.	Maturing tech firms see streaming as a growth market, and revenue models/goals vary (subscription/PPV/Download-to-own, advertising, to fuel hardware purchases). Cable channels and cable providers fear subscriber loss.	Many rivals are highly profitable in other industries/have resources for expansion and to sustain prolonged competition. Pay channels fear their content will be devalued if Netflix is both cheaper and has a greater selection. Cable providers/channels fear chord cutting/shaving customers.
Plans	Fixed price per month based on number of DVDs at a time. High volume customers that frequently return DVDs are unprofitable.	Unlimited monthly subscription to all content.	Rival plans vary and include: subscription, free/commercial-supported, rental, pay-per-view, download to own.
Innovation	Very limited since DVD content is fixed by the studios and burned onto a disc.	Opportunities for new content and revenue models.	Although Netflix states it will not consider anything beyond flat-rate subscriptions, streaming does offer the potential for mixed revenue streams (premium priced "windows," ad-supported offerings with ability to gather/leverage high-value customer data), and the ability to launch new content/services DVDs can't match (social, interactive premium content).
Availability	Any DVD that can be purchased (125,000 title long tail).	Limited to what studios will license (a shorter tail, fewer new/hit titles), or to new, original content that Netflix sponsors.	Content is licensed from studios (content owners) or cable channels (if channels have the right to relicense broadcast/streaming rights to others). HBO and others won't share. Pay channels get exclusives in "windows" that may require content to be pulled from streaming.
Delivery Infrastructure	Tough to duplicate (at one point as many as 58 warehouses). Staffed and maintained—require steady/increasing subscribers to keep margins high.	Currently uses public cloud (Amazon), but with proprietary technology.	Postal costs to increase while service may decrease (Saturday eliminated, delivery speed slowed). Public cloud use means rivals have access to similar delivery infrastructure assets. ISPs threaten end-user bandwidth caps that may lower streaming appeal.

	Netflix DVD-by-Mail	Netflix Streaming	Notes
Delivery To	Any device with a DVD player. Selected on Web, delivery in about a day.	Any network-connected screen (TV, PC, mobile) with a Netflix client. Instantly browse, preview, watch, and rate content.	Blu-ray likely the last physical standard. The future is streaming and Netflix has the largest partner platform, integrating in game consoles, TVs, DVD players, mobile devices, and more. Device partnerships are not exclusive to Netflix and rivals are expanding streaming reach with similar integration.
Global Expansion	Expensive to replicate infrastructure regionally.	Can be served from the cloud, but reliant on local backbone and last-mile broadband.	DVD-by-mail needs cheap/fast local postal networks. Streaming costs are mostly dropping worldwide, but availability limited in some areas, quality varies, and bandwidth caps may limit appeal.
Market Outlook/ Challenges	US DVD-by-mail is mature and likely to decrease. Profit margins associated with running a nationwide warehouse network will go down if subscribers drop/ shift to streaming.	A growing but highly unpredictable business in terms of future costs, content availability, rival intensity, appeal vs. alternatives, and more. Key is in creating strategic assets that others can't match, but what are they? Brand, scale advantages, and data drove DVD-by-mail dominance.	Uncertain if Netflix will continue to gain streaming subscribers ahead of rivals.

KEY TAKEAWAYS

- The shift from atoms to bits is impacting all media industries, particularly those relying on print, video, and music content. Content creators, middlemen, retailers, consumers, and consumer electronics firms are all impacted.

- Netflix's shift to a streaming model (from atoms to bits) is limited by access to content and in methods to get this content to televisions.

- The firm is right to be concerned that it needs to quickly transition to a new business model and that there are many potential advantages to the early mover who can create dominance in that space; however, the firm also made several blunders in its Qwikster attempt at this migration, and the failure of the firm to execute this shift effectively offers many lessons for firms considering customer-impacting changes.

- While the "First Sale Doctrine" allows Netflix to send out physical DVDs to subscribers, this law doesn't apply to streaming.

- Windowing, exclusives, and other licensing issues limit available content, and inconsistencies in licensing rates make profitable content acquisitions a challenge. Although the marginal cost for digital goods is zero, this benefit doesn't apply to licensees.

- Licensing issues will make it impossible to create a long tail as long as it is enjoyed in the DVD-by-mail business. Its new model is about providing a "long enough tail" to attract and retain subscribers.

- Netflix is attempting to secure exclusive content and to fund the creation of original programming for first-window rights. This makes the new, streaming-centric Netflix seem more like a premium pay channel (e.g., HBO or Showtime).

- Netflix offers more programming than pay channels, has a larger customer base and more viewing hours than these channels, is available in more countries worldwide, can stream to customers who don't have a cable TV subscription, and is less expensive than most premium cable channels.

- Streaming allows the firm to collect and leverage data for improved customer targeting, to help build models on content value, to promote original content in highly targeted ways, to allow for "binge-watching," and to potentially serve the needs of original content producers who are freed from distribution timing and content length constraints that conventional networks place on their work.

- Netflix makes its streaming technology available to hardware firms, and it has facilitated the development of streaming apps for a host of consumer electronics devices. As a result, Netflix streaming is available on more devices than any competing rival service.

- Netflix competitors in streaming are large, deep pocketed, and may have different motivations for offering streaming content (such as generating ad revenue, pay-per-view content sales, or as an incentive to make existing hardware platforms more attractive).

- International expansion offers the prospect of significant growth but is complicated by many issues, including increased licensing costs and disparate legal requirements.

- Netflix also faces threats from ISPs, including bandwidth caps and additional charges to ensure the quality of streaming efforts.

- The massive networks streaming delivery and operations infrastructure are largely hosted on the Amazon Web Services (AWS) cloud computing platform. This platform is available to all competitors, and it represents a cost that is potentially more variable as the firm grows than would be the case with a series of fixed-cost data centers. However, Netflix frees itself from dealing with many operational issues by contracting with Amazon, and it frees the firm to focus on proprietary systems that are a source of competitive advantage for the firm.

- Netflix is a significant creator of and contributor to software offerings—especially those that can be used to support cloud computing. The firm also uses crowdsourcing and code contests to fuel innovation. Both of these efforts also help the firm identify potential staffers and partners.

- The Netflix work culture is in many ways radically different from that of peers. The firm has shared its approach toward corporate culture, and this is increasingly having an influence on many firms—especially those in Silicon Valley.

QUESTIONS AND EXERCISES

1. Contrast Netflix's two businesses: DVD-by-mail and streaming. How do costs differ? How are these costs likely to change over time? How is subscriber interest in these services likely to change over time? What factors influence the reliability of each service? What threats are each of these businesses likely to face?

2. Who are the rivals to the Netflix streaming effort? Do any of these firms have advantages that Netflix lacks? What are these advantages?

3. Why would a manufacturer of DVD players be motivated to offer the Netflix "Watch Now" feature in its products?

4. Make a chart of the various firms offering video-streaming services. List the pros and cons of each, along with its revenue model. Which efforts do you think will survive a shakeout? Why?

5. Is Netflix a friend or foe to the studios? Make a list of reasons why they would "like" Netflix, and why studios might be fearful of the firm. What is disintermediation, and what incentives do studios have to try to disintermediate Netflix?

6. Why can't Netflix secure a long tail of streaming content that is the same size as its content catalog in the DVD-by-mail business? What is Netflix doing to make its streaming catalog more appealing than rival offerings?

7. Is streaming content provided by studios a commodity or differentiated good? How does this influence supplier power? How has this changed in the shift from DVD-by-mail to streaming subscriptions?

8. What advantages does Netflix have over premium cable television channels? What advantages do these channels have over Netflix? Do you think this is a winner-take-all market, or is there room enough for multiple players?

9. How does Netflix build its data asset? In what ways does it leverage this data asset? Why is the data asset stronger under streaming than it was for the DVD-by-mail business?

10. Why is streaming potentially better for consumers and for content producers? Why is Netflix a potentially attractive partner for content creators (producers, writers, directors)?

11. Can scale be achieved in the streaming industry? If so, how? Or if not, why not?

12. What is disintermediation, and what incentives do studios have to try to disintermediate Netflix?

13. What challenges does Netflix face as it expands internationally? What advantages does international expansion offer?

14. Why didn't Netflix vertically integrate and offer its own set-top box for content distribution?

15. What has been the impact of Netflix's move from single plan pricing to separate pricing for streaming and DVD-by-mail? What factors motivated this move? Do you think splitting the service into separate plans was a wise move? Why or why not? What errors did the firm make in the "Qwikster debacle"? What could the firm have done differently? Do you think this would have had a positive impact on the firm? Why or why not?

16. How does Netflix rank in terms of customer satisfaction today? What factors do you suppose are behind this ranking?

17. Investigate the current state of net neutrality. What is the current status of ISPs right to offer a fast lane or impose bandwidth caps? Who would you side with, Netflix or the large ISPs? Why?

18. Investigate Netflix stock price. One of the measures of whether a stock is "expensive" or not is the price-earnings ratio (share price divided by earnings per share). P/Es vary widely, but historic P/Es are about fifteen. What is the current P/E of Netflix? Do you think the stock is fairly valued based on prospects for future growth, earnings, and market dominance? Why or why not? How does the P/E of Netflix compare with that of other well-known firms, both in and out of the technology sector? Arrive in class with examples you are ready to discuss.

19. What are the risks and benefits to Netflix in using Amazon's cloud computing platform?

20. How has Netflix leveraged crowdsourcing and code contests?

21. In what ways do Netflix employee policies differ from those of most other firms? Does Netflix seem like the kind of firm you'd like to work for? Why or why not?

ENDNOTES

1. A. Vance, "Netflix, Reed Hastings Survive Missteps to Join Silicon Valley's Elite," *BusinessWeek*, May 9, 2013.

2. While Hastings stepped down from Microsoft's board in late 2012, as of this writing he continues to serve on Facebook's board.

3. J. Poggi, "3 Reasons Netflix Reed Hastings Shouldn't Be Fired…Yet," *TheStreet.com*, October 24, 2011.

4. M. Boyle, "Questions for…Reed Hastings," *Fortune*, May 23, 2007.

5. M. Boyle, "Questions for…Reed Hastings," *Fortune*, May 23, 2007.

6. M. Conlin, "Netflix: Flex to the Max," *BusinessWeek*, September 24, 2007.

7. M. Copeland, "Reed Hastings: The Leader of the Pack," *Fortune*, November 18, 2010.

8. B. McCarthy, "Netflix, Inc." (remarks, J. P. Morgan Global Technology, Media, and Telecom Conference, Boston, May 18, 2009).

9. Netflix Investor Day presentation, 2008, accessed via http://ir.netflix.com/events.cfm.

10. S. Reda and D. Schulz, "Concepts That Clicked," *Stores*, May 2008.

11. M. Hoffman, "Netflix Tops 23 Million Subscribers," *Inc.*, April 25, 2011; T. Hals and L. Baker, "Dish Expands Scope with Blockbuster Win," *Reuters*, April 6, 2011; infrastructure cost estimates from S. Reda and D. Schulz, "Concepts That Clicked," *Stores*, May 2008.

12. "Final Transcript: NFLX—Q1 2011 Netflix Inc. Earnings Conference Call," *Thompson StreetEvents*, April 25, 2011.

13. Netflix Investor Day presentation, May 2008, accessed via http://ir.netflix.com/events.cfm.

14. N. MacDonald, "Blockbuster Proves It's Not Dead Yet," *Maclean's*, March 12, 2008.

15. T. Hals and L. Baker, "Dish Expands Scope with Blockbuster Win," *Reuters*, April 6, 2011.

16. M. Hamblen, "Amazon: E-Books Now Outsell Print Books," *Computerworld*, May 19, 2011.

17. C. Edwards, "GameStop Shares Tumble 20% as Weak Sales Hurt Profit," *Bloomberg News*, Jan. 14, 2014.

18. K. Kezar, "GameStop sees decrease in Q4 sales but remains optimistic," *Dallas Business Journal*, March 26, 2015.

19. A. Silwinski, "GameStop closing 250 'unprofitable' stores, opening over 60 locations in 2013," *Engadget*, Feb. 13, 2013. And A. Elise, "Goodbye GameStop? 120 Locations Closing; Retailer To Focus On Mobile Gaming," *International Business Times*, April 25, 2014.

20. T. Team, "Where Is Netflix's DVD Business Headed?" *Forbes*, April 16, 2013.

21. Data reported by Statista: *Number of Netflix DVD subscribers in the United States from 3rd quarter 2011 to 1st quarter 2015 (in millions)*, Statista 2015 (via http://www.statista.com/statistics/250940/quarterly-number-of-netflix-dvd-subscribers-in-the-us/).

22. J. Roettgers, "The Slow but Inevitable Decline of Netflix's DVD Business," *GigaOM*, October 21, 2013.

23. J. Roettgers, "Responding to DVD subscription decline, Netflix closes call center," *GigaOm*, Oct. 23, 2014.

24. J. Fox, "Netflix and DVDs, Still Together," *Bloomberg View*, Jan. 21, 2015.

25. S. Steinberg, "Is Qwikster the Worst Product Launch Since New Coke?" *Rolling Stone*, October 3, 2011; and A. Goth and J. Yarrow, "15 Disastrous Product Launches That Were Quickly Killed," *Business Insider*, October 11, 2011.

26. D. Pogue, "Why Netflix Raised Prices," *New York Times*, July 14, 2011; E. Mack, "'Dear Netflix': Price Hike Ignites Social-Media Fire," *CNET*, July 12, 2011; and G. Sandoval, "Don't Call Netflix's CEO 'Greed' Hastings Just Yet," *CNET*, July 25, 2011.

27. R. Hastings, "How to Set Your Employees Free," *BusinessWeek*, April 12, 2012.

28. J. Kastrenakes, "Netflix Raises Streaming Price by $1 for New Subscribers," *The Verge*, May 9, 2014.

29. A. Brandenberger and B. Nalebuff, *Co-opetition: A Revolution Mindset That Combines Competition and Cooperation: The Game Theory Strategy That's Changing the Game of Business* (New York: Broadway Business, 1997); and S. Johnson, "The Frenemy Business Relationship," *Fast Company*, November 25, 2008.

30. D. Roth, "Netflix Everywhere: Sorry Cable, You're History," *Wired*, September 21, 2009.

31. A. Lutz, "These 6 Corporations Control 90% of the Media in America," *Business Insider*, June 14, 2012.

32. W. Donckles, "Netflix and Starz Can't Strike a Deal over Streaming," *Technorati*, September 7, 2011.

33. T. Cheredar, "Netflix's Hastings Says Amazon Prime Losses $1B Annually," *VentureBeat*, November 17, 2012.

34. S. Portnoy, "Netflix News: Starz Catalog Added to Online Service, Streaming to PS3, Xbox 360 through PlayOn Beta Software," *ZDNet*, October 2, 2008, http://blogs.zdnet.com/home-theater/?p=120.

35. J. Pepitone, "Netflix's Vanished Sony Films Are an Ominous Sign," *Fortune*, July 11, 2011.

36. P. Kafka, "HBO's Amazon Haul Is Big—But Not as Big as You Might Think," *Re/code*, April 23, 2014.

37. Netflix Investor Relations Document, "Netflix Long Term View," April 25, 2013.

38. M. Rich and B. Stone, "Publisher Wins Fight with Amazon over E-Books," *New York Times*, January 31, 2010.

39. R. Lawler, "Netflix CEO Reed Hastings on *Arrested Development*, Managing Content Licenses, and Coming Back from the Qwikster Debacle," *TechCrunch*, June 2, 2013.

40. V. Luckerson, "Star Wars Is Coming to Netflix," *Time*, February 13, 2014.

41. K. Stock, "Netflix Backs a Dead Show for TV's Future," *BusinessWeek*, April 4, 2013.

42. L. Cruz, "*Marco Polo*: Netflix's Critical Flop That Dared to Be Diverse," *The Atlantic*, Dec. 20, 2014.

43. M. Berniker, "Netflix Gaining Momentum, Subscribers, But Not Transparency," *Forbes*, April 20, 2015.

44. R. Hastings and D. Wells, "Letter to Shareholders," *Netflix*, April 15th, 2015. And D. Wallenstein, "Credit Netflix Originals Splurge for Surge in Subscribers, Stock," *Variety*, April 16, 2015.

45. P. Cohan, "How Netflix Reinvented Itself," *Forbes*, April 23, 2013.

46. P. Kafka, "Netflix Eats Into TV Ratings, With Help From the TV Industry," *Re/code*, April 23, 2015.

47. N. Laporte, "HBO to Netflix: Bring it On," *FastCompany*, April 7, 2015.

48. P. Kafka, "Netflix Eats Into TV Ratings, With Help From the TV Industry," *Re/code*, April 23, 2015.

49. L. Whitney, "Comcast to Offer 'House of Cards' to Xfinity Customers," *CNET*, March 10, 2014.

50. NC. Palermino, "Netflix is Finally Planning to Own Its Original Shows, Not Just License Them," *Digital Trends*, April 22, 2015.

51. P. Cohan, "How Netflix Reinvented Itself," *Forbes*, April 23, 2013.

52. L. H. Newman, "People Stream Netflix More than They Watch Any Cable Network," *Gizmodo*, April 14, 2013.

53. J. Gallaugher, "E-Commerce and the Undulating Distribution Channel," *Communications of the ACM* 45, no. 7 (July 2002).

54. P. Cohan, "How Netflix Reinvented Itself," *Forbes*, April 23, 2013.

55. L. Rose, "Netflix's Ted Sarandos Reveals His 'Phase 2' for Hollywood," *Hollywood Reporter*, May 22, 2013.

56. A. Madrigal, "How Netflix Reverse Engineered Hollywood," *Atlantic*, January 2, 2014.

57. D. Grandoni, "Netflix's New 'My List' Feature Knows You Better Than You Know Yourself (Because Algorithms)," *Huffington Post*, August 21, 2013.

58. Netflix Investor Relations Document, "Netflix Long Term View," April 25, 2013.

59. A. Vance, "Netflix, Reed Hastings Survive Missteps to Join Silicon Valley's Elite," *BusinessWeek*, May 9, 2013.

60. Netflix Investor Relations Document, "Netflix Long Term View," April 25, 2013.

61. A. Vance, "Netflix, Reed Hastings Survive Missteps to Join Silicon Valley's Elite," *BusinessWeek*, May 9, 2013.

62. A. Wallenstein, "Viacom and Netflix to Scale Down SVOD Deal," *Variety*, April 22, 2013.

63. L. Rose, "Netflix's Ted Sarandos Reveals His 'Phase 2' for Hollywood," *Hollywood Reporter*, May 22, 2013.

64. A. Vance, "How Netflix Delivers Movie Magic to Masses," *BusinessWeek*, May 9, 2013.

65. L. Rose, "Netflix's Ted Sarandos Reveals His 'Phase 2' for Hollywood," *Hollywood Reporter*, May 22, 2013.

66. S. Lacy, "Reed Hastings Won't Use Data to Mess with TV Plots, and That's Why Netflix Will Win," *PandoDaily*, May 29, 2014.

67. L. Rose, "Netflix's Ted Sarandos Reveals His 'Phase 2' for Hollywood," *Hollywood Reporter*, May 22, 2013.

68. S. Rosenbaum, "Why I Was Wrong about Netflix's *House of Cards*," *Forbes*, February 18, 2013.

69. M. Sweney, "Netflix's Ted Sarandos: 'We See an Incredible Appetite for TV,'" *Guardian*, May 26, 2013.

70. M. Guthrie, "'Arrested Development' Surpasses 'House of Cards' as Netflix's Biggest Hit," *Hollywood Reporter*, May 28, 2013.

71. A. Vance, "Netflix, Reed Hastings Survive Missteps to Join Silicon Valley's Elite," *BusinessWeek*, May 9, 2013.

72. "Netflix Long Term View," *Netflix Blog*, April 21, 2014.

73. L. Rose, "Netflix's Ted Sarandos Reveals His 'Phase 2' for Hollywood," *Hollywood Reporter*, May 22, 2013.

74. L. Brown, "In Conversation: Vince Gilligan on the End of Breaking Bad," *Vulture*, May 12, 2013.

75. Netflix Investor Relations Document, "Netflix Long Term View," April 25, 2013.

76. K. Flynn, "Netflix NetPromoter 2013 Benchmarks Released," *ResearchScape*, May 8, 2013.

77. B. Brouwer, "Netflix Will Reportedly Spend $5 Billion On Content In 2016," *Tubefilter*, Feb. 13, 2015.

78. R. Hastings and D. Wells, "Letter to Shareholders," Netflix Investor Relations Document, January 23, 2013.

79. M. Flancy, "Battle of the Streaming Giants: Which Streaming Service is Best for You?" Digital Trends, March 1, 2015. P. Kafka, "Netflix Still Dominates Streaming, but Amazon Is Picking Up Steam," *Re/code*, Nov. 20, 2014. And E. Steel, "Neilsen Charts Reach of Streaming Services," *The New York Times*, March 11, 2015.

80. C. Gayomali, "Redbox Instant Shuts Down," *FastCompany*, Oct. 6, 2014.

81. R. Hastings and D. Wells, "Letter to Shareholders," Netflix Investor Relations Document, January 23, 2013.

82. R. Hastings and D. Wells, "Letter to Shareholders," *Netflix Investor Relations Document*, January 23, 2013.

83. R. Empson, "With Overseas Subscribers Topping 6M, Netflix Puts a Hold on Expanding into International Markets," *TechCrunch*, January 23, 2013.

84. R. Empson, "With Overseas Subscribers Topping 6M, Netflix Puts a Hold on Expanding into International Markets," *TechCrunch*, January 23, 2013.

85. J. Greenberg, "Netflix Stock Hits Record as Wall St. Sees World Domination," *Wired*, May 19, 2015.

86. L. Edwards, "Netflix's Ted Sarandos Talks Arrested Development, 4K and Reviving Old Shows," *Stuff*, May 1, 2013.

87. "Netflix Faces Hurdles, Country by Country, in Bid to Expand in Europe," *New York Times*, May 21, 2014.

88. J. Greenberg, "Netflix Stock Hits Record as Wall St. Sees World Domination," *Wired*, May 19, 2015.

89. I. Lapowski, "Netflix Faces Tough Battles in its Push to Rule Europe," *Wired*, Aug. 12, 2014.

90. T. Spangler, "Netflix Adds Record 4.9 Million Subscribers in Q1," *Variety*, April 15, 2015.

91. P. Cohan, "How Netflix Reinvented Itself," *Forbes*, April 23, 2013.

92. B. Darrow, "Netflix: We Don't Need No Stinkin' Data Centers!" *GigaOM*, March 28, 2012.

93. A. Vance, "Netflix, Reed Hastings Survive Missteps to Join Silicon Valley's Elite," *BusinessWeek*, May 9, 2013.

94. A. Vance, "Netflix, Reed Hastings Survive Missteps to Join Silicon Valley's Elite," *BusinessWeek*, May 9, 2013.

95. A. Vance, "Netflix, Reed Hastings Survive Missteps to Join Silicon Valley's Elite," *BusinessWeek*, May 9, 2013.

96. See Netflix Open Connect Content Delivery Network, https://signup.netflix.com/openconnect (accessed June 13, 2013).

97. M. Aguilar, "How Netflix Makes 3.14 Petabytes of Video Feel like It's All for You," *Gizmodo*, May 9, 2013.

98. Y. Izrailevsky and A. Tseitlin, "The Netflix Simian Army," *The Netflix Blog*, July 19, 2011.

99. A. Vance, "Netflix, Reed Hastings Survive Missteps to Join Silicon Valley's Elite," *BusinessWeek*, May 9, 2013.

100. Controversially, one group of researchers claimed they were able to match anonymous Netflix ratings with identifiable IMDB submissions, determining the identity of raters in Netflix's anonymous data. See D. Demerjian, "Rise of the Netflix Hackers," *Wired*, March 15, 2007.

101. B. Patterson, "Netflix Prize Competitors Join Forces, Cross Magic 10-Percent Mark," *Yahoo! Tech*, June 29, 2009.

102. J. Ellenberg, "This Psychologist Might Outsmart the Math Brains Competing for the Netflix Prize," *Wired*, February 25, 2008.

103. A. Vance, "Netflix Announces $100,000 in Prizes for Coders," *BusinessWeek*, March 14, 2013.

104. P. Kafka, "Netflix CEO: Amazon Losing up to $1billion a Year on Streaming Video," *AllThingsD*, November 16, 2012.

105. L. Whitney, "Netflix Streaming Service Hit by Outage," *CNET*, July 18, 2011.

106. A. Vance, "Netflix, Reed Hastings Survive Missteps to Join Silicon Valley's Elite," *BusinessWeek*, May 9, 2013.

107. K. Hoban, "Why Wasn't There A Huge Outcry Against The FCC's Proposed Rules Against Net Neutrality?" *Forbes*, May 5, 2014.

108. W. Davis, "Netflix, Tumblr And Others Seek To Defend Net Neutrality Rules," *MediaPost*, May 14, 2015.

109. C. Stupp, "Netflix CEO: Europe needs strong net neutrality rules," *Euractive*, May 6, 2015.

110. R. Hastings, "How to Set Your Employees Free," *BusinessWeek*, April 12, 2012.

111. R. Hastings, "How to Set Your Employees Free," *BusinessWeek*, April 12, 2012.

112. R. Hastings, "How to Set Your Employees Free," *BusinessWeek*, April 12, 2012.

113. R. Hastings, "How to Set Your Employees Free," *BusinessWeek*, April 12, 2012.

114. R. Hastings, "How to Set Your Employees Free," *BusinessWeek*, April 12, 2012.

115. D. Lyons, "Advice on Corporate Culture from Netflix's Former Chief Talent Officer," *HubSpot Blog*, May 7, 2013.

116. J. Greenberg, "Netflix Stock Hits Record as Wall St. Sees World Domination," *Wired*, May 19, 2015.

CHAPTER 5
Moore's Law and More: Fast, Cheap Computing, and What This Means for the Manager

1. INTRODUCTION

LEARNING OBJECTIVES

1. Define Moore's Law and understand the approximate rate of advancement for other technologies, including magnetic storage (disk drives) and telecommunications (fiber-optic transmission).
2. Understand how the price elasticity associated with faster and cheaper technologies opens new markets, creates new opportunities for firms and society, and can catalyze industry disruption.
3. Recognize and define various terms for measuring data capacity.
4. Consider the managerial implication of faster and cheaper computing on areas such as strategic planning, inventory, and accounting.

Faster and cheaper—those two words have driven the computer industry for decades, and the rest of the economy has been along for the ride. Today it's tough to imagine a single industry not impacted by more powerful, less expensive computing. Faster and cheaper puts mobile phones in the hands of peasant farmers, puts a free video game in your Happy Meal, and drives the drug discovery that may very well extend your life.

1.1 Some Definitions

This phenomenon of "faster, cheaper" computing is often referred to as **Moore's Law**, after Intel cofounder, Gordon Moore. Moore didn't show up one day, stance wide, hands on hips, and declare "behold my law," but he did write a four-page paper for *Electronics Magazine* in which he described how the process of chip making enabled more powerful chips to be manufactured at cheaper prices.[1]

Moore's friend, legendary chip entrepreneur and CalTech professor Carver Mead, later coined the "Moore's Law" moniker. That name sounded snappy, plus as one of the founders of Intel, Moore had enough geek cred for the name to stick. Moore's original paper offered language only a chip designer would love, so we'll rely on the more popular definition: *chip performance per dollar doubles every eighteen months*. (Moore's original paper stated transistors per chip, a proxy for power, would double every two years, but many sources today refer to the *eighteen*-month figure, so we'll stick with that since managers are often blindsided by unanticipated rate of technology change. Some might note that Intel has recently speculated that Moore's Law may slow to a doubling every 2.5 years[2] —either way, we're still talking about ridiculously accelerating power and plummeting costs, a concept vital for managers to be aware of.)

Moore's Law

Chip performance per dollar doubles every eighteen months.

Hear Intel co-founder Gordon Moore, discuss Moore's Law at 50, and watch scenes showing the microprocessor manufacturing process.

View the video online at: http://www.youtube.com/embed/ylgk3HEyZ_g?rel=0

microprocessor

The part of the computer that executes the instructions of a computer program.

Moore's Law applies to chips—broadly speaking, to *processors* and chip-based storage: think of the stuff in your consumer electronics that's made out of silicon.[3] The **microprocessor** is the brain of a computing device. It's the part of the computer that executes the instructions of a computer program, allowing it to run a Web browser, word processor, video game, or virus. For processors, Moore's Law means that next generation chips should be twice as fast in about *eighteen* months, but cost the same as today's models (or from another perspective, in about a year and a half, chips that are same speed as today's models should be available for half the price).

random-access memory (RAM)

The fast, chip-based volatile storage in a computing device.

volatile memory

Storage (such as RAM chips) that is wiped clean when power is cut off from a device.

nonvolatile memory

Storage that retains data even when powered down (such as flash memory, hard disk, or DVD storage).

Random-access memory (RAM) is chip-based memory. The RAM inside your personal computer is **volatile memory**, meaning that when the power goes out, all is lost that wasn't saved to **nonvolatile memory** (i.e., a more permanent storage media like a hard disk or flash memory). Think of RAM as temporary storage that provides fast access for executing computer programs and files. When you "load" or "launch" a program, it usually moves from your hard drive or flash storage to those RAM chips, where it can be more quickly executed by the processor.

Cameras, MP3 players, USB drives, mobile phones, and even many lightweight notebook computers often use **flash memory** (sometimes called *flash RAM* or *flash storage*). It's not as fast as the RAM used in most traditional PCs, but holds data even when the power is off (so flash memory is also nonvolatile memory). You can think of flash memory as the chip-based equivalent of a hard drive. Apple's MacBook Air was one of the first commercial notebook computer to offer chip-based, nonvolatile memory as an alternative to laptop hard drives, although now several manufacturers and models also use the technology. The big advantage? Chips are **solid state electronics** (meaning no moving parts), so they're less likely to fail, and they draw less power. Data can also be accessed faster from flash memory than from conventional hard drives. For RAM chips and flash memory, Moore's Law means that in *eighteen* months you'll pay the same price as today for twice as much storage.

FIGURE 5.1 Advancing Rates of Technology (Silicon, Storage, Telecom)

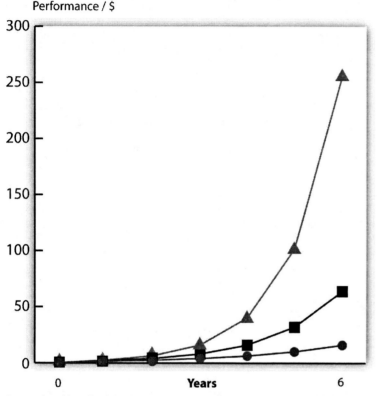

Performance / $

▲ Optical Fiber—
Doubles 9 months
(bits per second)

■ Data Storage—
Doubles 12 months
(bits per square inch)

● Moore's Law—
Doubles 18 months
(number of transistors)

Source: Adopted from Shareholder Presentation by Jeff Bezos, Amazon.com, 2006.

Computer chips are sometimes also referred to as **semiconductors** (a substance such as silicon dioxide used inside most computer chips that is capable of enabling as well as inhibiting the flow of electricity). So if someone refers to the *semiconductor industry*, they're talking about the chip business.[4]

Strictly speaking, Moore's Law does not apply to other technology components. But other computing components are also seeing their price versus performance curves skyrocket exponentially. Data storage doubles every twelve months. Networking speed is on a tear, too. With an equipment change at the ends of the cables, the amount of data that can be squirted over an **optical fiber line** can double every nine months.[5] These numbers should be taken as rough approximations and shouldn't be expected to be strictly precise over time. And predictability precision is tough to achieve. For example, some think the advance in hard drive storage (sometimes referred to as Kryder's Law[6]) is decelerating,[7] while others think it is poised to accelerate.[8] Others have claimed that network speeds are now doubling about every twenty-one months.[9] And as mentioned earlier, some say Moore's Law's doubling happens closer to every two and a half years.[10] Despite any fluctuation, it's clear that the price/performance curve for many technologies is exponential, offering astonishing improvement over time. While the pace of change may vary over time, these graphs (or recalibrated versions, if you like) are useful to managers as rough guides regarding future computing price/performance trends. As so many examples in this text have illustrated, managers without an eye on technology's advancing capabilities are often leading candidates for professional roadkill.

flash memory

Nonvolatile, chip-based storage, often used in mobile phones, cameras, and MP3 players. Sometimes called flash RAM, flash memory is slower than conventional RAM, but holds its charge even when the power goes out.

solid state electronics

Semiconductor-based devices. Solid state components often suffer fewer failures and require less energy than mechanical counterparts because they have no moving parts. RAM, flash memory, and microprocessors are solid state devices. Hard drives are not.

semiconductor

A substance such as silicon dioxide used inside most computer chips that is capable of enabling as well as inhibiting the flow of electricity. From a managerial perspective, when someone refers to semiconductors, they are talking about computer chips, and the semiconductor industry is the chip business.

optical fiber line

A high-speed glass or plastic-lined networking cable used in telecommunications.

1.2 Get Out Your Crystal Ball

price elasticity

The rate at which the demand for a product or service fluctuates with price change. Goods and services that are highly price elastic (e.g., most consumer electronics) see demand spike as prices drop, whereas goods and services that are less price elastic are less responsive to price change (think heart surgery).

Faster and cheaper makes possible the once impossible. As a manager, your job will be about predicting the future. First, consider how the economics of Moore's Law opens new markets. When technology gets cheap, **price elasticity** kicks in. Tech products are highly *price elastic*, meaning consumers buy more products as they become cheaper.[11] And it's not just that existing customers load up on more tech; entire *new markets* open up as firms find new uses for these new chips, technology becomes embedded in new products, and fast/cheap technology enables new services.

Just look at the *evolving waves of computing* we've seen over the previous decades.[12] In the *first wave* in the 1960s, computing was limited to large, room-sized mainframe computers that only governments and big corporations could afford. Moore's Law kicked in during the 1970s for the *second wave*, and minicomputers were a hit. These were refrigerator-sized computers that were as speedy as or speedier than the prior generation of mainframes, yet were affordable for work groups, factories, and smaller organizations. The 1980s brought *wave three* in the form of PCs, and by the end of the decade nearly every white-collar worker in America had a fast and cheap computer on their desk. In the 1990s, *wave four* came in the form of Internet computing; cheap servers and networks made it possible to scatter data around the world at the same time that fast, cheap PCs became mouse-click easy and PC ownership became common in the industrialized world. The previous decade saw mobile phones drive what can be considered *computing wave five*. Cheap processors enabled billions of low-end phones, while the march of Moore's Law is driving the smartphone revolution. Today many say this *sixth wave* of computing can be considered the era of *pervasive computing*, where technology is fast and so inexpensive that it is becoming ubiquitously woven into products in ways few imagined years before. Silicon is everywhere! It's in the throwaway radio frequency identification (RFID) tags that track your luggage at the airport. It's the brains inside robot vacuum cleaners, it's built into Legos, it's in the locks that allow Starwood hotel rooms to be opened with a guest's phone, it's in the iBeacon sensors that help you find a hot dog and beer at the ballpark, and it's empowering wearables from smartwatches to in-shirt sensors to Google Glass. These digital shifts can rearrange entire industries. Consider that today the firms that sell the most cameras aren't camera companies; they're phone manufacturers offering increasingly sophisticated chip-based digital cameras as a giveaway inside their main product offering. This shift has occurred with such sweeping impact that former photography giants Kodak and the now-merged Konica-Minolta have exited the conventional camera business.

Internet of Things

A vision where low-cost sensors, processors, and communication are embedded into a wide array of products and our environment, allowing a vast network to collect data, analyze input, and automatically coordinate collective action.

Tech Everywhere: From the Smart Thermostat to a Tweeting Diaper

Former Apple Vice President Tony Fadell has been called the "Father of the iPod," and he guided the first three iPhones through production. But his next act after Apple, Nest Labs, is decidedly sixth wave and seeks to smarten up the lowly thermostat with high-impact results. The Nest is loaded with Moore's Law smarts: motion sensors to tell if anyone's in a room, a temperature sensor, a Wi-Fi connection to grab weather conditions outside—it even runs Linux. The goal is to pay attention to you and the world around your home and to automatically and efficiently adjust your energy use to best fit your needs—no programming needed (although you can tinker with settings via smartphone app if you'd like). Current "dumb" thermostats control about half of the energy use in a typical U.S. home, so this is a big and important market with a potentially massive payoff for consumers and for the environment.[13] Nest users report shaving their heating and cooling bills by about 20 percent on average, saving a collective two billion kilowatt hours in two years.[14] Google believed in the less-than-four-year-old firm enough to buy it for $3.2 billion, making it Google's second most expensive acquisition ever.[15] Apple apparently also believes in the power of the connected home. The firm's HomeKit iOS extensions can control all sorts of Nest-like smart devices for the home, including thermostats, lighting, locks, home security systems, and more.

Nest is just one example of fast, cheap computing showing up in all sorts of products. Cambridge, Massachusetts–based Ambient Devices manufactures a smart umbrella that regularly receives wireless weather reports and will flash when rain is likely, as if to say, "You will soon require my services!" Smart billboards in Japan peer back at passersby to guess at their demographics and instantly change advertising for on-the-spot targeting.[16] And there are experimental efforts that range from the promising Airbus Bag2Go suitcases, which with RFID, GPS, and phone smarts offer quick check-in and never-lost luggage;[17] to the chuckle-worthy Huggies TweetPee, which can send a text or social media post when a child's diaper "activity" is detected.[18] Robust, low-cost hardware hacking is made easier with products like the Raspberry Pi and Arduino, credit card–sized computers that can run a full PC operating system and costs as little as $25.[19]

Some refer to these devices as the "**Internet of Things**," where low-cost sensors, computing, and communication put embedded smarts in all sorts of mundane devices so that these products can communicate with one another for data collection, analysis, and collective action.[20] We've already learned that when you buy a product from Zara that has an RFID tag attached to it, that act will trigger a message to restock shelves, ship more products from a warehouse, and spin up factories for a new order. And there's more to come. Imagine your Nest thermometer coordinating with the rest of your house: closing automated blinds when the sun is hot and high, turning off your water heater when you're away from home, and turning on lights to mimic activity while you're out of town. Smart tags in clothing could communicate with washing machines and dryers and warn the operator if settings could ruin a shirt.

IBM (you've seen those "Smarter Planet" ads) and General Electric (GE) are among firms pushing to create technology and common languages to turn this vision into a reality. Cities are using smart devices as constant monitors that share information on traffic, available parking spaces, and water quality. GE is outfitting almost everything it builds—from refrigerators to jet engines—with sensors and software so that these devices can share data and coordinate automatically to drive efficiency.[21] GE thinks efficiency gains across multiple sectors—transportation, health care, energy—could boost global GDP by as much as $10 to $15 trillion by 2030.[22] Research group Gartner predicts that there are already some 5 billion connected devices in use today, with an expected 25 billion to be in use by 2020.[23]

Moore's Law inside Your Medicine Cabinet

Moore's Law is coming to your medicine cabinet, and several early-stage efforts show the potential for low-cost computing to improve health care quality while lowering costs. The GlowCap from Vitality, Inc., is a "smart" pill bottle that will flash when you're supposed to take your medicine. It will play a little tune if you're an hour late for your dose and will also squirt a signal to a night-light that flashes as a reminder (in case you're out of view of the cap). GlowCaps can also be set to call or send a text if you haven't responded past a set period of time. And the device will send a report to you, your doc, or whomever else you approve. The GlowCap can even alert your pharmacy when it's time for refills. For other kinds of medicines such as inhalers, blister packs, and liquids, Vitality also sells a GlowPack—same concept, different form factor. The bottles sell for as little as $10 but in some cases are likely to be free. The business case for that? The World Health Organization estimates drug adherence at just 50 percent, and analysts estimate that up to $300 billion in increased medical costs and 125,000 annual deaths are due to patients missing their meds.[24] Vitality CEO David Rose (who incidentally also cofounded Ambient Devices) recently cited a test in which GlowCap users reported a 98 percent medication adherence rate.[25]

FIGURE 5.2

The GlowCap from Vitality, Inc., will flash, beep, call, and text you if you've skipped your meds. It can also send reports to you, your doctor, and your loved ones and even notify your pharmacy when it's time for a refill.

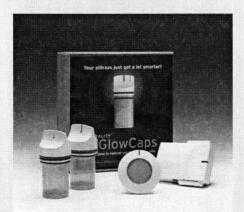

Source: Used with permission from Vitality, Inc.

And there might also be a chip inside the pills, too! Proteus, a Novartis-backed venture, has developed a sensor made of food and vitamin materials that can be swallowed in medicine. While there is a lot of talk about "wearable" technology, Proteus is an ingestible tech. The sensor is activated and powered by the body's digestive acids (think of your stomach as a battery). Once inside you, the chip sends out a signal with vitals such as heart rate, body angle, temperature, sleep, and more. A waterproof skin patch worn outside the body picks up the signal and can wirelessly relay the pill's findings when the patient walks within twenty feet of their phone. Proteus will then compile a report from the data and send it to their mobile device or e-mail account. The gizmo's already in clinical trials for heart disease, hypertension, and tuberculosis and for monitoring psychiatric illnesses.[26] And a pill with built-in smarts can identify itself to help guard against taking counterfeit drugs, a serious worldwide concern. Pills that chat with mobile phones could help promote telemedicine, bringing health care to hard-to-reach rural populations. And games and social apps based on this information can provide motivating, fun ways to nudge patients into healthy habits. The CEO of Proteus Health says that soon you may be able to think of your body as "the ultimate game controller."[27]

One of the most agile surfers of new generations of computing waves is Apple, Inc.—a firm with a product line that grew so broad, it dropped the word "Computer" from its name. Apple's keen insight on where trends in computing power and performance are headed is captured in this statement by the firm's cofounder, the late Steve Jobs: "There's an old Wayne Gretzky quote that I love. 'I skate to where the puck is going to be, not where it has been.' And we've always tried to do that at Apple."[28] The curves above aren't perfect, but they can point to where the puck is headed, helping the savvy manager predict the future, plan for the impossible to become possible, and act as the disruptor rather than the disrupted.

Apple's breakout resurgence owes a great deal to the iPod. At launch, the original iPod sported a 5 GB hard drive that Steve Jobs declared would "put 1,000 songs in your pocket." Cost? $399. Less than six years later, Apple's highest-capacity iPod sold for fifty dollars less than the original, yet held *forty times* the songs. By the iPod's tenth birthday, Apple was giving away 5 GB of storage (for music or other media) for free via its iCloud service. Apple's high-end iPod models have morphed into Internet browsing devices capable of showing maps, playing videos, and gulping down songs from Starbucks' Wi-Fi while waiting in line for a latte.

The original iPod has also become the jumping-off point for new business lines including the iPhone, Apple TV, Apple Watch, iPad, and iTunes. As an online store, iTunes is always open. The service regularly sells tens of millions of songs on Christmas Day alone, a date when virtually all of its offline competition is closed for the holiday. Just five years after its introduction, iTunes had sold over 4 billion songs and vaulted past retail giants Walmart, Best Buy, and Target to become the top music retailer in the world. Today's iTunes is a digital media powerhouse, streaming Internet radio and selling movies, TV shows, games, and other applications. And with podcasting, Apple's iTunes University even lets students at participating schools put their professors' lectures on their gym playlist for free. As high-bandwidth wireless had consumers switching from stored music to streaming, Apple again shifted, buying Beats for $1 billion not only for its high-end headphones business but also highly regarded Spotify-rivaling music service that streams tunes from the cloud.[29] Apple is late to the streaming party, and crafting a winning strategy here will be key. Tech's relentless advance has begun cut iTunes sales, and at least one major label has reported earning more revenue from streaming services than digital downloads.[30] Surfing the ever-evolving waves of computing has turned Apple into the most valuable company in the United States and the most profitable firm on the planet.[31] Ride these waves to riches, but miss the power and promise of Moore's Law and you risk getting swept away in its riptide. Apple's rise occurred while Sony, a firm once synonymous with portable music, sat on the sidelines unwilling to get on the surfboard. Sony's stock stagnated, barely moving in six years. The firm has laid off thousands of workers while ceding leadership in digital music (and video) to Apple.

TABLE 5.1 Top US Music Retailers

1992	2005	2006	2008
1. Musicland	1. Walmart	1. Walmart	1. **iTunes**
2. The Handleman	2. Best Buy	2. Best Buy	2. Walmart
3. Tower Records	3. Target	3. Target	3. Best Buy
4. Trans World Music	…7. **iTunes**	4. **iTunes**, Amazon tie	4. Amazon, Target tie
Moore's Law restructures industries. The firms that dominated music sales when you were born are now bankrupt, while one that had never sold a physical music CD now sells more than anyone else.			

Source: Michelle Quinn and Dawn C. Chmielewski, "Top Music Seller's Store Has No Door," Los Angeles Times, April 4, 2008.

TABLE 5.2 Tech's Price/Performance Trends in Action: Amazon Kindle and Apple Music Storage

Amazon Kindle		Apple	
First Generation	Fourth Generation	iPod	iCloud
250 MB	2 GB	5 GB	5 GB
November 2007	September 2011	October 2001	October 2011
$399	$79	$399	Free

Amazon's Kindle also dramatically demonstrates Moore's Law-fueled evolution. The first Kindle sold for nearly $400. Less than four years later, Amazon was selling an updated version for one-fifth that price. Other factors influence price drops, such as being able to produce products and their components at scale, but Moore's Law and related price/performance trends are clearly behind the price decreases we see across a wide variety of tech products and services. Apple's introduction of the iPad, complete with an iBook store, shows how Moore's Law rewrites the boundaries of competition, bringing a firm that started as a computer manufacturer and a firm that started as an online bookstore in direct competition with one another.

While the change in hard drive prices isn't directly part of Moore's Law (hard drives are magnetic storage, not silicon chips), as noted earlier, the faster and cheaper phenomenon applies to storage, too. Amazon provides another example of creating a once-impossible offering courtesy of the trajectory of price/performance technology curves. The firm's "Search Inside the Book" feature required digitizing the images and text from thousands of books in Amazon's catalog. Not only did making books searchable before purchase help customers; titles supporting "Search Inside the Book" enjoyed a 7 percent sales increase over nonsearchable books. Here's where fast/cheap technology comes in. When the feature launched, the database to support this effort was twenty *times* larger than *any* database used by any commercial firm just eight years earlier. For Amazon, the impossible had not just become possible; it became good business.

Bits and Bytes

Computers express data as bits that are either one or zero. Eight bits form a byte (think of a byte as being a single character you can type from a keyboard). A kilobyte refers to roughly a thousand bytes, or a thousand characters, megabyte = 1 million, gigabyte = 1 billion, terabyte = 1 trillion, petabyte = 1 quadrillion, and exabyte = 1 quintillion bytes.

While storage is most often listed in bytes, telecommunication capacity (bandwidth) is often listed in bits per second (bps). The same prefixes apply (Kbps = kilobits, or one thousand bits, per second, Mbps = megabits per second, Gbps = gigabits per second, and Tbps = terabits per second).

These are managerial definitions, but technically, a kilobyte is 2^{10} or 1,024 bytes, mega = 2^{20}, giga = 2^{30}, tera = 2^{40}, peta = 2^{50}, and exa = 2^{60}. To get a sense for how much data we're talking about, see the table below.[32]

TABLE 5.3 Bytes Defined

	Managerial Definition	Exact Amount	To Put It in Perspective
1 Byte	One keyboard character	8 bits	1 letter or number = 1 byte
1 Kilobyte (KB)	One thousand bytes	2^{10} bytes	1 typewritten page = 2 KB
			1 digital book (Kindle) = approx. 500—800 KB
1 Megabyte (MB)	One million bytes	2^{20} bytes	1 digital photo (7 megapixels) = 1.3 MB
			1 MP3 song = approx. 3 MB
			1 CD = approx. 700 MB
1 Gigabyte (GB)	One billion bytes	2^{30} bytes	1 DVD movie = approx. 4.7 GB
			1 Blu-ray movie = approx. 25 GB
1 Terabyte (TB)	One trillion bytes	2^{40} bytes	Printed collection of the Library of Congress = 20 TB
1 Petabyte (PB)	One quadrillion bytes	2^{50} bytes	Master copies of the shows and movies available on Netflix (2013) = 3.14 PB[33]
1 Exabyte (EB)	One quintillion bytes	2^{60} bytes	Estimated total data stored in the NSA's Bluffdale, Utah, data center (includes data from hard drives, overseas data centers, cell phones, and more) = 12 EB[34]
1 Zettabyte (ZB)	One sextillion bytes	2^{70} bytes	Estimated total annual amount of data transmitted over the Internet by 2018 = 1.6 ZB[35]

Here's another key implication for the curves shown earlier: if you are producing products subject to radically improving price/performance, then these products will rapidly fall in value over time. That's great when it makes your product cheaper and opens up new markets for your firm, but it can be deadly if you overproduce and have excess inventory sitting on shelves for long periods of time. Dell claims its inventory depreciates as much as a single percentage point in value each week.[36] That's a big incentive to carry as little inventory as possible, and to unload it, fast!

While the strategic side of tech may be the most glamorous, Moore's Law impacts mundane management tasks, as well. From an accounting and budgeting perspective, as a manager you'll need to consider a number of questions: How long will your computing equipment remain useful? If you keep upgrading computing and software, what does this mean for your capital expense budget? Your training budget? Your ability to make well-reasoned predictions regarding tech's direction will be key to answering these questions.

Tech for the Poor

Another tech product containing a microprocessor is transforming the lives of some of the world's most desperate poor—the cell phone. There are three billion people worldwide that don't yet have a phone, but they will, soon. In the ultimate play of Moore's Law opening up new markets, mobiles from Vodafone and Indian telecom provider Spice sell for $25 or less. While it took roughly twenty years to sell a billion mobile phones worldwide, the second billion sold in four years, and the third billion took just two years. Today, some 80 percent of the world's population lives within cellular network range (double the 2000 level), and the vast majority of mobile subscriptions are in developing countries.[37]

Why such demand? Mobiles change lives for the better. According to economist Jeffrey Sachs, "The cell phone is the single most transformative technology for world economic development."[38] A London Business School study found that for every ten mobile phones per one hundred people, a country's GDP bumps up 0.5 percent.[39] Think about the farmer who can verify prices and locate buyers before harvesting and transporting perishable crops to market; the laborer who was mostly unemployed but with a mobile is now reachable by those who have day-to-day work; the mother who can find out if a doctor is in and has medicine before taking off work to make the costly trek to a remote clinic with her sick child; or the immigrant laborer serving as a housekeeper who was "more or less an indentured servant until she got a cell phone" enabling new customers to call and book her services.[40]

Three-quarters of the world's poorest people get their food and income by farming.[41] But isolated rural farmers often suffer from an information asymmetry problem (see Chapter 2). These farmers traditionally don't have accurate information on what their products are worth, and in many communities, less scrupulous traders will buy up harvests at far-below-market rates, only to resell them and pocket the profits for themselves. Coming to the aid of farmers, the Ghanaian firm Esoko delivers market prices, farming tips, and other key information via text message on even the lowest-end cell phones. In one study, farmers using Esoko reported a 10 percent increase in revenue.[42] Other reports have revenue increases as high as 25 to 40 percent.[43] Esoko offers a breadth of services that range from helping farmers find transport services to helping buyers locate farmers with goods to sell.

Promotional Video of Esoko's Market Information System

View the video online at: //www.youtube.com/v/tcGuW-Mc48k

The Launch of Safaricom's M-PESA

This TechChange video is narrated by Michael Joseph, managing director of mobile money at Vodafone.

View the video online at: ://www.youtube.com/v/i0dBWaen3aQ

When phones can be used as currency for purchases or payments, who needs Visa or, for that matter, a wallet and cash? The M-PESA mobile banking service run by Kenya's Safaricom, allows customers to transfer cash using text messages. Nearly every Kenyan adult has an M-PESA account, paying for everything from groceries to cab rides to school tuition. The service can also allow family members to quickly and securely send cash across the country. Only 4 million Kenyans have traditional bank accounts, but 19 million use M-PESA, and upwards of 31 percent of Kenya's GDP flows through the service.[44] M-PESA is spreading to other regions and is even used in Afghanistan, while similar schemes are offered by firms such as WIZZIT in South Africa, Zaad in Somaliland, and GCASH in the Philippines. The "mobile phone as bank" may bring banking to a billion unserved customers in a few years.

KEY TAKEAWAYS

- Moore's Law applies to the semiconductor industry. The widely accepted managerial interpretation of Moore's Law states that for the same money, roughly eighteen months from now you should be able to purchase computer chips that are twice as fast or store twice as much information. Or over that same time period, chips with the speed or storage of today's chips should cost half as much as they do now.

- Nonchip-based technology also advances rapidly. Disk drive storage doubles roughly every twelve months, while equipment to speed transmissions over fiber-optic lines has doubled every nine months. While these numbers are rough approximations, the price/performance curve of these technologies continues to advance exponentially.

- These trends influence inventory value, depreciation accounting, employee training, and other managerial functions. They also help improve productivity and keep interest rates low.

- From a strategic perspective, these trends suggest that what is impossible from a cost or performance perspective today may be possible in the future. Fast/cheap computing also feeds a special kind of price elasticity where whole new markets are created. This fact provides an opportunity to those who recognize and can capitalize on the capabilities of new technology. As technology advances, new industries, business models, and products are created, while established firms and ways of doing business can be destroyed.

- Managers must regularly study trends and trajectory in technology to recognize opportunity and avoid disruption.

- Moore's Law (and related advances in fast/cheap technologies in things like storage and telecommunications) has driven six waves of disruptive, market-transforming computing. The sixth wave involves embedding intelligence and communications in all sorts of mundane devices. Some point to a future "Internet of Things" where objects will collect and share data and automatically coordinate collective action for radical efficiency improvements.

QUESTIONS AND EXERCISES

1. What is Moore's Law? What does it apply to?
2. Are other aspects of computing advancing as well? At what approximate rates? What is Kryder's Law?
3. What is a microprocessor? What devices do you or your family own that contain microprocessors (and hence are impacted by Moore's Law)?
4. What is a semiconductor? What is the substance from which most semiconductors are made?
5. How does flash memory differ from the memory in a PC? Are both solid state?
6. Which of the following are solid-state devices: an iPod shuffle, an iPhone, a USB flash drive, a TiVo DVR, a typical laptop PC?
7. Why is Moore's Law important for managers? How does it influence managerial thinking?
8. What is price elasticity? How does Moore's Law relate to this concept? What's special about falling chip prices compared to price drops for products like clothing or food?
9. Give examples of firms that have effectively leveraged the advancement of processing, storage, and networking technology.
10. What are the six waves of computing? Give examples of firms and industries impacted by the sixth wave.
11. As Moore's Law advances, technology becomes increasingly accessible to the poor. Give examples of how tech has benefited those who likely would not have been able to afford the technology of a prior generation.
12. How have cheaper, faster chips impacted the camera industry? Give an example of the leadership shifts that have occurred in this industry.
13. What has been the impact of "faster, cheaper" on Apple's business lines?
14. How did Amazon utilize the steep decline in magnetic storage costs to its advantage?
15. How does Moore's Law impact production and inventory decisions?
16. Research the impact of mobile phones on poor regions of the world. Come to class prepared to discuss examples that demonstrate the potential for fast/cheap technology to improve society, even for individuals with extremely low incomes.
17. The "Internet of Things" makes for compelling commercials, but what needs to happen before a world of interconnected, coordinating devices can become a reality? What implications does this raise for business and society with respect to issues such as privacy and security? If you were GE, would you seek to keep the communication language among smart devices proprietary or open? Why or why not?

2. THE DEATH OF MOORE'S LAW?

LEARNING OBJECTIVES

1. **Describe why Moore's Law continues to advance and discuss the physical limitations of this advancement.**
2. **Name and describe various technologies that may extend the life of Moore's Law.**
3. **Discuss the limitations of each of these approaches.**

fabs

Semiconductor fabrication facilities; the multibillion dollar plants used to manufacture semiconductors.

silicon wafer

A thin, circular slice of material used to create semiconductor devices. Hundreds of chips may be etched on a single wafer, where they are eventually cut out for individual packaging.

Moore simply observed that we're getting better over time at squeezing more stuff into tinier spaces. Moore's Law is possible because the distance between the pathways inside silicon chips gets smaller with each successive generation. While chip factories (semiconductor fabrication facilities, or **fabs**) are incredibly expensive to build, each new generation of fabs can crank out more chips per **silicon wafer**. And since the pathways are closer together, electrons travel shorter distances. If electronics now travel half the distance to make a calculation, that means the chip is twice as fast.

While shrinking silicon pathways creates better chips, packing pathways tightly together creates problems associated with three interrelated forces—*size*, *heat*, and *power*—that together are threatening to slow down Moore's Law's advance. When you make processors smaller, the more tightly packed electrons will heat up a chip—so much so that unless today's most powerful chips are cooled down, they will melt inside their packaging. To keep the fastest computers cool, many PCs, laptops, and video game consoles need fans, and most corporate data centers have elaborate and expensive air conditioning and venting systems to prevent a meltdown. A trip through the Facebook data center during its recent rise would show that the firm was a "hot" start-up in more ways than one. The firm's servers ran so hot that the Plexiglas sides of the firm's server racks were warped and melting![45] The need to cool modern data centers draws a lot of power and that costs a lot of money.

The chief eco officer at Sun Microsystems has claimed that computers draw 4 to 5 percent of the world's power. Google's chief technology officer has said that the firm spends more to power its servers than the cost of the servers themselves.[46] Apple, Facebook, Microsoft, Yahoo! and Google have all built massive data centers in the Pacific Northwest, away from their corporate headquarters, specifically choosing these locations for access to cheap hydroelectric power. Google's location in The Dalles, Oregon, is charged a cost per kilowatt hour less than one-fifth the rate the firm pays in Silicon Valley.[47] This difference means big savings for a firm that runs more than a million servers.

And while these powerful shrinking chips are getting hotter and more costly to cool, it's also important to realize that chips can't get smaller forever. At some point Moore's Law will run into the unyielding laws of nature. While we're not certain where these limits are, chip pathways certainly can't be shorter than a single molecule, and the actual physical limit is likely larger than that. Get too small and a phenomenon known as quantum tunneling kicks in, and electrons start to slide off their paths. Yikes! While the death of Moore's Law has been predicted for years, scientists continue to squeeze advancement through new manufacturing techniques. Many think that while Moore's Law has celebrated its fiftieth birthday, it may not make it to sixty.[48]

2.1   Buying Time

One way to address the problem of densely-packed, overheating chip designs is with **multicore microprocessors**, made by putting two or more lower power processor cores (think of a core as the calculating part of a microprocessor) on a single chip. Philip Emma, IBM's Manager of Systems Technology and Microarchitecture, offers an analogy. Think of the traditional fast, hot, single-core processors as a three hundred-pound lineman, and a dual-core processor as two 160-pound guys. Says Emma, "A 300-pound lineman can generate a lot of power, but two 160-pound guys can do the same work with less overall effort."[49] For many applications, the multicore chips will outperform a single speedy chip, while running cooler and drawing less power. Multicore processors are now mainstream.

Today, most smartphones, PCs, and laptops sold have at least a two-core (dual-core) processor. The Microsoft Xbox One and PlayStation 4 both have eight core processors. Intel has even demonstrated chips with upwards of fifty cores.

Multicore processors can run older software written for single-brain chips. But they usually do this by using only one core at a time. To reuse the metaphor above, this is like having one of our 160-pound workers lift away, while the other one stands around watching. Multicore operating systems can help achieve some performance gains. Versions of Windows or the Mac OS that are aware of multicore processors can assign one program to run on one core, while a second application is assigned to the next core. But in order to take full advantage of multicore chips, applications need to be rewritten to split up tasks so that smaller portions of a problem are executed simultaneously inside each core.

Writing code for this "divide and conquer" approach is not trivial. In fact, developing software for multicore systems is described by Shahrokh Daijavad, software lead for next-generation computing systems at IBM, as "one of the hardest things you learn in computer science."[50] Microsoft's chief research and strategy officer has called coding for these chips "the most conceptually different [change] in the history of modern computing."[51] Despite this challenge, some of the most aggressive adaptors of multicore chips have been video game console manufacturers. Video game applications are particularly well-suited for multiple cores since, for example, one core might be used to render the background, another to draw objects, another for the "physics engine" that moves the objects around, and yet another to handle Internet communications for multiplayer games.

Another approach that's breathing more life into Moore's Law moves chips from being paper-flat devices to built-up 3-D affairs. By building up as well as out, firms are radically boosting speed and efficiency of chips. Intel has flipped upward the basic component of chips—the transistor. Transistors are the supertiny on-off switches in a chip that work collectively to calculate or store things in memory (a high-end microprocessor might include over two billion transistors). While you won't notice that chips are much thicker, Intel says that on the miniscule scale of modern chip manufacturing, the new designs are 37 percent faster and half as power hungry as conventional chips.[52]

> **multicore microprocessors**
>
> Microprocessors with two or more (typically lower power) calculating processor cores on the same piece of silicon.

New Materials and Quantum Leaps? Thinking Beyond Moore's Law–Constraining Silicon

Think about it—the triple threat of size, heat, and power means that Moore's Law, perhaps the greatest economic gravy train in history, will likely come to a grinding halt in your lifetime. Multicore and 3-D transistors are here today, but what else is happening to help stave off the death of Moore's Law?

Every once in a while a material breakthrough comes along that improves chip performance. A few years back researchers discovered that replacing a chip's aluminum components with copper could increase speeds up to 30 percent. Now scientists are concentrating on improving the very semiconductor material that chips are made of. While the silicon used in chips is wonderfully abundant (it has pretty much the same chemistry found in sand), researchers are investigating other materials that might allow for chips with even tighter component densities. New processors made with silicon germanium, germanium, or grapheme have all been mentioned as next-gen candidates.[53] Hyperefficient chips of the future may also be made out of carbon nanotubes, once the technology to assemble the tiny structures becomes commercially viable.

Other designs move away from electricity over silicon. Optical computing, where signals are sent via light rather than electricity, promises to be faster than conventional chips, if lasers can be mass produced in miniature (silicon laser experiments show promise). Others are experimenting by crafting computing components using biological material (think a DNA-based storage device).

One yet-to-be-proven technology that could blow the lid off what's possible today is quantum computing. Conventional computing stores data as a combination of bits, where a bit is either a one or a zero. Quantum computers, leveraging principles of quantum physics, employ qubits that can be both one *and* zero at the same time. Add a bit to a conventional computer's memory and you double its capacity. Add a bit to a quantum computer and its capacity increases exponentially. For comparison, consider that a computer model of serotonin, a molecule vital to regulating the human central nervous system, would require 10^{94} bytes of information. Unfortunately there's not enough matter in the universe to build a computer that big. But modeling a serotonin molecule using quantum computing would take just 424 qubits.[54]

Some speculate that quantum computers could one day allow pharmaceutical companies to create hyperdetailed representations of the human body that reveal drug side effects before they're even tested on humans. Quantum computing might also accurately predict the weather months in advance or offer unbreakable computer security. Opportunities abound. Of course, before quantum computing can be commercialized, researchers need to harness the freaky properties of quantum physics wherein your answer may reside in another universe, or could disappear if observed (Einstein himself referred to certain behaviors in quantum physics as "spooky action at a distance").

Pioneers in quantum computing include IBM, HP, NEC, and a Canadian start-up named D-Wave, which has sold early-stage quantum computers to Google, NASA, and Lockheed-Martin.[55] If or when the full promise of quantum computing will become a reality is still unknown, but scientists and engineers are hoping that by the time Moore's Law runs into Mother Nature's limits, a new way of computing may blow past anything we can do with silicon, continuing to make possible the once impossible.

KEY TAKEAWAYS

- As chips get smaller and more powerful, they get hotter and present power-management challenges. And at some, point Moore's Law will stop because we will no longer be able to shrink the spaces between components on a chip.
- Multicore chips use two or more low-power calculating "cores" to work together in unison, but to take optimal advantage of multicore chips, software must be rewritten to "divide" a task among multiple cores.
- 3-D transistors are also helping extend Moore's Law by producing chips that require less power and run faster.
- New materials may extend the life of Moore's Law, allowing chips to get smaller, still. Entirely new methods for calculating, such as quantum computing, may also dramatically increase computing capabilities far beyond what is available today.

QUESTIONS AND EXERCISES

1. What three interrelated forces threaten to slow the advancement of Moore's Law?
2. Which commercial solutions, described in the section above, are currently being used to counteract the forces mentioned above? How do these solutions work? What are the limitations of each?
3. Will multicore chips run software designed for single-core processors?
4. As chips grow smaller they generate increasing amounts of heat that needs to be dissipated. Why is keeping systems cool such a challenge? What are the implications for a firm like Yahoo! or Google? For a firm like Apple or Dell?
5. What are some of the materials that may replace the silicon that current chips are made of?
6. Search online to assess the current state of quantum computing. What kinds of problems might be solved if the promise of quantum computing is achieved? How might individuals and organizations leverage quantum computing? What sorts of challenges could arise from the widespread availability of such powerful computing technology?

3.   BRINGING BRAINS TOGETHER: SUPERCOMPUTING, GRIDS, CLUSTERS, AND PUTTING SMARTS IN THE CLOUD

LEARNING OBJECTIVES

1. **Understand the differences between supercomputing, grid computing, cluster computing, and cloud computing.**
2. **Describe how grid computing can transform the economics of supercomputing.**
3. **Recognize that these technologies provide the backbone of remote computing resources used in cloud computing.**
4. **Understand the characteristics of problems that are and are not well suited for parallel processing found in modern supercomputing, grid computing, cluster computing, and multicore processors. Also be able to discuss how network latency places limits on offloading computing to the cloud.**

As Moore's Law makes possible the once impossible, businesses have begun to demand access to the world's most powerful computing technology. **Supercomputers** are computers that are among the fastest of any in the world at the time of their introduction.[56] Supercomputing was once the domain of governments and high-end research labs, performing tasks such as simulating the explosion of nuclear devices, or analyzing large-scale weather and climate phenomena. But it turns out with a bit of tweaking, the algorithms used in this work are profoundly useful to business.

Supercomputers

Computers that are among the fastest of any in the world at the time of their introduction.

Paging Doctor Watson

Perhaps the world's most famous supercomputer is the IBM-created, Jeopardy-playing Watson. Built to quickly answer questions posed in natural language, by the end of a televised three-day tournament Watson had put the hurt on prior Jeopardy champs Ken Jennings and Brad Rutter, trouncing the human rivals and winning one million dollars (donated to a children's charity). Watson's accomplishment represented a four-year project that involved some twenty-five people across eight IBM research labs, creating algorithms, in a system with ninety servers, "many, many" processors, terabytes of storage, and "tens of millions of dollars" in investment.[57] Winning Jeopardy makes for a few nights of interesting TV, but what else can it do? Well, the "Deep QA" technology behind Watson might end up in your doctor's office, and docs could likely use that kind of "exobrain." On average "primary care physicians spend less than twenty minutes face-to-face with each patient per visit, and average little more than an hour each week reading medical journals."[58] Now imagine a physician assistant Watson that could leverage massive diagnosis databases while scanning hundreds of pages in a person's medical history, surfacing a best guess at what docs should be paying attention to. A *JAMA* study suggested that medical errors may be the third leading cause of death in the United States,[59] so there's apparently an enormous and mighty troubling opportunity in health care alone. IBM is partnering with Massachusetts voice-recognition leader Nuance Communications (the tech that originally made Apple's Siri such a good listener) to bring Watson to the doc's office. Med schools at Columbia and the University of Maryland will help with the research effort. Of course, you wouldn't want to completely trust a Watson recommendation. While Watson was good enough to be tournament champ, IBM's baby missed a final Jeopardy answer of "Chicago" because it answered that Toronto was a US city.

Source: http://www.ibm.com/press.

IBM is aggressively encouraging others to take advantage of Watson technology. Today Watson tech has been applied to over 75 industries in 17 nations, with tens of thousands of people leveraging Watson-smarts to assist their own work.[60] The group's swanky new Manhattan digs provide a base for showcasing the tech to clients, and providing resources to third parties looking to bake Watson smarts into their own offerings using the "Watson Cloud," and other resources. IBM will even provide seed capital to efforts it deems most promising. A recent Watson Mobile App Challenge winner, the firm Elemental Path, is launching a dinosaur-shaped child's toy that uses Watson's Q&A smarts to answer kid questions, tell jokes and stories, and quiz kids as a learning buddy. The toy learns a child's interests and comprehension level, and tailors interaction as its understanding of its owner develops. A Kickstarter campaign for the product zoomed past its initial goal, and underscores how a few bright researchers can leverage cloud resources and plummeting costs to build something that was not just cost-prohibitive, it was impossible just a few years back.[61]

Kickstarter video for Elemental Path's Cognitoys Dinosaur, which interacts with children using Watson smarts accessed over the cloud. Moore's Law combined with savvy networking brings supercomputing-class technology into a sub-$90 child's toy.

View the video online at: http://www.youtube.com/embed/o1tm5Xs5vlw?rel=0

Corporate use of supercomputing varies widely. United Airlines used supercomputing to increase the number of flight-path combinations for scheduling systems from 3,000 to 350,000. Estimated savings through better yield management? Over $50 million! CIBC (the Canadian Imperial Bank of Commerce), one of the largest banks in North America, uses supercomputing to run its portfolio through

Monte Carlo simulations that aren't all that different from the math used to simulate nuclear explosions. The muscular mathematics CIBC performs allows the firm to lower capital on hand by hundreds of millions of dollars, a substantial percentage of the bank's capital, saving millions a year in funding costs. Also noteworthy: the supercomputer-enabled, risk-savvy CIBC was relatively unscathed by the subprime crisis.

Modern supercomputing is typically done via a technique called **massively parallel** processing (computers designed with many microprocessors that work together, simultaneously, to solve problems). The fastest of these supercomputers are built using hundreds or even thousands of microprocessors, all programmed to work in unison as one big brain. While supercomputers use special electronics and software to handle the massive load, the processors themselves are often of the off-the-shelf variety that you'd find in a computer at BestBuy. For example, the recent speed champ, China's Tianhe (or "Milky Way") 2, uses 32,000 Intel Xeon chips.[62]

massively parallel
Computers designed with many microprocessors that work together, simultaneously, to solve problems.

Another technology, known as **grid computing**, is further transforming the economics of high performance. With grid computing, firms place special software on its existing PCs or servers that enables these computers to work together on a common problem. While many firms set up grids in data centers from servers they've bought specifically to work together on corporate tasks, large organizations have also created grids by harnessing excess capacity from staff PCs when these computers aren't being used or aren't used to full capacity. With grid software installed, idle devices can be marshaled to attack portions of a complex task as if they collectively were one massively parallel supercomputer. *BusinessWeek* reports that while a middle-of-the-road supercomputer could run as much as $30 million, grid computing software and services to perform comparable tasks can cost as little as twenty-five thousand dollars, assuming an organization already has PCs and servers in place.

grid computing
A type of computing that uses special software to enable several computers to work together on a common problem as if they were a massively parallel supercomputer.

The biotech firm Monsanto uses this technology to explore ways to manipulate genes to create crop strains that are resistant to cold, drought, bugs, pesticides, or that are more nutritious. The fifty-fold time savings the firm achieved through grid computing lets Monsanto consider thousands of genetic combinations in a year.[63] Lower R&D time means faster time to market—critical to both the firm and its customers. Movie studios use grids for animation and special effects; Proctor & Gamble used the technology to redesign manufacturing for Pringles potato chips; Pratt and Whitney tests aircraft engine designs by employing grid technology; GM and Ford use grids to simulate crash tests; and JPMorgan Chase launched a grid effort that mimics CIBC's supercomputer, but at a fraction of the latter's cost. By the second year of operation, the JPMorgan Chase grid was saving the firm $5 million per year.

Another term you might hear is **cluster computing**. Computing clusters are also built with commodity servers, but they usually take advantage of special software and networking hardware to more tightly link them together to function as one. The geeky details of how tightly or loosely coupled devices are—and whether this classifies as a grid or cluster—are less important, but as a manager you should be able to recognize these terms and think critically about their potential use and limitations.

cluster computing
Connecting server computers via software and networking so that their resources can be used to collectively solve computing tasks.

Multicore, massively parallel, grid, and cluster computing are all related in that each attempts to lash together multiple computing devices so that they can work together to solve problems. Think of multicore chips as having several processors in a single chip. Think of massively parallel supercomputers as having several chips in one computer, and think of grid and cluster computing as using existing computers to work together on a single task (essentially a computer made up of multiple computers), with clusters being more "tightly coupled" with additional software and networking hardware to facilitate their coordination. While these technologies offer great promise, they're all subject to the same limitation: software must be written to divide existing problems into smaller pieces that can be handled by each core, processor, or computer, respectively. Some problems, such as simulations, are easy to split up, but for problems that are linear (where, for example, step two can't be started until the results from step one are known), the multiple-brain approach doesn't offer much help.

software as a service (SaaS)

A form of cloud computing where a firm subscribes to a third-party software and receives a service that is delivered online.

cloud computing

Replacing computing resources—either an organization's or individual's hardware or software—with services provided over the Internet.

server farms

A massive network of computer servers running software to coordinate their collective use. Server farms provide the infrastructure backbone to SaaS and hardware cloud efforts, as well as many large-scale Internet services.

latency

A term often used in computing that refers to delay, especially when discussing networking and data transfer speeds. Low-latency systems are faster systems.

Massive collections of computers running software that allows them to operate as a unified service also enable new service-based computing models, such as **software as a service (SaaS)** and **cloud computing**. In these models, organizations replace traditional software and hardware that they would run in-house with services that are delivered online. Google, Microsoft, Salesforce.com, and Amazon are among the firms that have sunk billions into these Moore's Law-enabled **server farms**, creating entirely new businesses that promise to radically redraw the software and hardware landscape while bringing gargantuan computing power to the little guy. (See Chapter 14) Technology such as the IBM Watson cloud act like a supercomputer for hire. Researchers have leveraged the technology to, as New Scientist states "make discoveries scientists can't" by scanning massive databases of research and hunting for patterns humans have missed.[64] Moving "brains" to the cloud can help increase calculating performance even when we can't pack more processing brawn into our devices, but the cloud requires a long-distance connection that's a lot slower and perhaps less reliable than the quick hop from storage to processor that occurs inside most consumer electronics. In tech circles, delay is sometimes referred to as **latency**—and low latency is good. It means communications are speedy. As an example of how latency limits what the cloud can do, consider the new generation of Xbox: the Xbox One. Microsoft has designed the gaming system so that it can offload some tasks to its massive 300,000-server gaming data centers if they don't require an immediate response. Latency-sensitive tasks that can't be shipped to the cloud might include reactions to bumping collisions in a racing game, or cross-fire in a shooter. But the cloud could easily handle complex calculations to load as needed, such as rendering a scene's background and lighting.[65]

Moore's Law will likely hit its physical limit in your lifetime, but no one really knows if this "Moore's Wall" is a decade away or more. What lies ahead is anyone's guess. Some technologies, such as still-experimental quantum computing, could make computers that are more powerful than all the world's conventional computers combined. Think strategically—new waves of innovation might soon be shouting "surf's up!"

KEY TAKEAWAYS

- Most modern supercomputers use massive sets of microprocessors working in parallel.
- The microprocessors used in most modern supercomputers are often the same commodity chips that can be found in conventional PCs and servers.
- Moore's Law means that businesses as diverse as financial services firms, industrial manufacturers, consumer goods firms, and film studios can now afford access to supercomputers.
- Grid computing software uses existing computer hardware to work together and mimic a massively parallel supercomputer. Using existing hardware for a grid can save a firm the millions of dollars it might otherwise cost to buy a conventional supercomputer, further bringing massive computing capabilities to organizations that would otherwise never benefit from this kind of power.
- Cluster computing refers to collections of server computers that are linked together via software and networking hardware so that they can function as a single computing resource.
- Massively parallel computing also enables the vast server farms that power online businesses like Google and Facebook, and which create new computing models, like software as a service (SaaS) and cloud computing.
- The characteristics of problems best suited for solving via multicore systems, parallel supercomputers, grid, or cluster computing are those that can be divided up so that multiple calculating components can simultaneously work on a portion of the problem. Problems that are linear—where one part must be solved before moving to the next and the next—may have difficulty benefiting from these kinds of "divide and conquer" computing. Fortunately many problems such as financial risk modeling, animation, manufacturing simulation, and gene analysis are all suited for parallel systems.
- Many computer tasks can be offloaded to the cloud, but networking speeds (latency)—that is, the time needed to send results back and forth—can limit instances where collections of off-site computing hardware can replace or augment local computing.

QUESTIONS AND EXERCISES

1. Show your familiarity with key terms: What are the differences between supercomputing, grid computing, and cluster computing? How are these phenomena empowered by Moore's Law?

2. How does grid computing using slack or excess computing resources change the economics of supercomputing?

3. Name businesses that are using supercomputing and grid computing? Describe these uses and the advantages they offer their adopting firms. Are they a source of competitive advantage? Why or why not?

4. What are the characteristics of problems that are most easily solved using the types of parallel computing found in grids, clusters, and modern-day supercomputers? What are the characteristics of the sorts of problems not well suited for this type of computing?

5. You can join a grid, too! Visit the SETI@Home Web site (http://setiathome.ssl.berkeley.edu/). What is the purpose of the SETI@Home project? How do you participate? Is there any possible danger to your computer if you choose to participate? (Read their rules and policies.) Do some additional research on the Internet. Are there other interesting grid efforts that you can load onto your laptop or even game console?

6. Search online to identify the five fastest supercomputers currently in operation. Who sponsors these machines? What are they used for? How many processors do they have?

7. What is "Moore's Wall"?

8. What is the advantage of using computing to simulate an automobile crash test as opposed to actually staging a crash?

9. Moore's Law may limit the amount of computing done on the PC, smartphone, or gaming console in front of you. How can cloud computing make these devices seem more powerful? Give examples of when using a powerful, remote, cloud computing resource might work well to enhance computing on a local device, and mention when the cloud might be less effective. What is the main constraint in your example?

4. E-WASTE: THE DARK SIDE OF MOORE'S LAW

LEARNING OBJECTIVES

1. **Understand the magnitude of the environmental issues caused by rapidly obsolete, faster and cheaper computing.**
2. **Explain the limitations of approaches attempting to tackle e-waste.**
3. **Understand the risks firms are exposed to when not fully considering the lifecycle of the products they sell or consume.**
4. **Ask questions that expose concerning ethical issues in a firm or partner's products and processes, and that help the manager behave more responsibly.**

We should celebrate the great bounty Moore's Law and the tech industry bestow on our lives. Costs fall, workers become more productive, innovations flourish, and we gorge at a buffet of digital entertainment that includes music, movies, and games. But there is a dark side to this faster and cheaper advancement. A laptop has an expected lifetime of around two to four years. A cell phone? Eighteen months or less.[66] Rapid obsolescence means the creation of ever-growing mountains of discarded tech junk, known as electronic waste or **e-waste**. In 2012, the United States alone generated over 9.4 million metric tons of e-waste[67] and the results aren't pretty. Consumer electronics and computing equipment can be a toxic cocktail that includes cadmium, mercury, lead, and other hazardous materials. Once called the "effluent of the affluent," e-waste will only increase with the rise of living standards worldwide.

The quick answer would be to recycle this stuff. Not only does e-waste contain mainstream recyclable materials we're all familiar with, like plastics and aluminum, it also contains small bits of increasingly valuable metals such as silver, platinum, and copper. In fact, there's more gold in one pound of discarded tech equipment than in one pound of mined ore.[68] But as the sordid record of e-waste management shows, there's often a disconnect between consumers and managers who *want* to do good and those efforts that are *actually* doing good. The complexities of the modern value chain, the vagaries of international law, and the nefarious actions of those willing to put profits above principle show how difficult addressing this problem will be.

The process of separating out the densely packed materials inside tech products so that the value in e-waste can be effectively harvested is extremely labor intensive, more akin to reverse manufacturing than any sort of curbside recycling efforts. Sending e-waste abroad can be ten times cheaper than

e-waste

Discarded, often obsolete technology; also known as electronic waste.

dealing with it at home,[69] so it's not surprising that up to 80 percent of the material dropped off for recycling is eventually exported.[70] Much of this waste ends up in China, South Asia, or sub-Saharan Africa, where it is processed in dreadful conditions.

Consider the example of Guiyu, China, a region whose poisoning has been extensively chronicled by organizations such as the Silicon Valley Toxics Coalition, the Basel Action Network (BAN), and Greenpeace. Workers in and around Guiyu toil without protective equipment, breathing clouds of toxins generated as they burn the plastic skins off of wires to get at the copper inside. Others use buckets, pots, or wok-like pans (in many cases the same implements used for cooking) to sluice components in acid baths to release precious metals—recovery processes that create even more toxins. Waste sludge and the carcasses of what's left over are most often dumped in nearby fields and streams. Water samples taken in the region showed lead and heavy metal contamination levels some four hundred to six hundred times greater than what international standards deem safe.[71] The area is so polluted that drinking water must be trucked in from eighteen miles away. Pregnancies are six times more likely to end in miscarriage, and 70 percent of the kids in the region have too much lead in their blood.[72]

FIGURE 5.3 Photos from Guiyu, China[73]

Source: © 2006 Basel Action Network (BAN).

China cares about its environment. The nation has banned the importing of e-waste since 2000.[74] But corruption ensures that e-waste continues to flow into the country. According to one exporter, all that's required to get e-waste past customs authorities is to tape a one-hundred-dollar bill on the side of the container.[75] Well-meaning US recyclers, as well as those attempting to collect technology for reuse in poorer countries, are often in the dark as to where their products end up.

The trade is often brokered by middlemen who mask the eventual destination and fate of the products purchased. BAN investigators in Lagos, Nigeria, documented mountains of e-waste with labels from schools, US government agencies, and even some of the world's largest corporations. And despite Europe's prohibition on exporting e-waste, many products originally labeled for repair and reuse end up in toxic recycling efforts. Even among those products that gain a second or third life in developing nations, the inevitable is simply postponed, with e-waste almost certain to end up in landfills that lack the protective groundwater barriers and environmental engineering of their industrialized counterparts. The reality is that e-waste management is extraordinarily difficult to monitor and track, and loopholes are rampant.

Thinking deeply about the ethical consequences of a firm's business is an imperative for the modern manager. A slip up (intentional or not) can, in seconds, be captured by someone with a cell phone, uploaded to YouTube, or offered in a blog posting for the world to see. When Dell was caught using Chinese prison labor as part of its recycling efforts, one blogger chastised the firm with a tweak of its marketing tagline, posting "Dude, you're getting a cell."[76] The worst cases expose firms to legal action and can tarnish a brand for years. Big firms are big targets, and environmentalists have been quick to push the best-known tech firms and retailers to take back their products for responsible recycling and to eliminate the worst toxins from their offerings.

Consider that even Apple (where Al Gore sits on the firm's board of directors), has been pushed by a coalition of environmental groups on all of these fronts. Critics have shot back that singling out Apple is unfair. The firm was one of the first computer companies to eliminate lead-lined glass monitors from its product line, and has been a pioneer of reduced-sized packaging that leverage recyclable materials. And Apple eventually claimed the top in Greenpeace's "Greener Electronics" rankings.[77] But if the firm that counts Al Gore among its advisors can get tripped up on green issues, all firms are vulnerable.

Environmentalists see this pressure to deal with e-waste as yielding results: Apple and most other tech firms have continually moved to eliminate major toxins from their manufacturing processes. All this demonstrates that today's business leaders have to be far more attuned to the impact not only of their own actions, but also to those of their suppliers and partners. How were products manufactured? Using which materials? Under what conditions? What happens to items when they're discarded? Who provides collection and disposal? It also shows the futility of legislative efforts that don't fully consider and address the problems they are meant to target.

Finding Responsible E-waste Disposers

A recent sting operation led by the US Government Accountability Office (US GAO) found that forty-three American recyclers were willing to sell e-waste illegally to foreign countries, without gaining EPA or foreign country approval. Appallingly, at least three of them held Earth Day electronics-recycling events.[78]

So how can firms and individuals choose proper disposal partners? Several certification mechanisms can help shed light on whether the partner you're dealing with is a responsible player. The Basel Action Network e-Stewards program certifies firms via a third-party audit, with compliant participants committing to eliminating e-waste export, land dumping, incineration, and toxic recycling via prison labor. The International Association of Electronics Recyclers (IAER) also offers audited electronics recycler certification. And firms certified as ISO 9001 and ISO 14001 compliant attest to quality management and environmental processes. Standards, techniques, and auditing practices are constantly in flux, so consult these organizations for the latest partner lists, guidelines, and audit practices.[79]

FIGURE 5.4

The e-Stewards program can help you find a vetted, responsible recycler.

Which brings us back to Gordon Moore. To his credit, Moore is not just the founder of the world's largest microprocessor firm and first to identify the properties we've come to know as Moore's Law, he has also emerged as one of the world's leading supporters of environmental causes. The generosity of the Gordon and Betty Moore foundation includes, among other major contributions, the largest single gift to a private conservation organization. Indeed, Silicon Valley, while being the birthplace of products that become e-waste, also promises to be at the forefront of finding solutions to modern environmental challenges. The Valley's leading venture capitalists, including Sequoia and Kleiner Perkins (where Al Gore is now a partner), have started multimillion-dollar green investment funds, targeted at funding the next generation of sustainable, environmental initiatives.

KEY TAKEAWAYS

- E-waste may be particularly toxic since many components contain harmful materials such as lead, cadmium, and mercury.
- Managers must consider and plan for the waste created by their products, services, and technology used by the organization. Consumers and governments are increasingly demanding that firms offer responsible methods for the disposal of their manufactured goods and the technology used in their operations.
- Managers must audit disposal and recycling partners with the same vigor as their suppliers and other corporate partners. If not, an organization's equipment may end up in environmentally harmful disposal operations.

QUESTIONS AND EXERCISES

1. What is e-waste? What is so dangerous about e-waste?
2. What sorts of materials might be harvested from e-waste recycling?
3. Many well-meaning individuals thought that recycling was the answer to the e-waste problem. But why hasn't e-waste recycling yielded the results hoped for?
4. What lessons do the challenges of e-waste offer the manager? What issues will your firm need to consider as it consumes or offers products that contain computing components?
5. Why is it difficult to recycle e-waste?
6. Why is e-waste exported abroad for recycling rather than processed domestically?
7. What part does corruption play in the recycling and disposal of e-waste?
8. What part might product design and production engineering play in the reduction of the impact of technology waste on the environment?
9. What are the possible consequences should a US firm be deemed "environmentally irresponsible"?
10. Name two companies that have incurred the wrath of environmental advocates. What might these firms have done to avoid such criticism?

5. MICKEY'S WEARABLE: DISNEY'S MAGIC BAND

LEARNING OBJECTIVES

1. Illustrate the value that Disney accrued from embedding technology in otherwise manual experiences.
2. Recognize how the experience improved the value of the customer's Disney World experience.
3. Understand some of the issues involved in deploying large-scale information systems in a corporate environment.

Plan a trip to Disney World in Orlando, Florida, and the park is armed to leverage tech to streamline your experience, delight you at every turn, and keep you spending money. The centerpiece is the MagicBand, a stylish, rubberized, waterproof wristband mailed in advance to guests' homes. Bands can be used for park and attraction admission, for keyless entry into your Disney hotel room, to pay for rides, and to locate your group to deliver restaurant meals, personalized greetings, match you to photos taken by park photographers and attraction cameras, and more. And of course, the tech is tied to your credit card, so you can pay for everything from an in-park Starbucks fix to gourmet restaurant meals to mouse ears and *Frozen* dolls, all with a wave of your wrist.

Family members choose the color of their individual band from a rainbow of options, and a band box arrives for the family with each guest's names etched inside their custom wearable. Each band is packed with low-cost, high-powered tech, courtesy of Moore's Law. Bands have both an RFID chip and a 2.4 GHz radio, akin to what you'd find in many cordless phones. MagicBands can transmit in a radius of 40 feet. Embedded batteries last two years.[80]

A video by Orlando Attractions Magazine shows the MagicBand in action in a variety of settings.

View the video online at: http://www.youtube.com/embed/l3ojftUvWWU?rel=0

MagicBands are part of a broader set of technologies that Disney calls MyMagic+ that link together various systems that include the Web and mobile MyDisneyExperience to plan and share your vacation itinerary, manage your schedule, and deliver GPS-park maps and schedules to smartphone apps; the FastPass+ ride reservation system; and the Disney PhotoPass that stitches together a custom media album gathered from your visit (with an option to purchase prints, of course).[81] The mandate from Meg Crofton, previous president of Walt Disney World Resort, was to remove the friction in the Disney World experience. Says another Disney exec, "If we can get out of the way, our guests can create more memories."[82]

A band that tracks users and contains payment information can lead to privacy concerns, but Disney seems to have this covered. The band doesn't store any personal information; instead, it contains a code that identifies users within Disney's internal encrypted databases. Lose a band and it can be disabled and replaced. Purchases also require a PIN, and parents concerned with free-spending children can disable purchasing on their bands, or set a spending limit.[83]

5.1 Experience Examples

Band up as soon as you arrive in Orlando, then just hop a shuttle and head to your hotel or directly to the park. Your band is your room key, your park admission ticket, the pass to zip into any rides you've reserved in advance, and your payment method. No need to delay the fun waiting for baggage claim carousels; Disney's systems will also make sure your luggage is delivered to your room.

The MagicBand rollout in Disney World's *Be Our Guest* restaurant, inspired by the fairy-tale dining experience in *Beauty and the Beast*, launched to glowing reviews. Guests arriving at the restaurant are greeted by name by a hostess that gets a heads-up on her modified iOS device. The welcome is followed by a suggestion to sit wherever you want. The kitchen already has the order you've made online. Wireless receivers on the table and in the walls know where you are, so your food is whisked right to you, as if you were Belle herself. All in all, a seamless experience that won top innovation honors from the National Restaurant Association.[84]

MagicBand can also turn a long ride wait into a time-filling interactive experience. The popular Epcot Test Track ride is notorious for its lines, but clever design fills the wait with a touch-screen auto-design session where users create their own car for integration into the attraction when they're ready to roll. Guests can also create a custom car commercial. Disney survey data suggests a 35-minute wait time for Test Track feels like it's only been 15 to 20 minutes.[85]

5.2 Big Data and Big Benefits

Disney World is really more of a city than a resort. It occupies twice as much land as Manhattan, contains four major theme parks, some 140 attractions, 300 dining locations, and 36 hotels. The 15-mile monorail alone hosts an average of 150,000 rides each day.[86] Driving far-reaching delight alongside efficiency at scale is the major goal of the MyMagic+ system that contains the magic band plus trip planning and operations technology.

Guests use the park's website and apps before they show up in Orlando so that they can reserve their favorite rides for priority seating. They can also select shows, parades, choose to attend fireworks displays, and set up character greetings. Information from these systems, when coupled with real-time data collected from MagicBand wearing guests, delivers more insight to tailor many more service improvements, than if guests were free-ranging around Disney World without prior planning.[87] Disney analysts saw that some guests were traversing the park upwards of 20 times a day to see all the rides they were most interested in, but with MyMagic+, park systems crunch data so the Mouse House can craft a custom guest itinerary that eliminates a frustrating zigzag across the many realms of the Magic Kingdom. MyMagic+ books ride reservations to minimize wait and spread out guests to further cut line time. With an average of 8,000 to 10,000 guests flowing through the park's main entrance every hour, big data analytics and efficient scheduling algorithms keep everyone happier.[88]

Data helps Disney know when to add more staff at rides and restaurants; how to stock restaurants, snack bars, and souvenir stands; and how many costumed cast members should be roaming in various areas of the park. If a snafu arises, such as an unexpectedly long line or a restaurant menu change, a custom-crafted alert with alternative suggestions can go out via text or e-mail.[89] At some point, systems might be able to detect when guests have waited too long or otherwise had an unexpectedly frustrating experience, offering a treat coupon or a pass to another ride. These kinds of systems have allowed casinos to turn negative experiences (losing big in slots) into positive ones.[90]

Disney says the MagicBand and supporting systems have cut turnstile transaction time by 30 percent, guests are spending more money, and systems have increased efficiency to the point where Disney World can serve 3,000 to 5,000 additional guests per day.[91] Another benefit to satisfied customers? They're less likely to decamp for nearby rival parks such as Universal Studios, Sea World, and Legoland.[92]

5.3 Magical Experiences Cost Serious Coin

These systems don't come cheap. It's estimated that Disney spent $1 billion on MyMagic+. Over 100 systems needed to be integrated to make the park function in a unified, guest-delighting way.[93] The cost just to redesign and integrate the DisneyWorld.com website with MyMagic+ is said to have cost about $80 million.[94]

Moore's Law turns embedded technology at scale, a once impossible proposition, into a now justifiable business-enhancing expense (albeit a big one). More than 28,000 hotel doors needed replacement locks to work with MagicBand. Two dozen workers spent eight months upgrading 120 doors per day, trying to be unobtrusive in properties that boast an 80 percent average guest occupancy rate. Two hundred eighty-three park-entry points also had to be upgraded. More than 6,000 mobile devices (mostly iPod Touch and iPads with custom apps) were deployed to support new park systems. Disney World also needed to install more than 30 million square feet of Wi-Fi coverage.[95] According to a source in a *FastCompany* article, "It was a huge effort to wire a communications infrastructure that was basically the same size as San Francisco."[96] And you can't roll out a major tech initiative without making sure your staff knows how to use it. Over 70,000 "cast members" (Disney's name for its employees) received MyMagic+ training, with 15,000 skilled-up in specifics such as the FastPass+ ride reservation system and MagicBand merchandising.[97]

Putting tech on the wrist of every guest also adds a marginal cost to everyone coming through the door. The firm spent only four cents each to print paper tickets, but the early prototype for MagicBand came in at $35. Fortunately Moore's Law, savvy engineering, and buying at scale kicked in, and manufacturing costs for bands are now below $5,[98] a much more tolerable price when tallied against the myriad of benefits delivered to each visiting guest.

5.4 Magical Experiences can Require Magical Coordination

A *FastCompany* article on the development of MyMagic+ also underscores political challenges when designing and deploying large-scale systems. Lots of groups had a stake in the outcome, and coordinating differing ideas, opinions, and agendas can be taxing. The systems impacted park operations, infrastructure, hotels, and marketing, among many other areas. Disney's IT group would be heavily involved in systems development and operation, and would need to lead integration with many existing systems and the replacement of others. The powerful Imagineering team, the group that designs much of the theme park wizardry that puts the magic in the Magic Kingdom, was also deep into the decision-making. Add to this additional work from third-parties, including Frog Design, a renown high-end global design consultancy whose prior clients include Apple, Lufthansa, and UNICEF; and tech consulting from Accenture, HP, and Synapse among others.[99] In such a disparate group, conflict, even among the well-intended, was inevitable.

Fortunately, the project benefited from strong executive leadership–a key to many successful transformative projects. The effort had the full support and backing of Disney CEO Bob Iger, who regularly discussed the project with the firm's Board of Directors. Iger's involvement sent a clear message: we're doing this, and the resources will be there to support the effort. The exploratory team for the Next Generation Experience project, or NGE (the early name for what would develop into MyMagic+ and MagicBand), included some of the firm's most senior execs in theme park and Disney World management. The core team for project included senior execs in technology, Imagineering, theme parks, and business development.[100] Disney's COO has stated the project actually came in a bit under budget, although delays and a staged roll-out had left many of originally-envisioned features to be introduced over time.[101]

5.5   Look to the Future

Additional services on deck include sharing data so that hosts and costumed cast members can issue birthday greetings, and rollout of even more interaction, such as animatronics that call you by name as you walk up to them.[102] Disney's theme park and resort destinations are, collectively, a $14.1 billion business.[103] Full rollout at other parks is less clear, but the Disney attractions empire is massive and includes theme parks in Anaheim, Paris, Shanghai, Tokyo, and Hong Kong; cruise lines; adventure travel; arcades; and ESPN properties. It's suspected that MagicBand wouldn't roll out in Disneyland in Anaheim, because the restructuring costs for a much smaller park wouldn't be efficient. Shanghai users may opt for a mobile phone experience, given the higher penetration and usage pattern of smartphones.[104] However, learning and various system components are expected to show up worldwide, with the firm stating it plans to roll out "variations on MyMagic+."[105] Disney parks have an annual admission of over 120 million guests a year. At that scale, innovations and bar-setting experiences have a massive influence on overall customer expectations.[106] Expect players in other hospitality and entertainment markets to study Disney's magic in hopes of creating a bit of sorcery of their own.

KEY TAKEAWAYS

- The Disney MagicBand handles many tasks, including park and attraction admission, payment, staff notification for improved service, and security such as hotel room admission.

- Deploying a project like MagicBand involves integrating over one hundred existing and new systems in a broader effort called MyMagic+. Infrastructure needed to be upgraded, and employees trained. The experience cost roughly $1 billion to deploy.

- Many internal and external groups were involved. Differing opinions and agendas often make large projects politically challenging to coordinate. Having the CEO champion the effort, and senior executives from various groups lead development, helped reduce debilitating infighting and helped the project come in under budget.

QUESTIONS AND EXERCISES

1. What is the MagicBand? What technology is inside it and what does it do? How do the bands benefit the customer experience? What benefits does Disney realize from the system?

2. In addition to designing and creating bands, what else did Disney need to do to pull off this effort? How many systems were involved? What infrastructure needed to be upgraded?

3. There's a lot you can do with technology, but Disney is also crafting a very special, branded experience. Do you think Disney got it right, or does the technology seem like it would interfere with the experience? Why or why not?

4. What more can and should Disney do with this technology?

5. Large technical projects can be a challenge to design and deploy. Why? How did Disney cut through some of these challenges and eventually deliver a project within goals and within budget?

6. How does Disney deal with security and privacy concerns? Do you think these precautions are enough? Why or why not?

ENDNOTES

1. G. Moore, "Cramming More Components onto Integrated Circuits," *Electronics Magazine*, April 19, 1965.

2. K. Krewell, "The Slowing Of Moore's Law And Its Impact," *Forbes*, July 30, 2015.

3. Although other materials besides silicon are increasingly being used.

4. Semiconductor materials, like the silicon dioxide used inside most computer chips, are capable of enabling as well as inhibiting the flow of electricity. These properties enable chips to perform math or store data.

5. Fiber-optic lines are glass or plastic data transmission cables that carry light. These cables offer higher transmission speeds over longer distances than copper cables that transmit electricity.

6. C. Walter, "Kryder's Law," *Scientific American*, July 25, 2005.

7. D. Rosenthal, "Storage Will be a Lot Less Free than It Used to be," *DSHR Blog*, October 1, 2012; Gwern Branwen, "Slowing Moore's Law: How It Could Happen," *Gwern.net*, last modified June 03, 2014.

8. K. Fisher, "All or Nothing in 2014," *Forbes*, February 10, 2014.

9. G. Satell, "What We Can Expect from the Next Decade of Technology," *Business Insider*, July 7, 2013.

10. K. Krewell, "The Slowing Of Moore's Law And Its Impact," *Forbes*, July 30, 2015.

11. As opposed to goods and services that are *price inelastic* (like health care and housing), which consumers will try their best to buy even if prices go up.

12. M. Copeland, "How to Ride the Fifth Wave," *Business 2.0*, July 1, 2005.

13. N. Patel, "Inside the Nest: iPod Creator Tony Fadell Wants to Reinvent the Thermostat," *The Verge*, November 14, 2011.

14. M. Meeker, "Internet Trends 2014," *KPCB*, May 28, 2014.

15. J. Salter, "Tony Fadell, Father of the iPod, iPhone and Nest, on Why He Is Worth $3.2bn to Google," *Telegraph*, June 14, 2014.

16. M. Chui, M. Loffler, and R. Roberts, "The Internet of Things," *McKinsey Quarterly*, March 2010.

17. M. Brian, "Airbus Smart Luggage Prototype Offers iPhone Tracking, Faster Check-in," *The Verge*, June 7, 2013.

18. T. Nudd, "Huggies App Sends You a Tweet Whenever Your Kid Pees in His Diaper," *AdWeek*, May 8, 2013.

19. K. Komando, "Should You Buy a $25 Computer? Meet the Raspberry Pi," *USA Today*, June 14, 2013.

20. J. Manyika, M. Chui, J. Bughin, R. Dobbs, P. Bisson, and A. Marrs, "Disruptive Technologies: Advances That Will Transform Life, Business, and the Global Economy," *McKinsey Quarterly*, May 2013.

21. C. Boulton, "GE Launches Industrial Internet Analytics Platform," *Wall Street Journal*, June 18, 2013.

22. S. Higginbotham, "GE's Industrial Internet Focus Means It's a Big Data Company Now," *GigaOM*, June 18, 2013.

23. B. Cha, "A Beginner's Guide to Understanding the Internet of Things," *Re/code*, Jan. 15, 2015.

24. E. Gray, "CVS Wants to Be Your Doctor's Office," *Time*, Feb. 12, 2015.

25. D. Rose, presentation as part of "From Disruption to Innovation" at the MIT Enterprise Forum, Cambridge, MA, June 23, 2010.

26. E. Landau, "Tattletale Pills, Bottles Remind You to Take Your Meds," *CNN*, February 2, 2010.

27. K. Rozendal, "The Democratic, Digital Future of Healthcare," *Scope*, May 13, 2011.

28. H. Mitchell, "Steve Jobs Used Wayne Gretzky as Inspiration," *Los Angeles Times*, October 6, 2011.

29. J. Edwards, "Report: Apple Needed the Beats Deal Because Its iTunes Radio Team Was Clueless," *Business Insider*, June 6, 2014.

30. P, Kafka, "Warner Music Says Streaming Revenue Has Passed Downloads, and It Wants More," *Re/code*, May 11, 2015.

31. G. Kumparak, "Apple Just Had The Most Profitable Quarter of Any Company Ever," *TechCrunch*, Jan. 27, 2015.

32. E. Schuman, "At Walmart, World's Largest Retail Data Warehouse Gets Even Larger," *eWeek*, October 13, 2004; and J. Huggins, "How Much Data Is That?" *Refrigerator Door*, August 19, 2008.

33. A. Vance, "Netflix, Reed Hastings Survive Missteps to Join Silicon Valley's Elite," May 9, 2013.

34. M. Riley and D. Gambrell, "The NSA Spying Machine," *BusinessWeek*, April 3, 2014.

35. N. Myslewski, "Cisco: You Think the Internet Is Clogged with Video Now? Just Wait until 2018," *The Register*, June 13, 2014.

36. B. Breen, "Living in Dell Time," *Fast Company*, November 24, 2004.

37. S. Corbett, "Can the Cellphone Help End Global Poverty?" *New York Times Magazine*, April 13, 2008.

38. J. Ewing, "Upwardly Mobile in Africa," *BusinessWeek*, September 24, 2007, 64–71.

39. J. Ewing, "Upwardly Mobile in Africa," *BusinessWeek*, September 24, 2007, 64–71.

40. S. Corbett, "Can the Cellphone Help End Global Poverty?" *New York Times Magazine*, April 13, 2008.

41. Bill and Melinda Gates Foundation, *What We Do: Agricultural Development Strategy Overview*, accessed via http://www.gatesfoundation.org/What-We-Do/Global-Development/Agricultural-Development (accessed June 11, 2013).

42. Esoko Press Release, *Groundbreaking Study Confirms That Farmers Using Esoko Receive More for Their Crops*, December 15, 2011.

43. K. A. Domfeh, "Esoko Impact on Farmers Assessed for Expansion," *AfricaNews.com*, March 1, 2012.

44. C. Mims, "31% of Kenya's GDP Is Spent through Mobile Phones," *Quartz*, February 27, 2013.

45. E. McGirt, "Hacker, Dropout, C.E.O.," *Fast Company*, May 2007.

46. D. Kirkpatrick, "The Greenest Computer Company under the Sun," *CNN*, April 13, 2007.

47. S. Mehta, "Behold the Server Farm," *Fortune*, August 1, 2006. Also see Chapter 14 in this book.

48. A. Hesseldahl, "Moore's Law Hits 50, but It May Not See 60," *Re/code*, April 15, 2015.

49. A. Ashton, "More Life for Moore's Law," *BusinessWeek*, June 20, 2005.

50. A. Ashton, "More Life for Moore's Law," *BusinessWeek*, June 20, 2005.

51. M. Copeland, "A Chip Too Far?" *Fortune*, September 1, 2008.

52. K. Bourzac, "How Three-Dimensional Transistors Went from Lab to Fab," *Technology Review*, May 6, 2011.

53. A. Hesseldahl, "Moore's Law Hits 50, but It May Not See 60," *Re/code*, April 15, 2015.

54. P. Kaihla, "Quantum Leap," *Business 2.0*, August 1, 2004.

55. D. Love, "Quantum Computing Could Lead to a Gigantic Leap Forward," *Business Insider*, June 11, 2013.

56. A list of the current supercomputer performance champs can be found at http://www.top500.org.

57. L. Sumagaysay, "After Man vs. Machine on 'Jeopardy,' What's Next for IBM's Watson?" *Good Morning Silicon Valley*, February 17, 2011.

58. C. Nickisch, "IBM to Roll Out Watson, M.D.," *WBUR*, February 18, 2011.

59. B. Starfield, "Is U.S. Health Really the Best in the World?" *Journal of the American Medical Association*, July 26, 2000.

60. B. Wallace-Wells, "Boyhood," *New York Magazine*, May 20, 2015.

61. S. Perez, "Elemental Path Debuts The First Toys Powered By IBM Watson," *TechCrunch*, Feb. 16, 2015.

62. D. Clark, "Intel Reveals Details of Next Supercomputing Chip," *Wall Street Journal*, June 17, 2013.

63. P. Schwartz, C. Taylor, and R. Koselka, "The Future of Computing: Quantum Leap," *Fortune*, August 2, 2006.

64. H. Hodson, "Supercomputers make discoveries that scientists can't," *NewScientist*, Aug. 27, 2014.

65. K. Orland, "How the Xbox One Draws More Processing Power from the Cloud," *Ars Technica*, May 23, 2013.

66. L. Gilpin, "The Depressing Truth about e-Waste: 10 Things to Know," *TechRepublic*, June 11, 2014.

67. A. Romano, "49 Million Tons of Electronic Waste Generated in 2012," *Mashable*, May 22, 2014.

68. P. Kovessy, "How to Trash Toxic Tech," *Ottawa Business Journal*, May 12, 2008.

69. C. Bodeen, "In 'E-waste' Heartland, a Toxic China," *International Herald Tribune*, November 18, 2007.

70. E. Royte, "E-waste@Large," *New York Times*, January 27, 2006.

71. E. Grossman, "Where Computers Go to Die—and Kill," *Salon.com*, April 10, 2006, http://www.salon.com/news/feature/2006/04/10/ewaste.

72. *60 Minutes*, "Following the Trail of Toxic E-waste," November 9, 2008.

73. J. Biggs, "Guiyu, the E-waste Capital of China," *CrunchGear*, April 4, 2008.

74. E. Grossman, "Where Computers Go to Die—and Kill," *Salon.com*, April 10, 2006.

75. C. Bodeen, "In 'E-waste' Heartland, a Toxic China," *International Herald Tribune*, November 18, 2007.

76. J. Russell, "Dell under Attack over Using Prison Labour," *Inquirer*, January 10, 2003. See also http://laughingmeme.org/2003/03/23/dell-recycling-a-ways-to-go-still.

77. J. Dalrymple, "Apple Ranks Highest among Greenpeace's Top Tech Companies," *The Loop*, January 7, 2010.

78. U.S. Government Accountability Office (U.S. GAO), *Report to the Chairman: Committee on Foreign Affairs, House of Representatives: Electronic Waste*, August 2008.

79. Basal Action Network e-Stewards program accessed via http://www.e-stewards.org/certification-overview/; International Standards Organization accessed via http://www.iso.org/iso/home.htm; the IAER accessed via http://www.iaer.org/search; and G. MacDonald, "Don't Recycle 'E-waste' with Haste, Activists Warn," *USA Today*, July 6, 2008.

80. C. Kuang, "Disney's $1 Billion Bet on a Magical Wristband," *Wired*, March 10, 2015.

81. A. Carr, "The Messy Business of Reinventing Happiness," *FastCompany*, May 2015.

82. C. Kuang, "Disney's $1 Billion Bet on a Magical Wristband," *Wired*, March 10, 2015.

83. B. Cha, "Tomorrowland Today: Disney MagicBand Unlocks New Guest Experience for Park Goers," *AllThingsD*, May 29, 2013.

84. A. Carr, "The Messy Business of Reinventing Happiness," *FastCompany*, May 2015.

85. A. Carr, "The Messy Business of Reinventing Happiness," *FastCompany*, May 2015.

86. A. Carr, "The Messy Business of Reinventing Happiness," *FastCompany*, May 2015.

87. C. Kuang, "Disney's $1 Billion Bet on a Magical Wristband," *Wired*, March 10, 2015.

88. A. Carr, "The Messy Business of Reinventing Happiness," *FastCompany*, May 2015.

89. C. Palmeri, "Disney Bets $1 Billion on Technology to Track Theme Park Visitors," *BusinessWeek*, March 7, 2014.

90. C. Kuang, "Disney's $1 Billion Bet on a Magical Wristband," *Wired*, March 10, 2015.

91. A. Carr, "The Messy Business of Reinventing Happiness," *FastCompany*, May 2015. And C. Palmeri, "Disney Bets $1 Billion on Technology to Track Theme Park Visitors," *BusinessWeek*, March 7, 2014.

92. C. Palmeri, "Disney Bets $1 Billion on Technology to Track Theme Park Visitors," *BusinessWeek*, March 7, 2014.

93. C. Kuang, "Disney's $1 Billion Bet on a Magical Wristband," *Wired*, March 10, 2015.

94. A. Carr, "The Messy Business of Reinventing Happiness," *FastCompany*, May 2015.

95. A. Carr, "The Messy Business of Reinventing Happiness," *FastCompany*, May 2015.

96. A. Carr, "The Messy Business of Reinventing Happiness," *FastCompany*, May 2015.

97. A. Carr, "The Messy Business of Reinventing Happiness," *FastCompany*, May 2015.

98. A. Carr, "The Messy Business of Reinventing Happiness," *FastCompany*, May 2015.

99. A. Carr, "The Messy Business of Reinventing Happiness," *FastCompany*, May 2015.

100. C. Kuang, "Disney's $1 Billion Bet on a Magical Wristband," *Wired*, March 10, 2015.

101. A. Carr, "The Messy Business of Reinventing Happiness," *FastCompany*, May 2015.

102. A. Carr, "The Messy Business of Reinventing Happiness," *FastCompany*, May 2015.

103. C. Palmeri, "Disney Bets $1 Billion on Technology to Track Theme Park Visitors," *BusinessWeek*, March 7, 2014.

104. A. Carr, "The Messy Business of Reinventing Happiness," *FastCompany*, May 2015.

105. A. Carr, "The Messy Business of Reinventing Happiness," *FastCompany*, May 2015.

106. C. Kuang, "Disney's $1 Billion Bet on a Magical Wristband," *Wired*, March 10, 2015.

CHAPTER 6
Disruptive Technologies: Understanding the Giant Killers and Tactics for Avoiding Extinction

1. INTRODUCTION

LEARNING OBJECTIVES

1. Identify the two characteristics of disruptive innovations.
2. Understand why dominant firms often fail to capitalize on disruptive innovations.
3. Suggest techniques to identify potentially disruptive technologies and to effectively nurture their experimentation and development.

Kodak once had 145,000 employees, a market share near 90 percent,[1] and profit margins so good an executive once bragged that any products more lucrative than film were likely illegal.[2] No firm was closer to photographers. No brand was more synonymous with photographs. Emotionally moving images were known as "Kodak moments." And yet a firm with so much going for it was crushed by the shift that occurred when photography went from being based on chemistry to being based on bits. Today Kodak is bankrupt, it's selling off assets to stay alive, and its workforce is about one-fourteenth what it used to be.[3]

The fall of Kodak isn't unique. Many once-large firms fail to make the transition as new technologies emerge to redefine markets. And while these patterns are seen in everything from earthmoving equipment to mini-mills, the tech industry is perhaps the most fertile ground for disruptive innovation. The market-creating price elasticity of fast/cheap technologies acts as a catalyst for the fall of giants.

1.1 The Characteristics of Disruptive Technologies

The term *disruptive technologies* is a tricky one, because so many technologies create market shocks and catalyze growth. Lots of press reports refer to firms and technologies as disruptive. But there is a very precise theory of disruptive technologies (also referred to as *disruptive innovation*—we'll use both terms here) offered by Harvard professor Clayton Christensen that illustrates giant-killing market shocks, allows us to see why so many once-dominant firms have failed, and can shed light on practices that may help firms recognize and respond to threats.

In Christensen's view, true disruptive technologies have two characteristics that make them so threatening. First, they come to market with a set of performance attributes that existing customers don't value. Second, over time the performance attributes improve to the point where they invade established markets.[4] (See Figure 6.1.)

These attributes are found in many innovations that have brought about the shift from analog to digital. The first digital cameras were terrible: photo quality was laughably bad (the first were only black and white), they could only store a few images and did so very slowly, they were bulky, and they had poor battery life. It's not like most customers were lined up saying "Hey, give me more of that!" Much the same could be said about the poor performance of early digital music, digital video, mobile phones, tablet computing, and Internet telephony (Voice over IP, or VoIP), just to name a few examples. But today all of these digital products are having a market-disrupting impact. Digital cameras have all but wiped out film use, the record store is dead, mobile phones for many are their only phone, tablets are selling faster than laptops, Internet phone service is often indistinguishable from conventional calls, and Skype can be considered the world's largest long-distance phone company.[5] All of these changes were enabled by fast/cheap technologies, largely by the trends we see in the chart from the prior chapter labeled Figure 5.1.

FIGURE 6.1 The Giant Killer

Incumbent technologies satisfy a sweet spot of consumer needs. Incumbent technologies often improve over time, occasionally even overshooting the performance needs of the market. Disruptive technologies come to market with performance attributes not demanded by existing customers, but they improve over time until the innovation can invade established markets. Disruptive innovations don't need to perform *better* than incumbents; they simply need to perform *well enough* to appeal to their customers (and often do so at a lower price).

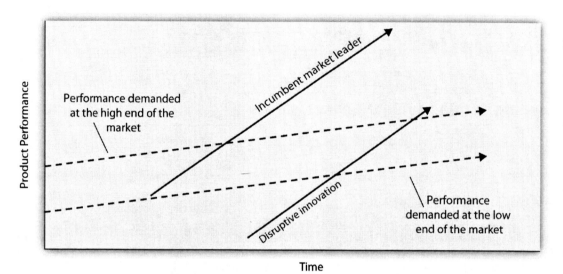

Source: Adapted from C. Christensen, The Innovator's Dilemma (Boston, MA: Harvard Business School Press, 2013).

1.2 Why Big Firms Fail

Those running big firms fail to see disruptive innovations as a threat not because they are dumb but, in many ways, because they do what executives at large, shareholder-dependent firms should do: they listen to their customers and focus on the bottom line. And because of the first characteristic mentioned, the majority of a firm's current customers don't want the initially poor-performing new technology. The most disruptive technologies also often have worse margins than the initially dominant incumbent offerings. Since these markets don't look attractive, big firms don't dedicate resources to developing the potential technology or nurturing the needs of a new customer base. Your best engineers are likely going to be assigned to work on cash-cow offerings, not questionable new stuff. This results in a sort of blindness created by an otherwise rational focus on customer demands and financial performance.

By the time the new market demonstrates itself, start-ups have been at it for quite some time. They have amassed expertise and often benefit from increasing scale and a growing customer base. The brands of firms leading in developing disruptive innovations may also now be synonymous with the new tech. If this happens, big firms are forced to play catch-up, and few ever close the gap with the new leaders.

1.3 Don't Fly Blind: Improve Your Radar

So how can a firm recognize potentially disruptive innovations? Paying attention to the trajectory of fast/cheap technology advancement and new and emerging technologies is critical. Seeing the future involves removing short-sighted, customer-focused, and bottom-line-obsessed blinders. Having conversations with those on the experimental edge of advancements is key. Top-tier scientific researchers and venture capitalists can be particularly good sources for information on new trends.

Increasing conversations across product groups and between managers and technologists can also be helpful. It's common for many firms to regularly rotate staff (both management and engineering) to improve idea sharing and innovation. Facebook, for example, requires employees to leave their teams for new assignments at least once every eighteen months.[6]

Note that many disruptive firms were started by former employees of the disrupted giants. The founders of Adobe, for example, came from Xerox; Apple's founders worked for Hewlett-Packard; Marc Benioff worked for Oracle before founding software-as-a-service giant Salesforce.com. Employees who feel so passionate about a trajectory for future technology that they are willing to leave the firm and risk it all on a new endeavor may be a signal that a development is worth paying attention to.

Yahoo! and the Squandered Mobile Opportunity

A *BusinessWeek* cover story on Yahoo! CEO Marissa Mayer's challenges stated that at the time Mayer took over, Yahoo! was a particularly weak player in mobile because it "ran into a classic Innovator's Dilemma"[7] (the name sometimes is ascribed to disruptive innovation theory, which is the title of one Clayton Christensen's books). Yahoo!'s success had been built on the desktop, browser-based web. While the firm had built a mobile team, the mobile group was disbanded by a former CEO who struggled to justify keeping talented engineers on underperforming projects. The mobile team leader left the company, while other members of the pioneering mobile unit were scattered to other teams and had trouble convincing browser-centric managers that mobile was the future. In many ways, Yahoo!'s mobile team was premature, but more importantly, it didn't have an executive champion to protect and nurture the team during the pioneering phase when financial results couldn't be realized. It couldn't show substantial results, so managers were reassigned while upstarts built multibillion-dollar businesses on increasingly powerful computers we carried in our pockets. Imagine if Yahoo!'s mobile team had been protected and allowed to experiment and grow. Could Flickr have morphed into Instagram? Could Yahoo! Messenger have become WhatsApp?

1.4   Potential Disruptor Spotted: Now What?

But all these conversations will simply expand a manager's radar. They don't necessarily offer insight on how to deal with *potentially* disruptive innovations once spotted. Navigating this next step is really tough. There's no guarantee that a potentially disruptive innovation will in fact become dominant. Trying to nurture new technology in-house is also a challenge. Top tech talent will often never be assigned to experimental products, or they may be pulled off emerging efforts to work on the firm's most lucrative offerings if the next version of a major product is delayed or in need of staff. And as disruptive technologies emerge, by definition they will eventually take market share away from a firm's higher-margin incumbent offerings. The result of the transition could include losses, contracting revenues, and lower profits—a tough thing for many shareholders to swallow.

Christensen suggests a few tactics to navigate the challenges. One is that a firm can build a portfolio of options on emerging technologies, investing in firms, start-ups, or internal efforts that can focus solely on what may or may not turn out to be the next big thing. An *option* is a right, but not the obligation, to make an investment, so if a firm has a stake in a start-up, it may consider acquiring the firm; or if it supports a separate division, it can invest more resources if that division shows promise. It's also important that these experimental efforts are nurtured in a way that is sufficiently separate from the parent—geographical distance helps, and it's critical to offer staff working on the innovation a high degree of autonomy. Christensen uses the analogy of the creosote bush to explain what often happens to new efforts in big firms that don't break out potentially disruptive innovations. The desert-dwelling creosote bush excretes and drops a toxin that kills nearby rival plants that might otherwise siphon away resources like water or soil nutrients. Threatened managers can act just like the bush—they'll pull high-quality engineers off emerging projects if a firm's top offerings need staff to grow. Lucrative old tech has a credible case for big budget allocations and is first in line when planning corporate priorities. But by nurturing potentially disruptive innovations in protected units (or even as separate firms), engineers and managers focusing on new markets can operate without distraction or interference from resource-coveting or threatened staff on other projects. This kind of separation can be vital for start-ups, but some firms maintain arms-length autonomy even as their investment in potential disruptors grows quite large. East-coast storage giant EMC is the majority owner of Silicon Valley's multibillion-dollar VMware but has left the latter largely free to innovate, nurture its customer base, and grow its own brands, even as some of the firm's products and partners threaten parent core products.

Intuit Pilots a Course through Disruption

One firm that appears to be successfully navigating the rough waters of disruptive innovation is Intuit. The highly profitable, multibillion-dollar firm is the leader in several packaged software categories, including personal finance (Quicken), small business (QuickBooks), and tax prep (TurboTax) software. But the future is in the cloud, and for conventional packaged software firms, this could be threatening. Acquisitions are one way Intuit has dealt with disruption. Mint.com is a personal finance offering delivered over the Web and in an app that wasn't just cheaper than Intuit's Quicken product—it was offered for free. (Mint makes money by making recommendations of ways to improve your finances—and takes a cut from these promotions.) Intuit decided to buy the upstart rival even though it was clearly cannibalizing Intuit's efforts. It even killed an internally developed but less successful rival product following the acquisition. Mint today remains as a separate brand and is helping inform the rest of the firm on how to succeed with alternatives to packaged software. The firm's TurboTax now has cloud-based offerings and a free SnapTax app—take a photo of your W2 and the app fills out your taxes for you automatically (you pay to electronically file). And engineers are able to use 10 percent of their work time to explore new, experimental ideas.[8] While so many firms have been thwarted by listening to existing customers and clinging to old models that are about to become obsolete, Intuit has managed to find growth through disruption. So-called connected services that either run in the cloud or enhance existing offerings make up over 65 percent of the firm's revenues.[9]

Intel and AMD's Low-Margin, Low-Power Threats

One firm threatened by disruptive innovation brought about by the advancement of Moore's Law is, ironically, processor giant Intel. The firm's most lucrative chips are the ones in servers—they cost a lot and have great margins. But a market in which Intel never had much success is now threatening to invade the server space. Chips based on Intel rival ARM power nearly all of the smartphones on the planet. Samsung, Apple, Motorola, LG, and Blackberry all use chips with ARM smarts. Unlike Intel, ARM doesn't manufacture chips itself—instead it licenses its hyperefficient designs to rivals who tweak them in their own offerings. ARM designs are especially attractive to smartphone manufacturers because they are far more power efficient than the chips Intel sells for PCs, laptops, and servers. The Intel chips were never designed for power efficiency; they evolved from markets where computers were always plugged in. As Moore's Law advances, ARM chips (once computational weaklings) are now fast enough to invade the established market for server chips. This has left Intel scrambling to create low-power chip offerings in an attempt to attack ARM in smartphones and satisfy the needs of its traditional customer base. Unlike Intel-compatible rival AMD, ARM chips can't run Intel software, so all of a firm's old code would need to be rewritten to work on any ARM-powered servers, laptops, or desktops. But the chips are also cheaper, threatening Intel margins.

HP offers a line of servers that will use ARM logic, and AMD, an Intel rival that has long made chips compatible with Intel's, has a new line of server chips based on the incompatible but power-stingy ARM logic. Meanwhile, Intel has developed lower-power chips to attack the smartphone market where ARM dominates. Another Intel chip architecture named Quark aims even lower, targeting the Internet of Things. To demonstrate possibilities, Intel's CEO has been wearing a "smart shirt" embedded with sensors that monitor heartbeat and other vitals.[10] Who wins remains to be seen, but Intel's battle cry comes from the title of a book written by former CEO Andy Grove—*Only the Paranoid Survive*. An adherent to the power of the Disruptive Innovation framework (Grove and Christensen once appeared together on the cover of *Forbes* magazine), Grove states, "[The] models didn't give us any answers, but they gave us a common language and a common way to frame the problem so that we could reach consensus around a counterintuitive course of action."[11]

Sometimes there aren't any easy answers for transitioning a firm that lies in the path of disruptive innovation. The newspaper industry has been gutted by Internet alternatives to key products, and online ad revenue for newspapers isn't enough to offset the loss of traditional sources of income. As an example of how bad things have been for newspapers, consider the *San Jose Mercury News*, the paper of record in Silicon Valley. In a span of five years, the *Merc* saw revenue from classified ads drop from $118 million to $18 million. Says Scott Herhold, a *Mercury News* columnist, "Craigslist has disemboweled us."[12] We can relate this chapter to the five-forces model covered previously: Fast/cheap technology fueled the Internet and created a superior substitute for newspaper classifieds—ads that were unlimited in length, could sport photos, link to an e-mail address, and be modified or taken down at a moment's notice, and were, in many cases, free. There aren't any easy answers for saving an industry when massive chunks of revenue evaporate overnight.

For every Kodak that suffers collapse, new wealth can be created for those who ride the wave of disruptive innovation. Consider the thirteen guys behind Instagram. In about eighteen months, they built a billion-dollar business that now has over 100 million users worldwide. Word to the wise—for your best bet at being a tech victor and not a tech victim, keep your disruption-detecting radar dialed up high and watch the trajectory of fast/cheap technology curves.

KEY TAKEAWAYS

- Many dominant firms have seen their market share evaporate due to the rise of a phenomenon known as disruptive technologies (also known as disruptive innovations). While this phenomenon occurs in a wide variety of industries, it often occurs when the forces of fast/cheap technology enable new offerings from new competitors.
- Disruptive technologies (also called disruptive innovations) come to market with a set of performance attributes that existing customers do not demand; however, performance improves over time to the point where these new innovations can invade established markets.
- Managers fail to respond to the threat of disruptive technologies, because existing customers aren't requesting these innovations and the new innovations would often deliver worse financial performance (lower margins, smaller revenues).
- Several techniques can help a firm improve its monitoring ability to recognize and surface potentially disruptive technologies. These include seeking external conversations with pioneers on the frontier of innovation (researchers and venture capitalists) and internal conversations with the firm's engineers and strategists who have a keen and creative eye on technical developments that the firm has not yet exploited.
- Once identified, the firm can invest in a portfolio of technology options—start-ups or in-house efforts otherwise isolated from the firm's core business and management distraction. Options give the firm the right (but not the obligation) to continue and increase funding as a technology shows promise.
- Having innovation separated from core businesses is key to encourage new market and technology development focus while isolating the firm from a "creosote bush" type of resource sapping from potentially competing cash-cow efforts.
- Piloting a firm through disruptive innovation is extremely difficult, as the new effort will cannibalize existing markets, may arrive with lower margins, and can compress revenues.

QUESTIONS AND EXERCISES

1. What are the two characteristics of disruptive innovations?
2. Make a list of recent disruptive innovations. List firms that dominated the old regime and firms that capitalized after disruption. Are any of the dominant firms from the previous era the same as those in the postdisruptive era? For those firms that failed to make the transition, why do you think they failed?
3. Why do leading firms fail to recognize and react to potentially disruptive innovations? How can a firm avoid the kind of blindness that leads to disruption?
4. Once a firm can detect disruptive technologies, what techniques can it use to nurture and develop these technologies?
5. Intuit seems to have successfully transitioned from a world of packaged software to one based in the cloud and in apps and that includes some free products. Are there other firms that have failed to make this transition? Others that haven't? Discuss the reasons for their success or failure.
6. Some say university education is about to be disrupted. Do you agree? Why or why not? What suggestions do you have for university administrators at your school for dealing with potential disruptions?
7. Research the role of 3D printers. Is this a disruptive technology? Which firms will be hurt as 3D printers advance? Which organizations will benefit from this transition? What advice do you have for firms that operate on a path that will be impacted by 3D printing?

2.   BITCOIN: A DISRUPTIVE INNOVATION FOR MONEY AND MORE?

LEARNING OBJECTIVES

1. **Understand what bitcoin is, to whom it appeals and why, its strengths, and its limitations.**
2. **Gain additional insights into evaluating the trajectory of technology and its disruptive capacity.**

Bitcoin

An open-source, decentralized payment system (sometimes controversially referred to as a digital, virtual, or cryptocurrency) that operates in a peer-to-peer environment, without bank or central authority.

FIGURE 6.2

The B symbol with two bars is used to refer to bitcoin.

Bitcoin is the transaction method favored by cybercriminals and illegal trade networks like the now shuttered Silk Road illegal drugs bazaar.[13] It's not backed by gold or government and appeared seemingly out of thin air as the result of mathematics performed by so-called "miners." It's been a wildly volatile currency, where an amount that could purchase a couple of pizzas today would be worth over $6 million a little over three years later.[14] Its one-time largest exchange handled millions in digital value, yet it was originally conceived as the "Magic: The Gathering Online card eXchange" (Mt. Gox), and that service suffered a massive breach where the digital equivalent of roughly $450 million disappeared.[15] Yet despite all this, many think bitcoin might upend money as we know it enough so that venture capitalists have been pouring their coin into bitcoin start-ups, totaling as much as $134 million by early 2014.[16]

Many don't even know what to call bitcoin. Is it a cryptocurrency, a digital currency, digital money, or a virtual currency?[17] The US government has ruled that bitcoin is property (US Marshals have auctioned off bitcoins seized from crooks).[18] While Goldman Sachs and UBS have been dismissive of bitcoin's future,[19] Deloitte has written that the negative hype has underestimated the technology's potential to revolution not just payments but all sorts of asset transactions.[20] The Bank of England has issued a report describing bitcoin as a "significant innovation" that could have "far-reaching implications."[21]

2.1   How It Works

Bitcoins are transferred from person to person like cash. Instead of using a bank as a middleman, transactions are recorded in a public ledger (known as a *blockchain* in bitcoin speak) and verified by a pool of users called *miners*. The miners get an incentive for being involved: they can donate their computer power in exchange for the opportunity to earn additional bitcoins, and sometimes, some modest transaction fees (this means bitcoin is peer-produced finance. For more on peer production, see Chapter 10). While the ledger records transactions, no one can use your bitcoins without a special password (called a *private key* and usually stored in what is referred to as a user's *bitcoin wallet*, which is really just an encrypted holding place). The technology behind this is open-source and considered rock solid. Passwords are virtually impossible to guess; and verification makes sure no one spends the same bitcoins in two places at once.

2.2   Benefits

Much of bitcoin's appeal comes from the fact that bitcoins are transferred from person to person like cash, rather than using an intermediary like banks or credit card companies. Getting rid of card companies **cuts out transaction fees** (usually by 10 to 20 cents), which can top 3 percent. Overstock.com was one of the first large online retailers to accept bitcoin. Its profit margins? Just 2 percent. Needless to say, Overstock's CEO is a bitcoin enthusiast.[22] Bitcoin also opens up the possibility of **micropayments** (or small digital payments) that are now impractical because of fees (think of everything from gum to bus fare to small donations).

Bitcoin could also be a boon for **international commerce**, especially for **cross-border remittance** and in **expanding e-commerce in emerging markets**. Family members working abroad often send funds home via services like Western Union or MoneyGram, but these can cost $10 to $17 for a $200 transfer and take up to five days to clear in some countries.[23] A bitcoin transfer would be immediate and could theoretically eliminate all transaction fees, although several firms are charging small fees to ease transactions and quickly get money moved from national currency to bitcoin and back. They're going after a big market, as global remittances total over half a trillion dollars.[24] Bitcoin might also lubricate the wheels of commerce between nations where credit card companies and firms like PayPal don't operate, and where internationally accepted cards are tough to obtain. Less than one-third of the population in emerging markets have any sort of credit card, but bitcoin could provide a vehicle to open this market up to online purchases.

Civil libertarians like the idea of transactions happening without the prying eyes of data miners inside card companies, having their transaction history shared by others, or the government. As *Wired* points out, bitcoin **straddles the line between transparency and privacy**. All transactions are recorded in the open, via the blockchain, but individuals can be anonymous. You can create your anonymous private key and have someone transfer funds to you or earn bitcoin via mining and no one can see who you are. While governments can try to shut down or legislate bitcoin activity within their borders, there's no bitcoin organization that controls money flows. It's been noted that following the revelations in WikiLeaks, Visa, Mastercard, and PayPal refused donations to WikiLeaks. In that aftermath, Bitcoin became the go-to vehicle for those supporting WikiLeaks' efforts.[25] There's was **no central organization to "freeze" a bitcoin account** or a central technical resource to impound or shut down. If a bitcoin transaction is not permitted in your country, go abroad and you've got full access to everything in your wallet.

A paper by Deloitte University sees bitcoin as far more than a replacement for money. At its core, bitcoin is a protocol for exchanging value over the Internet without an intermediary. This has the potential to disrupt all sorts of systems that rely on intermediaries, including the transfer of property, execution of contracts, and identity management. The paper's authors envision fractional bitcoin being attached to things like vehicles, where repair history and accidents can be referenced to an ownership-representing bitcoin fragment in the way that registry paperwork happens now, and where vehicle title can be transferred by passing bitcoin from one person to another—no lawyers, no notaries, no vehicle registration required.[26] Such innovation is less about the currency-aspect of bitcoin, and all about the blockchain. As the *Wall Street Journal* points out, "almost any document can be digitized, codified, and inserted into the blockchain, a record that is indelible, cannot be tampered with, and whose authenticity is verified by the consensus of a community of computer users rather than by the discretionary order of a centralized authority."[27] To get a sense of how seriously some in the finance industry view this emerging technology, consider that the Nasdaq stock exchange has tested Bitcoin's blockchain for transactions in its private market subsidiary, stating the exchange could eventually use the technology for Nasdaq trades in the public market.[28] If blockchain transactions are to emerge as mainstream, governments would likely want to link to such systems when ownership needs to be verified, but all this is technically possible to build, and if it works, the disruption across industries would be massive.[29]

2.3   Concerns

Bitcoin's future could be bright, or it could fizzle as another overhyped, underperforming technology. There are several challenges bitcoin needs to overcome before it makes it in the mainstream.

Consumer benefit needs to be stronger. While international remittance customers and those otherwise left out of the banking and credit card system can see immediate benefit from bitcoin, most of the population isn't impacted by this market. For most, bitcoin is a **difficult to understand** and often **difficult to use** technology that offers little benefit. Slick apps and firms offering streamlining support services that allow, for example, the easy and quick conversion from dollars (or other currencies) to bitcoin and back will help, but unless this offers consumer value beyond the credit card, few will bother to switch from plastic.

Bitcoin also has a **reputation problem**. Being embraced by drug dealers, tax evaders, and fringe libertarians doesn't instill a lot of confidence. And it doesn't help that bitcoin was created by a mysterious, unknown entity referred to as Satoshi Nakamoto.[30]

Security concerns also pose a problem. While bitcoin software is considered to be solid, it's not a guarantee that other entities are as secure. The multimillion dollar theft from Mt. Gox is a prime example.[31] The wallets that hold your private key are also potentially vulnerable. If your computer is wiped out by a virus and you haven't written down your password or saved a backup copy in another secure and accessible location, you're hosed; it's like money burned up in a fire. Hackers that steal passwords—whether they're on your computer or the cloud—effectively have access to anything in your bitcoin wallet; they can walk away with all your cash and it's unlikely that there'll be a way to recover the loot.

Many firms that hope to strengthen the bitcoin industry (wallet builders, exchanges, and payment processors) have struggled under an **ambiguous cloud of not knowing how they will be regulated** and what legal issues apply to them.[32] China has banned bitcoin,[33] but California has moved forward to legalize the use of alternative currencies.[34] New York has announced bitcoin-friendly initiatives.[35] The US government has also created regulations around bitcoin that make it less amorphous and safer for investors, while the IRS ruled that bitcoins are property.[36] Trends seem to be moving in the right direction, but financial institutions don't work well in environments of uncertainty, and clear operating guidelines and legal protections will be vital for bitcoin to thrive.

Volatility is also an issue. During a recent, less-than-twelve-month period, the value of a single bit-coin went from less than $100 to over $1,000 before losing half its value again. This kind of volatility makes bitcoin less useful as a dollar-like currency, limiting its appeal to speculators that often seem like get-rich-quick schemers or the much smaller legitimate market that is looking for in-and-out transactions such as cross-border payments. Some also worry about a bitcoin valuation bubble.[37] Fixes are possible and several have been proposed, but issuing a fix involves a massive upgrade of software, and certain factions of the community (including many in the large network of small-time bitcoin miners) are wary of the impact of any change.[38]

Increased **transaction volume** should help stabilize the market, increase liquidity, and bring some stability to the currency, but bitcoin has a long way to go. By mid-2014, bitcoin was seeing about 60,000 transactions per day, compared with the 150 million daily transactions that Visa processes.[39] And to get to that kind of volume, bitcoin will need more infrastructure support. During roughly this same period, Visa was handling 10,000 transactions in a second, while the entire bitcoin miner network could only handle seven. That's not seven thousand, that's one hand plus two fingers—a single digit.[40]

2.4 What Do You Think?

If all this sounds sketchy to you, consider how currencies have evolved. We've moved from precious materials (gold, silver, etc.) to a currency backed by precious materials (the gold standard), to one based largely on laws and governmental trust, to one allowing physical cash to be replaced by hand-signed paper receipts (checks), and then to bits—that is, credit cards and money transfers. Now, many of us use smartphone apps to snap photos of checks and have them electronically deposited into banks, rip up the check when you're done, and transaction is completed. With this evolution as context, does bitcoin seem like such an unlikely next step?

There are alternatives to bitcoin. You may have seen that NASCAR is sponsored by Dogecoin (the fact that this bitcoin rival was named after an Internet meme dog doesn't help credibility among the financially conservative). But bitcoin does have the early mover's advantage of getting the network effect of buyers and sellers working in its favor. However, Bitcoin is by far the most popular and had the highest valuation of any alternative currency network.[41]

What's your take? Do you see credible opportunity here? Disruptive threat? Or flash-in-the-pan hype that'll fizzle and go nowhere?

KEY TAKEAWAYS

- An open-source, decentralized payment system (sometimes controversially referred to as a digital, virtual, or cryptocurrency) that operates in a peer-to-peer environment without bank or central authority.
- Bitcoins are created and can be earned by miners who participate in verifying and recording transactions in a public ledger (the blockchain).
- Various exchanges have been developed to make it easier for consumers to trade conventional currency for bitcoin and vice versa. An increasingly long list of retailers and other providers have begun accepting bitcoin as cash.
- Since bitcoin provides technologies to exchange value over the Internet without an intermediary, the mechanism may one day move beyond cash-substitute uses and may evolve to facilitate the exchange of other types of property (autos, real estate, intellectual property, etc.). If the latter evolution takes place, bitcoin has the potential to disrupt not only financial institutions but also aspects of the legal system, government regulation, and more.
- Lower or no transaction costs appeal to retailers, and those wishing to exchange currency across borders. Bitcoin could lower retailer transaction costs, create an opportunity for the digital purchase of goods with small value (micropayments), and open up markets where credit card access is limited.
- Civil libertarians also like the fact that bitcoin transactions can happen without revealing the sorts of personal data that credit card companies and other financial institutions are gathering. Since it's a peer-to-peer transaction, there is no central authority that can freeze accounts or impose other policies on users.
- Limited consumer benefit, difficulty of use, reputation problems, security concerns, ambiguous regulation, volatility, transaction volume, and the scalability of current infrastructure are all concerns that may limit bitcoin's mainstream appeal.

QUESTIONS AND EXERCISES

1. Bitcoin's technology is in flux. Investigate how to get dollars into bitcoin, where you can pay for things using bitcoin, and how to get money out. Did you try this out? Why or why not?

2. Based on your experience in number 1, what will need to happen with bitcoin for it to gain mainstream consumer acceptance?

3. To whom does bitcoin appeal? Why? Do some exploring online. Where is bitcoin accepted? Have any of these firms commented on results (positive or negative) of accepting bitcoin? Share your findings with your class and discuss likely resulting market trends.

4. What can retailers do to encourage more customers to use bitcoin?

5. Members of the MIT bitcoin club each received $100 to experiment with the technology. Perform some additional research. What have they done? Come to class prepared to discuss their results and the value of this initiative.

ENDNOTES

1. *Economist*, "The Last Kodak Moment," January 14, 2012.

2. *Knowledge@Wharton*, "What's Wrong with This Picture: Kodak's 30-Year Slide into Bankruptcy," February 1, 2012.

3. M. Daneman, "Kodak Selling Two Businesses to Pension Plan," *USA Today*, April 29, 2013.

4. J. Bower and C. Christensen, "Disruptive Technologies: Catching the Wave," *Harvard Business Review*, January–February 1995.

5. O. Malik, "Skype, Now the World's Largest Long-Distance Phone Company," *GigaOM*, March 24, 2009.

6. M. Helft and J. Hempel, "Inside Facebook," *Fortune*, March 1, 2012.

7. B. Stone, "Can Marissa Mayer Save Yahoo?" *BusinessWeek*, August 1, 2013.

8. C. Farr, "How Intuit Plans to Help Main Street Fight Big Business with 'Big Data,'" *GigaOM*, December 14, 2012.

9. H. Clancy, "Intuit's Secret to Going Global Lies in Thinking Locally," *ZDNet*, September 19, 2012.

10. J. Burt, "Intel CEO Krzanich Shows Off Smart Shirt, Robot," *eWeek*, May 28, 2014.

11. J. Euchner, "Managing Disruption: An Interview with Clayton Christensen," *Managers at Work, Industrial Research Institute*, January–February 2011.

12. *Knowledge@Wharton*, "All the News That's Fit to… Aggregate, Download, Blog: Are Newspaper's Yesterday's News?" March 22, 2006.

13. P. Vigna and M. Casey, "BitBeat: Who Won the FBI's Bitcoin Auction?" *Wall Street Journal*, June 30, 2014.

14. John Biggs, "May 22 Is Bitcoin Pizza Day," *TechCrunch*, May 21, 2014.

15. R. McMillan, "The Inside Story of Mt. Gox, Bitcoin's $460 Million Disaster," *Wired*, May 3, 2014.

16. R. Wile, "Why VCs Are Still Planning To Pour Tons of Money Into Bitcoin," *Business Insider*, April 7, 2014.

17. T. Wan and M. Hoblitzell, "Bitcoin: Fact. Fiction. Future," *Deloitte University Press*, June 26, 2014.

18. P. Vigna and M. Casey, "BitBeat: Who Won the FBI's Bitcoin Auction?" *Wall Street Journal*, June 30, 2014.

19. R. Wile, "Why VCs Are Still Planning to Pour Tons of Money into Bitcoin," *Business Insider*, April 7, 2014.

20. T. Wan and M. Hoblitzell, "Bitcoin: Fact. Fiction. Future," *Deloitte University Press*, June 26, 2014.

21. A. Irrera, "UBS CIO: Blockchain Technology Can Massively Simplify Banking," *The Wall Street Journal*, Oct. 27, 2014.

22. M. Carney, "For Retailers, Accepting Bitcoin Is all about the Margin," *PandoDaily*, January 13, 2014.

23. E. Ombok, "Bitcoin Service Targets Kenya Remittances with Cut-Rate Fees," *Bloomberg*, November 28, 2013.

24. T. Wan and M. Hoblitzell, "Bitcoin: Fact. Fiction. Future," *Deloitte University Press*, June 26, 2014.

25. R. Salam, "The Vice Podcast—Professor Bitcoin," *Vice*, January 8, 2014.

26. T. Wan and M. Hoblitzell, "Bitcoin: Fact. Fiction. Future," *Deloitte University Press*, June 26, 2014.

27. A. Irrera, "UBS CIO: Blockchain Technology Can Massively Simplify Banking," *The Wall Street Journal*, Oct. 27, 2014.

28. M. Orcutt, "Leaderless Bitcoin Struggles to Make Its Most Crucial Decision," *Technology Review*, May 19, 2015.

29. T. Wan and M. Hoblitzell, "Bitcoin: Fact. Fiction. Future," *Deloitte University Press*, June 26, 2014.

30. P. Schimdt, "Bitcoin: Understanding What It Is," *Guardian Liberty Voice*, June 15, 2014.

31. R. McMillan, "The Inside Story of Mt. Gox, Bitcoin's $460 Million Disaster," *Wired*, May 3, 2014.

32. R. McMillan, "The Fierce Battle for the Soul of Bitcoin," *Wired*, March 26, 2014.

33. S. Yang and S. Lee, "China Bans Financial Companies from Bitcoin Transactions," *Bloomberg*, December 5, 2013.

34. J. Kirk, "California Removes Ban on Alternative Currencies," *Computerworld*, June 30, 2014.

35. E. Sherman, "New York State to Welcome Regulated Bitcoin Exchanges," *CBS Market Watch*, March 12, 2014.

36. P. Rosenblum, "Bitcoin Draws Attention of Institutional Bidders and MasterCard," *Forbes*, June 30, 2014.

37. S. Shankland, "Bitcoin Gets Buy-in from Newegg, the Tech-Focused Retailer," *CNET*, July 1, 2014.

38. M. Orcutt, "Leaderless Bitcoin Struggles to Make Its Most Crucial Decision," *Technology Review*, May 19, 2015.

39. T. Wan and M. Hoblitzell, "Bitcoin: Fact. Fiction. Future," *Deloitte University Press*, June 26, 2014.

40. R. McMillan, "The Fierce Battle for the Soul of Bitcoin," *Wired*, March 26, 2014.

41. S. Shankland, "Bitcoin Gets Buy-in from Newegg, the Tech-Focused Retailer," *CNET*, July 1, 2014.

CHAPTER 7

Amazon: An Empire Stretching from Cardboard Box to Kindle to Cloud

1. INTRODUCTION

LEARNING OBJECTIVES

1. Appreciate the breadth of businesses in which Amazon competes.
2. Understand that Amazon's financial performance has not been consistent.
3. Begin to recognize the reasons for this performance inconsistency and set the stage for the examination unfolding in subsequent sections.

As CEO of tech industry research firm Forrester Research, George Colony is paid to predict the future. Firms spend big bucks for Forrester reports that cover trends and insight across the world of computing. So when, in the early years of Amazon's expansion, Colony turned his attention to the Internet retailer founded by Jeff Bezos, there were a lot of people paying attention. Colony proclaimed that the recently public firm would soon be "Amazon.toast" as larger traditional retailers arrived to compete online.[1] Colony wasn't the only Bezos-basher. *Fortune*, the *Guardian*, and *Barron's* were among the publications to have labeled the firm "Amazon.bomb." Bezos's personal favorite came from a pundit who suggested the firm should be renamed "Amazon.org," adopting the domain of a nonprofit since it'll never make any money.[2]

Amazon went seven whole years without turning a profit, losing over $3 billion during that time. The firm's stock price had fallen from a high of $100 a share to below $6. Conventional wisdom suggested that struggling dot-coms were doomed, as retail giants were poised to bring their strong offline brands and logistics prowess to the Internet, establishing themselves as multichannel dominators standing athwart the bloodied remains of the foolish early movers.

But during those seven years and through to this day, Bezos (pronounced "bay-zose") steadfastly refused to concentrate on the quarterly results Wall Street frets over. Instead, the Amazon founder has followed his best reckoning on where markets and technology were headed, postponing profit harvesting while expanding warehousing capacity, building e-commerce operations worldwide, growing one of the Internet's most widely used cloud computing platforms, leading the pack in e-readers, and developing the first credible threat to Apple's dominant iPad in tablets.

Tellingly, Amazon's first profit was posted the week one-time brick-and-mortar goliath Kmart went bankrupt. Kmart was also the former parent of another giant of the offline world, Borders, a firm that completely shuttered in the wake of Amazon's dominance. And for Amazon, profits continued. In a three-year period following the introduction of the Kindle, Amazon's net income climbed from $476 million to $1.15 billion. Barnes & Noble's fell from $150 million to $37 million before dipping into the red. Punditry is a dangerous business, but *Barron's* made up for the dot-bomb comment, putting Amazon on its cover under a headline proclaiming the firm the world's best retailer. *Fortune* atoned by naming Bezos the "Businessperson of the Year."[3]

Amazon's future continues to be hotly debated as the firm's profitability swings wildly. Massive investments crushed Amazon profits in 2012, and despite over $74 billion in 2013 sales, the firm only made $274 million. 2014 had Amazon back in the red, losing nearly a quarter of a billion dollars. Yet Amazon's highly valued stock with its nosebleed P/E ratio suggests that Wall Street expects a huge upside. And Amazon was recently named as having the "Best Reputation of any US corporation."[4] So is

Amazon the "unstoppable monster of the tech industry" or a "charitable organization run by elements of the investment community for the benefit of customers"?[5] Both? Neither?

Jeff Bezos and the Long Term

"Our first shareholder letter, in 1997, was called 'It's all about the long term.' If everything you do needs to work on a three-year time horizon, then you're competing against a lot of people. But if you're willing to invest on a seven-year time horizon, you're now competing against a fraction of those people, because very few companies are willing to do that. Just by lengthening the time horizon, you can engage in endeavors that you could never otherwise pursue. At Amazon we like things to work in five to seven years. We're willing to plant seeds, let them grow—and we're very stubborn. We say we're stubborn on vision and flexible on details."[6]

Just how far ahead is Bezos's time horizon? His personal investments (invested as Bezos Expeditions) include Blue Origin, a commercial rocketry and aviation firm that intends to send humans into space and which has already launched a suborbital capsule test.[7] Other investments include Twitter and Uber. In 2013, Bezos went old school and bought the *Washington Post*.[8] Bezos used a *60 Minutes* profile to announce and demonstrate Amazon Prime Air, an effort from the firm's next-generation R&D lab. Approved use seems a long way off, but the goal is to eventually use copter-style drones to deliver packages to consumers in thirty minutes or less. The firm has already gone through nine generations of drone design and has applied for special FAA exemptions so it can accelerate testing.[9] Bezos has also built a 10,000-year clock deep inside a mountain on his ranch in West Texas. The timepiece plays an elaborate cuckoo-like sequence, composed by musician Brian Eno, to mark every year, decade, century, millennium, and ten millennia. How's that for a symbol of long-term thinking?[10]

 Promotional Video Announcing Amazon Prime Air

Billed as an Amazon R&D effort targeted at getting packages into customer's hands in thirty minutes or less using unmanned aerial vehicles.

View the video online at: http://www.youtube.com/embed/98Blu9dpwHU?rel=0

1.1 Why Study Amazon?

Looking at the Internet's largest retailer provides a context for introducing several critical management concepts, such as cash efficiency and channel conflict. We see ways in which tech-fueled operations can yield above-average profits far greater than offline players. We can illustrate advantages related to scale, the data asset, and the brand-building benefits of personalization and other customer service enhancements. Amazon's Kindle business and its expanding forays into the tablet, set-top box, and smartphone markets allow us to look into the importance of mobile and multiscreen computing as a vehicle for media consumption, a distribution channel for increased sales and advertising, a creator of switching costs, a gathering point for powerful data, and a competitor for platform dominance. And the firm's AWS (Amazon Web Services) business allows us to see how the firm is building a powerhouse cloud provider, generating new competitive assets while engaging in competition where it sells services to firms that can also be considered rivals.

KEY TAKEAWAYS

- Amazon is the largest online retailer and has expanded to dozens of categories beyond books. As much of the firm's media business (books, music, video) becomes digital, the Kindle business (which has expanded to tablet, set-top box, and smartphone) is a conduit for retaining existing businesses and for growing additional advantages. And the firm's AWS cloud computing business is one of the largest players in that category.
- Amazon takes a relatively long view with respect to investing in initiatives and its commitment to grow profitable businesses. The roughly seven-year timeline is a difficult one for public companies to maintain amid the pressure for consistent quarterly profits.
- Amazon's profitability has varied widely, and analysts continue to struggle to interpret the firm's future. However, studying Amazon will reveal important concepts and issues related to business and technology.

QUESTIONS AND EXERCISES

1. Which firms does Amazon compete with?
2. Investigate Amazon's performance over the last five years. How has the firm done with respect to revenue, net income, and share price? How does this compare with competitors mentioned?
3. What are some of the advantages in having a longer time horizon? What are some of the challenges? What needs to happen to enable Amazon to continue to "think long term"? What could derail this approach?
4. What do you think of Amazon Prime Air? Is it all publicity stunt or might this eventually be available in the market? What would need to happen (think technical, regulatory, economic, and societal perspectives) for this to be a viable offering? Do you think you'll see something like this in your lifetime? If so, how long will it take? Be prepared to discuss your thoughts in class. Come to class with examples, quotes, or other data to bolster your argument.

2.   THE EMPEROR OF E-COMMERCE

LEARNING OBJECTIVES

1. **Recognize how Amazon's warehouse technology and systems are designed to quickly and cost effectively get products from suppliers to customers with a minimum of error.**
2. **Understand how high inventory turns and longer accounts payable periods help fuel a negative cash conversion cycle at Amazon, and why this is a good thing.**
3. **Gain insight into various advantages that result from the firm's scale and cost structure.**
4. **Appreciate how data can drive advantages not fully available to offline firms, ranging from increased personalization to innovation and service improvements.**
5. **Identify the two sides in Amazon Marketplace network effects, and why this is important in strengthening the firm's brand. Understand the financial advantages of goods sold through marketplace versus those that Amazon takes possession of and sells itself.**
6. **Appreciate how mobile access is influencing opportunities through additional changes in how, where, and when consumers shop.**

Everybody starts small, even Bezos. At first the firm focused exclusively on selling books over the Internet. An early office was in a modest space boasting a then-appealing 400-square-foot basement warehouse in a low-rent area of Seattle, where neighboring establishments included the local needle exchange, a pawn shop, and "WigLand."[11] Today the firm is decidedly larger. Its 155 fulfillment centers (Amazon's term for the firm's stocking warehouses) planned or deployed worldwide boast roughly 100 million square feet of warehouse space.[12] And Amazon is now the world's largest online retailer in dozens of categories. The stylized smile in the Amazon logo doubles as an arrow pointing from A to Z (as in "we carry everything from A to Z"). A new downtown Seattle headquarters will take up three full city blocks anchored by three signature office towers.

How does a firm that sells products that pretty much any other retailer can provide, grow and create competitive advantages that keep rivals at bay? Look to the napkin! The lobby of Amazon's headquarters sports the framed vision scribbled out by Amazon's chief, allegedly penned on the nearest writing surface while Bezos was noshing (see Figure 7.1).

FIGURE 7.1   Amazon's "Wheel of Growth," Adapted from a Jeff Bezos Napkin Scribble

At the heart are three pillars of Amazon's business: large selection, customer experience (sometimes referred to simply as "convenience"), and lower prices. Says Bezos, "I always get the question, what's going to change in ten years? I almost never get asked, what's NOT going to change in the next ten years? That's the more important question, because you can build a business around things that are stable. [Things like] low prices…faster delivery [offering customer convenience]…vast selection."[13]

The three pillars of selection, customer experience, and low prices reinforce one another and work together to create several additional assets for competitive advantage. Exceptional customer experience fuels a strong brand that makes Amazon the first place most consumers shop online. Having more customers allows the firm to provide more products, creating scale. Amazon also opens its website up to third-party sellers—and a dynamic where more customers attract more sellers, which attracts still more customers (and so on). That virtuous cycle of buyer-seller growth is a two-sided network effect, yet another source of competitive advantage. And all this activity allows Bezos and Company to further sharpen the business battle sword by gathering an immensely valuable data asset. Each digital movement is logged, and the firm is constantly analyzing what users respond to in order to further fine-tune the customer experience, squeeze out costs, and drive cash flow. Let's look at each of these items and see how Amazon's bold tech-based strategy is realizing additional advantages in the domain of marketing, accounting, and operations.

2.1   Fulfillment Operations—Driving Selection, Customer Convenience, and Low Price

Amazon has always sold direct to consumers, but it didn't always do this well. The firm's early warehousing was a shambles of inefficient, money-burning processes. Said one analyst, Amazon's "inventory, and warehouse operating costs, [were] so high they made old-fashioned retailers look efficient."[14] As a sign of how bad the situation was, Amazon had to issue more than $2 billion in bonds just to stay in business. To fix the problem, Amazon looked to others for talent, hiring away both the chief information officer (CIO) and chief logistics officer from the world's largest retailer, Walmart. (Walmart sued, and the two eventually settled out of court.) But raiding Walmart's talent pool wasn't enough. Amazon's warehouse and technology infrastructure are radically different than those of any conventional retailer. While Walmart warehouses that support its superstores ship large pallets of identical items in a single shipment (think crates of diapers or toothpaste) to thousands of its retail locations, Amazon warehouses pack boxes of disparate individual items, sending packages to millions of homes. To build a system that worked, Amazon focused on costs, data, and processes so that it could figure out what was wrong and how it could improve.

One effort, "Get the C.R.A.P. out," focused on products that "can't realize any profits." The firm's senior vice president of North American operations recalls visiting a Kentucky warehouse and watching a staffer spend twenty minutes packaging up a folding chair—a process way too inefficient for a firm with razor-thin margins. To fix the situation, Amazon worked with the vendor to get chairs in prepackaged, ready-to-ship boxes, keeping the product available to customers while cleaving costs.[15]

To automate profit-pushing hyperefficiency, Amazon warehouses are powered by at least as much code as the firm's website[16] —nearly all of it homegrown.[17] Technology lets a given Amazon warehouse send out over 2 million packages a week during the holiday season, all without elves or flying reindeer.[18] The firm's larger warehouses are upwards of a quarter mile in length, packed with aisles shelves. Technology choreographs thousands of workers and robots in what seems part symphony, part sprint.

When suppliers ship new products to Amazon, items are scanned and prepped so inventory is ready to fulfill customer orders as soon as possible. Dozens of workers examine the incoming shipments for defects. If a problem is spotted in the receiving area, the staffer flips an adjacent warning light from green to red, signaling a warehouse "problem solver" to swoop in, deal with the issue, and make sure additional items in the rest of the product supply can keep flowing in.[19] Amazon is always looking to cut errors and identify areas for potential process improvement. Other groups of problem solvers scuttle about the warehouse with wheel-mounted laptops, observing operations and offering coaching on how staff can do things better.[20] To foster improvement, warehouse movements are continuously logged and productivity is tracked and plotted. High-performing workers are praised throughout the day, with management calling out the names of workers who hit or exceeded goals.[21] Says one Amazon exec, "If we discover a better way of doing something, we can roll it out across the world."[22]

While problem solvers can pick up quick-to-implement process improvements, there are also massive tech-fueled changes underway. In the past, workers called "shelvers" constantly traversed fulfillment centers with carts full of newly arrived goods. Shelvers would place items on shelves, scanning each location where a product was stored so that the firm's software knew what was in stock and where to find it. When customer orders came in, another category of worker known as "pickers" would dart around wheeling plastic order fulfillment bins, carrying around a wireless device (a sort of scan gun) that issued step-minimizing instructions on precisely where to navigate to and which items to grab within the maze of numbered aisles and shelves.[23] The worker run-about was good for personal cardio, but it required wide lanes, and the management of potentially path-crossing, cart-pushing humans. While this process is still used in many Amazon fulfillment centers, a new robot army is being rolled out to further turbocharge fulfillment operations.

Robots powering redesigned fulfillment centers come from Kiva Systems, a Massachusetts-based firm that Amazon bought for over three quarters of a billion dollars.[24] Kiva robots don't look like C-3PO. They're squat, 320 lb, orange colored, rounded-rectangles on wheels, about the size of a mid-sized living room ottoman. Two years after the purchase, Amazon began upgrading fulfillment centers so that, instead of workers running to shelves, shelves automatically came to workers. Robots don't yet handle the bulkiest items such as flat-screen TVs or lawnmowers, but Kiva robots carry shelves stacked with upwards of 750 lb of goods, making them capable of handling the majority of what you're likely ordering from Amazon.[25]

In Kiva-equipped fulfillment centers, those items that are handled by Kivas are sent to one of four floors where the robots roam. A massive robot arm known as the "Robo-Stow" might be used to hoist pallets of products from one floor to another.[26] Shelvers stand on platforms while Kiva robots line up for restocking, bearing shelf towers with open bins stacked nine-or-more slots high along on all four sides. Robots position shelves to expose the correct side for inventory placement. Shelvers scan products that are added to inventory, placing each in specific location on a specific shelf that is also scanned. This tells Amazon's software exactly where a given item is stored. Next, the shelf is whisked away by a robot until one of the items on the shelf is needed for a customer order. The same items might be stored on dozens of different shelves throughout the warehouse. This allows different robots to simultaneously fulfill different orders for the same items. Amazon software enforces an additional rule when stocking shelves: No two similar products sit next to each other. While this makes Amazon's shelves look like an unorganized hodgepodge, when a product is the only one of its type in a given shelf, this actually reduces the chances that a picker will confuse a size or color or otherwise grab the wrong thing.[27] Reducing mistakes keeps customers happy in brand-building ways, and it reduces errors that can crush profits.

When an online order comes in to a fulfillment center, pickers wait for shelf-carrying robots to line up with precisely those items that the customer has requested. A monitor near the picker indicates the item that's needed and where it can be found on the robot-conveyed shelf.[28] Humans are still needed to grab an item off the shelf, do a second quality check, electronically scan items and shelves to record the item as moving out of inventory, and place items into yellow plastic order fulfillment bins. Once all items for a given order are picked, the bins containing orders are placed on conveyor belts where they're whisked away for packing. Software identifies the optimal size of smile-logoed Amazon cardboard box to use for a given order, and a different set of robots fold and prepare boxes.[29] Packed boxes are weighed, and the software does an additional check to see if the weight is what's expected. If an order is too light, that's a sign that a box is missing an item, too heavy and the wrong item may be in the order.[30]

Watch Amazon's Kiva robots, "robo-stow," and other elements of Amazon's logistics action at work inside a fulfillment center

View the video online at: http://www.youtube.com/embed/quWFjS3Ci7A?rel=0

Hear Amazon's SVP of Worldwide Operations discuss the advantages of Kiva robots from within an Amazon fulfillment center.

View the video online at: http://www.youtube.com/embed/g6DlFpaoI6A?rel=0

Systems only stamp names and addresses on boxes after orders are complete and boxes are sealed. No floor workers know who you are or what you've ordered. Packed boxes are then loaded onto separate trays that ride into another conveyor belt system, where they are scanned and tipped down the correct chute among dozens of choices so that the box is routed onto the appropriate truck for that order's shipping provider and destination. Some warehouses ship products so quickly that outbound trucks are dispatched with a less-than-three-minute window between them.[31]

A single warehouse, like the massive Tracy, California facility (which is about as large as fifty-nine football fields) has as many as 3,000 Kiva robots,[32] helping the firm ship as many as 21 million distinct products.[33] Motion sensors and floor-mounted guides help robots find their way. Shelf-carrying Kivas travel around 3 to 4 mph and never collide. The wireless, electric robots will run a couple hours on a charge, and they'll return for a recharge when needed.[34] Robots can't repair themselves, but repairmen are on site in the event of failure, with no more than ten robots in the fleet expected to be out of commission at any point in time.[35] Kivas keep getting better, too. Amazon claims the current generation is 50 percent more efficient at moving inventory than models that were produced at the time of acquisition.[36]

As for benefits, Kiva robots allow shelves to be slotted closer together and can be queued up for rapid, never-colliding, constant round-trips. This helps Amazon store as much as 50 percent more product in Kiva-equipped warehouses (greater selection at lower cost), it has reduced unload time for inbound inventory from "hours" to as little as 30 minutes,[37] and it has cut average order fulfillment time from about an hour and a half to as little as fifteen minutes.[38] While robot workers are cheaper than people, Kiva isn't a job-killer; in fact, Amazon has actually increased staff since deploying the robots. Says the firm's VP of Worldwide Operations, "Kiva's doing the part that's not that complicated. It's just moving inventory around. The person is doing the complicated work, which is reaching in, identifying the right product, making sure it's the right quality, and making sure it's good enough to be a holiday gift for somebody."[39]

Deploying robots isn't cheap. It's estimated that Amazon spends over $26 million on equipment and $46 million total getting a large warehouse on board with Kiva robots,[40] but systems also help the firm position itself for even more customer satisfaction. Faster delivery times through speedy fulfillment centers helped Amazon expand same-day delivery to 14 cities in Spring 2015.[41]

Keeping customers happy stems in part from setting expectations, so Amazon's systems receive weather reports as well. Order a product during a pre-Christmas snowstorm, and expect to see a message on the website indicating that "adverse weather conditions are impacting deliveries." A nice touch on the few times when a snag might cause problems. Those are quite rare: Amazon boasts on-time package delivery rates of up to 99.9 percent or more.[42]

Amazon's Warehouse inside a Warehouse

Amazon has been experimenting with a new logistics model where it runs Amazon-staffed fulfillment operations in special fenced-off areas of P&G warehouses worldwide. Diapers, razor blades, and other high-volume, fast-moving items are passed over from P&G to Amazon. While P&G warehouses are set up to ship pallets of diapers to Walmart, Walgreens, and other retailers, they're not configured for sending lots of product to individual consumers, but these kinds of activities are Amazon's superpower.

The program, known as Vendor Flex, is meant to cut costs and reduce warehousing and shipping time to help Amazon keep pace with Costco, Walmart, and others. Eliminating additional transit steps from supplier to Amazon and to you should also reduce environmental impact from carbon footprint and transit congestion. As for bottom line bonus, the *Wall Street Journal* suggests that if online orders of nonperishable staples hit 6 percent (the share the Internet commands of overall retail), Amazon would generate an extra $10 billion. Vendor Flex is also in warehouses of Kimberly Clark (Huggies, Kleenex, and Scott), Georgia Pacific (Brawny, Dixie, and Quilted Northern), and eco-friendly nonperishables firm Seventh Generation.[43]

2.2   Amazon's Cash Conversion Cycle—Realizing Financial Benefits from Speed

Quickly moving products out of warehouses is good for customers, but Amazon's speed also offers another critical advantage over most brick-and-mortar retailers: The firm is astonishingly efficient at managing cash. Here's how.

When incoming inventory shows up at most retailers—and this is certainly true for Amazon, Barnes & Noble, and Best Buy—those firms don't pay their suppliers right away. Instead, they log payment due for these goods as an **account payable**, a bill that says when payment is due sometime in the future. Accounts payable periods vary, but it's not uncommon for a big retailer to be able to hold products for a month or longer without having to pay for them. However, when customers buy from a retailer, they pay right away. Cash is collected immediately, and funds from credit cards and checks clear in no more than a few days. The firm's period between shelling out cash and collecting funds associated with a given operation is referred to as the **cash conversion cycle** (CCC). There are other factors that influence the CCC, but right now we'll concentrate on the hugely important time difference between paying for inventory and selling those goods. A retailer wants this number to be as small as possible; otherwise, unsold inventory is sitting on shelves and doesn't generate any cash until it's sold. Especially cash-crunched firms may even require short-term loans to pay suppliers, and those firms that can't generate cash quickly enough are referred to as having **liquidity problems**.

While a firm's CCC varies from quarter to quarter, Barnes & Noble has reported that its inventory has sat on shelves sixty-eight days on average before being purchased.[44] BestBuy has held inventory for as many as seventy days before a sale.[45] Costco and Walmart sell goods more quickly, but they also pay for inventory before it is sold.[46] When compared with these peers, however, Amazon alone consistently reports a negative CCC—it actually sells goods and collects money from customers weeks before it has to pay its suppliers. This gives the firm a special advantage since it has an additional pool of cash that it can put to work on things like expanding operations, making interest-bearing investments, and more.

account payable

Money owed for products and services purchased on credit.

cash conversion cycle

Period between distributing cash and collecting funds associated with a given operation (e.g., sales).

liquidity problems

Problems that arise when organizations cannot easily convert assets to cash. Cash is considered the most *liquid* asset—that is, the most widely accepted with a value understood by all.

FIGURE 7.2   Cash Conversion Cycle (in Days) among Select Major Retailers

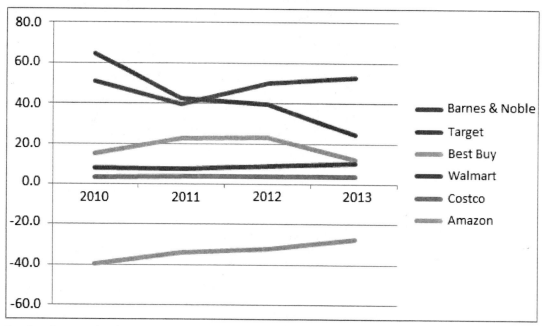

Note: Created using data from firm-published financial reports.

inventory turns

The number of times inventory is sold or used during a specific period (such as a year or quarter). A higher figure means a firm is selling products quickly.

The efficiency of a firm's cash cycle will vary over time. And numbers reported are an average for all products—some products are slow movers while others are sold very quickly. But the negative cash conversion cycle is another powerful benefit that Amazon's fast-fulfillment model offers over rivals. The goal for Amazon? Keep **inventory turns** high (e.g., sell quickly) and pay suppliers later.

Internet Economics, Scale, and Pricing Power

Selling more goods often gives Amazon bargaining power with suppliers. And the size (scale) of Amazon's business provides the firm with negotiating leverage to secure lower prices and longer payment terms. But Amazon's cost structure for operations is also superior to that of rivals. To be certain, Walmart's sales dwarf Amazon's. Walmart's 2014 sales figures were $473 billion. Amazon's $89 billion 2014 sales figures are about 17 billion ahead of Target's. But Walmart has 11,488 stores worldwide[47] and Target only has 1,795 stores.[48] Amazon has about 155 current or planned warehouses worldwide and (despite widespread, false rumors of an impending Manhattan location[49]) no conventional stores.[50] While Amazon spends significantly on software, automation, and expansion of its warehouses, its overall costs for things like real estate, energy, inventory, and security will be lower than costs experienced by brick-and-mortar rivals. And employee efficiency should be greater as well, since Amazon shift workers are working at fairly constant rates throughout the day while retailer activity fluctuates with the ebb and flow of customer visitation hours.

Amazon: Your Campus Bookstore

While Amazon does not have conventional retail stores, the firm's first consumer-oriented brick and mortar location opened at Purdue University in 2015, with similar facilities following at other schools. The Amazon-staffed Amazon@Purdue facility functions as a pickup and drop-off location for Amazon products. Students who buy an item and specify the store as their shipping address will receive an email or text alert once their shipment arrives. A link in the email or text generates a bar code to gain access to an in-store self-service lockers or pickup desk. A modified Amazon website shows class information and required texts for Purdue classes. Students receive free one-day shipping on Purdue textbooks shipped to Amazon@Purdue.[51] The partnership is assumed to have lowered textbook costs by 40 percent.[52]

Amazon@Purdue is Amazon's first consumer-facing brick and mortar facility.

View the video online at: //www.youtube.com/embed/bMRrMv0wnEE?rel=0

Retail can be a cutthroat business. The exact same products in one store are often available through competitors, so competition often boils down to whoever has the lowest price. Amazon's sales volume scale enables it to operate with thin margins and low prices. As former Amazon employee Eugene Wei puts it, this allows Amazon "to thin the oxygen" of competitors.[53] Amazon's breadth of operations brings in cash from other businesses giving the firm the stamina to endure the challenge of an unprofitable price war. Consider DVD Empire's reaction to the launch of the Amazon Video Store. DVD Empire was, at the time, the largest seller of online video. Feeling threatened by Amazon's arrival, DVD Empire lowered prices to an unsustainable 50 percent below retail. Amazon wouldn't make any money at 50 percent off, either, but Wei says, "Our leading opponent had challenged us to a game of who can hold your breath longer," and Amazon had "bigger lungs."[54] The lesson is clear: A smaller firm looking to pick a price fight with Amazon might not survive.

Amazon's retail prices aren't just cheaper than other e-commerce firms; they're usually cheaper than larger rival Walmart, too. Wells Fargo compared a diverse basket of products available at both firms and found that Walmart prices were actually 19 percent more expensive than Amazon prices. Target was 28 percent more expensive, while products purchased at specialty retailers cost 30 percent more. Even more impressive, Amazon seems to be monitoring the availability of products at competitor websites and using stockouts as an opportunity to earn more. The *Wall Street Journal* reports that "where rivals sold out of items, Amazon responded by raising its prices an average of 10 percent."[55] Firms should be careful—consumers have been known to react angrily to so-called **dynamic pricing** if they feel they are being taken advantage of.[56] But the insight does show how data can drive a nimble response to shifts in the competitive landscape.

Many analysts who are bullish on Amazon argue that the firm's drive to rapidly expand (so that it can leverage even greater scale over rivals) is the primary reason the firm's profits are often low to nonexistent.[57] Amazon generates a lot of cash, but instead of harvesting this as profits, for years it has been plowing nearly every penny back into the firm, mostly via investments in fulfillment center infrastructure and (as we'll see later in this chapter) capacity for the firm's dominant, higher-margin cloud computing business (visible in accounting statements by analyzing the sizeable gap between the firm's operating cash flow, which eliminates capital expenditures, and free cash flow, which includes them).[58] While Amazon has accelerated the build-out by taking on capital lease obligations (debt),[59] Bezos is playing the long game, thinking the opportunity to expand now will help the firm leverage scale to continue to dominate markets in the future. Larger warehouses, more warehouses closer to big cities, and more efficient warehouses all build a moat around the firm's existing businesses, making it less likely that any firm will be able to attack Amazon's three-pronged value trident of selection, service, and price.[60]

dynamic pricing

Pricing that shifts over time, usually based on conditions that change demand (e.g., charging more for scarce items).

FIGURE 7.3 Key Retailer Average Price Difference above Amazon.com[61]

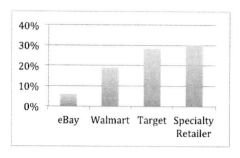

While not well known for its own brands beyond Kindle, Amazon's scale has allowed it to create several of its own branded product lines. Amazon's private-label brands include AmazonBasics (cables, batteries, and other consumer electronics accessories), Pinzon (kitchen gadgets), Strathwood (outdoor furniture), Pike Street (bath and home products), and Denali (tools).[62] An initial experiment with diapers under the Amazon Elements banner failed due to product quality concerns, but baby wipes continue to be offered under the Elements label while other products are in the works.[63]

Putting its own brand on high-volume products should allow Amazon to cut out some of the costs that would otherwise go to a branded supplier. The willingness to sell its own brands can also give Amazon even more negotiating leverage with suppliers. Firms unwilling to provide Amazon with the price breaks, payment terms, or complete product-line access it demands may see Amazon compete directly with them via a private-label product. And a scale-reinforced brand that screams "best price" in a space crowded with me-too retailers selling the exact same thing is a powerful asset and enormous barrier for competitors to try to overcome. Amazon can keep advertising spending down, as customers see the firm as the first and often only stop needed when moving from product research to purchase. Consider that Target (with billions less in sales than Amazon) is a member of that elite club of firms that spend over $1 billion in advertising ($1.62 billion in 2012), while Amazon didn't even make the list.[64]

Amazon also sees growth beyond consumers. AmazonBusiness (the evolution of a business formerly known as AmazonSupply) is going after the corporate procurement market, which Forbes generously estimates as being valued at $7.2 trillion.[65] Amazon's selection selling everything from paper to IT products to break room snacks to lab equipment may make the firm a first-choice destination for buying in many categories, especially given that the average business products wholesaler offers only about 50,000 products online.[66] Special features are targeted at business customers, including the ability to create multiple user accounts, integrate with corporate procurement systems, set up a purchase approval workflow, work with purchase orders, and even negotiate bulk discounts. A pass-through link will allow a visitor to Amazon to chat experts from firms selling technical products.[67] Getting most products in and out of a warehouse is the same regardless of category, so Amazon can quickly expand in any area where it thinks the model will work.

Customer Obsession

For a firm that does so much, Amazon's moves are largely motivated by one thing: relentless customer focus. Sure; every firm says they care about their customers. But consider this: In meetings, Bezos is known to insist that one seat be left open at the conference table as a symbol representing "the most important person in the room," the Amazon customer.[68] To keep even the most senior executives empathetic to the customer experience, every two years every employee, from Bezos on down, must spend two days on the service desk answering customer calls.[69]

It's an eye on improving the customer experience that has motivated so many of Amazon's pioneering efforts, among which include one-click ordering (which the firm patented), customer reviews, recommendations, bundles, look and search inside the book, where's my stuff, and free supersaver shipping. While pioneered by Amazon, many of these efforts are now accepted as must-have features across e-commerce categories.[70]

Amazon is also using the Amazon Prime subscription service to make customers happy, and along the way, to create habit-changing behaviors that fuel sales growth. Subscribers to Amazon Prime get free two-day shipping for unlimited qualifying purchases, so users don't have to bundle products in a shopping cart before they can qualify for free shipping. It also loads up Prime members with additional perks like a selection of thousands of videos and hundreds of thousands of songs that subscribers can stream for free. And when Amazon expanded same-day delivery to fourteen US cities, it waved fees for Prime subscribers (cementing a same-day Amazon habit may be important as firms that include Google, Macy's, and Nordstrom all experiment with same-day service for a fee).[71] Amazon hasn't shared how many customers are Prime subscribers, but third-party estimates suggest the number may exceed 50 million[72] (the firm did say it added 10 million Prime subscribers in Q4 2014).[73] Amazon also doesn't share spending habits of its Prime customers, but many estimates have Prime customers spending twice as much as non-Prime. Many on Wall Street have been critical of free shipping, but it's yet another way that Amazon improves the customer experience. Free shipping can cost Amazon upwards of $600 million in a single quarter,[74] and shipping costs have been rising as much as 25 percent a year since 2004. The firm's recent increase in Prime's subscription price (from $79 to $99 in the United States) coupled with increased volume and loyalty seem to be making the program worthwhile.

As we've mentioned earlier, strong brands are built largely through customer experience. As evidence of the strength of customer experience, Amazon has repeatedly scored the highest rating on the University of Michigan's American Customer Service Index (ACSI). Not only was it a rating that bested all other Internet retailers; it was the highest score of any firm in any service industry.

Leveraging the Data Asset—A/B Testing, Personalization, and Even an Ad Business

Moving early and having scale allow Amazon to amass that profoundly valuable tech-derived competitive resource—data. The more customers a firm has, the more accurately the firm can understand various patterns related to recommendations, preferences, customer segments, price tolerance, and more.

At Amazon, data win arguments, and the corporate culture gives employees the freedom to challenge even the most senior managers, all the way up to Bezos himself. When Amazon coder Greg Linden proposed that Amazon present "impulse buy" recommendations that match patterns associated with the consumer's shopping carts (e.g., customers who bought that also bought this), he was originally shot down by a senior vice president. Linden was undeterred; he ran an **A/B test**—capturing customer response for those who saw option "A" (recommendations) versus option "B" (no recommendations). The result overwhelmingly demonstrated that recommendations would drive revenue.[75]

Letter posted to Amazon's home page following the firm's second record-breaking ACSI score

amazon.com.

Dear Customers,

The American Customer Satisfaction Index is, by far, the most authoritative and widely followed survey of customer satisfaction. Last year, Amazon.com received an ACSI score of 84, the highest ever recorded -- not just online, not just in retailing -- but the highest score ever recorded in any service industry. This year, Amazon.com scored an 88 -- again the highest score ever recorded in any service industry.

In ACSI's words:

"Amazon.com continues to show remarkably high levels of customer satisfaction. With a score of 88 (up 5%), it is generating satisfaction at a level unheard of in the service industry...Can customer satisfaction for Amazon climb more? The latest ACSI data suggest that it is indeed possible. Both service and the value proposition offered by Amazon have increased at a steep rate".

Thank you very much for being a customer, and we'll work even harder for you in the future. (We already have lots of customer experience improvements planned for 2003.)

On behalf of everyone at Amazon.com,

Sincerely,

Jeff Bezos
Founder & CEO

Two-Pizza Teams: Keeping an Entrepreneurial Culture in a Big Firm

One challenge growing firms often face is that they become slow and less innovative as they expand.[76] In order to keep Amazon nimble and innovative, Bezos has mandated a rule known as "two-pizza teams," stating that any individual project team should be small enough that it can be fed by no more than two pizzas.[77] This helps ideas flourish, discourages the kind of "groupthink" that diminishes the consideration of alternative approaches, and even provides a mechanism where several efforts can compete to identify the best solution.

While the "abandoned shopping cart" problem plagues many Web retailers, Amazon is considered one of the best "converting" e-commerce sites, moving customers from product evaluation through completing checkout.[78] A/B tests drive this; the firm has relentlessly experimented with tests that modify and compare all sorts of variables, including the wording associated with images and buttons, screen placement, size, color, and more. Constantly measuring customer activity also helps the firm direct its investment in infrastructure. One test, for example, revealed that a tenth of a second's delay in page loading equaled a 1 percent drop in customer activity, pointing to a clear ROI (return on investment) for keeping server capacity scalable.[79]

While you're shopping on Amazon, you're likely part of some sort of experiment—perhaps several. While Amazon doesn't say how many A/B tests it runs, Google runs over seven thousand annually. Amazon has gotten so good at A/B testing that it launched a service offering scalable options for running simultaneous tests and gathering measured results for developers that use the Amazon app store. A/B testing is yet another advantage e-commerce firms have over conventional retailers. Constant experimentation, refinement, and retesting are far easier in the digital world when every user's click, delay, and back track can be measured and compared.

Amazon's data trove on you individually, and users collectively, fuels the firm's personalization effort (efficiently referred to internally as p13n, since there are thirteen letters between the p and the n in the word personalization). When visiting the Amazon home page, it's more accurate to say that you're visiting your Amazon home page at a given point in time. Your page may vary not only based on any ongoing A/B tests but also based on Amazon's best guess of what you'll want to see as well as any myriad of other sales and promotion goals. Behind the scenes, your Web browser receives a unique tracking string called a **cookie**, and Amazon tracks your surfing behavior as well as your buying history. Rate products? Even better! Amazon knows what you liked and what you didn't. The firm's proprietary **collaborative-filtering** software compares a user's data with others' data, mapping a best guess of what you'll like to see each time you visit. A parent who has searched for and bought items for young children will likely see recommendations for other age-appropriate kid products—maybe even guessing at your kid's gender and likes. Athletes, gamers, and romance novel fans should also expect interest revealed by surfing and purchasing to create a custom experience. Amazon has claimed that as much as 35 percent of product sales have come from the firm's recommendations.[80] Scale means the firm has more users doing more things, allowing the firm to collect more observations that fuel greater

A/B testing

A randomized group of experiments used to collect data and compare performance among two options studied (A and B). A/B testing is often used in refining the design of technology products, and A/B tests are particularly easy to run over the Internet on a firm's Web site. Amazon, Google, and Facebook are among the firms that aggressively leverage hundreds of A/B tests a year in order to improve their product offerings.

cookie

A line of identifying text assigned and retrieved by a given Web server and stored by your browser.

collaborative-filtering

A classification of software that monitors trends among customers and uses this data to personalize an individual customer's experience.

accuracy in tailoring the user experience. And this fuels that oh-so-important, brand-building positive customer experience.

All of this customer insight data also positions Amazon to grow a massive, Google-competing ad business. Amazon initially sold ads as a way to generate more sales through its website, but Amazon now offers advertisers the ability to advertise on Kindles, on other Amazon-owned sites like IMDb, within mobile apps, and via Amazon-targeted ads on third-party websites. Amazon ad offerings are feature rich, including things like the ability to play a movie trailer in an ad or embedding a discount coupon in a click-to-purchase offering. Amazon reportedly charges up to $1 million for ads placed on the welcome screen of the new Kindle Fire.[81] Don't like ads? You can pay $20 more for a Kindle without the "special offers." Have you also ever looked at a product on Amazon, didn't buy it, but then started seeing the product pop up in ads as you surfed the Web? That's called *retargeting*, and Amazon is building this business as well. Retargeting is especially attractive to suppliers since a click through brings you right to Amazon's cash register, a place where you've likely already got all of your account information online and where buying is just "1-Click" away.

FIGURE 7.4

In this retargeting example, a user visiting the Amazon page for a college-themed blanket (background) was tracked using a cookie, and the user's interest in this product was recorded. Advertisements for this product were shown when this same user visited other websites (foreground).

Selection and Network Effects

Amazon's radical focus on customer experience also caused it to take what many would consider a contrarian move—offering products provided by others alongside its own listings. Third-party products are referred to as being part of the Amazon Marketplace. Amazon doesn't own inventory of marketplace items. Sellers can warehouse and ship products themselves, or they can opt to use Amazon's warehouses as part of the Fulfilled by Amazon program. The latter lets Amazon handle logistics, storage, packaging, shipping, and customer service, while customers get Amazon shipping prices—including supersaver discounts and free shipping for customers enrolled in the Amazon Prime program. Customers also benefit if they already have credit card and other information on file with Amazon (a switching cost potentially deterring users from going to a new site).

two-sided network effect

Products or services that get more valuable as two distinct categories of participants expand (e.g., buyers and sellers).

As much as 40 percent of all units sold by Amazon are from the firm's 2 million participating Amazon Marketplace sellers worldwide.[82] Marketplace allows Amazon to build a *long tail* of product offerings without the costly risk of having to take ownership of unproven or slow-moving inventory, while the firm gets fat and happy in the middle of a **two-sided network effect** (i.e., more buyers attract more sellers, and more sellers attract more buyers). Some Marketplace products compete directly with Amazon's own offerings, but the firm doesn't shy away from allowing competitive listings, new or used, even if they're cheaper. Competition among sellers reinforces low price and lowers the chance that customers will look first to sites like PriceGrabber, Shopping.com, Google, or eBay. Even if a rival wins a sale, all products sold through Amazon allow Bezos's firm to collect a fee. Third-party sellers may send a signal to Amazon that a certain product category may be worth entering itself, all while sellers pick up the initial risk of inventory ownership. And when Amazon sells third-party goods through its site, it continues to "own" much of the customer relationship for that sale, gathering data that would have otherwise been lost if customers went elsewhere. Amazon also won't hesitate to kick out sellers with bad ratings to ensure quality and protect the Amazon brand.

Scale from Selection: The Long Tail

Much of Amazon's appeal as a first-choice shopping destination comes from the firm's selection. Internet businesses are free of what *Wired* editor Chris Anderson calls the limitations of shelf space and geography, which trouble traditional retailers.[83] Traditional retailers stock their limited shelves with the most popular items, and consumers are limited to the selection available in the stores that they are willing to travel to. Amazon's warehouses and third-party seller selection offer the equivalent of virtually limitless shelf stock, something you'd never find in a store. This selection is delivered by US mail or package shippers, so geography is no longer a concern. This allows the firm to leverage what is often called the long tail (as introduced in Chapter 4, the tail refers to the large number of products unavailable through conventional retail stores, see Figure 7.5, depicted below, and also shown in Chapter 4). The cost to house and ship a popular book, or a more obscure one, should be the same. While popular items make up traditional retailer inventory (the area on the left-hand side of the curve in Figure 7.5 "The Long Tail"), it turns out there's actually *more money* to be made selling obscure stuff (the stretched-out but larger area on the right-hand side of the curve) if you can reach a greater customer base over the Internet. As evidence, consider that at Amazon, roughly 60 percent of books sold are titles that aren't available in even the biggest Barnes & Noble Superstores.[84] Amazon is also moving from distribution of the "atoms" of books and video to digital distribution of media products via the Kindle. This eliminates the cost to warehouse and ship the atoms of physical goods.

FIGURE 7.5   The Long Tail

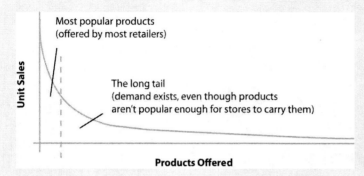

Not only does Amazon allow others to sell products through its site, it allows others to market for the firm. The Amazon Associates program is the world's largest **affiliate marketing program**, offering a sort of "finder's fee" for generating sales. Website operators can recommend Amazon products on their site, and Amazon gives the affiliate a percentage of sales generated from these promotions. For Amazon, fees paid are pay for performance—associates get a commission only if their promotions generate sales.

Acquisitions and Category Expansion: Fewer Rivals, More Markets, and More Customer Choice

Acquisition of other firms and the growth of new internal businesses has allowed Amazon to accomplish several things, including broadening the firm's product offerings to underscore Amazon as the "first choice" shopping destination; absorbing potentially threatening competitors before they get too big; experimenting with new product offerings and services; and integrating value-added businesses and technologies into the Amazon empire. *BusinessWeek* once ran a cover story titled "What Amazon Fears Most," featuring a diaper-clad toddler. The implication was that New Jersey-based Quidsi, operator of diapers.com, could grow brand and scale in staple products, drawing customers away from Amazon. Amazon's response? They bought the firm for over half a billion dollars. Today the Quidsi subsidiary has seven brands that can deliver a range of goods, from cosmetics to green cleaning products, in some cases within the same day. While Amazon hasn't yet made the decision to integrate Quidsi completely into the Amazon experience, they are now full owners of what was once regarded as one of the biggest threats to grabbing high-growth markets that Amazon didn't dominate.[85] Same thing with Zappos, which Amazon paid nearly $1 billion for, and which continues to operate as a separate brand.[86] Other acquired firms include Alexa, a Web analytics and tools provider; Audible, the leading provider of digital audio books; GoodReads and Shelfari, social networking sites for book readers; Woot, a **flash-sales** site; and LoveFilm, often described as the "Netflix of Europe."

Amazon is also growing its own brands in new categories. Examples include MyHabit, a fashion flash-sales site competing with the likes of Gilt Groupe and Rue La La. Amazon Instant Video offers streaming television and movie titles for rental or purchase, and some are included free with an Amazon Prime subscription. And Amazon Fresh is a FreshDirect-like competitor, offering same-day or next-day delivery of groceries and more.

Amazon is working to put inexpensive, specialty tech into the hands of its customers to make ordering even easier. The firm's Amazon Dash scanner helps Amazon Fresh customers build grocery lists; see the video clip in this section. Not convenient enough for you? The free Amazon Dash Button can be scattered about your home, allowing automatic ordering of high volume staples—things like

affiliate marketing program

Marketing practice where a firm rewards partners (affiliates) who bring in new business, often with a percentage of any resulting sales.

flash-sales

Offering deep discounts of a limited quantity of inventory. Flash sales often run for a fixed period or until inventory is completely depleted. Players include Guilt Groupe and Amazon's MyHabit in fashion, and OneKingsLane in home décor.

Keurig cups, Kraft Macaroni and Cheese, Gillette razors, and Huggies diapers, via a single, branded, Wi-Fi-enabled press. Amazon has also begun building warehouses close to major metropolitan areas, a move that many think is targeted at growing same-day delivery. (Walmart, eBay, and even Google also offer same-day delivery services in some areas.) The move is a departure for Amazon, which for years built warehouses in low-population states to avoid tax laws that require sales tax collection where the firm has a physical location.[87] As Amazon gives in on sales taxes, it's poised to launch an all-out assault on markets handled by local retailers.

 ### The Amazon Dash Scanner

The Amazon Dash scanner lets Amazon Fresh customers build simple grocery lists for some 500,000 items simply by speaking into the device or using the barcode scanner.

View the video online at: https://www.youtube.com/embed/aFYs9zqYpdM?rel=0

 ### The Amazon Dash Button

The Amazon Dash Button links to your Amazon account over Wi-Fi and provides one-touch ordering of popular brands at the touch of a button.

View the video online at: https://www.youtube.com/embed/EHMXXOB6qPA

KEY TAKEAWAYS

- Amazon's sophisticated fulfillment operations speed products into and out of inventory, reinforcing brand strength through speed, selection, and low prices.

- Rapid inventory turnover and long payment terms enable Amazon to consistently post a negative cash conversion cycle. The firm sells products and collects money from customers in most cases before it has paid suppliers for these products.

- The cost structure for online retailers can be far less than that of offline counterparts that service similarly sized markets. Savings can come from employee costs, inventory, energy usage, land, and other facilities-related expenses.

- Amazon's scale is a significant asset. Scale gives Amazon additional bargaining leverage with suppliers, and it allows the firm to offer cheaper prices in many categories than nearly every other firm, online or off. Scale through multiple warehouses allows Amazon to offer more products, a greater product selection, and same-day delivery for urban areas near warehouses. Amazon financials suggest that the firm is deferring profitability due to its increased investment in capital expenditures such as its warehouse and data center buildout.

- Around 40 percent of products sold on Amazon are offerings sold through Amazon Marketplace by third parties. Amazon gets a cut of each sale, maintains its control of the customer interface, and retains the opportunity to collect customer data that would be lost if users went elsewhere for a purchase.

- Amazon takes advantage of the *long tail*, a concept where firms can profitably offer a selection of less popular products. Amazon's enormous product selection—with offerings from the firm and from third parties—reinforces its position as the first-choice shopping destination.

- Amazon's ability to acquire and leverage data further allows the firm to enhance customer experience and drive sales. Internet retailers have a greater ability to gather personal data on consumers than do offline counterparts. Data is used in personalization and in innovation fueled by the result of A/B experiments.

QUESTIONS AND EXERCISES

1. When you walk into a conventional retailer, similar items are stacked next to each other. But Amazon tries not to do this in its warehouses. Why?

2. How do Amazon warehouse staff know where to find items? How does technology help make the process most efficient?

3. How have robots changed the way Amazon warehouses operate? What are the benefits these robots bring to Amazon? Which firm supplies Amazon's shelving robots and why might this be important for Amazon?

4. Does Amazon buy most of its warehouse automation software from others, or is most of the software written in house? Why do you suppose this is the case?

5. In what other ways do Amazon's information systems reduce errors? Why is error reduction so critical to firm performance?

6. Which requires more code—the firm's customer-facing website, or warehouse automation?

7. Although Amazon is investing in robotics, human beings still do most of the product picking. How does Amazon ensure that customer privacy is protected despite heavy human involvement? Do you think it needs to go to such great lengths? Why or why not?

8. What is the cash conversion cycle (CCC)? What factors enable Amazon to have a CCC that is negative? Why are offline rivals unable to match these efficiencies? What advantage does this give Amazon over rivals?

9. How do Amazon's prices compare with rivals' prices? What gives Amazon such advantages? What other pricing advantages does Amazon have that a conventional retailer might not be able to take advantage of?

10. What is dynamic pricing, and why might this be risky?

11. What are private-label products, and what advantages do they offer Amazon?

12. Log into Amazon (or pull up a page if you "remain" logged in). Compare it to a classmate's page. What similarities do you notice? What differences? Why do you think Amazon made the choice to show you the things that it did? Do you think it guessed accurately regarding your interests? Why or why not?

13. Amazon's unique customer data have allowed the firm to enter the advertising business. Which firms does this bring Amazon into competition with? Research Amazon's role in matching advertisers to consumers. How big a player is Amazon? How do you feel about a firm using your personal data on purchases, product browsing, and recommendations for advertising? Under what circumstances (if any) are you comfortable with such targeting, and under what circumstances are you concerned?

14. How does Amazon keep management focused on customer issues and "putting the customer first"?

15. Describe how Amazon Marketplace offers two-sided network effects.

16. Besides network effects, what additional benefits does Amazon gain by allowing other retailers to sell potentially competing products on Amazon?

17. What is the long tail? How does the long tail change retail economics? How does it influence shoppers' choice of where to look for products? What firms, other than Amazon, are taking advantage of the long tail in their industries?

18. How is scale important to Amazon? What advantages does scale offer Amazon over its smaller rivals?

19. Amazon's operations are a marvel of automation and procedural efficiency, but the firm has also been subject to criticism regarding its warehouse work environment. Investigate these criticisms on your own. Do you feel they are valid? Are any of the critics also worthy of criticism? If so, how? Do you feel Amazon has responded appropriately to this criticism? How would you have responded if you were CEO of the firm? What takeaways from your own investigation will inform your own actions as a manager?

3.   KINDLE ON FIRE: THE RISE OF DIGITAL, THE EVERYWHERE STORE, AND NEW OPPORTUNITIES FROM E-BOOK, TABLET, TV, AND PHONE

LEARNING OBJECTIVES

1. **Understand the motivation behind Amazon's Kindle business.**
2. **Recognize the various ways that Amazon earns money and strengthens its competitiveness via the Kindle platform.**
3. **Examine the changes Amazon's digital media offerings have brought to the traditional publishing industry value chain.**
4. **Understand key concepts such as channel conflict, wholesale pricing, and agency pricing.**

While Amazon has built solid advantages by selling a broad array of products, media (books, music, and video) still represents about a quarter of the firm's revenue,[88] and nearly all of that business is going to shift from atoms to bits, shipped not in physical packaging but through the Internet. Losing this market would be a blow that any publicly traded company, especially one with razor-thin margins, would find difficult to sustain. This is what has prompted the creation of the Kindle. While many refer to the Kindle as an e-reader, the Kindle isn't as much about reading digital books as it is about putting a store in the hands of the firm's over 244 million customers[89] not only allowing them to lap up goods from an increasingly massive digital trough, but also instantly linking those customers with the firm's entire inventory of physical products. What started as an e-book reader has now expanded to Kindle and Fire product lines that span categories that include tablet, television set-top box, and smartphone. Beyond media consumption and sales, Kindle and Fire devices are also data gathering conduits, arming Amazon to collect more customer insight to power existing and new initiatives.

3.1   The Kindle Line: Igniting Possibilities on e-Book and Tablet

The first Kindle was optimized for book reading and featured a black-and-white display that used E Ink. That display can't refresh fast enough for animation or video, but it is legible in sunlight and only draws power when flipping a dot from black to white or vice versa, offering exceptionally long battery life. Thanks to Moore's Law, Kindles, originally offered at $399, grew in power while plummeting in price, with a low-end model selling for just $69 five years after introduction. The success of the Kindle is staggering. By the holiday season of the product's second year, the Kindle was Amazon's top-selling product in both dollar volume and unit sales.[90] That means Amazon was selling more Kindles than any single book, CD, movie title, or toy—or any other product among the millions that it offers. Consumer Intelligence Research Partners estimates that some 20 percent of Amazon's US customers own some form of Kindle device, an astounding rate.[91]

Up next is the high-resolution, color, and touch-screen Kindle Fire tablet. In its introduction, the Kindle Fire came to market for half the price of the competing iPad and quickly became the second best-selling tablet on the market. The Kindle is also a cloud machine. The first Fire came with half the RAM of the iPad, the thought being that your media would be snugly stored on Amazon's servers, downloaded when you need it, creating a big sticky switching cost in the process.

Even more noteworthy for competitors in the e-book and tablet space, Amazon doesn't look to make money directly from Kindle hardware sales; various Kindle versions are regularly sold at or below costs.[92] But any Kindle device ordered from Amazon arrives linked to your Amazon account. That means the device comes, out of the box, as a preconfigured cash register with a vacuum attached firmly to the credit card in your wallet. Roughly 1 million titles are offered in the Kindle "always-open" bookstore, with "search inside the book" features and the first chapter downloadable for free. Estimates of the firm's Kindle-generated revenue bump vary, but all point to positive Kindle-fueled sales gains. RBC Capital estimates that despite being sold at a loss, each Kindle Fire generates over $136 in operating income, with operating margins above 20 percent over the lifetime of the device.[93] Kindle owners buy three to four times more books than they did prior to owning the device.[94] And Amazon today sells more electronic books overall than their print counterparts.[95] In terms of fueling overall sales, *SmartMoney* reported that Amazon customers who don't own a Kindle spend an average of $87 each . month while those with a Kindle spend $136 and Kindle Fire owners spend over $150.[96]

3.2   Amazon for Your TV . . . and Your Speaker

fork

In software development (sometimes also called project fork). When developers start with a copy of a project's program source code, but modify it, creating a distinct and separate product from the original base.

The e-book and tablet Kindles were followed by Fire TV. The tiny $99 device attaches to a television and offers fast streaming from Amazon's library. A $39 Fire TV stick offers most of the features in a device the size of a USB drive that plugs directly into your TV's HDMI port. Fire TV also runs apps for a host of other services, including Netflix and Hulu Plus. Voice search is enabled through a mic in the remote. An optional game controller opens up another world of entertainment. While Fire OS is based on Android, it's what is referred to as a modified Android '**fork**', with differences significant enough that fire runs only a subset of Android apps. During its launch, Fire TV only had 180 apps in total, while the competing Roku device, which had been on the market for years, was offering over 1,200 apps.[97]

The market for television streaming media players is crowded. Apple TV, Google TV, Google Chromecast, and Roku all have a head start, yet none of these has achieved any real scale. Just 8 percent of consumers in the United States own any kind of television-streaming media box.[98] That may mean TV is still anyone's game to win, but Amazon will need to convince customers to add yet another device to media stand clutter and octopus cabling that likely already includes a cable set-top box, game console, and DVD player.

While Fire TV lets you talk to your remote to search for video entertainment, Amazon Echo is the wireless speaker that you can talk to. In yet another slow-rollout consumer electronics experiment, the Echo is a high-quality speaker equipped with seven far-field-listening microphones that taps into Amazon's cloud. Call it by the name "Amazon" or "Alexa" and you can ask it questions ("How many teaspoons in a tablespoon?"); set a timer; inquire about the weather, traffic, or sports; ask it to tell you jokes; summon up a news briefing; dispatch it to play songs on Amazon Prime Music, TuneIn, or other services ("Play 80s music"); control *smart home* devices like the Belkin WeMo and Philips Hue lighting ("Turn off the living room lamp");[99] read back your Google calendar appointments;[100] create reminders; and of course, create shopping lists and place shopping orders.[101] Voice recognition can be tricky (early versions would mistakenly think they were summoned with the name "Amazon" when you asked the kids to get their "pajamas on") but with most of its brains in the cloud, Echo will only get smarter over time and consumers will instantly see improvements the next time they talk to their device.

3.3   Fire Phone: A Cash Register in Your Pocket and Much More

Amazon followed Fire TV with Fire Phone. The high-end smartphone comes with several innovative features. The phone is designed to enable several functions to be performed by one hand: just flick a wrist or tilt the phone to pull up menus, turn pages, or scroll. Tilting also changes the perspective on the phone's 3-D map. The phone's signature feature is Firefly, a software program that uses the camera to recognize all sorts of objects: bar codes, QR codes, books, artwork, and grocery items. Point the camera at a phone number, and you can dial with a tap. The phone also recognizes songs and movies, Shazam style. There's a dedicated Firefly button on the phone that pops up the fast-acting feature even if you're outside the lock screen. That means your pocket-holstered Fire Phone is now trigger-ready for the quickest of draws to make an impulse buy. Why create a shopping list? Out of a household item? Just scan, hit 1-Click order, and you're done. The phone comes with a free, one-year Amazon Prime subscription to help build your addiction. Amazon mobile executive Sam Hall puts it this way: "We're trying to remove the barrier between 'I want that' and 'I have it.'"[102]

Firefly is really a search service: scan a bag of chips and nutritional details will show up, which can then be sent to your health-tracking app; scan a wine bottle and get food pairing recommendations; and scan a song and listen to related music in a streaming music app. Amazon provides an API so developers can plug in, but think strategically about the possibilities. Firefly can be more than Amazon's cash register, it may be Amazon's Google. A restaurant logo could pull up OpenTable as well as a Yelp review. *Wired* states, "if you're listening to a song on the radio, Firefly might give you the option to buy the album from Amazon, buy a concert ticket on Stubhub, create an iHeartRadio playlist of that artist, and in time, much more."[103] Given the wealth of data a phone could assemble about a user (location, shopping, searching, and other Firefly scanned interests), the possibilities for advertising and partner service targeting are significant.

That is, if anyone buys it. The initial price of $199 with contract for the base phone placed it in line with Apple and Samsung's smartphone pricing, not the value-pricing Amazon customers have enjoyed on profitless Kindle hardware. The phone came bundled with a year of Prime, which equates to another $100 in value, but many of the customers Amazon hoped to appeal to were already wedded to iOS or Android, and getting them to break up means overcoming switching costs. In less than one year the price was cut to 99 cents, or $189 out of contract. By all accounts the launch was a flop, with Amazon declaring a $170 million write-off by Fall.[104] Like Fire TV, the Fire Phone's OS is an Android fork that doesn't run the vast majority of Android apps—that means Fire Phone is fighting against switching costs with a malnourished network effect. Apparently, version one of Fire Phone's nifty features and shopping convenience weren't enough. A *New York Times* piece reminds us that "phones are a grave-yard of tech dreams." Google struggled with the Nexus and sold off Motorola. Microsoft been at it for years and has never gotten phones right. Blackberry is withering. Apple and Samsung are the only play-ers making money in hardware. Amazon claims its not done with smartphones[105] — whether this means more Amazon-branded models, or Firefly-like apps on Android and iOS remains to be seen. Having a successful phone would be nice, but hardware almost certainly isn't the end game—sales and advertising are likely where Amazon hopes for a payoff.

3.4 Amazon Gets into Content Publishing

As device and storefront, Amazon has begun to vertically integrate, capturing several segments in the traditional book value chain. The printed book, or "dead-tree," publication value chain involved a pub-lisher, bookstore, agent, and author. Publishers typically get half of a physical book's retail price, the bookstore takes about 30 percent, and the author keeps about 20 percent as a royalty but shares 15 to 20 percent of this with his or her agent. At the time of the Kindle's rise, six (then consolidated to five) large publishers controlled about 60 percent of the US book business commonly referred to as "trade publishing" (that means most of the books you'd find in a typical bookstore but not books such as edu-cational, scientific, and medical texts).[106] While most Kindle titles are from publishers that sell both print and digital versions, Amazon has gotten into the book publishing business as well, creating sever-al of its own "imprints" (publishing divisions that specialize in a genre, like foreign translations, ro-mance, or sci-fi). For authors wanting to bring books to market through Amazon instead of through traditional publishers, Amazon offers royalty options ranging from 35 to 70 percent. There's even a "Kindle Singles" program that allows authors to sell work too short for a stand-alone book (fiction, es-says, magazine articles).[107] And since digitally published work doesn't require printing, shipping, and shelf-stocking, these titles can often come to market far faster than physical offerings. Using Amazon as a publisher doesn't mean your titles will only be available through Kindle.[108] The firm will also pro-duce print books and even offer them to bookstores willing to carry the titles. But Amazon has in-centivized many authors to sell exclusively through the world's biggest e-commerce outlet and largest e-book platform. By March 2012, Bezos was proclaiming that sixteen of the firm's top one hundred best-selling titles were "exclusive to [their] store."[109]

And Amazon's digital publishing ambitions aren't limited to the printed word. The firm's Amazon Game Studios has released titles for Kindle Fire as well as Android, iOS, and Facebook.[110] Amazon has also recruited top-tier talent to beef up its game platform for Fire tablet, TV, and Phone. Many of the firm's staff have pedigrees from Microsoft's Xbox group and Nintendo USA, both located a short drive from Amazon HQ. The firm has also recruited industry stars Kim Swift (designer of the game *Portal*), Clint Hocking (designer of *Far Cry 2*), and Ian Vogel (senior designer on *Age of Empires On-line* and *BioShock*).[111]

Amazon has also spent lavishly to build up digital media offerings, especially for Prime customers. Amazon spent $300 million for exclusive streaming access for a subset of HBO back titles,[112] and has locked up content from Nickelodeon and others. The firm offers a Spotify-like music streaming ser-vices for Prime subscribers, as well. None of this comes cheap. Reed Hastings of Netflix claims Amazon may be losing as much as $1 billion a year in video licensing.[113] Amazon is also pulling a Netflix, mov-ing aggressively into original programming. Amazon Studios is touted by Bezos as a "completely new way of making movies" and television shows.[114] The firm has floated several feature film ideas and television pilots ranging from children's programming to adult comedies. Amazon Studios uses crowd feedback to drive what makes it to market.[115] Early efforts haven't garnered *House of Cards*-style buzz, but the renewed Amazon's comedy, *Alpha House*, is written by creator of the *Doonesbury* comic, Garry Trudeau, and boasts a cast that includes John Goodman, Wanda Sykes, and cameos by Bill Murray; the firm's *Transparent* series won a Golden Globe; and Woody Allen has signed on to direct another Amazon original series. Also planned are feature films that will debut in theaters, then join Amazon Prime's lineup a month or two later.[116]

Amazon is also spending big for non-conventional broadcast entertainment, buying the Twitch video game streaming site for roughly $1 billion. Twitch allows gamers to stream their gameplay live, and offer real-time commentary to viewers. Is watching other people play video games really a big busi-ness? You bet! The service boasted 55 million unique viewers before its third birthday, with 1.1 million broadcasters bringing in 16 billion minutes of total videos watched in a single month.[117] In terms of Internet traffic, only Netflix, Google, and Apple are bigger bandwidth hogs than Twitch.[118] The ser-vice has nearly as many viewers as the established cable networks MTV, Comedy Central, and MSNBC. Twitch shares ad revenue with broadcasting gamers, and while few are big earners, some Twitch stars have been known to pull in six figures a year.[119] The 32 million people who tuned in to watch the

"League of Legends" championships comprised an audience bigger than the finales of *Breaking Bad, 24,* and *The Sopranos* combined![120]

FIGURE 7.6

At the time of its acquisition by Amazon, Twitch boasted a viewership comparable to several established cable networks.

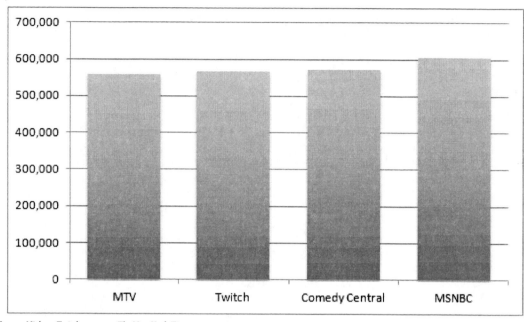

Source: Nielsen, Twitchapps.com, The New York Times

3.5 Channel Conflict and Consolidated Power

channel conflict

Exists when a firm's potential partners see that firm as a threat. This threat could come because it offers competing products or services via alternative channels or because the firm works closely with especially threatening competitors.

Amazon's ambitions to be a publisher that also sell e-readers, content, and just about everything else puts it at odds with partners who also increasingly see Amazon as a rival. **Channel conflict** exists when a firm's potential partners see that firm as a threat. This threat could come because it offers competing products or services via alternative channels or because the firm works closely with especially threatening competitors. Amazon has become a victim of channel conflict when other retailers have dropped its offerings. For example, Barnes & Noble and other book retailers have refused to carry titles from Amazon's publishing arm.[121] And Walmart and Target once carried the Kindle but have since stopped, fearing Amazon's e-reader would also be a conduit for stealing physical sales.[122] Authors and firms partnering with Amazon can also suffer channel conflict. When Amazon announced a partnership with DC Comics involving exclusive digital rights to Superman and Batman comics, Barnes & Noble and other book retailers pulled DC titles from their shelves.[123] The winner in channel conflict is the firm or group that offers greater value to conflicted partners.[124] As Amazon's scale grows to a seemingly insurmountable size and offers additional deal sweeteners like better author royalty rates, authors and providers of other goods may not care that working with Amazon will cut off other distribution channels. Those fearing that Amazon is achieving this kind of scale worry that the firm may gain near-monopoly market power.[125]

Amazon's power in the publishing industry again became an issue when the firm faced off with one of the big five book publishers, Hachette, over e-book terms. As a pressure tactic against Hachette, Amazon refused to allow customers to preorder Hachette books, it delayed sales (stating books that should ship in two days would usually ship in "1 to 2 months"), it refused to offer some Hachette e-books, and it even blocked the recognition of some of the firm's titles in the Fire Phone's Firefly feature.[126] Several big-name authors were impacted, including Harry Potter scribe J.K. Rowling. Comedian Stephen Colbert, whose books are also published by Hachette, skewered Amazon on his TV show, encouraging book patrons to shop at other websites. Amazon had enjoyed advocacy among some authors for helping spur sales and deliver greater author royalties, but the dispute eroded good will. Even worse, it called into question the firm's commitment to the customer.[127] The dispute was eventually settled with Hachette continuing to set its own prices for e-books, but gaining additional incentives (presumably in terms of the percentage of revenue it can keep) if it sets lower prices.[128] While Amazon's stated intentions were to lobby for lower e-book prices and hence, benefit the consumer, the short-term negative impact on customers (and authors) continues to raise concerns about power concentration. With Amazon controlling 41 percent of US new book sales and 61 percent of online sales,[129] the firm will need to tread carefully to avoid government inquiry and possible sanctions.

A lawsuit involving Apple and Amazon shows the uncertain terrain when a firm with feared dominance (Amazon) comes up against an oligopoly of suppliers seeking to balance the market by favoring a rival (Apple). Amazon's initial pricing agreement with many e-book publishers was what is often referred to as *wholesale pricing*, where Amazon paid publishers for titles and then sold those books at whatever price it wished. Jeff Bezos has stated that traditional trade books should not be priced at more than ten dollars,[130] and Amazon offered many digital titles near or even below the wholesale price in order to fuel the market for Kindle and cement its own dominant standard. When Apple introduced the iPad, five of the top publishers switched from wholesale pricing to *agency pricing*, where the publisher sets the price and the reseller gets a cut (usually around 30 percent). Agency pricing isn't illegal, but rivals colluding to set prices is. A lawsuit contends that publishers collectively introduce agency pricing to the iOS bookstore and shut out Amazon unless Bezos's firm agreed to switch to agency pricing, too.[131] Apple and the publishers have since settled the case, and Amazon has regained the ability to offer wholesale pricing, but the case shows challenging issues that arise as network effects, switching costs, scale, and standards in the digital world create radical power shifts. And even as publishers allow Amazon to resume wholesale pricing, Apple still has weapons to wield on its own devices. Apple legally charges app developers 30 percent for all revenue earned through in-app purchases, a fee that would further crater Amazon's thin-to-nonexistent margins on many e-books. As a result, Amazon dropped the "purchase" button from iOS Kindle apps. (You can still buy e-books to read in your iOS Kindle app, but you've got to exit the app and do so from the Web, a Kindle, or some other standard that Apple doesn't control).

KEY TAKEAWAYS

- About one-quarter of Amazon revenues come from the sale of media businesses that are rapidly shifting from atoms to bits.
- Moore's Law has allowed Amazon to radically drop the price of Kindle offerings while increasing device functionality.
- Amazon does not make money by selling Kindle hardware; instead it seeks to fuel media and e-commerce sales as well as side businesses such as on-Kindle and in-app advertising.
- It is estimated that 20 percent of Amazon's US customers own at least one Kindle device. The dominance of the platform potentially creates several advantages, including network effects (more Kindle users attract more Kindle-compatible titles and products), switching costs, and user data.
- The firm's Kindle Fire, Fire TV, Echo, and Fire Phone are additional platforms for deliver digital content, sales, and data gathering. These platforms face significant challenges in growing market share, and none has seen the success of the firm's e-book readers.
- Fire TV and Fire Phone have prompted Amazon to accelerate gaming efforts.
- Fire Phone's Firefly feature offers product search, image and symbol recognition, and may be a conduit for the firm to challenge Google, however the Fire Phone's initial launch is largely considered a flop.
- Amazon has upended the publishing value chain and significantly changed the cost structure of the industry.
- Amazon has also become a force in sponsoring original film and video series, creating video game, and has spent over $1 billion in the acquisition of the extremely popular Twitch video game broadcasting service.
- Amazon and partners have also been victims of channel conflict, stopping the sale of Kindles and blocking the sale of books published through Amazon imprints. But when channel conflict occurs, the winner will likely be the channel that offers the greatest aggregate value to its partners.
- Amazon's dominance of publishing, 41 percent of new US book sales and 61 percent of online sales, suggests inordinate market influence. The firm will need to be careful how aggressively it uses its bargaining power, as this could prompt domestic and international regulation and sanctions.

QUESTIONS AND EXERCISES

1. Roughly how big is Amazon's existing "media" business? What is happening to much of the physical media business?

2. Both Amazon and Apple would like you to store books, music, and other media in their "cloud." What critical key strategic advantage comes to a firm when consumers adopt one firm's cloud versus the other?

3. Amazon prices Kindle hardware at or below cost. Conduct research to find out Apple's margins on iPad hardware. How does Amazon make money from the Kindle? Which firm do you think will win the battle for tablet computing? Is it the same firm you think will win the battle for e-readers? Do you think there should be one winner? Why or why not?

4. Why is e-ink useful in an e-reader?

5. What operating system do Fire devices use? How does this impact the firm's network effects from complementary products?

6. Investigate the Amazon Echo online. Would you buy the product? Why or why not? Why will the Echo get 'smarter' and offer more features over time?

7. Why do you suppose Amazon's Fire Phone struggled in its first iteration? Do you think Amazon will ever be successful in Phones? Why not, or what will it take to be successful?

8. What is Firefly, and how might it offer competitive advantage? How does mobile (in general) and Firefly (in particular) change shopping habits?

9. How successful have Kindle e-book readers been? How about Fire tablet, Fire TV, and Fire Phone? What barriers does the firm face in competing? What advantages does Amazon have?

10. How has Kindle pricing changed over time? Would you expect similar changes with Amazon's other consumer electronics products? Why or why not?

11. How does the traditional publishing value chain differ from the Kindle value chain when Amazon is an author's publisher? List the rough percentages of revenue taken by each element in the value chain.

12. If you were an author, would you use Amazon as a publisher or not? What factors would influence this decision? What do you think will happen regarding trends and these factors over time?

13. How is Amazon acting as a hothouse for content creation beyond books? What other categories of media products is Amazon involved in developing? Investigate these—has Amazon done well, or have these products been flops? Does your research suggest why the firm has had success or struggled in various categories?

14. What is channel conflict, and how has Amazon been subject to channel conflict?

15. Is Amazon good or bad for the book business? Explain your answer.

16. What is Twitch? Why did Amazon buy it? Why is it a compelling service for the firm?

17. Why do you suppose Amazon has begun publishing video games? Producing more original video content?

18. Consider the e-book publishing case between Amazon and Apple, as well as the spat between Amazon and Hachette. Research the current state of these disputes and any court rulings. Is Amazon a monopoly? Does Amazon have too much power, and do you think it should be regulated? Is Amazon's pricing "predatory" in a way that unfairly disadvantages would-be competitors? Should Amazon be allowed to continue agency pricing without limitations? Do you think publishers were wrong to work with Apple? What is the current status of this case? (Note: similar cases in the United States and Europe may be at differing stages or have differing outcomes.) Are Amazon's actions with respect to Hachette fair? Do you believe they help or hurt consumers? How might this impact Amazon's brand? The firm's relationship with authors? Come to class prepared to discuss your opinions and findings.

4. AMAZON AND THE CLOUD: FROM PERSONAL STORAGE TO AWS

LEARNING OBJECTIVES

1. Identify several of Amazon's personal cloud offerings, how they are used, and the value they provide both users and Amazon.
2. Understand Amazon's cloud-computing offerings, the services provided, the firms that use AWS, the size of this business, and the firm's vision for its future growth.
3. Recognize why firms use cloud-computing platforms and some of the risks associated with giving up control of certain infrastructure.

Amazon's shift from selling media atoms to selling media bits has led to its expansion into consumer cloud-based offerings that store and serve up digital content over the Internet. It's already been pointed out that the Kindle can load a customer's "virtual bookshelf" and other content on demand, even if you delete purchases from your device. The same is true with Kindle Fire apps. Amazon Cloud Drive offers file storage similar to Dropbox and Google Drive. Amazon Prime users get free, unlimited photo storage in the Amazon cloud. And Amazon Cloud Player will stream music purchases through a Web browser or smartphone app. Amazon has even negotiated rights with major labels, retroactively loading digital copies of a customer's CD and even vinyl record purchases into a customer's Cloud Player account.[132] But Amazon's biggest cloud push comes in offering access to corporate-quality computing as a service.

AWS, or Amazon Web Services, allows firms, and really anyone with a credit card, to rent industrial-strength computing capacity on an as-needed basis. The best-known offerings are Amazon's EC2 (Elastic Computing Cloud), which provides the virtual equivalent of physical computing hardware; and S3 (Simple Storage Service), providing Web-based storage. But AWS provides dozens of service offerings, including various operating systems, database products, enterprise software, programming environments, networking services, and more. Amazon WorkSpaces provides access to fully-functional, remotely served, virtual Windows PCs through the cloud—offered up in a desktop browser window, or even on an iPad or Kindle Fire—for prices ranging from $35 to $75 a month. These kinds of products are great choices for clients that want securely locked down PCs, think call centers and law enforcement. Amazon AppStream is a cloud offering for game developers wanting to use Amazon's massive processing power for rendering complex images and gaming environments, squirting the results down to devices that would not otherwise be able to quickly create complex graphics on their own (think smartphones and tablets).[133] When it comes to AWS cloud offerings it seems the sky's the limit.

For years, big server firms like IBM, HP, and Sun worked at creating a market for so-called utility computing—a rent-not-buy model where consumers paid for technology as needed, similar to how one pays for water or electricity. But in true disruptive form, it wasn't enterprise-class hardware firms but rather a company originally launched as an online bookstore that managed to get real traction in this market. Today AWS powers hundreds of businesses, including Etsy, Airbnb, Pinterest, Yelp, and Zynga. It's Amazon's services that allowed thirteen guys to scale Instagram to tens of millions of users and a billion-dollar acquisition price in just fifteen months. And firms that might consider Amazon as a rival, including Netflix and Dropbox, rely on AWS as well. What's notable is that many of these firms aren't just big firms; they're the *largest* firms in their categories.[134] NASA, Eli Lilly, the New York Times Corporation, and ESPN have all used AWS for key tasks, too. Advantages of using the cloud are outlined in Chapter 14; they include allowing organizations to rent server capacity as needed—scaling up during high demand periods or intensive but short-term projects without having to over-invest in hardware, software, and personnel. And Amazon's deep experience in scalability, security, and fault tolerance are usually far better than a smaller firm could develop on its own. AWS isn't fool proof. Well-known outages have temporarily taken down or dramatically slowed several sites that have used the service, but most don't feel they could do a better job at a better price, even if this means relying on another firm to provide vital resources. Target provides a cautionary tale: The discount retailer had been relying on Amazon to power its website but left in an effort to create its own infrastructure. Three weeks later, an unexpectedly popular Target promotion crashed the firm's website.[135]

AWS was introduced in 2006, although some offerings were available as early as 2002. Google's competing AppEngine wasn't offered until 2008, and Microsoft's Windows Azure cloud platform came out in 2010. There are advantages to moving early as a platform provider. An early lead with a market-serving product creates a big share, customer lock-in, internal learning, and a network effect derived from complementary offerings ranging from the employment base provided by a growing number of

AWS-skilled developers to a rich assortment of software capable of using the platform. Even server providers like Rackspace and HP are playing catch-up with Amazon.[136] They've got a long way to go. Research firm Gartner estimates that "AWS offers five times the utilized compute capacity of the next 14 cloud providers combined!"[137]

AWS is only about seven percent of Amazon's overall revenue, but it is already a multibillion-dollar revenue generator, kicks off about $1 billion in profits, and it's the firm's fastest-growing business.[138] 2015 AWS revenues are estimated to be around $6 billion a year. That's about 10 times larger than Microsoft's Azure cloud business.[139] A Fall 2014 report estimated that Amazon's cloud business earned over seventy times the revenue of Google's corporate cloud.[140] Bezos has stated that he thinks AWS can eventually become as big as Amazon's retail business.[141] Why did Amazon decide to get into this business in the first place? Some have suggested that AWS came out of Amazon's desire to make money from the firm's excess computing capacity, but the firm's CTO has debunked that as a myth and a misconception. The real goal of AWS was to monetize the firm's *expertise* in scalability and reliability and turn this into a revenue-generating business. The benefits of having an entire skilled division of technicians creating reliable, standard platforms that Amazon can then use itself (instead of buying these services from others) is also seen as a key benefit.[142] Building this capacity doesn't come cheap. From 2005 through 2013, Amazon spent $12 billion building out the AWS infrastructure.[143] But long term, Bezos sees the future unfolding, and he wants to rake in billions more, not only by selling you just about everything you need, but also by powering any organization that is willing to farm out computing to the cloud.

KEY TAKEAWAYS

- Amazon offers personal cloud storage options for all forms of media, including books, games, music, and video. It even offers file storage akin to Dropbox and Google Drive. These personal cloud offerings allow users to access files from any app, browser, or device with appropriate access.

- Amazon Web Services (AWS) allows anyone with a credit card to access industrial-strength, scalable computing resources. Services include computing capability, storage, and many operating systems, software development platforms, and enterprise-class applications.

- Firms using cloud providers lose control of certain aspects of their infrastructure, and an error or crash caused by the cloud provider could shut off or scale back vital service availability. Amazon and other vendors have experienced outages that have negatively impacted clients. Despite these challenges, most firms believe they lack resources and scale to do a higher-quality or more cost-effective job than specialized cloud providers.

- AWS and competing cloud services offer several advantages, including increased scalability, reliability, security, lower labor costs, lower hardware costs, and the ability to shift computing from large fixed-cost investments to those with variable costs. Since Amazon also uses products developed by AWS, the firm's e-commerce and Kindle operations also benefit from the effort.

- Bezos believes that Amazon's AWS business can be at least as big as the firm's e-commerce efforts.

QUESTIONS AND EXERCISES

1. What other personal cloud products exist for vendors beyond Amazon?

2. Do you use personal cloud services? Do you use Amazon products, or products provided by rivals? Why have you made these choices regarding cloud platforms?

3. What is AWS, and what services are provided? Investigate online and report back on the costs associated with key services such as EC2 and S3.

4. Consider Amazon WorkSpaces: Why would a firm want a virtual version of Windows served in a browser? How might AWS AppStream help the firm's Fire efforts?

5. Which firms use AWS? What do they gain by using a cloud provider, and what do they give up? How might Amazon or other cloud firms reduce concerns potential and existing clients might have?

6. If there are alternatives available, why would firms that compete with Amazon in some businesses use Amazon anyway?

7. Are network effects at work in cloud platforms? How so? What kinds of complementary products might make AWS seem more attractive than a new cloud computing effort?

8. How big is this business relative to Amazon's other divisions? How big does Amazon think it can get?

9. Why did Amazon decide to get into cloud computing? This business is radically different from shipping books and other physical products. Do you think Amazon should continue to keep AWS as part of Amazon, or should it spin the firm out as a separate company? What would be the advantages to either approach? Search online to see if you can find opinions that analysts or journalists may have regarding AWS's growth prospects in Amazon or as a separate firm, and be prepared to report your findings back to class.

ENDNOTES

1. A. Deutschman, "Inside the Mind of Jeff Bezos," *Fast Company*, August 1, 2004.

2. K. Brooker, "Back to Being Amazon.bomb," *Fortune*, June 26, 2000; J. Martinson, "Amazon.bomb: How the Internet's Biggest Success Story Turned Sour," *Guardian*, June 26, 2000; L. Dignan, "What a Difference a Decade Makes: Barron's Proclaims Amazon Best Retailer," *ZDNet*, March 28, 2009; and D. Alef, *Jeff Bezos and the eBook Revolution* (Titans of Fortune Publishing, February 2011).

3. A. Lashinsky, "Amazon's Jeff Bezos: The Ultimate Disrupter," *Fortune*, November 16, 2012.

4. J. Yarrow, "Chart of the Day: Amazon Has the Best Reputation of Any Company in the U.S.," *Business Insider*, February 12, 2013.

5. T. Carmody, "Surprise! Jeff Bezos Explains to Amazon Investors Why No Profits Are a Good Thing," *Verge*, April 12, 2013.

6. S. Levy, "Jeff Bezos Owns the Web in More Ways than You Think," *Wired*, December 2011.

7. T. Malik, "Jeff Bezos' Blue Origin Launches Private Spaceship Test Flight (Photos, Video)," *Space.com*, April 30, 2015.

8. G. Sandoval, "Amazon's Jeff Bezos Buys *Washington Post* for $250 Million," *The Verge*, August 5, 2013.

9. G. McNeal, "Six Things You Should Know About Amazon's Drones," *Forbes*, July 11, 2014.

10. S. Woo, "What Makes Bezos Tick? A $42 Million Clock, for Starters," *Wall Street Journal*, June 19, 2012.

11. D. Carvajal, "The Other Battle over Browsers; Barnes & Noble and Other On-Line Booksellers Are Poised to Challenge Amazon.com," *New York Times*, March 9, 1998; and R. Brandt, "Birth of a Salesman," *Wall Street Journal*, October 15, 2011.

12. S. Wingo, "Update on Amazon's Fulfillment Center (FC) Network," *ChannelAdvisor*, Sept. 25, 2014. e

13. R. Hof, "Jeff Bezos: How Amazon Web Services Is Just Like the Kindle Business," *Forbes*, November 29, 2012.

14. F. Vogelstein, "Mighty Amazon Jeff Bezos Has Been Hailed as a Visionary and Put Down as a Goofball. He's Proved Critics Wrong by Forging a Winning Management Strategy Built on Brains, Guts, and above All, Numbers," *Fortune*, May 26, 2003.

15. G. Marino, "Geeking Out at Amazon," *Technology Review*, October 15, 2007.

16. F. Vogelstein, "Mighty Amazon Jeff Bezos Has Been Hailed as a Visionary and Put down as a Goofball. He's Proved Critics Wrong by Forging a Winning Management Strategy Built on Brains, Guts, and above All, Numbers," *Fortune*, May 26, 2003.

17. J. Salter, "Behind the Scenes at Amazon's Christmas Warehouse," *Telegraph*, November 13, 2012.

18. H. Hal Bernton and S. Kelleher, "Amazon Warehouse Jobs Push Workers to Physical Limit," *Seattle Times*, April 5, 2012.

19. J. Salter, "Behind the Scenes at Amazon's Christmas Warehouse," *Telegraph*, November 13, 2012.

20. H. Hal Bernton and S. Kelleher, "Amazon Warehouse Jobs Push Workers to Physical Limit," *Seattle Times*, April 5, 2012.

21. H. Hal Bernton and S. Kelleher, "Amazon Warehouse Jobs Push Workers to Physical Limit," *Seattle Times*, April 5, 2012.

22. J. Salter, "Behind the Scenes at Amazon's Christmas Warehouse," *Telegraph*, November 13, 2012.

23. H. Hal Bernton and S. Kelleher, "Amazon Warehouse Jobs Push Workers to Physical Limit," *Seattle Times*, April 5, 2012.

24. H. Hal Bernton and S. Kelleher, "Amazon Warehouse Jobs Push Workers to Physical Limit," *Seattle Times*, April 5, 2012.

25. D. Tam, "Meet Amazon's busiest employee -- the Kiva robot," *CNet*, Nov. 30, 2014.

26. M. Wohlsen, "Amazon Reveals the Robots at the Heart of its Epic Cyber Monday Operation," *Wired*, Dec. 1, 2014.

27. J. Salter, "Behind the Scenes at Amazon's Christmas Warehouse," *Telegraph*, November 13, 2012.

28. D. Tam, "Meet Amazon's busiest employee -- the Kiva robot," *CNet*, Nov. 30, 2014.

29. D. Tam, "Meet Amazon's busiest employee -- the Kiva robot," *CNet*, Nov. 30, 2014.

30. J. Salter, "Behind the Scenes at Amazon's Christmas Warehouse," *Telegraph*, November 13, 2012.

31. J. Salter, "Behind the Scenes at Amazon's Christmas Warehouse," *Telegraph*, November 13, 2012.

32. D. Tam, "Meet Amazon's busiest employee -- the Kiva robot," *CNet*, Nov. 30, 2014.

33. Unattributed, "Meet Amazon's New Robot Army Shipping Out Your Products," *Bloomberg Business*, Dec. 2, 2014.

34. E. Weise, "15,000 robots usher in Amazon's Cyber Monday," *USA Today*, Dec. 2, 2014.

35. D. Tam, "Meet Amazon's busiest employee -- the Kiva robot," *CNet*, Nov. 30, 2014.

36. D. Tam, "Meet Amazon's busiest employee -- the Kiva robot," *CNet*, Nov. 30, 2014.

37. Unattributed, "Meet the Robots Filling Your Cyber Monday Amazon Orders," *Bloomberg Business*, Dec. 1, 2014.

38. M. Wohlsen, "Amazon Reveals the Robots at the Heart of its Epic Cyber Monday Operation," *Wired*, Dec. 1, 2014.

39. M. Wohlsen, "Amazon Reveals the Robots at the Heart of its Epic Cyber Monday Operation," *Wired*, Dec. 1, 2014.

40. M. Wohlsen, "Amazon Reveals the Robots at the Heart of its Epic Cyber Monday Operation," *Wired*, Dec. 1, 2014.

41. S. Dent, "Amazon Prime same-day delivery is now free in 14 cities," *Engadget*, May 28, 2015.

42. J. Salter, "Behind the Scenes at Amazon's Christmas Warehouse," *Telegraph*, November 13, 2012.

43. S. Ng., "Soap Opera: Amazon Moves in with P&G," *Wall Street Journal*, October 14, 2013.

44. C. Loomis, "Amazon's Invisible Innovations," *Fortune*, November 11, 2004.

45. S. Distinguin, "Amazon.com: The Hidden Empire (2013 Update)," *faberNovel*, February 2013.

46. *Forbes*, "The Cash Conversion Cycle," March 10, 2012.

47. Walmart, "Our Locations: Interactive Map," *Walmart*, March 13, 2015, http://corporate.walmart.com/our-story/our-business/locations/.]

48. "Corporate Fact Sheet," *Target*, May 30, 2015, http://pressroom.target.com/corporate.

49. J. McDuling, "No, Amazon is not opening a physical store in New York for the holiday shopping season," *Quartz*, Dec. 3, 2014.

50. M. Wohlsen, "Amazon Takes a Big Step Toward Finally Making Its Own Deliveries," *Wired*, Sept. 25, 2014.

51. L. Whitney, "Amazon courts Purdue students with on-campus delivery center," *CNet*, Feb. 3, 2015.

52. Purdue Amazon Opens, Purdue University YouTube Channel, Feb. 3, 2015.

53. E. Wei, "Amazon, Apple and the Beauty of Lower Margins," *Remains of the Day*, November 28, 2012.

54. E. Wei, "Amazon, Apple and the Beauty of Lower Margins," *Remains of the Day*, November 28, 2012.

55. J. Jannarone, "Retailers Struggle in Amazon's Jungle," *Wall Street Journal*, February 22, 2011. Note: Study assumed no sales tax and free shipping on Amazon, common for purchases totaling $25 or more. The savings compared with Walmart were cut in half for purchases requiring standard shipping.

56. D. Streitfeld, "Amazon Flunks Pricing Test / Sliding Cost Angers Shoppers," *Washington Post*, September 28, 2000.

57. J. Fox, "At Amazon, It's All About the Cash Flow," *Harvard Business Review*, Oct. 20, 2014.

58. B. Evans, "Why Amazon Has No Profits (And Why It Works)," *Ben-Evans.com*, Sept. 5, 2014.

59. T. Green, "Amazon Just Admitted It's Making Less Than You Think," *Time*, Feb. 7, 2015.

60. B. Golden, "Amazon opens up about AWS revenues," *CIO*, May 12, 2015. B. Golden, "Amazon opens up about AWS revenues," *CIO*, May 12, 2015.

61. Adapted from J. Jannarone, "Retailers Struggle in Amazon's Jungle," *Wall Street Journal*, February 22, 2011; and S. Distinguin, "Amazon.com: The Hidden Empire (2013 Update)," *faberNovel*, February 2013.

62. D. Frommer, "10 Amazon Private-Label Products You Didn't Know Existed," *Business Insider*, November 19, 2009.

63. R. Yu, "Report: Amazon to launch private label food items," *USA Today*, May 28, 2015.

64. B. Goldman, "America's Billion-Dollar Advertisers in 2012," *Examiner*, December 30, 2012.

65. C. O'Connor, "Amazon Launches Amazon Business Marketplace, Will Close AmazonSupply," *Forbes*, April 28, 2015.

66. C. O'Connor, "Amazon's Wholesale Slaughter: Jeff Bezos' $8 Trillion B2B Bet," *Forbes*, May 7, 2014.

67. C. O'Connor, "Amazon Launches Amazon Business Marketplace, Will Close AmazonSupply," *Forbes*, April 28, 2015.

68. G. Anders, "Inside Amazon's Idea Machine: How Bezos Decodes the Customer," *Forbes*, April 4, 2012.

69. A. Elliott, "Amazon.com Facts: 10 Things You Didn't Know about the Web's Biggest Retailer," *Mashable*, June 22, 2011.

70. S. Distinguin, "Amazon.com: The Hidden Empire (2013 Update)," *faberNovel*, February 2013.

71. P. Wahba, "This Is the Best Amazon Prime Feature Yet," *Time*, May 28, 2015.

72. M. Wohlsen, "Amazon Prime is one of the Most Bizarre Good Business Ideas Ever," *Wired*, Feb. 19, 2015.

73. B. Molina, "Amazon adds 10M Prime subscribers during holiday," *USA Today*, Dec. 26, 2014.

74. J. Olshan, "The Elephant in Amazon's Mail Room," *MarketWatch*, November 29, 2012.

75. B. Christian, "The A/B Test: Inside the Technology That's Changing the Rules of Business," *Wired*, April 25, 2012.

76. M. Wessel, "How Big Companies Should Innovate," *Harvard Business Review Blog Network*, October 1, 2012.

77. R. Brandt, "Birth of a Salesman," *Wall Street Journal*, October 15, 2011.

78. B. Eisenberg, "Hidden Secrets of the Amazon Shopping Cart," *FutureNow*, February 26, 2008.

79. J. Salter, "Behind the Scenes at Amazon's Christmas Warehouse," *Telegraph*, November 13, 2012.

80. M. Marshall, "Aggregate Knowledge raises $5M from Kleiner, on a roll," *VentureBeat*, Dec. 10, 2006.

81. M. Learmonth, "Amazon: The Quietest Big Ad Business in Tech Would Like Your Brand Ads, Too," *AdAge*, April 11, 2013.

82. I. Steiner, "Amazon Sellers Achieve 40 Percent Unit Growth in Q4 2012," *eCommerce Bytes*, January 30, 2013.

83. C. Anderson, "The Long Tail," *Wired*, October 2004.

84. C. Anderson, "The Long Tail," *Wired*, October 2004.

85. A. Hines, "Amazon's Quidsi Lures Shoppers Online to Buy the Basics from Diapers to Pet Food," *Huffington Post*, September 28, 2012.

86. S. Lacy, "Amazon Buys Zappos, the Price Is $928 Million, Not $847 Million," *TechCrunch*, July 22, 2009.

87. F. Manjoo, "I Want It Today," *Slate*, July 11, 2012.

88. A. Lashansky, "In the Standoff between Amazon and Hachette, the Customer Comes Last," *Fortune*, May 27, 2014.

89. J. O'Toole, "Amazon Continues Assault on PayPal," *CNNMoney*, June 9, 2014.

90. J. Herman, "Kindle Outsells Every Other Product on Amazon (and What That Really Means)," *Gizmodo*, November 30, 2009.

91. J. Del Rey, "The Amazon Kindle Numbers that Jeff Bezos Must Really Care About," *AllThingsD*, December 12, 2013.

92. J. Yarow, "Amazon Is Not Doing a $99 Table, Despite Rumors," *Business Insider*, March 20, 2013.

93. J. Paczkowski, "Amazon Makes More than $100 off Each Kindle Fire," *AllThingsD*, January 19, 2012.

94. K. Auletta, "Publish or Perish," *New Yorker*, April 20, 2010; "Amazon Selling More Kindle Ebooks than Print Books," *BBC News*, August 8, 2012; and S. Malik, "Kindle Ebook Sales Have Overtaken Amazon Print Sales, Says Book Seller," *Guardian*, August 5, 2012.

95. *BBC News*, "Amazon Selling More Kindle Ebooks than Print Books," August 8, 2012.

96. Q. Forttrell, "10 Things that Amazon Won't Tell You," *SmartMoney*, June 26, 2012.

97. M. Wood, "Expressway to Amazon in a Box," *New York Times*, April 6, 2014.

98. M. Wood, "Expressway to Amazon in a Box," *New York Times*, April 6, 2014.

99. M. Dornbusch, "Amazon Echo review," *The Gadgeteer*, May 31, 2015.

100. D. Gewirtz, "Amazon Echo talks to Google Calendar (and you)," *ZDNet*, June 1, 2015.

101. J. Van Sack, "Booting Up: Echo listens so Amazon can learn everything about you," *The Boston Herald*, May 26, 2015.

102. D. Streitfeld, "With an Amazon Smartphone, the Retailer Seeks a Tether to Consumers," *New York Times*, June 15, 2014.

103. I. Lapowsky, "The Hidden Agenda of Amazon's New Phone," *Wired*, June 19, 2014.

104. A. Carr, "The Real Story Behind Jeff Bezos's Fire Phone Debacle and What it Mans for Amazon's Future," *FastCompany*, February 2015.

105. M. Sullivan, "A new Amazon Fire phone is in the works, but don't expect it in 2015," *VentureBeat*, Dec. 18, 2015.

106. A. Losowsky, "DRM Lawsuit Filed by Independent Bookstores against Amazon, 'Big Six' Publishers," *Huffington Post*, February 20, 2013.

107. F. Manjoo, "Don't Support Your Local Bookseller," *Slate*, December 13, 2011.

108. B. Stone, "Amazon's Hit Man," *BusinessWeek*, January 25, 2012.

109. B. Stone, "Why the Amazon Naysayers Should Be Scared," *BusinessWeek*, April 27, 2012.

110. D. Melanson, "Amazon Game Studios Releases Its First Mobile Game, Air Patriots, for iOS, Android, and Kindle Fire," *Engadget*, November 1, 2012.

111. C. Kohler, "Hands-on with Amazon's Fire TV, the Tiny Console that Could Transform Gaming," *Wired*, April 9, 2014.

112. J. D'Onfro, "Amazon Paid $300 Million for HBO's Old Shows," Business Insider, April 24, 2014.

113. P. Kafka, "Netflix CEO: Amazon Losing Up to $1 Billion a Year on Streaming Video," AllThingsD, November 16, 2012.

114. S. Levy, "Jeff Bezos Owns the Web in More Ways than You Think," Wired, December 2011.

115. J. Mitchell, "Amazon Studios Unveils 14 Pilots Online, Wants User Feedback to Determine Which Go to Series," Entertainment Weekly, April 19, 2013.

116. L. Sumagaysay, "Amazon to make movies for theaters, then streaming," *San Jose Mercury News*, Jan. 19, 2015.

117. N. Wingfield, "What's Twitch? Gamers Know, and Amazon Is Spending $1 Billion on It," *The New York Times*, Aug. 25, 2014.

118. D. Macmillan and G. Bensinger, "Amazon to Buy Twitch Video Site for $970 Million, *The Wall Street Journal*, Aug. 26, 2014.

119. N. Wingfield, "What's Twitch? Gamers Know, and Amazon Is Spending $1 Billion on It," *The New York Times*, Aug. 25, 2014.

120. D. Macmillan and G. Bensinger, "Amazon to Buy Twitch Video Site for $970 Million, *The Wall Street Journal*, Aug. 26, 2014.

121. N. Krug, "Amazon Finds Its Books Aren't Welcome at Many Bookstores," *Washington Post*, October 30, 2012.

122. L. Hazard Owen, "Following Target, Walmart Stops Selling Kindles," *GigaOM*, September 20, 2012.

123. D. Streitfeld, "Bookstores Drop Comics after Amazon Deal with DC," *New York Times*, October 18, 2011.

124. J. Gallaugher, "E-Commerce and the Undulating Distribution Channel," *Communications of the ACM* 45, no. 7 (July 2002).

125. B. Gladstone, "Is Amazon a New Monopoly?" *NPR's on the Media*, April 20, 2012.

126. B. Stelter, "Latest Victim of Amazon-Hachette Fight: J. K. Rowling," *CNNMoney*, June 19, 2014.

127. A. Lashansky, "In the Standoff between Amazon and Hachette, the Customer Comes Last," *Fortune*, May 27, 2014.

128. J. Trachtenberg and G. Bensinger, "Amazon, Hachette End Publishing Dispute," *The Wall Street Journal*, Nov. 13, 2014.

129. J. Milliot, "BEA 2014: Can Anyone Compete with Amazon?" *Publishers Weekly*, May 28, 2014.

130. S. Levy, "Jeff Bezos Owns the Internet in More Ways than You Think," *Wired*, November 13, 2011.

131. I. Luden, "Penguin Settles with the EU on Apple E-Book Pricing Case to 'Clear the Decks' for Random House Merger," *TechCrunch*, April 19, 2013; and B. Proffitt, "EBook Settlement Big Win for Amazon & Consumers," *ReadWrite*, September 7, 2012.

132. C. Warren, "Amazon Will Give You Free MP3s of Your Vinyl Record Purchases," *Mashable*, April 3, 2013.

133. Q. Hardy, "Amazon Web Services Gets Personal and Pretty," *New York Times*, November 14, 2013.

134. R. McMillan, "Why Amazon Hired a Car Mechanic to Run Its Cloud Empire," *Wired*, February 19, 2013.

135. S. Clifford, "Demand at Target for Fashion Line Crashes Site," *New York Times*, September 13, 2011.

136. S. Levy, "Jeff Bezos Owns the Web in More Ways than You Think," *Wired*, December 2011.

137. M. Asay, "Gartner: AWS Now Five Times the Size of Other Cloud Vendors Combined," *ReadWrite*, August 21, 2013.

138. L. Sun, "3 Things We Learned About Amazon.com Inc.'s Cloud Business," *The Motley Fool*, April 30, 2015.

139. L. Columbus, "Sizing Microsoft Azure And AWS Revenue," *Forbes*, April 15, 2015.

140. B. Butler, "How much bigger is Amazon's cloud vs. Microsoft and Google?" *NetworkWorld*, Oct. 24, 2014.

141. Deloitte, "Scaling the Edges: Amazon Case Study," http://www.deloitte.com/view/en_US/us/Industries/technology/e801d11accab9310VgnVCM2000001b56f00aRCRD.htm (accessed April 24, 2013).

142. A. Hesseldahl, "Should Amazon Spin Out Its Cloud Services?" *AllThingsD*, February 11, 2013.

143. M. Asay, "Gartner: AWS Now Five Times the Size of Other Cloud Vendors Combined," *ReadWrite*, August 21, 2013.

CHAPTER 8

Understanding Network Effects: Strategies for Competing in a Platform-Centric, Winner-Take-All World

1. INTRODUCTION

1. Define network effects.
2. Recognize products and services that are subject to network effects.
3. Understand the factors that add value to products and services subject to network effects.

Network effects are sometimes referred to as "Metcalfe's Law" or "network externalities." But don't let the dull names fool you—this concept is rocket fuel for technology firms. Bill Gates leveraged network effects to turn Windows and Office into virtual monopolies and, in the process, became the wealthiest man in America. Mark Zuckerberg of Facebook; Sergey Brin and Larry Page of Google; Pierre Omidyar of eBay; Kevin Systrom of Instagram; Jack Dorsey, Evan Williams and Biz Stone of Twitter; Nik Zennström and Janus Friis of Skype; Steve Chen and Chad Hurley of YouTube; Jan Koum and Brian Acton of WhatsApp; Evan Spiegel of SnapChat; Travis Kalanick of Uber; and the Airbnb triumvirate of Brian Chesky, Joe Gebbia, and Nathan Blecharczy—all these entrepreneurs have built massive user bases by leveraging the concept. When network effects are present, *the value of a product or service increases as the number of users grows.* Simply, more users = more value. Of course, most products aren't subject to network effects; you probably don't care if someone wears the same socks, uses the same pancake syrup, or buys the same trash bags as you. But when network effects are present, they're among *the most important* reasons you'll pick one product or service over another. You may care very much, for example, if others are part of your social network, if your video game console is popular, and if the Wikipedia article you're referencing has had previous readers. And all those folks who bought HD DVD players sure were bummed when the rest of the world declared Blu-ray the winner. In each of these examples, network effects are at work.

Network effects

Also known as Metcalfe's Law, or network externalities. When the value of a product or service increases as its number of users expands.

Not *That* Kind of Network

The term "network" sometimes stumps people when first learning about network effects. In this context, a network doesn't refer to the physical wires or wireless systems that connect pieces of electronics. It just refers to a common user base that is able to communicate and share with one another. So Facebook users make up a network. So do owners of Blu-ray players, traders that buy and sell stock over the NASDAQ, or the sum total of hardware and outlets that support the BS 1363 electrical standard.

KEY TAKEAWAY

- Network effects are among the most powerful strategic resources that can be created by technology-based innovation. Many category-dominating organizations and technologies, including Microsoft, Apple, NASDAQ, eBay, Facebook, and Visa, owe their success to network effects. Network effects are also behind the establishment of most standards, including Blu-ray, Wi-Fi, and Bluetooth.

QUESTIONS AND EXERCISES

1. What are network effects? What are the other names for this concept?
2. List several products or services subject to network effects. What factors do you believe helped each of these efforts achieve dominance?
3. Which firm do you suspect has stronger end-user network effects: Google's online search tool or Microsoft's Windows operating system? Why?
4. Network effects are often associated with technology, but tech isn't a prerequisite for the existence of network effects. Name a product, service, or phenomenon that is not related to information technology that still dominates due to network effects.

2. WHERE DOES ALL THAT VALUE COME FROM?

LEARNING OBJECTIVES

1. Identify the three primary sources of value for network effects.
2. Recognize factors that contribute to the staying power and complementary benefits of a product or service subject to network effects.
3. Understand how firms like Microsoft and Apple each benefit from strong network effects.

The value derived from network effects comes from three sources: exchange, staying power, and complementary benefits.

2.1 Exchange

Facebook for one person isn't much fun, and the first guy in the world with a fax machine didn't have much more than a paperweight. But as each new Facebook friend or fax user comes online, a network becomes more valuable because its users can potentially communicate with more people. These examples show the importance of *exchange* in creating value. Every product or service subject to network effects fosters some kind of exchange. For firms leveraging technology, this might include anything you can represent in the ones and zeros of digital storage, such as messaging, movies, music, money, video games, and computer programs. And just about any standard that allows things to plug into one another, interconnect, or otherwise communicate will live or die based on its ability to snare network effects.

Exercise: Graph It

Some people refer to network effects by the name Metcalfe's Law. It got this name when, toward the start of the dot-com boom, Bob Metcalfe (the inventor of the Ethernet networking standard) wrote a column in *InfoWorld* magazine stating that the value of a network equals its number of users squared. What do you think of this formula? Graph the law with the vertical axis labeled "value" and the horizontal axis labeled "users." Do you think the graph is an accurate representation of what's happening in network effects? If so, why? If not, what do you think the graph really looks like?

2.2   Staying Power

Users don't want to buy a product or sign up for a service that's likely to go away, and a number of factors can halt the availability of an effort: a firm could go bankrupt or fail to attract a critical mass of user support, or a rival may successfully invade its market and draw away current customers. Networks with greater numbers of users suggest a stronger **staying power**. The staying power, or long-term viability, of a product or service is particularly important for consumers of technology products. Consider that when someone buys a personal computer and makes a choice of Windows, Mac OS, or Linux, their investment over time usually greatly exceeds the initial price paid for the operating system. A user invests in learning how to use a system, buying and installing software, entering preferences or other data, creating files—all of which means that if a product isn't supported anymore, much of this investment is lost.

The concept of staying power (and the fear of being stranded in an unsupported product or service) is directly related to **switching costs** (the cost a consumer incurs when moving from one product to another) and switching costs can strengthen the value of network effects as a strategic asset. The higher the value of the user's overall investment, the more they're likely to consider the staying power of any offering before choosing to adopt it. Similarly, the more a user has invested in a product, the less likely he or she is to leave. Considering e-book readers? A user aware of Barnes & Noble's struggles might think twice about choosing the Nook over Amazon's thriving and dominant Kindle.

Switching costs also go by other names. You might hear the business press refer to products (particularly Web sites) as being "sticky" or creating "friction." Others may refer to the concept of "lock-in." And the elite Boston Consulting Group is really talking about a firm's switching costs when it refers to how well a company can create customers who are "barnacles" (that are tightly anchored to the firm) and not "butterflies" (that flutter away to rivals). The more friction available to prevent users from migrating to a rival, the greater the switching costs. And in a competitive market where rivals with new innovations show up all the time, that can be a very good thing!

staying power

The long-term viability of a product or service.

switching costs

The cost a consumer incurs when moving from one product to another. It can involve actual money spent (e.g., buying a new product) as well as investments in time, any data loss, and so forth.

TCO [Total Cost of Ownership]

An economic measure of the full cost of owning a product (typically computing hardware and/or software). TCO includes direct costs such as purchase price, plus indirect costs such as training, support, and maintenance.

Complementary benefits

Products or services that add additional value to the primary product or service that makes up a network.

How Important are Switching Costs to Microsoft?

"It is this switching cost that has given our customers the patience to stick with Windows through all our mistakes, our buggy drivers, our high **TCO [Total Cost of Ownership]***, our lack of a sexy vision at times, and many other difficulties [...] Customers constantly evaluate other desktop platforms, [but] it would be so much work to move over that they hope we just improve Windows rather than force them to move. [...] In short, without this exclusive franchise [meaning Windows] we would have been dead a long time ago."*

– Comments from a Microsoft General Manager in a memo to Bill Gates[1]

2.3   Complementary Benefits

Complementary benefits are those products or services that add additional value to the network. These products might include "how-to" books, software, and feature add-ons, even labor. You'll find more books about auctioning that focus on eBay, more video cameras that upload to YouTube, and more accountants who know Excel than other rival software. Why? Book authors, camera manufacturers, and accountants invest their time and resources where they're likely to reach the biggest market and get the greatest benefit. In auctions, video, and spreadsheet software, eBay, YouTube, and Excel each dwarf their respective competition.

platforms

Products and services that allow for the development and integration of software products and other complementary goods. Windows, the iPhone, the Wii, and the standards that allow users to create Facebook apps are all platforms.

APIs

Programming hooks, or guidelines, published by firms that tell other programs how to get a service to perform a task such as send or receive data. For example, Amazon provides application programming interfaces (APIs) to let developers write their own applications and Web sites that can send the firm orders.

Products and services that encourage others to offer complementary goods are sometimes called **platforms**.[2] Many firms do this by providing **APIs** or Application Programming Interfaces that allow third parties to integrate with their products and services. Allowing other firms to contribute to your platform can be a brilliant strategy because those firms will spend *their* time and money to enhance *your* offerings. Consider the billion-dollar hardware ecosystem that Apple has cultivated around iOS products. There are over ninety brands selling some 280 models of speaker systems.[3] Apple has begun to extend iOS into all sorts of products. CarPlay puts Siri on your steering wheel and allows auto manufacturers to integrate phone, maps, messaging, music, and other apps into automobile dashboards. Eighteen auto manufacturers from Ford to Ferrari committed to CarPlay at launch, and many more have been added since then. HealthKit allows Apple to use iOS as a platform for exercise and personal health measurement (products and services that measure fitness and health are sometimes referred to by the term "quantified self"), and HomeKit allows iOS to control home products including locks, lighting, and thermostats. Apple's CloudKit allows developers to plug into Apple's storage, hopefully creating greater bonds with iOS at the center instead of choosing rival storage platforms from Dropbox, Google, Microsoft, or others. AirPlay links Macs, iOS devices, and AppleTV. AppleWatch is designed as a tool that integrates and extends the iPhone. And ApplePay makes iOS platforms all the more valuable by integrating payments. Each add-on enhances the value of choosing iOS over rival platforms. Software-based ecosystems can grow very quickly. Less than one year after its introduction, the iTunes App Store boasted over fifty thousand applications, collectively downloaded over 1 billion times. Today, well over 1.2 million iOS apps have been downloaded over 75 billion times, collectively.[4]

Video of Apple's CarPlay in action

View the video online at: http://www.youtube.com/v/TQz64rhefqY

These three value-adding sources—*exchange, staying power,* and *complementary benefits*—often work together to reinforce one another in a way that makes the network effect even stronger. When users *exchanging* information attract more users, they can also attract firms offering *complementary* products. When developers of complementary products invest time writing software—and users install, learn, and customize these products—switching costs are created that enhance the *staying power* of a given network. From a strategist's perspective this can be great news for dominant firms in markets where network effects exist. The larger your network, the more difficult it becomes for rivals to challenge your leadership position.[5]

KEY TAKEAWAYS

- Products and services subject to network effects get their value from exchange, perceived staying power, and complementary products and services. Tech firms and services that gain the lead in these categories often dominate all rivals.
- Many firms attempt to enhance their network effects by creating a platform for the development of third-party products and services that enhance the primary offering.

QUESTIONS AND EXERCISES

1. What are the factors that contribute to the value created by network effects?

2. Why is staying power particularly important to many technology products and services?

3. Think about the kinds of technology products that you own that are subject to network effects. What sorts of exchange do these products leverage (e.g., information, money, software, or other media)?

4. Think about the kinds of technology projects you own. What sorts of switching costs are inherent in each of these? Are these strong switching costs or weak switching costs? What would it take for you to leave one of these services and use a rival? How might a competitor try to lessen these switching costs to persuade you to adopt their product?

5. Which other terms are sometimes used to describe the phenomenon of switching costs?

6. Think about the kinds of technology products that you own that are subject to network effects. What sorts of complementary benefits are available for these products? Are complementary benefits strong or weak (meaning, do people choose the product primarily based on these benefits, or for some other reason)?

7. Identify firms that you believe have built a strong platform. Can you think of firms that have tried to develop a platform, but have been less successful? Why do you suppose they have struggled?

3. ONE-SIDED OR TWO-SIDED MARKETS?

LEARNING OBJECTIVES

1. **Recognize and distinguish between one-sided and two-sided markets.**
2. **Understand same-side and cross-side exchange benefits.**

3.1 Understanding Network Structure

To understand the key sources of network value, it's important to recognize the structure of the network. Some networks derive most of their value from a single class of users. An example of this kind of network is instant messaging (IM). While there might be some add-ons for the most popular IM tools, they don't influence most users' choice of an IM system. You pretty much choose one IM tool over another based on how many of your contacts you can reach. Economists would call IM a **one-sided market** (a market that derives most of its value from a single class of users), and the network effects derived from IM users attracting more IM users as being **same-side exchange benefits** (benefits derived by interaction among members of a single class of participant).

one-sided market

A market that derives most of its value from a single class of users (e.g., instant messaging).

same-side exchange benefits

Benefits derived by interaction among members of a single class of participant (e.g., the exchange value when increasing numbers of IM users gain the ability to message each other).

two-sided market

Network markets comprised of two distinct categories of participant, both of which that are needed to deliver value for the network to work (e.g., video game console owners and developers of video games).

cross-side exchange benefit

When an increase in the number of users on one side of the market (console owners, for example) creates a rise in the other side (software developers).

But some markets are comprised of two distinct categories of network participant. Consider video games. People buy a video game console largely based on the number of really great games available for the system. Software developers write games based on their ability to reach the greatest number of paying customers, so they're most likely to write for the most popular consoles first. Economists would call this kind of network a **two-sided market** (network markets comprised of two distinct categories of participant, both of which that are needed to deliver value for the network to work). When an increase in the number of users on one side of the market (console owners, for example) creates a rise in the other side (software developers), that's called a **cross-side exchange benefit**.

The Positive Feedback Loop of Network Effects: One-Sided, Two-Sided, and Sometimes a Bit of Both

Messaging is considered a one-sided market (or one-sided network), where the value-creating, positive-feedback loop of network effects comes mostly from same-side benefits from a single group (messaging members who attract other members who want to communicate with them). Mobile payment efforts like Square, Apple Pay, and Android Pay, however, are considered to be two-sided markets, where significant benefits come from two distinct classes of users that add value by attracting each other. In the case of mobile payments, the more people that use a given payment platform, the more attractive that platform will be to storefronts and other businesses, and if more businesses accept these forms of mobile payment, then this in turn should attract more end consumers (and so on). Jumpstarting a two-sided network can be tricky. Square has partnered with Starbucks, which brings lots of Square-accepting coffee shops that Square hopes will prompt consumers to use the firm's payment app. (The problem is, Starbucks had its own highly successful mobile app launched prior to the Square deal, and few customers seem ready to switch.) Google hopes that its presence on Android and its ad relationship with many retailers will help it jumpstart Android Pay–accepting merchant adoption. iTunes and the App store helped Apple have over 800 million credit cards on file at the launch of Apple Pay for iOS.[6] And Walmart, BestBuy, and Target are among big-name retailers pooling their collective store footprint to introduce yet another mobile payment mechanism.

It's also possible that a network may have both same-side and cross-side benefits, too. Microsoft's Xbox benefits from cross-side benefits in that more users of that console attract more developers writing more software titles and vice versa. However, the Xbox Live network that allows users to play against each other has same-side benefits. If your buddies use Xbox Live and you want to play against them, you're more likely to buy an Xbox.

KEY TAKEAWAYS

- In one-sided markets, users gain benefits from interacting with a similar category of users (think instant messaging, where everyone can send and receive messages to and from one another).
- In two-sided markets, users gain benefits from interacting with a separate, complementary class of users (e.g., in the mobile-payment business, payment app–wielding consumers are attracted to a platform because there are more merchants offering convenient payment, while merchants are attracted to a payment system that others will actually use and that yields clear benefits over cash).

QUESTIONS AND EXERCISES

1. What is the difference between same-side exchange benefits and cross-side exchange benefits?
2. What is the difference between a one-sided market and a two-sided market?
3. Give examples of one-sided and two-sided markets.
4. Identify examples of two-sided markets where both sides pay for a product or service. Identify examples where only one side pays. What factors determine who should pay? Does paying have implications for the establishment and growth of a network effect? What might a firm do to encourage early network growth?
5. The Apple iOS Developer Program provides developers access to the App Store where they can distribute their free or commercial applications to millions of iPad, iPhone and iPod touch customers. Would the iPhone market be considered a one or two-sided market? Why?

4.   HOW ARE THESE MARKETS DIFFERENT?

LEARNING OBJECTIVES

1. Understand how competition in markets where network effects are present differ from competition in traditional markets.
2. Understand the reasons why it is so difficult for late-moving, incompatible rivals to compete in markets where a dominant, proprietary standard is present.

When network effects play a starring role, competition in an industry can be fundamentally different than in conventional, nonnetwork industries.

First, network markets experience *early, fierce competition*. The positive-feedback loop inherent in network effects—where the biggest networks become even bigger—causes this. Firms are very aggressive in the early stages of these industries because once a leader becomes clear, *bandwagons* form, and new adopters begin to overwhelmingly favor the leading product over rivals, tipping the market in favor of one dominant firm or standard. This tipping can be remarkably swift. Once the majority of major studios and retailers began to back Blu-ray over HD DVD, the latter effort folded within weeks.

These markets are also often winner-take-all or winner-take-most, *exhibiting monopolistic tendencies* where one firm dominates all rivals. Look at all of the examples listed so far—in nearly every case the dominant player has a market share well ahead of all competitors. When, during the U.S. Microsoft antitrust trial, Judge Thomas Penfield Jackson declared Microsoft to be a **monopoly** (a market where there are many buyers but only one dominant seller), the collective response should have been "of course." Why? The *natural state* of markets where strong network effects are present (and this includes operating systems and Office software) is for there to be one major player. Since bigger networks offer more value, they can charge customers more. Firms with a commanding network effects advantage may also enjoy substantial bargaining power over partners. For example, Apple, which controls over 75 percent of digital music sales, for years was able to dictate song pricing, despite the tremendous protests of the record labels.[7] In fact, Apple's stranglehold was so strong that it leveraged bargaining power even though the "Big Four" record labels (Universal, Sony, EMI, and Warner) were themselves an **oligopoly** (a market dominated by a small number of powerful sellers) that together provide over 85 percent of music sold in the United States.

Finally, it's important to note that the best product or service doesn't always win. PlayStation 2 dominated the original Xbox in a prior generation's game console war, despite the fact that nearly every review claimed the Xbox was hands-down a more technically superior machine. Why were users willing to choose an inferior product (PS2) over a superior one (Xbox)? The power of network effects! PS2 had more users, which attracted more developers offering more games.

monopoly

A market where there are many buyers but only one dominant seller.

oligopoly

A market dominated by a small number of powerful sellers.

FIGURE 8.1

Battling a leader with network effects is tough.[8]

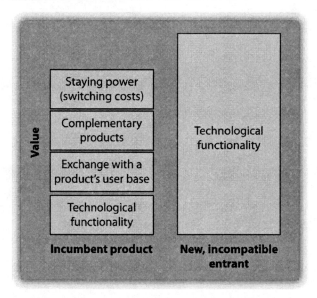

technological leapfrogging

Competing by offering a new technology that is so superior to existing offerings that the value overcomes the total resistance that older technologies might enjoy via exchange, switching cost, and complementary benefits.

This last note is a critical point to any newcomer wishing to attack an established rival. Winning customers away from a dominant player in a network industry isn't as easy as offering a product or service that is better. Any product that is incompatible with the dominant network has to exceed the value of the technical features of the leading player, plus (since the newcomer likely starts without any users or third-party product complements) the value of the incumbent's exchange, switching cost, and complementary product benefit (see Figure 8.1). And the incumbent must not be able to easily copy any of the newcomer's valuable new innovations; otherwise the dominant firm will quickly match any valuable improvements made by rivals. As such, **technological leapfrogging**, or competing by offering a superior generation of technology, can be really tough.[9]

Is This Good for Innovation?

Critics of firms that leverage proprietary standards for market dominance often complain that network effects are bad for innovation. But this statement isn't entirely true. While network effects limit competition *against* the dominant standard, innovation *within* a standard may actually blossom. Consider Windows. Microsoft has a huge advantage in the desktop operating system market, so few rivals try to compete with it. Apple's Mac OS and the open source Linux operating system are the firm's only credible rivals, and both have tiny market shares. But the dominance of Windows is a magnet for developers to innovate within the standard. Programmers with novel ideas are willing to make the investment in learning to write software for Windows because they're sure that a Windows version can be used by the overwhelming majority of computer users.

By contrast, look at the mess we initially had in the mobile phone market. With so many different handsets containing differing computing hardware, offering different screen sizes, running different software, having different key layouts, and working on different carrier networks, writing a game that's accessible by the majority of users is nearly impossible. Glu Mobile, a maker of online games, launched fifty-six reengineered builds of Monopoly to satisfy the diverse requirements of just one telecom carrier.[10] As a result, entrepreneurs with great software ideas for the mobile market were deterred because writing, marketing, and maintaining multiple product versions is both costly and risky. It wasn't until Apple's iPhone arrived, offering developers both a huge market and a consistent set of development standards, that third-party software development for mobile phones really took off. The fact that there are many different Android devices with different hardware specs running different versions of Google's mobile operating system also creates a challenge for developers. Hong Kong mobile app developer Animoca does quality assurance testing with about four hundred Android devices on every app the firm offers.[11]

FIGURE 8.2 Innovation in Fractured Standards

Because Android runs on so many different devices using various versions of the OS, game developers like Hong Kong-based Animoca test each product released on as many as four hundred devices.

Source: TechCrunch, http://techcrunch.com/2012/05/11/this-is-what-developing-for-android-looks-like/.

KEY TAKEAWAYS

- Unseating a firm that dominates with network effects can be extremely difficult, especially if the newcomer is not compatible with the established leader. Newcomers will find their technology will need to be so good that it must leapfrog not only the value of the established firm's tech, but also the perceived stability of the dominant firm, the exchange benefits provided by the existing user base, and the benefits from any product complements. For evidence, just look at how difficult it's been for rivals to unseat the dominance of Windows.
- Because of this, network effects might limit the number of rivals that challenge a dominant firm. But the establishment of a dominant standard may actually encourage innovation within the standard, since firms producing complements for the leader have faith the leader will have staying power in the market.

QUESTIONS AND EXERCISES

1. How is competition in markets where network effects are present different from competition in traditional markets?
2. What are the reasons it is so difficult for late-moving, incompatible rivals to compete in markets where a dominant, proprietary standard is present? What is technological leapfrogging and why is it so difficult to accomplish?
3. Does it make sense to try to prevent monopolies in markets where network effects exist?
4. Are network effects good or bad for innovation? Explain.
5. What is the relationship between network effects and the bargaining power of participants in a network effects "ecosystem"?
6. Cite examples where the best technology did not dominate a network effects-driven market.

5. COMPETING WHEN NETWORK EFFECTS MATTER

LEARNING OBJECTIVES

1. **Plot strategies for competing in markets where network effects are present, both from the perspective of the incumbent firm and the new market entrant.**
2. **Give examples of how firms have leveraged these strategies to compete effectively.**

Why do you care whether networks are one-sided, two-sided, or some sort of hybrid? Well, when crafting your plan for market dominance, it's critical to know if network effects exist, how strong they might be, where they come from, and how they might be harnessed to your benefit. Here's a quick rundown of the tools at your disposal when competing in the presence of network effects.

Strategies for Competing in Markets with Network Effects (Examples in Parentheses)

- Move early (Yahoo! Auctions in Japan).
- Subsidize product adoption (PayPal).
- Leverage viral promotion (Skype, WhatsApp, Facebook and Twitter feeds, Uber).
- Expand by redefining the market to bring in new categories of users (Nintendo Wii). or through convergence (iPhone).
- Form alliances and partnerships (NYCE vs. Citibank).
- Establish distribution channels (Java with Netscape; Microsoft bundling Media Player with Windows).
- Seed the market with complements (Blu-ray; Nintendo; thredUp).
- Encourage the development of complementary goods—this can include offering resources, subsidies, reduced fees, market research, development kits, venture capital (Facebook fbFund).
- Maintain backward compatibility (Apple's Mac OS X Rosetta translation software for PowerPC to Intel).
- For rivals, be compatible with larger networks (Apple's move to Intel; Live Search Maps).

- For incumbents, constantly innovate to create a moving target and block rival efforts to access your network (Apple's efforts to block access to its own systems).
- For large firms with well-known followers, make preannouncements (Microsoft).

5.1 Move Early

In the world of network effects, this is a biggie. Being first allows your firm to start the network effects snowball rolling in your direction. In Japan, worldwide auction leader eBay showed up just five months after Yahoo! launched its Japanese auction service. But eBay was never able to mount a credible threat and ended up pulling out of the market. Being just five months late cost eBay billions in lost sales, and the firm eventually retreated, acknowledging it could never unseat Yahoo!'s network effects lead.

Another key lesson from the loss of eBay Japan? Exchange depends on the ability to communicate! EBay's huge network effects in the United States and elsewhere didn't translate to Japan because most Japanese aren't comfortable with English, and most English speakers don't know Japanese. The language barrier made Japan a "greenfield" market with no dominant player, and Yahoo!'s early move provided the catalyst for victory.

Timing is often critical in the video game console wars, too. Sony's PlayStation 2 enjoyed an eighteen-month lead over the technically superior Xbox (as well as Nintendo's GameCube). That time lead helped to create what for years was the single most profitable division at Sony. By contrast, the technically superior PS3 showed up months after Xbox 360 and at roughly the same time as the Nintendo Wii, and has struggled in its early years, racking up multibillion-dollar losses for Sony.[12]

What If Microsoft Threw a Party and No One Showed Up?

Microsoft launched the Zune media player with features that should be subject to network effects—the ability to share photos and music by wirelessly "squirting" content to other Zune users. The firm even promoted Zune with the tagline "Welcome to the Social." Problem was the Zune Social was a party no one wanted to attend. The late-arriving Zune garnered a market share of just 3 percent, and users remained hard pressed to find buddies to leverage these neat social features.[13] A cool idea does not make a network effect happen.

5.2 Subsidize Adoption

Starting a network effect can be tough—there's little incentive to join a network if there's no one in the system to communicate with. In one admittedly risky strategy, firms may offer to subsidize initial adoption in hopes that network effects might kick in shortly after. Subsidies to adopters might include a price reduction, rebate, or other giveaways. PayPal, a service that allows users to pay one another using credit cards, gave users a modest rebate as a sign-up incentive to encourage adoption of its new effort (in one early promotion, users got back fifteen dollars when spending their first thirty dollars). This brief subsidy paid to early adopters paid off handsomely. EBay later tried to enter the market with a rival effort, but as a late mover its effort was never able to overcome PayPal's momentum. PayPal was eventually purchased by eBay for $1.5 billion, and the business unit is now considered one of eBay's key drivers of growth and profit.

Gilt Groupe, a high-end fashion flash deals site, used subsidies to increase adoption of the firm's mobile app "Gilt on the Go"—fueling the growth of a new and vital distribution channel. Gilt knew that getting its app into the purses and pockets of more of its users would increase the chance that a customer would view more deals and act on them. To encourage mobile owners to download the Gilt app, the company offered instant membership (as opposed to its normal invitation-only model) and a ten-dollar credit to the first ten thousand new subscribers. Awareness of Gilt on the Go spread virally, and apps grew in a flash, accounting for 15 percent of the firm's revenue within months.[14] Some of the best approaches to competing in network markets will simultaneously leverage several of the strategies we're outlining here, and in the case of Gilt, the *subsidy* helped create *viral* promotion that in turn helped establish a new *distribution channel*. Mobile is especially important for Gilt, since the firm offers flash sales. Making sure the firm can message users on their nondesktop screens increases the chances for the firm to reach and engage consumers, and rack up more sales.

FIGURE 8.3 Gilt Groupe iPad App

Gilt's ten-dollar iPad subsidy and instant membership offer helped fuel adoption of the iPad app. Mobile apps now account for 15 percent of the high-end fashion site's sales.

When Even Free Isn't Good Enough

Subsidizing adoption after a rival has achieved dominance can be an uphill battle, and sometimes even offering a service for free isn't enough to combat the dominant firm. When Yahoo! introduced a US auction service to compete with eBay, it initially didn't charge sellers at all (sellers typically pay eBay a small percentage of each completed auction). The hope was that with the elimination of seller fees, enough sellers would jump from eBay to Yahoo! helping the late-mover catch up in the network effect game.

But eBay sellers were reluctant to leave for two reasons. First, there weren't enough buyers on Yahoo! to match the high bids they earned on much-larger eBay. Some savvy sellers played an arbitrage game where they'd buy items on Yahoo!'s auction service at lower prices and resell them on eBay, where more users bid prices higher.

Second, any established seller leaving eBay would give up their valuable "seller ratings," and would need to build their Yahoo! reputation from scratch. Seller ratings represent a critical switching cost, as many users view a high rating as a method for reducing the risk of getting scammed or receiving lower-quality goods.

Auctions work best for differentiated goods. While Amazon has had some success in peeling away eBay sellers who provide commodity products (a real danger as eBay increasingly relies on fixed-price sales), eBay's dominant share of the online auction market still towers over all rivals.[15] While there's no magic in the servers used to create eBay, the early use of technology allowed the firm to create both network effects and switching costs—a dual strategic advantage that has given it a hammerlock on auctions even as others have attempted to mimic its service and undercut its pricing model.

5.3   Leverage Viral Promotion

Since all products and services foster some sort of exchange, it's often possible to leverage a firm's customers to promote the product or service. Internet calling service Skype (now owned by Microsoft) has over 600 million registered users yet has spent almost nothing on advertising. Neither has WhatsApp (now part of Facebook) with over half a billion monthly active users. Most Skype and WhatsApp users were recruited by others who shared the word on free and low-cost Internet calls and text messaging. And rise of social media has made viral promotion a tool that many firms can exploit. Facebook, Twitter, and mobile app integration with a phone's address book all act as a catalyst for friends to share deals, spread a good word, sign up for services, and load applications.

Viral promotions are also often linked to subsidies (e.g., recruit a new customer and you both get money to spend), but they can also provide the additional benefit of leveraging a trusted friend to overcome adoption inertia. PayPal and Uber are firms that have both used these incentives as trust proxies, or what is sometimes referred to as **social proof**. When a friend sends an invite to a service where users may otherwise have trust concerns (e.g., PayPal and sharing of financial information, Uber and stepping into a car driven by a stranger), an endorsement by a friend can ease concerns.

social proof

The positive influence created when someone finds out that others are doing something.

5.4   Expand by Redefining the Market

If a big market attracts more users (and in two-sided markets, more complements), why not redefine the space to bring in more users? Nintendo did this when launching the Wii. While Sony and Microsoft focused on the graphics and raw processing power favored by hard-core male gamers, Nintendo chose to develop a machine to appeal to families, women, and age groups that normally shunned alien shoot-'em ups. By going after a bigger, redefined market, Nintendo was able to rack up sales that exceeded the Xbox 360, even though it followed the system by twelve months.[16]

blue ocean strategy

An approach where firms seek to create and compete in uncontested "blue ocean" market spaces, rather than competing in spaces and ways that have attracted many, similar rivals.

Seeking the Blue Ocean? Better Think Strategically

Reggie Fils-Aimé, the president of Nintendo of America, has described the Wii Strategy as a Blue Ocean effort.[17] The concept of **blue ocean strategy** was popularized by European Institute of Business Administration (INSEAD) professors W. Chan Kim and Renée Mauborgne (authors of a book with the same title).[18] The idea—instead of competing in *blood-red* waters where the sharks of highly competitive firms vie for every available market scrap, firms should seek the *blue waters* of uncontested, new market spaces.

For Nintendo, the granny gamers, moms, and partygoers who flocked to the Wii represented an undiscovered feast in the Blue Ocean. Talk about new markets! Consider that the best-selling video game following the Wii's breakout launch was Wii Fit—a genre-busting title that comes with a scale so you can weigh yourself each time you play. That's a far cry from Grand Theft Auto IV, the title ranking fifth in 2008 sales, and trailing four Wii-only exclusives.

Blue ocean strategy often works best when combined with strategic positioning described in Chapter 2 If an early mover into a blue ocean can use this lead to create defensible assets for sustainable advantage, late moving rivals may find markets unresponsive to their presence. Of course, if your firm's claim in the blue ocean is based on easily imitated resources (like technology features), then holding off rivals will be tougher. For holiday season 2010, Microsoft showed up with its own motion-gaming controller, the Kinect video camera system. Kinect was such a hit with generation Wii that it became the fastest-selling consumer electronics product in history, pumping up Xbox 360 console sales and goosing Microsoft's entertainment division from zero to a billion dollars in profits in just two years.[19]

convergence

When two or more markets, once considered distinctly separate, begin to offer features and capabilities. As an example: the markets for mobile phones and media players are converging.

envelopment

When one market attempts to conquer a new market by making it a subset, component, or feature of its primary offering.

Market expansion sometimes puts rivals who previously did not compete on a collision course as markets undergo **convergence** (when two or more markets, once considered distinctly separate, begin to offer similar features and capabilities). Consider the market for portable electronic devices. Separate product categories for media players, cameras, gaming devices, phones, and global positioning systems (GPS) are all starting to merge. Rather than cede its dominance as a media player, Apple leveraged a strategy known as **envelopment**, where a firm seeks to make an existing market a subset of its product offering. Apple deftly morphed the iPod into the iPhone, a device that captures all of these product categories in one device. But the firm went further; the iPhone is Wi-Fi capable, offers browsing, e-mail, and an application platform based on a scaled-down version of the same OS X operating system used in Macintosh computers. As a "Pocket Mac," the appeal of the device broadened beyond just the phone or music player markets, and within two quarters of launch, iPhone became the second-leading smartphone in North America—outpacing Palm, Microsoft, Motorola and every other rival, except RIM's BlackBerry,[20] and it was only a matter of time before that rival was vanquished, as well.

5.5   Alliances and Partnerships

Firms can also use partnerships to grow market share for a network. Sometimes these efforts bring rivals together to take out a leader. In a classic example, consider ATM networks. Citibank was the first major bank in New York City to offer a large ATM network. But the Citi network was initially proprietary, meaning customers of other banks couldn't take advantage of Citi ATMs. Citi's innovation was wildly popular and being a pioneer in rolling out cash machines helped the firm grow deposits fourfold in just a few years. Competitors responded with a partnership. Instead of each rival bank offering another incompatible network destined to trail Citi's lead, competing banks agreed to share their ATM operations through NYCE (New York Cash Exchange). While Citi's network was initially the biggest, after the NYCE launch a Chase bank customer could use ATMs at a host of other banks that covered a geography far greater than Citi offered alone. Network effects in ATMs shifted to the rival bank alliance, Citi eventually joined NYCE and today, nearly every ATM in the United States carries a NYCE sticker.

Also, as mentioned earlier in this chapter, many of the nation's largest retailers are also working together on mobile payments standards. Backers of the MCX (Merchant Customer Exchange) standard include otherwise fierce rivals Walmart, Target, and Kmart, as well as BestBuy, Gap, and many others. What brings them all together? Hope that they can collectively set a standard through their collective network size, remain the primary customer interface in mobile payments, have access to data, and perhaps even make a bit of money or reduce costs from the effort—all prospects that are seen as more attractive than ceding these markets to Google, Apple, or other dominant tech firms.[21] That said, pulling off such a goal is difficult. MCX's CurrentC standard has been slow to launch, prompting BestBuy to break with the Apple-blocking consortium and accept Apple Pay.[22]

Share or Stay Proprietary?

Defensive moves like the ones above are often meant to diffuse the threat of a proprietary rival. Sometimes firms decide from the start to band together to create a new, more open standard, realizing that collective support is more likely to jumpstart a network than if one firm tried to act with a closed, proprietary offering. Examples of this include the coalitions of firms that have worked together to advance standards like Bluetooth and Wi-Fi. While no single member firm gains a direct profit from the sale of devices using these standards, the standard's backers benefit when the market for devices expands as products become more useful because they are more interoperable.

5.6   Leverage Distribution Channels

Firms can also think about novel ways to distribute a product or service to consumers. Sun faced a challenge when launching the Java programming language—no computers could run it. In order for Java to work, computers need a little interpreter program called the Java Virtual Machine (JVM). Most users weren't willing to download the JVM if there were no applications written in Java, and no developers were willing to write in Java if no one could run their code. Sun broke the logjam when it *bundled* the JVM with Netscape's browser. When millions of users downloaded Netscape, Sun's software snuck in, almost instantly creating a platform of millions for would-be Java developers. Today, even though Netscape has failed, Sun's Java remains one of the world's most popular programming languages. Indeed, Java was cited as one of the main reasons for Oracle's 2009 acquisition of Sun, with Oracle's CEO saying the language represented "the single most important software asset we have ever acquired."[23]

And when you don't have distribution channels, create them. That's what Apple did when it launched the Apple retail stores a little over a decade ago. At the time of launch, nearly every pundit expected the effort to fail. But it turns out, the attractive, high-service storefronts were the perfect platform to promote the uniqueness of Apple products. Apple's more than four hundred stores worldwide now bring in over $21 billion in revenue[24] and are among the world's most successful retail outlets on a sales-per-square-foot basis.[25]

As mentioned in Chapter 2 Microsoft is in a particularly strong position to leverage its products as distribution channels. The firm often bundles its new products into its operating systems, Office suite, Internet Explorer browser, and other offerings. The firm used this tactic to transform once market-leader Real Networks into an also-ran in streaming audio. Within a few years of bundling Windows Media Player (WMP) with its other products, WMP grabbed the majority of the market, while Real's share had fallen to below 10 percent.[26]

FIGURE 8.4 Apple's Retail Stores

Most pundits expected Apple retail to fail. Instead the stores provided a wildly successful channel to reach customers, explain products, and make sales. The Apple Store on Fifth Avenue in Manhattan was recently named the most photographed landmark in New York City.

Source: Photo courtesy of Samantha Marx, http://www.flickr.com/photos/spam/4414006602/.

Caution is advised, however. Regional antitrust authorities may consider product bundling by dominant firms to be anticompetitive. European regulators have forced Microsoft to unbundle Windows Media Player from its operating system and to provide a choice of browsers alongside Internet Explorer. Over the past decade the EU has slapped Microsoft with penalties that have amounted to over 2 billion euros in total.[27]

5.7   Seed the Market

When Sony launched the PS3, it subsidized each console by selling at a price estimated at three hundred dollars below unit cost.[28] Subsidizing consoles is a common practice in the video game industry—game player manufacturers usually make most of their money through royalties paid by game developers. But Sony's subsidy had an additional benefit for the firm—it helped sneak a Blu-ray player into every home buying a PS3 (Sony was backing the Blu-ray standard over the rival HD DVD effort). PS3 has struggled with fierce competition, but initially seeding the market with low-cost Blu-ray players at a time when that hardware sold at a very high price gave eventual winner Blu-ray some extra momentum. Since Sony is also a movie studio and manufacturer of DVD players and other consumer electronics, it had a particularly strong set of assets to leverage to encourage the adoption of Blu-ray over rival HD DVD.

Giving away products for half of a two-sided market is an extreme example of this kind of behavior, but it's often used. In two-sided markets, you charge the one who will pay. Adobe gives away the Acrobat reader to build a market for the sale of software that creates Acrobat files. Firms with Yellow Page directories give away countless copies of their products, delivered straight to your home, in order to create a market for selling advertising. And Google does much the same by providing free, ad-supported search.

Consignment firm thredUp buys clothing from one group of customers, then photographs and warehouses them for resale to others. Sending high-quality used clothes to thredUp can be a quick way to earn cash, but it can also lead to a lopsided market, where supply exceeds demand. In order to seed the "buy" side for its duds by encouraging sellers to become buyers, too; thredUp will give clothes sellers immediate purchase credit for any resale items that thredUp accepts for sale. Want cash instead? You'll get it, but you'll have to wait two weeks.

5.8   Encourage the Development of Complementary Goods

There are several ways to motivate others to create complementary goods for your network. These efforts often involve some form of developer subsidy or other free or discounted service. A firm may charge lower royalties or offer a period of royalty-free licensing. It can also offer free software development kits (SDKs), training programs, co-marketing dollars, or even start-up capital to potential suppliers. Microsoft and Apple both allow developers to sell their products online through Xbox LIVE Marketplace and iTunes, respectively. This channel lowers developer expenses by eliminating costs associated with selling physical inventory in brick-and-mortar stores and can provide a free way to reach millions of potential consumers without significant promotional spending.

Venture funds can also prompt firms to create complementary goods. The venture firm Highland Capital backed gesture detection start-up Leap Motion, a low-cost, bubblegum-pack-sized hardware add-on that is some two hundred times more sensitive than Xbox Kinect. Leap's success will be based on its ability to create a thriving two-sided market (more applications that use Leap Motion fuel more user demand and vice-versa), so Highland Capital also announced a fund to invest in start-ups building on Leap's technology. Those working with the platform today include game makers, health care providers, and other industrial firms.[29]

5.9   Leverage Backward Compatibility

backward compatibility

The ability to take advantage of complementary products developed for a prior generation of technology.

Those firms that control a standard would also be wise to ensure that new products have **backward compatibility** with earlier offerings. If not, they reenter a market at installed-base zero and give up a major source of advantage—the switching costs built up by prior customers. For example, when Nintendo introduced its 16-bit Super Nintendo system, it was incompatible with the firm's highly successful prior generation 8-bit model. Rival Sega, which had entered the 16-bit market two years prior to Nintendo, had already built up a large library of 16-bit games for its system. Nintendo entered with only its debut titles, and no ability to play games owned by customers of its previous system, so there was little incentive for existing Nintendo fans to stick with the firm.[30] iTunes users also found migration to Spotify made particularly easy since the latter offered the option of importing iTunes playlists.

Backward compatibility was the centerpiece of Apple's strategy to revitalize the Macintosh through its move to the Intel microprocessor. Intel chips aren't compatible with the instruction set used by the PowerPC processor used in earlier Mac models. Think of this as two entirely different languages—Intel speaks French, PowerPC speaks Urdu. To ease the transition, Apple included a free software-based **adaptor**, called Rosetta, that automatically emulated the functionality of the old chip on all new Macs (a sort of Urdu to French translator). By doing so, all new Intel Macs could use the base of existing software written for the old chip; owners of PowerPC Macs were able to upgrade while preserving their investment in old software; and software firms could still sell older programs while they rewrote applications for new Intel-based Macs.

Even more significant, since Intel is the same standard used by Windows, Apple developed a free software adaptor called Boot Camp that allowed Windows to be installed on Macs. Boot Camp (and similar solutions by other vendors) dramatically lowered the cost for Windows users to switch to Macs. Within two years of making the switch, Mac sales skyrocketed to record levels. Apple now boasts a commanding lead in notebook sales to the education market,[31] and a survey by Yankee Group found that 87 percent of corporations were using at least some Macintosh computers, up from 48 percent at the end of the PowerPC era two years earlier.[32]

> **adaptor**
>
> A product that allows a firm to tap into the complementary products, data, or user base of another product or service.

5.10 Rivals: Be Compatible with the Leading Network

Companies will want to consider making new products compatible with the leading standard. Microsoft's Live Maps and Virtual Earth 3D arrived late to the Internet mapping game. Users had already put in countless hours building resources that meshed with Google Maps and Google Earth. But by adopting the same keyhole markup language (KML) standard used by Google, Microsoft could, as *TechCrunch* put it, "drink from Google's milkshake." Any work done by users for Google in KML could be used by Microsoft. Voilà, an instant base of add-on content!

5.11 Incumbents: Close Off Rival Access and Constantly Innovate

Oftentimes, firms that control dominant networks will make compatibility difficult for rivals who try to connect with their systems. For example, while many firms offer video conferencing and Internet calling, the clear leader is Skype, a product that for years had been closed to unauthorized Skype clients.

Firms that constantly innovate make it particularly difficult for competitors to become compatible. Again, we can look to Apple as an example of these concepts in action. While Macs run Windows, Windows computers can't run Mac programs. Apple has embedded key software in Mac hardware, making it difficult for rivals to write a software emulator like Boot Camp that would let Windows PCs drink from the Mac milkshake. And if any firm gets close to cloning Mac hardware, Apple sues. The firm also modifies software on other products like the iPhone and iTunes each time wily hackers tap into closed aspects of its systems. And Apple has regularly moved to block competing third-party hardware products from plugging into iTunes.[33] Even if firms create adaptors that emulate a standard, a firm that constantly innovates creates a moving target that's tough for others to keep up with.

Apple has been far more aggressive than Microsoft in introducing new versions of its software. Since the firm never stays still, would-be cloners never get enough time to create a reliable emulator that runs the latest Apple software.

5.12 Large, Well-Known Followers: Preannouncements

Large firms that find new markets attractive but don't yet have products ready for delivery might *preannounce* efforts in order to cause potential adaptors to sit on the fence, delaying a purchasing decision until the new effort rolls out. Preannouncements only work if a firm is large enough to pose a credible threat to current market participants. While Apple rarely preannounces products, it previewed Apple Watch roughly eight months before it was ready to ship. Rivals from the Kickstarter darling, Pebble, to Google's Android Wear were courting developers, but Apple's early product demonstration caused many customers considering wearables to hold off until Apple Watch was out. Developers also knew that, unlike fragmented Android Wear offerings with varying watch face shapes and capabilities, Apple Watch would provide a uniform standard offered by the industry's biggest player. While large, respected firms may be able to influence markets through preannouncements, start-ups often lack credibility to delay user purchases. The tech industry acronym for the impact firms try to impart on markets through preannouncements is *FUD,* for fear, uncertainty, and doubt.

The Osborne Effect

When a firm preannounces a forthcoming product or service and experiences a sharp and detrimental drop in sales of current offerings as users wait for the new item.

The Osborne Effect

Preannouncers, beware. Announce an effort too early and a firm may fall victim to what's known as **"The Osborne Effect."** It's been suggested that portable computer manufacturer Osborne Computer announced new models too early. Customers opted to wait for the new models, so sales of the firm's current offerings plummeted. While evidence suggests that Osborne's decline had more to do with rivals offering better products, the negative impact of preannouncements has hurt a host of other firms.[34] Among these, Sega, which exited the video game console market entirely after preannouncements of a next-generation system killed enthusiasm for its Saturn console.[35]

congestion effects

When increasing numbers of users lower the value of a product or service.

Too Much of a Good Thing?

When network effects are present, more users attract more users. That's a good thing as long as a firm can earn money from this virtuous cycle. But sometimes a network effect attracts too many users, and a service can be so overwhelmed that it becomes unusable. These so-called **congestion effects** occur when increasing numbers of users lower the value of a product or service. This most often happens when a key resource becomes increasingly scarce. *Fortune* reported how the recent launch of a new version of the hit EA game SimCity fell victim to congestion effects, stating that "thanks to what the company called 'overwhelming demand,' players experienced a myriad of problems like failures to load the game entirely and wait times of twenty minutes to log in. Gameplay became so problematic that Amazon temporarily halted sales of the game, and EA offered users the option of downloading a free game from its online store."[36] Twitter's early infrastructure was often unable to handle the demands of a service in hypergrowth (leading to the frequent appearance of a not-in-service graphic known in the Twitter community as the "fail whale"). Facebook users with a large number of friends may also find their attention is a limited resource, as feeds push so much content that it becomes difficult to separate interesting information from the noise of friend actions.

And while network effects can attract positive complementary products, a dominant standard may also be the first place where virus writers and malicious hackers choose to strike.

FIGURE 8.5   The Twitter Fail Whale

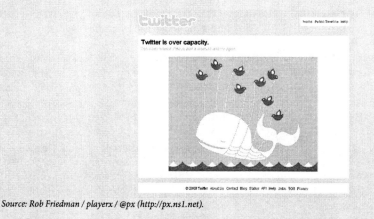

Source: Rob Friedman / playerx / @px (http://px.ns1.net).

Feel confident! Now you've got a solid grounding in network effects, the key resource leveraged by some of the most dominant firms in technology. And these concepts apply beyond the realm of tech, too. Network effects can explain phenomena ranging from why some stock markets are more popular than others to why English is so widely spoken, even among groups of nonnative speakers. On top of that, the strategies explored in the last half of the chapter show how to use these principles to sniff out, create, and protect this key strategic asset. Go forth, tech pioneer—opportunity awaits!

KEY TAKEAWAYS

- Moving early matters in network markets—firms that move early can often use that time to establish a lead in users, switching costs, and complementary products that can be difficult for rivals to match.

- Additional factors that can help a firm establish a network effects lead include subsidizing adoption; leveraging viral marketing, creating alliances to promote a product or to increase a service's user base; redefining the market to appeal to more users; leveraging unique distribution channels to reach new customers; seeding the market with complements; encouraging the development of complements; and maintaining backward compatibility.

- Established firms may try to make it difficult for rivals to gain compatibility with their users, standards, or product complements. Large firms may also create uncertainty among those considering adoption of a rival by preannouncing competing products.

QUESTIONS AND EXERCISES

1. Is market entry timing important for network effects markets? Explain and offer an example to back up your point.
2. How might a firm subsidize adoption? Give an example.
3. Give an example of a partnership or alliance targeted at increasing network effects.
4. Is it ever advantageous for firms to give up control of a network and share it with others? Why or why not? Give examples to back up your point.
5. Do firms that dominate their markets with network effects risk government intervention? Why or why not? Explain through an example.
6. How did Sony seed the market for Blu-ray players?
7. What does backward compatibility mean and why is this important? What happens if a firm is not backward compatible?
8. What tactic did Apple use to increase the acceptability of the Mac platform to a broader population of potential users?
9. How has Apple kept clones at bay?
10. What are preannouncements? What is the danger in announcing a product too early? What is the term for negative impacts from premature product announcements?
11. How did PayPal subsidize adoption?
12. Why is viral adoption especially important to PayPal and Uber?
13. Name two companies that leveraged viral promotion to compete.
14. Name a product that is the result of the *convergence* of media players, cameras, and phones.
15. What is bundling? What are the upsides and downsides of bundling?
16. Why does Adobe allow the *free* download of Acrobat Reader?
17. How does thredUp leverage its seller payout policy to balance sell-side supply with buy-side demand?
18. What tactic might an established firm employ to make it impossible, or at least difficult, for a competitor to gain access to, or become compatible with, their product or service?
19. How do Apple, Microsoft, and Facebook encourage the development of complementary products?
20. What is the "congestion effect"? Give an example.
21. Do network effects apply in nontech areas? Give examples.

ENDNOTES

1. M. Parsons, "Microsoft: 'We'd Have Been Dead a Long Time Ago without Windows APIs,'" ZDNet UK, April 22, 2004, http://news.zdnet.co.uk/software/0,1000000121,39152686,00.htm.

2. T. Eisenmann, G. Parker, and M. Van Alstyne, "Strategies for Two-Sided Markets," *Harvard Business Review*, October 2006.

3. S. Hansell, "The iPod Economy and C.E.S.," *New York Times*, January 7, 2008.

4. T. Cook, keynote address at Apple World Wide Developer Conference, San Francisco, California, June 2, 2014.

5. Content in this section sourced to: M. Parsons, "Microsoft: 'We'd Have Been Dead a Long Time Ago without Windows APIs,'" ZDNet UK, April 22, 2004, http://news.zdnet.co.uk/software/0,1000000121,39152686,00.htm

6. A. Jeffries, "Apple Pay allows you to pay at the counter with your iPhone 6," *The Verge*, Sept. 9, 2014

7. B. Barnes, "NBC Will Not Renew iTunes Contract," *New York Times*, August 31, 2007.

8. Adapted from J. Gallaugher and Y. Wang, "Linux vs. Windows in the Middle Kingdom: A Strategic Valuation Model for Platform Competition" (paper, Proceedings of the 2008 Meeting of Americas Conference on Information Systems, Toronto, CA, August 2008), extending M. Schilling, "Technological Leapfrogging: Lessons from the U.S. Video Game Console Industry," *California Management Review*, Spring 2003.

9. M. Schilling, "Technological Leapfrogging: Lessons from the U.S. Video Game Console Industry," *California Management Review*, Spring 2003.

10. N. Hutheesing, "Answer Your Phone, a Videogame Is Calling," *Forbes*, August 8, 2006.

11. K. Cutler, "This Is What Developing for Android Looks Like," *TechCrunch*, May 11, 2012.

12. C. Null, "Sony's Losses on PS3: $3 Billion and Counting," *Yahoo! Today in Tech*, June 27, 2008, http://tech.yahoo.com/blogs/null/96355.

13. R. Walker, "AntiPod," *New York Times*, August 8, 2008.

14. B. Gutman, "Gilt Groupe Reveals Its Success with Mobile and Social," *Forbes*, May 17, 2011.

15. B. Stone, "Amid the Gloom, an E-commerce War," *New York Times*, October 12, 2008.

16. M. Sanchanta, "Nintendo's Wii Takes Console Lead," *Financial Times*, September 12, 2007.

17. R. Fils-Aimé (presentation and discussion, Carroll School of Management, Boston College, Chestnut Hill, MA, April 6, 2009).

18. W. C. Kim and R. Mauborgne, *Blue Ocean Strategy: How to Create Uncontested Market Space and Make Competition Irrelevant* (Cambridge, MA: Harvard Business Press, 2005). See http://www.blueoceanstrategy.com.

19. S. Kessler, "Microsoft Kinect Sales Top 10 Million, Set New Guinness World Record," *Mashable*, March 9, 2011; D. Goldman, "Microsoft Profit Soars 31% on Strong Office and Kinect Sales," *CNNMoney*, April 28, 2011.

20. R. Kim, "iPhone No. 2 Smartphone Platform in North America," *The Tech Chronicles—The San Francisco Chronicle*, December 17, 2007.

21. L. Johnson, "MCX Makes Bid to Win Over Small Merchants as Rollout Date Nears," *Mobile Commerce Daily*, July 18, 2013.

22. J. Del Rey, "Apple Pay Coming to Best Buy Stores as Retailer Breaks Ranks From Walmart-Led Rival," *Re/code*, April 27, 2015.

23. A. Ricadela, "Oracle's Bold Java Plans," *BusinessWeek*, June 2, 2009.

24. Data from Statista.com: "Apple's revenue from company-owned retail stores from 2005 to 2014 (in billion U.S. dollars)" and "Number of Apple stores worldwide from 2005 to 2014"

25. P. Wahba, "Apple extends lead in U.S. top 10 retailers by sales per square foot," *Fortune*, March 13, 2015.

26. Normal 0 false false false EN-US X-NONE X-NONE /* Style Definitions */ table.MsoNormalTable {mso-style-name:"Table Normal"; mso-tstyle-rowband-size:0; mso-tstyle-colband-size:0; mso-style-noshow:yes; mso-style-priority:99; mso-style-qformat:yes; mso-style-parent:""; mso-padding-alt:0in 5.4pt 0in 5.4pt; mso-para-margin:0in; *BusinessWire*, "Media Player Format Share for 2006 Confirms Windows Media Remains Dominant with a 50.8% Share of Video Streams Served, Followed by Flash at 21.9%—'CDN Growth and Market Share Shifts: 2002–2006,'" December 18, 2006; and T. Eisenmann, G. Parker, and M. Van Alstyne, "Strategies for Two-Sided Markets," *Harvard Business Review*, October 2006

27. L. Sumagaysay, "A $733M 'Error' Message: EU Fines Microsoft over Browser-Choice Deal," *SiliconBeat*, March 6, 2013.

28. C. Null, "Sony's Losses on PS3: $3 Billion and Counting," *Yahoo! Today in Tech*, June 27, 2008, http://tech.yahoo.com/blogs/null/96355.

29. R. Lawler, "Highland Capital Partners Commits to Invest $25 Million in Leap Motion Developers," *TechCrunch*, June 20, 2013.

30. M. Schilling, "Technological Leapfrogging: Lessons from the U.S. Video Game Console Industry," *California Management Review*, Spring 2003.

31. P. Seitz, "An Apple for Teacher, Students: Mac Maker Surges in Education," *Investor's Business Daily*, August 8, 2008.

32. P. Burrows, "The Mac in the Gray Flannel Suit," *BusinessWeek*, May 1, 2008.

33. Notably, Apple repeatedly blocked smartphone maker Palm from accessing music in iTunes. Apple appealed to the consortium behind the USB standard to get Palm to stop unauthorized access. C. Metz, "USB supreme court backs Apple in Palm Pre kerfuffle," *The Register*, Sept. 24, 2009.

34. A. Orlowski, "Taking Osborne out of the Osborne Effect," *The Register*, June 20, 2005.

35. M. Schilling, "Technological Leapfrogging: Lessons from the U.S. Video Game Console Industry," *California Management Review*, Spring 2003.

36. J. Mangalindan, "4 Moves Electronic Arts Must Make Now," *Fortune*, March 20, 2013.

CHAPTER 9
Social Media, Peer Production, and Web 2.0

1. INTRODUCTION

LEARNING OBJECTIVES

1. Recognize the unexpected rise and impact of social media and peer production systems, and understand how these services differ from prior generation tools.
2. List the major classifications of social media services.

Over the past few years, a fundamentally different class of Internet services has attracted users, made headlines, and increasingly garnered breathtaking market valuations. Originally grouped under the poorly defined umbrella term "**Web 2.0**," these new services are targeted at harnessing the power of the Internet to empower users to collaborate, create resources, and share information in a distinctly different way than the static websites and transaction-focused storefronts that characterized so many failures in the dot-com bubble. While much of what was once often called Web 2.0 is now categorized as social media or the even broader classification of peer production, the precision of definitions in a category that is constantly evolving is less important. What is significant is how quickly the social media revolution came about, how unexpected it was, and how deeply impactful these efforts have become for individuals, businesses, and society. Consider the following:

- Half of the world's top ten most heavily trafficked Internet sites are social: Facebook, YouTube, Wikipedia, Tencent QQ (China), and Twitter.[1] US users now spend more time with social media than on any other category of Internet use.[2]

- It took just three years for the number of social sites to dominate the top ten. However, the list is volatile, and half of the top social sites (MySpace, Hi5, Orkut) fell out of this list, replaced by new entrants.[3] The turnover applies to social apps, too. Anonymous messaging app, Secret, only survived 18 months, despite having raised over $35 million and being valued at over $100 million.[4]

- With only seven full-time employees and an operating budget of less than $1 million, the nonprofit site Wikipedia became the fifth most visited site on the Internet.[5] The site boasts well over 30 million articles in over 280 different languages, all of them contributed, edited, and fact-checked by volunteers.

- Just twenty months after its founding, YouTube was purchased by Google for $1.65 billion. Over three hundred hours of video are uploaded to YouTube each minute. The site has emerged as the Web's leading destination for video, hosting everything from apologies from CEOs for service gaffes to questions submitted as part of presidential debates. Every day, YouTube's over 1 billion users watch hundreds of millions of hours of video and generate billions of views. Mobile revenue on YouTube is up over 100 percent year over year, and half of the site's views come from mobile devices, with an increasing number watching from non-PC devices, including mobile phones, tablets, and televisions.[6]

- The population of Facebook users is now so large that it could be considered the largest "nation" in the world. Half the site's users log in at least once a day, spending an average of fifty-two minutes a day on the site. Facebook is solidly profitable and revenues have been growing with astonishing speed (more than $12.47 billion in revenues and $2.9 billion in profits in 2014).[7] US users spend more time on Facebook than on any other app; a full 42 percent of app time on smart mobile devices is spent in the Facebook app. Telcos in emerging economies often compete by

Web 2.0

A term broadly referring to Internet services that foster collaboration and information sharing; characteristics that distinctly set "Web 2.0" efforts apart from the static, transaction-oriented Web sites of "Web 1.0." The term is often applied to Web sites and Internet services that foster social media or other sorts of peer production.

offering Facebook as a free service, usually via so-called text-based "dumb" phones. Says Kenya-based tech guru Erik Hersman, "That means that for those people in Africa with mobile phones but likely no computer access, Facebook is their Internet."[8]

- After acquiring 18-month-old Instagram for $1 billion and 5-year-old WhatsApp for $19 billion, Facebook now owns two of the fastest growing, most used apps in their respective categories. These two, along with the Facebook and Messenger apps, give Facebook the top four most used smartphone apps, globally.[9] Instagram has 300 million monthly active users (MAUs) who have shared over 30 billion photos total. Seventy million photos are shared on the service each day, recording 2.5 *billion* daily likes. WhatsApp is the world's most popular messaging client. The service has over 700 million MAUs. Each day WhatsApp users send over 700 million photos, 100 million videos, and 50 percent more messages than the entire worldwide SMS messaging standard.[10]

- Six of the top ten apps used globally are messaging apps: WhatsApp, Facebook Messenger, Line, Viber, KakaoTalk, and WeChat. It's worth nothing that while one global winner in social networking has emerged (Facebook has won in all but a few notable places such as China and Russia) the market for messaging apps is fragmented, with many players worldwide boasting hundreds of millions of active users.[11]

- All of the top ten most-used apps worldwide are social. The remaining three apps are Facebook, Instagram, and Twitter. Only Clash of Clans isn't what one would call conventional social media, but it's a social game.

- The trend extends to business. By its first birthday, workgroup productivity app Slack had over half a million daily active users sending 300 million messages each month on the platform, making it the fastest growing business app, ever. The firm was valued at over $1 billion after a $120 million funding round in October 2014. An April 2015 round raised another $160 million at a $2.8 billion valuation, with daily users soaring to three quarters of a million.[12] Slack's success is based largely on corporate users finding it wildly effective at reducing the glut of internal emails.[13]

- While WhatsApp is the global king of messaging, SnapChat, a service that reportedly spurned a $3 billion offer from Facebook,[14] is tops for messaging in the United States. SnapChat reports its users send a combined 1.2 billion photos and videos a day.[15] SnapChat posts vanish shortly after they're viewed, creating a service with a fundamentally different value proposition than Facebook and other permanent-post, wide-sharing-circle services.

- For many, social media is the "newspaper," the "news magazine," or the "news program." Pew Research reports that 35 percent of all news is discovered via social networks. Media brands that have learned to appeal to social media users have prospered. At less than 10 years old, the Huffington Post and BuzzFeed both attract significantly more monthly online users than the digital versions of the venerable stalwarts of American media, The New York Times and The Wall Street Journal.[16]

- Facebook and Twitter have become activist tools and have played vital roles in supporting protest movements worldwide. China and Iran are among the governments so threatened by the power of these services that each has, at times, blocked Facebook and Twitter access within their borders.

- Twitter has emerged as a major force that can break news and shape public opinion. By the time Twitter was five years old, the service boasted a population of over 200 million users that were collectively posting more than 1 billion tweets (Twitter messages) each week.[17] In another nod to the service's significance, the US Library of Congress announced plans to archive every tweet ever sent.[18]

- After just five years, Tumblr, founded by then-twenty-one-year-old David Karp, emerged as one of the top ten most visited websites in the United States.[19] One year later, the site was purchased by Yahoo! for over $1 billion.[20]

- The websites Stack Overflow and GitHub have emerged as critically important software developer learning tools and effective ways to establish and strengthen one's reputation. Roughly 3 million developers participate on the Stack Overflow question-and-answer site worldwide,[21] with 92 percent of posted questions receiving an answer and answers posted in an average of just 11 minutes.[22] With its roots as a collaborative software development resource, GitHub is now the world's largest online storage space for collaborative works.[23] Participants are free to download, study, enhance, and share anything in the network. As of March 2015, there were 8.8 million GitHub users collaborating on 20.7 million project repositories. As *Forbes* declares, "Software Engineers Are in Demand, and GitHub Is How You Find Them."[24]

- Image curating and sharing site Pinterest became the fastest growing website of all time,[25] with some studies suggesting the site has driven more sales than Facebook[26] and more blog traffic than Twitter.[27] A 2015 venture investment valued the firm at $11.5 billion.[28]

- Social media, especially Facebook, continues to reshape the online gaming landscape. Although Zynga has fallen from its once-lofty $10 billion valuation, app developers and games running on social sites continue to proliferate. Facebook integration is used by the majority of the most popular iOS games to drive traffic. Facebook claims that its mobile newsfeed alone drives over a quarter of a billion visits to the iOS app store and Google Play in a given month.[29] Spotify has leveraged Facebook to boost its growth to over 60 million worldwide, with 15 million paying subscribers.[30]

- Services such as Twitter, Yelp, and the highly profitable TripAdvisor have unleashed the voice of the customer so that gripes, praise, and ratings are now often captured and broadcast immediately at the point of service. Reviews are now incorporated into search results and maps, making them the first thing many customers see when encountering a brand online. TripAdvisor brings in over $1.2 billion in annual revenue and nearly a quarter of a billion dollars in profits.

- Google is looking to social media to improve maps and purchased the five-year-old Israeli crowdsourced traffic app, Waze, for $1 billion. At the time of acquisition, the service had 50 million users in 100 countries.[31]

- All sorts of mobile and social apps are garnering increased interest and sky-high valuations. At just over two years old, mobile dating site Tinder (majority owned by IAC, the parent of conventional dating site Match.com) has an estimated 22 million users,[32] processing 1.2 billion "swipes" and 15 million "matches" a day,[33] and has added SnapChat-style self-destructing images. The 27-person firm has grown 960 percent in just six months, with analysts projecting a valuation of $1.6 billion at mid 2015.[34]

FIGURE 9.1

The business messaging app Slack is called the "e-mail killer." The firm is the fastest growing business app ever, and was valued at $2.8 billion when it was barely a year old.

Slack

Top 10 Most Used Social Apps
1. Facebook
2. WhatsApp
3. Messenger
4. Instagram
5. LINE
6. Viber
7. Kakao Talk
8. Clash of Clans
9. WeChat
10. Twitter

Source: M. Meeker, "Internet Trends 2015 – Code Conference," KCPB, May 27, 2015, at: http://www.kpcb.com/internet-trends.

FIGURE 9.2   Mobile Continues to Drive Fast-Growing Social Services[35]

Managers must continually scan the social media landscape for new channels and potentially impactful trends. All of the top ten most-used apps worldwide are social. Six are messaging apps. Instagram, Pinterest, Tumblr, SnapChat, and WhatsApp are among the social media giants to grow rapidly, upend industries, and create new communication channels. Images from the mobile apps of some of these services are shown here.

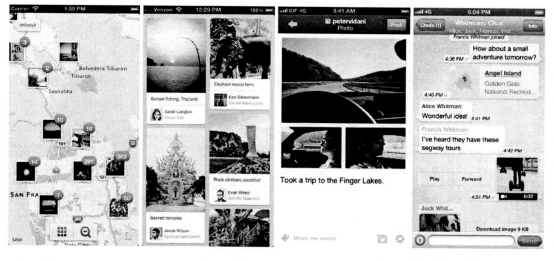

The old-school Web 2.0 moniker is a murky one because, like so many popular technology terms, there's not a precise definition. We'll add some precision to our discussion by focusing on social media efforts—technologies that support the creation of *user-generated content*, as well as content editing, commenting, curation, and sharing. Social media efforts include blogs, wikis, social networks, messaging services, Twitter, and photo and video sharing sites. The rise of social media has also coincided with the rise of mobile computing—meaning the worldwide Internet conversation is always in your pocket. Mobile and social also work together to fuel local discovery for everything from potential dates (Tinder) to regional gossip (Yik Yak) to a good place to get a bite to eat (Yelp).

The **peer production** leveraged by collaborating users isn't only used to create social media; it can be used to create *services*, too, and these are also considered to be part of Web 2.0. Skype and BitTorrent leverage users' computers instead of a central IT resource to forward phone calls and video. This ability saves their sponsors the substantial cost of servers, storage, and bandwidth. Peer production is also leveraged to create much of the open source software that supports many of the Web 2.0 efforts described above. Techniques such as crowdsourcing, where initially undefined groups of users band together to solve problems, create code, and develop services, are also a type of peer production. These efforts often seek to leverage the so-called wisdom of crowds, the idea that a large, diverse group often has more collective insight than a single or small group of trained professionals.

peer production

When users collaboratively work to create content, products, and services. Includes social media sites, open source software, and peer-produced services, such as Skype and BitTorrent, where the participation of users provides the infrastructure and computational resources that enable the service.

Related to peer production is the concept of the sharing economy, or **collaborative consumption**, where participants share access to products and services rather than having ownership. While the resources shared via collaborative consumption can be owned by a firm overseeing efforts (e.g., vehicles owned by the car-sharing service ZipCar, or the plane-sharing service NetJets), in other efforts participants come together to pool resources to provide a larger selection of services for customers. The latter is the case with RelayRides, which allows consumers to share their own cars ZipCar-style; Airbnb, which allows you to rent your entire home or a spare room in limited time periods whenever you'd like; and Uber, which provides an app to summon and pay for taxi-style service from a pooled, unused inventory provided by firm-vetted citizen suppliers. While some forms of collaborative consumption can be considered as relating to peer production, we'll cover the phenomenon distinctly and separately from the efforts in this chapter. For more on collaborative consumption, see Chapter 10.

Table 9.1 lists several examples typically considered to fall under the social media monikers, and each is offered alongside its first-generation Internet counterpart.[36] And while this table offers a description and examples of several major classifications of social media, many social media efforts exist outside these classifications and exert influence that exceeds the comparable size of their user base. For example, social news website Reddit is visited by only 6 percent of US Internet users yet is considered so important as a link-sharing virality catalyst that celebrities, CEOs, and even the president of the United States have held Reddit AMA (Ask Me Anything) events.[37] In 2014 alone, Reddit saw 71.25 billion pageviews on over eight thousand active subreddits, a 27 percent increase from 2013.[38] Other specialty sites, such as the question-and-answer site Quora, the programmer's Q&A site StackOverflow, and GitHub (the go-to site for code collaboration and sharing), are proving vital for learning and are well-trawled by those seeking technical talent.[39]

collaborative consumption

When participants share access to products and services rather than having ownership. Shared resources can be owned by a central service provider (e.g., ZipCar) or provided by a community that pools available resources (e.g., Airbnb, Uber).

TABLE 9.1   Web 1.0 versus Web 2.0 (Includes Social Media, Peer-Production Examples)

The Internet's First Phase (Web 1.0)	Social Media and Peer-Production Efforts (Web 2.0)
domain name speculation	→ search engine optimization, fans, and followers
publishing	→ participation
content management systems	→ wikis
directories (taxonomy)	→ tagging ("folksonomy")
Britannica Online, Encarta	→ Wikipedia
personal websites	→ blogging, status updates, and link sharing
Ofoto	→ Instagram, Flickr, Facebook, Twitter
instant messaging, SMS	→ Twitter, Facebook, SnapChat, WhatsApp
Monster.com	→ LinkedIn
RealNetworks	→ YouTube
YellowPages.com	→ Yelp
Travelocity	→ TripAdvisor
Vonage	→ Skype
Catalogs	→ Pinterest
CNN	→ Reddit
Expedia, Orbitz	→ Airbnb, Uber, RelayRides
Online personals	→ Tinder, Match.com, eHarmony
Gossip columns	→ Whisper, Yik Yak
MapQuest, Google Maps	→ Waze

Millions of users, billions of dollars, huge social impact, and most of these efforts grew to influence millions in less time than it takes the average freshman to complete college. When technology moves that quickly, even some of the world's most preeminent thought leaders can be sideswiped.

Consider that when management guru Michael Porter wrote a piece titled "Strategy and the Internet" at the end of the dot-com bubble, he lamented the high cost of building brand online, questioned the power of network effects, and cast a skeptical eye on ad-supported revenue models. Well, it turns out that social media, peer-produced efforts challenged *all* of these concerns. Among the efforts above, all built brand on the cheap with little conventional advertising, and each owes their hypergrowth and high valuation to their ability to harness the network effect.

This chapter can be considered in two parts. The first explains many technologies behind the social media/peer production/Web 2.0 movement, and we provide several examples of their use and impact. The final part of this chapter describes how firms should organize to engage with and take advantage of social media—specifically detailing how to "Get SMART" (with a social media awareness and response team). After going through both sections you should have a solid overview of major social technologies, how businesses are leveraging them, and how firms can organize for effective use while avoiding pitfalls.

TABLE 9.2   Major Social Media Tools

	Description	Features	Technology Providers
Blogs	Short for "Web log"—an online publication that keeps a running chronology of entries. Readers can comment on posts. Can connect to other blogs through blog rolls or trackbacks. **Key uses:** Share ideas, obtain feedback, mobilize a community.	■ Immediate publication and distribution ■ Reverse chronology ■ Comment threads ■ Persistence ■ Searchability ■ Tags ■ Trackbacks	■ Blogger (Google) ■ WordPress ■ Tumblr
Wikis	A website that anyone can edit directly from within the browser. **Key uses:** Collaborate on common tasks or to create a common knowledge base.	■ Collaborative content creation ■ All changes are attributed ■ Revision history, with the ability to roll back changes and revert to earlier versions ■ Automatic notification of updates ■ Searchability ■ Tags ■ Monitoring	■ Socialtext ■ PBWorks ■ Google Sites ■ Atlassian ■ Jive ■ Microsoft (SharePoint) ■ Apple OS X Server
Electronic Social Network	Online community that allows users to establish a personal profile, link to other profiles (i.e., friends), share content, and communicate with members via messaging, posts. Most personal relationships are reciprocal (i.e., both parties agree to be "friends"). **Key Uses:** Discover and reinforce affiliations; identify experts; message individuals or groups; virally share media.	■ Detailed personal profiles using multimedia ■ Affiliations with groups, organizations, and individuals ■ Messaging and public discussions ■ Media sharing ■ "Feeds" of recent activity among members	Open/Public ■ Facebook ■ LinkedIn ■ Google+ Enterprise/Private Platforms ■ Ning ■ Lithium ■ SelectMinds ■ LiveWorld ■ IBM/Lotus Connections ■ Salesforce.com ■ Socialtext

	Description	Features	Technology Providers
Microblogging	Short, asynchronous messaging system. Users send messages to "followers" who aren't required to follow back. **Key Uses:** Distribute time-sensitive information, share opinions, virally spread ideas, run contests and promotions, solicit feedback, provide customer support, track commentary on firms/products/issues, organize protests.	■ 140-character messages sent and received from mobile devices ■ Ability to respond publicly or privately ■ Can specify tags to classify discussion topics for easy searching and building comment threads ■ Follower lists	Open/Public ■ Twitter ■ Google+ Enterprise Platforms ■ Slack ■ HipChat ■ Socialtext Signals ■ Yammer ■ Salesforce.com (Chatter)
Messaging Services	**Key Uses:** Communicate with individuals or groups of users using short-format text, graphics, and video. Most messaging is done using mobile devices.	■ Communication can be public or private, identifying or anonymous ■ Some focus on a specific media type (e.g., photos/Instagram, video/Vine) ■ Others focus on ephemeral, nonpermanent posts that go away, typically after they are read (e.g., SnapChat)	SMS Replacement ■ WhatsApp ■ SnapChat ■ Viber ■ WeChat Photo ■ Instagram (permanent) ■ SnapChat (ephemeral) Enterprise ■ Slack ■ Hip Chat Anonymous ■ Whisper ■ Yik Yak
Question-and-Answer Sites	**Key Uses:** Knowledge sharing, discovery, learning, reputation building.	■ Public, member-posted questions ■ Permanent listing, searchable repository ■ Community voting on "best" or most appropriate answer ■ Reputation building, ranking, badging to encourage active participation	■ Quora (general) ■ Stack Exchange/ Stack Overflow (favored by technical professionals)

KEY TAKEAWAYS

- A new generation of Internet applications is enabling consumers to participate in creating content and services online. While the term Web 2.0 was once widely used, these efforts are now being categorized as social media (creating, sharing, curating, and commenting on content), peer-production (when users collaboratively work to create content, products, and services, which includes social media as well as user-created services like Skype and BitTorrent), and collaborative consumption (participants share access to products and services rather than having ownership). Shared resources can be owned by a central service provider (e.g., ZipCar) or provided by a community that pools available resources (e.g., Airbnb, Uber).

- These efforts have grown rapidly, most with remarkably little investment in promotion. Nearly all of these new efforts leverage network effects to add value and establish their dominance and viral marketing to build awareness and attract users.

- Experts often argue whether Web 2.0 is something new or merely an extension of existing technologies, but it's more important to appreciate the magnitude of the impact of the current generation of services.

- Many of these services often leverage the wisdom of crowds to provide insight, products, or ideas that can be far more accurate or valuable than those provided by a smaller group of professionals. Question-and-answer sites like Quora and Stack Overflow are both learning tools and methods to establish one's reputation and authority while helping the broader user community.

- Microblogging is a channel for sharing and consuming short pieces of content. The category is dominated by Twitter, although many private and public services exist.

- Services aren't limited to consumer use. Firms advertise, promote, and engage with customers over social networks. Other tools, such as Slack, Stack Overflow, and GitHub are considered essential in many modern enterprises.

- Messaging services have exploded with the advent of mobile devices. Many efforts are now preferred to SMS and offer rich exchange of media, specialization in media topic, public or private posting, and public or anonymous identity.

- Network effects play a leading role in enabling these efforts. Many of these services also rely on ad-supported revenue models and open source software.

QUESTIONS AND EXERCISES

1. What distinguishes the various technologies and services that fall under the old-school Web 2.0 moniker (social media and peer production) from the prior generation of Internet sites?

2. Several examples of rapidly rising Web 2.0 efforts are listed in this section. Make your own list of Web 1.0 and Web 2.0 services and technologies. Would you invest in them? Why or why not? Are there cautionary tales of efforts that may not have lived up to their initial hype or promise? Why do you suppose they failed?

3. In what ways do social, peer-produced efforts challenge the assumptions that Michael Porter made regarding Strategy and the Internet?

4. Trends in computing platforms and Internet services change quickly. How have the firms profiled in the bullet points above fared? Has each increased in use, value, and impact or shrunk? Are there other efforts or updates that you think are worthy of making the list in the next edition of this book?

5. How has social media changed the way you consume entertainment, play games, and learn about news? How important are these services to your generation versus the way your parents consume such information? What do these trends mean for managers and marketers?

6. If you have a smartphone, try more than one of the major messaging products. Be sure to explore one that is popular outside of your own country. Why do you suppose the products you've examined are popular? Are there major differences that you've noticed? Would you use the products you tested that were new to you? Why or why not?

7. Try Slack or other enterprise-oriented social productivity tool. Use it for group project work, a campus club, or in your own work environment. Share your experiences (good and/or bad) with your class. Would you recommend this to others? Why or why not?

2.   BLOGS

LEARNING OBJECTIVES

1. **Know what blogs are and how corporations, executives, individuals, and the media use them.**
2. **Understand the benefits and risks of blogging.**
3. **Appreciate the growth in the number of blogs, their influence, and their capacity to generate revenue.**

Blogs (short for Web logs) first emerged almost a decade ago as a medium for posting online diaries. As of early 2015, Tumblr reported hosting nearly 228 million sites.[40] WordPress is said to power nearly a quarter of Internet sites.[41] This is clearly a **long tail** phenomenon, loaded with niche content that remains "discoverable" through search engines and that is often shared via other types of social media like Facebook and Twitter. **Trackbacks** (citation links back to the original blog post) and **blog rolls** (a list of a blogger's favorite sites—a sort of shout-out to blogging peers)—as well as link-sharing on sites like Facebook, Twitter, Google+, LinkedIn, and Reddit—also help distinguish and reinforce the reputation of widely read blogs.

Most blogs offer a two-way dialogue, allowing users to comment (a sort of "letters to the editor" section for each post). The running dialogue can read like an electronic bulletin board and can be an effective way to gather opinion, brainstorm, and vet ideas. Comments also help keep a blogger honest—a vigorous community of commenters will quickly expose a blogger's errors of fact or logic.

Blogging can have significant appeal for an organization looking to be heard. Corporations that blog can enjoy *immediate* and *unfiltered* distribution of their ideas, with no limits on page size, word count, or publication deadline. And they can gather immediate *feedback* from readers via comments. Corporate blogs can be published directly to the public, skipping what bloggers call the mainstream media (MSM) and presenting their words without a journalist filtering their comments or an editor cutting out key points they'd hoped to make. That appeal has attracted some of the most senior executives to blogging. Hotel chief Bill Marriott, Zappos' Tony Hsieh, Virgin Group's Richard Branson, and venture capitalist Ben Horowitz are among those senior leaders who have used their blogs for purposes that have included a combination of marketing, sharing ideas, gathering feedback, press response, image shaping, and reaching consumers directly.

Most mainstream news outlets also supplement their content with blogs that offer greater depth, more detail, and an immediacy for breaking news that is unavailable in print. And many leading online news outlets got their start, first being called blogs: *The Huffington Post* and Tech Crunch (now both owned by Verizon) are prime examples.

Blogs

While the feature set of a particular blog depends on the underlying platform and the preferences of the blogger, several key features are common to most blogs:

- *Immediate and unfiltered publication.* The ability to reach the public without limits on publication size and without having posts filtered, edited, or cut by the mainstream media.
- *Ease of use.* Creating a new post usually involves clicking a single button.
- *Comment threads.* Readers can offer comments on posts.
- *Reverse chronology.* Posts are listed in reverse order of creation, making it easy to see the most recent content.
- *Persistence.* Posts are maintained indefinitely at locations accessible by permanent links.
- *Searchability.* Current and archived posts are easily searchable.
- *Tags.* Posts are often classified under an organized tagging scheme.
- *Trackbacks.* Allows an author to acknowledge the source of an item in their post, which allows bloggers to follow the popularity of their posts among other bloggers.

Despite this increased popularity, blogging has its downside. Blog comments can be a hothouse for spam and the disgruntled. Ham-handed corporate efforts (such as poor response to public criticism or bogus "praise posts") have been ridiculed. Employee blogging can be difficult to control and public postings can "live" forever in the bowels of an Internet search engine or as content pasted on other websites. Bloggers, beware: there are dozens of examples of workers who have been fired for what

---

Blogs

Online journal entries, usually made in a reverse chronological order. Blogs typically provide comment mechanisms where users can post feedback for authors and other readers.

long tail

In this context, refers to an extremely large selection of content or products. The long tail is a phenomenon whereby firms can make money by offering a near-limitless selection.

Trackbacks

Links in a blog post that refer readers back to cited sources. Trackbacks allow a blogger to see which and how many other bloggers are referring to their content. A "trackback" field is supported by most blog software and while it's not required to enter a trackback when citing another post, it's considered good "netiquette" to do so.

blog rolls

A list of a blogger's favorite blogs. While not all blogs include blog rolls, those that do are often displayed on the right or left column of a blog's main page.

employers viewed as inappropriate posts. The voice of the blogosphere can also wield significant influence. While not all blogosphere commentary deserves a response, firms ignore social media at their own peril (see the sidebar called "The New Marketing Lexicon: Owned, Paid, and Earned Media, and Inbound Marketing"). Tips on how firms should organize for social media engagement, issues to consider when developing corporate social media policy, and examples of effective and poor social media use are covered in Section 8

Like any Web page, blogs can be public, or isolated for internal use by being tucked behind a corporate firewall or password protected. Third-party blogging services include Google Blogger, WordPress, and Tumblr, with most offering a combination of free and premium features. The most popular platform for organizations choosing to host their own blog server is the open source WordPress system. Firms often choose this option to gain more control over security and formatting. Tumblr is built for speed and sharing.

The New Marketing Lexicon: Owned, Paid, and Earned Media, and Inbound Marketing

Online marketers and social media executives often refer to owned, paid, and earned media, so some definitions are in order:[42]

Owned media are communication channels that an organization controls. These can include firm-run blogs and websites, any firm-distributed corporate mobile website or app, and organization accounts on social media such as Twitter, Facebook, Pinterest, YouTube, and Instagram. Visit the Starbucks website? That's media owned by Starbucks.

Paid media refers to efforts where an organization pays to leverage a channel or promote a message. Paid media efforts include things such as advertisement and sponsorships. See a Starbucks ad online? That's paid media.

Earned media are promotions that are not paid for or owned but rather grow organically from customer efforts or other favorable publicity. Social media can be a key driver of earned media (think positive tweets, referring Facebook posts, and pins on Pinterest). Other forms of earned media include unsolicited positive press and positive customer word of mouth. View unsolicited praise of Starbucks in your Twitter feed by folks you follow? That's earned media.

Inbound marketing refers to leveraging online channels to draw consumers to the firm with compelling content rather than conventional forms of promotion such as advertising, e-mail marketing, traditional mailings, and sales calls.

Successful inbound marketers produce interesting content that acts as a magnet for the attention of potential customers. Inbound marketers look to attract traffic that is converted to leads that result in sales and hopefully repeat business.[43] Popular blog posts and other forms of social media play a critical role here, as do other online material such as free whitepapers and eBooks. Material deemed useful is likely to gain more Web links and cause firm-affiliated content to rise in **SEO** rankings, making your firm easy to find, pushing your firm higher in search results than your rivals, and solidifying perception of your firm as an expert. A catchy viral campaign can also bring in customers to an owned channel and gain earned media referrals. P&G's Old Spice Man (which included paid media advertisements as well as owned content on the firm's YouTube channel) eventually brought in 40 million YouTube views and is credited with a 107 percent increase in body wash sales in the thirty days following the campaign launch.[44] Many firms with sophisticated inbound marketing programs leverage social media analytic platforms (see Section 8). In fact, the term inbound marketing (sometimes called permission marketing) was coined by Brian Halligan, cofounder and CEO of HubSpot, a provider of social media and other analytics tools.

Owned media

Communication channels that an organization controls. These can include firm-run blogs, Web sites, apps, and organization accounts on social media such as Twitter, Facebook, Pinterest, YouTube, and Instagram.

Paid media

Refers to efforts where an organization pays to leverage a channel or promote a message. Paid media efforts include things such as advertisement and sponsorships.

Earned media

Promotions that are not paid for or owned but rather grow organically from customer efforts or other favorable publicity. Social media, word of mouth, and unsolicited positive press mentions are all examples of earned media.

Inbound marketing

Leveraging online channels to draw consumers to the firm with compelling content rather than conventional forms of promotion such as advertising, e-mail marketing, traditional mailings, and sales calls.

SEO

Search Engine Optimization. The process of improving a page's organic page rankings (rank in search results).

The Old Spice Man (which included paid media advertising as well as content on the firm's owned YouTube channel) created a viral sensation (lots of earned media referrals), leading to over 45 million YouTube views. The campaign is credited with contributing to more than doubling body wash sales in the month after the campaign's launch.

Old Spice | The Man Your Man Could Smell Like

Old Spice · 427 videos

Subscribe   365,104

45,871,724

👍 163,201   👎 3,258

KEY TAKEAWAYS

- Blogs provide a rapid way to distribute ideas and information from one writer to many readers.
- Search engines, social media sharing, and trackbacks allow a blogger's community of readers to spread the word on interesting posts and help distinguish and reinforce the reputations of widely read blogs.
- The comments section in blogs can create a conversation to gather opinion, vet ideas, and brainstorm. Public commentary can also apply pressure to correct inaccuracies and keep a blogger honest.
- Well-known blogs can be powerfully influential, acting as flashpoints on public opinion.
- Firms ignore influential bloggers at their peril, but organizations should also be cautious about how they use and engage blogs and avoid flagrantly promotional or biased efforts.
- Senior executives from several industries use blogs for business purposes, including marketing, sharing ideas, gathering feedback, press response, image shaping, and reaching consumers directly without press filtering.
- Blogs are a type of "owned" media, but when users online share blog posts from an organization, this constitutes a type of "earned" that generates even more awareness at no additional cost.
- Effective blogs can improve a firm's SEO (search engine rankings results), making the firm easier to find and possibly pushing online visibility ahead of rivals.

QUESTIONS AND EXERCISES

1. Search online to find out which blogs are currently the most popular. Why do you suppose the leaders are so popular?

2. How are popular blogs discovered? How is their popularity reinforced?

3. Are blog comment fields useful? If so, to whom or how? What is the risk associated with allowing users to comment on blog posts? How should a blogger deal with comments that they don't agree with?

4. Why would a corporation, an executive, a news outlet, or a college student want to blog? What are the benefits? What are the concerns?

5. Identify firms and executives that are blogging online. Bring examples to class and be prepared to offer your critique of their efforts. Show what you feel are effective examples, as well as those that you think are weak. How can the bad ones improve?

6. Investigate blogs that aren't corporate but that you still find useful. Share your list of favorites with your professor. Why do you like the blogs on your list? Are there blogs that are particularly useful for students of this course? Which ones?

7. Investigate current US Federal Trade Commission laws (or the laws in your home country) that govern bloggers and other social media use. How do these restrictions impact how firms interact with bloggers? What are the penalties and implications if such rules aren't followed? Are there unwritten rules of good practice that firms and bloggers should consider as well? What might those be?

8. What advantage do blogs have over the MSM? What advantage does the MSM have over the most popular blogs?

9. Start a blog using Tumblr, Blogger.com, WordPress.com, or some other blogging service. Post a comment to another blog. Look for the trackback field when making a post—if it's available, be sure to enter the trackback for any content you cite in your blog.

10. Gather examples of paid, earned, and owned media. Share with your class. Indicate whether you find this media effective or ineffective and if you've got suggestions for improvement, share them with your class.

3. WIKIS

LEARNING OBJECTIVES

1. **Know what wikis are and how they are used by corporations and the public at large.**
2. **Understand the technical and social features that drive effective and useful wikis.**
3. **Suggest opportunities where wikis would be useful and consider under what circumstances their use may present risks.**
4. **Recognize how social media such as wikis and blogs can influence a firm's customers and brand.**

A **wiki** is a website anyone can edit directly within a Web browser (provided the site grants the user edit access). Wikis derive their name from the Hawaiian word for "quick." Wikis can be one of the speediest ways to collaboratively create content online.

Many popular online wikis serve as a shared knowledge repository in some domain. The largest and most popular wiki is Wikipedia, but there are hundreds of publicly accessible wikis that anyone can participate in, with examples ranging from Wine Wiki for oenophiles to Wookieepedia, the Star Wars wiki. Wikis can also be used for any collaborative effort—from meeting planning to project management. And in addition to the hundreds of public wikis, there are many thousand more that are hidden away behind firewalls, used as proprietary internal tools for organizational collaboration. Many wikis also serve as knowledge management systems that act as a sort of collective corporate memory that's vital for sharing skills, learning, and preserving expertise even when employees leave the firm.

wiki

A Web site that can be modified by anyone, from directly within a Web browser (provided that user is granted edit access).

what you see is what you get (WYSIWYG)

A phrase used to describe graphical editing tools, such as those found in a wiki, page layout program, or other design tool.

roll back

The ability to revert a wiki page to a prior version. This is useful for restoring earlier work in the event of a posting error, inaccuracy, or vandalism.

Want to add to or edit a wiki entry? On most sites you just click the "Edit" link. Wikis support **what you see is what you get (WYSIWYG)** editing that, while not as robust as traditional word processors, is still easy enough for most users to grasp without training or knowledge of arcane code or markup language. Users can make changes to existing content and can easily create new pages or articles and link them to other pages in the wiki. Wikis also provide a version history. Click the "History" link on Wikipedia, for example, and you can see when edits were made and by whom. This feature allows the community to **roll back** a wiki to a prior state, in the event that someone accidentally deletes key info, or intentionally defaces a page. While the downside of most wikis is that only one person at a time can edit a page, many users find the version history and roll back features of wikis to be more clear than collaborating simultaneously in a tool such as Google Docs or Office365.

Wikis are available both as software (commercial as well as open source varieties) that firms can install on their own computers and as hosted online services (subscription or ad-supported) where software and content are housed 'in the cloud' by third parties that run the technology for wiki users. Since wikis can be started without the oversight or involvement of a firm's IT department, their appearance in organizations often comes from grassroots user initiative.

Wikis

As with blogs, a wiki's features set varies depending on the specific wiki tool chosen, as well as administrator design, but most wikis support the following key features:

- All changes are *attributed*, so others can see who made a given edit.
- A complete *revision history* is maintained so changes can be compared against prior versions and rolled back as needed.
- There is automatic *notification* and *monitoring* of updates; users subscribe to wiki content and can receive updates via e-mail or RSS feed when pages have been changed or new content has been added.
- All the pages in a wiki are *searchable*.
- Specific wiki pages can be classified under an organized *tagging* scheme.

wikimasters

Individuals often employed by organizations to review community content in order to delete excessive posts, move commentary to the best location, and edit as necessary.

griefers

Internet vandal and mischief maker; also sometimes referred to as a troll.

Jump-starting a wiki can be a challenge, and an underused wiki can be a ghost town of orphan, out-of-date, and inaccurate content. Fortunately, once users see the value of wikis, use and effectiveness often snowballs. The unstructured nature of wikis is also both a strength and weakness. Some organizations employ **wikimasters** to "garden" community content: "prune" excessive posts, "transplant" commentary to the best location, and "weed" as necessary.

The larger and more active a wiki community, the more likely it is that content will be up to date and that errors or vandalism will be quickly corrected (again, we see the influence of network effects, where products and services with larger user bases become more valuable). At Wikipedia, for example, **griefers** and partisans regularly alter pages (in one noteworthy stretch, the page of former US President Jimmy Carter was regularly replaced with a photo of a "scruffy, random unshaven man with his left index finger shoved firmly up his nose.")[45] But the Wikipedia community is so large and attentive that such changes are often recognized in seconds and rolled back, and mischief makers soon give up and move on. Several studies have shown that large community wiki entries are as or more accurate than professional publication counterparts.[46]

Wikis can make workers more productive and informed, and kill corporate time-wasters. At Disney's Pixar, wikis are used to improve meeting efficiency, with agendas and key materials distributed in advance. Posting corrections, comments, goals, deadlines, and completion keeps everyone involved and aware of expectations and progress.[47] Sony uses wikis for cross-functional collaboration on projects (finance, engineering, marketing), with secure access making sure that information is released on a need-to-know basis. Non-profits, investment banks, law offices, even the US intelligence services all take advantage of the power of wikis.[48]

neutral point of view (NPOV)

An editorial style that is free of bias and opinion. Wikipedia norms dictate that all articles must be written in NPOV.

Don't Underestimate the Power of Wikipedia

Not only is the nonprofit Wikipedia, with its enthusiastic army of unpaid experts and editors, replacing the three-hundred-year reference reign of *Encyclopedia Britannica*, Wikipedia entries can impact nearly all large-sized organizations. Wikipedia is the go-to, first-choice reference site for a generation of "netizens," and Wikipedia entries are invariably one of the top links, often the first link, to appear in Internet search results.

This position means that anyone from top executives to political candidates to any firm large enough to warrant an entry has to contend with the very public record of Wikipedia. In the same way that firms monitor their online reputations in blog posts and Twitter tweets, they've also got to keep an eye on wikis.

But firms that overreach and try to influence an entry outside of Wikipedia's mandated **neutral point of view (NPOV)** risk a backlash and public exposure. Version tracking means the wiki sees all. Users on computers at right-leaning Fox News were embarrassingly caught editing the wiki page of the lefty pundit and politician Al Franken (a nemesis of Fox's Bill O'Reilly)[49]; Sony staffers were flagged as editing the entry for a version of the exclusive Xbox game Halo 3[50]; and none other than Wikipedia founder Jimmy Wales was criticized for editing his own Wikipedia biography[51]—acts that some consider bad online form at best, and dishonest at worst.

One last point on using Wikipedia for research. Remember that according to its own stated policies, Wikipedia isn't an original information source; rather, it's a clearinghouse for verified information. So citing Wikipedia as a reference usually isn't considered good form. Instead, seek out original (and verifiable) sources, such as those presented via the links at the bottom of Wikipedia entries.

KEY TAKEAWAYS

- Wikis can be powerful tools for many-to-many content collaboration, and can be ideal for creating resources that benefit from the input of many such as encyclopedia entries, meeting agendas, and project status documents.
- The greater the number of wiki users, the more likely the information contained in the wiki will be accurate and grow in value.
- Wikis can be public or private.
- The availability of free or low-cost wiki tools can create a knowledge clearinghouse on topics, firms, products, and even individuals. Organizations can seek to harness the collective intelligence (wisdom of crowds) of online communities, and create a living knowledge repository. The openness of wikis also acts as a mechanism for promoting organizational transparency and accountability.

QUESTIONS AND EXERCISES

1. Visit a wiki, either an established site like Wikipedia, or a wiki service like Socialtext, PBWorks, or Atlassian Confluence. Make an edit to a wiki entry or use a wiki service to create a new wiki for your own use (e.g., for a class team to use in managing a group project). Be prepared to share your experience with the class.

2. What factors determine the value of a wiki? Which key concept, first introduced in Chapter 2 drives a wiki's success?

3. If anyone can edit a wiki, why aren't more sites crippled by vandalism or by inaccurate or inappropriate content? Are there technical reasons not to be concerned? Are there "social" reasons that can alleviate concern?

4. Give examples of corporate wiki use, as well as examples where firms used wikis to engage their customers or partners. What is the potential payoff of these efforts? Are there risks associated with these efforts?

5. Do you feel that you can trust content in wikis? Do you feel this content is more or less reliable than content in print encyclopedias? Than the content in newspaper articles? Why?

6. Have you ever run across an error in a wiki entry? Describe the situation.

7. Is it ethical for a firm or individual to edit their own Wikipedia entry? Under what circumstances would editing a Wikipedia entry seem unethical to you? Why? What are the risks a firm or individual are exposed to when making edits to public wiki entries? How do you suppose individuals and organizations are identified when making wiki edits?

8. Would you cite Wikipedia as a reference when writing a paper? Why or why not?

4. SOCIAL NETWORKS

LEARNING OBJECTIVES

1. Know what social networks are, be able to list key features, and understand how they are used by individuals, groups, and corporations.
2. Understand the difference between major social networks such as Facebook, Google+, and LinkedIn.
3. Recognize the benefits and risks of using social networks.
4. Be aware of trends that may influence the evolution of social networks.

Social networks

An online community that allows users to establish a personal profile and communicate with others. Large public social networks include Facebook, LinkedIn, and Google+, and Pinterest.

Social networks allow you to set up a profile, share content, comment on what others have shared, and follow the updates of particular users, groups, firms, and brands that may also be part of those networks. Many also are platforms for the deployment of third-party applications. The two most dominant public social networks are Facebook and LinkedIn, sites often described as the personal and professional networks, respectively. But there are also several other potentially high-value social networks that firms should consider. Google+ is smaller and has less engaged users than Facebook, but it is also integrated into the Google toolbar, the search feature, Gmail, and many of the Web giant's other services. And the Hangouts feature of Google+ (a video chat and broadcast platform with integrated messaging) is considered an "unmitigated success"[52] that is transforming workplace collaboration and webinars[53] while providing a platform for everything from online education to hosting live concerts.[54] And a host of third-party networks, including Ning, Lithium, and SelectMinds (now part of Oracle), allow firms to "roll their own" private networks.

Another example is the visually oriented social network Pinterest, which is driving cool-hunting, high-value buyers. Web-based home furnishings provider One Kings Lane benefits greatly from the viral sharing of Pinterest fans. Since offering "Pin It" buttons next to all items sold on its website, Pinterest traffic has nearly exceeded that of Facebook, while referrals from Pinterest are three times more likely to result in a sale than visits from the site's typical visitor.[55] The Pinterest buy button is an obvious evolution, moving the firm from public scrapbook to shopping cart.[56] Some see Pinterest as a powerful vehicle for e-commerce, since it focuses on the interest graph (what I like) rather than simply the social ties of "who I know."

Hundreds of firms have established pages on major social networks, and these are now legitimate customer- and client-engagement platforms. Social networks are a hothouse for "earned" media, where enthusiast-consumers can help spread the word about products and services. Much of the activity that takes place on social networks, spread via feed (or news feed). Pioneered by Facebook but now adopted by most services, feeds provide a timely list of the activities of and public messages from people, groups, and organizations that an individual has an association with.

viral

In this context, information or applications that spread rapidly between users.

Feeds are inherently **viral**. By seeing what others are doing on a social network, and by leveraging the power of others to act as word-of-mouth evangelists, feeds can rapidly mobilize populations, prompt activism, and offer low-cost promotion and awareness of a firm's efforts. Many firms now see a Facebook presence and social engagement strategy as vital. Facebook's massive size and the viral power of spreading the word through feeds, plus the opportunity to invite commentary and engage consumers in a dialogue, rather than a continual barrage of promotion, is changing the way that firms and customers interact (indeed, you'll hear many successful social media professionals declare that social media is more about conversations with customers than about advertising-style promotion).

Feeds are also controversial. Many users have reacted negatively to a public broadcast of their online activity, and feed mismanagement can create accusations of spamming, public relations snafus, a reduction in the likelihood that a firm's message will appear in a given fan's feed, and user discontent and can potentially open up a site to legal action. And some networks are curating user feeds, so it's not guaranteed that what you're posting on social networks will even be seen. Want more reach? Firms like Facebook will sell you this through its advertising products.

Social Networks

The foundation of a social network is the user profile, but utility goes beyond the sort of listing found in a corporate information directory. Typical features of a social network include support for the following:

- Detailed personal profiles

- Affiliations with *groups* (e.g., alumni, employers, hobbies, fans, health conditions, causes); with *individuals* (e.g., specific "friends"); and with *products*, *firms*, and other *organizations*
- Private *messaging* and public *discussions*
- Media *sharing* (text, photos, video)
- Discovery-fueling feeds of recent activity among members (e.g., status changes, new postings, photos, applications installed)

While Facebook was originally targeted at the social lives of college students (see Chapter 11), LinkedIn was conceived from the start as a social network for business users. On LinkedIn, members post profiles and contact information, list their work history, and can be "endorsed" by others on the network. It's sort of like having your resumé and letters of recommendation in a single location. Users can pose questions to members of their network, engage in group discussions, and ask for introductions through mutual contacts. The site has also introduced a variety of additional services, including messaging, information sharing, and news and content curation—yes, LinkedIn will help you find stuff you're likely to be most interested in (wasn't that Google's job?). Services owned by LinkedIn include SlideShare, a great place to discover educational presentations (and for individuals and firms to showcase their best work); and Lynda.com, an online education platform where users can learn all sorts of new skills.[57] Want tips on how to best use the service? Look online for "LinkedIn for Students." LinkedIn also makes money from online ads, premium subscriptions, and hiring tools for recruiters.

Active members find the site invaluable for maintaining professional contacts, seeking peer advice, networking, and even recruiting. The manager of enterprise staffing at Starbucks has stated that LinkedIn is "one of the best things for finding mid-level executives"[58] while others claim it is a far better place to uncover quality candidates than sites like Monster.com or CareerBuilder.[59] Such networks are also putting increasing pressure on firms to work particularly hard to retain top talent. While once HR managers fiercely guarded employee directories for fear that a list of talent may fall into the hands of rivals, today's social networks make it easy for anyone to gain a list of a firm's staff, complete with contact information and a private messaging channel.

FIGURE 9.3

LinkedIn also owns SlideShare, where you can find all sorts of interesting educational content, like this presentation about LinkedIn. SlideShare is a great way for students and professionals to showcase their own work, helping build a portfolio online that potential employers can reference.

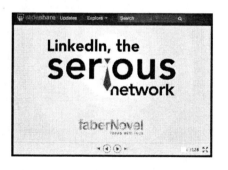

4.1   Corporate Use of Social Networks

Social networks have also become organizational productivity tools. While LinkedIn can help network all of a firm's employees, and Facebook has introduced a similar "Facebook at Work" service, many firms are choosing to implement their own internal social network platforms that they hope are more secure and tailored to firm needs. At the most basic level, these networks have supplanted the traditional employee directory. Social network listings are easy to update and expand, and employees are encouraged to add their own photos, interests, and expertise to create a living digital identity.

Firms such as Deloitte, Dow Chemical, and Goldman Sachs have created social networks for "alumni" who have left the firm or retired. These networks can be useful in maintaining contacts for future business leads, rehiring former employees (20 percent of Deloitte's experienced hires are so-called *boomerangs*, or returning employees), or recruiting retired staff to serve as contractors when labor is tight.[60] Maintaining such networks will be critical in industries like IT and health care that are likely to be plagued by worker shortages for years to come.

Social networking can also be important for organizations like IBM, where some 42 percent of employees regularly work from home or client locations. IBM's social network makes it easier to locate employee expertise within the firm, organize virtual work groups, and communicate across large distances.[61] As a dialogue catalyst, a social network transforms the public directory into a font of knowledge sharing that promotes organization flattening and value-adding expertise sharing.

While IBM has developed their own social network platforms, firms are increasingly turning to third-party vendors like SelectMinds (adopted by Deloitte, Dow Chemical, and Goldman Sachs) and LiveWorld (adopted by Intuit, eBay, the NBA, and Scientific American). With more robust corporate tools now offered by LinkedIn and Facebook, we might see proprietary, in-house efforts start to migrate there over time. The corporate messaging service, Slack, also looks like it's emerging as a major enterprise networking player. Channels are archived, easily searchable, and accessible across desktop and mobile. Entrepreneurs take note: Slack (started by Flickr co-founder Stewart Butterfield) shows that an elegant, easy-to-use solution that delivers value can grow big, even as social giants bulk up their services. *The New York Times* calls the tool the "App that may finally kill email."[62] They should know, the *Times* is a user, along with other biggies that include Walmart, HBO, and even the US State Department.[63]

A Little Too Public?

As with any type of social media, content flows in social networks are difficult to control. Embarrassing disclosures can emerge from public systems or insecure internal networks. Employees embracing a culture of digital sharing may err and release confidential or proprietary information. Networks could serve as a focal point for the disgruntled (imagine the activity on a corporate social network after a painful layoff). Publicly declared affiliations, political or religious views, excessive contact, declined participation, and other factors might lead to awkward or strained employee relationships. Users may not want to add a coworker as a friend on a public network if it means they'll expose their activities, lives, persona, photos, sense of humor, and friends as they exist outside of work. And many firms fear wasted time as employees surf the musings and photos of their peers.

All are advised to be cautious in their social media sharing. Employers are trawling the Internet, mining Facebook, and scouring YouTube for any tip-off that a would-be hire should be passed over. A word to the wise: those Facebook party pics, YouTube videos of open mic performances, or blog postings from a particularly militant period might not age well and may haunt you forever in a Google search. Think twice before clicking the upload button! As *Socialnomics* author Erik Qualman puts it, "What happens in Vegas stays on YouTube (and Flickr, Twitter, Facebook…)."

Firms have also created their own online communities to foster brainstorming and customer engagement. Dell's IdeaStorm.com forum collects user feedback and is credited with prompting line offerings, such as the firm's introduction of a Linux-based laptop.[64] At MyStarbucksIdea.com, the coffee giant has leveraged user input to launch a series of innovations ranging from splash sticks that prevent spills in to-go cups, to new menu items. Both IdeaStorm and MyStarbucksIdea run on a platform offered by Salesforce.com that not only hosts these sites but also provides integration into Facebook and other services. Starbucks (35.5 million Facebook "fans"[65]) has extensively leveraged the site, using Facebook as a linchpin in the "Free Pastry Day" promotion (credited with generating one million in-store visits in a single day) and promotion of the firm's AIDS-related RED campaign, which garnered an astonishing three hundred ninety million "viral impressions" through feeds, wall posts, and other messaging.[66]

Social Networks and Health Care

The mother of a fourteen-year-old boy returned to his doctor after her son coughed up a strange "branch-like" mass. The boy had no sore throat, pains, or fever. His lungs were clear, and he reported feeling better after expectorating the mass. The boy's doctor prepped the specimen to send out for lab analysis, but doc first took a photo of it, and posted it to Sermo, a social network for physicians. He invited other doctors to comment and included a survey asking colleagues what they thought it was. Answers started coming in within thirty minutes, and the consensus prompted urgent action. One doc posted, "He needs to see cardiology urgently for plastic bronchitis" (ultimately proved to be the correct diagnosis). Another shared that a three-year-old patient had died recently when a similar plastic bronchitis incident went undiagnosed. Plastic bronchitis is an extremely rare respiratory illness and most primary care physicians have never encountered it. Thanks to Sermo, the boy was referred to specialists before any lab results came back, and he was treated successfully.[67]

A photo posted to the physicians' social network, Sermo, of a mass coughed up by an otherwise healthy fourteen-year-old patient prompted life-saving treatment to get underway even before lab results were returned.

Source: Courtesy of Sermo

Sermo (which means conversation in Latin) is a godsend to physicians looking to gain peer opinion on confounding cases or other medical questions. Sermo claims most doctors receive responses within an hour and a half of posting, and most cases are solved within twenty-four hours. Eighty-five percent of posting physicians say they received information they were looking for. More than 340,000 doctors in the US and UK are Sermo members, although a much smaller percentage is active on the site. Member physicians are first screened and verified to maintain the integrity of the service. Harnessing the wisdom of the medical crowd can be powerful. The US National Center on Policy Analysis reports that from 10 to 20 percent of cases are misdiagnosed annually, and 28 percent of those are life-threatening, contributing to some 40,000 diagnostic error deaths each year, just in US intensive care units. In a recent year, member physicians posted 3,500 challenging patient cases the site, which were viewed 700,000 times and received 50,000 total comments.[68] Sermo posts can also send valuable warning signals on issues such as disease outbreaks or unseen drug side effects. And doctors have also used the service to rally against insurance company policy changes.[69]

FIGURE 9.4

These are some of the rich health monitoring and sharing tools available on PatientsLikeMe. Note that treatments, symptoms, and quality-of-life measures can be tracked over time.

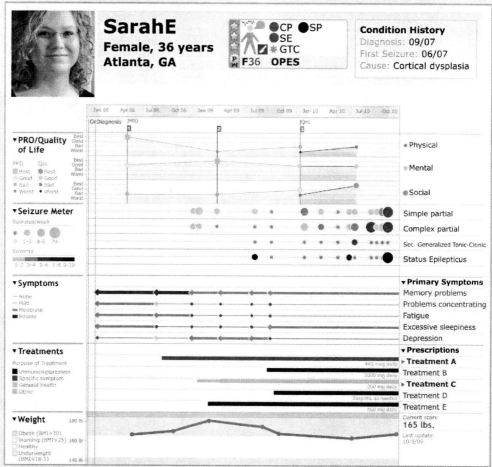

Source: PatientsLikeMe, 2011.

While Sermo focuses on the provider side of the health care equation, PatientsLikeMe (PLM) offers a social network empowering chronically ill patients across a wide variety of disease states. The firm's "openness policy" is in contrast to privacy rules posted on many sites and encourages patients to publicly track and post conditions, treatments, and symptom variation over time, using the site's sophisticated graphing and charting tools. The goal is to help others improve the quality of their own care by harnessing the wisdom of crowds.

Todd Small, a multiple sclerosis sufferer, used the member charts and data on PLM to discover that his physician had been undermedicating him. After sharing site data with his doctor, his physician verified the problem and upped the dose. Small reports that the finding changed his life, helping him walk better than he had in a decade and a half and eliminating a feeling that he described as being trapped in "quicksand."[70] In another example of PLM's people power, the site ran its own clinical trial–like experiment to rapidly investigate promising claims that the drug Lithium could improve conditions for ALS (amyotrophic lateral sclerosis) patients. While community efforts did not support these initial claims, a decision was arrived at in months, whereas previous efforts to marshal researchers and resources to focus on the relatively rare disease would have taken many years, even if funding could be found.[71]

Both Sermo and PatientsLikeMe are start-ups that are still exploring the best way to fund their efforts for growth and impact. Regardless of where these firms end up, with the rise of new methods for users to track and share health and fitness information (e.g., Apple's HealthKit and ResearchKit, and Google's Fit), it should be clear from these examples that social media will remain a powerful force on the health care landscape.

KEY TAKEAWAYS

- Electronic social networks help individuals maintain contacts, discover and engage people with common interests, share updates, and organize as groups.
- Modern social networks are major messaging services, supporting private one-to-one notes, public postings, and broadcast updates or "feeds."
- Social networks also raise some of the strongest privacy concerns, as status updates, past messages, photos, and other content linger, even as a user's online behavior and network of contacts changes.
- Network effects and cultural differences result in one social network being favored over others in a particular culture or region.
- Information spreads virally via news feeds. Feeds can rapidly mobilize populations, and dramatically spread the adoption of applications. The flow of content in social networks is also difficult to control and sometimes results in embarrassing public disclosures.
- Feeds have a downside and there have been instances where feed mismanagement has caused user discontent, public relations problems, and the possibility of legal action.
- The use of public social networks within private organizations is growing, and many organizations are implementing their own, private, social networks. LinkedIn is seen as a key recruiting, contact maintenance, and learning tool, while corporate messaging tools like Slack are used to increase employee productivity.
- Firms are also setting up social networks for customer engagement and mining these sites for customer ideas, innovation, and feedback.

QUESTIONS AND EXERCISES

1. Visit the major social networks (Facebook, LinkedIn, Google+, Pinterest). What distinguishes one from the other? Are you a member of any of these services? Why or why not?

2. How are organizations like Deloitte, Goldman Sachs, and IBM using social networks? What advantages do they gain from these systems?

3. What factors might cause an individual, employee, or firm to be cautious in their use of social networks?

4. How do you feel about the feed feature common in social networks like Facebook? What risks does a firm expose itself to if it leverages feeds? How might a firm mitigate these kinds of risks?

5. Investigate Facebook for Work. Would you want to use this service? Would it concern you? Why or why not?

6. What sorts of restrictions or guidelines should firms place on the use of social networks or the other Web 2.0 tools discussed in this chapter? Are these tools a threat to security? Can they tarnish a firm's reputation? Can they enhance a firm's reputation? How so?

7. Why do information and applications spread so quickly within networks like Facebook? What feature enables this? What key promotional concept (described in Chapter 2) does this feature foster?

8. Investigate social networks on your own. Look for examples of their use for fostering political and social movements; for their use in health care, among doctors, patients, and physicians; and for their use among other professional groups or enthusiasts. Identify how these networks might be used effectively, and also look for any potential risks or downside. How are these efforts supported? Is there a clear revenue model, and do you find these methods appropriate or potentially controversial? Be prepared to share your findings with your class.

9. Investigate the Hangouts feature of Google+ and come to class prepared to discuss how it can be effectively used to improve your education experience. Consider inviting a guest speaker to have a Hangout with the class. Search online for tips on running an effective hangout, and share them with the speaker and your classmates before running the event. If the program is a success, share your experiences and recommendations with other faculty, your dean, and others at your university.

10. Visit Quora, Stack Exchange, or another popular question-and-answer site (considered a subset of social networks by some). Search the website. Did you find that a question you were interested in was already answered? Do you trust answers on these websites and would you return to use them in the future? Why or why not?

11. Visit LinkedIn for Students. Use information on this page to create or enhance your own LinkedIn page. Share what you've learned with your class. Identify a "best practice" LinkedIn page and be prepared to share with your class why you think the page is so effective and what others can learn from the person profiled.

12. Visit SlideShare and browse on topics of interest. Do you find the site useful? Would you publish your own content here? Why or why not?

13. Firms often rely on young people to bring new social technologies into the firm. Keep pace with products: try an enterprise messaging tool like Slack, HipChat, or other social service (most have free trials or are free for a small number of users). Use it for a club or group project. Report back to your class on your experiences and offer a review.

5. TWITTER AND THE RISE OF MICROBLOGGING

LEARNING OBJECTIVES

1. **Appreciate the rapid rise of Twitter—its scale, scope, and broad appeal.**
2. **Understand how Twitter is being used by individuals, organizations, and political movements.**
3. **Contrast Twitter and microblogging with Facebook, conventional blogs, and other social media efforts.**
4. **Understand how organizations use Twitter for organic as well as paid promotion.**
5. **Consider the commercial viability of the effort, its competitive environment, and concerns regarding growth.**

Twitter is a microblogging service that allows users to post 140-character messages (tweets) via the Web, SMS, or a variety of third-party desktop and smartphone applications. Originally spawned as a side project at the now-failed podcasting start-up Odeo (an effort backed by Blogger.com founder Evan Williams), Twitter has morphed into one of the most influential channels for public, global, instant communications. Today virtually every significant website and mobile app has some form of Twitter integration, and it's rare to listen to a news or entertainment broadcast without hearing how you can "follow" or "connect" via the service. Twitter has 300 million monthly active users (MAUs)[72] and its influence (with tweets picked up in the news, published in media, and leveraged for activism) extends far beyond its base of regular users. Over 500 million tweets are sent each day—80 percent or more via smartphones.[73] The firm went public in fall 2013, with a market cap at the end of its first day of trading of roughly $25 billion.

The site also allows for the direct posting of images, video (captured and edited within the Twitter app, or through Twitter-owned Vine for short-length looping video clips), and Twitter also owns the Periscope real-time video streaming and video archiving service. The microblog moniker is a bit of a misnomer. The service actually has more in common with Facebook's status updates and news feeds than it does with traditional blogs. But unlike Facebook, where most users must approve "friends" before they can see status updates, Twitter's default setting allows for asymmetrical following (although it is possible to set up private Twitter accounts and to block followers).

Twitter leadership has described the service as communicating "The Pulse of the Planet."[74] Sure, there's a lot of inane "tweeting" going on, but for many, Twitter is a discovery engine; a taste-making machine; a critical source of market intelligence; a source of breaking news; a learning channel; a feedback source; an educational tool; a way to stay connected with family, friends, colleagues, and thought leaders; and an instantaneous way to plug into the moment's zeitgeist.

Users can classify comments on a given topic using **hashtags** (keywords preceded by the "#" or "hash" symbol), allowing others to quickly find related tweets (e.g., #iranelection, #oscars, #BringBackOurGirls, #sxsw). Any user can create a hashtag—just type it into your tweet (you may want to search Twitter first to make sure that the tag is not in use by an unrelated topic and that if it is in use, it appropriately describes how you want your tweet classified).

Twitter is also emerging as a legitimate business tool. Organizations have found Twitter useful for real-time promotions, for time-sensitive information, for scheduling and yield management, for customer engagement and support, for promotion, for intelligence gathering, for idea sourcing, and as a sales channel.

Consider the following commercial examples:

- Starbucks uses Twitter in a variety of ways. It has run Twitter-based contests and used the service to allow customers to request free samples of new products, such as its VIA instant coffee line. Twitter has also been a way for the company to engage customers in its cause-based marketing efforts, such as (Starbucks) RED, which supports (Product) RED. The firm has recruited staff via Twitter and was one of the first firms to participate in Twitter's advertising model featuring "promoted tweets." Starbucks even allows you to "Tweet a Coffee," sending a valid eGift card to anyone using the service.

- Twitter is becoming a commercial platform. Amazon allows Twitter users to mark items for order using the hashtag #AmazonCart. Dominoes has experimented with allowing users to order a pizza via hashtag or pizza emoji. In a more practical example, the Twitter "Buy" button launched with initial examples tied to sports jerseys and event tickets.

- Dell used Twitter to uncover an early warning sign indicating poor design of the keyboard on one of its portable computers. After a series of tweets from early adopters indicated that the apostrophe and return keys were positioned too closely together, the firm dispatched design change orders quickly enough to correct the problem when the next version of the product was launched just three months later.[75]

- Twitter is credited with having raised millions via Text-to-Donate and other fundraising as part of global disaster relief. Services now allow users to donate directly via tweeting a specific hash tag after linking the service to a payment method.[76]

- Twitter can be a boon for sharing time-sensitive information. The True Massage and Wellness Spa in San Francisco tweets last-minute cancellations to tell customers of an unexpected schedule opening. With Twitter, appointments remain booked solid. Gourmet food trucks are also using Twitter to share location and create hipster buzz. Los Angeles's Kogi Korean Taco Truck now has over 134,000 followers and uses Twitter to reveal where it's parked, ensuring long lines of BBQ-craving foodies. Of the firm's success, owner Roy Choi says, "I have to give all the credit to Twitter."[77]

hashtags

A method for organizing tweets where keywords are preceded by the # character.

FIGURE 9.5 Bin Laden's Neighbor Accidentally Tweets the US Raid

Tweets (topmost is most recent) by Abbottabad, Pakistan-based IT consultant Sohaib Athar (Twitter handle @ReallyVirtual), who had no idea (1) that Osama Bin Laden was his neighbor and (2) that his tweets about the neighborhood disturbance were actually a live account of a US raid.

@ReallyVirtual
Sohaib Athar

Uh oh, now I'm the guy who liveblogged the Osama raid without knowing it.

2 May via TweetDeck   ☆ Favorite   ⇄ Retweet   ↩ Reply

@ReallyVirtual
Sohaib Athar

A huge window shaking bang here in Abbottabad Cantt. I hope its not the start of something nasty :-S

1 May via TweetDeck   ☆ Favorite   ⇄ Retweet   ↩ Reply

@ReallyVirtual
Sohaib Athar

Helicopter hovering above Abbottabad at 1AM (is a rare event).

1 May via TweetDeck   ☆ Favorite   ⇄ Retweet   ↩ Reply

Retweeted by Davidbtweet and 100+ others

Source: J. O'Dell, "One Twitter User Reports Live from Osama Bin Laden Raid," Mashable, May 2, 2011.

FIGURE 9.6

Twitter's Buy button allows firms to embed promotions within tweets. Such efforts may be especially effective for time-sensitive promotions and expiring inventory.

Organizations are well advised to monitor Twitter activity related to the firm, as it can act as a sort of canary-in-a-coal mine uncovering emerging events. Users are increasingly using the service as a way to form flash protest crowds. Amazon.com, for example, was caught off-guard over a holiday weekend when thousands used Twitter to rapidly protest the firm's reclassification of gay and lesbian books (#amazonfail). Others use the platform for shame and ridicule. BP has endured withering ridicule from the satire account @BPGlobalPR (followed by roughly 200,000 people two months after the spill).

5.1 Organic Reach and Advertising

Facebook posts are curated by the firm's algorithms, and not every post to a fan page is seen by people who have "liked" a page. In fact, Facebook's algorithms have continually decreased the reach of fan page posts, meaning that firms are reaching fewer and fewer of their fans (although Facebook will gladly sell firms ad products to improve reach).[78] By contrast, Twitter posts appear chronologically in the feed of any follower. This means that as long as followers have Twitter open, any organically shared content will scroll by—no gate keepers, although for infrequent visitors to Twitter, the firm will first present the "best tweets" based on user engagement under the heading "While you were away."[79] And it's free to tweet. Engaging users with something interesting? You may get retweeted, ensuring that your post is broadcast out to all accounts that follow the person that's retweeting the post. Savvy firms have realized that tweeting during televised events that have a high degree of Twitter chatter (e.g., awards shows, sporting events) increases the chances that followers will see a post and react to it, promoting the viral spread of a message. When the power went out in the New Orleans Superdome during Super Bowl XLVII, the fast-acting Oreo social-media team mocked up an image that garnered thousands of retweets and favorites and went on to be subsequently mentioned in hundreds of media outlets discussing game events.

FIGURE 9.7

Oreo's clever tweet during an unexpected power outage during Super Bowl XLVII created timely buzz while many fans were engaged on second screens.

The bulk of Twitter's business is in advertising, and the firm offers mechanisms to promote tweets. Users don't have to be following a firm to see its ad, which can be served whenever a user visits Twitter, and the service offers extensive targeting. All ads are targeted as "promoted," but they appear in the user's Twitter stream—exactly in the screen space that users are focusing on. Advertisers can promote tweets to any user based on a host of criteria, including geography, language, keywords, interests, and device type, even matching e-mail addresses to those in their CRM (customer relationship management systems) to reach prospects they already know. Also, like Google, these ads are billed on pay per performance. Advertisers pay only when users engage by clicking on a tweet, retweeting a promotion, replying, favoriting, or following. The firm also offers promoted account products, also charging only when action is taken (i.e., someone new follows the promoted account).

Twitter's Amplify advertising product runs brief video highlights from major live broadcasts, with advertisers' names and messages playing before the clip. Twitter earns money for the ads, while networks gain promotion by having their clips targeted and placed by Twitter into the streams of users most likely to be interested in an event (say a PGA clip from someone who tweets about golf or follows golf-related accounts). Rights-holding TV networks offering an interesting clip of a close game, a snappy celebrity quip, or a major news event could attract a wider audience to tune in and benefit from increased viral reach as videos are retweeted. All major US and many European networks have signed up to share content with Twitter Amplify,[80] as well as professional sports leagues, including the NFL, NBA, MLB, and PGA,[81] and an automated service allows any Twitter advertiser to upload and promote video using Amplify.[82] To get a sense of Twitter's role as a second-screen conversation during televised events, consider that the firm reported 3.3 billion Oscar-related Tweets during the 2014 Academy Awards. Host Ellen DeGeneres got into the act, tweeting a selfie with the crowd that was retweeted 2.4 million times within the first twelve hours.

Twitter's fast-growing MoPub service connects advertisers that use ad networks like Google's AdMob, Apple's iAd, and Facebook's Audience Network with firms that want to auction off ad space in their apps and services (and it can use Twitter data for better ad targeting).[83] This is great for Twitter since it leverages data to make money without running more ads on its own service.[84]

5.2   The Twitter You May Not Know: Tools Empowering Mobile Developers

Twitter's new software development kit (**SDK**), Fabric, could be the way the company captures more revenues and broadens Twitter's reach. The set of mobile developer tools offer a highly useful set of products for those building apps, things like bug reporting, usage monitoring, easy sign-on, etc. The idea is to build a great set of tools that all app developers want, and you can also easily offer up features to integrate Twitter and Twitter's advertising products into their apps, too. The SDK encompasses a number of different tools with a backbone of functionality from a variety of apps. Crashlytics offers mobile crash-reporting, allowing developers to track when their apps crash, gain insight into crash causes, and distribute their apps to beta testers before launching them in the app store. The Digits tool enable users to sign up for their application with a mobile number—why let Zuckerberg win with "Log in using your Facebook ID"? MoPub will allow developers to easily add mobile ads served by Twitter's products, with Twitter sharing a cut of any revenue earned in apps. And the Answers product allows coders to easily build analytics into their apps so they can monitor how their products are being used and gain insights on who's using them. You can also easily add features, such as logging in using your Twitter ID, embed tweets, and integrate tweets into the service (like sharing a high score in a game, or tweeting to encourage friends to download the product).

SDK

Software Development Kit. Tools that allow the creation of products or add-ons for a specific operating system or other computing platform.

5.3   Twitter and Platform Challenges

Twitter also shows the challenges many firms face when weighing the advantages of being an open platform rather than a walled garden. Twitter initially made its data available for free to other developers via **API (application programming interface)**. Exposing data can be a good move as it spawned an ecosystem of over one hundred thousand complementary third-party products and services that enhance Twitter's reach and usefulness (generating *network effects* from complementary offerings similar to other "platforms" like Windows, iPhone, and Facebook). But there are potential downsides to such openness. If users don't visit Twitter.com, that makes it difficult to count users, serve profiling technologies such as tracking cookies (see Chapter 17), collect additional data on service use, and make money by serving ads or offering promotions on the website. All this creates what is known as the "**free rider problem**," where others benefit from a service while offering no value in exchange.

When users don't visit a service, it makes it difficult to spread awareness of new products and features. It can also create branding challenges and customer frustration. Twitter execs lamented that customers were often confused when they searched for "Twitter" in the iPhone App Store and were presented with scores of offerings but none from Twitter itself.[85] Twitter's purchase of the iPhone app Tweetie (subsequently turned into the free "Twitter for iPhone" app), its acquisition of TweetDeck, and the launch of its own URL-shortening service (limiting opportunities for bit.ly and others) allowed the firm to bring in-house efforts that might otherwise lead to "user leakage" to other services. Twitter has also blocked users of Instagram, Tumblr, and live-streaming app Meerkat (which competed with the firm's Periscope acquisition)[86] from easily searching for friends who are on Twitter, nixed an agreement that fostered tweet syndication and other sharing on LinkedIn, and disconnected the popular Web automation service IFTTT (If This Then That).[87] Why help other firms grow at the expense of time spent on Twitter?

API (application programming interface)

Programming hooks, or guidelines, published by firms that tell other programs how to get a service to perform a task such as send or receive data. For example, Amazon.com provides APIs to let developers write their own applications and Web sites that can send the firm orders.

free rider problem

When others take advantage of a user or service without providing any sort of reciprocal benefit.

5.4   Challenges: So How Big Is This Thing Gonna Be?

Since Twitter went public, the firm has regularly outperformed financial expectations. Revenue in Q4 2014 was $479 million, up 97 percent from the same quarter a year earlier.[88] Innovative ad products such as those described earlier should boost future revenue. The firm's November 2013 IPO was well received, jumping 73 percent above offering price,[89] but in the months that followed, the stock sank. Wall Street is concerned that user growth hasn't matched rival social media sites. A 300 million plus users may sound impressive, but by mid 2015, Twitter was still far short of CEO Dick Costolo's reported goal of 400 million total users by year end 2013, and Costolo resigned shortly thereafter.[90] Some have claimed certain Twitter concepts—retweeting, finding accounts to follow, direct messaging—are confusing to new users, and more private messaging apps have proven to be the primary communication mechanism for many. Several key executives have departed from the firm, including the company's head of engineering and its chief operating officer.

Microblogging does appear to be here to stay, and the impact of Twitter has been deep, broad, stunningly swift, and at times humbling in the power that it wields. But whether Twitter will be a durable, profit-gushing powerhouse remains to be seen. And beyond Twitter, several firms have commercialized microblogging services for internal corporate use. Salesforce.com's Chatter, Microsoft's Yammer, HipChat, and Slack are all services that have been billed as "Twitter for the Enterprise." Such efforts allow for Twitter-style microblogging that is restricted for participation and viewing by firm-approved accounts.

KEY TAKEAWAYS

- While many public and private microblogging services exist, Twitter remains by far the dominant service.

- Unlike status updates found on services like Facebook and LinkedIn, Twitter's default supports asymmetric communication, where someone can follow updates without first getting their approval. This function makes Twitter a good choice for anyone cultivating a following—authors, celebrities, organizations, and brand promoters.

- You don't need to tweet to get value. Many Twitter users follow friends, firms, celebrities, and thought leaders, quickly gaining access to trending topics.

- Twitter hash tags (keywords preceded by the # character) are used to organize "tweets" on a given topic. Users can search on hash tags, and many third-party applications allow for tweets to be organized and displayed by tag.

- Organizations are leveraging Twitter in a variety of ways, including for real-time promotions, for time-sensitive information, for scheduling and yield management, for customer engagement and support, for promotion, for intelligence gathering, for idea sourcing, and as a sales channel.

- Like other forms of social media, Twitter can serve as a hothouse that attracts opinion and forces organizational transparency and accountability.

- Activists have leveraged the service worldwide, and it has also served as an early warning mechanism in disasters, terror, and other events.

- Unlike Facebook posts, Twitter does not restrict tweets (although it will surface what its algorithms think you'll be most interested in under the "While you were away" heading). Any follower will see a posted tweet in their feed, provided Twitter is open at the time a tweet is sent. Because of this, many feel Twitter is more friendly and conducive for organic media sharing. Twitter also sells ad products to increase the reach of posts and to recruit new followers.

- Many organizations engage Twitter followers during major events, hoping to increase the likelihood that a post is seen and spread virally. Firms should use caution so as not to be perceived as exploiting tragedy or potentially sensitive events.

- Ad revenue is on the rise at Twitter. Short ads served in the tough-to-ignore stream of tweets are well suited for mobile offerings. Ad formats incorporating video and a platform for connecting advertisers with properties outside Twitter are novel mechanisms to leverage Twitter's strengths as a conversation platform and a data-driven targeting mechanism.

- Despite strong revenue growth, Twitter remains unprofitable and end-user growth has not kept pace with other social media offerings, straining the firm's stock performance and creating pessimism among some in the investment community.

- Twitter used to make its data available via an API, and this helped the firm grow a rich ecosystem of Twitter-supporting products and services. But by making data available to third parties, firms may suffer from the free rider problem where others firms benefit from a service without providing much benefit back to the sponsor itself. Twitter's acquisitions (particularly of popular third-party clients that had used its API) and moves to block rival social efforts from using Twitter data have switched the firm from a platform sponsor to one that has aggressively taken control of its ecosystem.

- Twitter's set of developer tools, known as Fabric, offers app coders several services they'd find useful, including analytics, crash reporting, and login. It also makes it easier for Twitter to embed Twitter functionality (e.g. Tweet your score) and revenue-earning Twitter ad products (where developers get a cut) into mobile apps.

QUESTIONS AND EXERCISES

1. If you don't already have one, set up a Twitter account and "follow" several others. To get more from Twitter, consider installing the free TweetDeck or using the Twitter smartphone app. Follow a diverse group—corporations, executives, pundits, or other organizations. Do you trust that account holders are who they say they are? Why? Which examples do you think use the service most effectively? Which provide the weaker examples of effective Twitter use? Why? Have you encountered Twitter "spam" or unwanted followers? What can you do to limit such experiences? Be prepared to discuss your experiences with your class.

2. Visit search.twitter.com. Which Twitter hash tags are most active at this time? Are there other "trending topics" that aren't associated with hash tags? What do you think of the activity in these areas? Is there legitimate, productive activity happening? Search Twitter for topics, firms, brand names, and issues of interest to you. What do you think of the quality of the information you've uncovered on Twitter? Who might find this to be useful? You can target your search with greater detail using "Advanced Search."

3. Why would a person or organization choose to use Twitter over Facebook's status update or other services? Which (if either) do you prefer and why?

4. What do you think of Twitter's revenue prospects? Is the firm a viable independent service or simply a feature to be incorporated into other social media activity? Advocate where you think the service will be in two years, five, ten. Would you invest in Twitter? Would you suggest that other firms do so? Why?

5. How does Twitter Amplify appeal to content right holders, to advertisers, and to Twitter? What advantages does this ad product offer to each?

6. Perform some additional research on Twitter's ad model. How have Twitter's attempts to grow revenues fared recently? How has user growth been trending? Has the firm's estimated value increased or decreased from the offer figures cited in this chapter? Why?

7. Assume the role of a manager for your firm. Advocate how the organization should leverage Twitter and other forms of social media. Provide examples of effective use, and cautionary tales, to back up your recommendation.

8. As an app developer, would you use the tools that Twitter provides free via "Fabric"? What does Twitter hope to get from providing these tools?

9. Some instructors have mandated Twitter for classroom use. Do you think this is productive? Would your professor advocate tweeting during lectures? What are the pros and cons of such use? Work with your instructor to discuss a set of common guidelines for in-class and course use of social media.

10. Follow this book's author at http://twitter.com/gallaugher. Tweet him if you run across interesting examples that you think would be appropriate for the next version of the book.

6. PREDICTION MARKETS AND THE WISDOM OF CROWDS

LEARNING OBJECTIVES

1. **Understand the concept of the wisdom of crowds as it applies to social networking.**
2. **List the criteria necessary for a crowd to be smart.**

Many social software efforts leverage what has come to be known as the **wisdom of crowds**. In this concept, a group of individuals (the crowd often consists mostly of untrained amateurs), collectively has more insight than a single or small group of trained professionals. Made popular by author James Surowiecki (whose best-selling book was named after the phenomenon), the idea of crowd wisdom is at the heart of wikis and many other online efforts. An article in the journal *Nature* positively comparing Wikipedia to *Encyclopedia Britannica* lent credence to social software's use in harnessing and distilling crowd wisdom.[91]

The crowd isn't always right, but in many cases where topics are complex, problems are large, and outcomes are uncertain, a large, diverse group may bring collective insight to problem solving that one smart guy or a professional committee lacks. One technique for leveraging the wisdom of crowds is a **prediction market**, where a diverse crowd is polled and opinions aggregated to form a forecast of an eventual outcome. The concept is not new. The stock market is arguably a prediction market, with a stock price representing collective assessment of the discounted value of a firm's future earnings. But Internet technologies are allowing companies to set up prediction markets for exploring all sorts of problems.

wisdom of crowds

The idea that a group of individuals (the crowd), often consisting of untrained amateurs, will collectively have more insight than a single or small group of trained professionals.

prediction market

Polling a diverse crowd and aggregating opinions in order to form a forecast of an eventual outcome.

Consider Best Buy, where employees are encouraged to leverage the firm's TagTrade prediction market to make forecasts, and are offered small gifts as incentives for participation. The idea behind this incentive program is simple: the "blue shirts" (Best Buy employees) are closest to customers. They see traffic patterns and buying cycles, can witness customer reactions first hand, and often have a degree of field insight not available to senior managers at the company's Minneapolis headquarters. Harness this collective input and you've got a group brain where, as wisdom of crowds proponents often put it, "the we is greater than the me." When Best Buy asked its employees to predict gift card sales, the "crowd's" collective average answer was 99.5 percent accurate; experts paid to make the prediction were off by 5 percent. Another experiment predicting holiday sales was off by only 1/10 of 1 percent. The experts? Off by 7 percent![92]

In an article in the *McKinsey Quarterly*, Surowiecki outlined several criteria necessary for a crowd to be "smart."[93] The crowd must

- be *diverse*, so that participants are bringing different pieces of information to the table,
- be *decentralized*, so that no one at the top is dictating the crowd's answer,
- offer *a collective verdict* that summarizes participant opinions,
- be *independent*, so that each focuses on information rather than the opinions of others.

Google, which runs several predictive markets, underscored these principles when it found that predictions were less accurate when users were geographically proximate, meaning folks in the same work group who sat near one another typically thought too much alike.[94] Poorer predictive outcomes likely resulted because these relatively homogeneous clusters of users brought the same information to the table (yet another reason why organizations should hire and cultivate diverse teams).

Feeling sick? Tweet about it!

Public health researchers will thank you. Research out of Cornell University indicates that due to their real-time nature, your tweets can better predict the spread of the flu virus than Google can. Researchers collected 3.6 million tweets from nearly 1 million Twitter users over a two-year span from June 2008 to June 2010, filtered out tweets according to their relevance, and mapped the data against data from the US Centers for Disease Control and Prevention (CDC). The results show an impressive 95.8 percent correlation between flu-related tweets and CDC diagnosis data, versus 91.7 percent correlation with the query search-based approach.[95] This data is of immense value to government and health organizations seeking to predict, prevent, and deploy resources to curb the spread of the flu virus.

Many firms run predictive markets to aid in key forecasts, and with the potential for real financial payoff. But University of Chicago law professor Todd Henderson warns predictive markets may also hold legal and ethical challenges. The US Securities and Exchange Commission may look askance at an employee who gets a heads-up in a predictive market that says a certain drug is going to be approved or fail clinical trials. If she trades on this information is she an insider, subject to prosecution for exploiting proprietary data? Disclosure issues are unclear. Gambling laws are also murky, with Henderson uncertain as to whether certain predictive markets will be viewed as an unregulated form of betting.[96]

Publicly accessible prediction markets are diverse in their focus. The Iowa Electronic Market attempts to guess the outcome of political campaigns, corporate performance, and other world events, with mixed results. Farecast (now part of Microsoft's Bing knowledge engine) claims a 75 percent accuracy rate for forecasting the future price of airline tickets.[97] The Hollywood Stock Exchange allows participants to buy and sell prediction shares of movies, actors, directors, and film-related options. The exchange, now owned by investment firm Cantor Fitzgerald, has picked Oscar winners with 90 percent accuracy.[98] And at HedgeStreet.com Nadex (formerly HedgeStreet), participants can make microbets on binary options (where outcomes are one of two options, such as true or false), wagering as little as ten dollars on the outcome of economic events, including predictions on the prices of homes, gold, foreign currencies, oil, and even the economic impact of hurricanes and tropical storms. Nadex is considered a market and is subject to oversight by the Commodity Futures Trading Commission.[99]

KEY TAKEAWAYS

- Many social media efforts allow firms to tap the wisdom of crowds, identifying collective intelligence.
- Prediction markets tap crowd opinion with results that are often more accurate than the most accurate expert forecasts and estimates.
- Prediction markets are most accurate when tapping the wisdom of a diverse and variously skilled and experienced group, and are least accurate when participants are highly similar.

QUESTIONS AND EXERCISES

1. What makes for a "wise" crowd? When might a crowd not be so wise?
2. Find a prediction market online and participate in the effort. Be prepared to share your experience with your class, including any statistics of predictive accuracy, participant incentives, business model of the effort, and your general assessment of the appeal and usefulness of the effort.
3. Brainstorm on the kinds of organizations that might deploy prediction markets. Why might you think the efforts you suggest and advocate would be successful?
4. In what ways are legal issues of concern to prediction market operators?

7. CROWDSOURCING

LEARNING OBJECTIVES

1. **Understand the value of crowdsourcing.**
2. **Identify firms that have used crowdsourcing successfully.**

The power of Web 2.0 also offers several examples of the democratization of production and innovation. Need a problem solved? Offer it up to the crowd and see if any of their wisdom offers a decent result. This phenomenon, known as **crowdsourcing**, has been defined by Jeff Howe, founder of the blog crowdsourcing.com and an associate editor at *Wired*, as "the act of taking a job traditionally performed by a designated agent (usually an employee) and outsourcing it to an undefined, generally large group of people in the form of an open call."[100]

Can the crowd really do better than experts inside a firm? At least one company has literally struck gold using crowdsourcing. As told by Don Tapscott and Anthony Williams in their book *Wikinomics*, mining firm Goldcorp was struggling to gain a return from its 55,000-acre Canadian property holdings. Executives were convinced there was gold "in them thar hills," but despite years of efforts, the firm struggled to strike any new pay dirt. CEO Rob McEwen, a former mutual fund manager without geology experience who unexpectedly ended up running Goldcorp after a takeover battle then made what seemed like a Hail Mary pass—he offered up all the firm's data, on the company's Web site. Along with the data, McEwen ponied up $575,000 from the firm as prize money for the Goldcorp Challenge to anyone who came up with the best methods and estimates for reaping golden riches. Releasing data was seen as sacrilege in the intensely secretive mining industry, but it brought in ideas the firm had never considered. Taking the challenge was a wildly diverse group of "graduate students, consultants, mathematicians, and military officers." Eighty percent of the new targets identified by entrants yielded "substantial quantities of gold." The financial payoff? In just a few years a $100 million firm grew into a $9 billion titan. For Goldcorp, the crowd coughed up serious coin.

Israeli firm Waze has used crowdsourcing to build a better map. The firm's growing community of over 50 million users shares anonymous, live driving data by default. This helps build extremely accurate maps of real-time traffic flow. Another 70,000 plus in the Waze community actively edit maps for increased accuracy.[101] Google won the bidding war for the firm, reportedly beating out interest from both Apple and Facebook. The eventual acquisition price? $1 billion. Apparently there's not just wisdom in the crowds; there's also big bucks!

crowdsourcing

The act of taking a job traditionally performed by a designated agent (usually an employee) and outsourcing it to an undefined generally large group of people in the form of an open call.

FIGURE 9.8

Waze has used crowdsourcing to build a better map app. Over 50 million users contribute real-time traffic data from their smartphones, while more than 70,000 actively edit maps. Google was so impressed it bought the firm for $1 billion.

FIGURE 9.9

The GE Aros air conditioner was born from ideas shared via the crowdsourcing platform at Quirky.com. View more products from the effort at https://www.quirky.com/shop/quirky-ge

Nine of the world's top ten brands have engaged in some form of crowdsourcing. In Germany, McDonald's challenged consumers to build a burger recipe, culminating in the launch of the Pretzelnator.[102] Netflix famously offered anonymous data to any takers, along with a one-million-dollar prize to the first team that could improve the accuracy of movie recommendations by 10 percent. Top performers among the over thirty thousand entrants included research scientists from AT&T Labs, researchers from the University of Toronto, a team of Princeton undergrads, and the proverbial "guy in a garage" (and yes, that was his team name). Frustrated for nearly three years, it took a coalition of four teams from Austria, Canada, Israel, and the United States to finally cross the 10 percent threshold. The winning team represented an astonishing brain trust that Netflix would never have been able to harness on its own.[103]

Other crowdsourcers include Threadless.com, which produces limited run t-shirts with designs users submit and vote on. Marketocracy runs stock market games and has created a mutual fund based on picks from the 100 top-performing portfolios. Just under seven years into the effort, the firm's m100 Index reports a 75 percent return versus 35 percent for the S&P 500. The St. Louis Cardinals baseball team is even crowdsourcing. The club's One for the Birds contest calls for the fans to submit scouting reports on promising players, as the team hopes to broaden its recruiting radar beyond its classic recruiting pool of Division I colleges. General Electronic has partnered with citizen-innovator site Quirky for a GE "inspiration platform," making patents available to would-be inventors and encouraging community votes on submitted ideas.[104] The GE app-powered Aros air conditioner is one of the first products to come out of this effort.[105]

There are several public markets for leveraging crowdsourcing for innovation, or as an alternative to standard means of production. Waltham, Massachusetts-based InnoCentive allows "seekers" to offer cash prizes ranging from $10 to $100,000. Over 250,000 "solvers" have registered to seek solutions for tasks put forward by seekers that include Dow Chemical, Eli Lilly, and Procter & Gamble.[106] Among the findings offered by the InnoCentive crowd are a biomarker that measures progression of ALS. Amazon.com has even created an online marketplace for crowdsourcing called Mechanical Turk. Anyone with a task to be completed or problem to be solved can put it up for Amazon, setting their price for completion or solution. For its role, Amazon takes a small cut of the transaction. And alpha geeks looking to prove their code chops can turn to TopCoder, a firm that stages coding competitions that deliver real results for commercial clients, such as ESPN. TopCoder contests have attracted roughly 300,000 participants from 200 countries.[107]

Not all crowdsourcers are financially motivated. Some benefit by helping to create a better service. Facebook leveraged crowd wisdom to develop versions of its site localized in various languages. Facebook engineers designated each of the site's English words or phrases as a separate translatable object. Members were then invited to translate the English into other languages, and rated the translations to determine which was best. Using this form of crowdsourcing, 1,500 volunteers cranked out Spanish Facebook in a month. It took two weeks for 2,000 German speakers to draft Deutsch Facebook. How does the Facebook concept of "poke" translate around the world? The Spaniards decided on "dar un toque," Germans settled on "anklopfen," and the French went with "envoyer un poke."[108] Vive le crowd!

KEY TAKEAWAYS

- Crowdsourcing tackles challenges through an open call to a broader community of potential problem solvers. Examples include Goldcorp's discovering of optimal mining locations in land it already held, Facebook's leverage of its users to create translations of the site for various international markets, and Netflix's solicitation of improvements to its movie recommendation software.
- Several firms run third-party crowdsourcing forums, among them InnoCentive for scientific R&D, TopCoder for programming tasks, and Amazon's Mechanical Turk for general work.

1. What is crowdsourcing? Give examples of organizations that are taking advantage of crowdsourcing and be prepared to describe these efforts.
2. What ethical issues should firms be aware of when considering crowdsourcing? Are there other concerns firms may have when leveraging this technique?
3. Assume the role of a manager or consultant. Recommend a firm and a task that would be appropriate for crowdsourcing. Justify your choice, citing factors such as cost, breadth of innovation, time, constrained resources, or other factors. How would you recommend the firm conduct this crowdsourcing effort?

8. GET SMART: THE SOCIAL MEDIA AWARENESS AND RESPONSE TEAM

LEARNING OBJECTIVES

1. Illustrate several examples of effective and poor social media use.
2. Recognize the skills and issues involved in creating and staffing an effective social media awareness and response team (SMART).
3. List and describe key components that should be included in any firm's social media policy.
4. Understand the implications of ethical issues in social media such as "sock puppetry" and "astroturfing" and provide examples and outcomes of firms and managers who used social media as a vehicle for dishonesty.
5. List and describe tools for monitoring social media activity relating to a firm, its brands, and staff.
6. Understand issues involved in establishing a social media presence, including the embassy approach, openness, and staffing.
7. Discuss how firms can engage and respond through social media, and how companies should plan for potential issues and crises.

For an example of how outrage can go viral, consider Dave Carroll.[109] The Canadian singer-songwriter was traveling with his band, Sons of Maxwell, on a United Airlines flight from Nova Scotia to Nebraska when, during a layover at Chicago's O'Hare International Airport, Carroll saw baggage handlers roughly tossing his guitar case. The musician's $3,500 Taylor guitar was in pieces by the time it arrived in Omaha. In the midst of a busy tour schedule, Carroll didn't have time to follow up on the incident until after United's twenty-four-hour period for filing a complaint for restitution had expired. When United refused to compensate him for the damage, Carroll penned the four-minute country ditty "United Breaks Guitars," performed it in a video, and uploaded the clip to YouTube (sample lyrics: "I should have flown with someone else or gone by car…'cuz United breaks guitars"). Carroll even called out the unyielding United rep by name. Take that, Ms. Irlwig! (Note to customer service reps everywhere: you're always on.)

The clip went viral, receiving 150,000 views its first day and five million more by the next month. Well into the next year, "United Breaks Guitars" remained the top result on YouTube when searching the term "United." No other topic mentioning that word—not "United States," "United Nations," or "Manchester United"—ranked ahead of this one customer's outrage.

Video

Dave Carroll's ode to his bad airline experience, "United Breaks Guitars," went viral, garnering millions of views.

View the video online at: http://www.youtube.com/embed/5YGc4zOqozo

Scarring social media posts don't just come from outside the firm. Earlier that same year employees of a Domino's Pizza outlet in Conover, North Carolina, created what they thought would be a funny gross-out video for their friends. Posted to YouTube, the resulting footage of the firm's brand alongside vile acts of food prep was seen by over one million viewers before it was removed. Over 4.3 million references to the incident can be found on Google, and many of the leading print and broadcast outlets covered the story. The perpetrators were arrested, the Domino's storefront where the incident occurred was closed, and the firm's president made a painful apology (on YouTube, of course).

Not all firms choose to aggressively engage social media. But your customers are there and they're talking about your organization, its products, and its competitors. Your employees are there, too, and without guidance, they can step on a social grenade with your firm left to pick out the shrapnel. Soon, nearly everyone will carry the Internet in their pocket. Phones and MP3 players are armed with video cameras capable of recording every customer outrage, corporate blunder, ethical lapse, and rogue employee. Social media posts can linger forever online, like a graffiti tag attached to your firm's reputation. Get used to it—that genie isn't going back in the bottle.

As the "United Breaks Guitars" and "Domino's Gross Out" incidents show, social media will impact a firm whether it chooses to engage online or not. An awareness of the power of social media can shape customer support engagement and crisis response, and strong corporate policies on social media use might have given the clueless Domino's pranksters a heads-up that their planned video would get them fired and arrested. Given the power of social media, it's time for all firms to get **SMART**, creating a social media awareness and response team. While one size doesn't fit all, this section details key issues behind SMART capabilities, including creating the social media team, establishing firmwide policies, monitoring activity inside and outside the firm, establishing the social media presence, and managing social media engagement and response.

SMART

The social media awareness and response team. A group tasked with creating policies and providing support, training, guidance, and development expertise for and monitoring of a firm's social media efforts.

8.1 Creating the Team

Firms need to treat social media engagement as a key corporate function with clear and recognizable leadership within the organization. Social media is no longer an ad hoc side job or a task delegated to an intern. When McDonald's named its first social media chief, the company announced that it was important to have someone "dedicated 100 percent of the time, rather than someone who's got a day job on top of a day job."[110] Firms without social media baked into employee job functions often find that their online efforts are started with enthusiasm, only to suffer under a lack of oversight and follow-through. One hotel operator found franchisees were quick to create Facebook pages, but many rarely monitored them. Customers later notified the firm that unmonitored hotel Facebook pages contained offensive messages—a racist rant on one, paternity claims against an employee on another.

Organizations with a clearly established leadership role for social media can help create consistency in firm dialogue; develop and communicate policy; create and share institutional knowledge; provide training, guidance, and suggestions; offer a place to escalate issues in the event of a crisis or opportunity; and catch conflicts that might arise if different divisions engage without coordination.

While firms are building social media responsibility into job descriptions, also recognize that social media is a team sport that requires input from staffers throughout an organization. The social media team needs support from public relations, marketing, customer support, HR, legal, IT, and other groups, all while acknowledging that what's happening in the social media space is distinct from traditional roles in these disciplines. The team will hone unique skills in technology, analytics, and design, as well as skills for using social media for online conversations, listening, trust building, outreach, engagement, and response. As an example of the interdisciplinary nature of social media practice, consider that the social media team at Starbucks (regarded by some as the best in the business) is organized under the interdisciplinary "vice president of brand, content, and online."[111]

Also note that while SMARTs (social media teams) provide leadership, support, and guidance, they don't necessarily drive all efforts. GM's social media team includes representatives from all the major brands. The idea is that employees in the divisions are still the best to engage online once they've been trained and given operational guardrails. Says GM's social media chief, "I can't go in to Chevrolet and tell them 'I know your story better than you do, let me tell it on the Web.'"[112] Similarly, the roughly fifty Starbucks "Idea Partners" who participate in MyStarbucksIdea are specialists. Part of their job is to manage the company's social media. In this way, conversations about the Starbucks card are handled by card team experts, and merchandise dialogue has a product specialist who knows that business best. Many firms find that the social media team is key for coordination and supervision (e.g., ensuring that different divisions don't overload consumers with too much or inconsistent contact), but the dynamics of specific engagement still belong with the folks who know products, services, and customers best.

8.2   Responsibilities and Policy Setting

In an age where a generation has grown up posting shoot-from-the-hip status updates and YouTube is seen as a fame vehicle for those willing to perform sensational acts, establishing corporate policies and setting employee expectations are imperative for all organizations. The employees who don't understand the impact of social media on the firm can do serious damage to their employers and their careers (look to Domino's for an example of what can go wrong).

Many experts suggest that a good social media policy needs to be three things: "short, simple, and clear."[113] Fortunately, most firms don't have to reinvent the wheel. Several firms, including Best Buy, IBM, Intel, The American Red Cross, and Australian telecom giant Telstra, have made their social media policies public.

Most guidelines emphasize the "three Rs": representation, responsibility, and respect.

- *Representation.* Employees need clear and explicit guidelines on expectations for social media engagement. Are they empowered to speak on behalf of the firm? If they are, it is critical that employees transparently disclose this to avoid legal action. US Federal Trade Commission rules require disclosure of relationships that may influence online testimonial or endorsement. On top of this, many industries have additional compliance requirements (e.g., governing privacy in the health and insurance fields, retention of correspondence and disclosure for financial services firms). Firms may also want to provide guidelines on initiating and conducting dialogue, when to respond online, and how to escalate issues within the organization.

- *Responsibility.* Employees need to take responsibility for their online actions. Firms must set explicit expectations for disclosure, confidentiality and security, and provide examples of engagement done right, as well as what is unacceptable. An effective social voice is based on trust, so accuracy, transparency, and accountability must be emphasized. Consequences for violations should be clear.

- *Respect.* Canadian communications firm, Mitel reminds employees that respect includes the firm, its customers, and its competitors.[114] ?Best Buy's policy explicitly states participants must "honor our differences" and "act ethically and responsibly." Many employees can use the reminder. Sure customer service is a tough task and every rep has a story about an unreasonable client. But there's a difference between letting off steam around the water cooler and venting online. Virgin Atlantic fired thirteen of the airline's staffers after they posted passenger insults and inappropriate inside jokes on Facebook.[115]

Policies also need to have teeth. Remember, a fourth "R" is at stake—reputation (both the firm's and the employee's). Violators should know the consequences of breaking firm rules and policies should be backed by action. Best Buy's policy simply states, "Just in case you are forgetful or ignore the guidelines above, here's what could happen. You could get fired (and it's embarrassing to lose your job for something that's so easily avoided)."

Despite these concerns, trying to micromanage employee social media use is probably not the answer. At IBM, rules for online behavior are surprisingly open. The firm's code of conduct reminds employees to remember privacy, respect, and confidentiality in all electronic communications. Anonymity is not permitted on IBM's systems, making everyone accountable for their actions. As for external postings, the firm insists that employees not disparage competitors or reveal customers' names without permission and asks that any employee posts from IBM accounts or that mention the firm also include disclosures indicating that opinions and thoughts shared publicly are the individual's and not Big Blue's.

Some firms have more complex social media management challenges. Consider hotels and restaurants where outlets are owned and operated by franchisees rather than the firm. McDonald's social media team provides additional guidance so that regional operations can create, for example, a Twitter handle (e.g., @mcdonalds_cincy) that handles a promotion in Cincinnati that might not run in other regions.[116] A social media team can provide coordination while giving up the necessary control. Without this kind of coordination, customer communication can quickly become a mess.

Training is also a critical part of the SMART mandate. GM offers an intranet-delivered video course introducing newbies to the basics of social media and to firm policies and expectations. GM also trains employees to become "social media proselytizers and teachers." GM hopes this approach enables experts to interact directly with customers and partners, allowing the firm to offer authentic and knowledgeable voices online.

Tweets from the Untrained

Followers of Kenneth Cole, founder, chairman, and chief creative officer of the eponymous fashion label, know when he has has tweeted via the corp—Cole signs these tweets with his initials KC. But it looks like KC could have used a bit of SMART training when he offered up a meant-to-be-light-hearted quip comparing Egypt's historic Mubarak-ousting protests (where several citizens were killed and injured) to enthusiasm for his firm's "new spring collection." Although the tweet was quickly deleted, screenshots (see below) linger forever, and the media widely reported on the big brand's insensitive gaffe.

Several firms have ended up with social media egg on their face after attempting to capitalize on trending topics and major news events. Some refer to commercial communication linked to tragic events as the social media "ambulance chasing trap."[117] Memorials for 9/11,[118] superstorm Sandy,[119] Pearl Harbor Day,[120] and the Boston Marathon bombing[121] are just a few examples that have garnered public ridicule and made brands appear callous, opportunistic, and insensitive. At a South by Southwest panel on social media crises, reporter Neal Mann of *The Wall Street Journal* stated flat-out that many journalists are on alert to "identify and exploit" gaffes committed in the name of organizations. The Schadenfreude also offers compelling coverage as a teachable moment, warning professionals what not to do. As Professor Jerry Kane of Boston College states, "Just because a topic is trending does not mean it's necessarily a good opportunity to promote a brand."[122]

Even though gaffes can be scary, well-trained employees engaging online can prove to be a valuable asset. Adobe realized that the collective reach of the firm's employees on LinkedIn was more than seven time greater than those connected with Adobe brand pages, plus 91 percent of the engagements employees were having regarding Adobe on LinkedIn were with people who weren't connecting with the firm's brand pages. Dispatching employees to indiscriminately spam contacts with firm propaganda is not the approach to take. But Adobe trains employees on social judgment, assessing sample social media conversations, and helping employees understand best approaches in situations where online advocacy makes sense. If you believe in a firm, its products, and its benefits, this can be natural, and persuasive.[123]

Training should also cover information security and potential threats. Social media has become a magnet for phishing, virus distribution, and other nefarious online activity. Over one-third of social networking users claim to have been sent malware via social networking sites (see Chapter 17). The social media team will need to monitor threats and spread the word on how employees can surf safe and surf smart.

Since social media is so public, it's easy to amass examples of what works and what doesn't, adding these to the firm's training materials. The social media team provides a catch point for institutional knowledge and industry best practice; and the team can update programs over time as new issues, guidelines, technologies, and legislation emerge. A savvy team will use tools such as wikis and blogs to capture and share findings.

The social media space introduces a tension between allowing expression (among employees and by the broader community) and protecting the brand. Firms will fall closer to one end or the other of this continuum depending on compliance requirements, comfort level, and goals. Expect the organization's position to move. Firms will be cautious as negative issues erupt; others will jump in as new technologies become hot and early movers generate buzz and demonstrate results. But it's the SMART responsibility to avoid knee-jerk reaction and to shepherd firm efforts with the professionalism and discipline of other management domains.

Astroturfing and Sock Puppets

Social media can be a cruel space. Sharp-tongued comments can shred a firm's reputation and staff might be tempted to make anonymous posts defending or promoting the firm. Don't do it! Not only is it a violation of FTC rules, IP addresses and other online breadcrumbs often leave a trail that exposes deceit.

Whole Foods CEO John Mackey fell victim to this kind of temptation, but his actions were eventually, and quite embarrassingly, uncovered. For years, Mackey used a pseudonym to contribute to online message boards, talking up Whole Foods stock and disparaging competitors. When Mackey was unmasked, years of comments were publicly attributed to him. The *New York Times* cited one particularly cringe-worthy post where Mackey used the pseudonym to complement his own good looks, writing, "I like Mackey's haircut. I think he looks cute!"[124]

Fake personas set up to sing your own praises are known as **sock puppets** among the digerati, and the practice of lining comment and feedback forums with positive feedback is known as **astroturfing**. Do it and it could cost you. The firm behind the cosmetic procedure known as the Lifestyle Lift was fined $300,000 in civil penalties after the New York Attorney General's office discovered that the firm's employees had posed as plastic surgery patients and wrote glowing reviews of the procedure.[125]

Review sites themselves will also take action. TripAdvisor penalizes firms if it's discovered that customers are offered some sort of incentive for posting positive reviews. The firm also employs a series of sophisticated automated techniques as well as manual staff review to uncover suspicious activity. Violators risk penalties that include being banned from the service.

Your customers will also use social media to keep you honest. Several ski resorts have been embarrassed when tweets and other social media posts exposed them as overstating snowfall results. There's even an iPhone app skiers can use to expose inaccurate claims.[126] Firms including MTV and Chipotle have faked a hack on their social media accounts to gain attention, and were later ridiculed when this was discovered. Be warned–customers aren't keen on feeling duped.[127]

So keep that ethical bar high—you never know when technology will get sophisticated enough to reveal wrongdoings.

sock puppets

A fake online persona created to promote a particular point of view, often in praise of a firm, product, or individual. Be aware that the use of undisclosed relationships in endorsements is a violation of U.S. Federal Trade Commission rules.

astroturfing

Engineering the posting of positive comments and reviews of a firm's product and services (or negative ones of a firm's competitors). Many ratings sites will penalize firms that offer incentives for positive feedback posts.

8.3   Monitoring

Concern over managing a firm's online image has led to the rise of an industry known as **online reputation management**. Firms specializing in this field will track a client firm's name, brand, executives' names, or other keywords, reporting online activity and whether sentiment trends toward the positive or negative.

But social media monitoring is about more than managing one's reputation; it also provides critical competitive intelligence, it can surface customer support issues, and it can uncover opportunities for innovation and improvement. Firms that are quick to lament the very public conversations about their brands happening online need to embrace social media as an opportunity to learn more.

Resources for monitoring social media are improving all the time, and a number of tools are available for free. All firms can take advantage of Google Alerts, which flags blog posts, new Web pages, and other publicly accessible content, regularly delivering a summary of new links to your mailbox (for more on using Google for intelligence gathering, see Chapter 18). Twitter search and Twitter clients like TweetDeck can display all mentions of a particular term. And more advanced commercial tools, such as SalesForce Radian6, HubSpot, and HootSuite, monitor a wide variety of social media mentions, provide metrics for ongoing campaigns and practices, and gauge sentiment and spot opportunities for sales leads or customer service.

online reputation management

The process of tracking and responding to online mentions of a product, organization, or individual. Services supporting online reputation management range from free Google Alerts to more sophisticated services that blend computer-based and human monitoring of multiple media channels.

FIGURE 9.10

Tools, such as those provided by HubSpot (depicted here), track social media mentions by key word or phrase. Savvy organizations can mine comments for competitive intelligence, insight, and product ideas or to coordinate follow-up and thoughtful customer service.

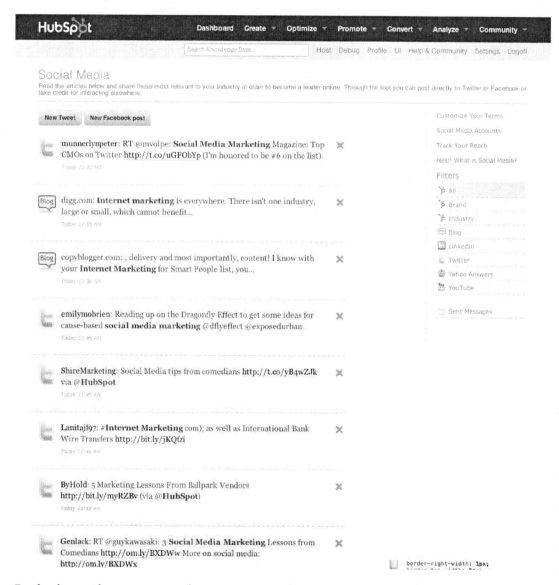

Facebook provides a summary of page activity to administrators (including stats on visits, new fans, wall posts, etc.), while Facebook's Audience Insights tool measures user demographics, exposure, actions, and response behavior relating to a firm's Facebook pages and ads. TripAdvisor provides an analytics dashboard enabling vendors to track their most important visitors, competitors and market trends,[128] and Yelp offers tools for business owners that also include analytics, as well as notifications of new review posts, and tools for public and private review response.[129] And you'll find similar dashboards at sites such as Pinterest and Foursquare, among others.

Bit.ly and many other URL-shortening services allow firms to track Twitter references to a particular page. Since bit.ly applies the same shortened URL to all tweets pointing to a page, it allows firms to follow not only if a campaign has been spread through "retweeting" but also if new tweets were generated outside of a campaign. Graphs plot click-throughs over time, and a list of original tweets can be pulled up to examine what commentary accompanied a particular link.

Monitoring should also not be limited to customers and competitors. Firms are leveraging social media both inside their firms and via external services (e.g., corporate groups on Facebook and LinkedIn), and these spaces should also be on the SMART radar. This kind of monitoring can help firms keep pace with employee sentiment and insights, flag discussions that may involve proprietary information or other inappropriate topics, and provide guidance for those who want to leverage social media for the firm's staff—that is, anything from using online tools to help organize the firm's softball league to creating a wiki for a project group. Social media are end-user services that are particularly easy to deploy but that can also be used disastrously and inappropriately, so it's vital for IT experts and other staffers on the social media team to be visible and available, offering support and resources for those who want to take a dip into social media's waters.

8.4   Establishing a Presence

Firms hoping to get in on the online conversation should make it easy for their customers to find them. Many firms take an **embassy** approach to social media, establishing presence at various services with a consistent name. Think facebook.com/starbucks, twitter.com/starbucks, youtube.com/starbucks, flickr.com/starbucks, instagram.com/starbucks, pinterest.com/starbucks, and so on. Corporate e-mail and Web sites can include icons linking to these services in a header or footer. The firm's social media embassies can also be highlighted in physical space such as in print, on bags and packaging, and on store signage. Firms should try to ensure that all embassies carry consistent design elements, so users see familiar visual cues that underscore they are now at a destination associated with the organization.

> **embassy**
>
> In the context of social media, an established online presence where customers can reach and interact with the firm. An effective embassy approach uses a consistent firm name in all its social media properties.

As mentioned earlier, some firms establish their own communities for customer engagement. Examples include Dell's IdeaStorm and MyStarbucksIdea. Not every firm has a customer base that is large and engaged enough to support hosting its own community. But for larger firms, these communities can create a nexus for feedback, customer-driven innovation, and engagement.

Customers expect an open dialogue, so firms engaging online should be prepared to deal with feedback that's not all positive. Firms are entirely within their right to screen out offensive and inappropriate comments. Noting this, firms might think twice before turning on YouTube comments (described as "the gutter of the Internet" by one leading social media manager).[130] Such comments could expose employees or customers profiled in clips to withering, snarky ridicule. However, firms engaged in curating their forums to present only positive messages should be prepared for the community to rebel and for embarrassing cries of censorship to be disclosed. Firms that believe in the integrity of their work and the substance of their message shouldn't be afraid. While a big brand like Starbucks is often a target of criticism, social media also provides organizations with an opportunity to respond fairly to that criticism and post video and photos of the firm's efforts. In Starbucks' case, the firm shares its work investing in poor coffee-growing communities as well as efforts to support AIDS relief. A social media presence allows a firm to share these works without waiting for conventional public relations (PR) to yield results or for journalists to pick up and interpret the firm's story. Starbucks executives have described the majority of comments the company receives through social media as "a love letter to the firm." By contrast, if your firm isn't prepared to be open or if your products and services are notoriously subpar and your firm is inattentive to customer feedback, then establishing a brand-tarring social media beachhead might not make sense. A word to the self-reflective: Customer conversations will happen online even if you don't have any social media embassies. Users can form their own groups, hash tags, and forums. A reluctance to participate may signal that the firm is facing deeper issues around its product and service.

While firms can learn a lot from social media consultants and tool providers, it's considered bad practice to outsource the management of a social media presence to a third-party agency. The voice of the firm should come *from* the firm. In fact, it should come from employees who can provide authentic expertise. Starbucks' first Twitter feed was managed by a former barista, while the firm's director of environmental affairs tweets and engages across social media channels on the firm's green efforts.

8.5   Engage and Respond

Having an effective social media presence offers "four Ms" of engagement: it's a *megaphone* allowing for outbound communication; it's a *magnet* drawing communities inward for conversation; and it allows for *monitoring* and *mediation* of existing conversations.[131] This dialogue can happen privately (private messaging is supported on most services) or can occur very publicly (with the intention to reach a wide audience). Understanding when, where, and how to engage and respond online requires a deft and experienced hand.

Many firms will selectively and occasionally retweet praise posts, underscoring the firm's commitment to customer service. Highlighting service heroes also reinforces exemplary behavior to employees who may be following the firm online, too. Users are often delighted when a major brand retweets their comments, posts a comment on their blog, or otherwise acknowledges them online—just be sure to do a quick public profile investigation to make sure your shout-outs are directed at customers you want associated with your firm. Escalation procedures should also include methods to flag noteworthy posts, good ideas, and opportunities that the social media team should be paying attention to. The customer base is often filled with heartwarming stories of positive customer experiences and rich with insight on making good things even better.

Many will also offer an unsolicited apology if the firm's name or products comes up in a disgruntled post. You may not be able to respond to all online complaints, but selective acknowledgement of the customer's voice (and attempts to address any emergent trends) is a sign of a firm that's focused on customer care. Getting the frequency, tone, and cadence for this kind of dialogue is more art than science, and managers are advised to regularly monitor other firms with similar characteristics for examples of what works and what doesn't.

Many incidents can be responded to immediately and with clear rules of engagement. For example, Starbucks issues corrective replies to the often-tweeted urban legend that the firm does not send coffee to the U.S. military because of a corporate position against the war. A typical response might read, "Not true, get the facts here" with a link to a Web page that sets the record straight.

Reaching out to key influencers can also be extremely valuable. Prominent bloggers and other respected social media participants can provide keen guidance and insight. The goal isn't to create a mouthpiece, but to solicit input, gain advice, gauge reaction, and be sure your message is properly interpreted. Influencers can also help spread accurate information and demonstrate a firm's commitment to listening and learning. In the wake of the Domino's gross-out, executives reached out to the prominent blog The Consumerist.[132] Facebook has solicited advice and feedback from MoveOn.org months before launching new features.[133] Meanwhile, Kaiser Permanente leveraged advice from well-known health care bloggers in crafting its approach to social media.[134]

However, it's also important to recognize that not every mention is worthy of a response. The Internet is filled with PR seekers, the unsatisfiably disgruntled, axe grinders seeking to trap firms, dishonest competitors, and inappropriate groups of mischief makers commonly referred to as *trolls*. One such group hijacked *Time* Magazine's user poll of the World's Most Influential People, voting their twenty-one-year-old leader to the top of the list ahead of Barack Obama, Vladimir Putin, and the pope. Prank voting was so finely calibrated among the group that the rankings list was engineered to spell out a vulgar term using the first letter of each nominee's name.[135]

To prepare, firms should "war game" possible crises, ensuring that everyone knows their role, and that experts are on call. A firm's social media policy should also make it clear how employees who spot a crisis might "pull the alarm" and mobilize the crisis response team. Having all employees aware of how to respond gives the firm an expanded institutional radar that can lower the chances of being blindsided. This can be especially important as many conversations take place in the so-called dark Web beyond the reach of conventional search engines and monitoring tools (e.g., within membership communities or sites, such as Facebook, where only "friends" have access).

In the event of an incident, silence can be deadly. Consumers expect a response to major events, even if it's just "we're listening, we're aware, and we intend to fix things." When director Kevin Smith was asked to leave a Southwest Airline flight because he was too large for a single seat, Smith went ballistic on Twitter, berating Southwest's service to his thousands of online followers. Southwest responded that same evening via Twitter, posting, "I've read the tweets all night from @ThatKevinSmith—He'll be getting a call at home from our Customer Relations VP tonight."

In the event of a major crisis, firms can leverage online media outside the social sphere. In the days following the Domino's incident, the gross-out video consistently appeared near the top of Google searches about the firm. When appropriate, companies can buy ads to run alongside keywords explaining their position and, if appropriate, offering an apology.[136] Homeopathic cold remedy Zicam countered blog posts citing inaccurate product information by running Google ads adjacent to these links, containing tag lines such as "Zicam: Get the Facts."[137]

Review sites such as Yelp and TripAdvisor also provide opportunities for firms to respond to negative reviews. This can send a message that a firm recognizes missteps and is making an attempt to address the issue (follow-through is critical, or expect an even harsher backlash). Sometimes a private response is most effective. When a customer of Farmstead Cheeses and Wines in the San Francisco Bay area posted a Yelp complaint that a cashier was rude, the firm's owner sent a private reply to the poster pointing out that the employee in question was actually hard of hearing. The complaint was subsequently withdrawn and the critic eventually joined the firm's Wine Club.[138] Private responses may be most appropriate if a firm is reimbursing clients or dealing with issues where public dialogue doesn't help the situation. One doesn't want to train members of the community that public griping gets reward. For similar reasons, in some cases store credit rather than reimbursement may be appropriate compensation.

Who Should Speak for Your Firm? The Case of the Cisco Fatty

Using the Twitter handle "TheConnor," a graduating college student recently offered full-time employment by the highly regarded networking giant Cisco posted this tweet: "Cisco just offered me a job! Now I have to weigh the utility of a fatty paycheck against the daily commute to San Jose and hating the work." Bad idea. Her tweet was public and a Cisco employee saw the post, responding, "Who is the hiring manager. I'm sure they would love to know that you will hate the work. We here at Cisco are versed in the Web." Snap!

But this is also where the story underscores the subtleties of social media engagement. Cisco employees are right to be stung by this kind of criticism. The firm regularly ranks at the top of *Fortune*'s list of "Best Firms to Work for in America." Many Cisco employees take great pride in their work, and all have an interest in maintaining the firm's rep so that the company can hire the best and brightest and continue to compete at the top of its market. But when an employee went after a college student so publicly, the incident escalated. The media picked up on the post, and it began to look like an old guy picking on a clueless young woman who made a stupid mistake that should have been addressed in private. There was also an online pile-on attacking TheConnor. Someone uncovered the woman's true identity and posted hurtful and disparaging messages about her. Someone else set up a website at CiscoFatty.com. Even Oprah got involved, asking both parties to appear on her show (the offer was declined). A clearer social media policy highlighting the kinds of issues to respond to and offering a reporting hierarchy to catch and escalate such incidents might have headed off the embarrassment and helped both Cisco and TheConnor resolve the issue with a little less public attention.[139]

It's time to take social media seriously. We're now deep into a revolution that has rewritten the rules of customer-firm communication. There are emerging technologies and skills to acquire, a shifting landscape of laws and expectations, a minefield of dangers, and a wealth of unexploited opportunities. Organizations that professionalize their approach to social media and other Web 2.0 technologies are ready to exploit the upside—potentially stronger brands, increased sales, sharper customer service, improved innovation, and more. Those that ignore the new landscape risk catastrophe and perhaps even irrelevance.

KEY TAKEAWAYS

- Customer conversations are happening and employees are using social media. Even firms that aren't planning on creating a social media presence need to professionalize the social media function in their firm (consider this a social media awareness and response team, or SMART).

- Social media is an interdisciplinary practice, and the team should include professionals experienced in technology, marketing, PR, customer service, legal, and human resources.

- While the social media team provides guidance, training, and oversight, and structures crisis response, it's important to ensure that authentic experts engage on behalf of the firm. Social media is a conversation, and this isn't a job for the standard PR-style corporate spokesperson.

- Social media policies revolve around "three Rs": representation, responsibility, and respect. Many firms have posted their policies online so it can be easy for a firm to assemble examples of best practice.

- Firms must train employees and update their knowledge as technologies, effective use, and threats emerge. Security training is a vital component of establishing social media policy. Penalties for violation should be clear and backed by enforcement.

- While tempting, creating sock puppets to astroturf social media with praise posts violates FTC rules and can result in prosecution. Many users who thought their efforts were anonymous have been embarrassingly exposed and penalized. Customers are also using social media to expose firm dishonesty.

- Many tools exist for monitoring social media mentions of an organization, brands, competitors, and executives. Google Alerts, Twitter search, TweetDeck, Twitrratr, bit.ly, Facebook, and Foursquare all provide free tools that firms can leverage. For-fee tools and services are available as part of the online reputation management industry (and consultants in this space can also provide advice on improving a firm's online image and engagement).

- Social media are easy to adopt and potentially easy to abuse. The social media team can provide monitoring and support for firm-focused efforts inside the company and running on third-party networks, both to improve efforts and prevent unwanted disclosure, compliance, and privacy violations.

- The embassy approach to social media has firms establish their online presence through consistently named areas within popular services (e.g., facebook.com/starbucks, twitter.com/starbucks, youtube.com/starbucks). Firms can also create their own branded social media sites using tools such as Salesforce.com's "Ideas" platform.

- Social media provides "four Ms" of engagement: the megaphone to send out messages from the firm, the magnet to attract inbound communication, and monitoring and mediation—paying attention to what's happening online and selectively engage conversations when appropriate. Engagement can be public or private.

- Engagement is often more art than science, and managers can learn a lot by paying attention to the experiences of others. Firms should have clear rules for engagement and escalation when positive or negative issues are worthy of attention.

QUESTIONS AND EXERCISES

1. The "United Breaks Guitars" and "Domino's Gross Out" incidents are powerful reminders of how customers and employees can embarrass a firm. Find other examples of customer-and-employee social media incidents that reflected negatively on an organization. What happened? What was the result? How might these incidents have been prevented or better dealt with?

2. Hunt for examples of social media excellence. List an example of an organization that got it right. What happened, and what benefits were received?

3. Social media critics often lament a lack of ROI (return on investment) for these sorts of efforts. What kind of return should firms expect from social media? Does the return justify the investment? Why or why not?

4. What kinds of firms should aggressively pursue social media? Which ones might consider avoiding these practices? If a firm is concerned about online conversations, what might this also tell management?

5. List the skills that are needed by today's social media professionals. What topics should you study to prepare you for a career in this space?

6. Search online to find examples of corporate social media policies. Share your findings with your instructor. What points do these policies have in common? Are there aspects of any of these policies that you think are especially strong that other firms might adopt? Are there things in these policies that concern you?

7. Should firms monitor employee social media use? Should they block external social media sites at work? Why or why not? Why might the answer differ by industry?

8. Use the monitoring tools mentioned in the reading to search your own name. How would a prospective employer evaluate what they've found? How should you curate your online profiles and social media presence to be the most "corporate friendly"?

9. Investigate incidents where employees were fired for social media use. Prepare to discuss examples in class. Could the employer have avoided these incidents?

10. Use the monitoring tools mentioned in the reading to search for a favorite firm or brand. What trends do you discover? Is the online dialogue fair? How might the firm use these findings?

11. Consider the case of the Cisco Fatty. Who was wrong? Advise how a firm might best handle this kind of online commentary.

ENDNOTES

1. Via Alexa.com, June 2014.

2. "What Americans Do Online: Social Media and Games Dominate Activity," *NielsenWire,* August 2, 2010.

3. Morgan Stanley, *Internet Trends Report,* March 2008.

4. L. Chapman, "Anonymous Social-Networking App 'Secret' Shuts Down," *The Wall Street Journal,* April 29, 2015.

5. G. Kane and R. Fichman, "The Shoemaker's Children: Using Wikis for Information Systems Teaching, Research, and Publication," *MIS Quarterly,* March 2009.

6. http://www.youtube.com/yt/press/statistics.html

7. "Facebook Reports Fourth Quarter and Full Year 2014 Results," Facebook, January 28, 2015.

8. L. Sumagaysay, "Facebook's First Billion Users, and Other Key Numbers," *SiliconBeat,* October 4, 2012.

9. M. Meeker, "Internet Trends 2015 – Code Conference," KCPB, May 27, 2015. M. Meeker, "Internet Trends 2015 – Code Conference," *KCPB,* May 27, 2015.

10. B. Evans, "Whatsapp sails past SMS, but where does messaging go next?" Benedict Evans, January 11, 2015.

11. M. Meeker, "Internet Trends 2015 – Code Conference," *KCPB,* May 27, 2015.

12. D. Primack, "Why Slack just raised $160 million at a $2.8 billion valuation," *Fortune,* April 16, 2015.

13. J. Linshi, "This 1-Year-Old Startup Says It's the Fastest-Growing Business App Ever," *Time,* Feb. 12, 2015.

14. E. Rusli and D. MacMillan, "Snapchat Spurned $3 Billion Acquisition Offer from Facebook," *The Wall Street Journal,* November 13, 2013.

15. Morgan Stanley, *Internet Trends Report,* May 28, 2014.

16. S. Decker, "Digital Content and the Social Flywheel,"*Re/code,* Feb. 23, 2015.

17. P. Kafka, "Twitter CEO Dick Costolo Talks about His New Photo Service, but Not about Profits," *AllThingsD,* June 1, 2011.

18. N. Bolton, "Chirp, Twitter's First Developer Conference, Opens Its Doors," *New York Times,* April 14, 2010; M. Shaer, "Google Launches Archive Search for Twitter," *Christian Science Monitor,* April 15, 2010.

19. J. Van Grove, "Tumblr Is Now the 9th Most Popular Site in the U.S.," *VentureBeat,* November 26, 2012.

20. J. Wortham and N. Bilton, "Before Tumblr, Founder Made Mom Proud. He Quit School," *New York Times,* May 20, 2013.

21. User count, *Stack Overflow,* June 16, 2014.

22. L. Mamykina, B. Manoim, M. Mittal, G. Hripcsak, and B. Hartmann, "Design Lessons from the Fastest Q&A Site in the West," Proceedings of the SIGCHI Conference on Human Factors in Computing Systems, Vancouver, BC, May 7–12, 2011.

23. L. Orsini, "GitHub for Beginners: Don't Get Scared, Get Started," *ReadWriteWeb,* September 30, 2013.

24. A. Kosner, "Software Engineers Are in Demand, and GitHub Is How You Find Them," Forbes, October 10, 2012.

25. J. Constine, "Pinterest Hits 10 Million U.S. Monthly Uniques Faster than Any Standalone Site Ever—comScore," *TechCrunch,* February 7, 2012.

26. D. Moth, "Pinterest Drives More Sales than Facebook: Stats," *eConsultancy,* May 8, 2012.

27. L. Indvik, "Pinterest Drives More Traffic to Blogs than Twitter," *Mashable,* March 8, 2012.

28. T. Huddleston, "Pinterest Now Valued at $11 Billion," *Time,* March 16, 2015.

29. B. Evangelista, "Facebook Finds Balance with Social Games after Zynga Breakup," *San Francisco Chronicle,* March 26, 2013.

30. Spotify Statistics, *Spotify,* March 18, 2015.

31. Unattributed, "Street Plan: Google Buys Waze," *The Economist,* June 15, 2013.

32. "InterActiveCorp's Tinder Catches Fire," *Barron's,* February 2, 2015.

33. K. Kokalitcheva, "Swipe right if you'd like to pay for this 'romantic' match on Tinder," *VentureBeat,* October 20, 2014.

34. J. Cook, "Tinder would be worth $1.6 billion as a standalone business," *Business Insider,* April 1, 2015.

36. Adapted and modified from the original list presented in T. O'Reilly, "What Is Web 2.0?" *O'Reilly,* September 30, 2005.

37. E. Zuckerman, "Reddit: A Pre-Facebook Community in a Post-Facebook World," *Atlantic,* July 8, 2013.

38. E. Protalinski, "Reddit's 2014 stats: Pageviews grow 27% to 71B, unique visitors not disclosed," *VentureBeat,* December 31, 2014.

39. H. Fawcett, "3 Unusual Q&A Sites to Source IT Talent From—Quora, GitHub, Stack-Overflow," *SocialTalent,* September 5, 2012.

40. Stats from http://tumblr.com/about, accessed March 18, 2015.

41. "Usage of content management systems for websites," *W3Techs,* March 18, 2015.

42. Adapted from S. Corcoran, "Defining Earned, Owned, and Paid Media," *Forrester Research,* December 16, 2009.

43. C. Pollitt, "The New 5 Step Inbound Marketing Methodology," *Business2Community,* October 21, 2011.

44. M. Kagan, "The Top 10 Most Remarkable Marketing Campaigns EVER," *HubSpot,* January 10, 2013.

45. D. Pink, "The Book Stops Here," *Wired,* March 2005.

46. S. Robert Lichter, *Are Chemicals Killing Us?* Statistical Assessment Service, May 21, 2009; J. Kane, R. Fichman, J. Gallaugher, and J. Glaser, "Community Relations 2.0," *Harvard Business Review,* November 2009.

47. M. Chui, A. Miller, R. Roberts, "Six ways to make Web 2.0 work," *McKinsey Quarterly,* Feb. 2009.

48. D. Carlin, "Corporate Wikis Go Viral," *BusinessWeek,* March 12, 2007. And M. Calabrese, "Wikipedia for Spies: The CIA Discovers Web 2.0," *Time,* April 8, 2009.

49. A. Bergman, "Wikipedia Is Only as Anonymous as Your I.P.," *O'Reilly Radar,* August 14, 2007.

50. I. Williams, "Sony Caught Editing Halo 3 Wikipedia Entry," *Vnunet.com,* September 5, 2007.

51. E. Hansen, "Wikipedia Founder Edits Own Bio," *Wired,* December 19, 2005.

52. R. Tate, "Hangouts Feature Emerges as Big Bright Spot for Google+," *Wired,* May 17, 2013.

53. G. Marks, "How Google Is Forever Changing the Webinar," *Forbes,* January 14, 2013.

54. R. Tate, "Hangouts Feature Emerges as Big Bright Spot for Google+," *Wired,* May 17, 2013.

55. M. Chafkin, "Can Ben Silbermann Turn Pinterest into the World's Greatest Shopfront?" *Fast Company,* October 2012.

56. T. Simonite, "EmTech Digital: Pinterest's Bid to Reinvent Online Shopping,"*Technology Review,* June 1, 2015.

57. K. Wagner, "Three Reasons LinkedIn Broke the Bank for Lynda.com," *Re/code,* April 9, 2015.

58. R. King, "No Rest for the Wiki," *BusinessWeek,* March 12, 2007.

59. O. Kharif, "Job Recruiters Eschew Monster to Find Hidden Talent on LinkedIn," *Bloomberg,* Dec. 13, 2012.

60. R. King, "Social Networks: Execs Use Them Too," *BusinessWeek,* November 11, 2006.

61. W. Bulkley, "Playing Well with Others," *Wall Street Journal,* June 18, 2007.

62. F. Majoo. "Slack, the Office Messaging App That May Finally Sink Email," *The New York Times,* March 11, 2015.

63. I. Lunden, "Used Daily By 750K Workers, Slack Raises $160M, Valuing Collaboration Startup At $2.8B," *TechCrunch,* April 16, 2015.

64. D. Greenfield, "How Companies Are Using I.T. to Spot Innovative Ideas," *InformationWeek,* November 8, 2008.

65. Starbucks, Facebook, April 16, 2015.

66. J. Gallaugher and S. Ransbotham, "Social Media and Customer Dialog Management at Starbucks," *MIS Quarterly Executive* 9, no. 4 (December 2010): 197–212.

67. K. Lant, "How A Social Network Can Help Dish Out a Diagnosis to Save a Life," *The Science Times,* May 22, 2015.

68. Unattributed, "When Every Second Counts: How Medical Crowdsourcing Saves Lives," *Sermo Blog,* May 20, 2015. And K. Lant, "How A Social Network Can Help Dish Out a Diagnosis to Save a Life," *The Science Times,* May 22, 2015.

69. G. Kane, R. Fichman, J. Gallaugher, and J. Glasser, "Community Relations 2.0," *Harvard Business Review,* Nov. 2009.

70. T. Goetz, "Practicing Patients," *New York Times Magazine,* March 23, 2008.

71. J. Kane, R. Fichman, J. Gallaugher, and J. Glaser, "Community Relations 2.0," *Harvard Business Review,* November 2009.

72. Twitter Usage / Company Facts, Accessed on June 6, 2015 from: https://about.twitter.com/company

73. About Twitter: Company, *Twitter,* March 18, 2015.

74. E. Schonfeld, "Twitter's Internal Strategy Laid Bare: To Be 'The Pulse of The Planet,'" *TechCrunch,* July 19, 2009.

75. K. Eaton, "Twitter Really Works: Makes $6.5 Million in Sales for Dell," *Fast Company,* December 8, 2009; J. Abel, "Dude—Dell's Making Money off Twitter!" *Wired News,* June 12, 2009.

76. A. Isaac, "Twitter users can now donate to charity with a hashtag," *The Guardian,* April 17, 2015.

77. A. Romano, "Now 4 Restaurant 2.0," *Newsweek,* February 28, 2009.

78. J. Constine, "Why Is Facebook Page Reach Decreasing? More Competition and Limited Attention," *TechCrunch,* April 3, 2014.

79. C. Shu, "Twitter's "While You Were Away" Feature Launches On Android," *TechCrunch,* Feb. 23, 2015.

80. G. Capon, "Twitter Amplify Will Create Enormous Value for Broadcasters and Brands," *The Guardian,* May 23, 2014.

81. J. Ourand and E. Fisher, "Leagues Embrace Twitter, with Eye on Future Revenue," *Sports Business Daily*, October 21, 2013.

82. K. Chaykowski, "Twitter Automates 'Amplify', As It Pushes The Live-Video Ad Product Into News, Entertainment," *Forbes*, May 28, 2015.

83. G. Stone, "Twitter's MoPub Welcomes Facebook's Mobile Ads into Its Platform. All Networks Plug In," *AdWeek*, May 1, 2014.

84. J. Constine, "Twitter Plans to Use What You Follow and Tweet to Target MoPub Ads on Other Apps. Here's How," *TechCrunch*, October 14, 2013.

85. D. Goldman, "Twitter Grows Up: Take a Peek Inside," *CNN*, April 16, 2010.

86. N. Mediati, "Twitter cuts off Meerkat, won't let it import who you follow on Twitter," *PC World*, March 19, 2015.

87. L. Duggan, "After LinkedIn, Instagram, Tumblr, the Latest to Get Disconnected from Twitter Is IFTTT," *MediaBistro*, September 21, 2012.

88. S. Kovach & J. Yarow, "Twitter crushes revenue and EPS, but whiffs on users. Stock still up though," *Business Insider*, February 5 2015.

89. J. Pepitone, "#WOW! Twitter soars 73% in IPO," CNN, November 7, 2013.

90. Y. Koh, "Meet Twitter's Mr. Fix-It: Ali Rowghani," *The Wall Street Journal*, April 29, 2014.

91. J. Giles, "Special Report: Internet Encyclopedias Go Head to Head," *Nature* 438, no. 15 (December 14, 2005): 900–901.

92. P. Dvorak, "Best Buy Taps 'Prediction Market,'" *Wall Street Journal*, September 16, 2008; and Renée Dye, "The Promise of Prediction Markets: A Roundtable," *McKinsey Quarterly* 2 (2008): 83–93.

93. R. Dye, "The Promise of Prediction Markets: A Roundtable," *McKinsey Quarterly* 2 (2008): 83–93.

94. B. Cowgill, J. Wolfers, and E. Zitzewitz, "Using Prediction Markets to Track Information Flows: Evidence from Google," working paper accessed November 30, 2009, via http://bocowgill.com/GooglePredictionMarketPaper.pdf.

95. "Twitter Datastream Used to Predict Flu Outbreaks," *MIT Technology Review*, October 9, 2013.

96. R. Dye, "The Promise of Prediction Markets: A Roundtable," *McKinsey Quarterly* 2 (2008): 83–93.

97. "Audit Reveals Farecast Predictive Accuracy at 74.5 Percent," *farecast.live.com*, May 18, 2007, http://www.prnewswire.com/news-releases/farecast-launches-new-tools-to-help-savvy-travelers-catch-elusive-airfare-price-drops-this-summer-58165652.html.

98. J. Surowiecki, "Crowdsourcing the Crystal Ball," *Forbes*, October 15, 2007.

99. V. Golvchenko, "Platform Review: Nadex Exchange-Traded Binary Options in the US," *Finance Magnates*, June 1, 2015.

100. J. Howe, "The Rise of Crowdsourcing," *Wired*, June 2006.

101. L. Gannes, "After Waze, What Else Can Mobile Crowdsourcing Do?," *AllThingsD*, June 19, 2013.

102. C. McNamara, "Nine of the World's Top 10 Brands are Crowdsourcing. So um…What Are You Waiting For?" *Australian Anthill*, June 5, 2013.

103. S. Lohr, "And the Winner of the $1 Million Netflix Prize (Probably) Is…" *New York Times*, June 26, 2009.

104. L. Seagall, "GE Gets Quirky," *CNN Money*, April 12, 2014.

105. C. Velazco, "Quirky and GE Cook Up a Smarter, Prettier Air Conditioner," *Engadget*, March 19, 2014.

106. "Frequently Asked Questions," *Innocentive*, April 16, 2015.

107. M. Brandel, "Should Your Company 'Crowdsource' Its Next Project?" *Computerworld*, December 6, 2007; M. Brandel, "Crowdsourcing: Are You Ready to Ask the World for Answers?" *Computerworld*, March 3, 2008; and TopCoder, 2011, http://topcoder.com/home.

108. D. Kirkpatrick, "Help Wanted: Adults on Facebook," *Fortune*, March 21, 2008.

109. The concepts in this section are based on work by J. Kane, R. Fichman, J. Gallaugher, and J. Glasser, many of which are covered in the article "Community Relations 2.0," *Harvard Business Review*, November 2009.

110. E. York, "McDonald's Names First Social-Media Chief," *Chicago Business*, April 13, 2010.

111. Starbucks was named the best firm for social media engagement in a study by Altimeter Group and WetPaint. See the 2009 ENGAGEMENTdb report at http://engagementdb.com.

112. C. Barger, talk at the Social Media Club of Detroit, November 18, 2009. Also available via UStream and DigitalMarketingZen.com.

113. J. Soat, "7 Questions Key to Social Networking Success," *InformationWeek*, January 16, 2010.

114. G. Kane, "Can You Really Let Employees Loose on Social Media?" *Sloan Management Review*, Nov. 6, 2014.

115. L. Conway, "Virgin Atlantic Sacks 13 Staff for Calling Its Flyers 'Chavs,'" *The Independent*, November 1, 2008.

116. E. York, "McDonald's Names First Social-Media Chief," *Chicago Business*, April 13, 2010.

117. O. Parker, "Food Website Posts Tasteless Social Media about Boston Marathon Tragedy," *Red Banyan Group*, February 8, 2014.

118. H. Tsukayama, "AT&T Removes, Apologizes for 9/11 Tribute Tweet," *The Washington Post*, September 11, 2013, http://www.washingtonpost.com/business/technology/atandt-removes-apologizes-for-911-tribute-tweet/2013/09/11/6d8f8806-1b06-11e3-a628-7e6dde8f889d_story.html.

119. L. Stampler, "The Nine Biggest Brand Fails Exploiting Hurricane Sandy," November 1, 2012, http://www.businessinsider.com/the-9-biggest-brand-fails-exploiting-hurricane-sandy-2012-11?op=1.

120. C. Choi, "SpaghettiOs Apologizes for Pearl Harbor Tweet," December 7, 2013, http://www.usatoday.com/story/money/business/2013/12/07/spaghettios-apologizes-for-pearl-harbor-tweet/3904843.

121. M. McGee, "Epicurious Becomes Latest Brand to Suffer Social Backlash from Tragedy-Related Tweets," April 16, 2013, http://marketingland.com/epicurious-becomes-latest-brand-to-suffer-social-backlash-from-tragedy-related-tweets-4

122. G. Kane, "How to Avoid a Social Media Fiasco," *Sloan Management Review Blog*, April 8, 2014.

123. Re/code, April 13, 2015. C. Edwards, "The Social Media Megaphone Every Brand Forgets," *Re/code*, April 13, 2015.

124. A. Martin, "Whole Foods Executive Used Alias," *New York Times*, July 12, 2007.

125. C. Cain Miller, "Company Settles Case of Reviews It Faked," *New York Times*, July 14, 2009.

126. L. Rathke, "Report: Ski Resorts Exaggerate Snowfall Totals," *USA Today*, January 29, 2010.

127. J. Fell, "Chipotle Jeopardizes Customer Trust With Fake Twitter Hack Stunt," *Entrepreneur*, July 25, 2013.

128. D. Schael, "TripAdvisor Has a New Analytics Dashboard Aimed at Tourism Boards," *Skift*, May 26, 2015

129. G. Sterling, "Yelp Upgraded Business Owner App Brings Mobile-First Account Management," *MarketingLand*, May 20, 2015.

130. Brad Nelson, presentation at the Social Media Conference NW, Mount Vernon, WA, March 25, 2010.

131. J. Gallaugher and S. Ransbotham, "Social Media and Dialog Management at Starbucks" (presented at the MISQE Social Media Workshop, Phoenix, AZ, December 2009).

132. A. Jacques, "Domino's Delivers during Crisis: The Company's Step-by-Step Response after a Vulgar Video Goes Viral," *The Public Relations Strategist*, October 24, 2009.

133. B. Stone, "Facebook Aims to Extend Its Reach across the Web," *New York Times*, December 2, 2008.

134. J. Kane, R. Fichman, J. Gallaugher, and J. Glaser, "Community Relations 2.0," *Harvard Business Review*, November 2009.

135. E. Schonfeld, "Time Magazine Throws Up Its Hands as It Gets Pawned by 4Chan," *TechCrunch*, April 27, 2009.

136. S. Gregory, "Domino's YouTube Crisis: 5 Ways to Fight Back," *Time*, April 18, 2009.

137. Zicam had regularly been the victim of urban legends claiming negative side effects from use; see Snopes.com, "Zicam Warning," http://www.snopes.com/medical/drugs/zicam.asp. However, the firm subsequently was cited in an unrelated FDA warning on the usage of its product; see S. Young, "FDA Warns against Using 3 Popular Zicam Cold Meds," *CNN.com*, June 16, 2009.

138. K. Paterson, "Managing an Online Reputation," *New York Times*, July 29, 2009.

139. H. Popkin, "Twitter Gets You Fired in 140 Characters or Less," *MSNBC*, March 23, 2009.

CHAPTER 10
The Sharing Economy, Collaborative Consumption, and Creating More Efficient Markets through Technology

1. INTRODUCTION

LEARNING OBJECTIVES

1. Recognize firms often categorized as part of the "sharing economy" or participating in "collaborative consumption." Test
2. Gain a sense of market size, impact, investment, and business valuation in these sectors.

In recent years, technology has enabled staggeringly diverse groups of product and service providers to connect with consumers, offering far greater reach and efficiency than traditional markets. Many of these new tech-fueled marketplaces are allowing millions of users to turn to private individuals—in effect, strangers instead of corporations—to meet some kind of demand. These efforts are also enabling a generation of "citizen suppliers" to go into business for themselves. Product owners are becoming providers of rentals, offering up their rooms (Airbnb), cars (RelayRides), boats (Boatbound), and power tools (Zilok). Others are empowering a whole new class of micro-entrepreneurs with possessions and skills to provide personal services. Car rides (Uber, Lyft), pet sitting (DogVacay), meal prep (Feastly), home services (Care.com, Angie's List, HandyBook), freelance business services (oDesk), and errand runners (TaskRabbit) are just some of the segments getting a high-octane, tech-fueled boost. Some firms are buying inventory and renting it out (RentTheRunway with dresses, ZipCar with autos, Chegg with textbooks). These firms are moving whole categories of products from something an individual owns outright to something that is "collaboratively consumed," wherein an individual takes possession of an item for a period of time, then returns it for use by others. Consumers are even collaborating as financiers, pooling capital to back projects (KickStarter, GoFundMe, Indiegogo) and provide loans (LendingClub, Prosper, Kiva). Most of these Internet-enabled market makers can trace their roots back to once-pioneering, now massively influential firms like eBay and CraigsList, which empowered all sorts of individual sellers and service providers.[1]

Author Rachel Botsman coined the term "collaborative consumption" to describe these efforts.[2] Economist Thomas Friedman, author of *The World Is Flat*, prefers the phrase "sharing economy."[3] Still others may refer to the "collaboration economy," "peer-to-peer commerce," or even "re-commerce."[4] Many have lamented that these terms lack clear definitions.[5] Trying to bring precision to the term, Boston College sociologist Juliet Schor says the sharing economy can involve the recirculation of goods, increased utilization of durable assets, exchange of services, or the sharing of productive assets.[6] A great start, but even this is tricky. Is a public library part of the sharing economy? Airbnb is a poster child for the effort, but why don't traditional bed and breakfasts get the same respect? Tech analyst Dan Schutzer adds that much of what we call "sharing economy" standouts differ from earlier efforts in that their efficiency is enhanced through streamlined coordination and broader reach by leveraging the Internet.[7] Even as we struggle for a precise definition, it's worth examining what's happening across this group of provider-pooling, tech-powered market places. These firms fuel more efficient matching of supply and demand, lower costs, enable more efficient resource use, and provide a level of reach and services heretofore unavailable.

Today, billions of dollars in commerce is flowing through these marketplaces. Some are currently addressing smaller, niche markets. For example, the market for hourly car-sharing services (e.g., ZipCar or RelayRides) is thought to be just one-sixtieth the size of the market for traditional car rentals (e.g., Hertz, Enterprise, and ZipCar parent Avis). However, others are building Goliaths. For example, as of mid-2015, taxi-alternative Uber was larger than any cab firm on the planet, operating in 311 cities in fifty-eight countries,[8] and fast-growing Airbnb had more property listings than Hilton, the biggest hotel chain on earth, has hotel rooms.[9] Given the potential for disruption, some very deep-pocketed investors are placing massive bets on the upstarts. Peer loan firm Lending Club was California's biggest IPO of 2014, raising $870 million at a nearly $8.9 billion valuation.[10] Airbnb raised $450 million at a $10 billion valuation. In 2015, the number two car service, Lyft, raised a massive $530 million financing round, but this isn't even half of what the leading player, Uber, had raised a few months earlier. The 2014 $1.2 billion Uber round was, at the time, the largest investment round in the history of technology firms[11] and one that pegged the firm's value at north of $18 billion, making it worth more than Hertz or Avis.[12] Chegg went public and has a half-billion-dollar market cap. ZipCar went public and was acquired by Avis, also for about half a billion dollars. And consumers are solidly on board with the sharing economy revolution. If we include the peer-to-peer selling in eBay and CraigsList within our broad categorization, then some 40 percent of the population of the United States and Canada already participates in the so-called sharing economy as either buyers or sellers.[13]

Some Examples of Firms Often Characterized as Part of the "Sharing Economy" or "Collaborative Consumption"

- Goods:
  - Pre-owned: eBay, CraigsList (peer-to-peer supplied); thredUp (firm-owned inventory).
  - Loaner products: Zilok (peer-to-peer supplied); RentTheRunway, Chegg (firm-owned inventory).
  - Custom products: Etsy, CustomMade.
- Services:
  - Professional services: oDesk, eLance, CrowdSpring.
  - Personal services: Angie's List, TaskRabbit.
  - Delivery: DoorDash, Dashed, Deliv, Instacart, Postmates (self-employed drivers for restaurant or grocery delivery), Drizly (drivers and alcohol inventory owned by suppliers).
- Transportation:
  - Transportation Services: Uber, Lyft, HailO (cars supplied by drivers).
  - Loaner Vehicles: Relay Rides (peer-to-peer supplied), ZipCar (firm-owned inventory).
- Office Space:
  - Office Space: LiquidSpace, ShareDesk (peer-to-peer supplied inventory).
  - Places to Stay: Airbnb, HomeAway, Couchsurfing (peer-to-peer supplied inventory).
- Money and Finance:
  - Money Lending: LendingClub, Kiva, Prosper (peer-to-peer loans).
  - CrowdFunding: KickStarter, GoFundMe, Indiegogo (peer-to-peer capital).

KEY TAKEAWAYS

- The sharing economy is allowing firms to pool resources, products, and services in ways that create new markets and market opportunities.
- Citizen suppliers are offering services and renting out their own goods, while other firms are taking possession of inventory to organize resale or rental markets.
- Definitions of the sharing economy are imprecise, but a common set of dynamics, which we'll explore in this chapter, underpin market competition and growth.

2. BOOM TIMES AND LOOMING CHALLENGES IN THE SHARING ECONOMY

LEARNING OBJECTIVES

1. Identify the factors that have contributed to the rise of the sharing economy.
2. Understand the competitive factors that influence success in marketplaces that support collaborative consumption.

2.1 Share On! Factors Fueling the Rise of Collaborative Consumption

Several factors have come together to create a perfect storm for market disruption in market making. A prolonged, worldwide economic recession and stagnant wages have boosted consumer interest in low-cost alternatives to conventional products and services, and it encouraged a whole new class of laypeople to try their hand at offering services for hire. Need money? Rent out your spare room, your truck, the belt sander in your basement, find a market for your crafts or handyman skills, or run an errand in your free time.

While inviting strangers into your home, lending them your stuff, or hiring them for personal services might creep out an earlier generation, apps and social technologies help allay fears by collecting and sharing ratings (of both buyers and suppliers), ensuring payment, and offering increased scheduling convenience. Many of the services also have an environmental benefit by fostering reuse and diminished consumption.

2.2 Winning in Electronic Markets

All of these efforts are two-sided markets, and network effects are in effect. Showing up early has the advantage of creating a critical mass of buyers that will attract sellers and vice versa. Early players gain scale, brand, and financial resources to help expand and reinforce assets for competitive advantage. Want to start a sharing economy marketplace? As in any market effort, understand that value needs to be realized on both sides of the transaction equation. Suppliers without buyers or buyers without suppliers is a lopsided recipe for failure.

Consider Lyft's struggles in Boston. Lyft allows anyone with a car to operate like a taxi, and for weeks after launch the city was filled with a distinctive fleet of cars sporting the fuzzy pink mustaches that Lyft drivers initially attached to their car grills when on duty (the grill stache is no longer a Lyft requirement). Lyft had subsidized the driver side of the market by providing a minimum hourly fee, even if drivers didn't pick up any customers. While drivers showed up, customers didn't follow as quickly, and when Lyft removed the wage floor, drivers began abandoning the service during non-peak times. As a result, customers looking for a Boston Lyft would often open the app only to be greeted by an empty map and an "All drivers are currently busy" message. Several Lyft drivers reported moving to Uber, a more popular service that also offers surge pricing to encourage more drivers to come out and satisfy customers during periods of peak demand.[14] Timing is at work in fueling the network effect. Uber started in 2009, Lyft in 2012. And Uber intends to keep its lead; the firm's CEO Travis Kalanick has declared that he'll be using the firm's gargantuan recent funding round to "fight Lyft."[15]

FIGURE 10.1

Lyft drivers use their own automobiles, but initially branded their participation by attaching pink mustaches to their car grills

Source: Scott Kirsner—Twitter @scottkirsner

Marketplaces are especially attractive to citizen-suppliers who want to make use of expensive items they've purchased but that are not regularly used. Technology allows exchange operators to coordinate a peer-to-peer supply, substituting information for real estate and other types of expensive inventory that traditional firms usually own outright. Airbnb doesn't own its hotel rooms; Uber and Lyft don't own cars. And in most cases, citizen-suppliers have already paid for the assets they use to earn money in the sharing economy. Airbnb's founder points to the wisdom of rental firm Zilok when stating, "There are 80 million power drills in America that are used an average of thirteen minutes. Does everyone really need their own drill?"[16] Capital investment, utilities, and maintenance are just some of the costs that sharing economy upstarts save over their competitors.

For some marketplaces, end users simply can't be relied on to consistently manage inventory and logistics. In these cases, successful "collaborative consumption" efforts own inventory to ensure quality and gain more control over the customer experience. Rent the Runway meticulously oversees its dress inventory, packing product for delivery, running a massive in-house garment cleaning effort, and retiring dresses that are noticeably worn. The goal is to ensure that an experience with the firm will bring customers a "Cinderella moment" filled with delight, rather than disappointment.[17] While some startups have attempted to allow women to rent dresses to others, none has achieved anything close to the scale of Rent the Runway's four million members.[18] For the same reason Chegg oversees textbook inventory for the timely delivery students demand. A service where college students rented textbooks to others could never consistently deliver on quality. And used clothing marketplace thredUp started as a peer-to-peer firm where consumers sold to each other similar to eBay, but it has since evolved into an online consignment store that curates and warehouses inventory, provides high-quality photography of items for sale, and attentively packages goods for delivery. All this is meant to raise the bar and create a used-clothing purchase experience that rivals new item retail while saving customers big bucks.[19]

Highly fragmented markets are especially ripe for rollup in electronic marketplaces. Lots of suppliers in a traditional market mean customer search costs are high. But ratings in marketplaces help you quickly size up high-quality providers and make a lower-risk choice. Why look at the yellow pages when Handybook can show you five-star plumbers, all vetted in background checks with insurance verified? Once a critical mass of buyers turns to a market as a first-choice for shopping, the supply side knows they've got to show up, but suppliers can also use these markets to lower other costs. Directories like Angie's List and Etsy also take the place of conventional advertising, marketing, or storefronts, so suppliers reduce overhead and marketplaces offer margins that traditional firms can't match.[20]

In highly-fragmented markets, marketplaces oftentimes extend the value chain by getting between suppliers and customers that would otherwise connect directly. This is contrary to what we think of when disintermediation removes organizations from the distribution channel in order to increase efficiency, but if the network offers value through search and discovery, use of otherwise underutilized assets, scheduling, payment, reputation management and more, then a longer value chain can be a more efficient one. Publicly traded Care.com screens fragmented networks of providers of child care, elder care, pet care, and home upkeep services. Alcohol delivery app Drizly doesn't actually employ any drivers, nor does it take possession of any hooch (saving it from liquor industry regulation). Instead it simply connects those looking for a booze delivery with an existing yet underutilized network of existing drivers working for independent (and highly fragmented) liquor stores.[21] While not quite a network of citizen suppliers, the same economics are at work here. The fragmented, small, independent suppliers are brought together by Drizly's market-making app to create what looks like a unified national brand, and this brings in new customers who seek the app-tap convenience of adult beverages brought right to their doorstep.

While Drizly rolls up the fragmented market for booze, ClassPass does the same for fitness classes. Customers pay a cancel-any-time monthly fee and can choose and schedule yoga, spin, Pilates, and more from a host of providers. Customers get choice, while providers bring in new customers and get a cut of ClassPass revenue while helping keep instructors and facilities full.

2.3   Social Media for Virality and Trust Strengthening

Word of mouth sharing and the virality offered by social media accelerate the growth of sharing economy marketplaces. Firms that can turn customers into brand ambassadors can see lower advertising and customer acquisition costs. One survey reported that 47 percent of participants in the sharing economy learned about the services they used via word of mouth.[22] Uber has proved inherently viral. Every seven riders attracts one new Uber user.[23] The firm regularly offers customers discounts for sharing Uber coupons to attract friends as new riders. Such programs aren't simply a subsidy to recruit customers, they are a trust-conveying **social proof** endorsement from an acquaintance that state "getting rides from a stranger isn't scary—I do it and here's money so you can try it, too!" Another factor that fuels virality? A satisfied customer base. One study found that 91 percent of sharing economy participants would recommend the last service they used to a friend or colleague.[24]

Lyft provides another good example of using social media to instill trust between drivers and customers. Both parties link to Lyft through their Facebook accounts.[25] Profile photos pop up as part of ride requests, so you know who you're going to be meeting. And both drivers and passengers rate each other. Drivers can skip fares with deadbeats ratings, while passengers get an endorsement that they're not about to step into a car driven by a sketchy rip-off artist, or worse.[26] Payment is guaranteed through the app. Consumers get an audit trail to call out any driver who tries to scam them or makes them feel uncomfortable, while drivers are ensured a fare won't pull the "no-cash dash," leaving them without pay for services. By leveraging technology this way, a service like Lyft can offer both parties in a transaction the kind of security that goes way beyond what one would get from a conventional taxi operation.

Online provider ratings can provide a lot more insight than you'd get when stepping into a conventional cab, or responding to a Yellow Pages ad, but online ratings aren't perfect. Boston College's Juliet Schor, who studied the sharing economy for the MacArthur Foundation, discovered evidence that some highly rated TaskRabbit suppliers leveraged the corresponding large volume of service requests to farm out their work to subcontractors, while taking a cut for themselves (such market-making within the market is against TaskRabbit terms of service).[27]

Crowdsourced ratings can also reflect the crowd's bias and reinforce discrimination. Allegations in an Uber driver forum suggest that college students rate older drivers lower, male riders give lower ratings to female drivers who don't respond to their flirtatiousness, drivers with disabilities also experience lower ratings, and black drivers have a lower acceptance rate than whites. A working paper published by Harvard researchers reports bias in Airbnb, claiming that after controlling for factors like location, rental characteristics, and quality, non-black Airbnb hosts in New York City were still able to charge 12 percent more than their black counterparts,[28] and black hosts received a larger penalty for having a poor location when compared to comparable non-black hosts.[29] Fighting this bias is tricky. Lyft doesn't track race or gender out of "a desire to be non-intrusive," but the firm will monitor things

FIGURE 10.2

Uniting fragmented markets: The smartphone app for Care.com pools citizen-suppliers for services such as childcare, eldercare, pet care, and home cleaning. Drizly allows independent liquor stores to collaborate to create a nationwide network for local alcohol delivery.

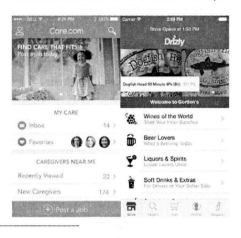

FIGURE 10.3

ClassPass provides choice and variety for fitness customers.

Source: Image courtesy of ClassPass.

social proof

Positive influence created when someone finds out that others are doing something.

like request denials. To prevent drivers from denying rides to minority neighborhoods, many ride-sharing firms also don't share passenger destinations until the passenger has accepted the ride or even is in the vehicle.[30]

2.4 Can You Share Nice? Challenges of Safety and Regulation

Instilling trust doesn't mean that firms are without safety issues, and participants in the sharing economy are continuing to evolve their policies as a result. Airbnb has had rare incidents where guests have trashed homes or otherwise misbehaved, and Uber comes under criticism in those extremely rare circumstances where drivers commit crimes or get into injurious or even fatal accidents.

Participating in the sharing economy raises questions for insurers. Will firms pay out if there is a "sharing economy" incident with a supplier, or will they try to refuse, saying, in effect, "your policy doesn't cover operating a business." Homes, cars and other insured items will experience more use, wear and tear, likely a greater risk for the insurer, than if the insured item was only for personal use. Some sharing economy firms offer service providers additional coverage and protection guarantees, but the environment is still fluid. California is threatening additional insurance regulation for sharing economy participants.[31] Attempts to further regulate the industry could arise from legislator concern, or lobbying from the insurance industry or entrenched incumbents threatened by sharing economy competition.

Many local firms also benefit from taxes and regulatory fees from industries threatened by the sharing economy, and groups opposed to new, rival efforts can represent very powerful lobbies. Firms usually pay for the right to operate a cab service within a municipal district. In New York City, companies need a so-called medallion, an operating privilege that can cost over $1 million for a single vehicle.[32] Firms that have made this kind of investment don't want to see new competitors, especially if newcomers don't have to shell-out for the same expenses. Thousands of cab drivers in major European cities snarled traffic to protest Uber and other ride-sharing services,[33] and Seattle's city council has voted to limit ride sharing services.[34] Most large cities also tax and regulate hotels and other industries that these new models threaten. Airbnb has actually offered to pay $21 million in annual taxes to New York City, and has even sponsored a NY State bill to allow it to collect taxes. But opposition threatened by sharing economy firms is strong. Taxi and hotel owners represent powerful lobbies, and they'd love to see competition from the sharing economy go away. Hotel unions fear the growth of non-union jobs. Neighborhood associations are concerned that family homes are now located side-by-side next to operating commercial properties that bring a large group of unknown, non-neighbors into their apartment buildings, condo complexes, and neighborhoods. Tenant lobbies worry that Airbnb encourages buying apartments as investment properties, contributing to a lack of affordable housing (San Francisco passed legislation to limit Airbnb-style short-term rentals to no more than 90 days a year).[35]

The road to citizen-led finance has also been filled with obstacles. Leading peer-to-peer lending sites Prosper and Lending Club shut down for a period of time to work with the SEC and develop an oversight plan, which eventually involved securitizing loans made on the site so that they could be bought and sold on the open market,[36] and requiring both companies to make their financials public, even when they were privately held.[37] It's also worth noting that a good thing for consumers might be a great thing for institutions, as well. While Prosper and Lending Club were founded on the vision of peer-to-peer finance fueled by an army of citizen lenders, the reality is now that much of the money in these systems comes from hedge funds, other big institutional investors, and the wealthy.[38]

Another major concern for firms in the sharing economy is uncertainty around the ability of these firms to continue to consider their workers as independent contractors and not employees. An administrator for the US Dept. of Labor wrote: "When employers improperly classify employees as independent contractors, the employees may not receive important workplace protections such as the minimum wage, overtime compensation, unemployment insurance, and workers' compensation. Misclassification also results in lower tax revenues for government and an uneven playing field for employers who properly classify their workers."[39] The CEO of HomeJoy shut down the sharing economy home cleaning firm, claiming that pending lawsuits had made it difficult for his firm to raise additional capital (the firm had already raised over $40 million from investors, including Google Ventures).[40] Other sharing economy firms, including Shyp (couriers) and Instacart (grocery delivery) have moved to reclassify independent contractors as employees.[41] The issue has gained the attention of state and federal agencies and presidential candidates, and raises the specter of class action lawsuits. Any move from independents (so called 1099 workers after the US tax form they fill out) to firm employees (that are issued a W-2 form) won't come cheap. A reclassification could raise wages by 20 percent, add upwards of 14 percent more for workers' compensation premiums that employers are required to pay, and employers will need to provide healthcare contributions.[42]

Not all authorities are opposed. Boston's mayor has voiced support for Uber, seeing it as a safe and popular service among citizens and city visitors.[43] Colorado and California have passed legislation largely supportive of ride sharing services, while requiring some regulation to ensure public safety.[44] With a mixed regulatory reception in many markets, sharing economy innovators should recognize that even though they can build "an app for that," it doesn't mean that technology efforts will be allowed to circumvent incumbent protections, and we're likely to see a wide variation in support and regulation for years to come.

WePay Winning Big: Processing Payments and Taming the Crowd through "Social" Security

Bringing together buyers and sellers can seem like a great business, but dealing with payment collection can cause migraine-inducing challenges. Credit card firms often take 3 percent or more from any transaction that accepts plastic, so many firms view payments as a despised, margin-narrowing expense.[45] Firms that run their own payments platforms also risk attack from hackers, vulnerabilities from software bugs and security crises, a complex regulatory environment, and more. Payments are rarely a source of competitive advantage in a marketplace—everyone needs to collect money—so firms are anxious to shed payment responsibility if they can.

On top of all this, processing payments in marketplace environments can prove especially challenging. Suppliers want to get up and running, accepting payments right away, but fraud is common. Crooks have been known to set up bogus storefronts or service providers and use stolen credit cards to "buy" from their own fake shops, in effect laundering money through these marketplaces. New merchant verification can be a slow, multistep process and has often resulted in inappropriately frozen merchant accounts (a complaint frequently made against payment leader PayPal).[46]

WePay is a firm that has stepped up to offer simple payment solutions that specifically target the challenges of buyer/seller platform operators. The firm's hundreds of clients include sharing economy standouts like service provider Care.com, goods marketplace CustomMade, and crowdfunding site GoFundMe. WePay combats challenges in several ways: first, the firm's Veda fraud fighting technology analyzes social profiles to get firms up and running with payments in a streamlined process, far faster than rivals.[47] By linking to social media accounts (Facebook, LinkedIn, Yelp, TripAdvisor), WePay can gain a fast read on whether founders and businesses are legitimate. It's extremely difficult to fake any history accrued over time. WePay has also been processing payments since 2008 and has transaction history from hundreds of thousands of customers currently sending billions of dollars a year through the firm's systems.[48] Each transaction adds to the firm's "big data" smarts used to separate the stand-up vendors from the sketchy. WePay makes adding payment capabilities to any site as easy as embedding a YouTube video, with a cut-and-paste of pre-generated code. The firm initially started as a group payments tool where clubs and friends could pool cash for purchases, but servicing businesses proved a much more lucrative market, with less support and other overhead needed for a focused group of high-volume clients. That **pivot** proved a winner. The firm now powers payments on eight of the top fifteen crowdfunding sites and is seeing growth balloon as new US regulations make crowdfunding more attractive. Early on, founders Bill Clerico and Rich Aberman took WePay through the elite Y-Combinator program (where the Airbnb team also gained mentors and connections). The duo have been named to *BusinessWeek*'s Best Young Tech Entrepreneurs list, and their firm has been named a "Top Five" financial technology company by *Forbes*. PayPal (which bought competitor Braintree) and Stripe present worthy competition, but WePay revenues are enjoying triple-digit growth, and the firm has raised nearly $75 million in capital to fuel expansion in the United States and abroad.[49]

pivot

A change in a firm's business model. Usually referring to a startup that targets a new market or makes a fundamentally new product offering.

KEY TAKEAWAYS

- Recession, wage stagnation, social media, environmental concerns, and the proliferation of smartphones are some of the factors that have helped fuel a rise in collaborative consumption.
- Two-sided network effects are at work in collaborative consumption marketplaces, and in order to be successful, firms must offer value to both buyers and suppliers.
- Firms that move early may get a jumpstart on the creation of key assets, such as network effects, brand, scale, and financial resources.
- Marketplaces allow suppliers to leverage underutilized assets, while marketplace operators can reduce overhead associated with conventional transactions by eliminating storefronts, utilities, staff, capital expense, and more.
- Some firms may choose to take control of inventory to maximize quality and customer experience.
- Fragmented markets are especially well-suited for roll up in electronic marketplaces.
- While we often talk about disintermediation that shrinks a distribution channel, channel-extending-intermediaries such as sharing economy exchanges, can position themselves between buyers and sellers, but add value for both parties. Suppliers gain reach and encourage discovery at a lower marketing spend, consumers see search costs lowered, and both sides can benefit from services such as scheduling and payment. Consumers see dramatically lowered search costs.
- Virality can lower advertising and customer acquisition costs, increase reputation, and lower the perception of risk.
- While crowdsourced participant ratings and social profiles can help improve trust, this technology can also reinforce bias and discriminatory tendencies of the crowd. Some firms audit data to try to uncover and address bias. Others hold back key information, such as destination information, if rides to a minority neighborhood might cause some suppliers to deny service to certain customers.
- Although incidents are rare, safety of the public and safety of service providers remains a concern in the sharing economy.
- Insurers may be reluctant to cover individuals or assets (homes, autos, or other high-value possessions) if they are being used commercially, instead of for standard, personal use as specified in most policies. As a result, some sharing economy firms have stepped up to offer their own supplemental insurance and safety coverage.
- Many entrenched interests will challenge the legality of the sharing economy and lobby for its regulation or curtailment.

QUESTIONS AND EXERCISES

1. What problems did Lyft face when trying to expand in the Boston market? Why do you suppose Uber is winning in Boston and many other cities?

2. Make a list of products that many people own, but that are underutilized. Are there sharing economy start-ups for these categories? If so, conduct some research to try to determine how they're doing. If not, do you think a market should be established? Why or why not? What challenges might such marketplaces face?

3. Give examples of firms that provide supply through peer-to-peer efforts, and collaborative consumption firms that take ownership of inventory.

4. Why do some collaborative consumption firms choose to take possession of inventory rather than allow the "crowd" to provide it peer-to-peer style?

5. Why do many collaborative consumption marketplaces work well in fragmented markets? What advantages do they offer buyers and sellers over traditional mechanisms of dealing with fragmented markets?

6. It sounds counterintuitive to gain efficiencies by adding a firm to the distribution channel, but how are some collaborative consumption marketplaces thriving as channel extending intermediaries? Give examples and discuss the value they add to both sides.

7. Why is social media important for many collaborative consumption efforts? Give examples of efforts that are effectively using social media for growth and success.

8. What sorts of legal risks are sharing economy firms exposed to? Conduct research online and identify examples of incidents that have put firms, customers, or suppliers at risk. Do you think these incidents will occur with greater or less frequency in sharing economy firms vs. traditional rivals? Why or why not?

9. Why do you suppose San Francisco passed a law to limit home owners to cap Airbnb (and similar) property rental to 90 days or less?

10. What can sharing economy firms do to reduce safety risks? Give examples of best practices.

11. Social profiles and crowdsourced ratings can improve trust, but they can also create opportunities for fraud and discrimination. Give examples of where this technology may have negative ethical implications, and discuss how the provider of a sharing economy marketplace can minimize risks and discriminatory bias.

12. Give examples of the kinds of entrenched interests that will lobby against expansion of the sharing economy? Why are each of these groups opposed to sharing economy efforts?

13. How do crooks try to use sharing economy marketplaces to commit fraud? How can social media help combat online fraud?

3. FUTURE OUTLOOK: ESTABLISHED PLAYERS GET COLLABORATIVE

LEARNING OBJECTIVES

1. **Identify and give examples of how large firms are investing in, partnering with, and building their own collaborative consumption efforts.**
2. **Gain insight into the advantages of collaborative consumption firms for traditional industry players, and enhance brainstorming skills for identifying possibilities for other firms.**

While the sharing economy has risen more rapidly than many expected, larger firms have also stepped up with investment, partnerships, and experiments of their own, underscoring a broad belief in the power and importance of the space. The following are some examples.

Google is a substantial investor in Uber, backing the firm with over a quarter of a billion dollars in capital, thus far.[50] Many see an obvious synergy between Uber's growing logistics prowess and Google's work on self-driving cars. Sharing economy standout, Rent the Runway, has also scored an investment by Condé Nast, the publisher behind *Vogue, Lucky, Glamour,* and other designer-friendly media properties. The firm has also evolved into an important industry partner. While some designers were originally worried that the service would cannibalize sales, many now realize that Rent the Runway has opened up a whole new tier of customers. An affinity with a designer gained from renting a more daring dress for a special occasion often translates into purchasing a staple, like a black cocktail dress, at a later date. Rent the Runway's social media engagement of its customer base also provides partners with valuable insights they'd otherwise not have access to.[51]

Other innovative partnerships include Walgreens and Task Rabbit, which will work together on drug store deliveries.[52] IBM also has its own delivery deal with collaborative commerce firm, Deliv. IBM offers software that powers many large retailers, and it works with Deliv to make same-day delivery services available to its clients, as well.[53] A W Hotel in New York City has partnered with the workspace sharing site Desks Near Me to offer business traveller guests access to places to work while in Manhattan.[54]

Some experiments will fail to achieve desired results. General Motors cancelled its OnStar-enabled partnership with car-sharing service RelayRides. But other automakers continue to explore their options. GM and Toyota give discounts on new-car purchases to Uber drivers; Mercedes Benz has invested in car-sharing service, car2go[55]; and Avis saw enough value in ZipCar to acquire the firm.

And expect some firms to enter as outright competitors. Amazon Home Services marketplace will put licensed professionals as well as small-time citizen service suppliers within the same massive discovery engine where millions search for physical products.[56]

While just a few years old, the sharing economy has accelerated in a wave of network effect-fueled technology efficiency and service enhancement that will impact industries for years to come. Hopefully this chapter has helped expose what's happening, why, and how managers can think about planning for a space where new electronic marketplaces empower and shift power from smartphone to supply chain.

KEY TAKEAWAYS

- Google and Condé Nast are among the large firms that have taken an investment stake in collaborative consumption start-ups.
- Walgreens, IBM, and the W Hotel are just a few firms that have enhanced customer offerings by partnering with sharing economy pioneers.
- Firms as diverse as auto manufacturers and Amazon are plotting independent collaborative consumption efforts as well.

QUESTIONS AND EXERCISES

1. Which collaborative consumption firms have Google and Condé Nast invested in? Why are these firms potentially attractive to their corporate investors?
2. Give examples of traditional firms that have partnered with collaborative consumption players. What does each hope to gain from the partnership?
3. Name traditional firms that have experimented with their own collaborative consumption efforts. Conduct additional research online. Are these efforts successful, failed, or is it too early to tell? What do you think of future prospects?

4. AIRBNB—HEY STRANGER, WHY DON'T YOU STAY AT MY PLACE?

LEARNING OBJECTIVES

1. **Understand how Airbnb has built a multibillion dollar sharing economy firm.**
2. **Recognize the appeal the firm has for suppliers and consumers.**
3. **Identify sources of competitive advantage and additional challenges as the firm continues to grow.**
4. **Understand how technology can build trust, even in an area as sensitive as selling stays in private homes.**

Brian Chesky, a graduate of the Rhode Island School of Design, had recently moved in with a friend in San Francisco and he couldn't make rent. Brainstorming on ideas, Chesky and his roomie, RISD classmate Joe Gebbia, realized an industrial designers conference was in town, and that all of the hotel rooms were booked solid. Sensing opportunity, the two inflated three air mattress and offered each one up for $80 a night. The duo earned enough to cover rent, and in the process, took their first step toward the creation of a multibillion dollar hospitality industry empire.[57]

Airbnb is now the poster child for the sharing economy. Put a single room or your entire property online, and you can become a citizen hotelier. A third cofounder, Nathan Blecharczyk, joined as CTO, the team gained admission to the elite Y-Combinator start-up finishing school, and Airbnb has since attracted several rounds of capital to fuel its meteoric growth. The firm's backers include Sequoia Capital, the storied Silicon Valley venture firm that invested in Apple, Cisco, Google, Oracle, and YouTube, among many others. Airbnb has raised over three quarters of a billion dollars so far, is valued at some $10 billion, and *Forbes* declared the firm's founding triumvirate as "The First Sharing Economy Billionaires."[58]

A guest checks into Airbnb every two seconds[59] and over 20 million have stayed with Airbnb with growth doubling in 2014.[60] Nightly guest stays were averaging 500,000 by mid 2015, heading toward a predicted 800,000 average during summer's high travel season.[61] The guest-to-listing ratio is eleven to one.[62] With listings in 34,000 cities and 192 countries, there is no other single hotel group that approaches the firm's worldwide reach.[63]

Airbnb has rallied the sharing economy to produce the longest accommodations tail in the lodging industry. According to founders, the firm's listings include over 600 castles, dozens of yurts, caves, tepees, water towers, clock towers, private islands, lighthouses, trains, environmentally-friendly "green" homes, igloos, glass houses, and more. Some of the exotic, high-end tree houses listed on Airbnb have six-month or more waiting lists for occupancy (but browse around, there are hundreds of tree houses offered through the site).[64] Want to stay in a home Charles Dickens, John Steinbeck, or Jim Morrison used to live in? Airbnb can set you up.

FIGURE 10.4

A sampling of some of the more unique properties available for rent on Airbnb.

Airbnb adds big value to both the supply and buy side of a transaction, and it's one of the few large players that can take a cut on each end of the deal. It charges guests a 6 to 12 percent fee, and hosts a 3 percent fee, paid after the first night.[65] During major events when hotels are booked to capacity, private citizens have turned on a money spigot courtesy of Chesky, Gebbia, and Blecharczyk, simultaneously saving travelers' bacon at political conventions, festivals, inaugurations, Olympics, and more. Airbnb was the largest short-term rental site of its kind in China before it even had any staff there. Such are the viral and ultralean dynamics of winning sharing economy marketplaces. You might even consider Airbnb a platform that nurtures an ecosystem of sharing economy value-added services. All sorts of citizen-suppliers are finding work from before an Airbnb listing is posted to after guests leave. This includes listing photographers, key-exchange coordinators, in-home chefs, house cleaners, and taxi-replacing ride-sharing services.[66]

Trust is essential for the sharing economy to work, especially on a service based on the intimacy of inviting strangers into your home. As a result, no one is anonymous on Airbnb. Guest identity is verified via a two-step process. The site is integrated with Facebook, and users can also share their LinkedIn profiles. Airbnb examines the length an online profile has been up and makes sure it matches additional information provided by the user, such as a driver's license and passport. IDs are only used to verify identity and the site stores this data securely. Verified identities should also discourage bad apples who are booted out of the system from trying to reapply with new accounts.[67] Transacting parties are otherwise on their own to work out the exchange of keys and other access information, but communication has to happen through Airbnb. Airbnb also arranged for high-quality photography of many early listings (in some cases the founders showed up to photograph sites themselves, using the opportunity to further interview property listers for feedback on their service). Chesky has even lived out of Airbnb rentals full time to gather more field intelligence.[68] Collective insight helped hone the firm's product-market fit in a way that delighted both renters and customers and gave the firm an early edge, and sometimes that's all you need to get the dynamo of two-sided network effects churning in your favor. As *Inc.* magazine reports, "improvements and refinements helped Airbnb do something previous sharing companies hadn't managed—to acquire an aura of style, respectability, safety, and trustworthiness."[69]

Negative incidents have occurred, and they've gotten the firm lots of unwanted press. In the days before verified identify, one San Francisco-based Airbnb host had her home ransacked by "guests" who stole her jewelry, consumer electronics, passport, and credit cards. Police eventually nabbed the perp.[70] In another incident, New York-based comedian Ari Teman reports renting his home to someone who self-described themselves as arranging wedding accommodations for a brother and sister-in-law, only to return to furniture damage and the discovery that his house had been used for a ticket-selling sex party that had attracted some fifty creepy strangers to his place.[71] An incident like this is never good news, but when it happens to a big-city comedian, it goes viral and becomes a top trending story on social media. In the unlikely event of an incident, the firm offers a $1 million guarantee for hosts, secure payment guarantees, and 24/7 support phone service backed up by a staff of six hundred in the firm's customer service and trust and safety departments. Despite headline-grabbing anomalies, the firm reports that of the 6 million guests who stayed with the firm in 2013, only 700 host claims were made—an incident rate of less than .012 percent.[72]

Airbnb is able to monitor transactions and communication at a fairly deep level. Reservations, payment, communication between host and guest, and subsequent reviewers are all handled through the firm's technology platform. In addition to helping with verification and transaction auditing, the firm also monitors to see if hosts are trying to arrange a stay and payment outside of the system (scanning communication for the names of alternate electronic payment methods like "Western Union"). The firm's technology also hunts for signals of fake positive reviews, money laundering, and other scams, and when suspicious activity is flagged, human monitors can take a closer look and follow up, as needed.

It's worth noting that in many areas where Airbnb operates, providers of the service are breaking the law. Many municipalities prohibit people from running a business, hostel, or hotel in a residential area or property not zoned for business. Health and safety laws governing hotels usually require things like sprinkler systems, exit signs, and clean towels. And of course, many Airbnb rentals exchange services outside conventional lodging taxes that hotel guests pay.[73] Malibu, New Orleans, and San Francisco are among the cities that have investigated Airbnb for violations. Barcelona has fined the firm. The New York State Attorney General claims Airbnb's unpaid tax bill tops $33 billion. New York City has sued owners of the site's highest volume listers, going after them for running illegal hotels out of apartment buildings they owned.[74]

Despite operating outside the law, it looks like many cities are looking to rewrite legislation for efforts that, ultimately, offer many benefits including added income for local property owners, additional capacity during major events and the high travel season, a bulwark against hotel price gouging, and a mechanism to widen travel and ultimately bring in the economic benefit of more tourist dollars. Portland, Oregon, and San Francisco (home town of Airbnb) are among the cities that have already legalized sharing economy property listings in exchange for tax revenue and other concessions.[75]

Competition looms and includes the publicly traded HomeAway as well as a host of international copycats. But a two-sided network effect keeps property listers and guests coming back to an experienced, trusted source likely to offer more choice than competitors.

KEY TAKEAWAYS

- Airbnb empowers citizen hoteliers who make rooms, properties, or other accommodations available online.
- The firm has arranged over 20 million guest stays in some 34,000 cities and 192 countries. Many accommodations are truly unique, offering consumers a long-tail of lodging options.
- The firm verifies the identify of both parties, monitors all communications between property listers and guests, provides twenty-four-hour support, and additional insurance coverage, all in an effort to reduce transaction friction stemming from a lack of trust.

QUESTIONS AND EXERCISES

1. How do Airbnb's total number of accommodations compare to the room count for Hilton?
2. How does Airbnb ensure safety and encourage trust among transacting parties? What role does technology play in trust assurance?
3. How does the firm limit the likelihood that it will be ripped off by unscrupulous operators?
4. What sort of legal trouble has Airbnb run into? Put yourself in the shoes of city lawmakers. List the pros and cons of allowing Airbnb or other property sharing services to operate in your city. Would you allow these services? Why or why not? If you would approve the service, would you extract concessions or write laws that force some changes that impact how Airbnb and its partners do business?
5. Visit Airbnb and browse properties at a vacation destination you'd like to visit, and listings in the area where you live. Would you rent a stay through Airbnb? Why or why not? Would you make your own property available? Why or why not?
6. How might Airbnb be considered a platform? Diagram the ecosystem that would surround an Airbnb transaction and identify various sharing economy firms that could provide services to help property listers or their guests. Could Airbnb create additional businesses by facilitating these transactions? Do some additional research—does Airbnb partner with any specific sharing economy firms?

5.   UBER: SHARING ECONOMY SUCCESS FROM TECH-FUELED SUPERIOR SERVICE

LEARNING OBJECTIVES

1. **Understand the appeal of Uber both to drivers and consumers.**
2. **Discuss how Uber leverages technology to radically improve on the service and cost structure of traditional cab and limo services.**
3. **Recognize how technology also empowers a data-driven enterprise that crafts strong and deepening competitive advantage over time.**

Just four years after Travis Kalanick cofounded Uber, the San Francisco-based car service was operating in 128 cities in 37 countries worldwide. How's that for the productivity achieved in what is basically the time it takes to earn an undergraduate degree! By mid 2015 the numbers were up to 58 countries and over 300 cities.[76] The firm has already offered a high-end "black car" service, the low-end taxi-competing UberX and an SUV service (UberXL) and has experimented with all sorts of promotions. At times over the past few years you could order a helicopter ride via the Uber app, call over a boat, arrange for Christmas tree delivery, cool off your home with an air conditioner delivery, order an ice cream truck, or summon forth a car full of puppies for a cuddle fix. 2015 revenues are expected to come in at around $2 billion, with Uber keeping about 20 percent of each transaction.[77] The firm's stable of big-believing investors, includes Google, which has incorporated Uber into Google Maps. Uber's $1.2 billion Spring 2014 fundraising round was the biggest single amount raised by any privately held tech start-up, ever. Investors valued the firm at a bit more than $18 billion.[78] Six months later another fundraising round valued the firm at $41 billion,[79] and a new round at a reported $50 billion valuation could make Uber the tech industry's most valuable startup.[80]

Uber also wants you to know it's a job creator. CEO Kalanick claims the firm's growth is minting over 50,000 new jobs a month (nearly all are drivers, who are considered independent contractors and not Uber employees).[81] The bar for drivers is high—each undergoes a rigorous county, federal, and multistate background check that looks back the maximum length of time allowed by law.[82] And while cars are supplied by drivers, only certain late-model cars are allowed in Uber's fleet,[83] and only then after a company inspection (no smoke-billowing clunkers here).[84] Those who make the cut can do much better than their conventional taxi industry counterparts. The median annual salary for a San Francisco-based UberX driver working at least forty hours a week was reported to be $74,191; in New York City the figure was $90,766. The average Big Apple cabbie makes just $30,000 a year.[85] Some have questioned whether average driver earnings are really that high, but with taxi drivers paying $70 to $140 a day in fees even if they earn no fares,[86] estimates consistently show that Uber drivers make more.[87] Further, job satisfaction among Uber drivers hovers around 80 percent. Nearly half of Uber drivers have a college degree (about two times that of the overall work force),[88] with most drivers reporting that they use Uber income to supplement earnings, not as their primary salary.[89] Uber claims it's also improving the environment, reducing DUI rates and making cities more appealing by reducing parking and road congestion.[90]

Uber isn't just taking away the current taxi market; it's expanding the overall market for metered consumer transportation. Many people who would not otherwise take a cab are now out on the town in an Uber. This is an effort that grows the economic pie. An Uber-commissioned study claims the firm's impact on the US economy tops $2.8 billion a year.[91]

While Uber services are often comparable to conventional cab rates, the real draw is trust and convenience. Instead of standing in potentially bad weather, competing with curb-straddling rivals trying to hail a cab for an indeterminate length of time, or phoning a surly human dispatcher who may or may not answer the phone after putting you on hold, Uber customers simply summon their ride with the tap of a smartphone app. A map shows the cab's approach and an alert tells you when your driver has arrived, so you can stay sheltered until it's time to leave. Riders can also set their pickup and drop off destination to get a fare quote for their trip, eliminating the fear many travelers have that an unscrupulous cabbie will overcharge them on an unnecessarily scenic route to their destination. Out of cash, fearful your driver can't make change, or worried that the credit card machine or fare meter in the cab might not work? No problem with Uber. All payment is handled through the app. The app even allows fare-splitting among passengers that share a ride. Says one Uber driver "No one ever gets in my car and says, 'Gee, I wish I were taking a cab.'"[92] Drivers use their own app to screen and accept fares. Drivers and riders rate each other, keeping both sides of the two-sided market satisfied. City drivers prefer Uber's phone-delivered dispatches to the taxi alternative of having to hunt for fares by driving around, scanning sidewalks.[93] Chapter 2 "Strategy and Technology: Concepts and Frameworks for Understanding What Separates Winners from Losers" discussed that brand is built through customer experience. From a service perspective Uber beats conventional cabs on almost all metrics (with big advantages offered to both drivers and passengers). Alternatives simply cannot compete.

Uber runs a lean cost of doing business by eliminating human dispatchers, eliminating the capital cost of a fleet (cars are owned by drivers, not Uber), and working around the expensive "medallion" system that grants cab rights in major cities worldwide. In addition to the firm's own screening techniques, customer feedback also reduces the cost associated with auditing driver quality and provides a continual evaluation of performance. Drivers who fall below 4.7 stars on a five point scale risk being fired.[94]

Customers do regularly complain of one downside—surge pricing. Uber pricing operates on a supply and demand scale. If there's a big event in town or some other condition where driver supply doesn't meet demand, Uber will raise prices using a "surge pricing" multiple. One particularly bad New York City snowstorm caused the surge pricing multiple to shoot as high as 8.25 times the normal rate. You'll see this before summoning your car, so riders shouldn't be surprised by a big bill. The firm states the goal isn't to gouge the consumer, rather it's to send a signal to potential drivers to hop in their cars, satisfy pent up demand, and make a quick buck.[95] Price setting occurs where supply and demand meet, so more drivers should lower prices. If you leave the stadium after the game gets out, don't expect a standard Uber fare, but if you can grab a drink and wait a few minutes, you'll likely see prices fall closer to normal over time. Dynamic pricing helps Uber's first customer commitment—to offer a reliable service (i.e., make sure you've got a ride). Competitive pricing is important, but first up is making sure there are enough rides for those willing to pay for the service. Without surge pricing, the real alternative is no service. Uber has since agreed to cap surging during emergencies at a price that is below the three highest-priced non-emergency days during the preceding two months. During record snowfall in the northeast, this resulted in major city price caps just below three times the normal rate, but it remains to be seen if this will be enough to put drivers on the road when they are most needed. Uber has also stated that during a disaster or state of emergency, the firm will donate all of its proceeds earned in the area during that period to the American Red Cross.[96]

Tragedy, Bad press, and Bad Behavior, but Tech raises the Safety Bar

No system can keep out all negative incidents in a worldwide firm this big, and a company that grows so quickly with such public fascination will likely see an amplification of any bad press. While a criminal cabbie or taxi-caused pedestrian fatality would likely not gain worldwide media attention, all eyes are on Uber and any negative incident seems to make headlines. And there have been horrendous incidents: accusations of price gouging during an Australian hostage standoff, a rape in India, a kidnapping and sexual assault in Boston, a driver hitting and killing a child in San Francisco.[97] All horrific, and certainly not incidents to be shunted aside as a cost of doing business. But amidst tragedy, a closer look shows that technology actually helps Uber keep a high safety bar, and to continue to raise that bar even higher. Committing a crime and taking risks as an Uber driver is incredibly stupid. The app knows who you are at all times, knows who you've picked up and where you took them, and these digital eyes are always on you, with bad performance exposed and customers (and drivers) empowered to shine a spotlight on what might have been previously hidden. Collectively, this offers a safety bar conventional cabs simply don't offer. Uber continues to invest in new technologies, exploring voice recognition and biometrics to further strengthen driver verification,[98] and implementing a panic button (rolled out first in India) that sends data directly to police.[99]

Unfortunately for Uber, apps can't stop management gaffes. The firm's executives have suffered bad press from a series of incidents that have included promoting Uber in France with scantily-clad female drivers,[100] and an executive who appeared to threaten journalists who criticized the firm.[101] Let this be a lesson to high-growth execs who get a bit too cocky–you're under the microscope! Double-audit your behavior and don't let success cascade into a brash, repugnant behavior. The firm has since hired high-ranking communication execs from the White House to Google to help Uber craft a more positive image,[102] and it has continued to grow its corporate social responsibility efforts.[103] CEO Kalanick seems to understand the firm's missteps, vowing to "make the firm a smarter and more humble company."[104]

5.1   Driven by Data

While participants in the sharing economy drive Uber cars, data drives Uber's growth and success. To pull off the firm's goal of getting you a ride within minutes of an app tap, Uber employs a team of mentally muscular mathematicians who have earned PhDs in data-crunching fields that include nuclear physics, astrophysics, and computational biology (true to cliché, some members of the data team have had prior careers and training as actual rocket scientists).[105] The staff constantly optimizes algorithms powering a whole host of activities: determining how many drivers the firm needs, identifying when and how to alert drivers of projected demand, pointing a subset of drivers to locations to best meet demand, setting dynamic pricing, and more.

Kalanick calls it "really fun, sexy math."[106] The firm supplements its own rich and growing trove of data with traffic influencing feeds such as weather-forecasts, and staff in each city closely track special events that could impact expectations (conventions, parades, large university commencements, a packed stadium for the home team). The latter, human element is vital, since even the best math and richest data set can't predict with perfect accuracy.

A visitor to an Uber office may get a glimpse of the "God View," a software system showing tiny car icons crawling around a map of the city, and little cartoon eyeballs scattered about, representing every location where a customer is looking at the Uber app.[107] Uber also produces "heat maps" of demand, using mathematical precision to coax additional demand from its driver pool. Information is offered in targeted release; you don't want to give this to every driver at once, or you'll create an imbalance as too many cars rush to cash in on surge pricing, leaving the rest of the city underserved. Data even helps the firm expand into new cities. Each time a user opens an app, even if it's in a location Uber hasn't operated in before, data is collected showing user interest. According to the firm, "we take this into account when we're working out which cities to dominate next." And the firm is prepared when they arrive, stating "we can build a prediction of where our cars need to be before we even get there."[108]

FIGURE 10.5

Uber's so-called "God View" shows every Uber car operating in a city, and every user looking at the Uber app.

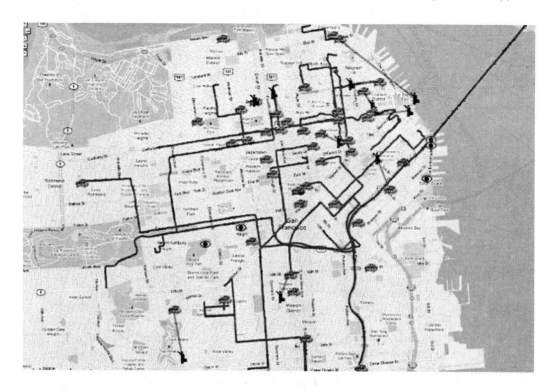

Source: Uber Blog, http://blog.uber.com/2011/05/16/uberdata-mapping-san-francisco-new-york-and-the-world/

Uber's massive data haul allows it to cut prices and attract drivers to power continued growth and expansion. Some markets have seen as many as six Uber price cuts in two years. One effort made simultaneous price cuts in 48 cities, while also offering income guarantees for drivers (they need to keep both sides of the two-sided network happy). Uber can make these kinds of bold moves because its massive database reliably reveals supply and demand curves at different price points, demonstrating price elasticity and pointing strongly to how markets behave as pricing changes. Uber upped the ante even more when it introduced Uber Pool, a car pooling service that gives you a cheaper ride if you share the car with someone else who's also headed in the same direction. Cheaper fares mean users will ride more, and even at lower prices, drivers will come out ahead if demand keeps them busy and constantly earning.[109]

5.2   APIs to Expand Reach

One way of making Uber appear as if it's everywhere in the physical world is embedding Uber everywhere in the digital world. Uber offers an API (application programming interface) that is essentially a published guideline on how other developers can embed Uber into their own apps. The service launched with eleven partners, including OpenTable, United Airlines, TripAdvisor, and Hyatt Hotels. Made a dinner reservation? Summon an Uber. Flight arrived? Skip the airport cab line and take one of Travis' drivers with a United app tap. Other ridesharing services can do this, too, but if you're a firm looking for a partner, you're going to choose the top firm rather than clog your app with every available choice. Once again, network effects help solidify a firm as a winning platform. And as we've pointed out earlier, data and the algorithms that refine their accuracy are improved over time, so as an early player, Uber simply has more smarts than anyone else operating in this space. Strategists, be aware that the firm that uses tech to build assets for competitive advantage early may also see these assets significantly strengthened over time.

5.3   How Big Can This Thing Get?

Analysts differ on whether Uber is worth its current valuation. That's not uncommon. Facebook, Google, and other tech giants have had their fair share of pundits and analysts who cried "bubble." But Uber's dominance is by no means a given. Regulatory concerns, the maintenance of a quality service, and the uncertainty of expanding in global markets where competitors exist are all challenges the firm will face. The firm's bubble-crying doubters include the data experts at the well-known Five Thirty Eight blog (known for their poll-besting accuracy in US presidential election predictions).[110] The Uber true believers includes *Business Insider*, which claims Uber is on its way to being "the next $100 billion company."[111]

Uber's mission statement is "Transportation as reliable as running water, everywhere for everyone."[112] The firm is doubling in size every six months with its current offerings, but Kalanick and Company are looking to a future with expansion way beyond taxi rides. Uber's CEO has stated that he sees the firm as essentially a "software platform for shipping and logistics."[113] Uber investor Shervin Pishevar describes the firm's potential, saying: "Uber is creating a digital mesh—a power grid which goes within the metropolitan areas. After you have that power grid running, in everyone's pockets, there's lots of possibility of what you could build like a platform. Uber is incorporated in the empire-building phase."[114]

The firm has experimented with several offerings, including a bike messenger service, a restaurant delivery service, and a same-day retail delivery service.[115] In addition to Google's big investment in Uber, another backer is someone else who knows a lot about serving customer demand by getting things from one location to the other, Amazon founder and CEO Jeff Bezos. Kalanick cites Bezos as "an entrepreneurial inspiration."[116] The Google investment has become more interesting, as several Uber moves seem as if they may point to areas where the firms might compete. Uber is expanding same-day delivery even as Google does the same through Google Express. While Uber is incorporated into Google maps, Uber also bought the mapping firm deCarta, a company once used by Google, and which has sold services to major industry players including BlackBerry, Verizon, OnStar, EBay, and Samsung.[117] And while Google famously has a self-driving car initiative that has seen several generations of test vehicles put thousands of miles on the road, Uber has begun to test its own self-driving car technology developed at Uber's Advanced Technology Center in Pittsburgh, partnering heavily with advanced robotics experts from Carnegie Mellon University.[118] While no one would call Google and Uber direct rivals today, it is an interesting development given the history of Google's former close partnership with Apple, and its unraveling. Android caused then Google CEO Eric Schmidt to leave Apple's board, Siri favored Bing, Apple created its own Maps and dropped YouTube from the pre-installed iPhone apps.

Kalanick is already on his third start-up, so he's been around the block a few times. His first firm, Scour, started when he was just twenty-one, was a Napster-like bust after media firms threatened to sue the firm out of existence. His second firm, Red Swoosh, served digital media over the Internet and was eventually acquired for $19 million by the Cambridge, Massachusetts-based content serving giant, Akamai. Uber's cofounders include Garrett Camp, who created StumbleUpon, a firm that eBay bought for $75 million.[119]

As for fighting regulation, San Francisco provides just one example of the Uber leader's iron-willed determination. When the city's transportation agency sent the firm, then known as UberCab, a cease-and-desist letter, stating it was running an unlicensed taxi service, the firm dropped "Cab" from its name, but vehemently argued that it was simply a software firm that connected drivers and riders.[120] Uber continued offering rides to a largely tech-centric following, a constituency San Francisco pols don't want to alienate if they want to remain in elected office. The California Public Utilities Commission eventually voted to create a permanent category of "Transportation Network Companies," encompassing Uber, as well as rivals such as Lyft and SideCar.[121] When you have such loyal customers and strong product-market fit, you can enlist an army to help you to bend legislators to make way for progress. Uber fans have firehosed Washington, DC officials with more than 50,000 emails in support of allowing the service to operate in the nation's capital. In Denver, an Uber rally attracted hundreds of supporters.

In markets as varied as Chicago, Mexico City, Paris, and Delhi, cabbies have protested, and many governments have been antagonistic toward the firm.[122] While Uber has flouted regulation, effectively operating illegally in many markets, it has also worked with local officials to be legitimate and has a stated goal of becoming explicitly legal everywhere it operates.[123] Uber has improved in areas of concern such as making sure that wheel-chair accessible vehicles are available (a standard taxi firms are held to). The firm went legit in New York City by complying with restrictions imposed by the local Taxi and Limousine Commission, even as it tries to change local rules.[124] And on top of claims that Uber boosts the economy and quality of life, the firm can also offer big data insights to cozy up as a government ally. An Uber partnership with the City of Boston provides data analysis to better understand commuting patterns and inform decisions on road construction and street maintenance. Pothole get fixed? Maybe you've got Uber to thank.[125]

Uber's global expansion leverages corporate-provided technology, learning, and data insights, but teams in new markets act as ground-floor entrepreneurs. Kalanick says the firm's growth teams are "parachuting in with machetes," doing what needs to be done to attract drivers, raise customer awareness kickstart usage, work with local legislators, and otherwise build the supply and demand side of the market from scratch.[126] Uber is growing, but the world's two most populous markets will present challenges. In China, local competition already has an estimated 90 percent of the market. To compete, Uber has been paying Chinese drivers more in bonuses than they collect in fares, trying to subsidize their way to a strong network effect. In China, Uber also faces a nation with strict regulation often considered among the hardest for US tech firms to crack (Google left, eBay was crushed, and Facebook still hasn't been allowed in).[127] In India, Uber's second-biggest market in terms of cities served, the firm faced an outright ban in Delhi. Said the firm's Head of Expansion in India, "We have no intention of stepping away."[128] Indian growth during this period had been climbing at a rate of about 40 percent a month, with huge additional promise in a nation with low car ownership and a rising middle class. Expansion continues with customized local products, including one targeted at three-wheeled auto-rickshaws popular throughout South Asia. While resisting shut-down, Uber has simultaneously applied for an official radio-dispatched-taxi license and has been in repeated talks with authorities drafting national legislation for ride summoning services.[129] Gaining brand, scale, and network effects are easy when you show up first. But arrive late and local rivals may have built advantages leaders enjoy elsewhere. A big chunk of all that cash Uber has raised is specifically targeted at global expansion. Just in China, Uber plans to invest over $1 billion a year to try to establish itself as a major player in the world's most populous nation.[130]

Kalanick speaks about Uber's rivals with the maniacal passion of the most successful entrepreneurs, stating "If you've got something to compete, bring it—I'm not sleeping. If you're sleeping, I'm gonna kick your ass."

Uber co-founder and CEO Travis Kalanick discusses the firm, its advantages in enabling city transformation, and its goals for future expansion.

View the video online at: http://www.youtube.com/embed/iayagHygV0Q?rel=0

(Under)estimating the Market for Disruption

Figuring out how big Uber will be, and how much it's worth, is a challenge. Many have suggested Uber is way overvalued because investors think it's worth more than the entire taxi industry.[131] Uber may indeed be overvalued—time will tell—but comparing Uber to the historical taxi industry misses key points about how a novel and disruptive new player grows the market with increased demand. A cheaper service with faster car arrival times (five minutes or less) and assured payment, trust and convenience are causing expansion into markets underserved by conventional taxis, and are prompting users to ride with Uber far more than they did with taxis or limos. Uber investor Bill Gurley points to several examples prompting increased usage: Uber replacing Mom's mini-van to shuttle kids to practices and events, Uber helping adult children transition elderly parents to give up driving but not give up on being able to get about town, Uber becoming the smart choice for a couple that wants to enjoy a bottle of wine with dinner, and Uber creating a genuine alternative to car-ownership in cities and suburbs.[132]

A blog post by Professor Angel Lozano of UPF in Barcelona provides a powerful historical example of failing to see a bigger market when none existed previously: "In 1980, McKinsey & Company was commissioned by AT&T (whose Bell Labs had invented cellular telephony) to forecast cell phone penetration in the United States by 2000. The consultant's prediction of 900,000 subscribers was less than 1 percent of the actual figure: 109

million. Based on this legendary mistake, AT&T decided there was not much future to these toys. A decade later, to rejoin the cellular market, AT&T had to acquire McCaw Cellular for $12.6 billion. By 2011, the number of subscribers worldwide had surpassed 5 billion and cellular communication had become an unprecedented technological revolution."[133]

Is the firm on a luxury lift to a $100 billion future, or is it an overvalued expectations wreck-in-waiting about to hit the wall of reality? Leverage what you've learned about network effects and the sharing economy to make your own predictions. Buckle up—it's sure to be a wild ride!

KEY TAKEAWAYS

- Uber's $1.2 billion investment round was the largest single investment ever in a private technology firm. This investment valued the firm at over $18 billion. Investors include Google, which has incorporated Uber's service into Google Maps. Later estimates have the firm valued at $50 billion.
- Uber's advantages over traditional taxi services include scheduling, service speed, reliability, increased trust, ease of payment, and car availability.
- The firm's disruptive model is creating growth that is outpacing the size of the taxi industry. Despite bad press, Uber's technology should offer far more safety and security than the conventional taxi industry, and the company continues to invest in furthering safety intiatives.
- Surge pricing is controversial, but surge prices are clearly communicated before users commit to a ride. Surge pricing is used by Uber to help maintain supply/demand equilibrium. It is hoped that higher surge prices attract more drivers to the Uber system, and that prices will eventually flatten out.
- Uber leverages data to power the firm's operational model, alert drivers, improve service, set pricing, and even identify possible cities to enter.
- APIs have allowed Uber to become a platform, expanding its reach through partnerships that make Uber available in other apps.
- Expansion to large markets such as China and India are complicated by regulations and by early-moving local rivals. Showing up late allows competitors to create assets such as brand, scale, and network effects that are difficult to overcome. Uber is spending big to establish a competitive position in these markets.
- Analysts differ on Uber's valuation, but some speculate the firm may be laying the groundwork for expansion into a variety of logistics businesses.

QUESTIONS AND EXERCISES

1. What do you think Google sees in Uber? Do you think the firm should have invested in Uber? Why or why not?
2. Is Uber good for the economy or bad? Justify your answer.
3. How might Uber impact cities? Impact car ownership? Should municipalities embrace Uber? Ban it? Regulate it? Have local authorities acted on ride-sharing services like Uber? Do you think their action was appropriate? Develop recommendations for your region and present it to class.
4. Lyft has tried to compete with Uber by undercutting the firm's surge pricing. Will this tactic work? Why or why not?
5. How does Uber ensure rider and passenger quality? As a rider or passenger, how would do you feel about these efforts? How does this change the service dynamic compared with traditional cab rides?
6. How does Uber cut costs compared with traditional taxi and limo fleet operators?
7. How does Uber leverage data in its service? What aspects of the firm's operations are improved through data analytics? Does this provide the firm with sustainable competitive advantage? Why or why not?
8. What is UberPool? What will need to happen for this to be a "win" for both customers and drivers? Why does Uber management think it can pull this off?
9. Uber has been described as creating a "mesh" that may serve as a utility for urban areas. If Uber is able to grow to scale, what other kinds of businesses might Uber expand into? What firms would be threatened by this, and which firms might consider Uber to be a good partner?
10. Why do some think Uber deserves a valuation in excess of the entire taxi and limo market? Do you feel this is justified? Why or why not?
11. Why has Uber received bad press? Is the coverage fair? What could the firm have done to present some of this coverage? Is the firm doing enough? Why or why not?

ENDNOTES

1. J. Tanz, "How Airbnb and Lyft Finally Got Americans to Trust Each Other," *Wired*, April 23, 2014.

2. R. Botsman, What's Mine is Yours: The Rise of Collaborative Consumption, *HarperBusiness*, 2010.

3. T. Friedman, "Welcome to the Sharing Economy," *New York Times*, July 20, 2013.

4. J. Reinhart, "Why the Success of 'Sharing Economy' Startups Hinges on Who Owns the Inventory," *Business Insider*, February 6, 2014.

5. R. Botsman, "The Sharing Economy Lacks a Shared Definition," *Fast Company*, November 21, 2013; A. Hagiu and J. Wright, "Marketplace or Resller?" *Harvard Business School Working Paper*, No. 13–092, May 2013 (Revised July 2013, January 2014).

6. J. Schor, "Debating the Sharing Economy," The Great Transition Initiative, Oct. 2014.

7. D. Schutzer, "Sharing Economy," FS Roundtable, Oct. 2014.D. Schutzer, "Sharing Economy," FS Roundtable, Oct. 2014.

8. Unattributed, "Five Years And 311 Cities Later," *Uber.com*, June 1, 2015.

9. T. Friedman, "Welcome to the Sharing Economy," *New York Times*, July 20, 2013.

10. N. Athwal, "LendingClub And Billion-Dollar Valuations Are Just The Beginning For Online Lending," *Forbes*, Dec. 18, 2014.

11. M. DeCambre, "Uber Just Had the Biggest Funding Round of All Time," *Quartz*, June 7, 2014.

12. A. Sorkin, "Why Uber Might Well Be Worth $18 Billion," June 9, 2014.

13. J. Owyang, A. Samuel, and A. Greenville, *Sharing Is the New Buying*, Report by Vision Critical and Crowd Companies, March 2, 2014.

14. J. Justin, "The Fall of Lyft and the Pink Mustaches in Boston," *Harvard Business School Digital Innovation and Transformation*, March 6, 2014.

15. L. Gomes, "Travis Kalanick: Uber Is Raising More Money to Fight Lyft and the 'Asshole' Taxi Industry," *Re/code*, May 28, 2014.

16. T. Friedman, "Welcome to the Sharing Economy," *New York Times*, July 20, 2013.

17. R. Grant, "Fashion Fairy Godmother Rent the Runway Raises $20M for Cinderella Moments," *Venture Beat*, November 30, 2012.

18. B. Moore, "Rent the Runway heads to Vegas' Cosmopolitan," *Los Angeles Times*, December 17, 2013.

19. J. Reinhart, "Why the Success of 'Sharing Economy' Startups Hinges on Who Owns the Inventory," *Business Insider*, February 6, 2014.

20. A. Sorkin, "Why Uber Might Well Be Worth $18 Billion," June 9, 2014.

21. C. Reidy, "Drizly, with its 'liqour store on a smartphone' app, rasies an additional $2.5m," *Boston Globe*, May 21, 2014.

22. J. Owyang, A. Samuel, and A. Greenville, *Sharing Is the New Buying*, Report by Vision Critical and Crowd Companies, March 2, 2014.

23. M. Sinanian, "On heels of new funding and global expansion, car service Uber launches in D.C. today," *Venture Beat*, December 15, 2011.

24. J. Owyang, A. Samuel, and A. Greenville, *Sharing Is the New Buying*, Report by Vision Critical and Crowd Companies, March 2, 2014.

25. K. Hill, "Lyft's Moment of Truth As Passenger Breaks Seattle Driver's Nose," *Forbes*, May 21, 2014.

26. J. Tanz, "How Airbnb and Lyft Finally Got Americans to Trust Each Other," *Wired*, April 23, 2014.

27. W. Alden, "The Business Tycoons of Airbnb," *The New York Times*, Nov. 25, 2014.

28. A. Sifferlin, "Harvard Study Suggests Racial Bias Among Some Airbnb Renters," Airbnb, *Time*, Jan. 27, 2014.

29. G. Harman, "The sharing economy is not as open as you might think," *The Guardian*, Nov. 12, 2014.

30. G. Harman, "The sharing economy is not as open as you might think," *The Guardian*, Nov. 12, 2014.

31. R. Swan, "Uber, Lyft, and Their Ilk Facing New State Insurance Regulations," *SF Weekly*, June 11, 2014.

32. M. Grynbaum, "2 Taxi Medallions Sell for $1 Million Each," *New York Times*, October 20, 2011.

33. L. Fleischer, "Thousands of European Cab Drivers Protest Uber, Taxi Apps," *Wall Street Journal*, June 11, 2014.

34. J. Kaminsky, "Seattle Council Votes to Limit Rideshare Firms UberX, Lyft, Sidecar," *Reuters*, March 18, 2014.

35. E. Green, "2 supervisors want to tighten 'Airbnb law' on short-term rentals," *SF Gate*, March 23, 2015.

36. P. Renton, "A Look Back at the Lending Club and Prosper Quiet Periods," *LendAcademy*, Dec. 19, 2011.

37. H. Somerville, "Prosper Marketplace, 2nd-largest online lender, raises $165 million," *SiliconBeat*, April 10, 2014.

38. N. Buhayar, "Peer-to-Peer Lending," *Bloomberg Review*, June 2, 2015.

39. E. Sherman, "Uber, TaskRabbit And Sharing Economy Giveth To Workers, But Also Taketh Away," *Forbes*, Aug. 4, 2015.

40. C. DeAmicis, "Homejoy Shuts Down After Battling Worker Classification Lawsuits," *Re/code*, July 17, 2015.

41. C. Zillman, "As Uber faces regulatory heat, yet another startup turns its contract workers into employees," *Fortune*, July 1, 2015.

42. Unattributed opinion piece, "Shackling the Sharing Economy," *The Wall Street Journal*, Aug. 2, 2015

43. M. Farrell, "Uber Gets Some Support from New Mayor," *Boston Globe*, March 01, 2014.

44. L. Gannes, "Uber Valued at $17 Billion in New "Record-Breaking" Round," *Re/code*, June 6, 2014.

45. M. Casey and P. Vigna, "BitBeat: Coinbase Promotes Bitcoin Discounts; Ripple Hits LatAm," *Wall Street Journal*, June 12, 2014.

46. J. Kincaid, "WePay Drops 600 Pounds of Ice in Front of PayPal Conference, Hilarity Ensues," *TechCrunch*, October 26, 2010.

47. C. Desmarais, "How Big Data Can Help Squash $35 Billion in Online Fraud," *Inc.*, April 29, 2014.

48. L. Rao, "Payments company WePay raises $40 million to go global," *Fortune*, May 201, 2015.

49. T. Geodfrey, "WePay's Triple Digit Growth Attracts Leading Investors," *PaymentWeek*, May 20, 2015.

50. A. Wilhelm and A. Tsotsis, "Google Ventures Puts $258M into Uber, Its Largest Deal Ever," *TechCrunch*, August 22, 2013.

51. V. Kansara, "Rent the Runway Raises $2.4 Million," *The Business of Fashion*, March 11, 2013.

52. T. Wasserman, "Walgreens Taps TaskRabbit to Deliver Cold Medicine to Shut-Ins," *Mashable*, January 6, 2014.

53. J. Del Ray, "With Amazon in Sight, IBM Will Offer Retail Clients Same-Day Delivery Tool," *Re/code*, June 10, 2014.

54. J. Owyang, A. Samuel, and A. Greenville, *Sharing Is the New Buying*, Report by Vision Critical and Crowd Companies, March 2, 2014.

55. L. Ram, "The End of Driving (As We Know It)," *Fortune*, June 12, 2014.

56. G. Bensinger, "Amazon Wants to Be Your Home Services Middleman," *The Wall Street Journal*, March 20, 2015.

57. T. Friedman, "Welcome to the Sharing Economy," *New York Times*, July 20, 2013.

58. A. Konrad and R. Mac, "Airbnb Cofounders to Become First Sharing Economy Billionaires As Company Nears $10 Billion Valuation," *Forbes*, March 20, 2014.

59. T. Friedman, "Welcome to the Sharing Economy," *New York Times*, July 20, 2013.

60. B. Helm, "Airbnb Is Inc.'s 2014 Company of the Year," *Inc.*, Dec. 2014/Jan. 2015.

61. K. Wagner, "Airbnb Is Approaching One Million Guests Per Night," *Re/code*, May 27, 2015.

62. M. Meeker, Internet Trends 2014, *KPCB*, May 28, 2014.

63. T. Friedman, "Welcome to the Sharing Economy," *New York Times*, July 20, 2013.

64. T. Friedman, "Welcome to the Sharing Economy," *New York Times*, July 20, 2013.

65. N. Kleinfeld, "Airbnb Host Welcomes Travelers From All Over," *New York Times*, April 15, 2014.

66. T. Friedman, "Welcome to the Sharing Economy," *New York Times*, July 20, 2013.

67. T. Geron, "Airbnb Adds Identity Verification to End Anonymity In Sharing Economy," *Forbes*, April 30, 2013

68. J. Bort, "Brian Chesky Talks About His Biggest Mistake With Airbnb," *BusinessInsider*, July 18, 2012.

69. B. Helm, "Airbnb Is Inc.'s 2014 Company of the Year," *Inc.*, Dec. 2014/Jan. 2015.

70. E. Mills, "SF Police Arrest Suspect in Trashing of Airbnb Rental," *CNET*, July 29, 2011.

71. J. Abbruzzese, "A New York Airbnb Trip Turns into 'XXX Freak Fest'," *Mashable*, March 17, 2014.

72. J. Tanz, "How Airbnb and Lyft Finally Got Americans to Trust Each Other," *Wired*, April 23, 2014.

73. B. Helm, "Airbnb Is Inc.'s 2014 Company of the Year," *Inc.*, Dec. 2014/Jan. 2015.

74. M. Masnick, "NYC Says Renting Out Your Place Via Airbnb Is Running An Illegal Hotel," *TechDirt*, May 21, 2013.

75. B. Helm, "Airbnb Is Inc.'s 2014 Company of the Year," *Inc.*, Dec. 2014/Jan. 2015.

76. D. Kerr, "Uber celebrates its fifth birthday with tears," *CNet*, June 3, 2015.

77. D. MacMillan and T. Demos, "Uber Eyes $50 Billion Valuation in New Funding," *The Wall Street Journal*, May 9, 2015.

78. M. DeCambre, "Uber Just Had the Biggest Funding Round of All Time," *Quartz*, June 7, 2014.

79. D. MacMillan and T. Demos, "Uber Eyes $50 Billion Valuation in New Funding," *The Wall Street Journal*, May 9, 2015.

80. K. Anderson, "Uber IPO Update: What a $50 Billion Valuation Means for Uber," *Money Morning*, May 12, 2015.

81. E. Cushing, "The Smartest Bro in the Room," *San Francisco Magazine*, Nov. 21, 2014.

82. Lane (only single name offered), "Uber Background Checks," *Uber Blog*, April 24, 2014.

83. M. Wohlsen, "What Uber Will Do with All That Money from Google," *Wired*, January 3, 2014.

84. E. Kirchner, D. Paredes, and S. Pham, "Is Uber Keeping Riders Safe?" *NBC Bay Area*, April 25, 2014.

85. M. McFarland, "Uber's Remarkable Growth Could End the Era of Poorly Paid Cab Drivers," *Washington Post*, May 27, 2014.

86. M. Tobias, "How Taxi Companies Rip Off Their Drivers," *Forbes*, Nov. 18, 2011. And P. Mazzei, "Miami-Dade County's taxicab industry: few dollars for drivers, poor service for passengers," *The Miami Herald*, Jan. 25, 2014.

87. D. Thompson, "The Uber Economy," *The Atlantic*, Jan. 23, 2015.

88. S. Frizell, "Uber Just Answered Everything You Want to Know About Your Driver," *Time*, Jan. 22, 2015.

89. J. Davidson, "Uber Reveals How Much Its Drivers Really Earn…Sort Of," *Time*, Jan. 22, 2015.

90. B. Gurley, "Uber's New BHAG: UberPool," *Above the Crowd*, Jan. 30, 2015.

91. M. McFarland, "Uber's Remarkable Growth Could End the Era of Poorly Paid Cab Drivers," *Washington Post*, May 27, 2014.

92. E. Cushing, "The Smartest Bro in the Room," *San Francisco Magazine*, Nov. 21, 2014.

93. R. Miller, "Airbnb and Uber Face Some Harsh Realities," *TechCrunch*, Oct. 8, 2014.

94. J. Kann, "Taxi Drivers Face Uber Trouble," *Labor Notes*, June 10, 2014.

95. A. Lowrey, "Is Uber's Surge-Pricing an Example of High-Tech Gouging?" *New York Times*, January 10, 2014.

96. S. Kim, "How Uber Chooses Its Surge Price Cap in Emergencies," *ABC News*, Jan. 26, 2015.

97. C. Scolaro, "Bad press continues to hammer Uber," *CNBC*, Dec. 18, 2014.

98. T. Lien, "Uber plans to use biometrics and 'scientific analysis' to screen drivers," *The Los Angeles Times*, Dec. 17, 2014.

99. D. Alba, "Uber's New Panic Button Beams Real Time Updates to Police," *Wired*, April 30, 2015.

100. S. Raphelson, "Tech Week: Uber Under Fire, The Vision Behind Google's Lollipop," *NPR*, Nov. 22, 2014.

101. J. Kastrenakes, "Uber executive casually threatens journalist with smear campaign," *The Verge*, Nov. 18, 2014

102. M. Isaac, "Uber Lures Top Google Executive and Shifts David Plouffe's Duties," *The New York Times*, May 13, 2015.

103. M. Isaac, "Uber Lures Top Google Executive and Shifts David Plouffe's Duties," *The New York Times*, May 13, 2015.

104. T. Kalanick, "The Ride Ahead," *Uber*, Dec. 4, 2014. T. Kalanick, "The Ride Ahead," *Uber*, Dec. 4, 2014.

105. S. Lacy, "Uber Out-Maths Google on NYC ETAs," *TechCrunch*, June 15, 2011.

106. B. Chen, "App-Powered Car Service Leaves Cabs in the Dust," *Wired*, April 5, 2011.

107. Voytek (only one name listed), "Uberdata: Mapping San Francisco, New York, and The World," *Uber Blog*, May 15, 2011.

108. Voytek (only one name listed), "Uberdata: Mapping San Francisco, New York, and The World," *Uber Blog*, May 15, 2011.

109. B. Gurley, "Uber's New BHAG: UberPool," *Above the Crowd*, Jan. 30, 2015.

110. A. Damodaran, "Uber Isn't Worth $17 Billion," *Five Thirty Eight*, June 18, 2014.

111. A. Shontell, "Uber Is Going To Be The Next $100 Billion Company," *Business Insider*, May 18, 2014.

112. C. Sacca, "Why I'd never want to compete with Uber's Travis Kalanick," *Fortune*, Feb. 4, 2015.

113. A. Sorkin, "Why Uber Might Well Be Worth $18 Billion," *New York Times*, June 9, 2014.

114. M. McFarland, "Digital Mesh: The Concept behind Uber's Shot at an Empire," *Washington Post*, April 8, 2014.

115. G. Anderson, "Will UberEATS And UberRUSH Drive Company Value?" *Forbes*, May 4, 2014.

116. M. Wohlsen, "What Uber Will Do with All That Money from Google," *Wired*, January 3, 2014.

117. V. Luckerson, "Uber CEO Promises to Make Company 'More Humble' As it Raises $1.2B," *Time*, Dec. 4, 2014.

118. S. Gibbs, "Uber's first self-driving car spotted in Pittsburgh," *The Guardian*, May 22, 2015.

119. N. Gonzales, "eBay's StumbleUpon Acquisition: Confirmed at $75 Million," *TechCrunch*, May 30, 2007.

120. M. Wohlsen, "What Uber Will Do with All That Money from Google," *Wired*, January 3, 2014.

121. A. Ha, "California Regulator Passes First Ridesharing Rules, A Big Win For Lyft, SideCar, And Uber," *TechCrunch*, September 19, 2013.

122. D. Gilmore, "The Uber revolution is just beginning, and no cabbie protest can stop it," *The Guardian*, June 13, 2014.

123. D. MacMillan and L. Fleisher, "How Sharp-Elbowed Uber Is Trying to Make Nice," *The Wall Street Journal*, Jan. 29, 2015.

124. J. Brunstein, "Uber and Lyft Fight Proposed NYC Rules – and Each Other," *Insurance Journal*, May 28, 2015.

125. D. MacMillan and L. Fleisher, "How Sharp-Elbowed Uber Is Trying to Make Nice," *The Wall Street Journal*, Jan. 29, 2015.

126. T. Kalanick, "How Uber Taxi Rolls Out City by City," Inc., VIDEO (no date offered): http://www.inc.com/nicole-carter-and-tim-rice/how-uber-grows-internationally-city-by-city.html

127. P. Mozur and M Isaac, "Uber Spends Heavily to Establish Itself in China," *The New York Times*, June 8, 2015.

128. J. Sugden and A. Malhotra, "Hard Charging Uber Mixes In Softer Approach," *The Wall Street Journal*, April 12, 2015.

129. J. Sugden and A. Malhotra, "Hard Charging Uber Mixes In Softer Approach," *The Wall Street Journal*, April 12, 2015. .

130. R. Carew, "Uber Boosts China Bet," *The Wall Street Journal*, June 12, 2015.

131. H. Blodget, "Uber CEO Reveals Mind-Boggling New Statistic That Skeptics Will Hate," *Business Insider*, Jan. 19, 2015.

132. B. Gurley, "How to Miss By a Mile: An Alterantive Look at Uber's Potential Market Size," *Above the Crowd*, July 11, 2014.

133. A. Lozano, The Hall of Innovation, Accesed from http://www.dtic.upf.edu/~alozano/innovation/ on June 12, 2015.

CHAPTER 11

Facebook: A Billion-plus users, the High-Stakes Move to Mobile, and Big Business from the Social Graph

1. INTRODUCTION

LEARNING OBJECTIVES

1. Be familiar with Facebook's origins, rapid rise, and rocky first-year performance as a public company.
2. Understand how Facebook's rapid rise has impacted the firm's ability to raise venture funding and its founder's ability to maintain a controlling interest in the firm.

It's hard not to be awed by what Mark Zuckerberg has created. An effort launched from his college dorm is now a species-level phenomenon.[1] Roughly one in every seven people on the planet has a Facebook account—an amazing track record given that Facebook is technically banned in China (taking about 20 percent of the world population off the table).[2] Want to connect to customers? Facebook is increasingly the place to be. The firm's daily traffic is three times larger than the viewership of the Super Bowl.[3] The firm runs the most visited site in the United States,[4] and global growth is on a tear, with over 85 percent of Facebook users coming from abroad.[5]

1.1 The Rise of Facebook and Growing Concerns

Facebook founder Mark Zuckerberg looked like a social media pioneer from the start. Consider this: During the weeks he spent working on Facebook as a Harvard sophomore, he didn't have time to study for a course he was taking, "Art in the Time of Augustus," so he built a website containing all of the artwork in class and pinged his classmates to contribute to a communal study guide. Within hours, the wisdom of crowds produced a sort of custom CliffsNotes for the course, and after reviewing the Web-based crib sheet, he aced the test. Turns out he didn't need to take that exam, anyway. Zuck (that's what the cool kids call him)[6] dropped out of Harvard later that year.

By the age of twenty-three, Mark Zuckerberg had graced the cover of *Newsweek*, been profiled on *60 Minutes*, and was discussed in the tech world with a reverence previously reserved only for the late Steve Jobs and the Google guys, Sergey Brin and Larry Page. Zuckerberg went on to be named *Time*'s "Person of the Year," and *The Social Network*, a (mostly fictionalized) account of Facebook's founding[7], was a box-office smash, nominated for a Best Picture Academy Award. Facebook's controversial 2012 public offering valued the firm at over $100 billion, and the $16 billion raised in the offering made it (at the time) the biggest tech **IPO** in history and the third biggest IPO ever.[8] Zuckerberg's net worth topped $19 billion.[9]

Post IPO many analysts were concerned Facebook wouldn't realize its growth potential, and the stock began to fall. No longer. 2014 revenues were nearly $12.5 billion. Profits were nearly $3 billion. Mobile was an early concern—the firm made no money on mobile at the time of its IPO. Today mobile

IPO

Initial public stock offering, the first time a firm makes shares available via a public stock exchange, also known as 'going public.'

brings in over 70 percent of Facebook advertising revenue,[10] and Facebook's stock has gone up alongside Zuck's ability to prove his firm can mint cash.

Yet despite growth and rosy outlook, concerns loom. Facebook, a firm that has built its reputation on desktop dominance, is seeing new competition, especially in mobile apps where the competitive dynamics differ significantly. Facebook was built on public sharing (at times controversially pushing consumers toward public sharing as default) but one of the most significant mobile competitors, fast-growing Snapchat is based on private sharing and disappearing posts.[11] Amid the stunning speed of social media evolution, Facebook continues to relentlessly hunt for innovations showing both patience with new efforts and a high tolerance for failure. And the firm is spending billions on acquisitions, bringing emerging competitors and high-potential platforms into the Facebook fold. Facebook also finds that in a voraciously competitive high-end technical job market, the firm no longer has the promise of a massive IPO pay-day as a recruiting lure. As a result, the firm has become one of Silicon Valley's most aggressive practitioners of the acqui-hire—acquiring start-ups as a means of securing new talent.[12] And all this comes while trying to balance concerns over user privacy with the potential for delivering products that are both lucrative for the firm and valued by its customers. Zuckerberg has built a colossus, but as the boy-wonder enters his 30s, does Facebook have what it takes to remain one of the global Internet's most successful and influential firms?

1.2 Why Study Facebook?

short

Short selling is an attempt to profit from a falling stock price. Short sellers sell shares they don't own with an obligation of later repayment. They do so in the hope that the price of sold shares will fall. They then repay share debt with shares purchased at a lower price and pocket the difference (spread) between initial share price and repayment price.

Trying to distinguish the reality from the hype is a critical managerial skill. In Facebook's case, there are a lot of folks with a vested interest in figuring out where the firm is headed. If you want to work there, are you signing on to a firm where your *stock options* and *401k* contributions are going to be worth something or worthless? If you're an investor, should you **short** the firm or increase your holdings? Would you invest in or avoid firms that rely on Facebook's business? Should your firm rush to partner with Facebook? Does Facebook deserve your firm's ad dollars and staff attention ahead of other methods of consumer engagement? If you're a banker, examining the strengths and weaknesses of Facebook may help you make better decisions on whether or not you'd extend a firm like this credit. Should you offer it better terms to secure its growing business, or worse terms because you think it's a risky bet? Let's look at the fundamentals with an eye to applying what we've learned about tech industry strategy, competition, and competitive advantage. No one has a crystal ball, but we do have some key concepts that can guide our analysis. There are a lot of broadly applicable managerial lessons that can be gleaned by examining Facebook's successes, missteps, and continuing evolution. Studying the firm provides a context for understanding network effects, platforms, partnerships, issues in the rollout of new technologies, privacy, ad models, the business value of social media, the differences between desktop and mobile markets, and more.

Zuckerberg Rules

Many entrepreneurs accept start-up capital from venture capitalists (VCs), investor groups that provide funding in exchange for a stake in the firm and often (especially in early-stage investments), a degree of managerial control (this may be in the form of a voting seat or seats on the firm's board of directors). Typically, the earlier a firm accepts VC money, the more control these investors can exert (earlier investments are riskier, so VCs can demand more favorable terms). VCs usually have deep entrepreneurial experience and a wealth of contacts and can often offer important guidance and advice, but strong investor groups can oust a firm's founder and other executives if they're dissatisfied with the firm's performance.

At Facebook, however, the firm's extraordinary growth left potential investors salivating to back a firm perceived as being less risky but carrying the potential of a huge upside. Early backers ceded control; at a time when Facebook's board had only five directors, Zuckerberg appointed three of them. When Facebook filed to go public, Zuckerberg's ownership stake stood at 28 percent, but Facebook created two classes of shares, ensuring that Zuckerberg maintains a majority of voting rights in the public company and virtually guaranteeing that his control of the firm continues, regardless of what investors say. Maintaining this kind of control is unusual (although not unprecedented—Google's founders have a similar ownership and voting structure).[13] Zuckerberg's influence is a testament to the speed with which Facebook expanded. When investors' demand to get in on "the next big thing" remains high, a firm's owner can extract extraordinary terms for the privilege of coming along for the ride. It also empowers Zuckerberg to make bold, long-term, potentially money-losing bets with less shareholder scrutiny than a typical public company. As *Slate* puts it, Facebook is "conducting an experiment in corporate dictatorship nearly without precedent for such a large and high-profile company." All hail Emperor Zuckerberg![14]

Facebook's Copilot

Don't let Zuck get all the credit. While Facebook's founder is considered the firm's visionary, chief operating officer Sheryl Sandberg is often depicted as the person who runs the place: the coach, the seasoned mentor, the drill sergeant, and the voice of experience in a workforce that skews remarkably young despite its vast, global influence. With her successful track record at Facebook she can add another powerful descriptor: billionaire.[15]

Regularly named to *Fortune* magazine's "Most Powerful Women in Business" list, Sandberg came to Facebook from Google (before that, she was chief of staff to US Treasury secretary Larry Summers). In just three years, she's helped steer Facebook to almost unimaginable heights. Users increased ten-fold, she's helped devise an advertising platform that has attracted the world's largest brands, she's developed a sales organization that can serve a customer base ranging from the *Fortune* 100 to mom-and-pop stores, and she's helped the firm through several crises, all while turning a profit and pushing revenue higher.

Sandberg, a Harvard grad, left the school with a geeky legacy akin to Zuckerberg's. When she was a student conducting economics research she ran so much data on Harvard's network that she choked the system. Zuckerberg would have much the same impact more than a decade later.[16]

Sheryl Sandberg is a powerful speaker and a leading advocate for increasing the ranks of women in senior management, and her book on the topic, *Lean In*, became a bestseller.[17]

View the video online at: //www.youtube.com/v/18uDutylDa4

KEY TAKEAWAYS

- Facebook was founded by a nineteen-year-old college sophomore and eventual dropout.
- It is currently the largest social network in the world, boasting roughly 1.4 billion members and usage rates that would be the envy of most media companies.
- Despite the firm's rapid growth and initially high stock market valuation, Facebook faces several challenges, including generating more revenue from its customer base, growing advertising, monetizing mobile, transitioning to a mobile-centric world where competitive conditions differ, protecting user privacy, and competing with a slew of new competitors some challenging Facebook's openness edict—all amid rising personnel and infrastructure costs.
- The firm's rapid growth and high user engagement allowed Facebook's founder to demand and receive an exceptionally high degree of control over the firm—even as the firm went public.

QUESTIONS AND EXERCISES

1. Who started Facebook? How old was he then? Now? How much control does the founding CEO have over his firm? Why?

2. Who is Facebook's COO? What is their role, responsibilities, and accomplishments?

3. Firms' values fluctuate over time. How much is Facebook "worth" today? Has the firm's value gone up or down since its IPO? Why? Was investing in Facebook at IPO a move that paid off or that has resulted in losses? Look for business press stories and analyst quotes at or shortly after the time Facebook went public. Did analysts get it right or wrong? Why? What are key take-aways does looking back at how Facebook has performed, that you might use as a manager when sizing up firms, competitiveness, and technology evolution?

4. Why was Zuckerberg able to demand and receive control of Facebook, even as the firm went public? What strategic factors were at work in Facebook's rise that gave the founder such leverage?

5. Some have stated that Facebook's appeal is waning. Has your Facebook use remained more, less, or the same over time? What trends do you observe in others (parents, older or younger friends and relatives)? What other services occupy your non-Facebook social media time, and how does your usage of these services compare with the time you spend on Facebook? Which of these services do you think you'll be using five years from now? Do you think new services are a threat to Facebook? Why or why not?

6. Facebook received several lucrative buyout offers before the firm went public. Why was Zuckerberg able to turn down these offers, even though they stood to make the firm's early investors very rich in a short amount of time? Was Zuckerberg wise to have turned down early acquisition offers? Why or why not?

7. Snapchat has also reportedly received lucrative buyout offers (including reportedly rejecting a $3 billion offer from Facebook). Do you think Snapchat should resist buyout or become acquired? Defend your answer.

8. Why study Facebook? Who cares if it succeeds? Why is it useful for managers and management students to study Facebook? Who cares if it succeeds?

2. DISRUPTING COMPETITION, BUILDING COMPETITIVE ADVANTAGE, AND THE CHALLENGING RISE OF MOBILE

LEARNING OBJECTIVES

1. **Identify the two strategic resources that are most critical to Facebook's competitive advantage and why Facebook was able to create resources with such strength.**

2. **Explain the concept of the "social graph," and explain how Facebook created a social graph stronger than that of its rivals.**

3. **Understand the role of features such as news feeds in reinforcing these strategic resources.**

4. **Recognize that Facebook's power in desktop services has allowed it to encroach on and envelop other Internet businesses.**

5. **Understand how mobile service offerings differ from desktop efforts and recognize that the dynamics that allowed Facebook to dominate on the desktop are substantially different than mobile.**

6. **Examine several of Facebook's recent acquisitions and the competitive motivations behind these purchases.**

7. **Understand the concept of the "dark Web" and why some feel this may one day give Facebook a source of advantage vis-à-vis Google.**

8. **Understand the basics of Facebook's infrastructure and the costs required to power an effort of such scale.**

Facebook's mission, as stated by Zuckerberg, is "to make the world more open and connected."[18] From a social network initially targeted at college students, Facebook has become a relentlessly advancing and evolving force, occupying large swaths of user time and expanding into all sorts of new markets.

2.1 The Social Graph and Why Facebook's Is So Strong

At the heart of Facebook's appeal is a concept Zuckerberg calls the **social graph**, which refers to Facebook's ability to collect, express, and leverage the connections between the site's users, or as some describe it, "the global mapping of everyone and how they're related."[19] Think of everything that's on Facebook as a node or endpoint that's connected to other stuff. You're connected to other users (your friends), photos about you are tagged, comments you've posted carry your name, you regularly declare your preferences and things that you "like," you're a member of groups, you're connected to applications you've installed—Facebook links them all.[20]

Facebook was established in the relatively safe cocoon of American undergraduate life and was conceived as a place where you could reinforce contacts among those who, for the most part, you already knew. The site was one of the first social networks where users actually identified themselves using their real names. Since "friending" (which is a link between nodes in the social graph) required both users to approve the relationship, the network fostered an incredible amount of trust. Today, many Facebook users post their cell phone numbers and their birthdays, offer personal photos, and otherwise share information they'd never share outside their circle of friends. Trust is one of Facebook's most distinguishing features—bringing along with it a degree of safety and comfort that enabled Facebook to become a true social utility and build out a solid social graph consisting of verified relationships.

There is also a strong **network effect** to Facebook (see Chapter 8). People are attracted to the service because others they care about are more likely to be on Facebook than anywhere else online. And that large user base has also attracted all sorts of firms and organizations looking to connect with Facebook's masses. Without the network effect, Facebook wouldn't exist. And it's because of the network effect that another smart kid in a dorm can't rip off Zuckerberg in any market where Facebook is the biggest player. Even an exact copy of Facebook would be a virtual ghost town with no social graph.

The **switching costs** for Facebook are also extremely powerful. A move to another service means recreating your entire social graph. The more time you spend on the service, the more you've invested in your graph and the less likely you are to move to a rival.

2.2 Facebook Feed: Viral Sharing Accelerated

While the authenticity and trust offered by Facebook was critical, offering News Feeds concentrated and released value from the social graph. With feeds, each time you perform an activity on Facebook—make a friend, upload a photo, joins a group—the feed offers the potential to blast this information to all of your connections. Corporations love feeds, too! Firms and products that you "Like" on Facebook can post messages that may appear in your news feed (where you can like and comment on their posts and share the messages virally), making Facebook a key channel for continued customer engagement.

Facebook continues to refine feeds in several ways, including categorizing sharing in several ways. You can find updates on the "News Feed" that Facebook actively curates by default; a "Timeline" on your personal page offers a sort of digital scrapbook of content that a user has shared online; and (on the desktop, Web version of Facebook) a "Ticker" for lighter content appears on the right side of the screen (e.g., sharing music, game activity, location updates). Not everyone sees every post to their feed; like Google, Facebook uses a secret and constantly refined algorithm that attempts to identify what you're most interested in, while cutting "spammy" content. Facebook's Engineering Manager for News Feed estimates that there are as many as "100,000 individual weights in the model" that determines if you'll see a post.[21] Some of the more significant factors include the past interest of a given user in the content's creator, a post's performance among other users, performance of past posts by the content creator, the type of posts a given user prefers (e.g., status, link, photo, etc.), and the regency of the post. And don't beg for likes or reshares. That'll get your post punished, decreasing its reach.[22] Users can also tweak their news feed settings, and opt to see posts based on recency rather than algorithmically determined "Top Stories." An awareness of key factors and "dos and don'ts" is critical to any organization looking to use Facebook for engagement. And of course, Facebook will gladly allow you to advertise to extend a post's reach. (Not surprisingly, as Facebook has significantly cut the organic reach of brand page postings, the firm's 'Promoted Post' ad business has increased).[23] Facebook's feed has also borrowed a page from Twitter, introducing trending topics and hash tags, which will help users discover conversation and encourage more public sharing of posts and other content.[24] The optional Facebook "Subscribe" feature also mimics Twitter's "Follow," allowing asymmetrical sharing where a user can view a person's updates in his or her feed without having to be friended back.

Facebook rules as kingmaker, opinion catalyst, and traffic driver, so media outlets are eager to be friends. While in the previous decade news stories would carry a notice saying "Copyright, do not distribute without permission," today's newspapers display Facebook icons alongside every copyrighted

social graph

The global mapping of users and organizations and how they are connected.

network effect

Also known as Metcalfe's Law, or network externalities. When the value of a product or service increases as its number of users expands.

switching costs

The cost a consumer incurs when moving from one product to another. It can involve actual money spent (e.g., buying a new product) as well as investments in time, any data loss, and so forth.

story, encouraging users to "share" the content on their profile pages. Great for Facebook, but a sharp elbow to Digg.com and Del.icio.us, which have both seen their link sharing appeal free-fall, even though they showed up first.[25] Facebook beats rivals in driving traffic to newspaper sites,[26] and it's also way ahead of Twitter and Pinterest in overall social traffic referrals.[27] Games firms, music services, video sites, daily deal services, publishers, and more all integrate with Facebook, hoping that posts to Facebook will spread their services virally.

2.3   Facebook's Dominance on the Desktop

Facebook has gradually turned on features that have allowed the firm to leverage its massive user base to encroach on a wide swath of Internet services. But even as we tally Facebook's successful envelopment of new product categories, there is increasing evidence that mobile presents new challenges where the old "turn on a feature and dominate" dynamics at play on the desktop simply aren't as strong.

First, let's look at desktop Facebook's past ability to envelop markets. In photos, Google, Yahoo!, and one-time standout MySpace all spent millions to acquire photo-sharing sites (Picasa, Flickr, and Photobucket, respectively). But to become the Web's leading photo-sharing service, Facebook didn't acquire anyone. The site simply turned on a substandard photo-sharing feature and quickly became the biggest photo-sharing site on the Web. Facebook users now post over 300 million photos each day.[28] When Facebook turned on chat, it become the first-choice communication service for many in its growing customer base, displacing instant messaging platforms that had massive early leads and millions of subscribers.[29] As mentioned earlier, Facebook's feed crushed the appeal of independent link-sharing services like Digg and Del.icio.us. Video is huge on Facebook, too. The firm serves as many views a day (4 billion) as YouTube.[30] Facebook even wants to be your better address book, business directory, and phone dialer. The firm's Android-only Hello App matches phone numbers of your calls to Facebook profiles so you get a better caller ID with more info about who you're talking to (e.g., a friendly heads-up it's the caller's birthday). The app can also block calls and search for businesses to call, plus links listings with Facebook Messenger for those times where you prefer text to voice.[31] Facebook has continued to experiment with all sorts of services, including partnerships to stream movies over Facebook,[32] offering users a Facebook.com e-mail address,[33] and creating a document collaboration service with Microsoft.[34] While many of these efforts have failed or did not achieve traction as initially hoped, they underscore Facebook's innovation culture, and the firm's relentless drive to experiment with new opportunities for social engagement. As Facebook is able to insert itself into new markets and envelop markets owned by other firms, we see a key advantage to Facebook's central role in the lives of consumers. Network effects, switching costs, and the firm's influence in catalyzing the spread of new products and services allow the company to quickly apply its installed base in key markets. Budding entrepreneurs beware: Are you building a *business* with sustainable advantage or a *feature* that will one day be wiped out by similar technology built into Facebook?

2.4   Facebook Takes on Search

dark Web

Internet content that can't be indexed by Google and other search engines.

Google, watch your back, Facebook is tinkering there, as well. Google indexes some Facebook content, but since much of Facebook is private, accessible only among friends, most Facebook activity represents a massive blind spot for Google search. Sites that can't be indexed by Google and other search engines are referred to as the **dark Web**. Early experiments incorporating Facebook with Microsoft Bing have been cancelled,[35] but while Google lacks access to Facebook's portion of the dark Web, some speculate that if Facebook can tie together standard Internet search with its dark Web content, this just might be enough for some to break the Google habit.

Facebook has introduced Graph Search, intending to evolve search beyond the keyword. With Graph Search, Facebook allows users to draw meaning from the site's social graph and to find answers from social connections. Planning an outdoorsy getaway and looking for ideas from friends you trust? Use Graph Search to collect photos of friends at National Parks. Some have claimed Graph Search could become a primary source for job placement, travel info, and even dating.[36]

Mark Zuckerberg Explains Graph Search

In this video, Mark Zuckerberg and other Facebook staff discuss the firm's Graph Search product. To try the product, visit https://www.facebook.com/about/graphsearch.

View the video online at: http://www.youtube.com/embed/U94DTrjAvuA?rel=0

Graph Search results are based in part on the connections in your social graph, but you also have access your past posts as well as any information that the billion-plus member Facebook community chooses to make public. Consider this when selecting your privacy settings. There's an active Tumblr account showing embarrassing Graph Search results.[37] Perhaps more seriously, critics have demonstrated how Graph Search could be used by foreign governments to uncover, say, members of China's banned Falun Gong movement or identify gays and lesbians in nations where homosexuality is outlawed and punishable.[38]

2.5 Why Mobile Is Different and in Some Ways Better than the Desktop

Up until now Facebook has been able to envelop all sorts of desktop services by simply adding a feature to its browser-based product, but with the rise of mobile, Facebook's dominance no longer looks like a given. It lost an early lead to mobile photo sharing to Instagram. WhatsApp and Snapchat have the preferred messaging clients for mobile, while others such as WeChat, Line, and Kakao Talk enjoy hundreds of millions of users in different locations throughout the world. Gaming firms, which once flocked to the Facebook platform as a fast path to riches, now see a more promising future in developing mobile apps.

Mobile *is* different. Many of the winner-takes-all dynamics of social on the desktop Web, which Facebook had leveraged so astutely to weave its way deeper into the lives of its users, do not appear to apply on mobile. Ben Evans, a partner at the venture firm Andreessen Horowitz, writes what many consider to be a must-read tech industry weekly newsletter (sign up at ben-evans.com). He points out that there are at least four areas where the competitive dynamics of smartphone apps differ from browser-based desktop services:

- Smartphone apps can access a user's address book. This makes it easier to rebuild the social graph for a new mobile service.
- Smartphones apps can access a phone's media library and can often plug into cloud storage. This makes it easier to share photos and video than on desktop services.
- Smartphone apps can use push notifications, a huge benefit for increasing engagement. While prior services needed to rely on e-mail notifications or hoped users remembered to return to a Web site, push notifications from a service instantly say, "Hey, there's something new here for you to pay attention to," and offer single-tap re-entry into a service.
- Smartphone apps also get an icon on the home screen. A constant visual reminder for a service. Single-tap access is also far better than bookmarking or typing in a URL.
- While a desktop site can crush a new competitor by adding a feature as a new menu item or icon, on mobile there isn't the screen real estate for this—another reason mobile seems to favor single-purpose, specialized apps.[39]

While many considered mobile platforms to be more limiting than the desktop—the screen size was smaller, typing was more difficult on a mobile device—there are plenty of things that a smartphone can do better than a laptop or desktop. As Evans states, "there's an old computer science saying that a computer should never ask you a question that it should be able to work out the answer to; a smartphone can work out much more."[40] The always-with-you phone can tell your location via GPS, iBeacons or other location-based service. Sensors, your address book, and usage patterns can reveal more. Are you in a store? Is there a deal close by? Where are you usually at this time a day? Is there anything close by that you may be interested in? Are you sitting, walking or running? What is the weather and traffic like where you're headed? Who are your friends and should we contact them? Services like Apple Pay and Android Pay allow not only one-click payment, but also one-click form fill-out, making buying easier on mobile. Custom keyboards, emoji, voice input, and other methods for creative and streamlined input came first and often work better via mobile. And APIs supplied to mobile app developers may be able to reveal or request even more. The savvy innovator doesn't lament what is lost with the desktop, they recognize all of the new that can be done in mobile and set to work building disruptive businesses.

2.6 Big Bets: Bringing Potential Rivals and Platform Powerhouses into the Facebook Family

While mobile is different, and Facebook hasn't always been a cross-category leader in mobile innovation, Facebook's profitability and IPO provide the firm with cash to try to ensure that it's *Facebook that's going to be the next Facebook*.[41] Three of the firm's acquisitions, each valued at $1 billion or more, demonstrate this.

Instagram

Facebook's dominance in photo sharing came largely from success over the Web, but photo sharing and many other activities went mobile, fast. At the time of Facebook's IPO, Instagram, an eighteen-month-old firm with thirteen employees, had fifty million users and was adding new ones at a rate of roughly five million a week.[42] Users loved the beautiful, artistic images Instagram's filters created, and photos were being shared not only on Instagram but also on Facebook's rival Twitter and other services. Analysts suggest mobile could have been Facebook's Achilles heel—allowing Instagram to open up and become a Facebook-rivaling platform (Insta-music? Insta-links? Insta-status updates?). Facebook even acknowledged its mobile vulnerabilities in pre-IPO regulatory filings.[43] But when Facebook acquired Instagram for a cool $1 billion, Facebook turned the potential rival into an asset for growth and another vehicle for the firm to remain central to users' lives.[44] Since the acquisition, Instagram has continued to operate a a separate brand, tripling its user base the year following acquisition. (and topping 300 million by Spring 2015).[45] Instagram now sports usage numbers larger than Twitter.[46] New features such as video were introduced, and with the introduction of ads, the app has also began to earn money.

FIGURE 11.1

Instagram was acquired on the eve of Facebook's IPO for $1 billion. Facebook maintains the app as a separate brand, and it now sports a user base larger than Twitter's.

Source: Image taken from Instagram's photos published on Apple's iTunes Store.

WhatsApp

Mobile messaging posed a bigger threat than smartphone photo sharing, so Facebook ended up writing an even bigger check. A potential acquisition of SnapChat was reported to have ended when that firm's twenty-three-year-old founder refused a Facebook offer of $3 billion,[47] but there was an even bigger prize out there. While less popular in the United States, WhatsApp had emerged as the global leader in mobile messaging, sending more total messages than the entire worldwide SMS text messaging standard![48] WhatsApp had 450 million monthly users, and a million more were signing up each day. A billion users for WhatsApp looked like a very real possibility. In the high-growth markets of India, Brazil, and Mexico, WhatsApp usage numbers were *twelve* to *sixty-four times* ahead of Facebook for mobile messaging![49] Seventy-two percent of WhatsApp account holders used the service each day, and collectively they shared over half a billion photos daily. While app switching costs may seem low, users were refining messaging with groups (e.g., "Family," "Project Team," "Running Club"), making it less likely they'd try something with fewer people that required re-creating messaging groups (network effects and switching costs strike again). Facebook began to realize that the only path to avoid being a messaging also-ran was to pony up and acquire WhatsApp, and to do it before it got any bigger.[50] The asking price for the fifty-five person firm with zero revenue:[51] $19 billion—$16 billion in cash, $3 billion in stock. The acquisition instantly turned cofounder Jan Koum into a billionaire, and in a rags-to-riches story, the self-taught programmer signed the deal papers on the door of the welfare office where he once collected food stamps.[52] Nineteen billion dollars seems like an incredible amount to pay for a firm that, at least in the short term, will add nothing to Facebook's bottom line. But this acquisition wasn't about increasing Facebook's total revenue; as TechCrunch stated, it was about surviving the global shift to mobile.[53] Yes, WhatsApp lost $138 million in 2014, but by Spring of 2015 the firm was at eight hundred MAUs (monthly active users) and growing.[54] From the perspective of securing a large user base and taking out a potentially threatening competitor, *Wired* labeled the Instagram and WhatsApp acquisitions as "two of the greatest bargains in recent tech history."[55]

FIGURE 11.2

WhatsApp has grown to over eight hundred monthly active users, with fans creating chat lists and sharing video, audio, photos, and location.

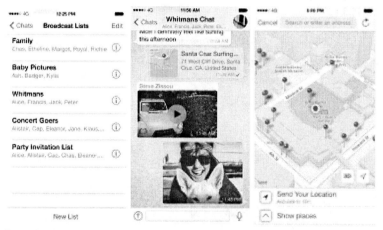

Source: Images from WhatsApp's public archive for news stories at: http://media.whatsapp.com/screenshots/iPhone/screens

Oculus VR

After the WhatsApp purchase, Mark Zuckerberg publicly stated: "After buying a company for $16 billion, you're probably done for a while,"[56] but within weeks he forked over the equivalent of two Instagrams to acquire a firm started by an eighteen-year-old that had no customers, no revenue, and no complete product. Facebook's $2 billion purchase of Oculus VR is a long-term bet at keeping the firm at the vanguard of computing's evolution. To the uninitiated, the first Oculus product, the Oculus Rift, looks weird. Still in prototype form at the time of acquisition, it's essentially a computing screen that you strap to your face. Two very high-resolution displays fill ski-goggle-like gear with a wraparound image covering your field of vision. Lenses and distortion algorithms tweak computer imagery at vision periphery to hack your visual cortex and send it the kind of images it would expect to encounter in the real world. Turn your head and the image moves in real time. The Rift's big breakthrough is that it doesn't make you puke. Previous VR efforts had so much latency (delay) in image rendering that users would become disoriented to the point of nausea. Early versions will integrate with PCs (which will provide computational heavy-lifting), will come bundled with a wireless Xbox controller, and can even stream Xbox games (although they'll need to be re-written to take advantage of the fully-immersive VR experience).[57] Oculus was founded by Palmer Luckey, a home-schooler who hacked together prototypes in his parents' garage in Long Beach, California. After experiencing an Oculus prototype, video game pioneer John Carmack (of Doom and Quake fame) was so impressed that he quit the firm he'd cofounded to join Oculus as CTO. Luckey launched a Kickstarter campaign to generate interest. Within hours the firm blew past its initial $250,000 goal and eventually hit $2.4 million in commitments. VCs lined up to invest. Gaming firms began working on prototypes. HBO showed an Oculus-enabled *Game of Thrones* experience at the South by Southwest festival. And Zuckerberg strapped on a Rift and saw the future. In a Facebook post announcing the acquisition, Zuckerberg wrote, "Imagine enjoying a courtside seat at a game, studying in a classroom of students and teachers all over the world, or consulting with a doctor face-to-face—just by putting on goggles in your home."[58] Justifying the acquisition, Zuckerberg has also said, "Strategically we want to start building the next major computing platform that will come after mobile."[59] Adds Luckey, "This isn't about sharing pictures. This is about being able to share experiences."[60] While Lucky and crew might have been able to build a multi-billion dollar firm on their own, many firms are circling VR, including deep-pocketed rivals with consumer experience (Samsung, Google, Sony, among them). Why sell out? Says Oculus CEO Brendan Iribe, Facebook's resources are allowing Oculus to faster and better weather the onslaught of rivals. In the year since the acquisition, the firm grew its employee base five-fold, from 50 engineers to roughly 250. Facebook provides the deep pockets for developing custom, high-resolution optics hardware, VR audio (that makes it seem like sound is above or below you), and offers deep in-house technical expertise as well as the ability to leverage hundreds of thousands of Facebook servers.[61]

FIGURE 11.3

Oculus Rift headset with Touch controllers.

Source: Image from Oculus PR Site Press Kit public image library: https://www.oculus.com/en-us/press-kit-hardware/

Time will tell if these acquisitions prove as strategically significant as Zuckerberg hoped. Facebook has launched several initiatives that failed completely or did not live up to initial promise. The shuttered Poke app; yet another photosharing app (Moments); the underperforming Paper (news reader), Slingshot (Snapchat competitor) and Rooms (anonymous chat rooms) apps[62]; the mostly unwanted Facebook Home smartphone platform[63]; and the firm's scuttled Gifts and Deals services are just a few examples. Buying promising innovations may be a savvy way for the now cash-rich firm to remain at the forefront of tech industry shifts.

So What's It Take to Run This Thing?

It takes some serious hardware to serve a billion people. As *BusinessWeek* reports, "each day, Facebook processes 2.7 billion 'Likes,' 300 million photo uploads, 2.5 billion status updates and check-ins, and countless other bits of data," plus the firm crunches much of what it has collected to customize feeds, estimate which ads to serve up, and refine and improve the Facebook experience.[64] Facebook has extraordinary data storage needs that are growing at breakneck speeds. Facebook's storage needs have grown by a factor of *4,000* in just four years,[65] and amount to a total storage well north of three hundred petabytes and growing at more than six hundred terabytes a day.[66]

The Facebook **cloud** (the big group of connected servers that power the site) is scattered across multiple facilities, including server farms in San Francisco, Santa Clara, northern Virginia, Oregon, North Carolina, Iowa, and Sweden.[67] The innards that make up the bulk of Facebook's massive multisite cloud aren't that different from what you'd find on a high-end commodity workstation: standard hard drives and multicore Intel or AMD processors—just a whole lot of them lashed together through networking and software. Like Google and Amazon, Facebook's servers are custom built, stripping out nonessential parts but adding in components when needed (such as massive and super-fast flash memory–based storage for some of its custom database servers).[68]

Much of what powers the site is **open source software (OSS)**. The service runs on the Linux operating system and Apache Web server software. A good portion of Facebook is written in PHP (a scripting language particularly well suited for Web site development), while some of the databases are in MySQL (a popular open source database). The firm is a major contributor to open source software efforts and was the force behind Hive, a product used to provide query support for big data projects, and Presto, another open source effort that's even speedier than Hive.[69] While a good portion of Facebook is written in the popular but slower-executing PHP language, the firm has written (and open sourced) a system it calls *HipHop Virtual Machine*, which takes PHP code and compiles (translates) it on the fly from something that a programmer can read to the machine language that a computer can more quickly execute.[70] The object cache that holds Facebook's frequently accessed objects is in chip-based RAM instead of on slower hard drives and is managed via an open source product called Memcache.

Other code components are written in a variety of languages, including C++, Java, Python, and Ruby, with access between these components managed by a code layer the firm calls Thrift (developed at Facebook, which was also turned over to the Apache Software Foundation). Facebook also developed its own media serving solution, called Haystack. Haystack coughs up photos 50 percent faster than more expensive, proprietary solutions, and since it's done in house, it saves Facebook costs that other online outlets spend on third-party **content delivery networks (CDN)** like Akamai. Facebook receives some 50 million requests per second,[71] yet 95 percent of data queries can be served from a huge, distributed server cache that lives in well over fifteen terabytes of RAM.[72]

All this technology is expensive. Facebook's annual spend on networking equipment and infrastructure was estimated to come in at $2.5 billion in 2014, an amount some 84 percent higher than 2013 levels. With users continuing to shovel data-heavy photos and video on the site (as well as through Facebook properties Instagram and WhatsApp), Facebook will likely be buying servers for years to come. And it'll pay a pretty penny just to keep things humming. Estimates suggest the firm spends over $1 million a month on electricity and another half million a month on telecommunications bandwidth to keep your feed full and your status updated.[73] Want to build your own server farm like Facebook? The firm will tell you how to do it. In an unprecedented move, Facebook made public the detailed specifications of its homegrown servers (including custom power supplies, chassis, and battery backup) as well as plans used in the Prineville site's building design and electrical and cooling systems. You can find details, photos, and video at http://www.opencompute.org. Facebook claims its redesigned servers are 38 percent more efficient and 24 percent cheaper than those sold by major manufacturers, and that these designs have resulted in yearly energy savings estimated about roughly $52 million, and infrastructure savings of more than $1 billion.[74] These kinds of savings will continue to be important with Facebook, WhatsApp, and Instagram users uploading roughly one billion photos each day.[75] Why give away the low-cost secrets? Says the firm's director of hardware, "Facebook is successful because of the great social product, not [because] we can build low-cost infrastructure. There's no reason we shouldn't help others out with this."[76]

cloud

A collection of resources available for access over the Internet.

open source software (OSS)

Software that is free and whose code can be accessed and potentially modified by anyone.

content delivery networks (CDN)

Systems distributed throughout the Internet (or other network) that help to improve the delivery (and hence loading) speeds of Web pages and other media, typically by spreading access across multiple sites located closer to users. Akamai is the largest CDN, helping firms like CNN and MTV quickly deliver photos, video, and other media worldwide.

KEY TAKEAWAYS

- Facebook's primary competitive advantages are grounded in network effects and switching costs.
- The social graph expresses the connections between individuals and organizations.
- Trust created through user verification and friend approval requiring both parties to consent encouraged Facebook users to share more and helped the firm establish a stronger social graph than other social networking rivals.
- Feeds catalyze virality and promote information sharing. Facebook's position as the digital center of its members' online social lives has allowed the firm to envelop related businesses such as photo and video sharing, messaging, bookmarking, and link sharing. Facebook has opportunities to expand into other areas as well.
- Facebook's dominance on the desktop has allowed the firm to encroach in new markets by essentially turning on features that, in many cases, allowed the firm to dominate categories pioneered by other firms.
- The mobile market differs from the desktop in many key ways that alter competition. Access to address books, media libraries, the cloud, push notifications, home screen icons, and limited screen real estate are enforcing a new competitive reality on Facebook and rivals.
- Many of the dynamics above caused Facebook to lose the lead in mobile photo sharing and messaging, but the firm's deep pockets have allowed it to acquire leading firms, removing threatening rivals and strengthening the firm's competitive assets.
- Facebook has also invested in Oculus VR, an unproven but promising start-up that may transform computing by making high-quality virtual reality accessible at a reasonable cost.
- Much of the site's content is in the dark Web, unable to be indexed by Google or other search engines. Some suggest this may create an opportunity for Facebook to challenge Google in search. Partnerships with Bing and Facebook's own Graph Search attempt to harness the firm's dark Web asset to answer questions.
- Facebook's growth requires a continued and massive infrastructure investment. The site is powered largely on commodity hardware, open source software, and proprietary code tailored to the specific needs of the service.

QUESTIONS AND EXERCISES

1. What is the social graph? Why is Facebook's social graph considered to be stronger than the social graph created by the sites of its early competitors?

2. Does Facebook have to worry about copycat firms from the United States? In overseas markets? Why or why not? If Facebook has a source (or sources) of competitive advantage, explain these. If it has no advantage, discuss why.

3. Which firms have seen Facebook enter their markets as a potential disrupter? What factors have allowed the firm to gain share in these markets at the expense of established firms? In what ways does it enjoy advantages that a traditional new entrant in such markets would not?

4. How does competition in services delivered in the browser on desktop computers differ from those delivered via smartphone app?

5. Consider Facebook's acquisitions of Instagram, WhatsApp, and Oculus VR. Was the firm smart to make these acquisitions, and did it pay a reasonable price? What were the risks in not acting?

6. Large firms in the tech industry are constantly making new acquisitions. Conduct some additional research online: Have Facebook or its rivals recently acquired firms that have the potential to alter the competitive landscape Zuckerberg's firm will compete in? If so, how?

7. What is the "dark Web," and why is it potentially an asset to Facebook? Why is Google threatened by Facebook's dark Web? How is Facebook harnessing the dark Web to provide potentially valuable search products? Do you think the dark Web is enough to draw users to a Facebook search product over Google? Why or why not?

8. Try Graph Search. Do you find it useful? When would you use it or why wouldn't you use it? Can Facebook turn Graph Search into a money maker? How could it do this, or why won't it accomplish this goal?

9. What privacy concerns are raised with Graph Search and other Facebook features? Do you think these concerns will hinder Facebook's ability to build new businesses using user data?

10. As Facebook grows, what kinds of investments continue to be necessary? What are the trends in these costs over time? Do you think Facebook should wait in making these investments? Why or why not?

11. How have media attitudes toward their copyrighted content changed over the past decade? Why is Facebook a potentially significant partner for firms like the *New York Times*? What does the *New York Times* stand to gain by encouraging "sharing" of its content? What do newspapers and others sites really mean when they encourage sites to "share"? What actually is being passed back and forth? Do you think this ultimately helps or undermines the *New York Times* and other newspaper and magazine sites? Why?

12. Research Facebook's smartphone apps. Which ones are successful and which have struggled or been shut down? Try those that are available on your own smartphone (or ask a friend to work with you to download the apps and given them a try). What factors are behind the success or failure of these products? Is it just user experience that drives success or failure, or are there other factors at work here, as well?

3.   LESSONS FROM FACEBOOK AS AN APPS PLATFORM: EARLY PROMISE, CONTINUED CHALLENGES, MOBILE MISSTEPS

L E A R N I N G   O B J E C T I V E S

1. **Understand the potential strategic value of evolving from a service to a platform. Learn from Facebook's platform successes as well as its missteps and lost opportunities.**
2. **Describe Facebook's efforts to integrate its service with other Web sites and the potential strategic benefit for Facebook and its partners.**
3. **Understand how Facebook's web-centric culture allowed for a degree of A/B testing, rapid refinement, and error correction that isn't as easy to obtain in an app-centric smartphone world and see how this may have led to several of the firm's struggles in developing and deploying mobile offerings.**
4. **Recognize how Facebook is evolving Messenger in ways far beyond an SMS replacement, so that it is now a platform for many additional services (and revenue-generating and strategic asset creating opportunities for the firm).**
5. **Highlight areas of opportunity and concern regarding Facebook's designs on emerging market growth.**

application programming interfaces

Programming hooks, or guidelines, published by firms that tell other programs how to get a service to perform a task such as send or receive data. For example, Amazon provides application programming interfaces (APIs) to let developers write their own applications and Web sites that can send the firm orders.

At the firm's first f8 developers conference, Facebook published a set of **application programming interfaces** (APIs) that specified how programs could be written to run within and interact with Facebook. Essentially Zuck was opening up Facebook screen real estate, user base and features like Feed to the world's developers. Now, any programmer could write an application that would live inside a user's profile. Developers could charge for their wares, offer them for free, or even run ads. Facebook lets developers keep earnings through their apps (Facebook does revenue share with app vendors for some services—for example, taking 30 percent of virtual goods sales transacted through the site). Apps could be cobbled together quickly; news feeds made them spread like wildfire and the early movers offered adoption rates never before seen by small groups of software developers. And for Facebook, becoming a platform meant that each new third-party app potentially added more value and features to the site without Facebook lifting a finger (which, in a prior chapter, we learned about as value-adding complementary benefits from network effects).

There were some missteps along the way. Some applications were accused of spamming friends with invites to install them (Facebook eventually put limits on viral communication from apps). There were also security concerns, privacy leaks, and apps that violated the intellectual property of other firms (see the "Errant Apps and the Challenges of Running a Platform" sidebar), but Facebook worked to quickly remove misbehaving apps, correct errors, improve the system, and encourage developers. Just one year in, Facebook had marshaled the efforts of some 400,000 developers and entrepreneurs, 24,000 applications had been built for the platform, 140 new apps were being added each day, and 95 percent of Facebook members had installed at least one Facebook application.

Errant Apps and the Challenges of Running a Platform

Rajat and Jayant Agarwalla, two brothers in Kolkata, India, who ran a modest software development company, decided to write a Scrabble clone as a Facebook application. The app, named Scrabulous, was social—users could invite friends to play or search for players looking for an opponent. Their application was a smash hit, snagging 3 million registered users and 700,000 players a day after just a few months. Scrabulous was featured in *PC World*'s 100 best products of the year; received coverage in the *New York Times*, *Newsweek*, and *Wired*; and was pulling in about $25,000 a month from online advertising. Way to go, guys![77] There is only one problem: the Agarwalla brothers didn't have the legal rights to Scrabble, and it was apparent to anyone, from the name to the tiles to the scoring, that this was a direct rip-off of the well-known board game. Hasbro owns the copyright to Scrabble in the United States and Canada, Mattel owns it everywhere else, and both Electronic Arts and RealNetworks had contracted with the firms to create online versions of the game.

While the Facebook Scrabulous app is long gone, the tale serves to illustrate some of the challenges faced when creating a platform. In addition to copyright violations, app makers have crafted apps that annoy, purvey pornography, step over the boundaries of good taste, and raise privacy and security concerns. The *Wall Street Journal* has reported that unscrupulous partners had scraped personal information from the profiles of Facebook users and then sold the information to third parties—a violation of Facebook's terms of service that created a firestorm in the media.[78] Other app firms were accused of scamming users into signing up for subscriptions or installing unwanted software in exchange for game credits.[79]

Firms from Facebook to Apple (through its iTunes Store) have struggled to find the right mix of monitoring, protection, and approval while avoiding cries of censorship and draconian control. Platform owners beware: developers can help you grow quickly and can deliver gobs of value, but misbehaving partners can create financial loss, damage the brand, and sow mistrust.

Despite the explosion of interest in Facebook platform, the top category Just for Fun was larger than the next four categories combined; and within that category, many of the early winners were starting to look like flash-in-the-pan fads. Once-promising start-ups Slide and iLike shriveled, eventually selling to Facebook rivals Google and MySpace for smaller figures than their one-time valuations.[80] Many developers would complain of being "Zucked over,"[81] claiming that Facebook became a poor partner making surreptitious platform changes, altering policies without consulting them, and taking away much of the virality that helped fuel the firm's initial app explosion;

Game maker Zynga's woes may have been unusually acute. The firm had scrapped an earlier agreement that gave it preferred status in the Facebook News Feed, and a revamp to Facebook's feed-ranking algorithm subsequently caused a significant portion of Zynga traffic to be screened out.[82] While Zynga's IPO debuted at $10 a share and was once one of the most valuable video game firms on the planet,[83] the firm's share price fell below $3 roughly a year and a half after its debut as a public firm. Nearly 20 percent of its workforce had been fired, users were fleeing games, and profits had vanished.[84] Still, while Zynga faltered, King.com (maker of Candy Crush Saga) surged. The firm had three of the four most popular games on Facebook in 2013;[85] it saw 150 million monthly active users and over a billion plays each day.[86]

Despite King's success, Facebook's mobile gaming revenues were down a full 11 percent compared to a year earlier;[87] Facebook itself admits the benefit of thinking beyond Facebook-only games. According to the firm, revenues are 3.3 times higher from cross-platform games than those developed only for Facebook's browser environment on the PC, and user engagement is 40 percent higher for games played on both mobile devices and PCs.[88] The shift to mobile, the inability to run Facebook apps within a Facebook mobile app, and changing expectations within the developer community have all conspired to stagnate the Facebook platform.

3.1   Mobile is Tougher, But Global Players Have Big Mobile Platforms

Certain technical aspects of the smartphone ecosystem put the brakes on Facebook's fast-paced "done is better than perfect" culture. On the Web, Facebook can test an innovation by rolling it out to a subset of users and gauging their reaction. But this so-called A/B testing is harder with mobile. Google and Apple release apps and updates to all of their users at once, so experimental feature testing with a subset of users is far more difficult to accomplish on a mobile phone. The app updating process is also usually slower than the instant "it's here" that occurs when visiting a Web page that automatically loads the latest version on a server, making fixes for app development mistakes more challenging to distribute.[89]

While Facebook suffered to bring its platform to mobile, it should be noted that several global messaging apps are directly accessing user address books and building their own app platforms from within iOS and Android. These include South Korea's KakaoTalk, Japan's Line, and most notably, China's massive WeChat. At roughly 550 million users in mid-2015, WeChat (owned by Shenzhen-based Tencent) is behind only to WhatsApp and Faceboko Messenger in messaging,[90] but the firm's open platform supports digital payments, shopping, gaming, banking, Uber-style taxi service,[91] and open access to third-party developers.[92] One analyst says "Weixin [what WeChat is called in China] is basically the mobile Internet for China." Food delivery startup Call-A-Chicken raised $1.6 million without a website; it doesn't need one because it does all of its business through Weixin.[93] It's worth noting that profitable Tencent had 2014 revenues of $12.9 billion, with a $200 billion market cap, numbers roughly in line with Facebook's size.[94]

FIGURE 11.4

China's fast-growing WeChat is not only the world's third largest mobile-messaging service behind WhatsApp and Facebook Messenger, it is also a platform offering digital payments, e-commerce, taxi services, and access to third-party developers.

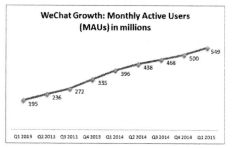

WeChat Growth: Monthly Active Users (MAUs) in millions

Source: "WeChat Monthly Active Users (MAUs)," Tech in Asia.

3.2 Messenger: A Pillar Business Building Facebook's Future

Zuckerberg claims messaging is "one of the few things that people actually do more than social networking" making it a must-win for his firm.[95] While Facebook ponied up some serious dinero for WhatsApp and Instagram, its home-grown Messanger is on a tear. Many questioned the firm's unbundling of Messenger, splitting it as a separate stand-alone from the Facebook app,[96] but today Messenger boasts 700 million users,[97] with over 1 billion downloads for Android alone.[98] In messaging, only WhatsApp is bigger.

To help Messenger realize its potential, Zuckerberg turned on the sales charm and did what many thought impossible: he poached the CEO of another thriving, high-growth, industry leading firm, PayPal. David Marcus left the helm of PayPal, where he led 15,000 employees to run Messenger's group of fewer than 100 employees. Marcus now runs PayPal like a separate business (not unlike Instagram, WhatsApp, or Oculus), but pulls in Facebook's scaled-for-a-billion-users resources when needed.[99]

The once-scrawny Messenger has bulked up, and now includes key features of other leading messaging apps: group messaging, stickers, location sharing, notifications if your message has been seen, recording and sending audio messages. It's also a Skype competitor, offering free VoIP (Voice over IP) Internet calls. Under Marcus, Messenger has also expanded to become a tool for corporations to communicate with customers. Firms can now use Facebook to send customer updates (receipts, shipping information), and can use Messenger for customer support chat. Firms are finding Messenger especially attractive in the wake of Gmail segregating "Promotions and Offers" to a separate tab, a function that often hides time-sensitive communication.[100] Such reasons may have motivated flash-sales site Zulily to sign up as one of the first firms working through Messenger.[101] If Messenger can find that delicate balance of service but not spam, it may evolve as a critical business-to-consumer communication channel.

With a PayPal guy at the helm, Messenger has also become a payments platform. The payments feature (phased in via a slow regional rollout) allows users to send and receive money with their contacts. To many this will sound a lot like Venmo, an effort that used to be under Marcus' supervision when he ran PayPal. Getting customer debit cards linked to Facebook accounts may also prime the pump for other fee-based services, such as in-ad purchases via a "Buy" button.[102]

The Payments feature in Facebook Messenger lets customers use their debit cards to exchange money with the simplicity of sending a text.

And taking a page from Asia's top messaging apps, such as WeChat and Line, Facebook has introduced a platform that allows developers to build their products that integrate directly via Messenger. The first implementation isn't great and adoption was sluggish.[103] Apps were initially tough to find, requiring users to click on the ellipses ("...") button during a chat session to uncover the Messenger app store. And offerings were skimpy (stickers, photo editors, sound-clips).[104] But games followed (first up was a Pictionary/DrawSomething-clone called Doodle Draw). The App store is overcrowded, so Messenger could help developers stand out, but only if they apply the lessons of limiting game spam learned from Facebook's maturity as a platform for browser games.[105] If Facebook can turn Messenger into a sort of must-use notification service for app and firm outreach it can also co-opt a key role of the OS and further cement the firm into all sorts of user experiences. If you can get shopping updates and info for your game-in-progress, why not travel, bank, breaking news, or anything else?

It's also worth noting that many of the lessons learned from Facebook's browser platform, and its mobile efforts, will help shed light on how to best build new platforms, like Oculus. It's pretty clear that Zuck is thinking beyond products to platforms as the bulwark of Facebook's value-add and future competitive strength.

3.3   APIs, Playing Well with Others, and Value Added: The Success and Impact of Open Graph

While Facebook's in-browser apps platform has stalled, and Facebook is looking to mobile and Messenger for further growth and innovation, another aspect of the Facebook platform, Facebook's Open Graph, continues to project Facebook's influence beyond the site itself. The initiative allows developers to link Web pages and app usage into the social graph, placing Facebook directly at the center of identity, sharing, and personalization—not only on Facebook but also across the Web. Consider some examples of what Open Graph can do.

With just a few lines of HTML code specified by Open Graph, any developer can add a Facebook "Like" button to his or her site and take advantage of the social network's power of viral distribution. When a user clicks that page's "Like" button, it would automatically send a link of that page to his or her news feed, where it has the potential to be seen by all of his or her friends. No additional sign-in is necessary as long as you logged into Facebook first (reinforcing Facebook's importance as the first stop in your Internet surfing itinerary). The effort was adopted with stunning speed. Facebook's "Like" button was served up more than one billion times across the Web in the first twenty-four hours, and over 50,000 websites signed up to add the "Like" button to their content within the first week. (Facebook now includes several new verb options beyond "Like.")[106]

Facebook also offered a system where website operators can choose to accept a user's Facebook credentials for logging in. Users like this because they can access content without the hurdle of creating a new account. Websites like it because with the burden of signing up out of the way, Facebook becomes an experimentation lubricant: "Oh, I can use my Facebook ID to sign in? Then let me try this out."

Other efforts allow firms to leverage Facebook data to make their sites more personalized. Firms around the Web can now show if a visitor's friends have "Liked" items on the site, posted comments, or performed other actions. Using this feature, Facebook users logging into Yelp can see a list of restaurants recommended by trusted friends instead of just the reviews posted by a bunch of strangers. Users of the music-streaming site Pandora can have the service customized based on music tastes pulled from their Facebook profile page. They can share stations with friends and have data flow back to update the music preferences listed in their Facebook profile pages. When you visit CNN.com, the site can pull together a list of stories recommended by friend.[107] Think about how this strengthens the social graph. While items in the news feed might quickly scroll away and disappear, that data can now be pulled up within a website, providing insight from friends when and where you're likely to want it most.

When taken together, these features enlist websites to serve as vassal states in the Facebook empire. Each of these ties makes Facebook membership more valuable by enhancing network effects, strengthening switching costs, and creating larger sets of highly personalized data to leverage.

3.4   Strategic Concerns for Platform Builders: Asset Strength, Free Riders, and Security

Facebook also allows third-party developers to create all sorts of apps to access Facebook data. Facebook feeds are now streaming through these devices: Samsung, Vizio, and Sony smart televisions; Xbox 360 and Wii game consoles; Verizon's FiOS pay-television service; and the Amazon Kindle. While Facebook might never have the time or resources to create apps that put its service on every gadget on the market, they don't need to. Developers using Facebook's access tools will gladly pick up the slack.

But there are major challenges with a more open approach—most notably, a weakening of strategic assets, revenue sharing, and security. First, let's discuss the potential for weakened assets. Mark Zuckerberg's geeks have worked hard to make their site the top choice for most of the world's social networkers and social network application developers. Right now, everyone goes to Facebook because everyone else is on Facebook. But Facebook, or any firm that opens up access to users and content, risks supporting efforts that undermine the critical assets of network effects and switching costs. If you can get Facebook content on other sites, why go to Facebook?

free rider problem

When others take advantage of a user or service without providing any sort of reciprocal benefit.

Related to asset weakening is the issue of revenue sharing. Hosting content (especially photos and rich media) is a very expensive proposition. What incentive does a site have to store data if it will just be sent to a third-party site that will run ads around this content and not share the take? Too much data portability presents a **free rider problem** in which firms mooch off of Facebook's infrastructure without offering much in return. As an example of this tension, Facebook and Twitter, firms once known for their openness, have begun to erect walls to make it more difficult for users to integrate their services. Twitter users used to be able to click on an Instagram photo and have it displayed directly in the Twitter app or in a pop-up window in Twitter-owned TweetDeck, but doing so prevents Facebook from wrapping Instagram content in messages, collecting "Likes," and—although it doesn't currently do so—running ads. Instagram also blocked user ability to find friends on Twitter, while Facebook blocked Twitter users from finding Facebook friends for the Twitter-owned video app, Vine.[108]

Finally, consider security. Allowing data streams that contain potentially private posts and photographs to flow through the Internet and have them land where you want them raise all sorts of concerns. What's to say an errant line of code doesn't provide a back door to your address book or friends list, to your messaging account, or to photos you'd hoped to only share with family? Security breaches can occur on any site, but once the data is allowed to flow freely, every site with access is, for hackers, the equivalent of a potential door to open or window to crawl through.

colossal walled garden

A closed network or single set of services controlled by one dominant firm. A closed network or single set of services controlled by one dominant firm.

Facebook's increasing dominance, long reach, and widening ambition have a lot of people worried, including the creator of the World Wide Web. Sir Tim Berners-Lee recently warned that the Web may be endangered by Facebook's **colossal walled garden**.[109] The fear is that if increasingly large parts of the Web reside inside a single (and, for the most part, closed) service, innovation, competition, and exchange may suffer.

KEY TAKEAWAYS

- Facebook has created a set of services and a platform for hosting and integrating with other services, helping the firm foster its stated mission to "make the world more open and connected."
- Facebook's platform allows the firm to further leverage the network effect. Developers creating applications create complementary benefits that have the potential to add value to Facebook beyond what the firm itself provides to its users.
- Most Facebook applications are focused on entertainment, and although Zynga's initial success has waned, several have built million-dollar-plus businesses.
- Despite the success of Facebook platform entertainment apps, the durable, long-term value of Facebook's apps platform remains to be seen. The shift to mobile and inconsistent policies toward developers has led to Facebook's app platform revenues stagnation and has fomented a degree of developer disappointment.
- Running a platform can be challenging. Copyright, security, appropriateness, free speech tensions, efforts that tarnish platform operator brands, privacy, and the potential for competition with partners can all make platform management more complex than simply creating a set of standards and releasing this to the public.
- Several major global messaging apps, including WeChat and Line, have evolved into platforms that host other apps and services, creating substantial revenue opportunities along the way.
- Facebook Messenger is evolving into a platform. Messenger now supports payments, while developers can create apps linked to Messenger and offered via the Messenger app store.
- Corporate communications via Messenger are especially attractive when e-mail may be segregated from a main inbox and quarantined in a "Promotions and Offers" folder.
- Facebook has extended its reach by allowing other Web sites to leverage the site. Using the firm's Open Graph tools, Facebook partners can add the "Like" button to encourage viral sharing of content, leverage Facebook user IDs for log-in, and tap a user's friend and feed data to personalize and customize a user's experience.
- These efforts come with risks, including enabling free riders that might exploit the firm's content without compensation and the potential for privacy and security risks.
- While Facebook's website is easy to update and push out to all users, or to test on a subset of users on a smaller scale, the firm does not have this kind of control over mobile apps.
- Some fear that Facebook may be an all-too-powerful walled garden that may stifle innovation, limit competition, and restrict the free flow of information.

QUESTIONS AND EXERCISES

1. Why is mobile app development more challenging from testing, experimentation, quality control, and maintenance perspective than browser-based services?

2. What competitive asset does the application platform initiative help Facebook strengthen? For example, how do apps make Facebook stronger when compared with rivals?

3. Have you used Facebook apps for the browser? For Messenger? Which are your favorites, or why don't you use them? What makes some Facebook apps successful?

4. Leverage your experience or conduct additional research. Are there developers who you feel have abused the Facebook app network? Why? What is Facebook's responsibility (if any) to control such abuse?

5. Why might some e-commerce firms be inclined to use Facebook Messenger to overcome limitations in e-mail? Explain.

6. How are global messaging apps like WeChat and Line behaving like platforms? Do additional research (online, with your own experience if you've used these services, or by interviewing a colleague who is a user), find examples and share them with your class.

7. How is Facebook Messenger evolving into a platform? Do you think they are doing a good job at this? Why or why not?

8. Cite effective examples you've seen of Facebook features being incorporated into other websites (or if you haven't seen any, do some background research to uncover such efforts). Why do the efforts you've highlighted "work" or why are they ineffective? Do they benefit users and if so, how? Does everyone benefit? Is anyone at risk? If so, explain the risks.

9. What risks does running a platform open up to a platform owner like Facebook? What challenges has it encountered, and how did it deal with these challenges?

10. Why have Facebook and Twitter been erecting walls that block users from integrating these services? What is the free rider problem? Give real examples of this phenomenon in social networks and digital media.

11. What is a walled garden? Facebook has been called a walled garden. Name other firms that might also be described in this term. In your opinion, is Facebook a walled garden? Why or why not? What might be the consequences if the firm is widely viewed as being more powerful and less open?

4. ADVERTISING AND SOCIAL NETWORKS: A CHALLENGING LANDSCAPE BUT A BIG PAYOFF

LEARNING OBJECTIVES

1. **Describe the differences between the Facebook and Google ad models.**
2. **Understand how content adjacency and user attention create challenges for social network operators and firms seeking to advertise on social networks.**
3. **Explain the hunt versus hike metaphor, contrast the relative success of ad performance on search compared to social networks, and understand the factors behind the latter's struggles.**
4. **Recognize how firms are leveraging social networks for brand building, product engagement, and driving purchase traffic.**
5. **Understand Facebook's considerable advantages and efforts with respect to ad targeting.**
6. **Compare Facebook's conventional advertising metrics with those of Google, as well as Facebook's mobile app install program. Understand the unique opportunity and potential challenges Facebook faces as it expands its app install program.**
7. **Recognize the challenges that mobile advertising presents for Facebook and understand why mobile is also a potential opportunity.**

If Facebook is going to continue to grow and give away its services for free, it needs to make money somehow. Right now the bulk of revenue comes from advertising. Fortunately for the firm, online advertising is hot. For years, online advertising has been the only major media category that has seen an increase in spending (see Chapter 18). Firms spend more advertising online than they do on radio, magazine, cable television, or newspaper ads.[110] But not all Internet advertising is created equal. For Facebook, the size of the firm's market has created a money-gushing bonanza, but we're not yet talking about Google money–not even close. Social has its challenges and we'll dive deeper into what's different, what's tougher, what's being tried, and what's working.

First a look at what's different about search advertising and social ads.

Firms face two key challenges when advertising on social media: **content adjacency** and user attention.

4.1 Content Adjacency Challenges: Do You Really Want Your Brand Next to *That*?

The *content adjacency* problem refers to concern over where a firm's advertisements will run. Consider all of the questionable titles in social networking groups. Do advertisers really want their ads running alongside conversations that are racy, offensive, illegal, or that may even mock their products? This potential juxtaposition is a major problem with any site offering ads adjacent to free-form social media. Summing up industry wariness, one Procter & Gamble manager said, "What in heaven's name made you think you could monetize the [screen] real estate in which somebody is breaking up with their girlfriend?" [111]

The issue of content adjacency came to a head when Facebook saw several blue-chip advertisers, including the UK media giant BSkyB and retail behemoth Marks and Spencer, pull their ads after they ran on a sexually themed Facebook page that may also have contained photos of minors.[112] Another campaign, led by several groups raising awareness of online hate speech and misogynistic content, resulted in tens of thousands of tweets and thousands of e-mails sent to firms whose advertisements were showing up next to "particularly vile content."[113] These crises caused Facebook to update its guidelines on hate speech; improve training for complaint reviewers; work more closely with groups concerned about hateful, graphic content on the social network; and restrict ads from appearing next to pages and groups that contain violent, graphic, or sexual content.[114] An IDC report suggests that it's because of content adjacency that "brand advertisers largely consider user-generated content as low-quality, brand-unsafe inventory" for running ads.[115] Dispelling concerns hinges on a combination of evolving public attitudes toward content adjacency issues in social media, as well as better technology and policing of the context in which ads appear.

4.2 Attention Challenges: *The Hunt* versus *the Hike*

Now let's look at the user attention problem and the difference between Google (search) and Facebook (social).

Users of Google and other search sites are on a hunt—a task-oriented expedition to collect information that will drive a specific action. Search users are expressing intent in search. They want to learn something, buy something, research a problem, or get a question answered. To the extent that the hunt overlaps with ads, it works. Just searched on a medical term? Google will show you an ad from a drug company. Looking for a toy? You'll see Google ads from eBay sellers and other online shops. Even better, Google only charges text advertisers when a user clicks through. No clicks? The ad runs at no cost to the advertiser. From a return on investment perspective, this is extraordinarily efficient. How often do users click on Google ads? Enough for this to be the single most profitable activity among any Internet firm. In 2014, Google revenue topped $66 billion. Profits were nearly $14.5 billion, almost all of this from pay-per-click ads (see **Chapter 18** for more details). That means Google earned as much in profit, as Facebook did in revenue, and is nearly five *times* more profitable.

While users go to Google to hunt, they go to Facebook as if they were going on a hike—they have a rough idea of what they'll encounter, but this often lacks the easy-to-monetize, directed intent of search. They're there to explore and look around and enjoy the sights (or site). They've usually allocated time for fun, and they don't want to leave the terrain when they're having conversations, looking at photos or videos, and checking out updates from friends. The owner of Superfly Kids, which pulls in over $2 million a year selling hero outfits to children and spends the bulk of the firm's online ad budget on Google, puts it this way "No one is searching Facebook for superhero capes."[116]

These usage patterns are reflected in click-through rates. Google users click on ads around one to two percent of the time (and at a much higher rate when searching for product information). At Facebook, click-throughs can register as low as 0.02 percent (although these can also go higher with targeting).[117] Such rates vary widely over time and by context, but most reports show a dramatic performance (one or two orders of magnitude) on CTR metrics when comparing Google and Facebook.[118]

Most banner ads don't charge per click but rather CPM, or cost per thousand impressions (the M representing the roman numeral for one thousand). An impression is measured each time an ad is served to a user for viewing, i.e. each time an ad appears on someone's screen. But Facebook banner ads performed so poorly that the firm pulled them in early 2010.[119] Facebook offers what one observer calls "the lowest cost per 1,000 impressions ad in history," often selling for 10 to 25 cents per 1,000 impressions.[120] That's a rate that's only about 1 percent of television ad rates (note that Facebook also offers advertisers cost-per-click and cost-per-action, as well as impression-based, or CPM, options).[121] As contrast, information and news-oriented sites do much better, particularly if these sites draw in a valuable and highly targeted audience. The social networking blog *Mashable* has CPM rates ranging between seven and thirty-three dollars. *Technology Review* magazine boasts a CPM of seventy dollars. *TechTarget*, a Web publisher focusing on technology professionals, has been able to command CPM rates of $100 and above, fueling that firm's IPO. Even other social sites show strong performance. Pinterest CPM rates are said to be between $30 and $40.[122] Facebook's low ad engagement rates are also reflected in chart in Figure 10.4, which shows average revenue per user (ARPU) figures for Google, Facebook, and Twitter. While a Facebook user is about twice as valuable in terms of revenue delivery as someone using Twitter, the chart also shows that all that time spent on Facebook is worth only about one-sixth on a per-user basis as time spent on Google.

FIGURE 11.5

Average revenue per user (2014).

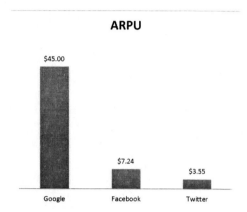

Source: P. Garner, *"Average revenue per user is an important growth driver,"* Market Realist, Feb. 11, 2015.

While Facebook has, at times, been the Web's most visited destination, its user base generates far less cash on a per-person basis than Google does. Facebook's ARPU is one-sixth Google's, but more than twice that of Twitter's.[123]

4.3   Facebook Ads: Amid Concerns, a Massive Potential Upside

Worries over Facebook's ad model were underscored when growth slowed in the two quarters prior to the firm's IPO.[124] There have also been significant concerns regarding the increasing shift in Facebook user traffic from the high-value ad real estate of the desktop, to the lower-value, lower-performing ads on mobile devices. There is also uncertainty as the firm tries to leverage the social graph. According to Facebook's own research, "an average Facebook user with five hundred friends actively follows the news on only forty of them, communicates with twenty, and keeps in close touch with about ten. Those with smaller networks follow even fewer."[125] That might not be enough critical mass to offer real, differentiable value to paying advertisers, and interest in deepening connections among users with "value-shallow" social graphs may in part have motivated Facebook's mishandled attempts to encourage more public data sharing. The advantages of leveraging the friend network hinge on increased sharing and trust, a challenge for a firm that has had so many high-profile privacy stumbles.

Despite these concerns, Facebook's recent performance seems to be dispelling doubt and silencing skeptics. By the end of 2014 Facebook had racked up ten straight quarters beating Wall Street earnings estimates. The first quarter of 2015 would have made it 11 straight, had there not been issues with foreign exchange rates.[126] Facebook's ability to better manage supply and demand to improve pricing, leverage data for targeting, and create lucrative new ad products and formats have kept growth engines oiled and fueled for expansion. And no one doubt's Facebook's mobile ad muscle now that mobile brings in more than 70 percent of the firm's ad revenue.[127]

4.4   Precise Targeting

First is the advertising appeal of precise targeting. Large advertising networks have tried to meticulously track users to develop a profile of their demographics, likes, and interests. Facebook knows all about you because you've told it the details—your age, the things you're enthusiastic about, where you live, your relationship status. This opens up all sorts of targeting opportunities to even the smallest of advertisers. In one example, a wedding photography studio targeted ads at women aged twenty-four to thirty whose relationship status was engaged—that's like sticking a flyer in front of precisely everyone you want to reach and not wasting a dime on anyone else. The firm, CM Photographics, reports that just $600 in Facebook ads resulted in nearly $40,000 in revenue.[128]

In a significant "big data" play for more accurate consumer targeting, Facebook now allows advertisers to combine externally collected data with Facebook's insights. Partnerships with third-party data providers Acxiom, Datalogix, and Epsilon (see Chapter 15 for more on such third-party data providers) allow data from offline purchases and loyalty programs to be used in targeting a vendors' ad campaigns that run on Facebook. As *AdAge* points out, "Use a loyalty card for discounts at the drug store? The ads you see on Facebook could start looking familiar."[129] Other Facebook initiatives will allow brands to upload e-mails, phone numbers, and addresses from their proprietary CRM (customer relationship management) databases to show ads to existing customers who are on Facebook. And while a big, combined database of offline and online activity may raise privacy concerns, Facebook claims it uses a technique called "hashing" that can find a match without allowing Facebook data to be intelligible to data vendors, or vice versa.[130]

Facebook, Help Get Me a Job!

The news is filled with stories about employers scouring Facebook to screen potential hires. But one creative job seeker turned the tables and used Facebook to make it easier for firms to find him. Recent MBA graduate Eric Barker, a talented former screenwriter with experience in the film and gaming industries, bought ads promoting himself on Facebook, setting them up to run only on the screens of users identified as coming from firms he'd like to work for. In this way, someone Facebook identified as being from Microsoft would see an ad from Eric declaring "I Want to Be at Microsoft" along with an offer to click and learn more. The cost to run the ads was usually less than $5 a day. Said Barker, "I could control my bid price and set a cap on my daily spend. Starbucks put a bigger dent in my wallet than promoting myself online." The ads got tens of thousands of impressions and hundreds of clicks, and dozens of people called offering assistance. Today, Eric Barker is gainfully employed at a "dream job" in the video game industry.[131]

FIGURE 11.6

Eric Barker used Facebook to advertise himself to prospective employers.

I want to be at Microsoft

Hi, my name is Eric and my dream is to work for Microsoft. I'm a MBA/MFA with a strong media background. Can you help me? Please click!

4.5   Mobile Revenue on the Upswing

Also despite concerns about mobile advertising, the story seems to be getting better. As of the first quarter of 2015, 87 percent of Facebook's monthly active users (MAUs) visited using mobile devices.[132] Fortunately Facebook has proven it can squeeze more money from mobile users, shrinking the gap between its mobile audience and mobile revenue (just 15 percentage points at the end of 2014, down from 38 percentage points just two years earlier).[133] By cracking the mobile ad code, Facebook has also been able to earn more from its global audience, with 51 percent of ad dollars now coming from outside the US.[134] Mobile users provide Facebook with a steadier flow of customer interaction throughout the day. One survey found that the average smartphone user checks Facebook fourteen times a day and that most check their phones immediately after waking up in the morning.[135] As for upside, also consider that Instagram only began running ads in November 2013,[136] and as of this writing, WhatsApp has yet to run an ad. That leaves a lot of room for new ad growth, and results in Facebook mobile suggest the firm understands how to run mobile ads without excessively annoying users.

4.6   Ads in Feeds: Better Performance Even as Fewer Ads are Shown

Facebook was initially reluctant to place ads in the news feed, but such ads have proven to be hugely successful for the firm. Unlike search ads, ads in the news feed move beyond the easy-to-ignore real estate on the right side of the desktop and instead put a message right in the middle of the exact screen real estate that a user is paying attention to. News feed ads have been shown to deliver a twenty-six times higher return on investment than sidebar ads.[137] And news feed ads are evolving with new video ad offerings. One survey found that more people age eighteen to twenty-four access Facebook during evening primetime hours than watch ABC, CBS, NBC, and Fox combined.[138] Advertisers that are losing audience reach in declining primetime numbers are likely to shift more ad dollars to channels where desirable demographics are spending more time.

Facebook has also leveraged a bit of Econ 101 to juice profits. Instead of annoying users by saturating their feeds with ads, Facebook has actually cut back on the percentage of ads that appear in feeds. This has created an inventory scarcity that allowed the firm to jack up prices as firms compete for a slot (i.e. more demand for limited supply). The net result: a better user experience and higher profits.[139] Layer on some data for targeting and firms will pay even more for what (hopefully) users find to be more appealing promotions.

4.7   Advertising Experiments Continue: Some Falter while New Winners Emerge

Facebook's ad growth continues even as the firm has decided to kill once-promising social ads known as sponsored stories (see this chapter's section titled "Reputation Damage, Increased Scrutiny, and Recovery—Learning from Facebook's Frequent Privacy Missteps"). These ads featured the usernames and photos of friends in ads for products they may have liked or interacted with online, but user concern combined with government ruling led Facebook to abandon the lucrative effort.[140] While sponsored stories have been pulled, a new, money-gushing ad line has emerged—one that draws directly from the explosion in mobile usage.

App Installs–Big Bucks, for Now…

Have you noticed an increase in Facebook ads prompting you to install an app? Turns out that while many advertisers pay Facebook CPM rates in the pennies, game app developers are "willing to pay as much as $8, $10 or $20" to run highly targeted ads. Such ads can be billed on cost per thousand impression (CPM), cost per click (CPC), or cost per install (CPI) models, and some Facebook customers are willing to regularly pay as much as $10 per app install. Firms such as King, Disney, and Warner Bros. are apparently "spending millions of dollars per month marketing their games" on Facebook.[141] The Facebook Mobile App Install program is led by Deborah Liu and is "hitting an annual run rate in the hundreds of millions of dollars."[142] Why spend so much? Targeted ads increase the chance that Facebook's data and reach can be used to catch a "whale," the gaming industry term for someone who spends big on in-app purchases. Whales make up only a small percentage of overall users, but they represent the vast majority of digital goods sales.[143] And Facebook has lots of whale-targeting data, including a history of which users have paid for in-app purchases on Facebook, who has installed apps, which apps they've installed, whether these apps are played in Facebook, and more. There are risks in relying too heavily on the app industry. Leaked e-mails from the Sony hack uncovered communication from Snapchat CEO Evan Spiegel warning these direct-response ads were funded by venture capitalists overfunding startups in their quest to find the next big thing.[144] Should interest in (or funding for) app markets wane, this now lucrative revenue stream could wither.

An Ad Network for Facebook. Can it Best Google?

Ad revenue is also likely to increase now that tweaks in Facebook's News Feed post-selection algorithm are limiting the reach of organic posts from firm fan pages.

Posts from fan pages used to be a free promotion source for any organization hoping to reach the news feeds of those who "liked" their product. While posts have long been curated by Facebook algorithms, such posts used to reach about 16 percent of a page's fans. Sources report that organic reach from fan posts has dropped to a range from 6.15 percent to as low as 2 percent.[145] While disappointing to marketers who have worked hard to cultivate a fan base on Facebook, it can't come as a surprise that Facebook would one day limit the free-ride on its service and attempt to commercialize fan pages by promoting post reach. Among the many ad products Facebook offers are "Promoted Posts," which increase the reach of an item that a firm shares. Expect firms with a substantial Facebook following, especially those that have seen solid results from past campaigns, to boost their advertising as a result.

More upside potential comes from Facebook's advertising network. Google earns about 20 percent of its revenue from ads it runs on third-party sites (referred to as the Google's ad network). Next time you search the Web, look for advertisements labeled "Ads by Google." Google serves up these ads and splits the take with website operators. Up until mid-2014, Facebook only ran ads within Facebook properties, but with the launch of the Facebook Audience Network, the firm can make money off its billion-plus users, even when they're not on Facebook's own sites and apps.[146] Mobile app developers can, too. All developers need to do is put a snippet of Facebook code into their apps. Zuckerberg's firm will line up advertisers, select and run targeted ads based on its massive knowledge of individual users and user preferences, measure ad performance, and collect payments to forward on to its partners (after taking a cut, of course). While your Facebook data will be used to target ads outside the service, the firm's ad network doesn't give advertisers or publishers any personal data, it simply performs matching on its own servers, then delivers the appropriately targeted ad to the app. And users can opt-out of any ad tracking, as well.[147] Some think that a Facebook ad network might be able to offer ad targeting that performs *better* than Google's AdSense product. Google targets ads on other Web sites based largely on keywords found on those sites, also using details it can glean from tracking a person's Web browsing history (see **Chapter 18** for details). Facebook can do all this, but it could also add in all sorts of data from the dark Web that Google can't see: data from a user's social activity, their highly accurate personal profile, and more. As an added bonus, Facebook can use its ad network to boost revenue without increasing the density of ads in its own products—another win for usability.

Content Providers, Step Deeper Inside My Walled Garden

Facebook has also offered to host and serve content on its own servers. The "Instant Articles" service helps vendors overcome the problem of slow page loads and content that's poorly formatted for mobile. Articles usually take an average of eight seconds to load, often enough to prompt users to quit, and causing content providers to miss out on the ad revenue from a page view. Caching articles on Facebook's servers allows pages to load ten times faster,[148] and articles are precisely formatted for display on a user's mobile device, even offering special formats like maps, zoomable photos, and video. Publishers have the option to fill their ad inventory themselves and keep all of the ad revenue (Facebook does have some guidelines on the format of ads that can be displayed), but the Facebook Audience Network will gladly line up advertisers for any unsold inventory the firm wants to make available, for a 30 percent cut for Zuck. Clicks will be recorded by comScore, reflecting traffic as if users visited a firm's site, and shared links will also refer back to a website rather than to the article cached on Facebook.[149] Initial big media partners include *The New York Times*, BuzzFeed, *The Atlantic*, *The Guardian*, NBC News, and National Geographic, but it's expected Facebook will open up "Instant Articles" to more firms. Facebook says it won't play favorites with "Instant Article" partners, but as TechCrunch speculates: "The animated Instant Article covers are certainly more eye-catching than traditional static blurbs, and those clicks tell the feed to show a story to more people."[150] Video on Facebook is booming and presents yet another content serving (and ad sales) opportunity that Facebook can develop and exploit. Facebook serves as many clips as YouTube in part because it's handled so well. Sound-off clips cut the annoyance while piquing interest, making the feed look "like a Harry Potter newspaper come to life."[151]

Some worry "Instant Articles" reinforce Facebook's walled garden and give the firm even more power over how journalism is distributed and seen, but if Facebook can placate concerns and deliver value to partners, it may be able to convince more to allow its ad network to serve ads on their content, as well.

Better Advertisement Everywhere. What's Up Next?

As for more speculative opportunities for ad market growth, consider the longer-term possibilities for social television. Facebook almost certainly wants to play a starring role in your living room, making the TV a platform for social activity: video chat, serving targeted ads, social entertainment recommend-ations, games, and all sorts of commerce. It will be tough to navigate the tensions of bandwidth-cap-ping cable guys, channel owners, and hardware firms keen to build their own platform, but Zuckerberg has Reed Hastings on his board. No one has built a further-reaching platform with consumer electron-ics firms than the Netflix CEO, and he should provide keen insight as Facebook spreads further. And don't count out Oculus. Those court-side immersive experiences Zuckerberg imagined would go great with deeply engaging ads, as well.

Facebook continues to refine its ad offerings, targeting, and reach potential, and the recent and continued surge in ad growth suggests that the firm's advertising customers are mostly satisfied and coming back for more. It's also worth noting that big advertisers aren't the only ones Facebook (and rivals) are after. Zuckerberg's firm has been used by over 1 million different advertisers, and many of these are small businesses using the firm's self-service ad platform.[152] Results-focused offerings for these clients, many of whom increasingly view a Facebook presence as being as important or more im-portant than a standard Web page, bode well for future revenue growth.[153] With more than half of Facebook's revenue comes from outside the United States[154] rising worldwide mobile engagement and a growing middle class in many emerging markets where Facebook operates, point to revenue forecasts that suggest the continued trajectory of up and to the right.

KEY TAKEAWAYS

- Issues of content adjacency and user attention can make social networking ads less attractive than ads running alongside search and professionally produced content sites.
- Google enjoys significantly higher click-through rates than Facebook. Rates are lower since users of social sites are there to engage friends, not to hunt for products. They are less likely to be drawn away by clicks.
- Display ads are often charged based on impression. Social networks also offer lower CPM rates than many other, more targeted websites. Facebook also sells ads on a cost-per-click, cost-per-action, and (with apps) a cost-per-install basis.
- Facebook ads can be precisely targeted since the firm has a large amount of actual data on users' self-expressed likes, interests, and demographics. Facebook has also taken steps to allow third-party databases to be incorporated into targeting ads on site while preventing the possibility that databases can be combined to reveal online information to offline partners or vice versa.
- Mobile traffic is growing, and despite initial concerns over Facebook's ability to find growth in this space, the firm's mobile ads in particular have grown at a tremendous rate and are solidly profitable.
- Ads in the news feed have the advantage of falling directly within the screen real estate that a consumer is focused on. As such, they are considered superior to ads that may occupy easy-to-ignore spaces on the right-hand side of a content window.
- Facebook has cut the number of ads it shows its users, and the scarcity this builds, along with better targeting, has allowed the firm to charge more. This has improved the user experience while improving profits.
- While Facebook has cancelled some experiments (notably "sponsored stories" ads that incorporated a user's profile information and actions into ad products), the firm has found success in mobile install ads. Some gaming firms are willing to spend as much as $10 per install for these ads.
- The Facebook Audience Network provide a way for firms to allow Facebook to gather advertisers, target and serve ads on third-party sites and apps, and collect revenue for them.
- "Instant Articles" allow Facebook to host, cache, and serve content from media firms. Faster article loads should increase article engagement and allow partners to make more money. Facebook hopes partners may be more inclined to use its ad network, as well. Video ads cached and served on Facebook are also booming, with Facebook serving as many videos a day as YouTube.
- Some are concerned that allowing Facebook to host and serve content reinforces Facebook's Walled Garden, where users rarely venture out, and where Facebook grows even more powerful as a vital partner in content distribution.

QUESTIONS AND EXERCISES

1. What is the content adjacency problem? Search for examples of firms that have experienced embarrassment due to content adjacency. Describe them, why they occurred, and if site operators could have done something to reduce the likelihood of these issues occurring.

2. What kinds of websites are most susceptible to content adjacency? Are news sites? Why or why not? What sorts of technical features might act as breeding grounds for content adjacency problems?

3. How are most display ads billed? What acronym is used to describe the pricing of most display ads?

4. How are most text ads on Google billed? What's the appeal for advertisers?

5. Contrast Facebook and Google click-through rates. Contrast Facebook's typical CPMs with CPMs at professional content sites. Why the discrepancy?

6. How do costs and billing models for mobile app installs differ from conventional ad costs on Facebook? Why are game firms willing to pay so much to acquire a customer?

7. If a firm removed user social media content because it was offensive to an advertiser, what kinds of problems might this create? When (if ever) should a firm remove or take down user content?

8. Has Facebook been improving the organic reach of brands online or reducing this reach? What are the implications for brands with fan pages and for Facebook?

9. Describe an innovative marketing campaign that has leveraged Facebook or other social networking sites. What factors made this campaign work? Are all firms likely to have this sort of success? Why or why not?

10. Have advertisers ever targeted you when displaying ads on Facebook? How were you targeted? What did you think of the effort?

11. How do you feel about Facebook allowing third-party databases to be used for ad targeting on the firm's site? Does this concern you? Why or why not? What is the upside and potential downside for Facebook, advertisers, and users for this sort of targeting?

12. What were the concerns with Facebook and mobile advertising, and how have Facebook mobile ads been performing for the firm?

13. Why do ads in feeds perform better than conventional display ads?

14. How has Facebook leveraged "Econ 101" to improve the user experience while improving ad profitability?

15. What are the benefits of Facebook hosting and serving content via "Instant Articles" and video caching? What are the concerns?

16. Why do some speculate that the Facebook Audience Network advertising network is potentially better at targeting users than Google's ad network?

5.   A PLATFORM PLAYER THAT MOVES FAST AND BREAKS THINGS: WHAT ALL MANAGERS CAN LEARN FROM FACEBOOK'S MISTAKES, RESPONSES, AND PURSUIT OF NEW OPPORTUNITIES

LEARNING OBJECTIVES

1. **Recognize how user issues and procedural implementation can derail even well-intentioned information systems efforts.**

2. **Recognize the risks in being a pioneer associated with new media efforts and understand how missteps led to Facebook and its partners being embarrassed (and in some cases sued) as a result of system design and deployment issues.**

3. **Examine the challenges that leveraging potentially sensitive consumer data, altering privacy settings, and changing terms of service may present to innovative firms. Understand the difference between opt-in and opt-out efforts, the breadth of possible consumer reaction, and impact of such policies on a business. Study Facebook's response to concern and crisis and learn tactics that may be employed to recover lost credibility with consumers, the government, and partners.**

4. **Highlight areas of opportunity and concern regarding Facebook's designs on emerging market growth.**

The road around Facebook's campus is named "Hacker Way," and concrete letters in the firm's central courtyard spell the word "HACK" (the term used by software engineers to refer to a clever solution, rather than the negative connotation used in security circles). Graffiti-laden walls underscore that Facebook is a creative and edgy place, and slogans like "Done is Better than Perfect" and "Move Fast, Break Things" are cultural signposts that direct staff to keep an eye on what has helped make the firm successful. This is, after all, a business built on network effects, and in Facebook's world, it's either be quick or be dead. And yes, sometimes things break. A mistake by one engineer once accidentally released all of Facebook's top-secret projects.[155] Oops! While the firm does strive to reduce errors, and Zuck has shifted slightly (crowing the less catchy "move fast with stable infrastructure"[156]), Facebook's "no-beta" culture tolerates mistakes on the road to progress. Even new hires in the firm's engineering boot camp work hands-on with the actual site. Code changes are rolled out to progressively larger groups so that user reaction and major bugs can be dealt with, but well-received updates can make it out to 1 billion users within hours. The willingness to take bold risks on new initiatives has allowed the firm to push forward with innovations that many users initially resisted but eventually embraced (e.g. the news feed, the messenger app). But moving fast with less forethought has also led to alienating gaffes that have damaged the firm's reputation. By examining some of Facebook's mistakes, managers can raise their internal awareness of pitfalls associated with implementing technology initiatives, and by watching Facebook's responses to missteps, managers can gain insight into effective course correction if initial efforts run into trouble.

FIGURE 11.7

Facebook's campus is full of signs and slogans to reinforce the firm's risk-taking, move-fast, hacker-centric culture.

Got a Great Team? Break 'Em Up and Spread 'Em Around!

Building such a great infrastructure requires a super-smart and super-creative talent base. In order to keep the ideas humming, Facebook regularly rotates technical staff. Every eighteen months employees are required to leave their teams and work on something different for at least a month. Getting people into new groups helps the firm's geniuses more broadly share their knowledge, generates idea flow, and prevents managers from developing fiefdoms. The firm also runs legendary hackathons, all-night sessions with one key rule: no one is allowed to work on what they normally do. Engineers blue-sky innovate on something new and show it to Zuckerberg and a senior staff brain trust, who then decide which projects go forward.[157]

5.1   Beacon Busted—Management Lessons on Tech Planning and Deployment

The launch, public outcry, resulting PR disaster, and eventual repeal of Facebook's high-touted "Beacon" platform provide a lesson for managers regarding the peril in introducing system modifications without considering their full implications. For all of Facebook's high-speed, innovation-fueled growth, moving fast does have a downside when things break.

The Beacon effort started from a simple question: Could the energy and virulent nature of social networks be harnessed to offer truly useful consumer information to its users? Word of mouth is considered the most persuasive (and valuable) form of marketing,[158] and Facebook was a giant word-of-mouth machine. What if the firm worked with vendors and grabbed consumer activity at the point of purchase to put it into the news feed and post it to a user's profile? If you watched a video, bought a cool product, or dropped something in your wish list, your buddies could get a heads-up, and they might ask you about it. The person being asked feels like an expert, the person with the question gets a frank opinion, and the vendor providing the data just might get another sale. The effort, named Facebook Beacon, looked like a homerun. Some forty e-commerce sites signed up, including Fandango, eBay, Blockbuster, Travelocity, Zappos, and the *New York Times*. Zuckerberg was so confident of the effort that he stood before a group of Madison Avenue ad executives and declared that Beacon would represent a "once-in-a-hundred-years" fundamental change in the way media works.

User reaction to Beacon was swift and brutal. The commercial activity of Facebook users began showing up without their consent. The biggest problem with Beacon was that it was "opt-out" instead of "opt-in." Facebook (and its partners) assumed users would agree to sharing data in their feeds. A pop-up box did appear briefly on most sites supporting Beacon, but it disappeared after a few seconds.[159] Many users, blind to these sorts of alerts, either clicked through or ignored the warnings. And, well, there are some purchases you might not want to broadcast to the world.

"Facebook Ruins Christmas for Everyone!" screamed one headline from MSNBC.com. Another, from *U.S. News and World Report*, read "How Facebook Stole Christmas." The *Washington Post* ran the story of Sean Lane, a twenty-eight-year-old tech support worker from Waltham, Massachusetts, who got a message from his wife just two hours after he bought a ring on Overstock.com. "Who is this ring for?" she wanted to know. Facebook had posted a feed not only that her husband had bought the ring but also that he got it for a 51 percent discount—making him look cheap!

Overstock.com quickly announced that it was halting participation in Beacon until Facebook changed its practice to opt in.[160] MoveOn.org started a Facebook group and online petition protesting Beacon. The Center for Digital Democracy and the U.S. Public Interest Research Group asked the Federal Trade Commission to investigate Facebook's advertising programs. And a Dallas woman sued Blockbuster for violating the Video Privacy Protection Act (a 1998 U.S. law prohibiting unauthorized access to video store rental records).

Zuckerberg would later say regarding Beacon, "We've made a lot of mistakes building this feature, but we've made even more with how we've handled them. We simply did a bad job with this release, and I apologize for it."[161] Beacon was eventually shut down, and $9.5 million was donated to various privacy groups as part of its legal settlement.[162] There's not much evidence that Beacon's failure had any notable impact on Facebook's growth. But perhaps a bigger problem was that many of those forty A-list e-commerce sites that took a gamble with Facebook now had their names associated with a privacy screw-up that made headlines worldwide. Not a good thing for one's career. A manager so burned isn't likely to sign up first for the next round of experimentation.

From the Prada example in Chapter 3 we learned that savvy managers look beyond technology and consider complete information systems—not just the hardware and software of technology but also the interactions among the data, people, and procedures that make up (and are impacted by) information systems. Beacon's failure is a cautionary tale of what can go wrong if users fail to broadly consider the impact and implications of an information system on all those it can touch. Technology's reach is often farther, wider, and more significantly impactful than we originally expect.

5.2 Reputation Damage, Increased Scrutiny, and Recovery: Learning from Facebook's Frequent Privacy Missteps

When Facebook pushes up against the average user's data creep-out tolerance, it creates a perception that the company acts brazenly, without considering user needs, and is fast and loose on privacy and user notification. And when a firm suffers damage to its reputation, brand, and credibility, future scrutiny will be even higher.

When Facebook changed its Terms of Service (TOS), *New York* magazine ran a cover story summarizing the changes: "We can do anything we want with your content, forever," even if a user deletes their account and leaves the service.[163] A similar backlash happened with another TOS change, this time when Facebook-acquired Instagram seemed to be informing users that the firm would now be allowed to incorporate user photos into advertisements.[164] In another dustup, the decision to launch many of the new Open Graph features as "opt-out" instead of "opt-in" immediately drew the concern of lawmakers.[165] And amid concerns of overstepping bounds with ad products, a US District judge has granted final approval to a settlement fining Facebook $20 million for using users' names and profile photos in its "Sponsored Stories" advertising program without their approval.[166]

In all cases, activists organized; the press crafted juicy, attention-grabbing headlines; and the firm was forced once again to backtrack. But here's where others can learn from Facebook's missteps and response. The firm was contrite and reached out to explain and engage users. In the case of Facebook's earlier TOS changes, old TOS were reinstated, and the firm posted a proposed new version that gave the firm broad latitude in leveraging user content without claiming ownership. The firm also renounced the right to use content if a user closed their Facebook account. Facebook also backpedaled on the Instagram TOS changes, and when announcing Instagram video, cofounder Kevin Systrom made it clear that users "will own the rights to the videos they create and can control how they are distributed by specifying who has permission to view the content."[167] Amid the crush of negative publicity over Open Graph's launch, the firm was forced to quickly roll out simplified privacy management controls. Facebook has also dropped "Sponsored Stories," advertising that used user photos and other information without their consent,[168] even though such ads were proving highly effective and bringing in north of $1 million in ad revenue a day.[169] And Facebook has backtracked from earlier policies that had set post sharing to "Public." Now new Facebook users' posts will automatically be set to "Friends," meaning only friends can see your information.[170] A "Privacy Shortcuts" menu now graces the upper right-hand corner of the desktop browser version of Facebook, and the firm has rolled out the "Privacy Checkup" feature, where a blue cartoon dinosaur pops up in a dialog-box audit stating "We just wanted to make sure you're sharing with the right people." Critics point out that Facebook was forced to take steps back from a stance that prodded users toward more public sharing as such policies became acutely at odds with user desires. Younger users, in particular, have begun spending more time outside Facebook.com, in privacy-friendly services like WhatsApp and Snapchat and anonymous-sharing apps like Secret and Whisper.[171] But customers that ignore the voice of the customer will suffer as more attractive alternatives come to market.

Facebook also experimented with allowing consumers to vote on proposed changes. Despite the uproar, only about 1 percent of Facebook users eventually voted on proposed changes, leading Facebook to table voting in favor of focus groups, Q&A sessions, and nonbinding polls.[172] While low voter turnout doesn't necessarily mean users don't care, these events also demonstrate that a tempest can be generated by a relatively small number of passionate users. Firms ignore the vocal and influential at their own peril!

In Facebook's defense, the broad TOS changes were probably more a form of legal protection than any nefarious attempt to annex and exploit user data. The US legal environment does require that explicit terms be defined and communicated to users, even if these are tough for laypeople to understand. But a "trust us" attitude toward user data doesn't work, particularly for a firm considered to have committed ham-handed gaffes in the past. Managers take note: in the era of social media, your actions are now subject to immediate and sustained review. Violate the public trust, and expect the equivalent of a high-powered investigative microscope examining your every move and a very public airing of the findings.

For Facebook, that microscope will be in place for at least the next two decades. In a deal with the US Federal Trade Commission, Facebook settled a series of governmental inquiries related to issues such as the ones outlined above—events that Zuckerberg admits added up to "a bunch of mistakes" made by the firm. Facebook agreed to undergo twenty years of regular third-party privacy audits, and to a host of additional restrictions including getting users' consent before making privacy changes and making content from deleted profiles unavailable after thirty days. If Facebook fails to comply with these terms, it will face fines of $16,000 per violation per day.[173]

Facebook's struggles show the tension faced by any firm that wants to collect data to improve the user experience (and hopefully make money along the way). Opt-out and immediately imposed policy changes can guarantee the largest possible reach for a given effort, and that's key in realizing the benefits of network effects, data, and scale. Making efforts opt-in creates the very real risk that not enough users will sign up and that the reach and impact of these kinds of initiatives will be limited.[174] *Fast Company* calls this the *paradox of privacy*, saying, "We want some semblance of control over our personal data, even if we likely can't be bothered to manage it."[175] Evidence suggests that most people are accepting some degree of data sharing as long as they know that they can easily turn it off if they want to. For example, when Google rolled out ads that tracked users across the network of websites running Google ads, the service also provided a link in each ad that allowed users to visit an "ad preferences manager" to learn how they were being profiled, to change settings, and to opt out (see Chapter 10). It turns out only one in fifteen visitors to the ad preferences manager ended up opting out completely.[176] However, a Pew Research study found that nearly nine in ten Internet users have taken steps online to remove or mask their digital footprints on some level.[177] Managers seeking to leverage data should learn from the examples of Facebook and Google and be certain to offer clear controls that empower user choice.

5.3 Challenges of Going Global: Low ARPUs, Legitimate Rivals, and Unreachable Users

crowdsourcing

The act of taking a job traditionally performed by a designated agent (usually an employee) and outsourcing it to an undefined generally large group of people in the form of an open call.

localization

Adapting products and services for different languages and regional differences.

With most of its revenue coming from outside the United States, Facebook is already massively global. Facebook's **crowdsourcing localization** effort, where users were asked to look at Facebook phrases and offer translation suggestions for their local language (see Chapter 7), helped the firm rapidly deploy versions in dozens of markets, blasting the firm past one-time rivals in global reach. But network effects are both quick and powerful, and late market entry can doom a business reliant on the positive feedback loop of a growing user base. And global competition is out there. Facebook wannabes worldwide include Vkontakte ("in contact"), Russia's most popular social networking site; Line, the app and platform which is tops in Japan and has a large following in many other countries; and QZone and WeChat (both owned by Tencent), which are wildly popular in China. And don't be surprised to see some of these well-capitalized overseas innovators making a move on US markets too. China's Tencent and Japan's Rakuten are among non-US firms that have acquired US-based Internet firms.

While global growth can seem like a good thing, acquiring global users isn't the same as making money from them. Free sites with large amounts of users from developing nations face real cost or revenue challenges. As the *New York Times* points out, fewer than half of global Internet users have disposable incomes high enough to interest major advertisers, meaning that in terms of average revenue per user (ARPU), these new social networking recruits are likely to be far less lucrative in the near future than the firm's current users.[178] In the first quarter of 2015, ARPU climbed 42 percent in the United States and Canada, but in Asia-Pacific ARPU grew just 27 percent, and in Latin America and Africa ARPU climbed just 14 percent.[179]

Making money in the face of this so-called international paradox requires an awareness of fast-and-cheap tech trends highlighted in Chapter 5 and an ability to make accurate predictions regarding regional macroeconomic trends. If you ignore a market that's unprofitable today, a rival could swoop in and establish network effects and other assets that are unbeatable tomorrow. But if you move too early, losses could drag you down. To make Facebook more appealing to low-end users, Facebook has built an app that requires just 1 percent of the computing resources used by its main smartphone app. Facebook Lite won't support video, and images will be compressed,[180] but users can post status updates and pictures, scroll through a news feed and get notifications.[181] The firm will sell ads through Facebook Lite, even though high-appeal video and hi-res images aren't on the platform.

Concerns aren't just financial and technical; they're also political and ethical. Facebook is officially banned in China (although many Chinese have used technical work-arounds to access the site), and Zuckerberg is clearly interested in the Chinese market. He reportedly spends an hour each day learning Chinese and has made several trips to China, addressing crowds in "halting, but passable" mandarin."[182] Some say even a censored Facebook would be a catalyst for Chinese democratic reform, while others see this as a compromise of the firm's belief in the power of exchange and promoting the free flow of information. The firm's COO Sheryl Sandberg said, "There are compromises on not being in China, and there are compromises on being in China. It's not clear to me which one is bigger."[183]

5.4 Internet.org: A Path to Billions?

Zuckerberg has also been thinking beyond short to mid-term profits, and has declared Internet access to be a "human right."[184] As announced in a cover story in *Time* magazine, his explicit goal is "to make sure that actually, literally every single human being on Earth has an Internet connection." Some 4.3 billion people are currently offline–about three times Facebook's current size.[185] To remedy the problem, Facebook has been actively working on schemes for providing Internet access to areas with no signal. For example, by purchasing a designer of solar-powered drone aircraft, Facebook hopes that one day these systems will circle underserved areas at altitudes above clouds and troubling weather, returning to earth only when they need maintenance.[186] While these efforts get lots of press, the reality is that about 85 percent of the world's population already lives within range of a cell tower with at least a 2G data network. So why are so many offline? Three reasons: 1) data is too expensive for many of the world's poorest citizens; 2) services aren't designed for emerging market use by populations who need ultra-low bandwidth services that run reliably on very low-end or old, recycled hardware; and 3) content is not compelling enough to draw in non-users. If done right, however, the impact of Internet could be life-changing. That device in a pocket is a tool to lubricate markets, educate, and connect citizens with government services and healthcare. A Deloitte study (albeit one commissioned by Facebook) posited that moving the population of India with Internet access from 15 percent to 75 percent would create 65 million jobs, cut extreme poverty by 28 percent, and reduce infant mortality by 85,000 deaths a year. Says Facebook COO Sheryl Sandberg "If the first decade was starting the process of connecting the world, the next decade is helping connect the people who are not yet connected and watching what happens."[187]

To get to Zuckerberg's goal of everyone online, Facebook has partnered in the creation of Internet.org, a nonprofit organization also supported by leading mobile phone firms (e.g., Ericsson, Nokia, Opera, Qualcomm, and Samsung).[188] Internet.org crafts non-exclusive partnerships with local carriers to offer a free tier of services, a sort of "Internet dial tone" that includes social networking (of course), as well as vital information such as weather, health care information, education, and food prices, all through a lightweight app that runs on very low end phones (often called 'feature phones' as opposed to app-installing smart phones).[189] With the commitment of local carriers providing free data for these services, Internet.org has launched in a dozen countries and brought millions online.[190] For carriers, these free services are a sort of gateway to the Internet, and users would have to pay if they clicked outside of the core offerings. The goal isn't to trick and exploit the poor, but there is hope among carrier partners that as incomes increase and smartphones proliferate, these unprofitable users will one day graduate and become revenue-generating customers, with some becoming a source of innovation, too. Some worry that for billions of low-income users, Facebook will come to represent the only Internet they know and have access to, deepening the roots and entanglement vines of the firm's walled garden. However Internet.org has been expanded and is now available to all developers who meet a set of core criteria (targeted largely at ensuring services serve low-end consumers and don't act as a free option for those who can afford to pay).[191] The organization hopes this is enough to quiet critics in Chile, India, and elsewhere who have claimed that Internet.org violates net neutrality laws. Given the positive benefits that potentially cut across education, health care, and economic development, should a deep-pocketed player (or players, Google has similar goals in mind) willing to catalyze access to billions be welcomed, or is this just a land-grab ploy pulled off by deep-pocketed tech giants? Counters Sandberg: "When we've been accused of doing this for our own profit, the joke we have is, God, if we were trying to maximize profits, we have a long list of ad products to build! We'd have to work our way pretty far down that list before we got to this."[192] Stay tuned, as Zuckerberg enters his thirties, it looks like he's just getting started.

Hear from a diverse group of Internet.org users in Zambia on how the service has impacted their lives.

View the video online at: http://www.youtube.com/embed/zS6xBV4ZwZY?rel=0

KEY TAKEAWAYS

- Facebook empowers its engineering staff to move quickly, at times releasing innovations before they are perfect. The hope is that this will foster innovation and allow the firm to gain advantages from moving early, such as network effects, switching costs, scale, and learning.

- While moving early has its advantages, Facebook has also repeatedly executed new initiatives and policy changes in ways that have raised public, partner, and governmental concern.

- Word of mouth is the most powerful method for promoting products and services, and Beacon was conceived as a giant word-of-mouth machine with win-win benefits for firms, recommenders, recommendation recipients, and Facebook.

- Beacon failed because it was an opt-out system that was not thoroughly tested beforehand and because user behavior, expectations, and system procedures were not completely taken into account. Partners associated with the rapidly rolled out, poorly conceived, and untested effort were embarrassed. Several faced legal action.

- Facebook also reinforced negative perceptions regarding the firm's attitudes toward users, notifications, and their privacy. This attitude served only to focus a continued spotlight on the firm's efforts, and users became even less forgiving.

- Activists and the media were merciless in criticizing the firm's terms of service (TOS) changes and other privacy missteps. Facebook's contrite response and user outreach while in crisis mode demonstrate lessons other organizations can learn from regarding user scrutiny, public reaction, and stakeholder engagement. The firm's policy shifts to default sharing "with friends" rather than "public," and the removal of the sponsored stories ad program are also examples of course correction in response to user concerns. The firm's revamped privacy settings and notification tools help raise awareness of issues and keep consumers in control of limits on their sharing.

- Global growth is highly appealing to firms, but expensive bandwidth costs and low prospects for ad revenue create challenges akin to the free rider problem.

- Despite concern, Facebook is investing in new technologies and access services that promise to dramatically lower Internet access barriers, with a goal to bring billions of customers online. Consumers not only represent potential ad revenue growth as markets develop and incomes increase but also entirely new product lines, such as mobile banking, may emerge from within emerging markets.

- The world population with no Internet access is roughly 3 times larger than the Facebook user base, however most of the world's population live within cell towers or other means to access the Internet. Cost, compelling content, and technical issues to make services available on low-end hardware are the three main factors that conspire to limit Internet use.

- Internet access has the potential to improve healthcare, education, and economic prosperity. To bring more users online, Facebook and other tech giants have formed Internet.org, a non-profit that partners non-exclusively with local carriers to free access to a set of basic services.

- Many have criticized Facebook and Internet.org as violating principles of net neutrality and extending Facebook's walled garden as a defacto proxy for the Intenret, however Internet.org has opened their services to any provider that can meet a basic set of criteria.

QUESTIONS AND EXERCISES

1. At Facebook, why is "done better than perfect," and why is it considered important to "move fast and break things"?

2. What was Beacon? Why was it initially thought to be a good idea? What were the benefits to firm partners, recommenders, recommendation recipients, and Facebook? Who were Beacon's partners, and what did they seek to gain through the effort?

3. Describe the biggest problem with Beacon. Would you use Beacon? Why or why not?

4. How might Facebook and its partners have avoided the problems with Beacon? Could the effort be restructured while still delivering on its initial promise? Why or why not?

5. Beacon shows the risk in being a pioneer—are there risks in being too cautious and not pioneering with innovative, ground-floor marketing efforts? What kinds of benefits might a firm miss out on? Is there a disadvantage in being late to the party with these efforts as well? Why or why not?

6. Why do you think Facebook changed its terms of service? Did these changes concern you? Were users right to rebel? What could Facebook have done to avoid the problem? Did Facebook do a good job in following up? How would you advise Facebook to apply lessons learned from the TOS controversy?

7. Visit Facebook and experiment with privacy settings. What kinds of control do you have over feeds and data sharing? Is this enough to set your mind at ease? Did you know these settings existed before being prompted to investigate features?

8. How did Facebook localize its site so quickly in various different regions of the world?

9. What factors encourage firms to grow an international user base as quickly as possible? Why is this a risk, and what is the so-called international paradox? What sorts of firms are at more risk than others?

10. List the pros, cons, and unknowns if Facebook were to seek a way for the Chinese government to allow its expansion into China. What are the risks if the firm remains out of the country? What do you think the firm should do?

11. How is Facebook seeking to reach the next billion Internet users? What technologies and service offerings is the firm hoping to leverage? How might the firm make money off of such users?

12. Do you agree with Mark Zuckerberg that "connectivity is a human right"? Why or why not? What goal do governments and the private sector aim for in helping empower disenfranchised populations?

13. What are the benefits of offering Intenret.org to low-income users worldwide? What are the concerns? Do you think Internet.org should be welcomed, halted, or limited with constraints? Be prepared to discuss with your class.

14. So you've had a chance to learn about Facebook, its model, growth, outlook, strategic assets, and competitive environment. Do you think the firm will dominate in the future or be swept aside by technology's relentless advance? Why?

ENDNOTES

1. L. Grossman, "Person of the Year: Mark Zuckerberg," *Time*, December 15, 2010.

2. V. Goel and J. Wortham, "Facebook Takes On Twitter with Video," *New York Times*, June 20, 2013.

3. L. Stampler, "Facebook Is Three Times Bigger than the Super Bowl, Every Day," *Business Insider*, October 23, 2012.

4. L. Sumagaysay, "Facebooking More than Googling," *Good Morning Silicon Valley*, December 30, 2010.

5. C. Smith, "7 Statistics about Facebook Users that Reveal Why It's Such a Powerful Marketing Platform," *Business Insider*, November 16, 2013.

6. For an insider account of Silicon Valley Web 2.0 start-ups, see S. Lacy, *Once You're Lucky, Twice You're Good: The Rebirth of Silicon Valley and the Rise of Web 2.0.* (New York: Gotham Books, 2008).

7. L. Grossman, "Person of the Year: Mark Zuckerberg," *Time*, December 15, 2010.

8. J. Pepitone, "Facebook Trading Sets Record IPO Volume," *Fortune*, May 18, 2012.

9. D. Netburn, "Facebook IPO Makes Mark Zuckerberg 29th Richest Person on Earth," *Los Angeles Times*, May 17, 2012.

10. K. Wagner, "More Than 70 Percent of Facebook Ad Revenue Now Comes From Mobile," *Re/code*, April 22, 2015.

11. V. Goel, "Some Privacy, Please? Facebook, under Pressure, Gets the Message," *New York Times*, May 22, 2014.

12. J. Abbruzzese, "Facebook's Formula: Buy Startups, Absorb Products, Keep Talent," *Mashable*, January 30, 2014.

13. S. Denning, "Is Google's Share-Split Evil?" *Forbes*, April 13, 2012.

14. M. Yglesias, "All Hail, Emperor Zuckerberg," *Slate*, February 3, 2012.

15. J. Weiner, "Sheryl Sandberg: Billionaire," *Washington Post*, March 19, 2014.

16. B. Stone, "Why Facebook Needs Sheryl Sandberg," *BusinessWeek*, May 16, 2011.

17. *USA Today*, "Book Buzz: Sheryl Sandberg's 'Lean In' Is No. 1," March 21, 2013.

18. J. Constantine, "Zuckerberg Receives Hoodie, Says 'Our Mission Isn't to Be a Public Company' in Pre-IPO Remarks," *TechCrunch*, May 18, 2012.

19. A. Zeichick, "How Facebook Works," *Technology Review*, July/August 2008.

20. S. Ante, "Facebook: Friends with Money," *BusinessWeek*, May 9, 2008.

21. M. McGee, "EdgeRank Is Dead: Facebook's News Feed Algorithm Now Has Close to 100K Weight Factors," *MarketingLand*, August 16, 2013.

22. J. Constine, "Facebook's Feed Now Punishes Pages that Ask for Likes or Share Reruns," *TechCrunch*, April 10, 2014.

23. A. Loten, A. Janofsky, and R. Albergotti, "New Facebook Rules Will Sting Entrepreneurs," *The Wall Street Journal*, Nov. 27, 2014.

24. B. Womack, "Facebook Adopts Hashtags in Nod to Twitter to Boost User Chatter," *BusinessWeek*, June 12, 2013.

25. B. Stone, "Why Facebook Needs Sheryl Sandberg," *BusinessWeek*, May 16, 2011.

26. J. Kincaid, "Facebook Users Uploaded a Record 750 Million Photos over New Year's," *TechCrunch*, January 3, 2011.

27. M. Beck, "Facebook Extends Its Lead in Social Referral Traffic, Shareaholic Data Shows," *MarketingLand*, April 21, 2014.

28. A. Vance, "Facebook: The Making of a Billion Users," *BusinessWeek*, October 4, 2012.

29. L. Leong, "Microsoft to Discontinue Messenger on March 15th, Forcing Users to Use Skype Instead," *Softonic*, January 9, 2013; D. Johnson, "WhatsApp 'Overtakes Facebook as Leading Mobile Message Service,'" Telegraph, November 29, 2013.

30. N. Carlson, "It's official: Google blew it with YouTube, and Facebook has caught up," *Business Insider*, June 3, 2015.

31. J. Constine, "'Hello' Is Facebook's New Android-Only Social Caller ID App," *TechCrunch*, April 22, 2015.

32. J. Pepitone, "Rent a Movie—On Your Facebook Page," *CNN*, March 8, 2011

33. E. Hamburger, "Facebook Retires Its Troubled @facebook.com Email Service," *The Verge*, February 24, 2014.

34. J. Schofield, "Facebook Introduces Docs, Based on Microsoft Web Office," *Guardian*, April 22, 2010.

35. J. Crook, "Facebook Dumps Bing, Will Introduce Its Own Search Tool," *TechCrunch*, Dec. 13, 2014.

36. V. Hernandez, "Friends, Photos Are Early Favorites on Facebook Graph Search," *CNN*, March 21, 2013.

37. Footnote: J. Krasny, "There's a Seedy Underbelly to Facebook's Graph Search," *Complex.com*, January 23, 2013.

38. K. Hill, "Facebook Graph Search Shows You 'Married People Who Like Prostitutes' and 'Employers of People Who Like Racism,'" *Forbes*, January 23, 2013.

39. B. Evans, "WhatsApp and $19bn," *Benedict Evans Blog*, February 19, 2014.

40. B. Evans, "Mobile First," *Ben-Evans.com*, May 14, 2015.

41. B. Evans, "WhatsApp and $19bn," *Benedict Evans Blog*, February 19, 2014.

42. C. Taylor, "Instagram Passes 50 Million Users, Adds Five Million a Week," *Mashable*, May 1, 2012.

43. D. Reisinger, "SEC Spooked by Facebook's Pre-IPO Mobile Numbers," *CNET*, June 15, 2012.

44. N. Carlson, "Here's the Chart That Scared Zuckerberg into Spending $1 Billion on Instagram," *Business Insider*, April 14, 2012; and K. Teare, "It's Not about Instagram—It's about Mobile," *TechCrunch*, April 18, 2012.

45. R. Reader, "WhatsApp now has 800M monthly active users," *VentureBeat*, April 18, 2015.

46. S. Ingram, "Facebook's (FB) Instagram Is Close to Twitter's (TWTR) User Numbers," *TheStreet*, March 26, 2014

47. M. McFarland, "Snapchat's 23-Year-Old CEO Was Smart to Turn Down a $3 Billion Offer," *Washington Post*, November 14, 2013.

48. T. Anazodo, "Why the Whatsapp Acquisition Was a Great Deal for Facebook," *The Medium*, February 23, 2014.

49. J. Constine and K. Cutler, "Why Facebook Dropped $19B On WhatsApp: Reach into Europe, Emerging Markets," *TechCrunch*, February 19, 2014.

50. B. Evans, "WhatsApp and $19bn," *Benedict Evans Blog*, February 19, 2014.

51. H. Blodget, "Everyone Who Thinks Facebook Is Stupid to Buy WhatsApp For $19 Billion Should Think Again," *Business Insider*, February 20, 2014.

52. P. Olson, "Exclusive: The Rags-To-Riches Tale of How Jan Koum Built WhatsApp into Facebook's New $19 Billion Baby," *Forbes*, February 19, 2014.

53. J. Constine and K. Cutler, "Why Facebook Dropped $19B on WhatsApp: Reach into Europe, Emerging Markets," *TechCrunch*, February 19, 2014.

54. R. Reader, "WhatsApp now has 800M monthly active users," *VentureBeat*, April 18, 2015.

55. M. Wohlsen, "I'm Too Old for Snapchat, Which is Exactly Why It Should Be Worth $19B," *Wired*, Feb. 23, 2015.

56. J. Pepitone, "Mark Zuckerberg: $19 Billion for WhatsApp Is Cheap!" *NBC News*, February 24, 2014.

57. D. Graziano, "Explained: How the Oculus Rift streams PC and Xbox One games," *CNet*, June 12, 2015.

58. G. Stahl, "Facebook Looks Ahead with Bet on Virtual Reality in Oculus Buy," *Wall Street Journal*, March 26, 2014.

59. S. Parkin, "What Zuckerberg Sees in Oculus Rift," *MIT Technology Review*, March 26, 2014.

60. P. Rubin, "The Inside Story of Oculus Rift and How Virtual Reality Became Reality," *Wired*, May 20, 2014.

61. B. Stone, "I Put on the New Oculus Rift Headset. This Is What I Saw," *BusinessWeek*, Jan. 8, 2015.

62. K. Wagner, "Facebook's New App Moments Lets You Share Photos Outside of Facebook," *Re/code*, June 15, 2015.

63. R. Cheng, "Here's why the Facebook phone flopped," *CNet*, May 8, 2013.

64. A. Vance, "Facebook: The Making of 1 Billion Users," *BusinessWeek*, October 4, 2012.

65. J. Novet, "Facebook Unveils Presto Engine for Querying 250 PB Data Warehouse," *GigaOM*, June 6, 2013.

66. T. Morgan, "How Facebook Compresses Its 300 PB Data Warehouse," *EnterpriseTech*, April 11, 2014.

67. D. Lyons, "Digg This: A Cautionary Tale for Web 2.0 Companies," *Newsweek*, October 24, 2010; and M. Arrington, "Yahoo Sells Delicious to YouTube Founders," *TechCrunch*, April 27, 2011.

68. C. Metz, "Facebook Shatters the Computer Server into Tiny Pieces," *Wired*, January 16, 2013.

69. J. Novet, "Facebook Unveils Presto Engine for Querying 250 PB Data Warehouse," *GigaOM*, June 6, 2013.

70. C. Metz, "How Three Guys Rebuilt Facebook's Foundations," *Wired*, June 11, 2013.

71. S. Kessler, "For Top News Sites, Facebook Drives More Traffic than Twitter," *Mashable*, May 9, 2011.

72. J. Kincaid, "What Is This Mysterious Facebook Music App?" *TechCrunch*, February 2, 2010; and R. Maher, "Facebook's New Payment System Off to Great Start, Could Boost Revenue by $250 Million in 2010," *TBI Research*, February 1, 2010.

73. A. Zeichick, "How Facebook Works," *Technology Review*, July/August 2008; J. Packzkowski, "Superpoke! Facebook Chooses N.C. for $450M Data Center," *AllThingsD*, November 11, 2010; and T. Simonite, "Facebook Opens Up Its Hardware Secrets," *Technology Review*, April 7, 2011.

74. J. Constine, "Facebook Saved over a Billion Dollars by Building Open Sourced Servers," *TechCrunch*, January 28, 2014.

75. M. Meeker, "2014 Internet Trends," *KPCB*, May 28, 2014.

76. S. Gaudin, "Facebook Rolls Out Storage System to Wrangle Massive Photo Stores," *Computerworld*, April 1, 2009, http://www.computerworld.com/s/article/9130959/Facebook_rolls_out_storage_system_to_wrangle_massive_photo_stores.

77. D. MacMillan, P. Burrows, and S. Ante, "Inside the App Economy," *BusinessWeek*, November 2, 2009.

78. B. Barnes and C. Cain Miller, "Disney Buys Playdom in $763 Million Deal, becoming Hollywood Leader in Social Games," *New York Times*, July 27, 2010.

79. Footnote: J. Guynn, "A Software Industry @ Facebook," *Los Angeles Times*, September 10, 2007.

80. H. McKenzie, "Move Fast, Break Things: The Sad Story of Platform, Facebook's Gigant-ic Missed Opportunity," *Pando Daily*, July 23, 2013.

81. H. McKenzie, "Move Fast, Break Things: The Sad Story of Platform, Facebook's Gigant-ic Missed Opportunity," *Pando Daily*, July 23, 2013.

82. "Facebook Changes Hitting Zynga Hard, Worrying Investors," *Reuters*, July 26, 2012.

83. Rusli, "Zynga's Value at $7 Billion, Is Milestone for Social Gaming," *Wall Street Journal*, December 15, 2011.

84. M. G. "The Chips Are Down," *Economist*, June 4, 2013.

85. T. Brugger, "Facebook Inc. Says 'Game On!'" *The Motley Fool*, March 22, 2014.

86. J. Constine, "Facebook's Cutesy Annual Report to Partners Reveals First Country-by-Country Mobile Stats," *TechCrunch*, December 29, 2013.

87. M. Minotti, "Facebook's Desktop Gaming Revenue Slips in the First Quarter of 2014," *Venture Beat*, April 24, 2014.

88. T. Brugger, "Facebook Inc. Says 'Game On!'" *The Motley Fool*, March 22, 2014.

89. A. Madrigal, "Why the Facebook Innovation Machine Doesn't Work on Mobile Devices," *Atlantic*, June 11, 2013.

90. S. Millward, "WeChat Grows to 549M Monthly Active Useres," *TechInAsia*, May 13, 2015.

91. L. Kuo, "WeChat Is Nothing Like WhatsApp—And that Makes It Even More Valuable"

92. T. Xiang, "WeChat Announced 70 million Overseas Users, Will Open up to Third-party Developers," *TechNode*, July 3, 2013.

93. J. Russell, "Facebook's Messenger Platform Must Go Beyond Apps And Embrace The Web," *TechCrunch*, March 30, 2015

94. Unattributed, "China's Tencent hits $200 billion market cap for first time," *Reuters*, April 13, 2015.

95. J. Hempel, "Why Facebook Has Trusted its Future to the CEO of PayPal," *Wired*, Nov. 10, 2014.

96. E. Niu, "Facebook Inc.'s Messenger Unbundling Strategy is Backfiring," *Fool.com*, August 11, 2014. V. Luckerson, "Here's How to Avoid Having to Use Facebook Messenger," *Time*, Aug. 12, 2014.

97. D. Reisinger, "Facebook Messenger chats its way to 700 million users," *CNet*, June 12, 2015.

98. J. Constine, "Facebook Messenger On Android Hits 1...Billion...Downloads," *TechCrunch*, June 9, 2015.

99. J. Hempel, "Why Facebook Has Trusted its Future to the CEO of PayPal," *Wired*, Nov. 10, 2014.

100. J. Del Rey, "Gilt Groupe's Very Cloudy Future," *Re/code*, March 16, 2015.

101. J. Del Rey, "Facebook Starts Turning Messenger Into a Shopping Platform," *Re/code*, March 25, 2015.

102. V. Goel, "Facebook Announces a Payments Feature for Its Messenger App," *The New York Times*, March 17, 2015.

103. T. Dotan, "With Messenger Apps Sluggish, Facebook Eyeing Games," *The Information*, May 18, 2015.

104. A. Heath, "Facebook Messenger's app store is here, and it sucks," *CultOfMac*, March 30, 2015.

105. J. Constine, "Facebook Plans To Turn Messenger Into A Platform," *TechCrunch*, March 19, 2015.

106. J. Brodkin, "Facebook Shuts Down Beacon Program, Donates $9.5 Million to Settle Lawsuit," *NetworkWorld*, December 8, 2009; and N. Devore, "Facebook Moves beyond the 'Like' Button, Introduces New Verbs to Timeline," *OBI*, January 25, 2012.

107. V. Grigoriadis, "Do You Own Facebook? Or Does Facebook Own You?" *New York*, April 5, 2009.

108. L. Sumagaysay, "Plans Personalized Internet, Facebook vs. Twitter et al., Plus Cisco, Square and the Woz," *SiliconBeat*, January 25, 2013.

109. M. Helft, "Facebook Offers New Messaging Tool," *New York Times*, November 15, 2010.]

110. D. Takahashi, "Internet Ads Finally Surpass Newspapers," *VentureBeat*, April 14, 2011.

111. B. Stone, "Facebook Aims to Extend Its Reach across Web," *New York Times*, December 1, 2008.

112. R. Cellan-Jones, "Facebook Removes Ads from Controversial Pages to Avoid Boycott," *BBC*, June 28, 2013.

113. J. Brustein, "To Change Facebook's Policies, Start with Its Advertisers," *BusinessWeek*, May 29, 2013.

114. A. Ha, "Facebook Announces New Review Policy to Prevent Ads from Running on Controversial Pages and Groups," *TechCrunch*, June 28, 2013.

115. D. Takahashi, "Internet Ads Finally Surpass Newspapers," *VentureBeat*, April 14, 2011.

116. A. Loten, A. Janofsky, and R. Albergotti, "New Facebook Rules Will Sting Entrepren-eurs," *The Wall Street Journal*, Nov. 27, 2014.

117. S. Mazaheri, "All About Click-Through Rate," AdStage, July 17, 2014. *Salesforce.com*, "The Facebook Ads Benchmark Report," June 2013; and C. Smith, "Facebook Ads Still Lag Paid Search in Click-Through Rates," *Business Insider*, June 13, 2013.

118. Y. He, "How Buying Ads on Google Can Give Small Companies Big Results," *SmartBusiness*, July 1, 2013.

119. C. McCarthy, "More Social, Please: Facebook Nixes Banner Ads," *CNET*, February 5, 2010.

120. M. Shields, "Why Mobile App Install Ads Are Suddenly Such a Huge Deal," *Wall Street Journal*, April 24, 2014.

121. B. Carter, "Why Every Business Should Spend at Least $1 per Day on Facebook Ads," *The Moz Blog*, February 19, 2014.

122. C. Delo, "Pinterest Launches First Paid Ads with Kraft, Gap and Others," *AdAge*, May 12, 2014.

123. P. Garner, "Average revenue per user is an important growth driver," *Market Realist*, Feb. 11, 2015.

124. H. Blodget, "Well, Now That Everyone Has Sobered Up, Let's Figure Out What Face-book Is Actually Worth..." *Business Insider*, May 21, 2012.

125. S. Baker, "Learning and Profiting from Online Friendships," *BusinessWeek*, May 21, 2009.

126. J. Constine, "Facebook Has Mixed Q1 Earnings With Miss On $3.54B Revenue, Beat On $0.42 EPS, User Growth Up To Hit 1.44B," *TechCrunch*, April 22, 2015.

127. K. Wagner, "More Than 70 Percent of Facebook Ad Revenue Now Comes From Mobile," *Re/code*, April 22, 2015.

128. M. Cowan, "Marketers Struggle to Get Social," *Reuters*, June 19, 2008, ht-tp://www.reuters.com/news/video?videoId=84894.

129. C. Delo, "Facebook to Partner with Acxiom, Epsilon to Match Store Purchases with User Profiles," *AdAge*, February 22, 2013.

130. C. Delo, "Facebook to Partner with Acxiom, Epsilon to Match Store Purchases with User Profiles," *AdAge*, February 22, 2013.

131. B. Urstadt, "The Business of Social Networks," *Technology Review*, July/August 2008; J. Hempel, "Finding Cracks in Facebook," *Fortune*, May 13, 2008; and E. Schonfeld, "Are Facebook Ads Going to Zero? Lookery Lowers Its Guarantee to 7.5-cent CMPs," *TechCrunch*, July 22, 2008.

132. H. King, "Facebook's mobile ad revenue jumps," *CNN Money*, April 22, 2015.

133. T. Peterson, "Facebook's Mobile Revenue Climbs to $2.5 Billion as Ad Prices Soar," *AdAge*, Jan. 28, 2015.

134. J. Saba, "Exclusive: Facebook earns 51 percent of ad revenue overseas – executives," *Reuters*, June 9, 2015.

135. M. Murphy, "Hooked on Facebook Mobile," *Silicon Beat*, March 29, 2013.

136. S. Martin, "Instagram Begins First Ads," *USA Today*, November 1, 2013.

137. J. Lafferty, "How Facebook Advertisers Are Getting the Most from News Feed Ads," *InsideFacebook*, June 26, 2013.

138. J. Bercovici, "Can Twitter Save TV? (And Can TV Save Twitter?)," *Forbes*, October 7, 2013.

139. T. Peterson, "Facebook's Mobile Revenue Climbs to $2.5 Billion as Ad Prices Soar," *AdAge*, Jan. 28, 2015.

140. D. Hendricks, "Facebook to Drop Sponsored Stories: What Does This Mean for Advert-isers?" *Forbes*, January 16, 2014.

141. M. Shields, "Why Mobile App Install Ads Are Suddenly Such a Huge Deal," *Wall Street Journal*, April 24, 2014.

142. M. Lynley, "Meet the Woman behind One of Facebook's Fastest-Growing and Most Lucrative New Businesses," *BuzzFeed*, February 12, 2014.

143. M. Shields, "Why Mobile App Install Ads Are Suddenly Such a Huge Deal," *Wall Street Journal*, April 24, 2014.

144. R. Hof, "Why Can't Facebook's App Install Ads Get Any Respect?" *Forbes*, Feb. 27, 2015.

145. A. Loten, A. Janofsky, and R. Albergotti, "New Facebook Rules Will Sting Entrepren-eurs," *The Wall Street Journal*, Nov. 27, 2014. And C. Delo, "Brands' Organic Facebook Reach Has Crashed Since October: Study," *AdAge*, March 6, 2014.

146. M. Isaac, "Here Comes Facebook's Ad Network: Mobile Ads Launching This Month," *Re/code*, April 20, 2014.

147. J. Constine, "Facebook Audience Network Mobile Ad Network Launches at F8," *TechCrunch*, April 30, 2014.]

148. T. Spanger, "Facebook launches 'Instant Articles' with NBC, NY Times, BuzzFeed -- and video publishers could be next," *The Boston Herald*, May 13, 2015.

149. L. Moses, "Publishers shrug off concerns, eager to publish on Facebook," *Digiday*, May 18, 2015.

150. J. Constine, "Facebook Starts Hosting Publishers' "Instant Articles"," *TechCrunch*, May 12, 2015.

151. N. Carlson, "It's official: Google blew it with YouTube, and Facebook has caught up," *Business Insider*, June 3, 2015.

152. R. Hof, "You Know What's Cool? 1 Million Advertisers on Facebook," *Forbes*, June 18, 2013.

153. E. Zimmerman, "Small Retailers Open Up Storefronts on Facebook," *New York Times*, July 25, 2012.

154. J. Saba, "Exclusive: Facebook earns 51 percent of ad revenue overseas – executives," *Reuters*, June 9, 2015.

155. A. Vance, "Facebook: The Making of a Billion Users," *BusinessWeek*, October 4, 2012.

156. D. Baer, "Mark Zuckerberg Explains Why Facebook Doesn't 'Move Fast And Break Things' Anymore," *Business Insider*, May 2, 2014.

157. A. Vance, "Facebook: The Making of 1 Billion Users," *BusinessWeek*, October 4, 2012.

158. M. D'Onofrio, "Social Networking Sites Using New Advertising," *BrandingIron*, November 18, 2010.

159. B. Stone, "Why Facebook Needs Sheryl Sandberg," *BusinessWeek*, May 16, 2011.

160. M. Walsh, "Facebook Drives 31% of Display Ads in Q1," *MediaPost*, May 4, 2011.

161. B. Stone, "Why Facebook Needs Sheryl Sandberg," *BusinessWeek*, May 16, 2011.

162. V. Kumar, J. Andrew Petersen, and R. Leone, "How Valuable Is Word of Mouth?" *Harvard Business Review* 85, no. 10 (October 2007): 139–46.

163. E. Nakashima, "Feeling Betrayed, Facebook Users Force Site to Honor Their Privacy," *Washington Post*, November 30, 2007.

164. J. Wortham, "Facebook Responds to User Anger over Proposed Instagram Changes," *New York Times*, December 18, 2012.

165. J. Kincaid, "A Look at the Future of Facebook Credits," *TechCrunch*, April 21, 2010.

166. Catherine Shu, "Judge Approves Facebook's $20M 'Sponsored Stories' Settlement," *TechCrunch*, August 26, 2013.

167. M. Chapman, "Facebook Adds Video to Instagram to Create 'Vine on Steroids,'" *MediaWeek*, June 21, 2013.

168. D. Hendricks, "Facebook to Drop Sponsored Stories: What Does This Mean for Advertisers?" *Forbes*, January 16, 2014.

169. Catherine Shu, "Judge Approves Facebook's $20M 'Sponsored Stories' Settlement," *TechCrunch*, August 26, 2013.

170. V. Goel, "Some Privacy, Please? Facebook, Under Pressure, Gets the Message," *New York Times*, May 22, 2014.

171. V. Goel, "Some Privacy, Please? Facebook, Under Pressure, Gets the Message," *New York Times*, May 22, 2014.

172. M. Murphy, "Quoted: Low Turnout Dooms Facebook Voting," *SiliconBeat*, December 12, 2012.

173. C. McCarthy, "Facebook's Zuckerberg: 'We Simply Did a Bad Job' Handling Beacon," *CNET*, December 5, 2007.

174. C. McCarthy, "Facebook to Developers: Get Ready for Credits," *CNET*, February 25, 2010.

175. M. Ingram, "Facebook's Two Deal Weapons: The Social Graph and Credits," *GigaOM*, April 26, 2011.

176. C. Nuttall, "Facebook Credits Bank of the Web," *Financial Times*, April 23, 2010.

177. V. Goel, "Some Privacy, Please? Facebook, Under Pressure, Gets the Message," *New York Times*, May 22, 2014.

178. F. Lardinois, "Is It Time for Facebook to Make Opt-In the Default?" Read Write Web, April 27, 2010.

179. A. Levy, "This Lightweight App Will Help Facebook Capture Its Next Billion Users," *The Motley Fool*, June 15, 2015.

180. A. Levy, "This Lightweight App Will Help Facebook Capture Its Next Billion Users," *The Motley Fool*, June 15, 2015.

181. D. Seetharaman, "Facebook Launches Lightweight App for Emerging Markets ," *The Wall Street Journal*, June 4, 2015.

182. L. Grossman, "Inside Facebook's Plan to Wire the World," *Time*, Dec. 15, 2014. And F. Manjoo, "Does Privacy on Facebook, Google, and Twitter Even Matter?" *Fast Company*, May 1, 2010

183. F. Manjoo, "Does Privacy on Facebook, Google, and Twitter Even Matter?" *Fast Company*, May 1, 2010.

184. J. Stern, "Mark Zuckerberg Reveals Plans to Bring the Internet to the Rest of the World," *ABC News*, August 21, 2013

185. L. Grossman, "Inside Facebook's Plan to Wire the World," *Time*, Dec. 15, 2014.

186. J. Garside, "Facebook Buys UK Maker of Solar-Powered Drones to Expand Internet," *Guardian*, March 28, 2014.

187. L. Grossman, "Inside Facebook's Plan to Wire the World," *Time*, Dec. 15, 2014.

188. D. Kerr, "Zuckerberg: Let's Make the Internet 100x More Affordable," *CNET*, September 30, 2013.

189. Unattributed, "Internet.org Myths and Facts," *Internet.org*, accessed June 16, 2015. And M. Dano, "Facebook's Zuckerberg Pushes for Free Tier of Wireless Internet Access During MWC Keynote," *FierceWireless*, February 24, 2014.

190. A. Levy, "This Lightweight App Will Help Facebook Capture Its Next Billion Users," *The Motley Fool*, June 15, 2015.

191. J. Russell, "Facebook Opens Internet.Org To All Developers In Response To Net Neutrality Concerns," *TechCrunch*, May 4, 2015.

192. L. Grossman, "Inside Facebook's Plan to Wire the World," *Time*, Dec. 15, 2014.

CHAPTER 12
Rent the Runway: Entrepreneurs Expanding an Industry by Blending Tech with Fashion

1. INTRODUCTION

LEARNING OBJECTIVE

1. Understand the Rent the Runway model and how the founders thought they could build a tech-fueled model to expand the market for high-end fashion.

There were serious problems in the fashion industry and Jenn Hyman and Jenny Fleiss knew it. Younger fashion fans were rabid for well-known designers but rarely could afford them. Designers wanted to reach the elusive younger demographic, too. They may be cash-strapped now but they also represent potentially lucrative lifelong customers. On top of this, social media was putting even more pressure on women to "wear something new" that hadn't already appeared in their Facebook and Instagram photos, making the problem of a full closet with nothing to wear even more acute.

Jenn and Jenny are recasting the relationship many women have to high-end fashion by delivering value to everyone who sees this hurt. Their solution is the fashion-rental powerhouse, Rent the Runway. The *New York Times* calls the firm "Netflix for Fashion."[1] Forbes calls it "Catch and Release Couture,"[2] and many of the firm's 5 million plus members[3] call it a fairy godmother that makes "Cinderella moments" happen. The firm has now moved far beyond the initial target of young consumers, delivering selection, convenience, value, and quality in a way that millions of women see as the best option for dressing to dazzle.

1.1 Here's How it Works

Customers browse the Rent the Runway site, select a dress (or other clothing item or accessory), and schedule a delivery date for a four-day loan (eight-day rentals are available for an added fee). Rentals are often only 10 percent of a dress's retail price.[4] That's like getting high-end designer garments at a fast-fashion price. Need help narrowing options or selecting a style? Stylists are available for phone calls, emails and online chat. Rent the Runway will send two sizes, to make sure that you receive a dress that fits. Customers who are on the fence about a choice can choose a second style as a backup, for an additional fee. Items will arrive in a branded garment bag that the customer can keep. The company uses reusable garment bags for shipping both ways. In an age where Uber, Airbnb, and Spotify change how we think about owning automobiles, homes, and music, Rent the Runway is going right after your closet.

1.2 A Fashion Company with a Technology Soul

The model sounds straightforward, but execution is astonishingly complex. This is a massive e-commerce company where 100 percent of the inventory is returned, needs to be inspected, cleaned, pressed, possibly mended, then packaged up for good-as-new send-out to the next precisely scheduled customer order.[5] Get this wrong and you've likely ruined an event that was weeks in the planning. Get it right and the client experiences the holy grail of business: full-blown customer delight. A woman is often wearing Rent the Runway at a time when she looks her best, her hair and makeup are done, she's with friends, and she's at a fantastic party where she's showered with complements. Says co-founder Fleiss, the firm "empowers women to feel confident and beautiful for the most memorable moments of their lives."[6]

The only way to pull this off is to build, as CEO Jenn Hyman puts it, a "fashion company with a technology soul."[7] Look beyond the exquisite, high-end fashion lovingly delivered to delighted customers and you'll see a massive, ultra-complex, precision-scheduled reverse logistics business, with deep industry partnerships, world-class analytics, a growing mobile- and social-enabled model that encourages return engagement, and more.[8] The complexity of the business helps keep away the competition; and competitive assets that include brand, scale, partnerships, and data are all strengthened the longer the firm operates. Says Juliet de Baubigny, a partner at venture firm Kleiner Perkins, a company that has invested in scores of tech firms, including Google, Twitter, SnapChat, Spotify, and Uber: "We didn't back [Rent the Runway] as a fashion start up. It's the sharing economy meets the Facebook–Instagram generation."[9]

KEY TAKEAWAYS

- Rent the Runway is a highlight of the sharing economy, enabling consumers to rent designer dresses at a fraction of the cost.
- The firm's CEO and co-founder, Jenn Hyman, describes the firm as a "fashion company with a technology soul." The firm leverages mobile, social, big data, and advanced tech-enabled logistics to deliver on the promise of "Cinderella Moments."

QUESTIONS AND EXERCISES

1. What sorts of customers was Rent the Runway designed to appeal to? Do you think these are the only customers who would find the model appealing? Why or why not?
2. What challenges do you think the entrepreneurs faced in going from idea to implementation? What challenges are customer-focused? Which are supplier-focused?
3. Have you or has anyone you know used Rent the Runway? If so, describe your experiences or interview a friend who has experience and share this with your class. If you can't find anyone who has used the firm, interview women you know and ask them if they've heard of the firm, what they think of the idea, and report back on their thoughts as well as why they would or wouldn't use the effort. What do these responses tell you about growing a new venture?

2. FOUNDING THE BUSINESS. ARE WE ON TO SOMETHING?

LEARNING OBJECTIVES

1. **Recognize key entrepreneurship and product development concepts of product/market fit, minimum viable product, and customer lifetime value.**
2. **Understand how the entrepreneurs behind Rent the Runway went about testing and refining their business thesis to gain confidence in their idea and approach.**
3. **Identify potential issues with customer and supplier perception, and how Rent the Runway counteracts these concerns.**

Time Magazine has called Rent the Runway one of the country's 50 Best Websites,[10] and Jenn Hyman and Jenny Fleiss have been named to FastCompany's list of Most Influential Women in Technology,[11] *Inc. Magazine's* 30 Under 30,[12] and *Fortune's* list of Most Promising Women Entrepreneurs,[13] yet all this started when both women were still in their twenties, hadn't yet finished their MBAs (both were students at Harvard), and had little fashion industry or technology expertise.

The "light bulb moment" that sparked the idea for the firm happened when Jenn Hyman's younger sister showed off a $2,000 Marchesa dress she'd bought for a wedding she'd be attending. For a young woman fresh out of college, price tags like that represent a big chunk of one's salary, spent on an item that has a limited shelf life. And yes, she had a full closet, but complained of nothing to wear. Blame Facebook, the outfit killer.[14]

Hyman teamed up with classmate Fleiss to immediately explore **product/market fit**—the idea that they were crafting a solution the market wants, one that customers are willing to pay for, and one that'll scale into a large, profitable business. The first step wasn't about building a website or a logistics system, it involved running low-tech tests to prove that they were really on to something. These tests amounted to quickly developing what entrepreneurs often call the **minimum viable product**, or **MVP**, a barebones offering that allows the team to collect customer feedback and to validate concepts and assumptions that underlie the business idea.[15] There were lots of unknowns: would women want to rent dresses? Would they return dresses in decent shape so they could be rented again? Would they rent from a website and trust delivery and product quality?

Jennifer Hyman and Jenny Fleiss, Founders of Rent the Runway

One test involved purchasing 100 dresses and setting up a popup rental shop for college students.[16] Hyman watched one undergrad slide into a silver-sequined Tory Burch minidress, twirl in front of the mirror and cry out to friends, "Oh my God, I look so hot!"[17] Initial evidence of customer interest and delight? Check! Later tests investigated how much customers were willing to pay, and verified that women were willing to rent from a photo even if they couldn't try the product on, first (in true MVP style, tests were conducted with PDF photos rather than building a full-blown website).[18] All this helped provide confidence in their concept and armed the founders for making a persuading pitch to investors.[19]

Source: © Abbey Drucker

2.1 Customers Like It—But What About Suppliers? Growing the Customer-base and Creating a Win-Win

Rent the Runway needed to buy from designers in bulk, and at a discount, in order for the model to work. But designers needed to be convinced it was worth taking a risk on two women with an unprofitable fledgling business and little direct domain experience. Some designers were initially concerned that rental would dilute their brand. Many also feared that rental would cannibalize retail sales.[20]

Being effective stewards of designer brands has always been important at Rent the Runway, and the care with which the firm showcases designer products extends from website to packaging. "We try to be brand ambassadors for the designers," says Hyman.[21] One way the firm does this is through landing pages dedicated to each designer. These include photos and bios, which educate women about individual brands and convey product quality, especially important for the new customer who may be migrating from fast-fashion retailers like Zara to high quality couture.[22] Stylists are also highly trained at effectively communicating garment quality and artistry. Shipped dresses arrive in customer homes nestled in a quality garment bag, not unlike if it were purchased in a store.

Rather than cannibalizing sales, Rent the Runway is now seen by many designers as a vital partner: an experiential marketing channel that introduces high-end designer brands to new customers. Rent the Runway clients are about a decade younger, on average, than the typical department store patron.[23] And while most e-commerce shoppers buy brands they are already familiar with, 98 percent of Rent the Runway customers rent brands they've never bought before.[24] The halo-effect from a positive experience renting a designer's more daring dresses may prompt a woman to purchase more frequently-worn staples like a little black cocktail dress, leather leggings, or accessories.[25] Some designers are now even testing new looks on Rent the Runway, while others are developing exclusive lines for the site.[26]

Technology also helps Rent the Runway improve customer service over time. Customers will browse and visit a website much more frequently than they'll visit a store, and this helps develop keen insights on her preferences. What is she paying attention to? What does she return to but hasn't yet rented? How are her tastes evolving and are these reflected in market, demographic, and regional trends? The firm also meets with each designer several times a year to learn concerns and share ideas.[27] Today, Rent the Runway carries apparel and accessories from over 300 designers, attracting customers and further delivering the scale and reach that designers wouldn't get solely through conventional sales channels.[28]

product/market fit

A key concept in entrepreneurship and new product development that conveys the degree to which a product satisfies market demand. Successful efforts should be desired by customers, and scale into large, profitable businesses.

minimum viable product

A bare-bones offering that allows entrepreneurs and product developers to collect customer feedback and to validate concepts and assumptions that underlie a business idea.

MVP

A bare-bones offering that allows entrepreneurs and product developers to collect customer feedback and to validate concepts and assumptions that underlie a business idea.

The Rent the Runway website helps deliver high value and high fashion to millions of women.

Source: © Rent the Runway

2.2   Customer Evolution

While the model was proven on cash-strapped college students, the firm's understanding of its target customer has evolved. The average Rent the Runway customer is actually someone who can afford to buy the dress. Average customer income is around $100,000.[29] For these savvy, affluent consumers that value experiences ahead of ownership, Rent the Runway is the smartest, most convenient way to shop.

While customers skew affluent, the young customer who gets hooked on the fashion rental experience may very well become a Rent the Runway lifer, delivering up what marketers refer to as high **customer lifetime value**. Someone who has a good first experience at a prom rental will move on to college events, graduate to weddings and engagement parties, use the firm for holiday parties or society events, she may rent a bridal dress, and use the site for high-end maternity fashions when baby is on the way.

Customer Lifetime Value

The concept of customer lifetime value (sometimes abbreviated as CLV, CLTV, or LTV) is vital when planning a profitable business. The idea is to predict the value of future profits that will accrue from acquired customers, so CLV is often stated as the **net present value** (NPV) of future profits from the customer relationship. It's an easy concept to state, but a much trickier one to predict, especially in a new industry that redefines customer relationship and engagement. Firms (especially new ones) don't really know how long a customer will remain with the firm (i.e., **churn rate**), how much it costs to maintain a customer, what is a reasonable rate for discounting the value of future profits into today's dollars, and how customer purchases will change over time, especially as tastes and product offerings evolve.

One key consideration is **customer acquisition costs**. The cost to acquire a customer must be less than reasonably estimated customer lifetime value (i.e., it should cost you less to bring in a customer than the value that customer will eventually return to your business). The greater this gap, the more profitable the customer.

Customer Acquisition Costs < CLV = NPV (future customer profits)

For all firms, but especially early-stage startups, low customer acquisition costs can be critical. Customer word-of-mouth and social media all help keep acquisition costs low. And firms more likely to generate repeat customers will see a CLV boost—key, since that regular cash flow is what's going to keep you in business!

customer lifetime value

Sometimes abbreviated as CLV, CLTV, or LTV. Refers to the current value of future profits that will accrue from acquired customers. CLV = NPV (future customer profits).

net present value

The value of future cash flows discounted into today's dollars (it is discounted because a dollar today should be worth more in the future assuming inflation or the potential to earn money on the dollar if it is invested).

churn rate

The rate at which consumers leave a product or service.

customer acquisition costs

The amount of money a firm spends to convince a customer to buy (or in the case of free products, try or use) a product or service.

KEY TAKEAWAYS

- The idea from Rent the Runway came from observing how an existing market was underserving a family member and other young women.
- Many uncertainties existed, and co-founders Hyman and Fleiss addressed these by launching a series of experiments to test product/market fit. They did many of these experiments with minimum viable products: running popup rental shops on college campuses, sharing PDFs with potential customers to see how women would respond to the prospect of renting without seeing and trying on a garment.
- Many supplier uncertainties existed, as well, but the firm worked closely with suppliers and demonstrated that they could actually grow the market and create a channel for reaching customers with a potential for high customer lifetime value.
- The co-founders have discovered that the model appeals not just to young, cash-strapped women, but to all women who seek convenience and value and who are interested in more broadly sampling high-end fashion.

QUESTIONS AND EXERCISES

1. How did the founders of Rent the Runway go about testing their original idea? Why was their approach especially efficient and useful when compared to building and deploying a website ready for a full launch?
2. What unknowns and concerns existed with respect to customer engagement with the concept? How did Rent the Runway's founders dispel these concerns?
3. What concerns did suppliers and designers have? How did Rent the Runway's founders dispel these concerns? Describe how the firm seeks to build deep and mutually beneficial industry partnerships.

3. CUSTOMER ENGAGEMENT (MOBILE, SOCIAL, AND PHYSICAL STOREFRONTS)

LEARNING OBJECTIVES

1. Understand how mobile and social are exceptionally useful for a firm like Rent the Runway.
2. Recognize why, although Rent the Runway is an e-commerce firm, it also benefits from having storefronts.

3.1 Mobile

As with many new efforts, the biggest challenge to adoption comes not from a given competitor, but rather from inertia. Firms need to develop ways of getting customers to try the experience, re-engage, and experiment with new offerings. While Rent the Runway began on the web, customer engagement via mobile is vital for the firm's future. Mobile represents even more customer convenience. Booked a calendar item on your phone? The same device can be used to select a dress and reserve it for the big event. A woman who has downtime and a smartphone can browse whenever she'd like—it's like having a closet in the cloud.[30] The firm's emphasis on mobile is clearly showing success. Shortly after Rent the Runway launched its first mobile app, mobile spiked to over 40 percent of firm traffic, and continues to rise.[31]

Despite the success of mobile, as mentioned in the Facebook chapter, many experimental features and A/B tests are more easily conducted on the Web. Changes on a firm's website are immediately available to all users the next time they visit the site, and it can be easier to run experiments by showing new features and design changes to a subset of users who access the site via a browser. For mobile apps, users may have to download a new version of the app, problems take longer to fix, and updates take longer to distribute for wide use.

3.2 Social

The mobile device isn't just the store—it's a world-connected camera to capture and share looks and fuel up a hyper-viral word of mouth machine leveraging the firm's biggest fans as its most persuasive marketers. As we've seen in other chapters, mobile is the key gateway to social.

Referrals matter. Rent the Runway sees a 75 percent higher conversion rate from friend referrals than from other marketing methods.[32] Experience from other retailers suggests that friend referrals result in better customers, as well. Online home goods retailer One Kings Lane reports that customers brought in through friend referrals have a customer lifetime value two times greater than those arriving from other channels.[33] Among friends, dress commentary is often the first icebreaker: "You look so good! What are you wearing?" "Oh, I Rented the Runway—have you heard of them?" Venture Capitalist Aileen Lee of Kleiner Perkins refers to the value of referrals in encouraging trial and purchase as **social proof**—positive influence created when someone finds out that others are doing something. And of course, social media magnifies the potential reach and impact of social proof.

Executives noted that Rent the Runway's Facebook page was a traffic magnet on Mondays. Women would post glowing, positive experiences with the firm, and they were changing their profile pictures to recently taken photos of them decked out in Rent the Runway dresses.[34] When it became clear that customers loved sharing their experiences online, the firm launched photo reviews on the Rent the Runway website. At first this seemed a bit of a risk. Would customers consider it icky to see other women in their dresses? Would there be inappropriate comments? It turns out the community was much more altruistic and supportive—pretty much the opposite of what one finds in YouTube comments. Any woman can submit a photo, the firm only screens for nudity and offensive images. These images are linked to the "Find Women Like Me" tool, which allows women to enter key parameters: height, bust size, dress size, and age, then combs through thousands of images to show social proof in the form of what real women are wearing. Members can also post questions to the women in the photos. Examples: "What heel height did you wear with that? Did you wear Spanx? Will that work as a maternity dress?"[35] Women who have viewed a user-generated photo are 200 percent more likely to rent than those who have viewed a product photographed on a model.[36] Rent the Runway has an ever-tuned ear to the customer, and has leveraged social in other ways, including Twitter chats and style councils held on Facebook, seeking input on straight from the catwalk couture.[37] Blogs are

social proof

Positive influence created when someone finds out that others are doing something.

earned media

Positive influence created when someone finds out that others are doing something.

paid media

Refers to efforts where an organization pays to leverage a channel or promote a message. Paid media efforts include things such as advertisement and sponsorships.

another way that user-generated content helps spread the word with lower costs and higher effectiveness. Customers arriving at the site via the **earned media** of a fashion blog have a 200 percent higher conversion rate than customers arriving via the **paid media** of search engine ads.[38] As a result, most of the firm's online growth is organic. Rent the Runway does very little paid advertising.

FIGURE 12.1

This sample customer comment on Rent the Runway shares that the dress reviewed is suitable for New Year's Eve, it offers details on fit and length, and it includes additional information about the sequin detailing.

★ ★ ★ ★ ★

"Fun, sparkly New Years dress!"

Height	5'4"	Size Worn	6
Weight	125 lbs	Usual Size	4
Bust	34C	Overall Fit	Small
Body Type	Hourglass	Worn To	Party
Age	27		

I rented this dress for New Years Eve and LOVED it! The dress was more form fitting than I anticipated from the picture, but it ended up fitting great. The sequins were so fun and I got a lot of compliments on it. The length was also good - short but not too short. I would definitely recommend!

– JENNIFER

Social not only helps spread the good word about Rent the Runway, as mentioned earlier it also helps fuel business demand. The firm's CEO has stated that today's Internet "creates pressure for women. Now you can't repeat outfits because your friends have seen that outfit on social media. As ridiculous as that sounds, that is what drives our business."[39]

3.3   Physical Retail—When Brick and Mortar Has a Role in an Online Business

At Amazon, being an Internet pure-play without physical storefronts brings clear advantages. Eliminating stores creates labor, real estate, energy, security, inventory and other cost efficiencies that flow right to the bottom line. Pure play works for Amazon because, for the most part, the firm sells commodity products that users are already familiar with and don't need to experience before feeling comfortable making a purchase.

Providers of experience goods, however, may need to spend more effort convincing customers to try their offerings. Any highly differentiated products that may be unfamiliar to consumers, might be able to benefit from in-person customer engagement. This was the idea behind the Apple store. Apple products offered at the Apple store give firm-trained employees an opportunity to present features and advantages of the company's unique products, how they work together, and offer free on-site customer support. For Apple this formula has resulted in the single most successful retail chain in the United States on a sales-per-square-foot basis, dwarfing not just consumer electronics categories, but also clothing retailers, high-end jewelers, and everyone else.[40]

Rent the Runway's move into physical retail locations allows the firm to continue to offer online efficiencies for most of its customers, but it also creates an opportunity for some customers to have a high-touch in person experience. According to Hyman, this can be especially important for "serving up a new customer behavior like renting clothes."[41] The physical retail experience can attract new customers, while underscoring the merits of the model, and laying the groundwork for an enduring customer relationship that can shift online, over time. A similar expansion into physical stores is also happening at clothier Bonobos and eyewear firm Warby Parker, both fashion-centric retailers that started online.[42]

Rent the Runway's stores are focused on customized, high-value customer engagement. Customers go online to book an appointment with an in-store stylist, and technology is leveraged to enhance the store visit. Customers give information in advance on the type of event they're planning to attend and they can share additional information that might allow stylists to pull product for their appointment and be best prepared for their arrival. The firm charges for booked appointments ($25 for single-event styling, $40 for longer, multiple-event appointments), but also allows walk-ins, as available. If a customer tries on ten dresses and likes several, this is data that can be used for later targeting and customer-focused follow-up, personalizing online shopping and e-mail marketing with styles she's most likely interested in. Stores also act as a way to offer a fit guarantee, and can function as mini-distribution centers with same-day rental of certain styles, plus dress pickup, and drop off. The high level of service offered by the firm prompts Hyman to quip, "We're more like a hotel company than a fashion company."[43] And for customers that are local, Rent the Runway retail can replace a last-minute department store run. Since an estimated 30 percent of purchases at retailers like Zara and H&M are for a last-minute need, the retail footprint means Rent the Runway can compete to capture sales from fast fashion, too.[44]

Retail was rolled out cautiously, with a limited MVP experience offered at the firm's South Village, Manhattan headquarters. A second physical retail trial was conducted in carve-out space inside the Fifth Avenue store of accessory retailer Henri Bendel (Bendel's was a good initial partner. The store didn't sell dresses so it didn't fear sales cannibalization, and Bendel's could benefit from increased traffic).

With the concept proven, Rent the Runway moved out of Bendel's, and now has several stand-alone stores in locations that include New York, Washington DC, Chicago, and at the Cosmopolitan Hotel in Las Vegas (Rent the Runway has also experimented with popup shops and a mobile road tour).[45] Customer rental patterns differ by location. A DC client will come with her calendar app open, planning for formal events throughout the year, while the Vegas customer is more likely to walk out with a dress to wear that evening (one goal: allow clients to go on vacation without packing a suitcase[46]). Even with these differences, each in-store engagement is an opportunity to delight the customer and gather data to strengthen the relationship so that she can be turned into a loyal, regularly-renting client. While retail has been successful for all of the reasons outlined above, Hyman envisions there being fifteen to twenty destination-style Rent the Runway retail locations in major metropolitan areas, not hundreds that a major retail brand would have.[47]

KEY TAKEAWAYS

- Mobile is an always-on store that encourages users to browse and engage with the site.
- Mobile also allows the firm to collect additional, valuable data on each user so that it can better understand her preferences and interests.
- The mobile camera and calendar also integrate with Rent the Runway—allow for scheduling and social sharing.
- Social media "kills" outfits, heightening interest in the kind of efficient, high-quality wardrobe rotation that Rent the Runway offers.
- Rent the Runway has leveraged the concept of social proof to spread the word about the firm, encourage others to sign up, and help customers gain additional information so that they can overcome inertia and rent a dress.
- Storefronts make sense when products are novel and customers may need additional education to help them get over inertia and actually try the new firm's offerings. Rent the Runway storefronts also act as mini-warehouses and additional points to gather experience-enhancing customer data.

QUESTIONS AND EXERCISES

1. Why is mobile especially important to Rent the Runway? How are customers using mobile devices to engage with the firm?
2. How has the rise of social media helped Rent the Runway?
3. What concerns do firms have when encouraging customers to socially share and publicly engage a brand online? Describe Rent the Runway's experience. Do you think this is typical or unique? Why?
4. In what ways do retail storefronts help the firm? In what ways are Rent the Runway stores like Apple stores?

4. DATA

LEARNING OBJECTIVES

1. Recognize the many ways that data can be collected and leveraged to enhance the Rent the Runway business model.
2. Understand the concept of agile software development and why it is important to Rent the Runway and the many other firms that practice this approach.

It was clear from the start that data would be the lifeblood of the business. The firm's Chief Analytics Officer was one of the firm's first hires,[48] and the team now includes top talent who honed their skill at Oracle, Netflix, and other data-crunching champs.[49] Consider the potential of data to drive efficiencies throughout the firm's unique value chain. When sourcing product, data helps uncover demand patterns—how popular are long dresses, short dresses, colors, designers, and styles? The firm can also gain a sense of how trends change over time by season, geography, and demographics.

For operations, data exposes bottom-line impacting variations such as, how long do certain materials last, how prone are they to needing repair, and how does this impact cost and any prep delay before certain types of dresses can be sent out again?[50] Analytics have helped inform the length of a rental period, expectations on turn-around time, slack inventory needed to cover for any dresses not returned on time, methods that can encourage on-time returns, selection of optimal shipping partners, the locations of the firm's warehouse and stores, and much, much more.[51]

The website and mobile app can then track online engagement and deliver a host of customer metrics—where a customer clicks, what she's searching on and which products she's returning to. Outside the website and mobile app, analytics inform which e-mail campaigns are working; how Facebook, Pinterest, Twitter, Instagram and other social media drive traffic; and what sorts of other marketing campaigns are most effective. The firm's recommendation engine is continually refined, not just for dress suggestions, but also as feedback is gathered on the conversion rate for accessories and other products offered for purchase.[52] Customers provide additional feedback on dress fit, comfort, and other satisfaction indicators. A/B testing is used to continually refine the firm's approach through constant experimentation.[53] More data will also provide even more insights on fit for a given body type—nudging customer satisfaction even higher.[54] All of this underpins an evolving personalization engine that presents products you're most likely to be interested in.

Like Uber, the airline industry, hotels, and other service providers with limited inventory and varying demand, Rent the Runway also leverages analytics for demand pricing.[55] A hot summer dress available in limited quantities may be higher priced from May to August, but data will also help expose value in underutilized inventory a customer is most likely to be interested in, maximizing return from the firm's vast dress library.[56]

Geek Up, Get Agile, and Innovate Faster

As non-technical founders, Fleiss and Hyman have nonetheless gained insight into ways to build key firm skills. Software development was initially outsourced, but it was quickly shifted in house as the firm was able to expand its technical team—vital since Rent the Runway's custom built systems underpin the firm's competitive advantage. To help inform technology decision-making, the firm's founders went to tech meet-ups, searched out engineers to chat up and recruit, and read widely—everything from software development books to coder blogs.[57]

Rent the Runway is one of the many practitioners of **agile software development**, a systems development technique that leverages cross-functional, self-organizing teams designed to rapidly leverage business knowledge and software development skills.[58] The new reality of software development has business people working in tandem with coders and system architects on continued innovation, iteration, and refinement; further underscoring the importance of tech in all careers.[59] Rent the Runway also practices **continuous deployment**, allowing the firm to have shorter release cycles on software updates.[60] This helps Rent the Runway rapidly push out bug fixes and new features when they're ready for release, rather than waiting for a slower-moving centrally-managed schedule.[61] One finds these techniques, which foster more autonomy and collaboration in software development, in use by many tech leaders, including Etsy, Facebook, Google, and Netflix.[62] At Rent the Runway, this is the kind of practice that's vital for a fast-paced startup that's inventing the future of commerce.

agile software development

A systems development method in which requirements and solutions rapidly and iteratively evolve through collaboration between self-organizing, cross-functional teams, rather than a top-down, centrally-managed, schedule-driven approach.

continuous deployment

A software development approach where an organization's developers release products, features, and updates in shorter cycles, when ready, rather than wait for centrally-managed delivery schedules.

QUESTIONS AND EXERCISES

1. In what ways is data collected at Rent the Runway?
2. How does data enhance the customer experience?
3. How does data enhance firm operations? How does it help cut costs and improve efficiency?
4. How does Rent the Runway price product? What other firms use this approach and why?
5. Describe the concepts of agile software development and continuous deployment. Why do they make sense in an entrepreneurial environment like Rent the Runway? What do these techniques imply about the skills set of technologists and managers?

5. OPERATIONS AND LOGISTICS

LEARNING OBJECTIVES

1. **Understand and appreciate the scale and breadth of the operations and logistics business that Rent the Runway needs to run its business.**
2. **Recognize the critical role that technology plays in implementing this model.**

A significant part of the firm's technology use and data analytics ends up focused on an operations and logistics model that is, at its core, people moving product—a one-of-a-kind orchestration of luxury good selection, cleaning, repair, packaging, shipping, return, and inspection that's executed over and over again. No one has done anything like this at the scale of Rent the Runway. Consider that the firm's Secaucus, New Jersey distribution center, about the size of two football fields, isn't just the firm's primary warehouse; it's the largest single dry cleaning operation in the United States.[63]

Extremes also apply to the Rent the Runway distribution center workweek. Most of the events that prompt client rentals occur on the weekend, so return envelopes flood in on Monday and Tuesday. Products need to be prepped, packaged, and out the door by an ultra-busy Wednesday to ensure that they'll arrive on time for the next set of weekend parties.[64] Tech points the way to prioritization. Receiving staff scan the outside of returned envelopes and a message pops up on-screen with each scan, immediately determining if an item needs to go out right away. Garments are placed into bins color coded for urgency: black can eventually be prepped for restocking, but red is for those high-priority items that need to be immediately turned-around for send-out to another customer.[65] The system will also identify mid-term priority items, as in "get to this if you have time after taking care of priority items—if we ship it today, we'll save money." It'll even prioritize return shipping based on inventory demands, printing a higher-priced but faster-shipping return label for a customer if product turn-around is especially acute.[66]

Next up for urgent items is a cleaning, but tech alone can't yet match the human touch that's sometimes needed. This isn't a simple rack 'em and steam 'em facility. Garments are expensive, materials are diverse, and stains potentially too varied for conveyor belt cleaning alone to meet Rent the Runway quality standards. Instead, highly skilled "spotters," some with decades of experience in the industry and earning over $100,000 a year, inspect garments, assess stains, and choose the right method for any problem issues needing an especially pristine clean.[67] Spotters are more like potion master chemists, each working alongside an assembly of bottles, vials, sprays, and air hoses that can be used to restore a good-as-new sparkle.[68]

After cleaning, a team of over four dozen seamstresses stand ready as the Navy Seals of dress repair. This same facility has a massive operation for jewelry mending and leather dyeing, too.[69] Any individual item might be matched with additional products such as a second dress size, or additional accessories, so technology dispatches warehouse workers to pick any other products needed for a complete order. Items are scanned for a pre-packaging double check, shipping labels are automatically printed, and items are boxed and ready to be sent out. Delivery firms drop by around 8 p.m. to get garments on their way.[70] The firm's operations are so efficient that many items arriving by 8 a.m. can be turned around in twelve hours for same-day send-out.[71]

The more times a dress is rented, the more revenue the firm generates, and despite the firm's exacting standards for maintaining product quality, dresses can be turned about thirty times during their rental life.[72] Even after a lifetime of partying, most dresses are still in pretty good shape. Much of the post-rental inventory is eventually sold via semi-annual inventory-clearing sales.[73]

Rent the Runway could have turned a profit already, but instead the firm has elected to expand its infrastructure and systems.[74] These investments help deliver the scale, data, and operational advantage likely to be essential to keeping challengers at bay. Overbuilding can make a lot of business sense. A large distribution facility doesn't just provide expansion capacity for growth, it also acts as a staging area for experimenting with new ideas and product lines.

KEY TAKEAWAYS

- Rent the Runway leverages technology to run a reverse logistics business in which every product that is sent out to a customer must also come back. Technology is used to schedule and prioritize inventory flow.
- Product must also be washed, perhaps repaired, and prepped for send-out in what is often a very small window of time for completion.
- Despite relying so heavily on technology, many aspects of Rent the Runway's business still need human participation.

QUESTIONS AND EXERCISES

- How does technology help Rent the Runway prioritize items to be sent out?
- How does technology help the firm optimize shipping rates?
- In what ways are human beings still necessary to the process? How does technology help here and how might new technology help more? Do you think the firm will the firm need this many workers in another ten years? Why or why not?

6. EXPANDING WITH NEW MODELS

LEARNING OBJECTIVE

1. **Recognize new business opportunities for Rent the Runway, why they are attractive, and what challenges the firm faces when exploring these initiatives.**

Rent the Runway's founders are ambitious. Jenn Hyman has declared the ultimate opportunity for Rent the Runway "is to build the Amazon of rental."[75] In addition to wedding dresses, maternity dresses, and plus-size fashions, the company's offerings now include jewelry, handbags, scarves, and even rentals of "ugly sweaters" for holiday parties. And Rent the Runway will suggest undergarments, makeup, and hair accessories to further enhance your look (all available for purchase).[76]

Next up, says Hyman, "We have a vision to create your closet on rotation."[77] Rent the Runway Unlimited really is the fashion equivalent of the old Netflix DVD-by-mail service. It's a flexible, subscription-based ownership model for accessories and clothing. For $99 a month, women create a queue of requested items. Customers choose the items they want first and can keep them as long as they'd like. Send an item back and choose the next item you want. The firm started with handbags, leather jackets, and jewelry (less risky categories since there are no sizing issues), but has now also moved into everyday fashion (daytime dresses, skirts, tops, outerwear). Love an item you've been sent? You can also buy it from Rent the Runway.

Unlimited is a startup inside a startup, expanding beyond the firm's special events rentals with a new service offering an every-day Rent the Runway use case. For many women, Unlimited makes solid financial sense. The average American woman buys 64 pieces of clothing a year, and half of those items will be worn only once.[78] Even frequently warn items, like a winter coat, might be better chosen as a six-month rental. And the ability to browse and manage a fashion queue on your phone is a potential time-saver for professional women, mothers, and anyone else with dwindling hours to dedicate to store shopping. Hyman's grand vision: "Every woman should have a subscription to fashion just like you have a subscription to music or entertainment and through that subscription you'll be able to have fun with this amazing industry."[79] Success will require convincing large numbers of customers to yet again rethink their perception of clothes ownership, but the appeal is clear: Your smartphone can mimic a magic trapdoor at the back of your closet where thousands of beautiful items can be summoned forth at the press of a button.

KEY TAKEAWAYS

- Rent the Runway has an opportunity to move to a subscription business, further enhancing the concept of the "closet in the cloud."
- Customers can buy items they like at a discount.
- Customers are currently not used to subscribing to fashion, so convincing them to try this model may be a challenge.

QUESTIONS AND EXERCISES

1. What is Rent the Runway Unlimited? Would you use this? Why or why not?
2. What other areas could Rent the Runway expand into? Would you recommend these? What about men's fashion? Casual fashion?
3. Why did Rent the Runway choose the initial product categories to focus on when testing the Unlimited service?

7. CONCLUSION

LEARNING OBJECTIVES

1. **Recognize potential sources of competitive advantage created by Rent the Runway that make it difficult for customers to challenge the firm.**
2. **Identify successful firms founded or led by women, and why having a female-led business can be an advantage for Rent the Runway.**

Rent the Runway's founders represent a new generation of entrepreneurs leveraging a collection of enabling technologies to fundamentally recast the consumer relationship in a multibillion dollar industry. Mobile, social, big data, tech-orchestrated operations, and collaborative consumption all come together in a market-growing set of services that create value for both customers and designers. Success is never a sure thing, and imitators exist in the United States and abroad, but the castle that makes Rent the Runway's Cinderella moments possible is protected by some pretty deep moats that potential competitors will find difficult to cross. This is a firm that has raised over $100 million in capital and is experiencing significant growth. While still a privately held firm, press reports have suggested that in 2014 the firm rented $809 million in retail value of dresses and accessories and shipped more orders than in the previous five years combined.[80] Some speculate that Rent the Runway is on their way to so-called **unicorn** status, the tech industry's name for those extraordinary startups valued at $1 billion or more.[81]

The rise of successful women entrepreneurs continues. The list of the world's youngest self-made billionaires includes Elizabeth Holmes, the Stanford dropout and founder of blood testing company

Theranos, which Holmes founded with money she'd saved for college.[82] Women have also been co-founders of multibillion-dollar giants like Cisco and HTC, as well as more recent startups including EventBrite, Poshmark, SlideShare, and Birchbox. And women execs have run some of tech's biggest firms, including HP, IBM, Oracle, and Yahoo!. Still, women remain underrepresented among venture-backed entrepreneurs, and in participating in the tech industry. Rent the Runway's founders are committed to changing this. The firm's Chicago storefront also serves as a platform to promote local women entrepreneurs. The store will host talks with Chicago businesswomen and selected entrepreneurs will also have their stories posted on the Rent the Runway website. All managers, technologists, and would-be startup captains can learn from the Rent the Runway story, but helping to mentor and inspire broader participation in innovation is a legacy from the firm's founders that boldly stands alongside crafting the new colossus of couture.

Creating a Magnet for Talent and Capital

Rent the Runway has also become a much-sought-after employer for talented women executives and technologists. While firms like Facebook and Twitter are about 70 percent male, the equation is flipped at Jenn and Jenny's shop. The CCO is a woman, so is the firm's Chief Technology Officer, and the second men's room was recently converted to a third ladies' room.[83] Among those cautious and weary of "gamer gate"[84] headlines and concern over a lack of gender diversity in the tech industry,[85] the female friendly and mentor-rich environment of Rent the Runway gives the firm a recruiting edge. The industry impacting opportunity from Rent the Runway has also attracted an eclectic set of backers, from top-tier venture capital firms that include Bain, Highland Capital Partners, and Kleiner Perkins, to an investment from Condé Nast Publications, the parent of the fashion bible *Vogue*.

KEY TAKEAWAYS

- Rent the Runway has the potential to grow a series of assets that will repell rivals, among them: brand, scale, deep industry partnerships, data, and more.
- There have been many tech firms founded by and led by women. These firms are often talent magnets for high-performing women who seek a supportive environment rich in mentors and led by leaders they find easier to identify with.

QUESTIONS AND EXERCISES

1. Why do you suppose so few women are involved in entrepreneurship and technology? What can industries, firms, universities, and other entities do to improve this situation.
2. Conduct research online. Which firms are considered as doing an exceptional job in attracting underrepresented talent to the workplace? Why are these efforts working?
3. How can firms increase the pipeline so that more people from underrepresented groups bring their minds to tech and entrepreneurship?
4. Research and find additional women-led or founded tech firms and share these with your class.
5. Describe the resources Rent the Runway is building for sustainable competitive advantage. Which of these do you think is exceptionally strong and will keep the firm at the top of the industry. Why? Is the firm vulnerable? If so, how so, and if not, why not?

ENDNOTES

1. J. Wortham, "A Netflix Model for Haute Couture," *The New York Times*, Nov. 8, 2009.

2. S. Bertoni, "How Mixing Data And Fashion Can Make Rent The Runway Tech's Next Billion Dollar Star," *Forbes*, Sept. 8, 2014.

3. J. D'Onfro, "This startup founder wants you to be able to go on a vacation without packing a suitcase," *BusinessInsider*, March 14, 2015.

4. L. Lazare, "Rent the Runway is bringing high fashion for rent to Chicago," *Chicago Business Journal*, March 30, 2015.

5. S. Bertoni, "The Secret Mojo Behind Rent The Runway's Rental Machine," *Forbes*, August, 26, 2014.

6. H. Turk, "Dress for Less in Las Vegas at Rent the Runway," *USA Today*, March 10, 2014.

7. R. King, "Q&A: How Rent the Runway dazzles shoppers with data," *ZDNet*, Feb. 20, 2015.

8. S. Bertoni, "The Secret Mojo Behind Rent The Runway's Rental Machine," *Forbes*, August, 26, 2014. And K. Ryssdal, "A Warehouse Dash with Rent the Runway," *Marketplace*, April 30, 2015.

9. S. Bertoni, "How Mixing Data And Fashion Can Make Rent The Runway Tech's Next Billion Dollar Star," *Forbes*, Sept. 8, 2014.

10. Time Staff, "50 Best Websites of 2010," Time, Aug. 25, 2010. Time Staff, "50 Best Websites of 2010," *Time*, Aug. 25, 2010.

11. S. Evans, "The Most Influential Women in Technology 2011 – Jennifer Hyman and Jennifer Fleiss," *FastCompany*, Jan. 10, 2011.

12. T. Black, "Jennifer Hyman and Jenny Fleiss, Founders of Rent the Runway," *Inc.*, July 19, 2010.

13. P. Sellers, "Fortune's most promising women entrepreneurs," *Fortune*, Sept. 13, 2011.

14. S. Bertoni, "How Mixing Data And Fashion Can Make Rent The Runway Tech's Next Billion Dollar Star," *Forbes*, Sept. 8, 2014.

15. E. Reis, The Lean Startup: How Today's Entrepreneurs Use Continuous Innovation to Create Radically Successful Businesses, *Crown Business*, New York, 2011.

16. H. Seligson, "The Startup Queens' Rules for Confidence at Work," *Glamour*, May 2011.

17. C. Binkley, "Fashion 101: Rent the Runway Targets Students," *The Wall Street Journal*, April 7, 2011.

18. N. Furr and J. Dyer, The Innovator's Method: Bringing the Lean Startup into Your Organization, *Harvard Business Review Press*, Boston, 2014.

19. S. Bertoni, "How Mixing Data And Fashion Can Make Rent The Runway Tech's Next Billion Dollar Star," *Forbes*, Sept. 8, 2014.

20. Unattributed, "Rent the Runway: Saving a Fortune on Fashion Indulgences," *Fox Business*, Sept. 15, 2013.

21. I. Lapowski, "The Way I Work: Jennifer Hyman, Rent the Runway," *Inc.*, Jan. 24, 2012.

22. Unattributed, "WWD CEO Summit," *The Baxter Consulting Group*, Oct. 30, 2014.

23. E. Griffith, "Rent the Runway Unveils a Netflix Subscription for Your Closet," *Fortune*, July 16, 2014.

24. I. Lapowski, "The Way I Work: Jennifer Hyman, Rent the Runway," *Inc.*, Jan. 24, 2012.

25. I. Lapowski, "The Way I Work: Jennifer Hyman, Rent the Runway," *Inc.*, Jan. 24, 2012.

26. Elle (unattributed), "Donna Karan Creates Capsule Collection for Rent the Runway," Feb. 11, 2013.

27. I. Lapowski, "The Way I Work: Jennifer Hyman, Rent the Runway," *Inc.*, Jan. 24, 2012.

28. E. Griffith, "Rent the Runway Unveils a Netflix Subscription for Your Closet," *Fortune*, July 16, 2014.

29. S. Asprea, "SXSW session notes: Defining the next-generation retail experience," *MSL Group*, March 14, 2015.

30. E. Griffith, "Rent The Runway unveils a Netflix subscription for your closet," *Fortune*, July 16, 2014.

31. S. Bertoni, "How Mixing Data And Fashion Can Make Rent The Runway Tech's Next Billion Dollar Star," *Forbes*, Sept. 8, 2014.

32. Lee, Aileen, "Social Proof is the New Marketing," *TechCrunch*, November 27, 2011.

33. Lee, Aileen, "Social Proof is the New Marketing," *TechCrunch*, November 27, 2011

34. A. Orley, "Rent the Runway Buys Into Social Media," *CNBC*, Aug. 16, 2012.

35. S. Clifford, "High Fashion, No Airbrushing," *The New York Times*, Oct. 19, 2012.

36. L. Rao, "Rent The Runway Turns Customers Into Models With New Search Feature," *TechCrunch*, Oct. 21, 2012.

37. A. Orley, "Rent the Runway Buys Into Social Media," *CNBC*, Aug. 16, 2012.

38. S. Clifford, "High Fashion, No Airbrushing," *The New York Times*, Oct. 19, 2012.

39. S. Bertoni, "How Mixing Data And Fashion Can Make Rent The Runway Tech's Next Billion Dollar Star," *Forbes*, Sept. 8, 2014.

40. B. Thau, "Apple And The Other Most Successful Retailers By Sales Per Square Foot," *Forbes*, May 20, 2014.

41. J. Hyman (as panelist), "Stowaway Cosmetics, Rent The Runway, and Spring on the End of Wholesale," *TechCrunch*, May 4, 2015.

42. J. Hyman (as panelist), "Stowaway Cosmetics, Rent The Runway, and Spring on the End of Wholesale," *TechCrunch*, May 4, 2015.

43. C. Binkley, "Fashion 101: Rent the Runway Targets Students," *The Wall Street Journal*, April 7, 2011.

44. J. Hyman (as panelist), "Stowaway Cosmetics, Rent The Runway, and Spring on the End of Wholesale," *TechCrunch*, May 4, 2015.

45. E. Brooke, "Rent The Runway Branches Further Offline, With A Permanent Showroom At Henri Bendel," *TechCrunch*, Oct. 17, 2013.

46. J. D'Onfro, "This startup founder wants you to be able to go on a vacation without packing a suitcase," *BusinessInsider*, March 14, 2015.

47. J. Hyman (as panelist), "Stowaway Cosmetics, Rent The Runway, and Spring on the End of Wholesale," *TechCrunch*, May 4, 2015.

48. J. Bell, "On the Ground at SXSW2015 > Redefining the Next Generation Retail Experience," *GPY&R*, March 17, 2015.

49. P. Marx, "The Borrowers," The New Yorker, Jan. 31, 2011. And J. Bell, "On the Ground at SXSW2015 > Redefining the Next Generation Retail Experience," *GPY&R*, March 17, 2015.

50. S. Galbraith, "The Secret Behind Rent the Runway's Success," *Forbes*, Dec. 3, 2013.

51. S. Galbraith, "The Secret Behind Rent the Runway's Success," *Forbes*, Dec. 3, 2013.

52. S. Bertoni, "How Mixing Data And Fashion Can Make Rent The Runway Tech's Next Billion Dollar Star," *Forbes*, Sept. 8, 2014.

53. G. Tong, "Experimenting With Alchemy," *Rent the Runway's Dress Code Blog*, July 30, 2014.

54. J. Dutcher, "Ask a Data Scientist at Rent the Runway," *datascience@berkeley*, Sept. 12, 2013.

55. J. Singer, "Rent the Runway: Fashion Meets the Sharing Economy," *The Robin Report*, May 18, 2015.

56. S. Galbraith, "The Secret Behind Rent the Runway's Success," *Forbes*, Dec. 3, 2013.

57. I. Lapowski, "The Way I Work: Jennifer Hyman, Rent the Runway," *Inc.*, Jan. 24, 2012.

58. J. Bloomberg, "Scaling Agile Software Development for Digital Transformation," *Forbes*, Sept. 8, 2014; and S. Denning, "Why Do Managers Hate Agile?" *Forbes*, January 28, 2015.

59. R. Fergueson, "Rent The Runway: Organizing Around Analytics," *MIT Sloan Management Review*, March 24, 2014.

60. M. Wunsch, "Continuous Delivery @RentTheRunway," Presented at the TimesOpen Transitioning to Continuous Delivery event, Slides published to SlideShare on July 22, 2014. M

61. E. Weinstein, "Deploying Daily," Rent the Runway's *The Dress Code blog*, May 8, 2014.

62. J. Humble, "The Case for Continuous Delivery," *ThoughtWorks*, Feb. 13, 2014.

63. R. Greenfield, "Inside Rent the Runway's Secret Dry Cleaning Empire," *FastCompany*, Oct. 28, 2014.

64. W. Schuster, "Camille Fournier on the Software and Data Science Behind Rent the Runway," *InfoQ*, May 21, 2015.

65. K. Ryssdal, "A Warehouse Dash with Rent the Runway," *Marketplace*, April 30, 2015.

66. W. Schuster, "Camille Fournier on the Software and Data Science Behind Rent the Runway," *InfoQ*, May 21, 2015.

67. R. Greenfield, "Inside Rent the Runway's Secret Dry Cleaning Empire," *FastCompany*, Oct. 28, 2014.

68. R. Greenfield, "Inside Rent the Runway's Secret Dry Cleaning Empire," *FastCompany*, Oct. 28, 2014. And K. Ryssdal, "A Warehouse Dash with Rent the Runway," *Marketplace*, April 30, 2015.

69. J. Hyman, "Borrowing is the New Owning," *FastCompany*, Sept. 9, 2014.

70. K. Ryssdal, "A Warehouse Dash with Rent the Runway," *Marketplace*, April 30, 2015.

71. J. Hyman, "Borrowing is the New Owning," *FastCompany*, Sept. 9, 2014.

72. S. Bertoni, "The Secret Mojo Behind Rent The Runway's Rental Machine," *Forbes*, August, 26, 2014.

73. R. Greenfield, "Inside Rent the Runway's Secret Dry Cleaning Empire," *FastCompany*, Oct. 28, 2014.

74. S. Bertoni, "How Mixing Data And Fashion Can Make Rent The Runway Tech's Next Billion Dollar Star," *Forbes*, Sept. 8, 2014.

75. S. Bertoni, "The Secret Mojo Behind Rent The Runway's Rental Machine," *Forbes*, August, 26, 2014.

76. S. Galbraith, "The Secret Behind Rent the Runway's Success," *Forbes*, Dec. 3, 2013.

77. J. Hyman, "Borrowing is the New Owning," *FastCompany*, Sept. 9, 2014.

78. E. Griffith, "Rent The Runway unveils a Netflix subscription for your closet," *Fortune*, July 16, 2014.

79. K. Ryssdal, "A Warehouse Dash with Rent the Runway," *Marketplace*, April 30, 2015

80. A. Elejalde-Ruiz, "Rent the Runway's new Chicago store to promote local women entrepreneurs," *The Chicago Tribune*, April 6, 2016.

81. C. Leahey, "How female founders can join the Unicorn Club," Jan. 30, 2015.

82. Forbes Staff, "Elizabeth Holmes: The World's Billionaires," *Forbes*, March 2, 2015.

83. S. Bertoni, "How Mixing Data And Fashion Can Make Rent The Runway Tech's Next Billion Dollar Star," *Forbes*, Sept. 8, 2014.

84. E. Klein, "GamerGate: A Closer Look At The Controversy Sweeping Video Games," *Forbes*, Sept. 4, 2014.

85. D. Dubinsky, "What Is Silicon Valley's Problem With Gender?" *Re/code*, March 25, 2015.

CHAPTER 13
Understanding Software: A Primer for Managers

1. INTRODUCTION

LEARNING OBJECTIVES

1. Recognize the importance of software and its implications for the firm and strategic decision making.
2. Understand that software is everywhere; not just in computers, but also cell phones, cars, cameras, and many other technologies.
3. Know what software is and be able to differentiate it from hardware.
4. List the major classifications of software and give examples of each.

We know **computing hardware** is getting faster and cheaper, creating all sorts of exciting and disruptive opportunities for the savvy manager. But what's really going on inside the box? It's **software** that makes the magic of computing happen. Without software, your PC would be a heap of silicon wrapped in wires encased in plastic and metal. But it's the instructions—the software code—that enable a computer to do something wonderful, driving the limitless possibilities of information technology.

Software is everywhere. An inexpensive cell phone has about 1 million lines of code.[1] Ford automobiles actually have more lines of code than Twitter and Facebook combined.[2] Software might even be in grandpa. The average pacemaker has between 80,000 and 100,000 of code.[3] In this chapter we'll take a peek inside the chips to understand what software is. A lot of terms are associated with software: operating systems, applications, enterprise software, distributed systems, and more. We'll define these terms up front, and put them in a managerial context. A follow-up chapter, Chapter 14 will focus on changes impacting the software business, including open source software, software as a service (SaaS), cloud computing, virtualization, and the rise of apps. These changes are creating an environment radically different from the software industry that existed in previous decades—confronting managers with a whole new set of opportunities and challenges.

Managers who understand software can better understand the possibilities and impact of technology. They can make better decisions regarding the strategic value of IT and the potential for technology-driven savings. They can appreciate the challenges, costs, security vulnerabilities, legal and compliance issues, and limitations involved in developing and deploying technology solutions. And since firms which cannot communicate will struggle to work in tandem, managers who understand software can appreciate the key role that technology plays in partnerships, merger and acquisitions, and firm valuation. Given the pervasiveness of tech in all managerial disciplines, a firm without technologists in the boardroom is setting itself up for failure. In the next two chapters we will closely examine the software industry and discuss trends, developments and economics—all of which influence decisions managers make about products to select, firms to partner with, and firms to invest in.

1.1 What Is Software?

When we refer to computer hardware (sometimes just hardware), we're talking about the physical components of information technology—the equipment that you can physically touch, including computers, storage devices, networking equipment, and other peripherals.

computer hardware

The physical components of information technology, which can include the computer itself plus peripherals such as storage devices, input devices like the mouse and keyboard, output devices like monitors and printers, networking equipment, and so on.

software

A computer program or a collection of programs. It is a precise set of instructions that tells hardware what to do.

Software refers to a computer program or collection of programs—sets of instructions that tell the hardware what to do. Software gets your computer to behave like a Web browser or word processor, lets your smartphone play music and video, and enables your bank's ATM to spit out cash.

It's when we start to talk about the categories of software that most people's eyes glaze over. To most folks, software is a big, incomprehensible alphabet soup of acronyms and geeky phrases: API, ERP, OS, SQL, to name just a few.

Don't be intimidated. The basics are actually pretty easy to understand. But it's not soup; it's more of a layer cake. Think about computer hardware as being at the bottom of the layer cake. The next layer is the **operating system**, the collection of programs that control the hardware. Windows, Mac OS X, iOS, and Linux are operating systems. On top of that layer are **applications**—a range of which include end-user programs like those in Office, apps that run on smartphones, and the complex set of programs that manage a business's inventory, payroll, and accounting. At the top of the cake are users.

The flexibility of these layers gives computers the customization options that managers and businesses demand. Understanding how the layers relate to each other helps you make better decisions on what options are important to your unique business needs, can influence what you buy, and may have implications for everything from competitiveness to cost overruns to security breaches. What follows is a Manager's Guide to the main software categories with an emphasis on why each is important.

operating system

The software that controls the computer hardware and establishes standards for developing and executing applications.

applications

Includes desktop applications, enterprise software, utilities, and other programs that perform specific tasks for users and organizations.

FIGURE 13.1 The Hardware/Software Layer Cake

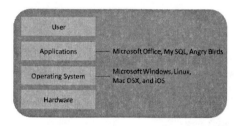

KEY TAKEAWAYS

- Software refers to a computer program or collection of programs. It enables computing devices to perform tasks.
- You can think of software as being part of a layer cake, with hardware at the bottom; the operating system controlling the hardware and establishing standards, the applications executing one layer up, and the users at the top.
- How these layers relate to one another has managerial implications in many areas, including the flexibility in meeting business demand, costs, legal issues and security.
- Software is everywhere—not just in computers, but also in cell phones, cars, cameras, and many other technologies.

QUESTIONS AND EXERCISES

1. Explain the difference between hardware and software.
2. Why should a manager care about software and how software works? What critical organizational and competitive factors can software influence?
3. What role has software played in your decision to select certain products? Has this influenced why you favored one product or service over another?
4. Find the *Fortune* 500 list online. Which firm is the highest ranked software firm? While the *Fortune* 500 ranks firms according to revenue, what's this firm's profitability rank? What does this discrepancy tell you about the economics of software development? Why is the software business so attractive to entrepreneurs?
5. Refer to earlier chapters (and particularly to Chapter 2): Which resources for competitive advantage might top software firms be able to leverage to ensure their continued dominance? Give examples of firms that have leveraged these assets, and why they are so strong.

2. OPERATING SYSTEMS

LEARNING OBJECTIVES

1. Understand what an operating system is and why computing devices require operating systems.
2. Appreciate how embedded systems extend Moore's Law, allowing firms to create "smarter" products and services

Computing hardware needs to be controlled, and that's the role of the operating system. The operating system (sometimes called the "OS") provides a common set of controls for managing computer hardware, making it easier for users to interact with computers and for programmers to write application software. Just about every computing device has an operating system—desktops and laptops, enterprise-class server computers, your mobile phone. Even specialty devices like iPods, video game consoles, and television set-top boxes run some form of OS.

Some firms, like Apple and Nintendo, develop their own proprietary OS for their own hardware. Microsoft sells operating systems to everyone from Dell to the ATM manufacturer Diebold (listen for the familiar Windows error beep on some cash machines). And there are a host of specialty firms, such as Wind River (purchased by Intel), that help firms develop operating systems for all sorts of devices that don't necessarily look like a PC, including cars, video editing systems, and fighter jet control panels.

Anyone who has used both a PC and a Mac and has noticed differences across these platforms can get a sense of the breadth of what an operating system does. Even for programs that are otherwise identical for these two systems (like the Firefox browser), subtle differences are visible. Screen elements like menus, scroll bars, and window borders look different on the Mac than they do in Windows. So do the dialogue boxes that show up when you print or save.

These items look and behave differently because each of these functions touches the hardware, and the team that developed Microsoft Windows created a system distinctly different from their Macintosh counterparts at Apple. Graphical **user interface (UI)** items like scroll bars and menus are displayed on the hardware of the computer display. Files are saved to the hardware of a hard drive or other storage device. Most operating systems also include control panels, desktop file management, and other support programs to work directly with hardware elements like storage devices, displays, printers, and networking equipment. The Macintosh Finder and the Windows Explorer are examples of components of these operating systems. The consistent look, feel, and functionality that operating systems enforce across various programs help make it easier for users to learn new software, which reduces training costs and operator error. See Figure 13.2 for similarities and differences.

user interface (UI)

The mechanism through which users interact with a computing device. The UI includes elements of the graphical user interface (or GUI, pronounced "*gooey*"), such as windows, scroll bars, buttons, menus, and dialogue boxes; and can also include other forms of interaction, such as touch screens, motion sensing controllers, or tactile devices used by the visually impaired.

FIGURE 13.2

Differences between the Windows and Mac operating systems are evident throughout the user interface, particularly when a program interacts with hardware.

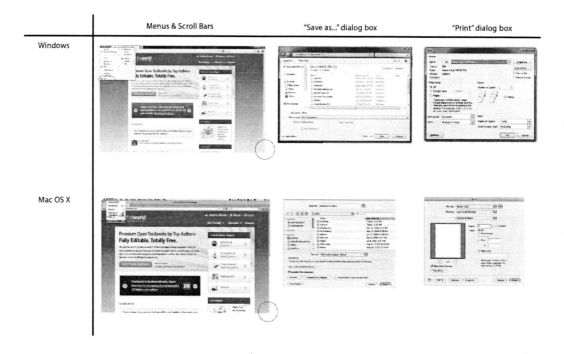

Operating systems are also designed to give programmers a common set of commands to consistently interact with the hardware. These commands make a programmer's job easier by reducing program complexity and making it faster to write software while minimizing the possibility of errors in code. Consider what an OS does for the Wii game developer. Nintendo's Wii OS provides Wii programmers with a set of common standards to use to access the Wiimote, play sounds, draw graphics, save files, and more. Without this, games would be a lot more difficult to write, they'd likely look differently, be less reliable, would cost more, and there would be fewer titles available.

Similarly, when Apple provided developers with a common set of robust, easy-to-use standards for the iPhone and (via the App Store) an easy way for users to install these applications on top of the iPhone/iPod touch/iPad's operating system (iOS), software development boomed, and Apple became hands-down the most versatile mobile computing device available.[4] In Apple's case, some fifty thousand apps became available through the App Store in less than one year, and well over 1.5 million apps in total are available today. A good OS and software development platform can catalyze network effects (see Chapter 8). While the OS seems geeky, its effective design has very strategic business implications!

FIGURE 13.3 Smartphone OS Market Share

Operating system market share is notoriously difficult to calculate and a search online will reveal widely varying numbers. That said, this interactive graphic will give you a sense of the variance in major mobile operating systems worldwide. A slider will allow you to compare how share has changed.

Source: http://www.kantarworldpanel.com/global/smartphone-os-market-share/

Firmware and Embedded Systems

Most personal computers have an operating system installed on their hard drives. This system allows the OS to be replaced or upgraded easily. But many smaller, special-purpose computing devices have their operating systems installed on nonvolatile memory, often on read-only memory (ROM) chips. Control programs stored on chips are sometimes referred to as **firmware**. The OS in an iPod, automobile, or your TV's set-top box is most likely stored as firmware. Your PC also has a tiny bit of firmware that allows it to do very basic functions like start-up (boot) and begin loading its operating system from disk.

Another term you might hear is **embedded systems**. As computing gets cheaper, special-purpose technology is increasingly becoming embedded into all sorts of devices like cars, picture frames, aircraft engines, photocopiers, and heating and air conditioning systems. The software programs that make up embedded systems are often stored as firmware too. Using microprocessors and embedded software to enable commonly encountered devices to communicate with one another (think of the Nest thermostat or app-controlled lighting and door locks by SmartThings) is sometimes referred to as the Internet of Things. Embedded systems are now found in everything from herd-tracking cow collars[5] to pipeline monitoring sensors, eliminating the need for workers to trek out and monitor operations.[6]

Moore's Law (see Chapter 5) enables embedded systems, and these systems can create real strategic value. The Otis Elevator Company, a division of United Technologies, uses embedded systems in its products to warn its service centers when the firm's elevators, escalators, and moving walkways need maintenance or repair. This warning provides Otis with several key benefits:

1. Since products automatically contact Otis when they need attention, these systems generate a lucrative service business for the firm and make it more difficult for third parties to offer a competing business servicing Otis products.

2. Products contact service technicians to perform maintenance based on exact needs (e.g., lubricant is low, or a part has been used enough to be replaced) rather than guessed schedules, which makes service more cost-effective, products less likely to break down, and customers happier.

3. Any product failures are immediately detected, with embedded systems typically dispatching technicians before a client's phone call.

4. The data is fed back to Otis's R&D group, providing information on reliability and failure so that engineers can use this info to design better products.

Collectively, software embedded on tiny chips yields very big benefits, for years helping Otis remain at the top of its industry.

firmware

Software stored on nonvolatile memory chips (as opposed to being stored on devices such as hard drives or removable discs). Despite the seemingly permanent nature of firmware, many products allow for firmware to be upgraded online or by connecting to another device.

embedded systems

Special-purpose software designed and included inside physical products (often on firmware). Embedded systems help make devices "smarter," sharing usage information, helping diagnose problems, indicating maintenance schedules, providing alerts, or enabling devices to take orders from other systems.

KEY TAKEAWAYS

- The operating system (OS) controls a computer's hardware and provides a common set of commands for writing programs.
- Most computing devices (enterprise-class server computers, PCs, phones, set-top boxes, video games, cars, the Mars Rover) have an operating system.
- Some products use operating systems provided by commercial firms, while others develop their own operating system. Others may leverage open source alternatives (see Chapter 14 "Software in Flux: Partly Cloudy and Sometimes Free").
- Embedded systems are special-purpose computer systems designed to perform one or a few dedicated functions, and are frequently built into conventional products like thermostats, door locks, cars, air conditioners, industrial equipment, and elevators.
- Embedded systems can make products and services more efficient, more reliable, more functional and can enable entire new businesses and create or reinforce resources for competitive advantage.

QUESTIONS AND EXERCISES

1. What does an operating system do? Why do you need an operating system? How do operating systems make a programmer's job easier? How do operating systems make life easier for end users?

2. What kinds of operating systems are used in the devices that you own? On your personal computer? Your mobile phone? The set-top box on top of your television? Are there other operating systems that you come into contact with? If you can't tell which operating system is in each of these devices, see if you can search the Internet to find out.

3. For your list in the prior question (and to the extent that you can), diagram the hardware/software "layer cake" for these devices.

4. For your list in the prior question (and to the extent that you can), diagram the hardware/software "layer cake" for these devices.

5. For this same list, do you think each device's manufacturer wrote all of the software that you use on these devices? Can you add or modify software to all of these devices? Why or why not? What would the implications be for cost, security, complexity, reliability, updates and upgrades, and the appeal of each device?

6. Operating system market share is notoriously difficult to calculate. Do some research on major OS markets (PCs, tablets, smartphones, or other products). Gather data and share with your class. Is your data inconsistent with classmates' data? Why do you suppose there are such discrepancies? Even if data are precisely inaccurate, are there rough trends that you can trust, and if so, what sorts of managerial decisions might these influence?

7. Which mobile OS has a larger global market share: Android or iOS? Which has returned more money to developers through its app store? Is this data what you'd expect? Why or why not?

8. Some ATM machines use Windows. Why would an ATM manufacturer choose to build its systems owing Windows? Why might it want to avoid this? Are there other non-PC devices you've encountered that were running some form of Windows?

9. What are embedded systems? When might firms want to install software on chips instead of on a hard drive? Why are embedded systems important for the Internet of Things?

10. It's important to understand how technology impacts a firm's strategy and competitive environment. Consider the description of Otis elevator's use of embedded systems. Which parts of the value chain does this impact? How? Consider the "five forces": How does the system impact the firm's competitive environment? Are these systems a source of competitive advantage? If not, explain why not? If they are, what kinds of resources for competitive advantage can these kinds of embedded systems create?

11. Can you think of other firms that can or do leverage embedded systems? Provide examples and list the kinds of benefits these might offer firms and consumers.

12. Research the Americans with Disabilities Act of 1990 (or investigate if your nation has a similar law), and the implications of this legislation for software developers and Web site operators. Have firms been successfully sued when their software or Web sites could not be accessed by users with physical challenges? What sorts of issues should developers consider when making their products more accessible? What practices might they avoid?

3.   APPLICATION SOFTWARE

LEARNING OBJECTIVES

1. Appreciate the difference between desktop and enterprise software.
2. List the categories of enterprise software.
3. Understand what an ERP (enterprise resource planning) software package is.
4. Recognize the relationship of the DBMS (database system) to the other enterprise software systems.
5. Recognize both the risks and rewards of installing packaged enterprise systems.

Operating systems are designed to create a **platform** so that programmers can write additional applications, allowing the computer to do even more useful things. While operating systems control the hardware, *application software* (sometimes referred to as *software applications*, *applications*, or even just *apps*) perform the work that users and firms are directly interested in accomplishing. Think of applications as the place where the users or organization's real work gets done. As we learned in Chapter 8 the more application software that is available for a platform (the more games for a video game console, the more apps for your phone), the more valuable it potentially becomes.

Desktop software refers to applications installed on a personal computer—your browser, your Office suite (e.g., word processor, spreadsheet, presentation software), photo editors, and computer games are all desktop software. **Enterprise software** refers to applications that address the needs of multiple, simultaneous users in an organization or work group. Most companies run various forms of enterprise software programs to keep track of their inventory, record sales, manage payments to suppliers, cut employee paychecks, and handle other functions. Another term you might hear is *apps*. While the definition of *apps* is somewhat fluid, most folks use the term *app* to refer to smaller pieces of software that are designed for a specific platform, such as the programs that are executed on a smartphone, tablet, television, or specialized platform like the Apple Watch or Oculus Rift.

Some firms write their own enterprise software from scratch, but this can be time consuming and costly. Since many firms have similar procedures for accounting, finance, inventory management, and human resource functions, it often makes sense to buy a **software package** (a software product offered commercially by a third party) to support some of these functions. So-called **enterprise resource planning (ERP)** software packages serve precisely this purpose. In the way that Microsoft can sell you a suite of desktop software programs that work together, many companies sell ERP software that coordinates and integrates many of the functions of a business. The leading ERP vendors include the firm's SAP and Oracle, although there are many firms that sell ERP software. A company doesn't have to install all of the modules of an ERP suite, but it might add functions over time—for example, to plug in an accounting program that is able to read data from the firm's previously installed inventory management system. And although a bit more of a challenge to integrate, a firm can also mix and match components, linking software the firm has written with modules purchased from different enterprise software vendors.

platform

Products and services that allow for the development and integration of software products and other complementary goods. Windows, iOS, Android, and the standards that allow users to create Facebook apps are all platforms.

Desktop software

Applications installed on a personal computer, typically supporting tasks performed by a single user.

Enterprise software

Applications that address the needs of multiple users throughout an organization or work group.

software package

A software product offered commercially by a third party.

enterprise resource planning (ERP)

A software package that integrates the many functions (accounting, finance, inventory management, human resources, etc.) of a business.

FIGURE 13.4 ERP in Action[7]

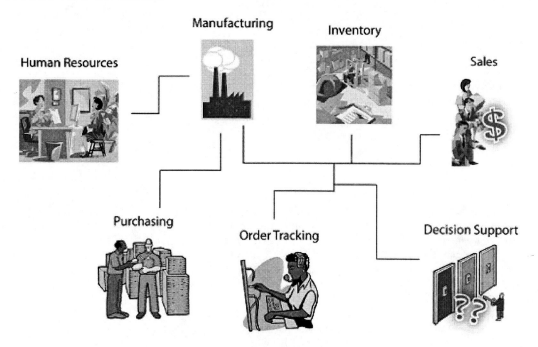

An ERP system with multiple modules installed can touch many functions of the business:

- *Sales*—A sales rep from Vermont-based SnowboardCo. takes an order for five thousand boards from a French sporting goods chain. The system can verify credit history, apply discounts, calculate price (in euros), and print the order in French.

- *Inventory*—While the sales rep is on the phone with his French customer, the system immediately checks product availability, signaling that one thousand boards are ready to be shipped from the firm's Burlington warehouse, the other four thousand need to be manufactured and can be delivered in two weeks from the firm's manufacturing facility in Guangzhou.

- *Manufacturing*—When the customer confirms the order, the system notifies the Guangzhou factory to ramp up production for the model ordered.

- *Human Resources*—High demand across this week's orders triggers a notice to the Guangzhou hiring manager, notifying her that the firm's products are a hit and that the flood of orders coming in globally mean her factory will have to hire more workers to keep up.

- *Purchasing*—The system keeps track of raw material inventories, too. New orders trigger an automatic order with SnowboardCo.'s suppliers, so that raw materials are on hand to meet demand.

- *Order Tracking*—The French customer can log in to track her SnowboardCo. order. The system shows her other products that are available, using this as an opportunity to cross-sell additional products.

- *Decision Support*—Management sees the firm's European business is booming and plans a marketing blitz for the continent, targeting board models and styles that seem to sell better for the Alps crowd than in the US market.

Other categories of enterprise software that managers are likely to encounter include the following:

- **customer relationship management (CRM)** systems used to support customer-related sales and marketing activities
- **supply chain management (SCM)** systems that can help a firm manage aspects of its value chain, from the flow of raw materials into the firm through delivery of finished products and services at the point-of-consumption
- **business intelligence (BI) systems**, which use data created by other systems to provide reporting and analysis for organizational decision making

Major ERP vendors are now providing products that extend into these and other categories of enterprise application software, as well.

Most enterprise software works in conjunction with a **database management system (DBMS)**, sometimes referred to as a "database system." The database system stores and retrieves the data that an application creates and uses. Think of this as another additional layer in our cake analogy. Although the DBMS is itself considered an application, it's often useful to think of a firm's database systems as sitting above the operating system, but under the enterprise applications. Many ERP systems and enterprise software programs are configured to share the same database system so that an organization's different programs can use a common, shared set of data. This system can be hugely valuable for a company's efficiency. For example, this could allow a separate set of programs that manage an inventory and point-of-sale system to update a single set of data that tells how many products a firm has to sell and how many it has already sold—information that would also be used by the firm's accounting and finance systems to create reports showing the firm's sales and profits.

Firms that don't have common database systems with consistent formats across their enterprise often struggle to efficiently manage their value chain. Common procedures and data formats created by packaged ERP systems and other categories of enterprise software also make it easier for firms to use software to coordinate programs between organizations. This coordination can lead to even more value chain efficiencies. Sell a product? Deduct it from your inventory. When inventory levels get too low, have your computer systems send a message to your supplier's systems so that they can automatically build and ship replacement product to your firm. In many cases these messages are sent without any human interaction, reducing time and errors. And common database systems also facilitate the use of BI systems that provide critical operational and competitive knowledge and empower decision making. For more on CRM and BI systems, and the empowering role of data, see Chapter 15

customer relationship management (CRM)

Systems used to support customer-related sales and marketing activities.

supply chain management (SCM)

Systems that can help a firm manage aspects of its value chain, from the flow of raw materials into the firm, through delivery of finished products and services at the point-of-consumption.

business intelligence (BI) systems

Systems that use data created by other systems to provide reporting and analysis for organizational decision making.

database management system (DBMS)

Sometimes referred to as database software; software for creating, maintaining, and manipulating data.

FIGURE 13.5

An organization's database management system can be set up to work with several applications both within and outside the firm.

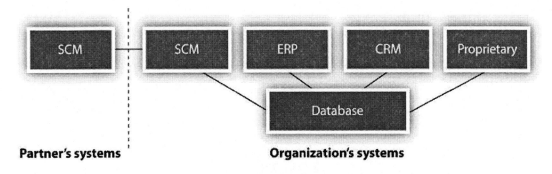

The Rewards and Risks of Packaged Enterprise Systems

When set up properly, enterprise systems can save millions of dollars and turbocharge organizations. For example, the CIO of office equipment maker Steelcase credited the firm's ERP with an eighty-million-dollar reduction in operating expenses saved from eliminating redundant processes and making data more usable. The CIO of Colgate Palmolive also praised their ERP, saying, "The day we turned the switch on, we dropped two days out of our order-to-delivery cycle."[8] Packaged enterprise systems can streamline processes, make data more usable, and ease the linking of systems with software across the firm and with key business partners. Plus, the software that makes up these systems is often debugged, tested, and documented with an industrial rigor that may be difficult to match with proprietary software developed in-house.

But for all the promise of packaged solutions for standard business functions, enterprise software installations have proven difficult. Standardizing business processes in software that others can buy means that those functions are easy for competitors to match, and the vision of a single monolithic system that delivers up wondrous efficiencies has been difficult for many to achieve. The average large company spends roughly $15 million on ERP software, with some installations running into the hundreds of millions of dollars.[9] And many of these efforts have failed disastrously.

FoxMeyer was once a six-billion-dollar drug distributor, but a failed ERP installation led to a series of losses that bankrupted the firm. The collapse was so rapid and so complete that just a year after launching the system, the carcass of what remained of the firm was sold to a rival for less than $80 million. Hershey Foods blamed a $466 million revenue shortfall on glitches in the firm's ERP rollout. Among the problems, the botched implementation prevented the candy maker from getting product to stores during the critical period before Halloween. Nike's first SCM and ERP implementation was labeled a "disaster"; their systems were blamed for over $100 million in lost sales.[10] Even tech firms aren't immune to software implementation blunders. HP once blamed a $160 million loss on problems with its ERP systems.[11] Manager beware—there are no silver bullets. For insight on the causes of massive software failures, and methods to improve the likelihood of success, see Section 6

Companies that have efficient, flexible information systems don't just see value through operations efficiency and cost savings. Technology can also influence a firm's options with respect to inter-firm partnerships, as well as merging with, acquiring, or getting acquired by other firms (M&A, or mergers and acquisitions). Firms that have systems that work smoothly internally may find it easier to partner with others. Consulting firm McKinsey suggests that many mergers don't live up to expectations because firms struggle when trying to combine complex and incompatible information systems. Efficient and integrated enterprise systems may also make firms more attractive acquisition targets or make it easier for a firm to acquire other firms and realize the benefit from acquisition. McKinsey suggests acquired firms may be more valuable and acquirers may be justified in bidding more for acquisition targets since efficient tech may allow firms to capture the 10 to 15 percent cost savings that successful mergers can usually realize by combining IT systems. McKinsey points to Oracle as an example of a firm whose efficiency has helped it win at M&A (mergers and acquisition). Oracle, which sells ERP systems, consolidated seventy of its own IS into a single ERP for the entire firm, saving an estimated $1 billion annually. Serious coin, but from a strategic perspective, it also created internal systems that were streamlined and simplified, making it easier to integrate acquired firms. Oracle bought over fifty firms in a four-year period and can now integrate most acquisitions in six months or less.[12]

KEY TAKEAWAYS

- Application software focuses on the work of a user or an organization.
- Desktop applications are typically designed for a single user. Enterprise software supports multiple users in an organization or work group.
- Popular categories of enterprise software include ERP (enterprise resource planning), SCM (supply chain management), CRM (customer relationship management), and BI (business intelligence) software, among many others.
- These systems are used in conjunction with database management systems, programs that help firms organize, store, retrieve, and maintain data.
- ERP and other packaged enterprise systems can be challenging and costly to implement, but can help firms create a standard set of procedures and data that can ultimately lower costs and streamline operations.
- The more application software that is available for a platform, the more valuable that platform becomes.
- The DBMS stores and retrieves the data used by the other enterprise applications. Different enterprise systems can be configured to share the same database system in order share common data.
- Firms that don't have common database systems with consistent formats across their enterprise often struggle to efficiently manage their value chain, and often lack the flexibility to introduce new ways of doing business. Firms with common database systems and standards often benefit from increased organizational insight and decision-making capabilities.
- Enterprise systems can cost millions of dollars in software, hardware, development, and consulting fees, and many firms have failed when attempting large-scale enterprise system integration. Simply buying a system does not guarantee its effective deployment and use.
- When set up properly, enterprise systems can save millions of dollars and turbocharge organizations by streamlining processes, making data more usable, and easing the linking of systems with software across the firm and with key business partners.
- Efficient enterprise systems may also make it easier for firms to partner with other organizations, and can give it advantages when considering mergers and acquisitions.

QUESTIONS AND EXERCISES

1. What is the difference between desktop and enterprise software?
2. Who are the two leading ERP vendors?
3. List the functions of a business that might be impacted by an ERP.
4. What do the acronyms ERP, CRM, SCM, and BI stand for? Briefly describe what each of these enterprise systems does.
5. Where in the "layer cake" analogy does the DBMS lie.
6. Name two companies that have realized multimillion-dollar benefits as result of installing enterprise systems.
7. Name two companies that have suffered multimillion-dollar disasters as result of failed enterprise system installations.
8. How much does the average large company spend annually on ERP software?
9. How do efficient enterprise systems help firms with respect to partnering with other organizations, as well as decisions around M&A?

4. DISTRIBUTED COMPUTING, WEB SERVICES, AND APIS

LEARNING OBJECTIVES

1. **Understand the concept of distributed computing and its benefits.**
2. **Understand the client-server model of distributed computing.**
3. **Know what Web services and APIs are and the benefits that these technologies bring to firms.**
4. **Appreciate the importance of messaging standards and understand how sending messages between machines can speed processes, cut costs, reduce errors, and enable new ways of doing business.**

When computers in different locations can communicate with one another, this is often referred to as **distributed computing**.[13] Distributed computing can yield enormous efficiencies in speed, error reduction, and cost savings and can create entirely new ways of doing business. Designing systems architecture for distributed systems involves many advanced technical topics. Rather than provide an exhaustive decomposition of distributed computing, the examples that follow are meant to help managers understand the bigger ideas behind some of the terms that they are likely to encounter.

Let's start with the term **server**. This is a tricky one because it's frequently used in two ways: (1) in a hardware context a server is a computer that has been configured to support requests from other computers (e.g., Dell sells servers), and (2) in a software context a server is a program that fulfills requests (e.g., the Apache open source Web server). Most of the time, server *software* resides on server-class *hardware*, but you can also set up a PC, laptop, or other small computer to run server software, albeit less powerfully. And you can use mainframe or super-computer-class machines as servers, too. Also note that many firms chose not to own some of their applications or any of their own server hardware at all. Instead, they pay third-party firms to host their software "in the cloud." This option is particularly attractive for smaller firms that can't or don't want to invest in the expense and expertise associated with owning and operating hardware, for firms looking for extra computing capacity, and for firms that want public servers (e.g., websites) to be in fast, reliable locations outside of a company's own private network.

The World Wide Web, like many other distributed computing services, is what geeks call a *client-server* system. Client-server refers to two pieces of software: a **client** that makes a request and a server that receives and attempts to fulfill the request. In our WWW scenario, the client is the browser (e.g., Internet Explorer, Chrome, Firefox, Safari). When you type a website's address into the location field of your browser, you're telling the client to "go find the Web server software at the address provided, and tell the server to return the website requested." Smartphone and tablet apps can also act as clients that make requests of more powerful server programs running elsewhere on the Web. Another example is smartphone voice recognition software, such as Apple's Siri. Voice recognition typically requires computing power far greater than that held on a smartphone, so Apple sends your voice to a more powerful collection of servers for processing and interpretation.

distributed computing

A form of computing where systems in different locations communicate and collaborate to complete a task.

server

A program that fulfills the requests of a client.

client

A software program that makes requests of a server program.

application server

Software that houses and serves business logic for use (and reuse) by multiple applications.

web services

Small pieces of code that are accessed via the application server which permit interoperable machine-to-machine interaction over a network.

It is possible to link simple scripting languages to a Web server for performing calculations, accessing databases, or customizing websites. But more advanced distributed environments may use a category of software called an **application server**. The application server (or app server) houses business logic for a distributed system. Individual software components or **web services** served up by the app server are programmed to perform different tasks: returning a calculation ("sales tax for your order will be $11.58"), accessing a database program ("here are the results you searched for"), or even making a request to another server in another organization ("Visa, please verify this customer's credit card number for me").

FIGURE 13.6

In this multitiered distributed system, client browsers on various machines (desktop, laptop, mobile) access the system through the Web server. The cash register doesn't use a Web browser, so instead the cash register logic is programmed to directly access the services it needs from the app server. Web services accessed from the app server may be asked to do a variety of functions, including perform calculations, access corporate databases, or even make requests from servers at other firms (for example, to verify a customer's credit card).

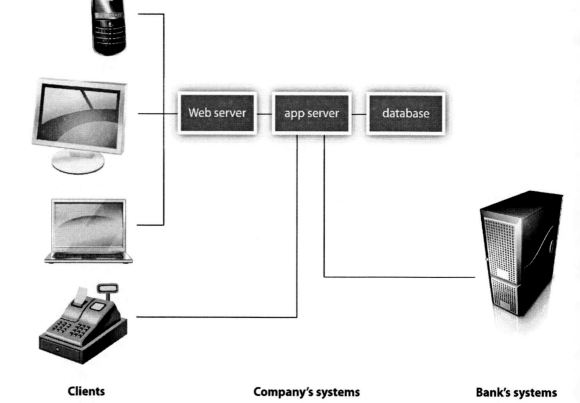

Clients   **Company's systems**   **Bank's systems**

API

Programming hooks, or guidelines, published by firms that tell other programs how to get a service to perform a task such as send or receive data. For example, Amazon provides APIs to let developers write their own applications and Web sites that can send the firm orders.

Those little chunks of code that are accessed via the application server are sometimes referred to as Web services. The World Wide Web consortium defines *Web services* as software systems designed to support interoperable machine-to-machine interaction over a network.[14] You might also hear the term **API** (or Application Programming Interface) used to describe the same concept. There are deeper technical issues that precisely define web services and the super-set of technologies known APIs (and even IBM says existing definitions aren't especially precise),[15] but for managerial purposes you can think of Web services and APIs as doing pretty much the same thing; they are referring to pieces of code, and the request/response standards so that this code be summoned by other programs to perform a task (the term API is more in vogue today, so expect to hear that more). Have you seen firms other than Google using Google Maps? They can do this because Google publishes APIs so that others can use this service. Uber's API allowed United Airlines to build an app that can summon an Uber driver (either by deep-linking to the Uber app, or by completing a transaction over United's website if the app isn't installed).[16] Spotify's API allowed Uber to modify its app to play a rider's playlist through the driver's smartphone-connected car speakers. Alcohol delivery service Drizly has published an API that allows the whisky recommendation app Distiller to order booze right from Distiller screens.[17]

Organizations that have created a robust set of Web services around their processes and procedures are said to have a **service-oriented architecture (SOA)**. Organizing systems like this, with separate applications in charge of client presentation, business logic, and database, makes systems more flexible. Code can be reused, and each layer can be separately maintained, upgraded, or migrated to new hardware—all with little impact on the others. And firms that invite other organizations to integrate with their systems via web services and APIs are often thought of as turning their products into **platforms**. Firms that create platforms have the potential to make their products and services more useful, widen their reach, create switching costs, and enhance network effects (for more on this, see the Network Effects chapter).

As an example of the business value of APIs in action, consider the Expedia Affiliate Network. Expedia sells a lot of travel through its own apps and website, but it realized that by sharing its inventory with partners (for a cute of the revenue), Expedia could sell even more. The Expedia Affiliate Network offers APIs that allow partner firms to integrate Expedia's technology and travel inventory into their own webites and apps. Partners that take advantage of these Expedia APIs include United,[18] Aer Lingus,[19] Greyhound,[20] and travel search tool Hipmunk.[21] These firms use the APIs so that their users can book hotel and other travel booking from within their own apps and websites, but without having to source inventory, work with suppliers, and create their own complete travel booking systems (all that's the stuff Expedia is so good at). For partners, this can be a great deal; they get to keep customers in their websites for a greater percentage of travel needs (booked your Aer Lingus flight to Ireland at aerlingus.com? Pick out a hotel and rental car, too). The partner firm's brand remains front and center with the customer. The partner firm continues to maintain the relationship with the customer (and gather critically important customer data), and they get a cut of Expedia's booking revenue. For its trouble, Expedia gets distribution—many more orders than it would otherwise get through its own sites and apps. How many? About $2 billion a year, even after sharing a percentage of bookings with API-using partners![22]

FIGURE 13.7

The Expedia Affiliate Network uses APIs to allow partner sites to book hotels and other travel services through their own apps and websites. This process lets partners provide more travel services to their customers, strengthen the customer relationship, gather additional data, and gain a cut of additional sales. Expedia gains some $2 billion in added sales funneled to it by partners that use its APIs.

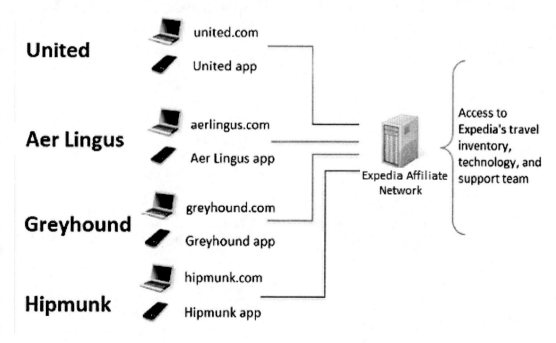

---

service-oriented architecture (SOA)

A robust set of Web services built around an organization's processes and procedures.

platforms

Products and services that allow for the development and integration of software products and other complementary goods. Windows, the iPhone, the Wii, and the standards that allow users to create Facebook apps are all platforms.

4.1   Formats to Facilitate Sharing Data

EDI (electronic data interchange)

A set of standards for exchanging messages containing formatted data between computer applications.

extensible markup language (XML)

A tagging language that can be used to identify data fields made available for use by other applications. Most APIs and Web services send messages where the data exchanged is wrapped in identifying XML tags.

Two additional terms you might hear within the context of distributed computing are EDI and XML. **EDI (electronic data interchange)** is a set of standards for exchanging information between computer applications. EDI is most often used as a way to send the electronic equivalent of structured documents between different organizations. Using EDI, each element in the electronic document, such as a firm name, address, or customer number, is coded so that it can be recognized by the receiving computer program. Eliminating paper documents makes businesses faster and lowers data entry and error costs. One study showed that firms that used EDI decreased their error rates by 82 percent, and their cost of producing each document fell by up to 96 percent.[23]

EDI is a very old standard, with roots stretching back to the 1948 Berlin Air Lift. While still in use, a new generation of more-flexible technologies for specifying data standards are taking its place. Chief among the technologies replacing EDI is **extensible markup language (XML)**. XML has lots of uses, but in the context of distributed systems, it allows software developers to create a set of standards for common data elements that, like EDI messages, can be sent between different kinds of computers, different applications, and different organizations. XML is often thought of as easier to code than EDI, and it's more robust because it can be extended—organizations can create formats to represent any kind of data (e.g., a common part number, photos, the complaint field collected by customer support personnel). In fact, most messages sent between Web services are coded in XML. Many computer programs also use XML as a way to export and import data in a common format that can be used regardless of the kind of computer hardware, operating system, or application program used. And if you design websites, you might encounter XML as part of the coding behind the cascading style sheets (CSS) that help maintain a consistent look and feel to the various Web pages in a given website.

Connectivity has made our systems more productive and enables entire new strategies and business models. But these wonderful benefits come at the price of increased risk. When systems are more interconnected, opportunities for infiltration and abuse also increase. Think of it this way: each "connection" opportunity is like adding another door to a building. The more doors that have to be defended, the more difficult security becomes. It should be no surprise that the rise of the Internet and distributed computing has led to an explosion in security losses by organizations worldwide.

KEY TAKEAWAYS

- Client-server computing is a method of distributed computing where one program (a client) makes a request to be fulfilled by another program (a server).
- Server is a tricky term and is sometimes used to refer to hardware. While server-class hardware refers to more powerful computers designed to support multiple users, just about any PC or notebook can be configured to run server software. Many firms chose to have their server software hosted "in the cloud" on the computers of third-party firms.
- Web servers serve up websites and can perform some scripting.
- Most firms serve complex business logic from an application server.
- Isolating a system's logic in three or more layers (presentation or user interface, business logic, and database) can allow a firm flexibility in maintenance, reusability, and in handling upgrades.
- Web services and APIs allow different applications to communicate with one another. The terms are imprecise and you'll often hear them used interchangeably. Web services and APIs define the method to call a piece of software (e.g., to get it to do something), and the kind of response the calling program can expect back.
- APIs and web services make it easier to link applications as distributed systems, and can make it easier for firms to link their systems across organizations. Expedia uses APIs to expand its reach and bring in some $2 billion from revenue-sharing partners that use its technology.
- Popular messaging standards include EDI (older) and XML. Sending messages between machines instead of physical documents can speed processes, drastically cut the cost of transactions, and reduce errors.
- Distributed computing can yield enormous efficiencies in speed, error reduction, and cost savings and can create entirely new ways of doing business.
- When computers can communicate with each other (instead of people), this often results in fewer errors, time savings, cost reductions, and can even create whole new ways of doing business.

QUESTIONS AND EXERCISES

1. Differentiate the term "server" used in a hardware context, from "server" used in a software context.
2. Describe the "client-server" model of distributed computing. What products that you use would classify as leveraging client-server computing?
3. How are firms using APIs to transform from being a product to being a platform? How can APIs and web services enhance a firm's competitive advantage?
4. List the advantages that APIs have brought to Expedia and its partners.
5. What are the security risks associated with connectivity, the Internet, and distributed processing?

5. WRITING SOFTWARE

LEARNING OBJECTIVES

1. **Understand, at a managerial level, what programming languages are and how software is developed.**
2. **Recognize that an operating system and microprocessor constrain the platform upon which most compiled application software will run.**
3. **Understand what Java is and why it is significant.**
4. **Know what scripting languages are.**

So you've got a great idea that you want to express in software—how do you go about creating a program? Programmers write software in a **programming language**. While each language has its strengths and weaknesses, most commercial software is written in a variant of the C programming language such as C++ (pronounced "see plus plus"), C# (pronounced "see sharp"), or Objective C (popular for iOS app development). Visual Basic (from Microsoft) and Java (from Sun) are also among the more popular of the dozens of programming languages available. Web developers may favor specialty languages like Ruby and Python, SQL is a popular special-purpose language used in databases. And languages are constantly evolving. Apple has created Swift, a new programming language to offer the power of Objective-C but in a language that has the simplicity and error handling of leaner, easier-to-use web programming languages.

Some programming languages are extended by frameworks. These are libraries, templates, and extensions that simplify and standardize common tasks, speeding software development, reducing errors, and prompting reuse. Programmers use frameworks to use a standardized set of code and techniques that others have developed and tested, rather than requiring every developer to create his or her own code for things many others have done before them (handle database interactions, manage cookies, etc.). Examples of popular frameworks used to develop websites include Rails (for Ruby), Django (for Python), AngularJS (for JavaScript), and ASP.NET (pronounced "ay-ess-pee dot net").

programming language

Provides the standards, syntax, statements, and instructions for writing computer software.

integrated development environment (IDE)

An application that includes an editor (a sort of programmer's word processor), debugger, and compiler, among other tools.

compile

Step in which program code written in a language that humans can more easily understand, is then converted into a form (expressed in patterns of ones and zeros) that can be understood and executed by a microprocessor. Programmers using conventional programming languages must compile their software before making it available for execution.

Most professional programmers use an **integrated development environment (IDE)** to write their code. The IDE includes a text editor, a debugger for sleuthing out errors, and other useful programming tools. The most popular IDE for Windows is Microsoft's Visual Studio (which also supports development for many other platforms, including Mac OS X, iOS, Android, Java, and cloud platforms), while Apple offers the Xcode IDE. Most IDEs can support several different programming languages. The IDE will also **compile** a programmer's code, turning the higher-level lines of instructions that are readable by humans into lower-level instructions expressed as the patterns of ones and zeros that are readable by a computer's microprocessor.

FIGURE 13.8

Microsoft's Visual Studio IDE supports desktop, server, mobile, and cloud computing software development.

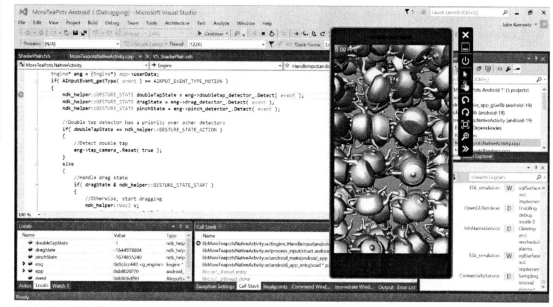

Source: Microsoft Visual Studio, used with permission from Microsoft.

Java

A programming language, initially developed by Sun Microsystems, designed to provide true platform independence ("write once, run anywhere") for application developers. In most cases, Java apps are developed to be executed by a Java Virtual Machine—an interpreting layer that translates code as it executes, into the format required by the operating system and microprocessor. Without Java, application developers have to write and compile software to execute natively by a specific operating system / microprocessor combination (e.g., Windows/Intel, Linux PowerPC, Mac/Intel, Linux/Intel).

Look at the side of a box or online order information from commercial software, and you're likely to see system requirements that specify the operating system and processor that the software is designed for (e.g., "this software works on computers with Windows 10 and Intel-compatible processors"). Wouldn't it be great if software could be written once and run everywhere? That's the idea behind **Java**—a programming language developed by Sun Microsystems.

Java programmers don't write code with specific operating system commands (say for Windows, Mac OS X, or Linux), instead they use special Java commands to control their user interface or interact with the display and other hardware. Java programs can run on any computer that has a Java Virtual Machine (JVM), a software layer that interprets Java code so that it can be understood by the operating system and processor of a given computer. Java's platform independence—the ability for developers to "write once, run everywhere"—is its biggest selling point. Many websites execute Java applets to run the animation you might see in advertisements or games. Java has also been deployed on over 6 billion mobile phones worldwide, and is popular among enterprise programmers who want to be sure their programs can scale from smaller hardware up to high-end supercomputers. As long as the machine receiving the Java code has a JVM, then the Java application should run. However, Java has not been popular for desktop applications. Since Java isn't optimized to take advantage of interface elements specific to the Mac or Windows, most Java desktop applications look clunky and unnatural. Java code that runs through the JVM interpreter is also slower than code compiled for the native OS and processor that make up a platform.[24]

Scripting languages are the final category of programming tool that we'll cover. **Scripting languages** typically execute within an application. Microsoft offers a scripting language called VB Script (a derivative of Visual Basic) to automate functions in Office. And most browsers and Web servers support JavaScript, a language that helps make the Web more interactive (despite its name, JavaScript is unrelated to Java). Scripting languages are **interpreted** within their applications, rather than compiled to run directly by a microprocessor. This distinction makes them slower than the kinds of development efforts found in most commercial software. But most scripting languages are usually easy to use, and are often used both by professional programmers and power users.

scripting languages

Programming tool that executes within an application. Scripting languages are interpreted within their applications, rather than compiled to run directly by a microprocessor.

interpreted

Languages where each line of written code is converted (by a software program, called an "interpreter") for execution at run-time. Most scripting languages are interpreted languages. Many programmers also write Java applications to be interpreted by the Java Virtual Machine.

KEY TAKEAWAYS

- Programs are often written in a tool called an IDE, an application that includes an editor (a sort of programmer's word processor), debugger, and compiler, among other tools.
- Compiling takes code from the high-level language that humans can understand and converts them into the sets of ones and zeros in patterns representing instructions that microprocessors understand.
- Popular programming languages include C++, C#, Visual Basic, and Java.
- Most software is written for a platform—a combination of an operating system and microprocessor.
- Java is designed to be platform independent. Computers running Java have a separate layer called a Java Virtual Machine that translates (interprets) Java code so that it can be executed on an operating system/processor combination. In theory, Java is "write once, run everywhere," as opposed to conventional applications that are written for an operating system and compiled for an OS/processor combination.
- Java is popular on mobile phones, enterprise computing, and to make websites more interactive. Java has never been a successful replacement for desktop applications, largely because user interface differences among the various operating systems are too great to be easily standardized.
- Scripting languages are interpreted languages, such as VB Script or Java Script. Many scripting languages execute within an application (like the Office programs, a Web browser, or to support the functions of a Web server). They are usually easier to program, but are less powerful and execute more slowly than compiled languages.

QUESTIONS AND EXERCISES

1. List popular programming languages.
2. What are programming frameworks, and why would you use one? Name some of the more popular programming frameworks used for web development, and name the programming languages they are used with.
3. What's an IDE? Why do programmers use IDEs? Name IDEs popular for Windows and Mac users.
4. What is the difference between a compiled programming language and an interpreted programming language?
5. Name one advantage and one disadvantage of scripting languages.
6. In addition to computers, on what other technology has Java been deployed? Why do you suppose Java is particularly attractive for these kinds of applications?
7. What's a JVM? Why do you need it?
8. What if a programmer wrote perfect Java code, but there was a bug on the JVM installed on a given computer? What might happen?
9. Why would developers choose to write applications in Java? Why might they skip Java and choose another programming language?
10. Why isn't Java popular for desktop applications?
11. Go to http://www.java.com. Click on "Do I have Java?" Is Java running on your computer? Which version?

6. UNDERSTANDING TECHNOLOGY BEYOND THE PRICE TAG: TOTAL COST OF OWNERSHIP (TCO) AND THE COST OF TECH FAILURE

LEARNING OBJECTIVES

1. List the different cost categories that comprise total cost of ownership.
2. Understand that once a system is implemented, the costs of maintaining and supporting the system continue.
3. List the reasons that technology development projects fail and the measures that can be taken to increase the probability of success.
4. Examine the failed launch and eventual fix associated with HealthCare.gov, understanding the factors associated with the system's botched rollout and techniques used to recover the effort.

Managers should recognize that there are a whole host of costs that are associated with creating and supporting an organization's information systems. Of course, there are programming costs for custom software as well as purchase, configuration, and licensing costs for packaged software, but there's much, much more.

There are costs associated with design and documentation (both for programmers and for users). There are also testing costs. New programs should be tested thoroughly across the various types of hardware the firm uses, and in conjunction with existing software and systems, *before* being deployed throughout the organization. Any errors that aren't caught can slow down a business or lead to costly mistakes that could ripple throughout an organization and its partners. Studies have shown that errors not caught before deployment could be one hundred times more costly to correct than if they were detected and corrected beforehand.[25]

Once a system is "turned on," the work doesn't end there. Firms need to constantly engage in a host of activities to support the system that may also include the following:

compliance

Ensuring that an organization's systems operate within required legal constraints, and industry and organizational obligations.

- providing training and end user support
- collecting and relaying comments for system improvements
- auditing systems to ensure **compliance** (i.e., that the system operates within the firm's legal constraints and industry obligations)
- providing regular backup of critical data
- planning for redundancy and disaster recovery in case of an outage
- vigilantly managing the moving target of computer security issues

total cost of ownership (TCO)

All of the costs associated with the design, development, testing, implementation, documentation, training and maintenance of a software system.

With so much to do, it's no wonder that firms spend 70 to 80 percent of their information systems (IS) budgets just to keep their systems running.[26] The price tag and complexity of these tasks can push some managers to think of technology as being a cost sink rather than a strategic resource. These tasks are often collectively referred to as the **total cost of ownership (TCO)** of an information system. Understanding TCO is critical when making technology investment decisions. TCO is also a major driving force behind the massive tech industry changes discussed in Chapter 14.

6.1 Why Do Technology Projects Fail?

Even though information systems represent the largest portion of capital spending at most firms, an astonishing one in three technology development projects fail to be successfully deployed.[27] Imagine if a firm lost its investment in one out of every three land purchases, or when building one in three factories. These statistics are dismal! Writing in *IEEE Spectrum*, risk consultant Robert Charette provides a sobering assessment of the cost of software failures, stating, "The yearly tab for failed and troubled software conservatively runs somewhere from $60 to $70 billion in the United States alone. For that money, you could launch the space shuttle one hundred times, build and deploy the entire twenty-four-satellite Global Positioning System, and develop the Boeing 777 from scratch—and still have a few billion left over."[28]

Why such a bad track record? Sometimes technology itself is to blame, other times it's a failure to test systems adequately, and sometimes it's a breakdown of process and procedures used to set specifications and manage projects. In one example, a multimillion-dollar loss on the NASA Mars Observer was traced back to a laughably simple oversight: Lockheed Martin contractors using English measurements, while the folks at NASA used the metric system.[29] Yes, a $125 million taxpayer investment was lost because a bunch of rocket scientists failed to pay attention to third grade math. When it comes to the success or failure of technical projects, the devil really is in the details.

Projects rarely fail for just one reason. Project post-mortems often point to a combination of technical, project management, and business decision blunders. The most common factors include the following:[30]

- Unrealistic or unclear project goals
- Poor project leadership and weak executive commitment
- Inaccurate estimates of needed resources
- Badly defined system requirements and allowing "feature creep" during development
- Poor reporting of the project's status
- Poor communication among customers, developers, and users
- Use of immature technology
- Unmanaged risks
- Inability to handle the project's complexity
- Sloppy development and testing practices
- Poor project management
- Stakeholder politics
- Commercial pressures (e.g., leaving inadequate time or encouraging corner-cutting)

Managers need to understand the complexity involved in their technology investments, and that achieving success rarely lies with the strength of the technology alone.

But there is hope. Information systems organizations can work to implement procedures to improve the overall quality of their development practices. Mechanisms for quality improvement include **capability maturity model integration (CMMI)**, which gauge an organization's process maturity and capability in areas critical to developing and deploying technology projects, and provides a carefully chosen set of best practices and guidelines to assist quality and process improvement.[31]

Firms are also well served to leverage established project planning and software development methodologies that outline critical businesses processes and stages when executing large-scale software development projects. The idea behind these methodologies is straightforward—why reinvent the wheel when there is an opportunity to learn from and follow blueprints used by those who have executed successful efforts. When methodologies are applied to projects that are framed with clear business goals and business metrics, and that engage committed executive leadership, success rates can improve dramatically.[32]

While software development methodologies are the topic of more advanced technology courses, the savvy manager knows enough to inquire about the development methodologies and quality programs used to support large scale development projects, and can use these investigations as further input when evaluating whether those overseeing large scale efforts have what it takes to get the job done.

capability maturity model integration (CMMI)

A process-improvement approach (useful for but not limited to software engineering projects) that can assist in assessing the maturity, quality, and development of certain organizational business processes, and suggest steps for their improvement.

Lessons Learned from the Failure and Rescue of HealthCare.gov

To say the Affordable Care Act was controversial is an understatement. What many regard as the signature legislation of President Obama's domestic agenda had barely passed the US Senate, squeaking by with just one vote. The US House of Representatives has voted at least fifty times to repeal or rollback parts of the law.[33] But politics aside, for the law to be successful, technology needed to work, and at roll-out it didn't.

The Affordable Care Act (a.k.a., Obamacare) called for a website, HealthCare.gov, that served as a national health care exchange where citizens could shop for, compare, and enroll in health care plans. The site would also offer subsidies for low-income enrollees and assist those eligible to sign up for Medicaid. Interest surged the first day the site went live.[34] Over 250,000 users were said to have visited HealthCare.gov on day one. What is the total enrollment after the first day? Eight.[35] That's not a typo. The system implementing HealthCare.gov was full of bugs and design flaws that it had enrolled very few people, the number of which is enough to count using your two hands. And this is for a system where the government had agreed to pay the lead contractor $292 million.[36]

FIGURE 13.9

The HealthCare.gov website

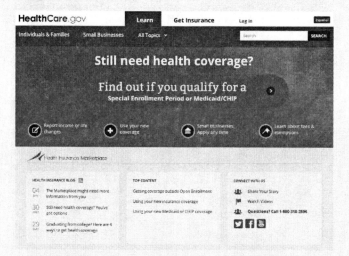

The Problems

Problems with the website could have been predicted by anyone who read the previous section. The most critical issue was a lack of clear authority. Consultants brought in to fix the problem claimed they couldn't figure out who was in charge of the HealthCare.gov launch. What was seen after the launch were "multiple contractors bickering with one another and no one taking ownership for anything."[37] Technologists were also not involved in top-level planning. The president regularly ended meetings on the Affordable Care Act by saying, "I want to remind the team that this only works if the technology works." However, no one in the meetings had any idea whether the technology worked.[38] In fact, in the months leading up to the site's launch, the White House health-reform director kept the White House CTO (an executive who had previously launched two commercial health care firms), "off the invitation list for the planning meetings."

Most large-scale systems will have clear stages: requirements definition, design, development, and testing phases, but consultants brought in to survey HealthCare.gov pointed out that these phases were started on top of one another, where design and development began before requirements definition was even complete.[39]

While so-called "agile software development" methodologies allow for iterative development, they also rely on regular testing of modules developed along the way, but there were no such precautions taken with HealthCare.gov. Predeployment testing was minimal or nonexistent,[40] and the system was implemented in a single big bang rollout. One of the executives brought in to help diagnose problems and consult on fixes was former Twitter CTO and current Kleiner Perkins partner Mike Abbott. Abbott knows how to fix websites in crisis. He's credited with getting Twitter past incessant "fail whale" site down messages. Abbott said, "You never open a service like this to everyone at once. You open it in small concentric circles and expand"—such as one state first, then a few more—"so you can watch it, fix it and scale it."[41] The lack of testing also led to no credible verification on project status. The administration was so clueless to potential problems that even thirty-six hours beforehand, White House Chief of Staff Denis McDonough told a friend that "when we turned it on we're going to knock your socks off."[42]

There were also several technical and design problems with the implementation of the site. It was immediately obvious that HealthCare.gov could not scale to handle national demands. At best, the site could tolerate 1,100 simultaneous users at launch, nowhere near the 50,000–60,000 that was expected, or the 250,000 that had been reported as visiting the first day.[43] The site also lacked common measurement and reporting systems. Most consumer websites report data to a dashboard used by their technical staff, a summary screen that provides a quick way for engineers to measure a website's performance, showing things like access traffic and the number of times the page was loaded, and helping to pinpoint where system problems are occurring. HealthCare.gov lacked even the most basic performance dashboard. Common practices like caching frequently accessed data (storing high-demand items in memory so databases don't need to be repeatedly accessed) also weren't implemented. Also, from a design perspective, the user experience was horrible. For example, consumers were required to create an account before being able to compare plans, and the registration process created a bottleneck that further exacerbated issues, increasing wait times. Using the browser's "Back" button frequently broke the site, and users who were kicked off mid-enrollment often had to restart efforts from scratch.

The Fix

Fixing HealthCare.gov in a few weeks' time was a daunting challenge. No one knew the extent of problems or even if the system could be saved or needed to be scrapped entirely. Fixing the site required bringing in experienced management with clear leadership authority and responsibility. The White House tapped Jeff Zients, a highly regarded businessman, who at the time was deputy director of the Office of Management and Budget. Zients had experience running large bureaucratic programs (among them the "Cash for Clunkers" effort that spurred car sales following the 2008 US recession). Zients was also scheduled to take over as director of the president's National Economic Council.

A team of seasoned technologists was also brought in to lead the system triage and site fixes. Todd Park, the White House CTO, took a front-and-center role in helping assemble the team. In addition to on-site and remote consulting from Abbot, the team harnessed the expertise of Mikey Dickerson, Google's Site Reliability engineer. Dickerson was an administration ally and had taken a leave from Google in 2012 to help Obama staffers develop big data systems deemed responsible for getting out the winning vote.[44] Also part of the effort was Gabriel Burt, CTO at Chicago-based Civis Analytics, the firm founded by many of the analytics specialists involved in the 2012 campaign. Both men showed up in October and stayed into December.

The team needed more than leadership, they needed developer commitment. Abbot said, "The first red flag you look for is whether there is a willingness by the people there to have outside help. If not, then I'd say it's simpler to write it new than to understand the code base as it is, if the people who wrote it are not cooperating. But they were eager to cooperate."[45]

At times, it seemed that bureaucracy was conspiring to halt goodwill. Government regulations don't allow for volunteers to work on government projects for sustained periods of time. So new leadership actually had to be put on the payroll of contractor QSSI as hourly workers, earning Dickerson what he reported was "a fraction" of his Google pay.[46]

Clear priority setting, results reporting, and coordination was implemented through stand-up meetings, which is common among practitioners of agile development and popular inside the development groups of many leading tech firms and start-ups. In a stand-up meeting, technologists stand up (no sitting, be quick and to the point), identify a problem or a set of problems they're facing, identify obstacles to gaining a solution, gain quick feedback from the group, then disperse to solve presented problems, reporting back at the end of the day at a recap stand-up. An open phone line would connect people working on the website at other locations. The stand-ups helped everyone feel progress toward common goals and offered coordination early project management lacked.

The Result

The nonpartisan Congressional Budget Office (CBO) originally projected 7 million enrollees, and revised that figure down to 6 million after persistent website glitches plagued HealthCare.gov. Despite what was likely the most disastrous and embarrassing roll-out of a consumer-facing government technology initiative, HealthCare.gov had actually signed up over 8 million insurance users by mid-April (roughly two weeks after the original deadline, which was extended due to roll-out problems).

While the system's failure was large and public, it was by no means an anomaly. Research firm the Standish Group estimates that in the past ten years, some 94 percent of large federal information technology projects were unsuccessful: "More than half were delayed, over budget, or didn't meet user expectations, and 41.4 percent failed completely." The United States isn't alone in government technology failures. United Kingdom's National Health Service wasted almost $20 billion to computerize medical records before eventually abandoning the project. Wise managers will learn from the lessons of HealthCare.gov.[47]

KEY TAKEAWAYS

- The care and feeding of information systems can be complex and expensive. The total cost of ownership of systems can include software development and documentation, or the purchase price and ongoing license and support fees, plus configuration, testing, deployment, maintenance, support, training, compliance auditing, security, backup, and provisions for disaster recovery. These costs are collectively referred to as TCO, or a system's total cost of ownership.

- Information systems development projects fail at a startlingly high rate. Failure reasons can stem from any combination of technical, process, and managerial decisions.

- IS organizations can leverage software development methodologies to improve their systems development procedures, and firms can strive to improve the overall level of procedures used in the organization through models like CMMI. However, it's also critical to engage committed executive leadership in projects, and to frame projects using business metrics and outcomes to improve the chance of success.

- System errors that aren't caught before deployment can slow down a business or lead to costly mistakes that could ripple throughout an organization. Studies have shown that errors not caught before deployment could be 100 times more costly to correct than if they were detected and corrected beforehand.

- Firms spend 70 to 80 percent of their IS budgets just to keep their systems running.

- IS organizations can employ project planning and software development methodologies to implement procedures to improve the overall quality of their development practices.

- A combination of managerial and technical issues conspired to undermine the roll-out of HealthCare.gov. While the website was effectively unusable at launch, a systematic effort of management authority, communication, coordination, and expertise rescued the effort, allowing the site to exceed enrollment projections.

ENDNOTES

1. R. Charette, "Why Software Fails," *IEEE Spectrum*, September 2005.

2. S. Lacy, "Is Atlassian the Next Big Enterprise Software IPO?" *Pando Daily*, February 22, 2012.

3. Z. Jiang and R. Mangharam, "University of Pennsylvania Develops Electrophysiological Heart Model for Real-Time Closed-Loop Testing of Pacemakers," *Mathworks Newsletter*, 2013 Edition.

4. The iPhone and iPod touch OS is derived from Apple's Mac OS X operating system.

5. C. Scott, "Why Farmers Are Connecting Their Cows to the Internet," *SingularityHub*, April 3, 2014.

6. M. Overfelt, "A $15 trillion dream of GE-Silicon Valley hybrid," *CNBC*, April 22, 2014.

7. Adapted from G. Edmondson, "Silicon Valley on the Rhine," *BusinessWeek International*, November 3, 1997.

8. A. Robinson and D. Dilts, "OR and ERP," *ORMS Today*, June 1999.

9. C. Rettig, "The Trouble with Enterprise Software," *MIT Sloan Management Review* 49, no. 1 (2007): 21–27.

10. C. Koch, "Nike Rebounds: How (and Why) Nike Recovered from Its Supply Chain Disaster," *CIO*, June 15, 2004.

11. R. Charette, "Why Software Fails," *IEEE Spectrum*, September 2005.

12. H. Sarrazin and A. West, "Understanding the strategic value of IT in M&A," *McKinsey Quarterly*, January 2011.

13. Note: the managerial definition is simplified. The discussion of virtual machines later in the book will show that separate virtual 'computers' for distributed computing can actually be housed in the same physical device. When talking about distributed computing, the collaborating components are location independent and usually not all within the same device.

14. W3C, "Web Services Architecture," *W3C Working Group Note*, February 11, 2004.

15. K. Clark, "Integration architecture: Comparing web APIs with service-oriented architecture and enterprise application integration," *IBM developerMix*, March 18, 2015.

16. United Hub Team, "United flies you, Uber drives you -- all in one app," *United Hub at United.com*, Aug. 20, 2014. And Unattributed, "Deep Linking," from dev.uber.com, accessed on June 20, 2015 from https://developer.uber.com/v1/deep-linking/

17. B. Basche, "From the Uber-Spotify Partnership to Drizly's API: The Rise of the Remix Economy," *Medium*, Dec. 8, 2014.

18. Unattributed, "Expedia and United Airlines sign new deal for air and hotel content," *Expedia Newsroom*, Dec. 6, 2011.

19. Unattributed, "Expedia Affiliate Network Signs Long Term Partnership With Aer Lingus," *PR Newswire*, Sept. 22, 2011.

20. Unattributed, "Greyhound Partners With Expedia Affiliate Network to Offer Hotel," *PR Newswire*, Jan. 5, 2011.

21. Unattributed, "Hipmunk Launches Direct Hotel Bookings on Web and Mobile Through Partnership With Expedia Affiliate Network," *Yahoo Finance*, May 9, 2013.

22. E. Thomas, "Amazon Outage Proof API Monitoring Approaches Need Overhaul," *Wired*, Oct. 25, 2012.

23. "Petroleum Industry Continues to Explore EDI," *National Petroleum News* 90, no. 12 (November 1998).

24. Some offerings have attempted to overcome the speed issues associated with interpreting Java code. Just-in-time compilation stores code in native processor-executable form after each segment is initially interpreted, further helping to speed execution. Other environments allow for Java to be compiled ahead of time so that it can be directly executed by a microprocessor. However, this process eliminates code portability—Java's key selling point. And developers preparing their code for the JVM actually precompile code into something called Java bytecode, a format that's less human friendly but more quickly interpreted by JVM software.

25. R. Charette, "Why Software Fails," *IEEE Spectrum*, September 2005.

26. C. Rettig, "The Trouble with Enterprise Software," *MIT Sloan Management Review* 49, no. 1 (2007): 21–27.

27. L. Dignan, "Survey: One in 3 IT Projects Fail; Management OK with It," *ZDNet*, December 11, 2007.

28. R. Charette, "Why Software Fails," *IEEE Spectrum*, September 2005.

29. R. Lloyd, "Metric Mishap Caused Loss of NASA Orbiter," *CNN*, September 20, 1999.

30. List largely based on R. Charette, "Why Software Fails," *IEEE Spectrum*, September 2005.

31. R. Kay, "QuickStudy: Capability Maturity Model Integration (CMMI)," *Computerworld*, January 24, 2005; and Carnegie Mellon Software Engineering Institute, *Welcome to CMMI*, 2009, http://www.sei.cmu.edu/cmmi.

32. A. Shenhar and D. Dvir, *Reinventing Project Management: The Diamond Approach to Successful Growth and Innovation* (Boston: Harvard Business School Press, 2007).

33. E. O'Keefe, "The House Has Voted 54 Times in Four Years on Obamacare: Here's the Full List," *Washington Post*, March 21, 2014.

34. K. Pallarito, "Design and Software Problems Plague Health Exchanges: Report," *HealthDay*, October 7, 2013.

35. S. Brill, "'Code Red': Steve Brill on HealthCare.gov, Video Excerpt from the Charlie Rose Show," *BloombergTV*, March 4, 2014.

36. G. Kessler, "How Much Did HealthCare.gov Cost?" *Washington Post*, October 24, 2013.

37. S. Brill, "Obama's Trauma Team," *Time*, February 27, 2014.

38. S. Brill, "Obama's Trauma Team," *Time*, February 27, 2014.

39. E. Hu, "This Slide Shows Why HealthCare.gov Wouldn't Work at Launch," *NPR*, November 19, 2013.

40. M. Kelley, "Why the Obamacare Website Failed in One Slide," *Business Insider*, November 19, 2013.

41. S. Brill, "Obama's Trauma Team," *Time*, February 27, 2014.

42. S. Brill, "'Code Red': Steve Brill on HealthCare.gov, Video Excerpt from the Charlie Rose Show," *BloombergTV*, March 4, 2014.

43. F. Thorp, "'Stress Tests' Show HealthCare.gov Was Overloaded," *NBC News*, November 6, 2013.

44. B. Hughes, "Michael Dickerson: The Invisible Man behind Obamacare's Tech Surge," *Washington Examiner*, December 6, 2013.

45. S. Brill, "Obama's Trauma Team," *Time*, February 27, 2014.

46. S. Brill, "Obama's Trauma Team," *Time*, February 27, 2014.

47. L. Woodhill, "The Obamacare Website Failed for the Same Reason the Soviet Union Did," *Forbes*, November 13, 2013.

CHAPTER 14
Software in Flux: Open Source, Cloud, Virtualized and App-driven Shifts

1. INTRODUCTION

LEARNING OBJECTIVES

1. Understand how low marginal costs, network effects, and switching costs have combined to help create a huge and important industry.
2. Recognize that the software industry is undergoing significant and broadly impactful change brought about by several increasingly adopted technologies including open source software, cloud computing, and software as a service.

For many, software has been a magnificent business. It is the $400 billion-per-year juggernaut[1] that placed Microsoft's Bill Gates and Oracle's Larry Ellison among the wealthiest people in the world. Increasingly, even defining the software industry is difficult. It powers everything from media consumption (Netflix, Spotify) to appliances (Nest, Apple HomeKit). It drives modern farming, scientific discovery, and even the most mundane task such as driving (self-parking features have become commonplace, software drives airbags to GPS). Once a successful software product has been written, the economics for a category-leading offering are among the best you'll find in any industry.[2] Unlike physical products assembled from raw materials, the **marginal cost** to produce an additional copy of a software product is effectively zero. Just duplicate, no additional input required. That quality leads to businesses that can gush cash. Microsoft generates one and a half billion dollars a month from Windows and Office alone.[3] Network effects and switching cost can also offer a leading software firm a degree of customer preference and lock in that can establish a firm as a standard, and in many cases creates winner-take-all (or at least winner-take-most) markets.

marginal cost

The cost of producing one more unit of a product.

open source software (OSS)

Software that is free and where anyone can look at and potentially modify the code.

cloud computing

Replacing computing resources—either an organization's or individual's hardware or software—with services provided over the Internet.

software as a service (SaaS)

A form of cloud computing where a firm subscribes to a third-party software and receives a service that is delivered online.

virtualization

A type of software that allows a single computer (or cluster of connected computers) to function as if it were several different computers, each running its own operating system and software. Virtualization software underpins most cloud computing efforts, and can make computing more efficient, cost-effective, and scalable.

But as great as the business has been, the fundamental model powering the software industry is under assault. **Open source software (OSS)** offerings—free alternatives where anyone can look at and potentially modify a program's code—pose a direct challenge to the assets and advantages cultivated by market leaders. Giants shudder—"How can we compete with free," while others wonder, "How can we make money and fuel innovation on free?" And if free software wasn't enough of a shock, the way firms and users think about software is also changing. A set of services referred to as **cloud computing** is making it more common for a firm to move software out of its own IS shop so that it is run on someone else's hardware. In one variant of this approach known as **software as a service (SaaS)**, users access a *vendor's software* over the Internet, usually by simply starting up a Web browser. With SaaS, you don't need to own the program or install it on your own computer. Hardware clouds can let firms take *their software* and run it on someone else's hardware—freeing them from the burden of buying, managing, and maintaining the physical computing that programs need. Another software technology called **virtualization** can make a single computer behave like many separate machines. This function helps consolidate computing resources and creates additional savings and efficiencies.

Perhaps equally remarkable are the firms that are pioneering these efforts. A few years back you might have expected giants like IBM, HP, Microsoft, and Sun to drive the future of computing. But if you look at the leading contributors to many of the most widely used open source efforts, or providers of widely used cloud infrastructure, you will see that major players include (as *BusinessWeek* put it) a retailer (Amazon), an entertainment company (Netflix), an advertiser (Google), a résumé site (LinkedIn), and a social network (Facebook).[4] And our notion of packaged software is also challenged by instant access to a cornucopia of offerings through device app stores, covering smartphones, tablets, televisions, and more. App offerings further change the underlying economics and possibilities of the software industry and have been a catalyst for the birth of several, innovative, billion-dollar-plus businesses.

These transitions are important. They mean that smaller firms have access to the kinds of burly, sophisticated computing power than only giants had access to in the past. Start-ups can scale quickly and get up and running with less investment capital. Existing firms can leverage these technologies to reduce costs. Got tech firms in your investment portfolio? Understanding what's at work here can inform decisions you make on which stocks to buy or sell. If you make tech decisions for your firm or make recommendations for others, these trends may point to which firms have strong growth and sustainability ahead, or which may be facing troubled times.

KEY TAKEAWAYS

- The software business is attractive due to near-zero marginal costs and an opportunity to establish a standard—creating the competitive advantages of network effects and switching costs.
- New trends in the software industry, including open source software (OSS), cloud computing, software as a service (SaaS), and virtualization are creating challenges and opportunities across tech markets. Understanding the impact of these developments can help a manager make better technology choices and investment decisions.

QUESTIONS AND EXERCISES

1. What major trends, outlined in the section above, are reshaping how we think about software? What industries and firms are potentially impacted by these changes? Why do managers, investors, and technology buyers care about these changes?
2. Which organizations might benefit from these trends? Which might be threatened? Why?
3. What are marginal costs? Are there other industries that have cost economics similar to the software industry?
4. Investigate the revenues and net income of major software players: Microsoft, Google, Oracle, Red Hat, and Salesforce.com. Which firms have higher revenues? Net income? Which have better margins? What do the trends in OSS, SaaS, and cloud computing suggest for these and similar firms?
5. How might the rise of OSS, SaaS, and cloud computing impact hardware sales? How might it impact entrepreneurship and smaller businesses?

2.   OPEN SOURCE

L E A R N I N G   O B J E C T I V E S

1. **Define open source software and understand how it differs from conventional offerings.**
2. **Provide examples of open source software and how firms might leverage this technology.**

Who would have thought a twenty-one-year-old from Finland could start a revolution that continues to threaten the Microsoft Windows empire? But Linus Torvalds did just that. During a marathon six-month coding session, Torvalds created the first version of Linux[5] marshaling open source revolutionaries like no one before him. Instead of selling his operating system, Torvalds gave it away. Now morphed and modified into scores of versions by hundreds of programmers, **Linux** can be found just about everywhere, and most folks credit Linux as being the most significant product in the OSS arsenal. Today Linux powers everything from cell phones to stock exchanges, set-top boxes to supercomputers. You'll find the OS on 16 to 30 percent of the servers in corporate America (depending on how you slice the numbers) and[6] on the majority of smartphones, tablets,[7] and supercomputers,[8] and supporting most Web servers (including those at Google, Amazon, and Facebook). Linux forms the core of the TiVo operating system, it underpins Google's Android and Chrome OS offerings, and it has even gone interplanetary. Linux has been used to power the Phoenix Lander and to control the Spirit and Opportunity Mars rovers.[9] Yes, Linux is even on Mars!

Linux

An open source software operating system.

n00b

Written with two zeros, pronounced "newb." Geek-slang (leet speak) derogatory term for an uninformed or unskilled person.

How Do You Pronounce Linux?

Most English speakers in the know pronounce Linux in a way that rhymes with *"cynics."* You can easily search online to hear video and audio clips of Linus (whose name is actually pronounced "Lean-us" in Finnish) pronouncing the name of his OS. In deference to Linux, some geeks prefer something that sounds more like *"lean-ooks."*[10] Just don't call it *"line-ucks,"* or the tech-savvy will think you're an open source **n00b**! Oh yeah, and while we're on the topic of operating system pronunciation, the Macintosh operating system OS X is pronounced "oh es ten."

FIGURE 14.1   Tux, the Linux Mascot

Open source software (OSS) is often described as free. While most OSS can be downloaded for free over the Internet, it's also "free" as in liberated (you may even see the acronym FLOSS for free/libre/open source software). The source code for OSS products is openly shared. Anyone can look at the source code, change it, and even redistribute it, provided the modified software continues to remain open and free.[11] This openness is in stark contrast to the practice of conventional software firms, who treat their intellectual property as closely guarded secrets and who almost never provide the source code for their commercial software products. As the movement began to pick up steam, many software industry execs became downright hostile toward OSS. The former president of SAP once referred to the open source movement as "socialism," while a former Microsoft CEO has called Linux a "cancer."[12]

But while execs at some firms saw OSS as a threat undermining the lifeblood of their economic model, other big-name technology companies are now solidly behind the open source movement. The old notion of open source being fueled on the contributions of loners tooling away for the glory of contributing to better code is now largely inaccurate. The vast majority of people who work on efforts like Linux are now paid to do so by commercially motivated employers.[13] Nearly every major hardware firm and a list of tech giants (e.g., Apple, Box, Facebook, Google, IBM, LinkedIn, Netflix, and Twitter) has paid staff contributing to open source projects[14]—an open source workforce collectively numbers in the thousands.[15] Most firms also work together to fund foundations that set standards and coordinate the release of product revisions and improvements. Such coordination is critical—helping, for example, to ensure that various versions of products can work alike and operate together.

LAMP

An acronym standing for **L**inux, the **A**pache Web server software, the **M**ySQL database, and any of several programming languages that start with **P** (e.g., Perl, Python, or PHP).

Turn on the LAMP—It's Free!

FIGURE 14.2

Open source is big on the Web. In fact, you'll often hear Web programmers and open source advocates refer to the LAMP stack. **LAMP** is an acronym that stands for the Linux operating system, the Apache Web server software, the MySQL database, and any of several programming languages that start with the letter "P"—Python, Perl, and PHP. From Facebook to YouTube, you'll find LAMP software powering many of the sites you visit each day.

KEY TAKEAWAYS

- OSS is not only available for free, but also makes source code available for review and modification (for the Open Source Initiatives list of the criteria that define an open source software product, see http://opensource.org/docs/osd).
- While open source alternatives are threatening to conventional software firms, some of the largest technology companies now support OSS initiatives and work to coordinate standards, product improvements, and official releases.
- The flagship OSS product is the Linux operating system, now available on all scales of computing devices from cell phones to supercomputers.
- The LAMP stack of open source products is used to power many of the Internet's most popular websites. Linux can be found on 30 percent of corporate servers; supports most Web servers, smartphones, tablets, and supercomputers; and is integral to TiVo and Android-based products.
- The majority of persons who work on open source projects are paid by commercially motivated employers.

QUESTIONS AND EXERCISES

1. Who developed Linux?
2. Who develops it today?
3. List the components of the LAMP stack. Which commercial products do these components compete with (investigate online, if necessary)?
4. Why do commercial firms contribute to open source consortia and foundations?
5. Free doesn't always win. Why might a firm turn down free software in favor of a commercial alternative?

3.   WHY OPEN SOURCE?

LEARNING OBJECTIVES

1. Know the primary reasons firms choose to use OSS.
2. Understand how OSS can beneficially impact industry and government.

There are many reasons why firms choose open source products over commercial alternatives:

Cost—Free alternatives to costly commercial code can be a tremendous motivator, particularly since conventional software often requires customers to pay for every copy used and to pay more for software that runs on increasingly powerful hardware. Banking giant Barclays has been able to reduce software costs by 90 percent by switching to open source products.[16] Online broker E*TRADE estimates that its switch to open source helped save over $13 million a year.[17] And Amazon claimed in SEC filings that the switch to open source was a key contributor to nearly $20 million in tech savings.[18] Firms like TiVo, which use OSS in their own products, eliminate a cost spent either developing their own operating system or licensing similar software from a vendor like Microsoft.

Reliability—There's a saying in the open source community, "Given enough eyeballs, all bugs are shallow."[19] What this means is that the more people who look at a program's code, the greater the likelihood that an error will be caught and corrected. The open source community harnesses the power of legions of geeks who are constantly trawling OSS products, looking to squash bugs and improve product quality. And studies have shown that the quality of popular OSS products outperforms proprietary commercial competitors.[20] In one study, Carnegie Mellon University's Cylab estimated the quality of Linux code to be less buggy than commercial alternatives by a factor of two hundred![21]

Security—OSS advocates also argue that by allowing "many eyes" to examine the code, the security vulnerabilities of open source products come to light more quickly and can be addressed with greater speed and reliability.[22] High-profile hacking contests have frequently demonstrated the strength of OSS products. In one event, laptops running Windows and Macintosh were both hacked (the latter in just two minutes), while a laptop running Linux remained uncompromised.[23] Government agencies and the military often appreciate the opportunity to scrutinize open source efforts to verify system integrity (a particularly sensitive issue among foreign governments leery of legislation like the USA PATRIOT Act of 2001).[24] Many OSS vendors offer **security-focused** (sometimes called *hardened*) versions of their products. These can include systems that monitor the integrity of an OSS distribution, checking file size and other indicators to be sure that code has not been modified and redistributed by bad guys who've added a back door, malicious routines, or other vulnerabilities.

> **security-focused**
>
> Also known as "hardened." Term used to describe technology products that contain particularly strong security features.

Scalability—Many major OSS efforts can run on everything from cheap commodity hardware to high-end supercomputing. **Scalability** allows a firm to scale from start-up to blue chip without having to significantly rewrite their code, potentially saving big on software development costs. Not only can many forms of OSS be migrated to more powerful hardware, packages like Linux have also been optimized to balance a server's workload among a large number of machines working in tandem. Brokerage firm E*TRADE claims that usage spikes following sweeping US Federal Reserve moves flooded the firm's systems, creating the highest utilization levels in five years. But E*TRADE credits its scalable open source systems for maintaining performance while competitors' systems struggled.[25]

> **Scalability**
>
> Ability to either handle increasing workloads or to be easily expanded to manage workload increases. In a software context, systems that aren't scalable often require significant rewrites or the purchase or development of entirely new systems.

Agility and Time to Market—Vendors who use OSS as part of product offerings may be able to skip whole segments of the software development process, allowing new products to reach the market faster than if the entire software system had to be developed from scratch, in-house. Motorola has claimed that customizing products built on OSS has helped speed time-to-market for the firm's mobile phones, while the team behind the Zimbra e-mail and calendar effort built their first product in just a few months by using some forty blocks of free code.[26]

When the Open Source Army Doesn't Show Up: Lessons from Heartbleed

Many open source projects are very well maintained with tightly coordinated contribution armies overseen by well-funded, paid professionals. For example, Red Hat is one of many private firms helping maintain and improve Linux, the firm EnterpriseDB is heavily involved in supporting the PostgreSQL database product, and Google's many open source efforts include stewardship of the Python programming language. But some widely used open source products have been woefully neglected, and this became abundantly clear with the exposure of the Heartbleed bug in spring 2014.

Heartbleed was an error in the OpenSSL security toolkit, a product used by some two-thirds of Internet Web sites, and underpinning security related to the little padlock many web browsers show when sending secure information over the Internet.[27] But for a product that handles a significant chunk of the thirty billion annual e-commerce transactions, OpenSSL was maintained by a pitifully under-sourced effort. Most of the work was done by "two guys named Steve" who had never met and didn't have much of a budget to speak of. A routine coding error in the widely distributed software opened a hole that could potentially have been used to allow hackers to gather passwords, encryption keys, and other sensitive information, triggering "the largest security breach in the history of the human race."[28]

In order to help funnel money and resources to underserved and high-value open source projects, the Linux Foundation, a multimillion-dollar project called the Core Infrastructure Initiative "to fund open source projects that are in the critical path for core computing functions." Big name and deep-pocketed backers include Google, IBM, Facebook, and Microsoft. An initial earmark of $3.9 million was committed for the first three years of the effort, with larger firms committed to pay in at least $100,000 into the annual funding pot. It shouldn't be surprising that OpenSSL is first up on the initiative's support list.

Heartbleed provides a cautionary tale to managers: just because a tool is used by many doesn't mean one shouldn't audit its software products to understand the strength of support and potential risks associated with use.

KEY TAKEAWAYS

- The most widely cited benefits of using OSS include low cost; increased reliability; improved security and auditing; system scalability; and helping a firm improve its time to market.
- Free OSS has resulted in cost savings for many large companies in several industries.
- OSS often has fewer bugs than its commercial counterparts due to the large number of persons who have looked at the code.
- The huge exposure to scrutiny by developers and other people helps to strengthen the security of OSS.
- "Hardened" versions of OSS products often include systems that monitor the integrity of an OSS distribution, checking file size and other indicators to be sure that code has not been modified and redistributed by bad guys who have added a back door, malicious routines, or other vulnerabilities.
- OSS can be easily migrated to more powerful computers as circumstances dictate, and also can balance workload by distributing work over a number of machines.
- Vendors who use OSS as part of product offerings may be able to skip whole segments of the software development process, allowing new products to reach the market faster.

QUESTIONS AND EXERCISES

1. What advantages does OSS offer TiVo? What alternatives to OSS might the firm consider and why do you suppose the firm decided on OSS?
2. What's meant by the phrase, "Given enough eyeballs, all bugs are shallow"? Provide evidence that the insight behind this phrase is an accurate one. How does this phrase relate to the Heartbleed bug?
3. How has OSS benefited E*TRADE? Amazon? Motorola? Zimbra? What benefits were achieved in each of these examples?
4. Describe how OSS provides a firm with scalability. What does this mean, and why does this appeal to a firm? What issues might a firm face if chosen systems aren't scalable?
5. The Web site NetCraft (http://www.netcraft.com) is one of many that provide a tool to see the kind of operating system and Web server software that a given site is running. Visit NetCraft or a similar site and enter the address of some of your favorite Web sites. How many run open source products (e.g., the Linux OS or Apache Web server)? Do some sites show their software as "unknown"? Why might a site be reluctant to broadcast the kind of software that it uses?

4.   EXAMPLES OF OPEN SOURCE SOFTWARE

LEARNING OBJECTIVES

1. Recognize that just about every type of commercial product has an open source equivalent.
2. Be able to list commercial products and their open source competitors.

Just about every type of commercial product has an open source equivalent. Want to take a look at what's out there, and get a gander at the code? Check out GitHub, where millions of projects are hosted and shared (coding students take note: today's employers assume you're GitHub savvy since this is a service many use for project collaboration). Many of these products come with the installation tools, support utilities, and full documentation that make them difficult to distinguish from traditional commercial efforts.[29] In addition to the LAMP products, some major examples include the following:

- Firefox—a Web browser that competes with Internet Explorer
- OpenOffice—a competitor to Microsoft Office
- Gimp—a graphic tool with features found in Photoshop
- Alfresco—collaboration software that competes with Microsoft Sharepoint and EMC's Documentum
- Marketcetera—an enterprise trading platform for hedge fund managers that competes with FlexTrade and Portware
- Zimbra—open source e-mail software that competes with Outlook server
- MySQL, Ingres, and PostgreSQL—open source relational database software packages that each go head-to-head with commercial products from Oracle, Microsoft, Sybase, and IBM
- HBase and Cassandra—nonrelational distributed databases used to power massive file systems (used to power key features on Facebook, Twitter, LinkedIn, and Amazon)
- SugarCRM—customer relationship management software that competes with Salesforce.com and Siebel
- Docker – tools for 'containerization', an evolution beyond virtualization.
- Asterix—an open source implementation for running a PBX corporate telephony system that competes with offerings from Nortel and Cisco, among others
- Free BSD and Sun's OpenSolaris—open source versions of the Unix operating system

KEY TAKEAWAYS

- There are thousands of open source products available, covering nearly every software category. Many have a sophistication that rivals commercial software products.
- Not all open source products are contenders. Less popular open source products are not likely to attract the community of users and contributors necessary to help these products improve over time (again we see network effects are a key to success—this time in determining the quality of an OSS effort).
- Just about every type of commercial product has an open source equivalent.

QUESTIONS AND EXERCISES

1. Make a brief list of commercial product categories that an individual or enterprise might use. Are there open source alternatives for these categories? Are well-known firms leveraging these OSS offerings? Which commercial firms do they compete with? Explore GitHub and do some additional research on top and rising open source projects. Report back to class with examples you find most interesting and promising.

2. Why is open source so important for software development and IS professionals? How should programming students leverage resources available to improve learning, job prospects, and their credibility when job hunting?

3. Are the OSS efforts you identified above provided by commercial firms, nonprofit organizations, or private individuals? Does this make a difference in your willingness to adopt a particular product? Why or why not? What other factors influence your adoption decision?

4. Download a popular, end-user version of an OSS tool that competes with a desktop application that you own, or that you've used (hint: choose something that's a smaller file or easy to install). What do you think of the OSS offering compared to the commercial product? Will you continue to use the OSS product? Why or why not?

---

5. WHY GIVE IT AWAY? THE BUSINESS OF OPEN SOURCE

LEARNING OBJECTIVES

1. **Understand the disproportional impact OSS has on the IT market.**
2. **Understand how vendors make money on open source.**

Open source is a $60 billion industry,[30] but it has a disproportionate impact on the trillion-dollar IT market. By lowering the cost of computing, open source efforts make more computing options accessible to smaller firms. More reliable, secure computing also lowers costs for all users. OSS also diverts funds that firms would otherwise spend on fixed costs, like operating systems and databases, so that these funds can be spent on innovation or other more competitive initiatives. Think about Google, a firm that some estimate has over 1.4 million servers. Imagine the costs if it had to license software for each of those boxes!

Commercial interest in OSS has sparked an acquisition binge. Red Hat bought open source application server firm JBoss for $350 million. Novell snapped up SUSE Linux for $210 million (and was later bought by Attachmate for $2.2 billion). And Sun plunked down over $1 billion for open source database provider MySQL.[31] And with Oracle's acquisition of Sun, one of the world's largest commercial software firms has zeroed in on one of the deepest portfolios of open source products. Open source firms that are valued in excess of $1 billion include now-public Hortonworks, Cloudera, and MapR (all provide big data tools built on open source Hadoop), MongoDB (an open source NoSQL database leader), and Docker (a virtualization technology known as 'containers').[32]

But how do *vendors* make money on open source? One way is by selling support and consulting services. While not exactly Microsoft money, Red Hat, the largest purely OSS firm, reported over a billion-and-a-half dollars in revenue from paying customers subscribing for access to software updates and support services.[33] Oracle, a firm that sells commercial ERP and database products, provides Linux for free, selling high-margin Linux support contracts for as much as $500,000.[34] The added benefit for Oracle? Weaning customers away from Microsoft—a firm that sells many products that compete head-to-head with Oracle's offerings. Service also represents the most important part of IBM's business. The firm now makes more from services than from selling hardware and software.[35] And every dollar saved on buying someone else's software product means more money IBM customers can spend on IBM computers and services. Many open firms also sell their premium add-ons on top of the free stuff. MongoDB, for example, charges firms that run its management software on more than eight servers. And others are leveraging the cloud, too. Docker will sell hosted services for firms that don't want to run its product in-house.[36]

Here's where we also can relate the industry's evolution to what we've learned about standards competition in our earlier chapters. In the pre-Linux days, nearly every major hardware manufacturer made its own, incompatible version of the Unix operating system. These fractured, incompatible markets were each so small that they had difficulty attracting third-party vendors to write application software. Now, much to Microsoft's dismay, all major hardware firms run Linux. That means there's a large, unified market that attracts software developers who might otherwise write for Windows.

To keep standards unified, several Linux-supporting hardware and software firms also back the Linux Foundation, the nonprofit effort where Linus Torvalds serves as a fellow, helping to oversee Linux's evolution. Sharing development expenses in OSS has been likened to going in on a pizza together. Everyone wants a pizza with the same ingredients. The pizza doesn't make you smarter or better. So why not share the cost of a bigger pie instead of buying by the slice?[37] With OSS, hardware firms spend less money than they would in the brutal, head-to-head competition where each once offered a "me too" operating system that was incompatible with rivals but offered little differentiation. Hardware firms now find their technical talent can be deployed in other value-added services mentioned above: developing commercial software add-ons, offering consulting services, and enhancing hardware offerings.

Linux on the Desktop?

While Linux is a major player in enterprise software, mobile phones, and consumer electronics, the Linux OS can only be found on a tiny fraction of desktop computers. There are several reasons for this. Some suggest Linux simply isn't as easy to install and use as Windows or the Mac OS. This complexity can raise the **total cost of ownership (TCO)** of Linux desktops, with additional end-user support offsetting any gains from free software. The small number of desktop users also dissuades third party firms from porting popular desktop applications over to Linux. For consumers in most industrialized nations, the added complexity and limited desktop application availability of desktop Linux just it isn't worth the one to two hundred dollars saved by giving up Windows.

But in developing nations where incomes are lower, the cost of Windows can be daunting. Consider the OLPC, Nicholas Negroponte's "one-hundred-dollar" laptop. An additional one hundred dollars for Windows would double the target cost for the nonprofit's machines. It is not surprising that the first OLPC laptops ran Linux. Microsoft recognizes that if a whole generation of first-time computer users grows up without Windows, they may favor open source alternatives years later when starting their own businesses. As a result, Microsoft has begun offering low-cost versions of Windows (in some cases for as little as seven dollars) in nations where populations have much lower incomes. Microsoft has even offered a version of Windows to the backers of the OLPC. While Microsoft won't make much money on these efforts, the low cost versions will serve to entrench Microsoft products as standards in emerging markets, staving off open source rivals and positioning the firm to raise prices years later when income levels rise.

Legal Risks and Open Source Software: A Hidden and Complex Challenge

Open source software isn't without its risks. Competing reports cite certain open source products as being difficult to install and maintain (suggesting potentially higher total cost of ownership, or TCO). Adopters of OSS without support contracts may lament having to rely on an uncertain community of volunteers to support their problems and provide innovative upgrades. Another major concern is legal exposure. Firms adopting OSS may be at risk if they distribute code and aren't aware of the licensing implications. Some commercial software firms have pressed legal action against the users of open source products when there is a perceived violation of software patents or other unauthorized use of their proprietary code.

For example, Microsoft once suggested that Linux and other open source software efforts violated some two hundred thirty-five of its patents.[38] The firm then began collecting payments and gaining access to the patent portfolios of companies that use the open source Linux operating system in their products, including Fuji, Samsung, and Xerox. Microsoft also cut a deal with Linux vendor Novell in which both firms pledged not to sue each other's customers for potential patent infringements.

Also complicating issues are the varying open source license agreements (these go by various names, such as GPL and the Apache License), each with slightly different legal provisions—many of which have evolved over time. Keeping legal with so many licensing standards can be a challenge, especially for firms that want to bundle open source code into their own products.[39] An entire industry has sprouted up to help firms navigate the minefield of open source legal licenses. Chief among these are products, such as those offered by the firm Black Duck, which analyze the composition of software source code and report on any areas of concern so that firms can honor any legal obligations associated with their offerings. Keeping legal requires effort and attention, even in an environment where products are allegedly "free." This also shows that even corporate lawyers had best geek-up if they want to prove they're capable of navigating a twenty-first-century legal environment.

total cost of ownership (TCO)

All of the costs associated with the design, development, testing, implementation, documentation, training and maintenance of a software system.

KEY TAKEAWAYS

- Business models for firms in the open source industry are varied, and can include selling support services and add-on products, offering hosting to run and maintain customer projects 'in the cloud', licensing OSS for incorporation into commercial products, and using OSS to fuel hardware sales.
- Many firms are trying to use OSS markets to drive a wedge between competitors and their customers.
- Linux has been very successful on mobile devices and consumer electronics, as well as on high-end server class and above computers. But it has not been as successful on the desktop. The small user base for desktop Linux makes the platform less attractive for desktop software developers. Incompatibility with Windows applications, switching costs, and other network effects-related issues all suggest that Desktop Linux has an uphill climb in more mature markets.
- OSS also has several drawbacks and challenges that limit its appeal. These include complexity of some products and a higher total cost of ownership for some products, concern about the ability of a product's development community to provide support or product improvement, and legal and licensing concerns.

QUESTIONS AND EXERCISES

1. Describe the impact of OSS on the IT market.
2. Show your understanding of the commercial OSS market. How do Red Hat, Oracle, Oracle's Sun division, and IBM make money via open source?
3. Visit Mozilla.org. Which open source products does this organization develop? Investigate how development of these efforts is financed. How does this organization differ from the ones mentioned above?
4. What is the Linux Foundation? Why is it necessary? Which firms are members, underwriting foundation efforts?
5. List the reasons why Linux is installed on only a very small fraction of desktop computers. Are there particular categories of products or users who might see Linux as more appealing than conventional operating systems? Do you think Linux's share of the desktop market will increase? Why or why not?
6. How is Microsoft combating the threat of open source software and other free tools that compete with its commercial products?
7. Conduct additional research online. What is the dominant open source database software product? How has stewardship of the leading OSS database effort changed in recent years? Who oversees the effort today? What questions does this raise for the product's future? Investigate the current status of this effort—reaction of the developer community, continued reception of the product—and be prepared to share your findings with class.
8. List some of the risks associated with using OSS. Give examples of firms that might pass on OSS software, and explain why.

6. DEFINING CLOUD COMPUTING

LEARNING OBJECTIVES

1. **Understand the concept of cloud computing.**
2. **Identify the major categories of cloud computing, including SaaS, PaaS, and IaaS.**

When folks talk about cloud computing they're really talking about replacing computing resources—either an organization's or an individual's hardware or software—with *services* provided over the Internet. The name actually comes from the popular industry convention of drawing the Internet or other computer network as a big cloud. The various businesses that fall under the rubric of cloud computing are predicted to continue to grow tremendously from an estimated $40.7 billion in 2011 to $241 billion in 2020.[40]

Cloud computing encompasses a bunch of different efforts. We'll concentrate on describing, providing examples of, and analyzing the managerial implications of two separate categories of cloud computing: (1) *software as a service (SaaS)*, where a firm subscribes to a third-party software-replacing service that is delivered online, and (2) models often referred to as **utility computing**, which can include variants such as *platform as a service* (PaaS) and *infrastructure as a service* (IaaS). Think of SaaS as delivering end-user software to a firm over the Internet instead of on the organization's own computing resources. PaaS delivers tools (a.k.a., a platform) so an organization can develop, test, and deploy software in the cloud. These could include programming languages, database software, product testing and deployment software, and an operating system. IaaS offers an organization a more bare-bones set of services that are an alternative to buying its own physical hardware—that is, computing, storage, and networking resources are instead allocated and made available over the Internet and are paid for based on the amount of resources used. With IaaS firms get the most basic offerings but can also do the most customization, putting their own tools (operating systems, databases, programming languages) on top. Typically, the further down this stack you go, the more support and maintenance services your own organization needs to perform (less for SaaS, the most for IaaS since that's where a firm heavily customizes and runs its own tech). A later section on virtualization will discuss how some organizations are developing their own private clouds, pools of computing resources that reside inside an organization and that can be served up for specific tasks as need arrives.

The benefits and risks of SaaS and the utility computing-style efforts are very similar, but understanding the nuances of each effort can help you figure out if and when the cloud makes sense for your organization. The evolution of cloud computing also has huge implications across the industry: from the financial future of hardware and software firms, to cost structure and innovativeness of adopting organizations, to the skill sets likely to be most valued by employers.

utility computing

A form of cloud computing where a firm develops its own software, and then runs it over the Internet on a service provider's computers.

KEY TAKEAWAYS

- Cloud computing refers to replacing computing resources—of either an organization or individual's hardware or software—with services provided over the Internet.
- Software as a service (SaaS) refers to a third-party software-replacing service that is delivered online.
- Platform as a service (PaaS) delivers tools (a.k.a. a platform) so an organization can develop, test, and deploy software in the cloud. These could include programming languages, database software, and product testing and deployment software.
- Infrastructure as a service (IaaS) offers an organization an alternative to buying its own physical hardware. Computing, storage, and networking resources are instead allocated and made available over the Internet and are paid for based on the amount of resources used. IaaS offers the most customization, with firms making their own choices on what products to install, develop, and maintain (e.g. operating systems, programming langauges, databases) on the infrastructure they license.
- SaaS typically requires the least amount of support and maintenance, IaaS requires the most, since firms choose the tech they want to install, craft their own solution, and run it on what is largely a 'blank canvas' of cloud-provided hardware.
- Cloud computing is reshaping software, hardware, and service markets and is impacting competitive dynamics across industries.

QUESTIONS AND EXERCISES

1. Define cloud computing.
2. Identify and contrast the categories of cloud computing. Which typically requires the most support and maintenance, why? Why would firms choose a platform that requires more support and maintenance?

7.   SOFTWARE IN THE CLOUD: WHY BUY WHEN YOU CAN RENT?

L E A R N I N G   O B J E C T I V E S

1. Know how firms using SaaS products can dramatically lower several costs associated with their information systems.
2. Know how SaaS vendors earn their money.
3. Be able to list the benefits to users that accrue from using SaaS.
4. Be able to list the benefits to vendors from deploying SaaS.

If open source isn't enough of a threat to firms that sell packaged software, a new generation of products, collectively known as SaaS, claims that you can now get the bulk of your computing done through your Web browser or app. Don't install software—let someone else run it for you and deliver the results over the Internet.

Software as a service (SaaS) refers to software that is made available by a third party online. You might also see the terms ASP (application service provider) or HSV (hosted software vendor) used to identify this type of offering, but those are now used less frequently. SaaS is potentially a very big deal. Firms using SaaS products can dramatically lower several costs associated with the care and feeding of their information systems, including software licenses, server hardware, system maintenance, and IT staff. Most SaaS firms earn money via a usage-based pricing model akin to a monthly subscription. Others offer free services that are supported by advertising, while others promote the sale of upgraded or premium versions for additional fees.

Make no mistake, SaaS is yet another direct assault on traditional software firms. The most iconic SaaS firm is Salesforce.com, an enterprise customer relationship management (CRM) provider. This "un-software" company even sports a logo featuring the word "software" crossed out, *Ghostbusters*-style.[41]

FIGURE 14.3

The antisoftware message is evident in the logo of SaaS leader Salesforce.com.

Other enterprise-focused SaaS firms compete directly with the biggest names in software. Some of these upstarts are even backed by leading enterprise software executives. Examples include NetSuite (funded in part by Oracle's Larry Ellison), which offers a comprehensive SaaS ERP suite; Workday (launched by founders of Peoplesoft), which has SaaS offerings for managing human resources; and Aravo, which offers supply chain management software as SaaS. Several traditional software firms have countered start-ups by offering SaaS efforts of their own. IBM offers an SaaS version of its Cognos business intelligence products, Oracle offers CRM On Demand, and SAP's Business ByDesign includes a full suite of enterprise SaaS offerings. Even Microsoft has gone SaaS, with a variety of Web-based services that include CRM, Web meeting tools, collaboration, e-mail, and calendaring.

SaaS is also taking on desktop applications. Intuit has online versions of its Quick-Books and TurboTax software, while the firm's cloud-based Mint is used by many instead of Intuit's Quicken desktop product. Adobe has an online version of Photoshop and offers cloud-based shareable storage for its products. Google, Apple, and Zoho offer office suites that compete with desktop alternatives, prompting Microsoft's own introduction of an online version of Office.

FIGURE 14.4

A look at Zoho's home page shows the diversity of both desktop and enterprise offerings from this SaaS upstart. Note that the firm makes its services available through browsers, phones, and even Facebook.

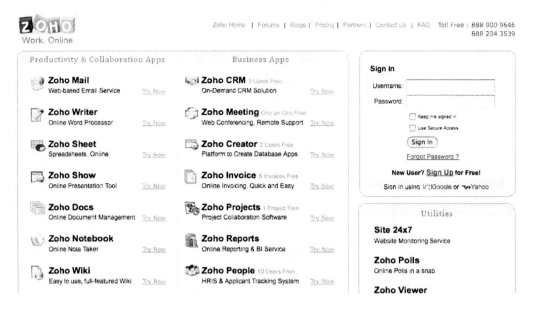

7.1   The Benefits of SaaS

Firms can potentially save big using SaaS. Organizations that adopt SaaS forgo the large upfront costs of buying and installing software packages. For large enterprises, the cost to license, install, and configure products like ERP and CRM systems can easily run into the hundreds of thousands or even millions of dollars. And these costs are rarely a one-time fee, with many products requiring an annual maintenance contract.[42]

Firms that adopt SaaS don't just save on software and hardware, either. There's also the added cost for the IT staff needed to run these systems. Forrester Research estimates that SaaS can bring cost savings of 25 to 60 percent if all these costs are factored in.[43]

There are also accounting and corporate finance implications for SaaS. Firms that adopt software as a service never actually buy a system's software and hardware, so these systems become a variable operating expense. This flexibility helps mitigate the financial risks associated with making a large capital investment in information systems. For example, if a firm pays Salesforce.com sixty-five dollars per month per user for its CRM software, it can reduce payments during a slow season with a smaller staff, or pay more during heavy months when a firm might employ temporary workers. At these rates, SaaS not only looks good to large firms, it makes very sophisticated technology available to smaller firms that otherwise wouldn't be able to afford expensive systems, let alone the IT staff and hardware required to run them.

In addition to cost benefits, SaaS offerings also provide the advantage of being highly scalable. This feature is important because many organizations operate in environments prone to wide variance in usage. Some firms might expect systems to be particularly busy during tax time or the period around quarterly financial reporting deadlines, while others might have their heaviest system loads around a holiday season. A music label might see spikes when an artist drops a new album. Using conventional software, an organization would have to buy enough computing capacity to ensure that it could handle its heaviest anticipated workload. But sometimes these loads are difficult to predict, and if the difference between high workloads and average use is great, a lot of that expensive computer hardware will spend most of its time doing nothing. In SaaS, however, the vendor is responsible for ensuring that systems meet demand fluctuation. Vendors frequently sign a **service level agreement (SLA)** with their customers to ensure a guaranteed uptime and define their ability to meet demand spikes.

When looking at the benefits of SaaS, also consider the potential for higher quality and service levels. SaaS firms benefit from economies of scale that not only lower software and hardware costs, but also potentially boost quality. The volume of customers and the diversity of their experiences mean that an established SaaS vendor is most likely an expert in dealing with all sorts of critical computing issues. SaaS firms handle backups, instantly deploy upgrades and bug fixes, and deal with the continual burden of security maintenance—all costly tasks that must be performed regularly and with care, although each offers little strategic value to firms that perform these functions themselves in-house. The breadth of an SaaS vendor's customer base typically pushes the firm to evaluate and address new technologies

service level agreement (SLA)

A negotiated agreement between the customer and the vendor. The SLA may specify the levels of availability, serviceability, performance, operation, or other commitment requirements.

as they emerge, like quickly offering accessibility from smartphones and tablets. And many contend that cloud computing can actually be greener. SaaS and other cloud firms often have data centers that are better designed to pool and efficiently manage computing resources, and they are often located in warehouse-style buildings designed for computers, not people. Contrast that with corporate data centers that may have wasteful excess capacity to account for service spikes and may be crammed inside inefficiently cooled downtown high-rises. For all but the savviest of IT shops, an established SaaS vendor can likely leverage its scale and experience to provide better, cheaper, more reliable standard information systems than individual companies typically can.

Software developers who choose to operate as SaaS providers also realize benefits. While a packaged software company like SAP must support multiple versions of its software to accommodate operating systems like Windows, Linux, and various flavors of Unix, an SaaS provider develops, tests, deploys, and supports just one version of the software executing on its own servers.

An argument might also be made that SaaS vendors are more attuned to customer needs. Since SaaS firms run a customer's systems on their own hardware, they have a tighter feedback loop in understanding how products are used (and why they fail)—potentially accelerating their ability to enhance their offerings. And once made, enhancements or fixes are immediately available to customers the next time they log in.

SaaS applications also impact distribution costs and capacity. As much as 30 percent of the price of traditional desktop software is tied to the cost of distribution—pressing CD-ROMs, packaging them in boxes, and shipping them to retail outlets.[44] Going direct to consumers can cut out the middleman, so vendors can charge less or capture profits that they might otherwise share with a store or other distributor. Going direct also means that SaaS applications are available anywhere someone has an Internet connection, making them truly global applications. This feature has allowed many SaaS firms to address highly specialized markets (sometimes called **vertical niches**). For example, the Internet allows a company writing specialized legal software, for example, or a custom package for the pharmaceutical industry, to have a national deployment footprint from day one. Vendors of desktop applications that go SaaS benefit from this kind of distribution, too.

Finally, SaaS allows a vendor to counter the vexing and costly problem of software piracy. It's just about impossible to make an executable, illegal copy of a subscription service that runs on an SaaS provider's hardware.

vertical niches

Sometimes referred to as vertical markets. Products and services designed to target a specific industry (e.g., pharmaceutical, legal, apparel retail).

KEY TAKEAWAYS

- SaaS firms may offer their clients several benefits including the following:
    - *lower costs* by eliminating or reducing software, hardware, maintenance, and staff expenses
    - *financial risk mitigation* since start-up costs are so low
    - potentially *faster deployment times* compared with installed packaged software or systems developed in-house
    - costs that are a *variable operating expense* rather than a large, fixed capital expense
    - *scalable systems* that make it easier for firms to ramp up during periods of unexpectedly high system use
    - *higher quality and service levels* through instantly available upgrades, vendor scale economies, and expertise gained across its entire client base
    - *remote access and availability*—most SaaS offerings are accessed through any Web browser, and often even by phone or other mobile device
- Vendors of SaaS products benefit from the following:
    - *limiting development to a single platform*, instead of having to create versions for different operating systems
    - *tighter feedback loop* with clients, helping fuel innovation and responsiveness
    - ability to *instantly deploy bug fixes and product enhancements* to all users
    - *lower distribution costs*
    - *accessibility* to anyone with an Internet connection
    - greatly *reduced risk of software piracy*
- SaaS (and the other forms of cloud computing) are also thought to be better for the environment, since cloud firms more efficiently pool resources and often host their technologies in warehouses designed for cooling and energy efficiency.

QUESTIONS AND EXERCISES

1. Firms that buy conventional enterprise software spend money buying software and hardware. What additional and ongoing expenses are required as part of the "care and feeding" of enterprise applications?

2. In what ways can firms using SaaS products dramatically lower costs associated with their information systems?

3. How do SaaS vendors earn their money?

4. Give examples of enterprise-focused SaaS vendors and their products. Visit the websites of the firms that offer these services. Which firms are listed as clients? Does there appear to be a particular type of firm that uses its services, or are client firms broadly represented?

5. Give examples of desktop-focused SaaS vendors and their products. If some of these are free, try them out and compare them to desktop alternatives you may have used. Be prepared to share your experiences with your class.

6. List the cost-related benefits to users that accrue from using SaaS.

7. List the benefits other than cost-related that accrue to users from using SaaS.

8. List the benefits realized by vendors that offer SaaS services instead of conventional software.

9. Why might cloud computing be greener than conventional computing alternatives? Research online and share examples suggesting that cloud firms could be less environmentally taxing than if a firm built and ran its own corporate data center.

8. SAAS: NOT WITHOUT RISKS

LEARNING OBJECTIVE

1. Be able to list and appreciate the risks associated with SaaS.

Like any technology, we also recognize there is rarely a silver bullet that solves all problems. A successful manager is able to see through industry hype and weigh the benefits of a technology against its weaknesses and limitations. And there are still several major concerns surrounding SaaS.

The largest concerns involve the tremendous dependence a firm develops with its SaaS vendor. While some claim that the subscription-based SaaS model means that you can simply walk away from a vendor if you become dissatisfied, in fact there is quite a bit of lock-in with SaaS vendors, too. And in addition to the switching costs associated with switching on conventional software platforms, switching SaaS vendors may involve the slow and difficult task of transferring very large data files over the Internet. Having all of your eggs in one basket can leave a firm particularly vulnerable. If a traditional software company goes out of business, in most cases its customers can still go on using its products. But if your SaaS vendor goes under, you're hosed. They've got all your data, and even if firms could get their data out, most organizations don't have the hardware, software, staff, or expertise to quickly absorb an abandoned function.

Beware with whom you partner. Any hot technology is likely to attract a lot of start-ups, and most of these start-ups are unlikely to survive. In just a single year, the leading trade association found the number of SaaS vendors dropped from seven hundred members to four hundred fifty.[45] One of the early efforts to collapse was Pandesic, a joint venture between SAP and Intel—two large firms that might have otherwise instilled confidence among prospective customers. In another example, Danish SaaS firm "IT Factory" was declared "Denmark's Best IT Company" by *Computerworld*, only to follow the award one week later with a bankruptcy declaration.[46] Indeed, despite the benefits, the costs of operating as an SaaS vendor can be daunting. NetSuite's founder claimed it "takes ten years and $100 million to do right"[47]—maybe that's why the firm still wasn't profitable, even three and a half years after going public.

Firms that buy and install packaged software usually have the option of sticking with the old stuff as long as it works, but organizations adopting SaaS may find they are forced into adopting new versions. This fact is important because any radical changes in an SaaS system's user interface or system functionality might result in unforeseen training costs, or increase the chance that a user might make an error.

Keep in mind that SaaS systems are also reliant on a network connection. If a firm's link to the Internet goes down, its link to its SaaS vendor is also severed. Relying on an Internet connection also means that data is transferred to and from an SaaS firm at Internet speeds, rather than the potentially higher speeds of a firm's internal network. Solutions to many of these issues are evolving as Internet speeds become faster and Internet service providers become more reliable. Many SaaS offerings also allow for offline use of data that is typically stored in SaaS systems. With these products a user can download a subset of data to be offline (say on a plane flight or other inaccessible location) and then sync the data when the connection is restored. Ultimately, though, SaaS users have a much higher level of dependence on their Internet connections.

And although an SaaS firm may have more security expertise than your organization, that doesn't mean that security issues can be ignored. Any time a firm allows employees to access a corporation's systems and data assets from a remote location, a firm is potentially vulnerable to abuse and infiltration. Some firms may simply be unacceptably uncomfortable with critical data assets existing outside their own network. There may also be contractual or legal issues preventing data from being housed remotely, especially if an SaaS vendor's systems are in another country operating under different laws and regulations. "We're very bound by regulators in terms of client data and country-of-origin issues, so it's very difficult to use the cloud," says Rupert Brown, a chief architect at Merrill Lynch.[48]

SaaS systems are often accused of being less flexible than their installed software counterparts—mostly due to the more robust configuration and programming options available in traditional software packages. It is true that many SaaS vendors have improved system customization options and integration with standard software packages. And at times a lack of complexity can be a blessing—fewer choices can mean less training, faster start-up time, and lower costs associated with system use. But firms with unique needs may find SaaS restrictive.

SaaS offerings usually work well when the bulk of computing happens at the server end of a distributed system because the kind of user interface you can create in a browser isn't as sophisticated as what you can do with a separate, custom-developed desktop program. A comparison of the first few iterations of the Web-based Google Docs office suite, which offers word processing, presentation software, and a spreadsheet, reveals a much more limited feature set than Microsoft's Office desktop software. The bonus, of course, is that an online office suite is accessible anywhere and makes sharing documents a snap. Again, an understanding of trade-offs is key.

Here's another challenge for a firm and its IT staff: SaaS means a greater *consumerization* of technology. Employees, at their own initiative, can go to firms such as Atlassian or PBworks and set up a wiki, WordPress to start blogging, and subscribe to an SaaS offering like Salesforce.com and start storing potentially sensitive corporate files in Dropbox all without corporate oversight and approval. This work can result in employees operating outside established firm guidelines and procedures, potentially introducing operational inconsistencies or even legal and security concerns.

The consumerization of corporate technology isn't all bad. Employee creativity can blossom with increased access to new technologies, costs might be lower than home grown solutions, and staff could introduce the firm to new tools that might not otherwise be on the radar of the firm's IS Department. But all this creates an environment that requires a level of engagement between a firm's technical staff and the groups that it serves that is deeper than that employed by any prior generation of technology workers. Those working in an organization's information systems group must be sure to conduct regular meetings with representative groups of employees across the firm to understand their pain points and assess their changing technology needs. Non-IT managers should regularly reach out to IT to ensure that their needs are on the tech staff's agenda. Organizations with internal IT-staff R&D functions that scan new technologies and critically examine their relevance and potential impact on the firm can help guide an organization through the promise and peril of new technologies. Now more than ever, IT managers must be deeply knowledgeable about business areas, broadly aware of new technologies, and able to bridge the tech and business worlds. Similarly, any manager looking to advance his or her organization has to regularly consider the impact of new technologies.

KEY TAKEAWAYS

The risks associated with SaaS include the following:

- *dependence on a single vendor.*
- concern about the long-term *viability of partner firms.*
- users *may be forced to migrate to new versions*—possibly incurring unforeseen training costs and shifts in operating procedures.
- *reliance on a network connection*—which may be slower, less stable, and less secure.
- *data asset stored off-site*—with the potential for security and legal concerns.
- *limited configuration, customization, and system integration options* compared to packaged software or alternatives developed in-house.
- *the user interface of Web-based software is often less sophisticated and lacks the richness of most desktop alternatives.*
- ease of adoption *may lead to pockets of unauthorized IT* being used throughout an organization.

QUESTIONS AND EXERCISES

1. Consider the following two firms: a consulting start-up, and a defense contractor. Leverage what you know about SaaS and advise whether each might consider SaaS efforts for CRM or other enterprise functions? Why or why not?

2. Think of firms you've worked for, or firms you would like to work for. Do SaaS offerings make sense for these firms? Make a case for or against using certain categories of SaaS.

3. What factors would you consider when evaluating an SaaS vendor? Which firms are more appealing to you and why?

4. Discuss problems that may arise because SaaS solutions rely on Internet connections. Discuss the advantages of through-the-browser access.

5. Evaluate trial versions of desktop SaaS offerings (offered by Adobe, Apple, Google, Microsoft, Zoho, or others). Do you agree that the interfaces of Web-based versions are not as robust as desktop rivals? Are they good enough for you? For most users?

9. UNDERSTANDING CLOUD COMPUTING MODELS: PAAS, IAAS, AND MOTIVATIONS AND RISKS

LEARNING OBJECTIVES

1. **Distinguish between SaaS and hardware clouds.**
2. **Provide examples of firms and uses of hardware clouds.**
3. **Understand the concepts of cloud computing, cloudbursting, and black swan events.**
4. **Understand the challenges and economics involved in shifting computing hardware to the cloud.**

While SaaS provides the software *and* hardware to replace an internal information system, sometimes a firm develops its own custom software but wants to pay someone else to run it for them. That's where cloud offerings such as PaaS and IaaS come in. In these models, a firm replaces software and hardware that it might otherwise run on-site with a service provided by a third party online. While the term utility computing was fashionable a few years back (and old timers claim it shares a lineage with terms like hosted computing or even time sharing), now most in the industry have begun referring to this as an aspect of cloud computing. Hardware and software used in such scenarios exists "in the cloud," meaning somewhere on the Internet. The costs of systems operated in this manner look more like a utility bill—you only pay for the amount of processing, storage, and telecommunications used. Tech research firm Gartner has estimated that 80 percent of corporate tech spending goes toward data center maintenance.[49] Hardware-focused cloud computing provides a way for firms to chip away at these costs.

Major players are spending billions building out huge data centers to take all kinds of computing out of the corporate data center and place it in the cloud. While cloud vendors typically host your software on their systems, many of these vendors also offer additional tools to help in creating and hosting apps in the cloud. Salesforce.com offers Force.com, which includes not only a hardware cloud but also several cloud-supporting tools, such as a programming environment (IDE) to write applications specifically tailored for Web-based delivery. Google's App Engine offers developers several tools, including a database product called Big Table. And Microsoft offers the Windows Azure cloud platform that runs several tools including the SQL Azure database. These efforts are often described by the phrase **platform as a service (PaaS)** since the cloud vendor provides a more complete platform (e.g., hosting hardware, operating system, database, and other software), which clients use to build their own applications.

platform as a service (PaaS)

Where cloud providers offer services that include the hardware, operating system, development tools, testing and hosting (i.e., the platform) that its customers use to *build their own applications* on the provider's infrastructure. In this scenario the cloud firm usually manages the platform (hosting, hardware, and supporting software), while the client has control over the creation and deployment of their application.

infrastructure as a service (IaaS)

Where cloud providers offer services that include running the remote hardware, storage, and networking (i.e., the infrastructure), but client firms can choose software used (which may include operating systems, programming languages, databases, and other software packages). In this scenario the cloud firm usually manages the infrastructure (keeping the hardware and networking running), while the client has control over most other things (operating systems, storage, deployed applications, and perhaps even security and networking features like firewalls and security systems).

Another alternative is called **infrastructure as a service (IaaS)**. This is a good alternative for firms that want even more control. In IaaS, clients can select their own operating systems, development environments, underlying applications like databases, or other software packages (i.e., clients, and not cloud vendors, get to pick the platform), while the cloud firm usually manages the infrastructure (providing hardware and networking). IaaS services are offered by a wide variety of firms, including Amazon, CSC, Rackspace, HP, IBM, and VMware.

FIGURE 14.5

Estimated Monthly Costs to Run a Website with 50 Million Monthly Page Views.

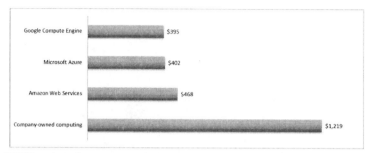

Source: "SADA Systems," Wall Street Journal

Still other cloud computing efforts focus on providing a virtual replacement for a subset of operational hardware like storage and backup solutions. These include the cloud-based backup efforts like EMC's Mozy, and corporate storage services like Box and Amazon's Simple Storage Solution (S3). Consumer services like Apple's iCloud that provide storage as a service and sync user data across devices (phone, multiple desktops) also fall into this camp. The common theme in all of this is leveraging computing delivered over the Internet to satisfy the computing needs of both users and organizations.

cloudbursting

Describes the use of cloud computing to provide excess capacity during periods of spiking demand. Cloudbursting is a scalability solution that is usually provided as an overflow service, kicking in as needed.

black swans

Unpredicted, but highly impactful events. Scalable computing resources can help a firm deal with spiking impact from Black Swan events. The phrase entered the managerial lexicon from the 2007 book of the same name by Nassim Taleb.

Clouds in Action: A Snapshot of Diverse Efforts

Large, established organizations, small firms and start-ups are all embracing the cloud. Examples are wide ranging. Consider that President Obama's reelection campaign was run almost entirely on Amazon's cloud and that a big chunk of the code they relied on included open source tools developed and shared with the world by Netflix.[50] The examples below illustrate the wide range of these efforts.

Journalists refer to the *New York Times* as, "The Old Gray Lady," but it turns out that the venerable paper is a cloud-pioneering whippersnapper. When the *Times* decided to make roughly one hundred fifty years of newspaper archives (over fifteen million articles) available over the Internet, it realized that the process of converting scans into searchable PDFs would require more computing power than the firm had available.[51] To solve the challenge, a *Times* IT staffer simply broke out a credit card and signed up for Amazon's EC2 cloud computing and S3 cloud storage services. The *Times* then started uploading terabytes of information to Amazon, along with a chunk of code to execute the conversion. While anyone can sign up for services online without speaking to a rep, someone from Amazon eventually contacted the *Times* to check in after noticing the massive volume of data coming into its systems. Using one hundred of Amazon's Linux servers, the *Times* job took just twenty-four hours to complete. In fact, a coding error in the initial batch forced the paper to rerun the job. Even the blunder was cheap—just two hundred forty dollars in extra processing costs. Says a member of the *Times* IT group: "It would have taken a month at our facilities, since we only had a few spare PCs....It was cheap experimentation, and the learning curve isn't steep."[52]

NASDAQ also uses Amazon's cloud as part of its Market Replay system. The exchange uses Amazon to make terabytes of data available on demand, and uploads an additional thirty to eighty gigabytes every day. Market Reply allows access through an Adobe AIR interface to pull together historical market conditions in the ten-minute period surrounding a trade's execution. This allows NASDAQ to produce a snapshot of information for regulators or customers who question a trade. Says the exchange's VP of Product Development, "The fact that we're able to keep so much data online indefinitely means the brokers can quickly answer a question without having to pull data out of old tapes and CD backups."[53] NASDAQ isn't the only major financial organization leveraging someone else's cloud. Others include Merrill Lynch, which uses IBM's Blue Cloud servers to build and evaluate risk analysis programs; and Morgan Stanley, which relies on Force.com for recruiting applications.

Sometimes organizations can't give up ownership of their own hardware, software, or data, so they create what are called "private clouds." These are pools of computing resources that an organization owns or leases and which it doesn't share with other customers. Private clouds still use cloud computing technologies for fast service provisioning (e.g., quickly spinning up servers and storage as demand spikes). Amazon has provided its own software and data center management expertise to the U.S. Central Intelligence Agency, allowing the CIA to run a private cloud that it owned and only it can occupy, but that could take advantage of Amazon tools, expertise, and management.[54]

Some firms provide so-called hybrid clouds, the ability to allocate computing assets from a pool of resources an organization owns (e.g., the private cloud) to resources provided off site by a cloud computing provider that serves other customers as well (e.g., the public cloud). IBM's cloud efforts, which count Elizabeth Arden and the U.S. Golf Association among their customers, offer several hybrid-cloud services, including so-called **cloudbursting**. In a cloudbursting scenario a firm's data center running at maximum capacity can seamlessly shift part of the workload to IBM's cloud, with any spikes in system use metered, utility style. Cloudbursting is appealing because forecasting demand is difficult and can't account for the ultrarare, high-impact events, sometimes called **black swans**. Planning to account for usage spikes explains why the servers at many conventional corporate IS shops run at only 10 to 20 percent capacity.[55] While Cloud Labs cloudbursting service is particularly appealing for firms that already have a heavy reliance on IBM hardware in-house, it is possible to build these systems using the hardware clouds of other vendors, too.

Salesforce.com's Force.com cloud is especially tuned to help firms create and deploy custom Web applications. The firm makes it possible to piece together projects using premade Web services that provide software building blocks for features like calendaring and scheduling. The integration with the firm's SaaS CRM effort, and with third-party products like Google Maps allows enterprise mash-ups that can combine services from different vendors into a single application that's run on Force.com hardware. The platform even includes tools to help deploy Facebook applications. Intuitive Surgical used Force.com to create and host a custom application to gather clinical trial data for the firm's surgical robots. An IS manager at Intuitive noted, "We could build it using just their tools, so in essence, there was no programming."[56] Other users include Jobscience, which used Force.com to launch its online recruiting site; and Caesars Entertainment, which uses Force.com applications to manage room reservations, air travel programs, and player relations.

9.1 Challenges Remain

Cloud computing efforts categorized as PaaS and IaaS share similar benefits and risk with SaaS, and as our discussion of SaaS showed, cloud efforts aren't for everyone. Some additional examples illustrate the challenges in shifting computing hardware to the cloud.

For all the hype about cloud computing, it doesn't work in all situations. From an architectural standpoint, most large organizations run a hodgepodge of systems that include both package applications and custom code written in-house. Installing a complex set of systems on someone else's hardware can be a brutal challenge and in many cases is just about impossible. For that reason we can expect most cloud computing efforts to focus on new software development projects rather than options for old software (sometimes called legacy systems). Even for efforts that can be custom-built and cloud-deployed, other roadblocks remain. For example, some firms face stringent regulatory compliance issues. To quote one tech industry executive, "How do you demonstrate what you are doing is in compliance when it is done outside?"[57]

Firms considering cloud computing need to do a thorough financial analysis, comparing the capital and other costs of owning and operating their own systems over time against the variable costs over the same period for moving portions to the cloud. For high-volume, low-maintenance systems, the numbers may show that it makes sense to buy rather than rent. Cloud costs can seem super cheap, and they're getting cheaper. The intensity of competition among leading cloud players including Google, Amazon, and Microsoft led each firm to cut various services by up to 85 percent in a single month.[58] A quarter a gigabyte a month may seem like a small amount, but system maintenance costs often include the need to clean up old files or put them on tape. If unlimited data is stored in the cloud, these costs can add up.

Firms should enter the cloud cautiously, particularly where mission-critical systems are concerned. Problems at Amazon have caused a cloud collapse, impacting a number of firms, especially start-ups looking to leanly ramp up by avoiding buying and hosting their own hardware.[59] An Adobe problem with the firm's Creative Cloud suite left graphics professionals locked out for over a day.[60] If a cloud vendor fails you and all your eggs are in one basket, then you're down, too. Vendors with multiple data centers that are able to operate with fault-tolerant provisioning, keeping a firm's efforts at more than one location to account for any operating interruptions, will appeal to firms with stricter uptime requirements, but even this isn't a guarantee. A human configuration error hosed Amazon's clients, despite the fact that the firm had confirmed redundant facilities in multiple locations.[61] Cloud firms often argue that their expertise translates into less downtime and failure than conventional corporate data centers, but no method is without risks.

KEY TAKEAWAYS

- It's estimated that 80 percent of corporate tech spending goes toward data center maintenance. Cloud computing helps tackle these cost by allowing firms to run their own software on the hardware of the provider, paying only for services that are used.
- Amazon, Google, IBM, Microsoft, Oracle/Sun, Rackspace, Salesforce.com, and VMware are among firms offering cloud computing services.
- Cloud computing varieties include platform as a service (PaaS), where vendors provide a platform (e.g., the operating system and supporting software like database management systems, a software development environment, testing, and application service) but where client firms write their own code; and infrastructure as a service (IaaS), where cloud vendors provide and manage the underlying infrastructure (hardware, storage, and networking), while clients can create their own platform, choosing operating systems, applications, and configurations.
- Some firms use cloud computing technology on hardware they own or lease as a sole customer. This is referred to as a private cloud. Other firms allocate resources between their own systems (the private cloud) and the public cloud (where resources may be shared with other clients). This is referred to as a hybrid-cloud strategy.
- Amazon provides software and services, helping the CIA build and maintain its own private cloud.
- Users of cloud computing run the gamut of industries, including publishing (the *New York Times*), finance (NASDAQ), and cosmetics and skin care (Elizabeth Arden).
- Benefits and risks are similar to those discussed in SaaS efforts. Benefits include the use of the cloud for handling large batch jobs or limited-time tasks, offloading expensive computing tasks, and cloudbursting efforts that handle system overflow when an organization needs more capacity.
- Most legacy systems can't be easily migrated to the cloud, meaning most efforts will be new efforts or those launched by younger firms.
- Cloud (utility) computing doesn't work in situations where complex legacy systems have to be ported or where there may be regulatory compliance issues.
- Some firms may still find TCO and pricing economics favor buying over renting—scale sometimes suggests an organization is better off keeping efforts in-house.

QUESTIONS AND EXERCISES

1. What is cloud computing? What kinds of services are described by this term? What are other names for this phenomenon?
2. Which firms are the leading providers of cloud computing services? How are clients using these efforts?
3. List the circumstances where cloud computing works best and where it works poorly. When would each alternative make more sense—SaaS, PaaS, and IaaS? What sorts of firms would use a private cloud? A hybrid cloud? What sorts of issues should firms consider, and what sorts of expertise would be necessary when adopting each alternative?
4. Research cloud-based alternatives for backing up your hard drive. Which are among the best reviewed product or services? Why? Do you or would you use such a service? Why or why not?
5. Can you think of "black swan" events that have caused computing services to become less reliable? Describe the events and its consequences for computing services. Suggest a method and vendor for helping firms overcome the sorts of events that you encountered.

10. CLOUDS AND TECH INDUSTRY IMPACT

LEARNING OBJECTIVES

1. Understand how cloud computing's impact across industries is proving to be broad and significant.
2. Know the effects of cloud computing on high-end server sales and the influence on the trend shifting from hardware sales to service.
3. Know the effects of cloud computing on innovation and the influence on the changes in the desired skills mix and job outlook for IS workers.
4. Know that by lowering the cost to access powerful systems and software, cloud computing can decrease barriers to entry.
5. Understand the importance, size, and metrics of server farms.

Although still a relatively recent phenomenon, cloud computing's impact across industries is already proving to be broad and significant.

Cloud computing is affecting the competitive dynamics of the hardware, software, and consulting industries. In the past, firms seeking to increase computing capacity invested heavily in expensive, high-margin server hardware, creating a huge market for computer manufacturers. But now, hardware firms find these markets may be threatened by the cloud. IBM saw server sales fall from 20 to 30 percent in recent years, finally selling its low-end server business off to Lenovo (the same firm that bought Big Blue's PC and laptop business years earlier).[62] Barclays estimates that for every dollar that flows into cloud computing, several dollars are cut out of traditional hardware sales and other IT end markets.[63] Michael Dell has stated that after taking his firm private, he will sell off several hardware businesses and refocus the firm on cloud computing, an area where Dell lags significantly behind rivals.

The shift to cloud computing also alters the margin structure for many in the computing industry. While Moore's Law has made servers cheap, deploying SaaS and operating a commercial cloud is still very expensive—much more so than simply making additional copies of conventional, packaged software. Microsoft surprised Wall Street when it announced it would need to pour at least $2 billion more than analysts expected into the year's **server farm** capital spending. The firm's stock—among the world's most widely held—sank 11 percent in a day.[64] As a result, many portfolio managers started paying closer attention to the business implications of the cloud.

Cloud computing can accelerate innovation and therefore changes the desired skills mix and job outlook for IS workers. If cloud computing customers spend less on expensive infrastructure investments, they potentially have more money to reinvest in strategic efforts and innovation. IT careers may change, too. Demand for nonstrategic skills like hardware operations and maintenance are likely to decrease. Organizations will need more business-focused technologists who intimately understand a firm's competitive environment, and can create systems that add value and differentiate the firm from its competition.[65] While these tech jobs require more business training, they're also likely to be more durable and less likely to be outsourced to a third party with a limited understanding of the firm.

By lowering the cost to access powerful systems and software, barriers to entry also decrease. Firms need to think about the strategic advantages they can create, even as technology is easily duplicated. This trend means the potential for more new entrants across industries, and since start-ups can do more with less, it's also influencing entrepreneurship and venture capital. The CTO of SlideShare, a start-up that launched using Amazon's S3 storage cloud, offers a presentation on his firm's site labeled "Using S3 to Avoid VC." Similarly, the CEO of online payments start-up Zuora claims to have saved between half a million and $1 million by using cloud computing: "We have no servers, we run the entire business in the cloud."[66] And the sophistication of these tools lowers development time. Enterprise firm Apttus claims it was able to perform the equivalent of six months of development in a couple of weekends by using cloud services. The firm scored its first million-dollar deal in three months, and was break-even in nine months, a ramp-up time that would have been unheard of, had they needed to plan, purchase, and deploy their own data center, and create from scratch the Web services that were provided by its cloud vendor.[67] Venture capitalist Mark Suster claims that the cost to start an Internet company has fallen from $5 million in 2000 to just $5,000 in 2011, due in large part to advances in cloud computing and open source software.[68]

server farm

A massive network of computer servers running software to coordinate their collective use. Server farms provide the infrastructure backbone to SaaS and hardware cloud efforts, as well as many large-scale Internet services.

So What's It Take to Run This Thing?

In the countryside surrounding the Columbia River in the Pacific Northwest, potato farms are yielding to server farms. Turns out the area is tailor made for creating the kinds of massive data installations that form the building blocks of cloud computing. The land is cheap, the region's hydroelectric power costs a fraction of Silicon Valley rates, and the area is served by ultrafast fiber-optic connections. Even the area's mild temperatures cut cooling costs.

Most major players in cloud computing have server farms in the region, each with thousands of processors humming away simultaneously. Microsoft's Quincy, Washington, facility is as big as ten American football fields and has nearly six hundred miles of wiring, 1.5 metric tons of battery backup, and three miles of chiller piping to keep things cool. Storage is big enough to store 6.75 trillion photos. Just a short drive away, Yahoo! has two facilities on fifty acres, including one that runs at a zero carbon footprint. Google has a thirty-acre site sprawled across former farmland in The Dalles, Oregon. The Google site includes two massive buildings, with a third on the way. And in Boardman, Oregon, Amazon has a three building petabyte palace that sports its own ten-megawatt electrical substation.[69]

While U.S. activity has been particularly intense in the Pacific Northwest, server farms that support cloud computing are popping up from Shanghai to São Paulo. Not only does a diverse infrastructure offer a degree of fault tolerance and disaster recovery (Oregon down? Shift to North Carolina), the myriad of national laws and industry-specific regulatory environments may require some firms to keep data within a specific country or region. To meet the challenge, cloud vendors are racing to deploy infrastructure worldwide and allowing customers to select regional availability zones for their cloud computing needs.

The build-out race has become so intense that many firms have developed rapid-deployment server farm modules that are preconfigured and packed inside shipping containers. Some of these units contain as many as three thousand servers each. Just drop the containers on-site, link to power, water, and telecom, and presto—you've got yourself a data center. More than two hundred containers can be used on a single site. One Microsoft VP claimed the configuration has cut the time to open a data center to just a few days, claiming Microsoft's San Antonio facility was operational in less time than it took a local western wear firm to deliver her custom-made cowboy boots![70] Microsoft's Dublin-based fourth generation data center will be built entirely of containers—no walls or roof—using the outside air for much of the cooling.[71]

FIGURE 14.6

This server-packed shipping container from Oracle's Sun unit is designed for rapid data center deployment.

While firms are buying less hardware, cloud vendors have turned out to be the computing industry's best customers. Amazon has spent well over $2 billion on its cloud infrastructure. Google reportedly has 1.4 million servers operating across three dozen data centers.[72] Demonstrating it won't be outdone, Microsoft plans to build as many as twenty server farms, at costs of up to $1 billion each.[73] Look for the clouds to pop up in unexpected places. Microsoft has scouted locations in Siberia, while Google has applied to patent a method for floating data centers on an offshore platform powered by wave motions.[74]

KEY TAKEAWAYS

- Cloud computing's impact across industries is proving to be broad and significant.
- Clouds can lower barriers to entry in an industry, making it easier for start-ups to launch and smaller firms to leverage the backing of powerful technology.
- Clouds may also lower the amount of capital a firm needs to launch a business, shifting power away from venture firms in those industries that had previously needed more VC money.
- Clouds can shift resources out of capital spending and into profitability and innovation.
- Hardware and software sales may drop as cloud use increases, while service revenues will increase.
- Cloud computing can accelerate innovation and therefore changes the desired skills mix and job outlook for IS workers. Tech skills in data center operations, support, and maintenance may shrink as a smaller number of vendors consolidate these functions.
- Demand continues to spike for business-savvy technologists. Tech managers will need even stronger business skills and will focus an increasing percentage of their time on strategic efforts. These latter jobs are tougher to outsource, since they involve an intimate knowledge of the firm, its industry, and its operations.
- The market for expensive, high margin, sever hardware is threatened by companies moving applications to the cloud instead of investing in hardware.
- Server farms require plenty of cheap land, low cost power, ultrafast fiber-optic connections, and benefit from mild climates.
- Google, Oracle's Sun, Microsoft, IBM, and HP have all developed rapid-deployment server farm modules that are preconfigured and packed inside shipping containers.

QUESTIONS AND EXERCISES

1. Describe how the shift to cloud computing may impact traditional computing hardware firms.
2. Describe the shift in skill sets required for IT workers that is likely to result from the widespread adoption of cloud computing.
3. Why do certain entry barriers decrease as a result of cloud computing? What is the effect of lower entry barriers on new entrants, entrepreneurship, and venture capital? On existing competitors?
4. What factors make the Columbia River region of the Pacific Northwest an ideal location for server farms?
5. Why did Microsoft's shift to cloud computing create an unexpected shock among stock analysts who cover the firm? What does this tell you about the importance of technology understanding among finance and investment professionals?
6. Why do cloud computing vendors build regional server farms instead of one mega site?
7. Why would a firm build a container-based data center?

11. VIRTUALIZATION: SOFTWARE THAT MAKES ONE COMPUTER ACT LIKE MANY

LEARNING OBJECTIVES

1. Know what virtualization software is and its impact on cloud computing.
2. Be able to list the benefits to a firm from using virtualization.

virtualization

A type of software that allows a single computer (or cluster of connected computers) to function as if it were several different computers, each running its own operating system and software. Virtualization software underpins most cloud computing efforts, and can make computing more efficient, cost-effective, and scalable.

Perhaps the most important software tool in the cloud computing toolbox is **virtualization**. Think of virtualization as being a kind of operating system for operating systems. A server running virtualization software can create smaller compartments in memory that each behave as a separate computer with its own operating system and resources. The key benefit: firms can stop buying separate servers for each application they want to run. Instead, organizations can create many virtual computers on a single machine (or cluster of machines that provide a pool of capacity) so hardware is used more efficiently.[75]

This means virtualization can save firms big bucks. Most server computers aren't running at anywhere near a full load. Some studies have shown that, on average, conventional data centers run at 15 percent or less of their maximum capacity. Since virtualization allows firms to cram more of their computing into this unused space, data centers using virtualization software have increased utilization to 80 percent or more.[76] This increased efficiency means cost savings in hardware, staff, and real estate. Plus it reduces a firm's IT-based energy consumption, cutting costs, lowering its carbon footprint, and boosting "green cred."[77] Using virtualization, firms can buy and maintain fewer servers, each running at a greater capacity. It can also power down servers until demand increases require them to come online. Virtualization also helps firms scale up. Find you need more capacity for a specific function, like a spike online orders sent by a new app? The virtual representation of any computer can be transferred to more burly hardware that has fewer additional virtual machines running on it so it can handle the load as demand spikes.

containers

A type of virtualization that allows for shared operating systems for more resource savings and faster execution. However containers still isolate applications so they execute and moved to different computing hardware, just like conventional virtualization.

There's another term that's increasingly appearing in the tech and business press, **containers**. This is a type of virtualization that allows applications to share an operating system, but it still lets resources be shuttled around from low-powered hardware to massive pools of servers if capacity spikes. Since containers don't need their own separate operating system, they use even less resources and execute faster.[78] The big dog in this space is the open-source firm Docker, a technology that's getting wide use from Silicon Valley to Wall Street.[79]

virtual desktop

When a firm runs an instance of a PC's software on another machine and simply delivers the image of what's executing to the remote device. Using virtualization, a single server can run dozens of PCs, simplifying backup, upgrade, security, and administration.

While virtualization is a key software building block that makes public cloud computing happen, it can also be used in-house to reduce an organization's hardware needs, and even to create a firm's own private cloud of scalable assets. Bechtel, BT, Merrill Lynch, and Morgan Stanley are among the firms with large private clouds enabled by virtualization.[80] Another kind of virtualization, **virtual desktops** allow a server to run what amounts to a copy of a PC—OS, applications, and all—and simply deliver an image of what's executing to a PC or other connected device. This allows firms to scale, back up, secure, and upgrade systems far more easily than if they had to maintain each individual PC. One game start-up hopes to remove the high-powered game console hardware attached to your television and instead put the console in the cloud, delivering games to your TV as they execute remotely on superfast server hardware. Virtualization can even live on your desktop. Anyone who's ever run Windows in a window on Mac OS X is using virtualization software; these tools inhabit a chunk of your Mac's memory for running Windows and actually fool this foreign OS into thinking that it's on a PC.

Interest in virtualization has exploded in recent years. VMware, the publicly traded firm that is majority-owned by software giant EMC, is the current leader in virtualization software, really defining the commercialization of the software category. But its niche is getting crowded. Microsoft has entered the market, building virtualization into its server offerings. Dell bought a virtualization software firm for $1.54 billion, and Xen is an open source virtualization product.[81] Containers champ Docker is also open source, and new funding valued the firm at over $1 billion.[82]

KEY TAKEAWAYS

- Virtualization software allows one computing device to function as many. The most sophisticated products also make it easy for organizations to scale computing requirements across several servers.
- Virtualization software can lower a firm's hardware needs, save energy, and boost scalability.
- Data center virtualization software is at the heart of many so-called private clouds and scalable corporate data centers, as well as the sorts of public efforts described earlier.
- Virtualization also works on the desktop, allowing multiple operating systems (Mac OS X, Linux, Windows) to run simultaneously on the same platform.
- Virtualization software can increase data center utilization to 80 percent or more.
- While virtualization is used to make public cloud computing happen, it can also be used in-house to create a firm's own private cloud.
- While traditional virtualization acts as a software representation of hardware where each virtual machine requires its own operating system, a type of virtualization known as containers performs many of the functions of virtualization without requiring a separate operating system. This saves even more power and computer space, and helps resources execute even faster.
- A number of companies, including Microsoft and Dell, have entered the growing virtualization market. Container startup Docker is seeing widespread adoption across industries and leading firms.

QUESTIONS AND EXERCISES

1. List the benefits to a firm from using virtualization.
2. What is the average utilization rate for conventional data centers?
3. List companies that have virtualization-enabled private clouds.
4. Give an example of desktop virtualization.
5. Name three companies that are players in the virtualization software industry.

12.   APPS AND APP STORES: FURTHER DISRUPTING THE SOFTWARE INDUSTRY ON SMARTPHONES, TABLETS, AND BEYOND

LEARNING OBJECTIVE

1. **Understand the benefits and challenges of app stores and how these products are also changing the way we conceive software and the opportunities for firms to offer value-added services to consumers.**

More monumental changes are being brought about by app stores, specifically the use of apps on smartphones. Smartphones have surpassed the one-billion-unit-sales-per-year milestone,[83] and costs are plummeting. For many worldwide, the smartphone is the primary screen for engaging in a series of tasks or entire new categories of software and services. And while smartphones use the web, most smartphone functionality is delivered via custom apps.

By 2015, Apple claimed its iOS app store has seen over 100 billion downloads of the over 1.5 million apps offered.[84] Apps have several advantages over packaged software and browser-based alternatives. The app store is *always open*, and apps are distributed at a fraction of the cost of conventional packaged software, completely cutting out costs associated with printing discs, boxes, and shipping product to retailers. Apps offer richer, more interactive interface options than simple web-based applications. Most smartphones also allow apps to integrate with the OS and send out direct message to users, whereas the Web provides no such OS-level integration. Many products will upgrade apps in the background, ensuring that users regularly have the latest features and bug-squashing editions on their devices, further lowering software maintenance costs. And several businesses simply would not exist without apps to engage with customers. Uber, Instagram, Rovio, and WhatsApp are among the billion-dollar firms that exist because of smartphones and the rapid proliferation of apps. Innovative retailers such as One Kings Lane and the high-fashion rental firm Rent the Runway are also leveraging apps to capture impulse orders when consumers have a top-of-mind task, not when they return to a desktop. And new offerings that leverage tools (such as the app-engaging, location-based technology, iBeacon) are allowing venues to guide consumers to deals, products, and even parking spaces.

While apps and smartphones are also contributing to "software in flux," some are critical of our app-centric future. Apps can lock a user into a given platform. They often require software developers to create a package using developer tools provided by mobile device manufacturers, further deepening switching costs. Apps also have software development disadvantages when compared to browser-based services. If a bug is detected, code served to users via a browser is available next time they visit the site, while apps need to be downloaded and installed, potentially allowing harmful bugs and security flaws to linger in the wild. Browser-based applications can also perform A/B testing easier, sending different versions to the browsers of different users. Smartphone users would require an app that can serve either option, again requiring a software update. Others lament the walled garden created within apps where data is more tightly controlled by a service provider and where firms must comply to the usage policies of the platform provided (e.g., Apple, Google, Amazon, or Microsoft). Finally, while the app store allows a firm, in theory, to reach millions, crowded app stores increasingly make it more challenging for a potential star to rise above the din of the crowd and get recognized.

While our app store discussion has focused on smartphones and tablets, it's important to realize these are not the only platforms for software distribution. Apple and Microsoft offer app stores for their desktop operating systems. Google has an app store for Chrome browser extensions. New computing platforms, such as Google Glass and Facebook's Oculus Rift also sport app stores that extend their offerings and provide new alternatives to entrepreneurs. Televisions, smart watches, and even automobiles will all provide new opportunities to reach consumers with innovative, app-powered offerings.

KEY TAKEAWAYS

- Over one billion smartphones are sold a year, providing a rich platform for app deployment.
- Compared with packaged software, apps lower the cost of software distribution and maintenance.
- Apps offer a richer user interface and integrate more tightly with a device's operating system, enabling more functionality and services such as app-delivered alerts.
- Several billion-dollar firms have leveraged smartphone apps as their only, or primary, interface with consumers.
- Mobile apps do provide additional challenges for developers, especially when compared against browser-based alternatives. Among them, more challenging updates, version control, and A/B testing.
- Critics of apps say they force consumers into smartphone walled gardens and raise consumer-switching costs.
- While development and distribution costs are cheaper for apps than packaged software, discovery poses a problem, and it can be increasingly difficult for high-quality firms to generate consumer awareness among the growing crowd of app offerings.

QUESTIONS AND EXERCISES

1. How big is the worldwide smartphone market? Do you use a smartphone? Which one and why did you choose that product?
2. How are smartphone cost trends and capabilities changing over time?
3. Are smartphones the only products with app stores? What other app stores are available? Do they have the same dynamics at work as those described above?
4. If you were developing a product or service today, would you go "mobile first," concentrating on an app as the customer interface rather than a web-based interface? Why or why not?
5. In what ways are apps superior to browser-based alternatives? In what ways is app development and maintenance more challenging that writing code for the browser?

13. MAKE, BUY, OR RENT

L E A R N I N G   O B J E C T I V E S

1. Know the options managers have when determining how to satisfy the software needs of their companies.
2. Know the factors that must be considered when making the make, buy, or rent decision.

So now you realize managers have a whole host of options when seeking to fulfill the software needs of their firms. An organization can purchase packaged software from a vendor, use open source offerings, leverage SaaS or other type of cloud computing, outsource development or other IT functions to another firm either domestically or abroad, or a firm can develop all or part of the effort themselves. When presented with all of these options, making decisions about technologies and systems can seem pretty daunting.

First, realize that that for most firms, technology decisions are not binary options for the whole organization in all situations. Few businesses will opt for an IT configuration that is 100 percent in-house, packaged, or SaaS. Being aware of the parameters to consider can help a firm make better, more informed decisions. It's also important to keep in mind that these decisions need to be continuously reevaluated as markets and business needs change. What follows is a summary of some of the key variables to consider.

Competitive Advantage—*Do we rely on unique processes, procedures, or technologies that create vital, differentiating competitive advantage?* If so, then these functions aren't good candidates to outsource or replace with a package software offering. Amazon had originally used recommendation software provided by a third party, and Netflix and Dell both considered third-party software to manage inventory fulfillment. But in all three cases, these firms felt that mastery of these functions was too critical to competitive advantage, so each firm developed proprietary systems unique to the circumstances of each firm.

Security—*Are there unacceptable risks associated with using the packaged software, OSS, cloud solution, or an outsourcing vendor? Are we convinced that the prospective solution is sufficiently secure and reliable? Can we trust the prospective vendor with our code, our data, our procedures and our way of doing business? Are there noncompete provisions for vendor staff that may be privy to our secrets? For off-site work, are there sufficient policies in place for on-site auditing?* If the answers to any of these questions is no, outsourcing might not be a viable option.

Legal and Compliance—*Is our firm prohibited outright from using technologies? Are there specific legal and compliance requirements related to deploying our products or services?* Even a technology as innocuous as instant messaging may need to be deployed in such a way that it complies with laws requiring firms to record and reproduce the electronic equivalent of a paper trail. For example, SEC Rule 17a-4 requires broker dealers to retain client communications for a minimum of three years. HIPAA laws governing health care providers state that electronic communications must also be captured and stored.[85] While tech has gained a seat in the board room, legal also deserves a seat in systems planning meetings.

Skill, Expertise, and Available Labor—*Can we build it?* The firm may have skilled technologists, but they may not be sufficiently experienced with a new technology. Even if they are skilled, managers must consider the costs of allocating staff away from existing projects for this effort.

Cost—*Is this a cost-effective choice for our firm?* A host of factors must be considered when evaluating the cost of an IT decision. The costs to build, host, maintain, and support an ongoing effort involve labor (software development, quality assurance, ongoing support, training, and maintenance), consulting, security, operations, licensing, energy, and real estate. Any analysis of costs should consider not only the aggregate spending required over the lifetime of the effort but also whether these factors might vary over time.

Time—*Do we have time to build, test, and deploy the system?*

Vendor Issues—*Is the vendor reputable and in a sound financial position? Can the vendor guarantee the service levels and reliability we need? What provisions are in place in case the vendor fails or is acquired? Is the vendor certified via the Carnegie Mellon Software Institute or other standards organizations in a way that conveys quality, trust, and reliability?*

The list above is a starter. It should also be clear that these metrics are sometimes quite tough to estimate. Welcome to the challenges of being a manager! At times an environment in flux can make an executive feel like he or she is working on a surfboard, constantly being buffeted about by unexpected currents and waves. Hopefully the issues outlined in this chapter will give you the surfing skills you need for a safe ride that avoids the organizational equivalent of a wipeout.

KEY TAKEAWAYS

- The make, buy, or rent decision may apply on a case-by-case basis that might be evaluated by firm, division, project or project component. Firm and industry dynamics may change in a way that causes firms to reassess earlier decisions, or to alter the direction of new initiatives.
- Factors that managers should consider when making a make, buy, or rent decision include the following: competitive advantage, security, legal and compliance issues, the organization's skill and available labor, cost, time, and vendor issues.
- Factors must be evaluated over the lifetime of a project, not at a single point in time.
- Managers have numerous options available when determining how to satisfy the software needs of their companies: purchase packaged software from a vendor, use OSS, use SaaS or utility computing, outsourcing development, or developing all or part of the effort themselves.
- If a company relies on unique processes, procedures, or technologies that create vital, differentiating, competitive advantages, the functions probably aren't a good candidate to outsource.

QUESTIONS AND EXERCISES

1. What are the options available to managers when seeking to meet the software needs of their companies?
2. What are the factors that must be considered when making the make, buy, or rent decision?
3. What are some security-related questions that must be asked when making the make, buy, or rent decision?
4. What are some vendor-related questions that must be asked when making the make, buy, or rent decision?
5. What are some of the factors that must be considered when evaluating the cost of an IT decision?
6. Why must factors be evaluated over the lifetime of a project, not at a single point in time?

ENDNOTES

1. R. Kelly, "DC: Worldwide IT Spending Growth to Slow in 2014," *Campus Technology*, February 5, 2014.

2. G. Winfrey, "The 5 Most Profitable Industries in the U.S.," *Inc.*, March 9, 2015.

3. F. Vogelstein, "Rebuilding Microsoft," *Wired*, October 2006.

4. A. Vance, "Netflix Announces $100,000 in Prizes for Coders," *BusinessWeek*, March 14, 2013.

5. D. Diamond, "The Good-Hearted Wizard—Linus Torvalds," *Virtual Finland*, January 2008.

6. S. Lacy, "Open Warfare in Open Source," *BusinessWeek*, August 21, 2006; "Worldwide Server Market Revenues Increase 12.1% in First Quarter as Market Demand Continues to Improve, according to IDC," *IDC*, May 24, 2011.

7. S. Vaughan-Nichols, "The Five Most Popular End-User Linux Distributions," *ZDNet*, May 30, 2014.

8. K. Noyes, "94 Percent of the World's Top 500 Supercomputers Run Linux," *Linux*, November 14, 2012.

9. J. Brockmeier, "NASA Using Linux," *Unix Review*, March 2004; and S. Barrett, "Linux on Mars," *Science News, Space News, Technology News*, June 6, 2008.

10. For examples, see http://mostlylinux.ca/pronounce/torvalds-says-linux.wav and http://suseroot.com/about-suse-linux/how-do-you-pronounce-linux.php.

11. A list of criteria defining open source software can be found at the Open Source Initiative at http://opensource.org/osr.

12. J. Fortt, "Why Larry Loves Linux (and He's Not Alone)," *Fortune*, December 19, 2007.

13. D. Woods, "The Commercial Bear Hug of Open Source," *Forbes*, August 18, 2008.

14. M. Hinkle, "No Longer Why Open Source, but How to Do Open Source," *BlackDuck Software Blog*, May 7, 2014.

15. C. Preimesberger, "Sun's 'Open'-Door Policy," *eWeek*, April 21, 2008

16. C. Stokel-Walker, "The Internet Is Being Protected by Two Guys Named Steve," *BuzzFeed*, April 25, 2014.

17. R. King, "Cost-Conscious Companies Turn to Open-Source Software," *BusinessWeek*, December 1, 2008.

18. S. Shankland, M. Kane, and R. Lemos, "How Linux Saved Amazon Millions," *CNET*, October 30, 2001.

19. E. Raymond, *The Cathedral and the Bazaar: Musings on Linux and Open Source by an Accidental Revolutionary* (Sebastopol, CA: O'Reilly, 1999).

20. J. Ljungberg, "Open Source Movements as a Model for Organizing," *European Journal of Information Systems* 9, no. 4 (December 2000): 208–16.

21. M. Castelluccio, "Enterprise Open Source Adoption," *Strategic Finance*, November 2007.

22. D. Wheeler, *Secure Programming for Linux and Unix*, 2003, http://www.dwheeler.com/secure-programs/Secure-Programs-HOWTO/index.html.

23. R. McMillan, "Gone in Two Minutes," *InfoWorld*, March 27, 2008.

24. S. Lohr, "Microsoft to Give Governments Access to Code," *New York Times*, January 15, 2003.

25. R. King, "Cost-Conscious Companies Turn to Open-Source Software," *BusinessWeek*, December 1, 2008.

26. R. Guth, "Virtual Piecework: Trolling the Web for Free Labor, Software Upstarts Are a New Force," *Wall Street Journal*, November 13, 2006.

27. D. Goodin, "Critical Crypto Bug in OpenSSL Opens Two-Thirds of the Web to Eavesdropping," *ArsTechnica*, April 7, 2014.

28. C. Stokel-Walker, "The Internet Is Being Protected by Two Guys Named Steve," *BuzzFeed*, April 25, 2014.

29. D. Woods, "The Commercial Bear Hug of Open Source," *Forbes*, August 18, 2008.

30. M. Asay, "Open Source Is a $60 Billion Industry," *CNET*, May 15, 2008.

31. A. Greenberg, "Sun Snaps Up Database Firm, MySQL," *Forbes*, January 16, 2008; G. Huang, "Attachmate Buys Novell for $2.2B—The End of an Era," *Xconomy*, November 22, 2010.

32. R. Waters, "New breed of open source start-ups eye rising revenues and IPOs," *Financial Times*, April 6, 2015.

33. A. Greenberg, "Sun Snaps Up Database Firm, MySQL," *Forbes*, January 16, 2008.

34. J. Fortt, "Why Larry Loves Linux (and He's Not Alone)," *Fortune*, December 19, 2007.

35. J. Robertson, "IBM Sees Better-than-Expected 2009 Profit, Earns US$4.4 Billion in Q4," *Associated Press*, January 20, 2009, http://humantimes.com/finance/business/sanfrancis/54853.

36. R. Waters, "New breed of open source start-ups eye rising revenues and IPOs," *Financial Times*, April 6, 2015.

37. S. Cohen, "Open Source: The Model Is Broken," *BusinessWeek*, December 1, 2008.

38. A. Ricadela, "Microsoft Wants to 'Kill' Open Source," *BusinessWeek*, May 15, 2007.

39. S. Lacy, "Open Warfare in Open Source," *BusinessWeek*, August 21, 2006.

40. L. Dignan, "Cloud Computing Market: $241 Billion in 2020," *ZDNet*, April 22, 2011.

41. J. Hempel, "Salesforce Hits Its Stride," *Fortune*, March 2, 2009.

42. S. Lacy, "On-Demand Computing: A Brutal Slog," *BusinessWeek*, July 18, 2008.

43. J. Quittner, "How SaaS Helps Cut Small Business Costs," *BusinessWeek*, December 5, 2008.

44. M. Drummond, "The End of Software as We Know It," *Fortune*, November 19, 2001.

45. M. Drummond, "The End of Software as We Know It," *Fortune*, November 19, 2001.

46. R. Wauters, "The Extraordinary Rise and Fall of Denmark's IT Factory," *TechCrunch*, December 2, 2008.

47. S. Lacy, "On-Demand Computing: A Brutal Slog," *BusinessWeek*, July 18, 2008.

48. G. Gruman, "Early Experiments in Cloud Computing," *InfoWorld*, April 7, 2008.

49. J. Rayport, "Cloud Computing Is No Pipe Dream," *BusinessWeek*, December 9, 2008.

50. A. Vance, "Netflix, Reed Hastings, Survive Missteps to Join Silicon Valley's Elite," *BusinessWeek*, May 9, 2013.

51. J. Rayport, "Cloud Computing Is No Pipe Dream," *BusinessWeek*, December 9, 2008.

52. G. Gruman, "Early Experiments in Cloud Computing," *InfoWorld*, April 7, 2008.

53. P. Grossman, "Cloud Computing Begins to Gain Traction on Wall Street," *Wall Street and Technology*, January 6, 2009.

54. B. Butler, "Amazon Hints at Details on Its CIA Franken-Cloud," *NetworkWorld*, November 14, 2013.

55. J. Parkinson, "Green Data Centers Tackle LEED Certification," *SearchDataCenter.com*, January 18, 2007.

56. G. Gruman, "Early Experiments in Cloud Computing," *InfoWorld*, April 7, 2008.

57. G. Gruman, "Early Experiments in Cloud Computing," *InfoWorld*, April 7, 2008.

58. S. Ovide, "A Price War Erupts in Cloud Services," *Wall Street Journal*, April 25, 2014.

59. A. Hesseldahl, "Amazon Details Last Week's Cloud Failure, and Apologizes," *AllThingsD*, April 29, 2011.

60. D. Goodin, "Outage of Adobe Creative Cloud, more than a day old, locked out app users," *Ars Technica*, May 15, 2014.

61. M. Rosoff, "Inside Amazon's Cloud Disaster," *Business Insider*, April 22, 2011.

62. J. Novet, "Why IBM Was Smart to Sell Off Its Low-End Server Business to Lenovo," *VentureBeat*, February 26, 2014.

63. D. Linthicum, "Yes, the Cloud Is Replacing Enterprise Hardware and Software," *InfoWorld*, December 3, 2013.

64. S. Mehta, "Behold the Server Farm," *Fortune*, July 28, 2006.

65. J. Fortt, "Tech Execs Get Sexy," *Fortune*, February 12, 2009.

66. E. Ackerman, "Forecast for Computing: Cloudy," *San Jose Mercury News*, December 23, 2008.

67. J. Rayport, "Cloud Computing Is No Pipe Dream," *BusinessWeek*, December 9, 2008.

68. M. Suster, "The State of Venture Capital and the Internet," *TechCrunch*, October 20, 2011.

69. R. Katz, "Tech Titans Building Boom," *IEEE Spectrum* 46, no. 2 (February 1, 2009): 40–43.

70. P. Burrows, "Microsoft to Google: Get Off of My Cloud," *BusinessWeek*, November 21, 2008.

71. T. Vanderbilt, "Data Center Overload," *New York Times*, June 8, 2009.

72. R. Katz, "Tech Titans Building Boom," *IEEE Spectrum* 46, no. 2 (February 1, 2009): 40–43.

73. P. Burrows, "Microsoft to Google: Get Off of My Cloud," *BusinessWeek*, November 21, 2008.

74. R. Katz, "Tech Titans Building Boom," *IEEE Spectrum* 46, no. 2 (February 1, 2009): 40–43.

75. D. Lyons, "A Mostly Cloudy Computing Forecast," *Washington Post*, November 4, 2008.

76. R. Katz, "Tech Titans Building Boom," *IEEE Spectrum* 46, no. 2 (February 1, 2009): 40–43.

77. K. Castro, "The Virtues of Virtualization," *BusinessWeek*, December 3, 2007.

78. K. Townsend, "Containers: The pros and the cons of these VM alternatives," *TechRepublic*, Feb. 20, 2015.

79. S. Vaughan-Nichols, "What is Docker and why is it so darn popular?" *ZDNet*, Aug. 4, 2014.

80. J. Brodkin, "Private Clouds Bring IT Mgmt. Challenges," *NetworkWorld*, December 15, 2008.

81. K. Castro, "The Virtues of Virtualization," *BusinessWeek*, December 3, 2007.

82. J. Clark, "Docker Said to Join $1 Billion Valuation Club With New Funding," *Bloomberg Business*, April 14, 2015.

83. C. Arthur, "Smartphone Sales Pass 1bn in 2013 as China Booms," *Guardian*, January 24, 2014.

84. I. Lunden, "iTunes App Store Passes 1.5M Apps, 100B Downloads, $30B Paid To Developers To Date," *TechCrunch*, June 8, 2015.

85. D. Shapiro, "Instant Messaging and Compliance Issues: What You Need to Know," *SearchCIO*, May 17, 2004.

CHAPTER 15

The Data Asset: Databases, Business Intelligence, Analytics, Big Data, and Competitive Advantage

---

1. INTRODUCTION

LEARNING OBJECTIVES

1. Understand how increasingly standardized data, access to third-party data sets, cheap, fast computing and easier-to-use software are collectively enabling a new age of decision making.
2. Be familiar with some of the enterprises that have benefited from data-driven, fact-based decision making.

The planet is awash in data. Cash registers ring up transactions worldwide. Web browsers leave a trail of cookie crumbs nearly everywhere they go. Fitness trackers, health monitors, and smartphone apps are collecting data on the behavior of millions. And with radio frequency identification (RFID), inventory can literally announce its presence so that firms can precisely journal every hop their products make along the value chain: "I'm arriving in the warehouse," "I'm on the store shelf," "I'm leaving out the front door."

A study by Gartner Research claims that the amount of data on corporate hard drives doubles every six months,[1] while IDC states that the collective number of those bits already exceeds the number of stars in the universe.[2] Walmart alone boasts a data volume well over 125 times as large as the entire print collection of the US Library of Congress, and rising.[3] It's further noted that the Walmart figure is just for data stored on systems provided by the vendor Teradata. Walmart has many systems outside its Teradata-sourced warehouses, too. You'll hear managers today broadly refer to this torrent of bits as "**big data**."

> **big data**
>
> Big data is a general term used to describe the massive amount of data available to today's managers. Big data are often unstructured and are too big and costly to easily work through use of conventional databases, but new tools are making these massive datasets available for analysis and insight.

business intelligence (BI)

A term combining aspects of reporting, data exploration and ad hoc queries, and sophisticated data modeling and analysis.

analytics

A term describing the extensive use of data, statistical and quantitative analysis, explanatory and predictive models, and fact-based management to drive decisions and actions.

machine learning

A type of artificial intelligence that leverages massive amounts of data so that computers can improve the accuracy of actions and predictions on their own without additional programming.

And with this flood of data comes a tidal wave of opportunity. Research has found that companies ranked in the top third of their industry in the use of data-driven decision making were on average 5 percent more productive and 6 percent more profitable than competitors.[4] Increasingly standardized corporate data, and access to rich, third-party data sets—all leveraged by cheap, fast computing and easier-to-use software—are collectively enabling a new age of data-driven, fact-based decision making. You're less likely to hear old-school terms like "decision support systems" used to describe what's going on here. The phrase of the day is **business intelligence (BI)**, a catchall term combining aspects of reporting, data exploration and ad hoc queries, and sophisticated data modeling and analysis. Alongside business intelligence in the new managerial lexicon is the phrase **analytics**, a term describing the extensive use of data, statistical and quantitative analysis, explanatory and predictive models, and fact-based management to drive decisions and actions (and in our ever-imprecise world of business buzzwords, you'll often hear business intelligence and analytics used interchangeably to mean the same thing—using data for better decision making).[5] Another trend, **machine learning**, refers to a sophisticated category of software applications known as artificial intelligence that leverage massive amounts of data so that computers can "learn" and improve the accuracy of actions and predictions on their own without additional programming.[6]

The benefits of all this data and number crunching are very real, indeed. Data leverage lies at the center of competitive advantage in many of the firms that we've studied, including Amazon, Netflix and Zara. Data mastery has helped vault Walmart to the top of the Fortune 500 list. It helps Spotify craft you a killer playlist for your run. And it helps make Google's voice recognition a better listener and Google search a better detective, so that the service can accurately show you what you've asked it to look up. There's even something here for Poli Sci majors, since data-driven insights are increasingly being credited with helping politicians win elections.[7] To quote from a *BusinessWeek* cover story on analytics, "Math Will Rock Your World!"[8]

Sounds great, but it can be a tough slog getting an organization to the point where it has a leveragable data asset. In many organizations data lies dormant, spread across inconsistent formats and incompatible systems, unable to be turned into anything of value. Many firms have been shocked at the amount of work and complexity required to pull together an infrastructure that empowers its managers. But not only can this be done, it must be done. Firms that are basing decisions on hunches aren't managing, they're gambling. And today's markets have no tolerance for uninformed managerial dice rolling.

While we'll study technology in this chapter, our focus isn't as much on the technology itself as it is on what you can do with that technology. Consumer products giant P&G believes in this distinction so thoroughly that the firm renamed its IT function as "Information and Decision Solutions."[9] Solutions drive technology decisions, not the other way around.

In this chapter we'll study the data asset, how it's created, how it's stored, and how it's accessed and leveraged. We'll also study many of the firms mentioned above, and more, providing a context for understanding how managers are leveraging data to create winning models, and how those that have failed to realize the power of data have been left in the dust.

Data, Analytics, and Competitive Advantage

Anyone can acquire technology—but data is oftentimes considered a defensible source of competitive advantage. The data a firm can leverage is a true strategic asset when it's rare, valuable, imperfectly imitable, and lacking in substitutes (see Chapter 2).

If more data brings more accurate modeling, moving early to capture this rare asset can be the difference between a dominating firm and an also-ran. But be forewarned, there's no monopoly on math. Advantages based on formulas, algorithms, and data that others can also acquire will be short-lived. Moneyball advances in sports analytics originally pioneered by the Oakland A's and are now used by nearly every team in the major leagues.

This doesn't mean that firms can ignore the importance data can play in lowering costs, increasing customer service, and other ways that boost performance. But differentiation will be key in distinguishing operationally effective data use from those efforts that can yield true strategic positioning.

That Seat Will Cost You $8—Wait, Make That $45.50

For some games it's tough to fill the stands. A Wednesday night game against a mediocre rival will prompt thousands to stay home unless they get a really compelling deal. But many fans are ready to pay big bucks for a rivalry game on a weekend. To optimize demand, over thirty teams in Major League Baseball (MLB), the National Basketball Association (NBA), National Hockey League (NHL), and Major League Soccer (MLS) are using data analytics from Austin-based Qcue to fill seats and maximize revenue.[10]

Take the San Francisco Giants as an example. The baseball standout draws big crowds when playing crosstown, interleague rivals, the Oakland As. A seat in the left field, upper deck of AT&T Park will cost above $45 for a Saturday afternoon game. But when the Diamondbacks are in town on a work or school night, that very same seat can be had for $8. Changing pricing based on demand conditions is known as dynamic pricing, and the Giants credits analytics-driven demand pricing with helping bump ticket revenues by at least 6 percent in a single year[11] and fuel a 250-plus sellout streak.[12] And getting fans in the stands is critical since once there, those fans usually rack up even more revenue in the form of concessions and merchandise sales. Dynamic pricing can be tricky. In some cases, it can leave consumers feeling taken advantage of (it is especially tricky in situations where consumers make repeated purchases and are more likely to remember past prices, and when they have alternative choices, like grocery or department store shopping). But dynamic pricing often works in markets where supply is constrained and subject to demand spikes. Firms from old-school airlines to app-savvy Uber regularly let data analytics set a supply-demand equilibrium through dynamic pricing, while also helping boost their bottom line. Sports teams are even leveraging weather insights and other data to drive the pricing of concession specials and to set the cost of a beer. New technologies, such as iBeacon (a tech that sends messages to iPhones using a low-energy Bluetooth signal) are being rolled out throughout MLB, making it easier to let consumers know a deal is in effect and guiding them to the quickest counter for quenching thirst and satisfying cravings.[13]

FIGURE 15.1

Major League Baseball's At the Ballpark app will use iBeacon technology to distribute deals and guide you to concessions.

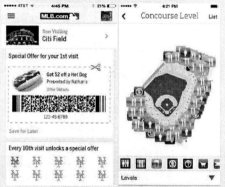

Source: Alex Colon, "MLB Completes iBeacon Installations at Dodger Stadium and Petco Park," GigaOM, February 14, 2014, https://gigaom.com/2014/02/14/mlb-completes-ibeacon-installations-at-dodger-stadium-and-petco-park.

KEY TAKEAWAYS

- The amount of data being created doubles every two years.
- In many organizations, available data is not exploited to advantage. However new tools supporting *big data*, business intelligence, and analytics are helping managers make sense of this data torrent.
- Data is oftentimes considered a defensible source of competitive advantage; however, advantages based on capabilities and data that others can acquire will be short-lived.

QUESTIONS AND EXERCISES

1. Name and define the terms that are supplanting discussions of decision support systems in the modern IS lexicon.
2. Is data a source of competitive advantage? Describe situations in which data might be a source for sustainable competitive advantage. When might data not yield sustainable advantage?
3. Are advantages based on analytics and modeling potentially sustainable? Why or why not?
4. Think about the amount of data that is collected about you every day. Make a list of various technologies and information systems you engage with and the organizations that use these technologies, systems, and services to learn more about you. Does this information serve you better as a consumer? What, if any, concerns does broad data collection leave you with?
5. What role do technology and timing play in realizing advantages from the data asset?
6. What do you think about dynamic pricing? Is it good or bad for consumers? Is it good or bad for businesses? Explain your answer.
7. Have you visited a retailer or other venue using iBeacons? If so, describe your experience. If not, research the technology and come to class prepared to discuss its implications for collecting data and for driving consumer actions.

---

2.   DATA, INFORMATION, AND KNOWLEDGE

LEARNING OBJECTIVES

1. **Understand the difference between data and information.**
2. **Know the key terms and technologies associated with data organization and management.**

data

Raw facts and figures.

information

Data presented in a context so that it can answer a question or support decision making.

knowledge

Insight derived from experience and expertise.

Data refers simply to raw facts and figures. Alone it tells you nothing. The real goal is to turn data into **information**. Data becomes information when it's presented in a context so that it can answer a question or support decision making. And it's when this information can be combined with a manager's **knowledge**—their insight from experience and expertise—that stronger decisions can be made.

Trusting Your Data

The ability to look critically at data and assess its validity is a vital managerial skill. When decision makers are presented with wrong data, the results can be disastrous. And these problems can get amplified if bad data is fed to automated systems. As an example, look at the series of man-made and computer-triggered events that brought about a billion-dollar collapse in United Airlines stock.

In the wee hours one Sunday morning, a single reader browsing several years of old back stories on the *Orlando Sentinel*'s website viewed a 2002 article on the bankruptcy of United Airlines (UAL went bankrupt in 2002, but emerged from bankruptcy four years later). That lone Web surfer's access of this story during such a low-traffic time was enough for the *Sentinel*'s Web server to briefly list the article as one of the paper's "most popular." Google crawled the site and picked up this "popular" news item, feeding it into Google News.

Early that morning, a worker in a Florida investment firm came across the Google-fed story, assumed United had yet again filed for bankruptcy, then posted a summary on Bloomberg. Investors scanning Bloomberg jumped on what looked like a reputable early warning of another United bankruptcy, dumping UAL stock. Blame the computers again—the rapid plunge from these early trades caused automatic sell systems to kick in (event-triggered, computer-automated trading is responsible for about 30 percent of all stock trades). Once the machines took over, UAL dropped like a rock, falling from twelve to three dollars. That drop represented the vanishing of $1 billion in wealth, and all this because no one checked the date on a news story. Welcome to the new world of paying attention![14]

2.1   Understanding How Data Is Organized: Key Terms and Technologies

A **database** is simply a list (or more likely, several related lists) of data. Most organizations have several databases—perhaps even hundreds or thousands. And these various databases might be focused on any combination of functional areas (sales, product returns, inventory, payroll), geographical regions, or business units. Firms often create specialized databases for recording transactions, as well as databases that aggregate data from multiple sources in order to support reporting and analysis.

Databases are created, maintained, and manipulated using programs called **database management systems (DBMS)**, sometimes referred to as *database software*. DBMS products vary widely in scale and capabilities. They include the single-user, desktop versions of Microsoft Access or Filemaker Pro, Web-based offerings like Intuit QuickBase, and industrial strength products from Oracle, IBM (DB2), Microsoft (SQL Server), the popular open-source product MySQL (also stewarded by Oracle), and others. Oracle is the world's largest database software vendor, and database software has meant big bucks for Oracle cofounder and CEO Larry Ellison. Ellison perennially ranks in the Top 10 of the *Forbes* 400 list of wealthiest Americans.

The acronym SQL (often pronounced *sequel*) also shows up a lot when talking about databases. **Structured query language (SQL)** is by far the most common language for creating and manipulating databases. You'll find variants of SQL inhabiting everything from lowly desktop software, to high-powered enterprise products. Given this popularity, if you're going to learn one language for database use, SQL's a pretty good choice. And for a little inspiration, visit LinkedIn, Monster.com, or another job site and search for openings that mention SQL. You'll find page after page of listings, suggesting that while database systems have been good for Ellison, learning more about them might be pretty good for you, too.

Even if you don't become a database programmer or **database administrator (DBA)**, you're almost surely going to be called upon to dive in and use a database. You may even be asked to help identify your firm's data requirements. It's quite common for nontech employees to work on development teams with technical staff, defining business problems, outlining processes, setting requirements, and determining the kinds of data the firm will need to leverage. Database systems are powerful stuff, and can't be avoided, so a bit of understanding will serve you well.

---

database

A single table or a collection of related tables.

database management systems (DBMS)

Sometimes called "database software"; software for creating, maintaining, and manipulating data.

structured query language (SQL)

A language used to create and manipulate databases.

database administrator (DBA)

Job title focused on directing, performing, or overseeing activities associated with a database or set of databases. These may include (but not necessarily be limited to): database design, creation, implementation, maintenance, backup and recovery, policy setting and enforcement, and security.

FIGURE 15.2 A Simplified Relational Database for a University Course Registration System

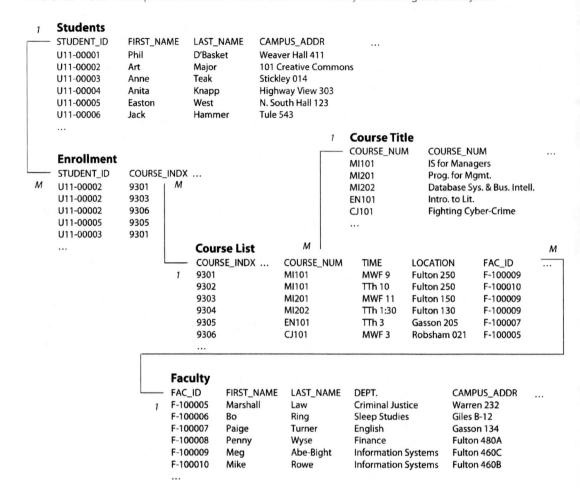

A complete discourse on technical concepts associated with database systems is beyond the scope of our managerial introduction, but here are some key concepts to help get you oriented, and that all managers should know.

- A **table or file** refers to a list of data.

- A *database* is either a single table or a collection of related tables. The course registration database above depicts five tables.

- A **column or field** defines the data that a table can hold. The "Students" table above shows columns for STUDENT_ID, FIRST_NAME, LAST_NAME, CAMPUS_ADDR (the "…" symbols above are meant to indicate that, in practice, there may be more columns or rows than are shown in this simplified diagram).

- A **row or record** represents a single instance of whatever the table keeps track of. In the example above, each row of the "Students" table represents a student, each row of the "Enrollment" table represents the enrollment of a student in a particular course, and each row of the "Course List" represents a given section of each course offered by the University.

- A key is the field or fields used to relate tables in a database. Look at how the STUDENT_ID key is used above. There is *one* unique STUDENT_ID for each student, but the STUDENT_ID may appear *many* times in the "Enrollment" table, indicating that each student may be enrolled in many classes. The "1" and "M" in the diagram above indicate the one-to-many relationships among the keys in these tables.

- These one-to-many relationships are sometimes referred to as a *primary key* and *foreign key*. There's only one unique STUDENT_ID value for each record (row) in the "Student" table, so STUDENT_ID is a *primary key* in the student table. But in the "Enrollment" table, STUDENT_ID is the *foreign key*. It appears several times and relates back to the primary key in the "Student" table, so we can find out more information about each unique student that is enrolled in a particular course.

Databases organized like the one above, where multiple tables are related based on common keys, are referred to as **relational databases**. There are many other database formats (sporting names like *hierarchical*, and *object-oriented*), but relational databases are far and away the most popular. And all SQL databases are relational databases.

Even though SQL and the relational model are hugely popular and dominate many corporate environments, other systems exist. An increasingly popular set of technologies known as NoSQL avoid SQL and the rigid structure of relational databases. NoSQL technologies are especially popular with Internet firms that rely on massive, unwieldy, and disparately structured data; and this technology is often at the heart of what are often characterized as "big data" efforts.

We've just scratched the surface for a very basic introduction. Expect that a formal class in database systems will offer you far more detail and better design principles than are conveyed in the elementary example above. But you're already well on your way!

relational database

The most common standard for expressing databases, whereby tables (files) are related based on common keys.

KEY TAKEAWAYS

- Data includes raw facts that must be turned into information in order to be useful and valuable.
- Databases are created, maintained, and manipulated using programs called database management systems (DBMS), sometimes referred to as database software.
- Relational database management systems (RDBMS) are the most common database standard by far, and SQL (or structured query language) is the most popular standard for relational database systems.
- In relational database systems, several data fields make up a data record, multiple data records make up a table or data file, and one or more tables or data files make up a database. Files that are related to one another are linked based on a common field (or fields) known as a key. If the value of a key is unique to a record in a table, and that value can never occur in that field while referring to another record in that table, then it is a primary key. If a key can occur many times over multiple records in a table but relates back to a primary key in another table, then it is a foreign key.

QUESTIONS AND EXERCISES

1. Define the following terms: table, record, field. Provide another name for each term along with your definition.

2. Answer the following questions using the course registration database system, diagramed above:

    a. Imagine you also want to keep track of student majors. How would you do this? Would you modify an existing table? Would you add new tables? Why or why not?

    b. Why do you suppose the system needs a "Course Title" table?

    c. This database is simplified for our brief introduction. What additional data would you need to keep track of if this were a real course registration system? What changes would you make in the database above to account for these needs?

    d. Why do you need a STUDENT_ID? Why don't you just use a student's last name?

    e. Could you use Social Security number as a STUDENT_ID? Why or why not? (Hint: feel free to search on the Internet for additional insights.)

3. Research to find additional examples of organizations that made bad decisions based on bad data. Report your examples to your class. What was the end result of the examples you're citing (e.g., loss, damage, or other outcome)? What could managers have done to prevent problems in the cases that you cited? What role did technology play in the examples that you cite? What role did people or procedural issues play?

4. Why is an understanding of database terms and technologies important, even for nontechnical managers and staff? Consider factors associated with both system use and system development. What other skills, beyond technology, may be important when engaged in data-driven decision making?

3. WHERE DOES DATA COME FROM?

LEARNING OBJECTIVES

1. Understand various internal and external sources for enterprise data.
2. Recognize the function and role of data aggregators, the potential for leveraging third-party data, the strategic implications of relying on externally purchased data, and key issues associated with aggregators and firms that leverage externally sourced data.

Organizations can pull together data from a variety of sources. While the examples that follow aren't meant to be an encyclopedic listing of possibilities, they will give you a sense of the diversity of options available for data gathering.

3.1 Transaction Processing Systems

transaction processing systems (TPS)

Systems that record a transaction (some form of business-related exchange), such as a cash register sale, ATM withdrawal, or product return.

transaction

Some kind of business exchange.

loyalty card

Systems that provide rewards and usage incentives, typically in exchange for a method that provides a more detailed tracking and recording of customer activity. In addition to enhancing data collection, loyalty cards can represent a significant switching cost.

For most organizations that sell directly to their customers, **transaction processing systems (TPS)** represent a fountain of potentially insightful data. Every time a consumer uses a point-of-sale system, an ATM, or a service desk, there's a **transaction** (some kind of business exchange) occurring, representing an event that's likely worth tracking.

The cash register is the data generation workhorse of most physical retailers, and the primary source that feeds data to the TPS. But while TPS can generate a lot of bits, it's sometimes tough to match this data with a specific customer. For example, if you pay a retailer in cash, you're likely to remain a mystery to your merchant because your name isn't attached to your money. Grocers and retailers can tie you to cash transactions if they can convince you to use a **loyalty card**. Use one of these cards and you're in effect giving up information about yourself in exchange for some kind of financial incentive. The explosion in retailer cards is directly related to each firm's desire to learn more about you and to turn you into a more loyal and satisfied customer.

Some cards provide an instant discount (e.g., the CVS Pharmacy ExtraCare card), while others allow you to build up points over time (Best Buy's Reward Zone). The latter has the additional benefit of acting as a switching cost. A customer may think "I could get the same thing at Target, but at Best Buy, it'll increase my existing points balance and soon I'll get a cash back coupon."

3.2 Enterprise Software (CRM, SCM, and ERP)

Firms increasingly set up systems to gather additional data beyond conventional purchase transactions or Web site monitoring. CRM or customer relationship management systems are often used to empower employees to track and record data at nearly every point of customer contact. Someone calls for a quote? Brings a return back to a store? Writes a complaint e-mail? A well-designed CRM system can capture all these events for subsequent analysis or for triggering follow-up events.

Enterprise software includes not just CRM systems but also categories that touch every aspect of the value chain, including supply chain management (SCM) and enterprise resource planning (ERP) systems. More importantly, enterprise software tends to be more integrated and standardized than the prior era of proprietary systems that many firms developed themselves. This integration helps in combining data across business units and functions, and in getting that data into a form where it can be turned into information (for more on enterprise systems, see Chapter 13).

3.3 Surveys

Sometimes firms supplement operational data with additional input from surveys and focus groups. Oftentimes, direct surveys can tell you what your cash register can't. Zara store managers informally survey customers in order to help shape designs and product mix. Online grocer FreshDirect (see Chapter 2) surveys customers weekly and has used this feedback to drive initiatives from reducing packaging size to including star ratings on produce.[15] Many CRM products also have survey capabilities that allow for additional data gathering at all points of customer contact.

Can Technology "Cure" US Health Care?

The U.S. health care system is broken. It's costly, inefficient, and problems seem to be getting worse. Estimates suggest that health care spending makes up a whopping 18 percent of U.S. gross domestic product.[16] U.S. automakers spend more on health care than they do on steel.[17] Even more disturbing, it's believed that medical errors cause as many as ninety-eight thousand unnecessary deaths in the United States each year, more than motor vehicle accidents, breast cancer, or AIDS.[18]

For years it's been claimed that technology has the potential to reduce errors, improve health care quality, and save costs. Now pioneering hospital networks and technology companies are partnering to help tackle cost and quality issues. For a look at possibilities for leveraging data throughout the doctor-patient value chain, consider the "event-driven medicine" system built by Dr. John Halamka and his team at Boston's Beth Israel Deaconess Medical Center (part of the Harvard Medical School network).

When docs using Halamka's system encounter a patient with a chronic disease, they generate a decision support "screening sheet." Each event in the system: an office visit, a lab results report (think the medical equivalent of transactions and customer interactions), updates the patient database. Combine that electronic medical record information with **artificial intelligence** on best practice, and the system can offer recommendations for care, such as, "Patient is past due for an eye exam" or, "Patient should receive pneumovax [a vaccine against infection] this season."[19] The systems don't replace decision making by doctors and nurses, but they do help to ensure that key issues are on a provider's radar.

More efficiencies and error checks show up when prescribing drugs. Docs are presented with a list of medications covered by that patient's insurance, allowing them to choose quality options while controlling costs. Safety issues, guidelines, and best practices are also displayed. When correct, safe medication in the right dose is selected, the electronic prescription is routed to the patients' pharmacy of choice. As Halamka puts it, going from "doctor's brain to patients vein" without any of that messy physician handwriting, all while squeezing out layers where errors from human interpretation or data entry might occur.

Nearly every major technology company now has a health solutions group. And with the rise of efforts such as Apple's HealthKit and ResearchKit, expect even more solutions to allow consumers to gather data on their own health, with organizations offering insights on data-driven lifestyle improvements. At the introduction of ResearchKit, five apps were launched in conjunction with leading US healthcare institutions, including Dana-Farber, Massachusetts General Hospital, Stanford Medicine, Weill Cornell Medical College, and the Mayo Clinic. Apps focused on studying Parkinson's disease, diabetes, breast cancer, and heart health. Users opt-in to share data with research institutions, which can come from user input, quizzes, smart phone monitoring, the Apple Watch or other external devices. Apple doesn't hold the data, it is encrypted, and names are not associated with results. Initial results suggest an influx of valuable data at a lower cost from these sorts of efforts. The asthma study app received more than 3,500 people within 72 hours, whereas it had previously taken about two years to recruit 500 to 1,000 participants in comparable efforts.[20] If systems like Halamka's, Apple's platform, and others realize their promise, big benefits may be just around the corner.

artificial intelligence

Computer software that seeks to reproduce or mimic (perhaps with improvements) human thought, decision making, or brain functions.

3.4 External Sources

Sometimes it makes sense to combine a firm's data with bits brought in from the outside. Many firms, for example, don't sell directly to consumers (this includes most drug companies and packaged goods firms). If your firm has partners that sell products for you, then you'll likely rely heavily on data collected by others.

Data bought from sources available to all might not yield competitive advantage on its own, but it can provide key operational insight for increased efficiency and cost savings. And when combined with a firm's unique data assets, it may give firms a high-impact edge.

Consider restaurant chain Brinker, a firm that runs seventeen hundred eateries in twenty-seven countries under the Chili's, On The Border, and Maggiano's brands. Brinker (whose ticker symbol is EAT), supplements their own data with external feeds on weather, employment statistics, gas prices, and other factors, and uses this in predictive models that help the firm in everything from determining staffing levels to switching around menu items.[21]

In another example, Carnival Cruise Lines combines its own customer data with third-party information tracking household income and other key measures. This data plays a key role in a recession, since it helps the firm target limited marketing dollars on those past customers that are more likely to be able to afford to go on a cruise. So far it's been a winning approach. For three years in a row, the firm has experienced double-digit increases in bookings by repeat customers.[22]

data aggregators

Firms that collect and resell data.

Who's Collecting Data about You?

There's a thriving industry collecting data about you. Buy from a catalog, fill out a warranty card, or have a baby, and there's a very good chance that this event will be recorded in a database somewhere, added to a growing digital dossier that's made available for sale to others. If you've ever gotten catalogs, coupons, or special offers from firms you've never dealt with before, this was almost certainly a direct result of a behind-the-scenes trafficking in the "digital you."

Firms that trawl for data and package them up for resale are known as **data aggregators**. They include Acxiom, a $1.3 billion a year business that combines public source data on real estate, criminal records, and census reports, with private information from credit card applications, warranty card surveys, and magazine subscriptions. The firm holds data profiling some two hundred million Americans[23] and works with both Facebook and Google to create shopping insights that combine online and offline data.[24]

Or maybe you've heard of Lexis-Nexis. Many large universities subscribe to the firm's electronic newspaper, journal, and magazine databases. But the firm's parent, Reed Elsevier, is a data sales giant, with divisions packaging criminal records, housing information, and additional data used to uncover corporate fraud and other risks. The firm became even more "data rich" when it purchased Acxiom competitor, ChoicePoint, for $4.1 billion. With that kind of money involved, it's clear that data aggregation is very big business.[25]

The Internet also allows for easy access to data that had been public but otherwise difficult to access. For one example, consider home sale prices and home value assessments. While technically in the public record, someone wanting this information previously had to traipse down to their Town Hall and speak to a clerk, who would hand over a printed log book. Not exactly a Google-speed query. Contrast this with a visit to Zillow.com. The free site lets you pull up a map of your town and instantly peek at how much your neighbors paid for their homes. And it lets them see how much you paid for yours, too.

Computerworld's Robert Mitchell uncovered a more disturbing issue when public record information is made available online. His New Hampshire municipality had digitized and made available some of his old public documents without obscuring that holy grail for identity thieves, his Social Security number.[26]

Then there are accuracy concerns. A record incorrectly identifying you as a cat lover is one thing, but being incorrectly named to the terrorist watch list is quite another. During a five-week period airline agents tried to block a particularly high profile US citizen from boarding airplanes on five separate occasions because his name resembled an alias used by a suspected terrorist. That citizen? The late Ted Kennedy, who at the time was the senior U.S. senator from Massachusetts.[27]

For the data trade to continue, firms will have to treat customer data as the sacred asset it is. Step over that "creep-out" line, and customers will push back, increasingly pressing for tighter privacy laws. Data aggregator Intellius used to track cell phone customers, but backed off in the face of customer outrage and threatened legislation.

Another concern—sometimes data aggregators are just plain sloppy, committing errors that can be costly for the firm and potentially devastating for victimized users. For example, ChoicePoint once accidentally sold records on 145,000 individuals to a cybercrime identity theft ring. The ChoicePoint case resulted in a $15 million fine from the Federal Trade Commission.[28] In another example, hackers stole at least 60 million e-mail addresses from marketing firm Epsilon, prompting firms as diverse as Best Buy, Citi, Hilton, and the College Board to go through the time-consuming, costly, and potentially brand-damaging process of warning customers of the breach. Epsilon faces liabilities charges of almost a quarter of a billion dollars, but some estimate that the total price tag for the breach could top $4 billion.[29] Just because you can gather data and traffic in bits doesn't mean that you should. Any data-centric effort should involve input not only from business and technical staff, but from the firm's legal team as well (for more, see the box "Privacy Regulation: A Moving Target").

Privacy Regulation: A Moving Target

New methods for tracking and gathering user information appear daily, testing user comfort levels. For example, the firm Umbria uses software to analyze millions of blog and forum posts every day, using sentence structure, word choice, and quirks in punctuation to determine a blogger's gender, age, interests, and opinions. While Google refused to include facial recognition as an image search product ("too creepy," said its chairman),[30] Facebook, with great controversy, turned on facial recognition by default.[31] It's quite possible that in the future, someone will be able to upload a photo to a service and direct it to find all the accessible photos and video on the Internet that match that person's features. And while targeting is getting easier, a Carnegie Mellon study showed that it doesn't take much to find someone with a minimum of data. Simply by knowing gender, birth date, and postal zip code, 87 percent of people in the United States could be pinpointed by name.[32] Another study showed that publicly available data on state and date of birth could be used to predict U.S. Social Security numbers—a potential gateway to identity theft.[33]

Some feel that Moore's Law, the falling cost of storage, and the increasing reach of the Internet have us on the cusp of a privacy train wreck. And that may inevitably lead to more legislation that restricts data-use possibilities. Noting this, strategists and technologists need to be fully aware of the legal environment their systems face (see Chapter 18 for examples and discussion) and consider how such environments may change in the future. Many industries have strict guidelines on what kind of information can be collected and shared.

For example, HIPAA (the U.S. Health Insurance Portability and Accountability Act) includes provisions governing data use and privacy among health care providers, insurers, and employers. The financial industry has strict requirements for recording and sharing communications between firm and client (among many other restrictions). There are laws limiting the kinds of information that can be gathered on younger Web surfers. And there are several laws operating at the state level as well.

International laws also differ from those in the United States. Europe, in particular, has a strict European Privacy Directive. The directive includes governing provisions that limit data collection, require notice and approval of many types of data collection, and require firms to make data available to customers with mechanisms for stopping collection efforts and correcting inaccuracies at customer request. Australia is among the nations mimic much of what it finds in European laws.[34] Data-dependent efforts plotted for one region may not fully translate to another effort if the law limits key components of technology use. The constantly changing legal landscape also means that what works today might not be allowed in the future.

Firms beware—the public will almost certainly demand tighter controls if the industry is perceived as behaving recklessly or inappropriately with customer data.

KEY TAKEAWAYS

- For organizations that sell directly to their customers, transaction processing systems (TPS) represent a source of potentially useful data.
- Grocers and retailers can link you to cash transactions if they can convince you to use a loyalty card which, in turn, requires you to give up information about yourself in exchange for some kind of financial incentive such as points or discounts.
- Enterprise software (CRM, SCM, and ERP) is a source for customer, supply chain, and enterprise data.
- Survey data can be used to supplement a firm's operational data.
- Data obtained from outside sources, when combined with a firm's internal data assets, can give the firm a competitive edge.
- Data aggregators are part of a multibillion-dollar industry that provides genuinely helpful data to a wide variety of organizations.
- Data that can be purchased from aggregators may not in and of itself yield sustainable competitive advantage since others may have access to this data, too. However, when combined with a firm's proprietary data or integrated with a firm's proprietary procedures or other assets, third-party data can be a key tool for enhancing organizational performance.
- Data aggregators can also be quite controversial. Among other things, they represent a big target for identity thieves, are a method for spreading potentially incorrect data, and raise privacy concerns.
- Firms that mismanage their customer data assets risk lawsuits, brand damage, lower sales, fleeing customers, and can prompt more restrictive legislation.
- Further raising privacy issues and identity theft concerns, recent studies have shown that in many cases it is possible to pinpoint users through allegedly anonymous data, and to guess Social Security numbers from public data.
- New methods for tracking and gathering user information are raising privacy issues which possibly will be addressed through legislation that restricts data use.

QUESTIONS AND EXERCISES

1. Why would a firm use a loyalty card? What is the incentive for the firm? What is the incentive for consumers to opt in and use loyalty cards? What kinds of strategic assets can these systems create?

2. Make a list of the kind of data you might give up when using a cash register, a website, or a loyalty card, or when calling a firm's customer support line. How might firms leverage this data to better serve you and improve their performance?

3. Are you concerned by any of the data-use possibilities that you outlined in prior questions, discussed in this chapter, or that you've otherwise read about or encountered? If you are concerned, why? If not, why not? What might firms, governments, and consumers do to better protect consumers?

4. What are some of the sources data aggregators tap to collect information?

5. Privacy laws are in a near constant state of flux. Conduct research to identify the current state of privacy law. Has major legislation recently been proposed or approved? What are the implications for firms operating in effected industries? What are the potential benefits to consumers? Do consumers lose anything from this legislation?

6. Self-regulation is often proposed as an alternative to legislative efforts. What kinds of efforts would provide "teeth" to self-regulation. Are there steps firms could take to make you believe in their ability to self-regulate? Why or why not?

7. What is HIPPA? What industry does it impact?

8. How do international privacy laws differ from US privacy laws?

---

4. DATA RICH, INFORMATION POOR

LEARNING OBJECTIVES

1. **Know and be able to list the reasons why many organizations have data that can't be converted to actionable information.**
2. **Understand why transactional databases can't always be queried and what needs to be done to facilitate effective data use for analytics and business intelligence.**
3. **Recognize key issues surrounding data and privacy legislation.**

Despite being awash in data, many organizations are data rich but information poor. A survey by consulting firm Accenture found 57 percent of companies reporting that they didn't have a beneficial, consistently updated, companywide analytical capability. Among major decisions, only 60 percent were backed by analytics—40 percent were made by intuition and gut instinct.[35] The big culprit limiting BI initiatives is getting data into a form where it can be used, analyzed, and turned into information. Here's a look at some factors holding back information advantages.

4.1 Incompatible Systems

legacy system

Older information systems that are often incompatible with other systems, technologies, and ways of conducting business. Incompatible legacy systems can be a major roadblock to turning data into information, and they can inhibit firm agility, holding back operational and strategic initiatives.

Just because data is collected doesn't mean it can be used. This limit is a big problem for large firms that have **legacy systems**, outdated information systems that were not designed to share data, aren't compatible with newer technologies, and aren't aligned with the firm's current business needs. The problem can be made worse by mergers and acquisitions, especially if a firm depends on operational systems that are incompatible with its partner. And the elimination of incompatible systems isn't just a technical issue. Firms might be under extended agreement with different vendors or outsourcers, and breaking a contract or invoking an escape clause may be costly. Folks working in M&A (the area of investment banking focused on valuing and facilitating mergers and acquisitions) beware—it's critical to uncover these hidden costs of technology integration before deciding if a deal makes financial sense.

Legacy Systems: A Prison for Strategic Assets

The experience of one *Fortune* 100 firm that your author has worked with illustrates how incompatible information systems can actually hold back strategy. This firm was the largest in its category, and sold identical commodity products sourced from its many plants worldwide. Being the biggest should have given the firm scale advantages. But many of the firm's manufacturing facilities and international locations developed or purchased separate, incompatible systems. Still more plants were acquired through acquisition, each coming with its own legacy systems.

The plants with different information systems used *different* part numbers and naming conventions even though they sold *identical* products. As a result, the firm had no timely information on how much of a particular item was sold to which worldwide customers. The company was essentially operating as a collection of smaller, regional businesses, rather than as the worldwide behemoth that it was.

After the firm developed an information system that standardized data across these plants, it was, for the first time, able to get a single view of worldwide sales. The firm then used this data to approach their biggest customers, negotiating lower prices in exchange for increased commitments in worldwide purchasing. This trade let the firm take share from regional rivals. It also gave the firm the ability to shift manufacturing capacity globally, as currency prices, labor conditions, disaster, and other factors impacted sourcing. The new information system in effect liberated the latent strategic asset of scale, increasing sales by well over a billion and a half dollars in the four years following implementation.

4.2   Operational Data Can't Always Be Queried

Another problem when turning data into information is that most transactional databases aren't set up to be simultaneously accessed for reporting and analysis. When a customer buys something from a cash register, that action may post a sales record and deduct an item from the firm's inventory. In most TPS systems, requests made to the database can usually be performed pretty quickly—the system adds or modifies the few records involved and it's done—in and out in a flash.

But if a manager asks a database to analyze historic sales trends showing the most and least profitable products over time, they may be asking a computer to look at thousands of transaction records, comparing results, and neatly ordering findings. That's not a quick in-and-out task, and it may very well require significant processing to come up with the request. Do this against the very databases you're using to record your transactions, and you might grind your computers to a halt.

Getting data into systems that can support analytics is where data warehouses and data marts come in, the topic of our next section.

KEY TAKEAWAYS

- A major factor limiting business intelligence initiatives is getting data into a form where it can be used (i.e., analyzed and turned into information).
- Legacy systems often limit data utilization because they were not designed to share data, aren't compatible with newer technologies, and aren't aligned with the firm's current business needs.
- Most transactional databases aren't set up to be simultaneously accessed for reporting and analysis. In order to run analytics the data must first be ported to a data warehouse or data mart.

QUESTIONS AND EXERCISES

1. How might information systems impact mergers and acquisitions? What are the key issues to consider?
2. Discuss the possible consequences of a company having multiple plants, each with a different information system using different part numbers and naming conventions for identical products.
3. Why does it take longer, and require more processing power, to analyze sales trends by region and product, as opposed to posting a sales transaction?

5. DATA WAREHOUSES, DATA MARTS, AND TECHNOLOGY BEHIND "BIG DATA"

LEARNING OBJECTIVES

1. Understand what data warehouses and data marts are and the purpose they serve.
2. Know the issues that need to be addressed in order to design, develop, deploy, and maintain data warehouses and data marts.
3. Recognize and understand technologies behind "Big Data," how they differ from conventional data management approaches, and how they are currently being used for organizational benefit.

Since running analytics against transactional data can bog down a system, and since most organizations need to combine and reformat data from multiple sources, firms typically need to create separate data repositories for their reporting and analytics work. Such data repositories act as a kind of staging area from which to turn that data into information.

FIGURE 15.3

Information systems supporting operations (such as TPS) are typically separate, and "feed" information systems used for analytics (such as data warehouses and data marts).

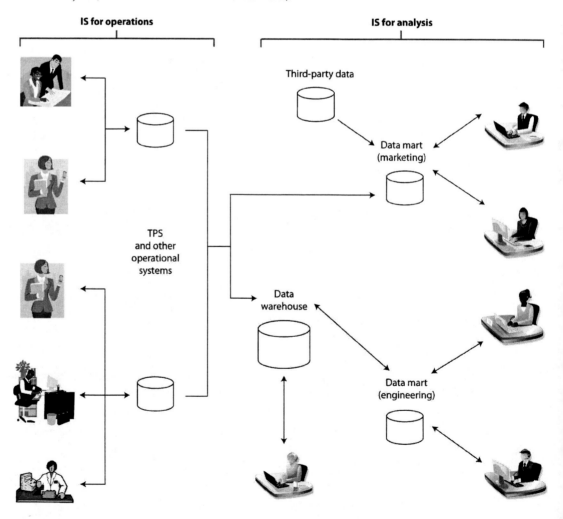

Two terms you'll hear for these kinds of repositories are **data warehouse** and **data mart**. A data warehouse is a set of databases designed to support decision making in an organization. It is structured for fast online queries and exploration. Data warehouses may aggregate enormous amounts of data from many different operational systems.

A data mart is a database focused on addressing the concerns of a specific problem (e.g., increasing customer retention, improving product quality) or business unit (e.g., marketing, engineering).

Marts and warehouses may contain huge volumes of data. For example, a firm may not need to keep large amounts of historical point-of-sale or transaction data in its operational systems, but it might want past data in its data mart so that managers can hunt for patterns and trends that occur over time.

It's easy for firms to get seduced by a software vendor's demonstration showing data at your fingertips, presented in pretty graphs. But as mentioned earlier, getting data in a format that can be used for analytics is hard, complex, and challenging work. Large data warehouses can cost millions and take years to build. Every dollar spent on technology may lead to five to seven more dollars on consulting and other services.[36]

Most firms will face a trade-off—do we attempt a large-scale integration of the whole firm, or more targeted efforts with quicker payoffs? Firms in fast-moving industries or with particularly complex businesses may struggle to get sweeping projects completed in enough time to reap benefits before business conditions change. Most consultants now advise smaller projects with narrow scope driven by specific business goals.[37]

Firms can eventually get to a unified data warehouse but it may take time. Even analytics king Walmart will take years to get to that point. The retail giant once reported having over seven hundred different data marts and hired Hewlett-Packard for help in bringing the systems together to form a more integrated data warehouse.[38]

The old saying from the movie *Field of Dreams*, "If you build it, they will come," doesn't hold up well for large-scale data analytics projects. This work should start with a clear vision with business-focused objectives. When senior executives can see objectives illustrated in potential payoff, they'll be able to champion the effort, and experts agree, having an executive champion is a key success factor. Focusing on business issues will also drive technology choice, with the firm better able to focus on products that best fit its needs.

Once a firm has business goals and hoped-for payoffs clearly defined, it can address the broader issues needed to design, develop, deploy, and maintain its system:[39]

- *Data relevance.* What data is needed to compete on analytics and to meet our current and future goals?
- *Data sourcing.* Can we even get the data we'll need? Where can this data be obtained from? Is it available via our internal systems? Via third-party data aggregators? Via suppliers or sales partners? Do we need to set up new systems, surveys, and other collection efforts to acquire the data we need?
- *Data quantity.* How much data is needed?
- *Data quality.* Can our data be trusted as accurate? Is it clean, complete, and reasonably free of errors? How can the data be made more accurate and valuable for analysis? Will we need to "scrub," calculate, and consolidate data so that it can be used?
- *Data hosting.* Where will the systems be housed? What are the hardware and networking requirements for the effort?
- *Data governance.* What rules and processes are needed to manage data from its creation through its retirement? Are there operational issues (backup, disaster recovery)? Legal issues? Privacy issues? How should the firm handle security and access?

For some perspective on how difficult this can be, consider that an executive from one of the largest US banks once lamented at how difficult it was to get his systems to do something as simple as properly distinguishing between men and women. The company's customer-focused data warehouse drew data from thirty-six separate operational systems—bank teller systems, ATMs, student loan reporting systems, car loan systems, mortgage loan systems, and more. Collectively these legacy systems expressed gender in *seventeen* different ways: "M" or "F"; "m" or "f"; "Male" or "Female"; "MALE" or "FEMALE"; "1" for man, "0" for woman; "0" for man, "1" for woman and more, plus various codes for "unknown." The best math in the world is of no help if the values used aren't any good. There's a saying in the industry, "garbage in, garbage out."

data warehouse

A set of databases designed to support decision making in an organization.

data mart

A database or databases focused on addressing the concerns of a specific problem (e.g., increasing customer retention, improving product quality) or business unit (e.g., marketing, engineering).

5.1 Hadoop: Big Insights from Unstructured "Big Data"

Having neatly structured data warehouses and data-marts are great—the tools are reliable and can often be turned over to end-users or specialists who can rapidly produce reports and other analyses. But roughly 80 percent of corporate data is messy and unstructured, and it is not stored in conventional, relational formats—think of data stored in office productivity documents, e-mail, call center conversations, and social media.[40] It's the three Vs of "Big Data"—volume, velocity, and variety—that distinguish it from conventional data analysis problems and require a new breed of technology. Big data is forcing companies to rethink both the technology infrastructure and the necessary skills needed to successfully interpret and act on the information.[41] Conventional tools often choke when trying to sift through the massive amounts of data collected by many of today's firms. The open-source project known as Hadoop was created to analyze massive amounts of raw information better than traditional, highly structured databases. While there are other technologies that can be leveraged for Big Data projects, Hadoop is the clear leader growing alongside big data trends to analyze massive amounts of unstructured data, so it merits distinct mention in this discussion.

Hadoop is made up of some half-dozen separate software pieces and requires the integration of these pieces to work. Hadoop-related projects have names such as Hive, Pig, and Zookeeper. Several commercial firms provide support, add-on products, or proprietary technology for big data implementations leveraging these technologies, including fast-growing Hadoop specialists such as Cloudera (which, after Red Hat, is only the second open source firm in history to crack $100 million in revenues), Hortonworks (which went public in 2014), and MapR. Amazon, IBM, and Pivotal (which is a venture by EMC and its VMWare subsidiary) are among established tech giants that provide Hadoop products and services. Hadoop use is catching on like wildfire, with some expecting that within five years, more than half of the world's data will be stored in Hadoop environments.[42]

There are four primary advantages to Hadoop, although these advantages may also apply to competing big data technologies, as well:[43]

- *Flexibility*: Hadoop can absorb any type of data, structured or not, from any type of source (geeks would say such a system is *schema-less*). But this disparate data can still be aggregated and analyzed.

- *Scalability*: Hadoop systems can start on a single PC, but thousands of machines can eventually be combined to work together for storage and analysis.

- *Cost effectiveness*: Since the system is open source and can be started with low-end hardware, the technology is cheap by data-warehousing standards. Many vendors also offer Hadoop as a cloud service, allowing firms to avoid hardware costs altogether.

- *Fault tolerance*: One of the servers running your Hadoop cluster just crashed? No big deal. Hadoop is designed in such a way so that there will be no single point of failure. The system will continue to work, relying on the remaining hardware.

Financial giant Morgan Stanley is a big believer in Hadoop. One senior technology manager at the firm contrasts Hadoop with highly structured systems, saying that in the past, "IT asked the business what they want, creates a data structure and writes structured query language, sources the data, conforms it to the table and writes a structured query. Then you give it to them and they often say that is not what they wanted." But with Hadoop overseeing a big pile of unstructured (or less structured) data, technical staff can now work with users to carve up and combine data in lots of different ways, or even set systems loose in the data to hunt for unexpected patterns (see the discussion of data mining later in this chapter). Morgan Stanley's initial Hadoop experiments started with a handful of old servers that were about to be retired, but the company has steadily ramped up its efforts. Now by using Hadoop, the firm sees that it is able to analyze data on a far larger scale ("petabytes of data, which is unheard of in the traditional database world") with potentially higher-impact results. The bank is looking at customers' financial objectives and trying to come up with investment insights to help them invest appropriately, and it is seeking "Big Data" insights to help the firm more effectively manage risk.[44]

FIGURE 15.4   The Hadoop Logo

The project was named after a toy elephant belonging to the son of Hadoop Developer Doug Cutting.

Other big name-firms using Hadoop for "Big Data" insights include Bank of America, Disney, GE, LinkedIn, Nokia, Twitter, and Walmart. Hadoop is an open source project overseen by the Apache Software Foundation. It has an Internet pedigree and is based on ideas by Google and lots of software contributed by Yahoo! (two firms that regularly need to dive into massive and growing amounts of unstructured data—Web pages, videos, images, social media, user account information, and more). IBM used Hadoop as the engine that helped power Watson to defeat human opponents on *Jeopardy*, further demonstrating the technology's ability to analyze wildly different data for accurate insight. Other tech firms embracing Hadoop and offering some degree of support for the technology include HP, EMC, and Microsoft.

Over 91 percent of *Fortune* 1000 senior executives surveyed said big data initiatives were planned or underway with half of these execs expecting efforts to cost $10 million or more.[45] Yet while success stories for big data abound, many organizations lack the skills required to exploit big data.[46] McKinsey estimates a US talent shortfall of 140,000 to 190,000 data scientists and a further need for 1.5 million more managers and analysts who will have to be savvy consumers of big data analytics.[47] Time to double-down on studying big data and analytics.

Spotify: Your DJ in the Cloud

In 2014, the top music streaming service in the world, Stockholm-based Spotify, plunked down undisclosed millions for The Echo Nest a Somerville, MA-based firm that had essentially created an automated music geek. While Apple's Beats 1 radio station uses a handful of charismatic human DJs to line up tracks,[48] Echo Nest is building a better hipster. According to CEO Jim Lucchese, the firm systems do "what a great deejay does, or the friend that you rely on musically: to better understand who you are as a fan, understand all the music that's out there and make that connection."[49]

The EchoNest was founded by the musically and technically talented team of Brian Whitman and Tristan Jehan, researchers who honed their craft at MIT's Media Lab. The duo built systems that could do two things: The first was to "listen" to music; analyze it to break down its characteristics: pitch, key, tempo, vocals or instrumental, live or studio, energy level, mood, and more.[50] While Pandora has human beings rating music, the idea struggles to scale and be consistent.[51] The Echo Nest, by contrast, created precision and speed. Over 30 million songs in that great musical catalog in the cloud[52] have been devoured and detailed, and 20,000 new ones are added each day.[53] And, with machine learning, the service only gets better the more data it's fed.[54]

The second big Echo Nest trick is to pay attention to what the world is saying about music. The firms software constantly scours the Web, "reading" music blogs, news reports, and more —as many as 10 million documents each day. The firm's homegrown technology analyzes descriptions of artists, albums, tracks, and developing insight into trends and genres. In this, the EchoNest has essentially built a cool hunting machine that listens to the world's music reviewers, music mavens and rabid fans, constantly and planet-wide.[55]

Using the Echo Nest, Spotify is helping to curate the cloud according to your taste. The plan is to have Spotify examine your playlists, your listening habits, and what it learns about its millions of other users to build "you radio," exactly what you want to hear when you want to hear it. New services hint at where this can go. If you run, Spotify's smartphone app can pay attention to your running tempo, examine your song preferences, and build a playlist cued up based on how fast move.[56] The future could be even more extraordinarily predictive. Does your phone tell Spotify you're at work? Queue up some non-distracting instrumental music to listen to in the background. Home cooking dinner? You'll get something smooth and relaxing. Gym patterns kicking in? Power mix. Big Data, droppin' beats.

With over 20 million paying subscribers and 75 million active users, Spotify is by far the world's most popular streaming music service. Big Data leveraged by the firm's subsidiary, The Echo Nest, promises to leverage everything the firm knows about music, and about you, to queue up the best listening experience at exactly the right time.

Source: Spotify's public archive for media use at: https://press.spotify.com/no/pictures/application/

E-discovery: Supporting Legal Inquiries

Data archiving isn't just for analytics. Sometimes the law requires organizations to dive into their electronic records. **E-discovery** refers to identifying and retrieving relevant electronic information to support litigation efforts. E-discovery is something a firm should account for in its archiving and data storage plans. Unlike analytics that promise a boost to the bottom line, there's no profit in complying with a judge's order—it's just a sunk cost. But organizations can be compelled by court order to scavenge their bits, and the cost to uncover difficult to access data can be significant, if not planned for in advance.

In one recent example, the Office of Federal Housing Enterprise Oversight (OFHEO) was subpoenaed for documents in litigation involving mortgage firms Fannie Mae and Freddie Mac. Even though the OFHEO wasn't a party in the lawsuit, the agency had to comply with the search—an effort that cost $6 million, a full 9 percent of its total yearly budget.[57]

KEY TAKEAWAYS

- Data warehouses and data marts are repositories for large amounts of transactional data awaiting analytics and reporting.
- Large data warehouses are complex, can cost millions, and take years to build.
- The open source Hadoop effort provides a collection of technologies for manipulating massive amounts of unstructured data. The system is flexible, scalable, cost-effective, and fault-tolerant. Hadoop grew from large Internet firms but is now being used across industries.

QUESTIONS AND EXERCISES

1. List the issues that need to be addressed in order to design, develop, deploy, and maintain data warehouses and data marts.
2. What is meant by "data relevance"?
3. What is meant by "data governance"?
4. What is the difference between a data mart and a data warehouse?
5. Why are data marts and data warehouses necessary? Why can't an organization simply query its transactional database?
6. How can something as simple as customer gender be difficult for a large organization to establish in a data warehouse?
7. What is Hadoop? Why would a firm use Hadoop instead of conventional data warehousing and data mart technologies?
8. Research the current state of "Big Data" analysis. Identify major firms leveraging Hadoop or similar technologies and share high-impact examples with your classmates and professor.

6. THE BUSINESS INTELLIGENCE TOOLKIT

LEARNING OBJECTIVES

1. **Know the tools that are available to turn data into information.**
2. **Identify the key areas where businesses leverage data mining.**
3. **Understand some of the conditions under which analytical models can fail.**
4. **Recognize major categories of artificial intelligence and understand how organizations are leveraging this technology.**

So far we've discussed where data can come from, and how we can get data into a form where we can use it. But how, exactly, do firms turn that data into information? That's where the various software tools of business intelligence (BI) and analytics come in. Potential products in the business intelligence toolkit range from simple spreadsheets to ultrasophisticated data mining packages leveraged by teams employing "rocket-science" mathematics.

6.1 Query and Reporting Tools

The idea behind query and reporting tools is to present users with a subset of requested data, selected, sorted, ordered, calculated, and compared, as needed. Managers use these tools to see and explore what's happening inside their organizations.

Canned reports provide regular summaries of information in a predetermined format. They're often developed by information systems staff and formats can be difficult to alter. By contrast, **ad hoc reporting tools** allow users to dive in and create their own reports, selecting fields, ranges, and other parameters to build their own reports on the fly. **Dashboards** provide a sort of heads-up display of critical indicators, letting managers get a graphical glance at key performance metrics. Some tools may allow data to be exported into spreadsheets. Yes, even the lowly spreadsheet can be a powerful tool for modeling "what if" scenarios and creating additional reports (of course be careful: if data can be easily exported, then it can potentially leave the firm dangerously exposed, raising privacy, security, legal, and competitive concerns).

canned reports

Reports that provide regular summaries of information in a predetermined format.

ad hoc reporting tools

Tools that put users in control so that they can create custom reports on an as-needed basis by selecting fields, ranges, summary conditions, and other parameters.

dashboards

A heads-up display of critical indicators that allow managers to get a graphical glance at key performance metrics.

FIGURE 15.5 The Federal IT Dashboard

The Federal IT dashboard offers federal agencies, and the general public, information about the government's IT investments.

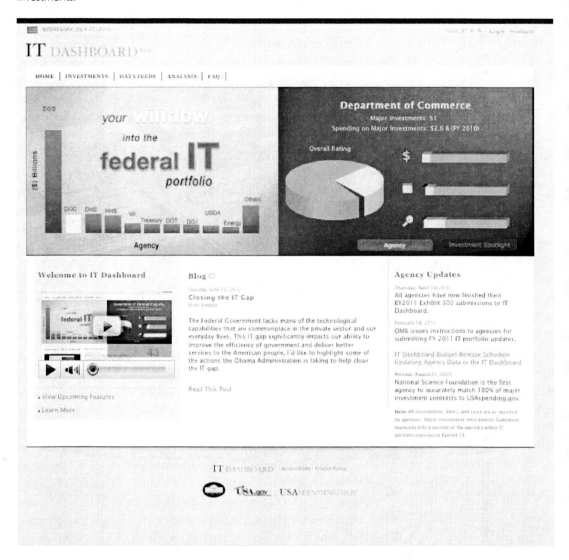

<dl>
<dt>online analytical processing (OLAP)</dt>
<dd>A method of querying and reporting that takes data from standard relational databases, calculates and summarizes the data, and then stores the data in a special database called a data cube.</dd>

<dt>data cube</dt>
<dd>A special database used to store data in OLAP reporting.</dd>
</dl>

A subcategory of reporting tools is referred to as **online analytical processing (OLAP)** (pronounced "oh-lap"). Data used in OLAP reporting is usually sourced from standard relational databases, but it's calculated and summarized in advance, across multiple dimensions, with the data stored in a special database called a **data cube**. This extra setup step makes OLAP fast (sometimes one thousand times faster than performing comparable queries against conventional relational databases). Given this kind of speed boost, it's not surprising that data cubes for OLAP access are often part of a firm's data mart and data warehouse efforts.

A manager using an OLAP tool can quickly explore and compare data across multiple factors such as time, geography, product lines, and so on. In fact, OLAP users often talk about how they can "slice and dice" their data, "drilling down" inside the data to uncover new insights. And while conventional reports are usually presented as a summarized list of information, OLAP results look more like a spreadsheet, with the various dimensions of analysis in rows and columns, with summary values at the intersection.

FIGURE 15.6

This OLAP report compares multiple dimensions. Company is along the vertical axis, and product is along the horizontal axis. Many OLAP tools can also present graphs of multidimensional data.

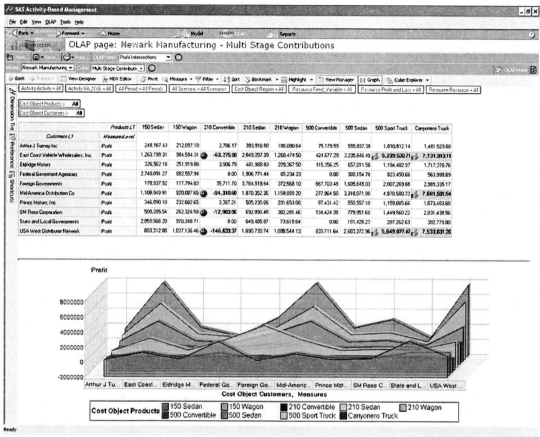

Source: Copyright © 2009 SAS Institute, Inc.

Public Sector Reporting Tools in Action: Fighting Crime and Fighting Waste

Access to ad hoc query and reporting tools can empower all sorts of workers. Consider what analytics tools have done for the police force in Richmond, Virginia. The city provides department investigators with access to data from internal sources such as 911 logs and police reports, and combines this with outside data including neighborhood demographics, payday schedules, weather reports, traffic patterns, sports events, and more.

Experienced officers dive into this data, exploring when and where crimes occur. These insights help the department decide how to allocate its limited policing assets to achieve the biggest impact. While IT staffers put the system together, the tools are actually used by officers with expertise in fighting street crime—the kinds of users with the knowledge to hunt down trends and interpret the causes behind the data. And it seems this data helps make smart cops even smarter—the system is credited with delivering a single-year crime-rate reduction of 20 percent.[58]

As it turns out, what works for cops also works for bureaucrats. When administrators for Albuquerque were given access to ad hoc reporting systems, they uncovered all sorts of anomalies, prompting excess spending cuts on everything from cell phone usage to unnecessarily scheduled overtime. And once again, BI performed for the public sector. The Albuquerque system delivered the equivalent of $2 million in savings in just the first three weeks it was used.[59]

omnichannel

Providing customers with a unified experience across customer channels, which may include online, mobile, catalog, phone, and retail. Pricing, recommendations, and incentives should reflect a data-driven, accurate, single view of the customer.

L.L. Bean: Data Master

For a look at data-driven prowess, head to Maine and visit the over 100-year-old clothing and equipment retailer, L.L. Bean. Bean's world has changed dramatically since the 1990s, when it had a highly-structured, mostly relational information system to support a single marketing channel (catalog sales). Today Bean has retail stores, an adventure travel business, websites, apps, buying through Google Shopping and affiliates, social media, loyalty programs, and more—engaging customers through roughly 30 different channels overall. All of this inflates data collection—website traffic, app stats, A/B testing, purchases, items viewed but not purchased, returns, repairs, ad impressions, online marketing response, to name just a few.

Structured data didn't cut it any more. The business was changing too fast and data was flooding in like water from a firehose. So the firm began shifting from structured SQL to massive stores of unstructured data harnessed with Hadoop technology. Outside consultants were brought in to help develop a new systems architecture with new technologies.[60] The firm's classic 10TB enterprise data warehouse, stored onsite, was augmented with a 100TB cloud-based system. The conversation changed from the cost-focused "what data can we afford to keep" to the value-focused "what data can we afford to throw away." IT staff learned new skills, with the firm "turning its SQL developers into Hive and Impala NoSQL experts."[61] Marketing managers and new analytics team members were schooled in "Big Data Boot Camps" to show them how to dive deep into unstructured data to hunt down valuable insights. OLAP cubes and easy-to-use reporting tools were also made available to non-technical team members. One goal was to empower Bean staff for better insight and decision-making, increasing the users of firm data by at least ten times those who had prior reporting access.

Automated tools were also developed to leverage this data in real-time (making it not just "big data" but also "fast data"), allowing Bean to serve customers online, on the phone or in stores based on what the firm knows about them. This kind of integrated shopping experience and unified customer view across channels is sometimes referred to as **omnichannel**. Bean's web and app stores leverage these insights for on-the-fly personalization with a sharp-shooter aim at what the customer wants. Additionally, iPad wielding store staff and info-armed phone reps now have access to a deeply-detailed real-time view of each customer, and these profiles are served up to create more relevant offers, better-received recommendations, and to deliver overall customer delight.[62] Need proof that customers see the benefit? Bean tied with Amazon as best in online retail customer satisfaction.[63]

Sources include: C. Wilson and D. Bryan, Talk: "Transitioning from Original Big Data to the New Big Data: L.L. Bean's Journey," at Strata+Hadoop World, Oct. 15-17, 2014, New York, NY (stream available at https://www.safaribooksonline.com/library/view/strata-conference-new/9781491900352/part110.html). And V. Heffernan, "Big Moose is Watching You," *Medium*, Oct. 31, 2014.

6.2 Data Mining

While reporting tools can help users explore data, modern data sets can be so large that it might be impossible for humans to spot underlying trends. That's where data mining can help. **Data mining** is the process of using computers to identify hidden patterns and to build models from large data sets.

Some of the key areas where businesses are leveraging data mining include the following:

data mining

The process of using computers to identify hidden patterns in, and to build models from, large data sets.

- *Customer segmentation*—figuring out which customers are likely to be the most valuable to a firm.

- *Marketing and promotion targeting*—identifying which customers will respond to which offers at which price at what time.

- *Market basket analysis*—determining which products customers buy together, and how an organization can use this information to cross-sell more products or services.

- *Collaborative filtering*—personalizing an individual customer's experience based on the trends and preferences identified across similar customers.

- *Customer churn*—determining which customers are likely to leave, and what tactics can help the firm avoid unwanted defections.

- *Fraud detection*—uncovering patterns consistent with criminal activity.

- *Financial modeling*—building trading systems to capitalize on historical trends.

- *Hiring and promotion*—identifying characteristics consistent with employee success in the firm's various roles.

For data mining to work, two critical conditions need to be present: (1) the organization must have clean, consistent data, and (2) the events in that data should reflect current and future trends. The recent financial crisis provides lessons on what can happen when either of these conditions isn't met.

First let's look at problems with using bad data. A report in the *New York Times* has suggested that in the period leading up to the 2008 financial crisis, some banking executives deliberately deceived risk management systems in order to skew capital-on-hand requirements. This deception let firms load up on risky debt, while carrying less cash for covering losses.[64] Deceive your systems with bad data and your models are worthless. In this case, wrong estimates from bad data left firms grossly overexposed to risk. When debt defaults occurred, several banks failed, and we entered the worst financial crisis since the Great Depression.

Now consider the problem of historical consistency: Computer-driven investment models can be very effective when the market behaves as it has in the past. But models are blind when faced with the equivalent of the "hundred-year flood" (sometimes called *black swans*); events so extreme and unusual that they never showed up in the data used to build the model.

We saw this in the late 1990s with the collapse of the investment firm Long Term Capital Management. LTCM was started by Nobel Prize–winning economists, but when an unexpected Russian debt crisis caused the markets to move in ways not anticipated by its models, the firm lost 90 percent of its value in less than two months. The problem was so bad that the Fed had to step in to supervise the firm's multibillion-dollar bailout. Fast forward a decade to the banking collapse of 2008, and we again see computer-driven trading funds plummet in the face of another unexpected event—the burst of the housing bubble.[65]

Data mining presents a host of other perils, as well. It's possible to **over-engineer** a model, building it with so many variables that the solution arrived at might only work on the subset of data you've used to create it. You might also be looking at a random but meaningless statistical fluke. In demonstrating how flukes occur, Tyler Vigen, a geospatial intelligence analyst for the US Army, has put together a hilarious website demonstrating high correlations among impossibly linked data, most trending in near lockstep over a ten-year period. One graph shows a ten-year trend in per-capita US sour cream consumption and motorcycle riders killed in noncollision transport accidents. An unskilled person drawing inferences from what appears to be a very consistent trend between the two might erroneously conclude that sour cream kills bikers. The number of people who drowned by falling into a swimming pool is also highly correlated with the number of films Nicolas Cage has appeared in. Someone stop the actor before his reign of swimming pool tragedy continues![66]

> **over-engineer**
>
> Build a model with so many variables that the solution arrived at might only work on the subset of data you've used to create it.

One way to test to see if you're looking at a random occurrence in the numbers is to divide your data, building your model with one portion of the data, and using another portion to verify your results. This is the approach Netflix has used to test results achieved by teams in the Netflix Prize, the firm's million-dollar contest for improving the predictive accuracy of its movie recommendation engine (see Chapter 4).

Analyst beware, it's also important to understand the source and consistency of data over time. Just because data may be expressed in a consistent format doesn't mean it was collected consistently or without distortive outside influence. Consider Google's initial success, then failure in identifying influenza trends from search data. Initial press trumpeted the fact that Google queries could identify the spread of the flu more quickly and at least as accurately as the Centers for Disease Control. Two years later, Google was making more bad predictions than accurate ones. Researches hunting for the breakdown point to the fact that Google regularly changes its search engine. For example, one update began recommending related search terms. Another began suggesting diagnoses. Suddenly Google was vastly overestimating CDC predictions, likely because its own tools accelerated the number of queries using flu-related terms.[67]

Finally, sometimes a pattern is uncovered but determining the best choice for a response is less clear. Data-mining wizards at European retailer, Tesco, uncovered that product sales data showed several money-losing products, including a type of bread known as "milk loaf." Drop those products, right? Not so fast. Further analysis showed milk loaf was a "destination product" for a loyal group of high-value customers, and that these customers would shop elsewhere if milk loaf disappeared from Tesco shelves. The firm kept the bread as a loss-leader and retained those valuable milk loaf fans.[68] Data miner, beware—first findings don't always reveal an optimal course of action.

This last example underscores the importance of recruiting a data mining and business analytics team that possesses three critical skills: information technology (for understanding how to pull together data, and for selecting analysis tools), statistics (for building models and interpreting the strength and validity of results), and business knowledge (for helping set system goals, requirements, and offering deeper insight into what the data really says about the firm's operating environment). Miss one of these key functions and your team could make some major mistakes.

While we've focused on tools in our discussion above, many experts suggest that business intelligence is really an organizational process as much as it is a set of technologies. Having the right team is critical in moving the firm from goal setting through execution and results.

neural networks

An AI system that examines data and hunts down and exposes patterns, in order to build models to exploit findings.

Expert systems

AI systems that leverage rules or examples to perform a task in a way that mimics applied human expertise.

Genetic algorithms

Model building techniques where computers examine many potential solutions to a problem, iteratively modifying (mutating) various mathematical models, and comparing the mutated models to search for a best alternative.

machine learning

Leverages massive amounts of data so that computers can act and improve on their own without additional programming.

Artificial Intelligence and the New World of Machine Learning

Data mining has its roots in a branch of computer science known as artificial intelligence (or AI). The goal of AI is to create computer programs that are able to mimic or improve upon functions of the human brain. Data mining can leverage **neural networks** or other advanced algorithms and statistical techniques to hunt down and expose patterns and build models to exploit findings. And massive amounts of data play a role here. Google leverages data it collects when users talk to and type into its search engine to improve its speech recognition algorithms, cutting errors by 25 percent in a single rollout.[69]

Expert systems are AI systems that leverage rules or examples to perform a task in a way that mimics applied human expertise. Expert systems are used in tasks ranging from medical diagnoses to product configuration.

Genetic algorithms are model building techniques where computers examine many potential solutions to a problem, iteratively modifying (mutating) various mathematical models, and comparing the mutated models to search for a best alternative. Genetic algorithms have been used to build everything from financial trading models to handling complex airport scheduling, to designing parts for the international space station.[70]

While AI is not a single technology, and not directly related to data creation, various forms of AI can show up as part of analytics products, CRM tools, transaction processing systems, and other information systems.

Another area of AI that's been getting a lot of attention in business circles is **machine learning** where software seems to learn on its own by applying algorithms and data to improve the accuracy of actions, insights, solutions and predictions on their own without additional programming.[71] Neural networks and other types of AI play a role in machine learning, but what's special is that computers themselves examine data, find insights, and improve.

Taken together we see machine learning and AI beginning to deliver on multiple fronts. The self-driving car is a reality today. Working concepts for the autonomous kitchen with robo-chefs preparing meals is thought to be something you'll see in your lifetime, perhaps within just a few years.[72] There's also a good chance you've been reading news items and other copy written by robo-journalists. The Associated Press uses software called Wordsmith by the firm Automated Insights to craft more than 3,000 financial reports per quarter, posting summaries online within minutes of their release. The *Los Angeles Times* uses "Quakebot" to analyze geological data, in one case breaking the story of a 4.7 magnitude earthquake in Southern California.[73] The Big Ten Network uses software from Narrative Science for updates of football and basketball games and for short recaps of collegiate baseball and softball. Box scores and other play-by-play data are all the inputs these systems need.[74] And while a computer didn't write a line of this textbook, Insead Management Science professor Philip M. Parker has created an algorithm that has generated more than 100,000 books that are available on Amazon (sample title The Official Patient's Sourcebook on Acne Rosacea).[75]

And it's not just text and numerical data that allow machines learn, breakthroughs are helping computers develop models to acquire abstract concepts on their own through visual data. In one experiment, software "taught" itself what a cat was by watching 10 million images on YouTube.[76] Goofy, right? But in a subsequent advance systems could, in plain English, describe the contents of photos (e.g., "A group of young people playing a game of Frisbee").[77]

A system developed by IBM and the Baylor College of Medicine "read" 100,000 research papers in two hours and "found completely new biology hidden in the data." Undiscovered needle-like insights buried in the existing massive haystacks of human-generated knowledge, but that no single researcher could digest and map. These specific insights "could provide routes to new cancer drugs."[78] Some hear about machine learning and have nightmares of Skynet from the Terminator movies (Elon Musk, Bill Gates, and Steven Hawking are among well known tech-forward crowds who have cautioned about AIs future),[79] but big brain insights from AI just might save your life one day.

KEY TAKEAWAYS

- Canned and ad hoc reports, digital dashboards, and OLAP are all used to transform data into information.
- OLAP reporting leverages data cubes, which take data from standard relational databases, calculating and summarizing data for superfast reporting access. OLAP tools can present results through multidimensional graphs, or via spreadsheet-style cross-tab reports.
- Modern data sets can be so large that it might be impossible for humans to spot underlying trends without the use of data mining tools.
- Businesses are using data mining to address issues in several key areas including customer segmentation, marketing and promotion targeting, collaborative filtering, and so on.
- Machine learning and other types of AI are being applied in all sorts of ways, including voice and image recognition, enabling self-driving cars, writing news articles and other content, and making scientific discovery.
- Models influenced by bad data, missing or incomplete historical data, and over-engineering are prone to yield bad results.
- One way to test to see if you're looking at a random occurrence in your data is to divide your data, building your model with one portion of the data, and using another portion to verify your results.
- Analytics may not always provide the total solution for a problem. Sometimes a pattern is uncovered, but determining the best choice for a response is less clear.
- A competent business analytics team should possess three critical skills: information technology, statistics, and business knowledge.

QUESTIONS AND EXERCISES

1. What are some of the tools used to convert data into information?
2. What is the difference between a canned report and ad hoc reporting?
3. How do reports created by OLAP differ from most conventional reports?
4. List the key areas where businesses are leveraging data mining.
5. What is market basket analysis?
6. What is customer churn?
7. For data mining to work, what two critical data-related conditions must be present?
8. Discuss occurrences of model failure caused by missing or incomplete historical data.
9. Why do researchers think Google's Flu predictions became less accurate over time? How does this inform managerial caution on business intelligence projects? How can one avoid making similar errors?
10. Discuss Tesco's response to their discovery that "milk loaf" was a money-losing product.
11. List the three critical skills a competent business analytics team should possess.
12. Do any of the products that you use leverage artificial intelligence? What kinds of AI might be used in Netflix's movie recommendation system, Apple's iTunes Genius playlist builder, or Amazon's website personalization? What kind of AI might help a physician make a diagnosis or help an engineer configure a complicated product in the field?
13. Research business applications of machine learning and come to class prepared to discuss new developments, organizations using this technology, and their current plus potential long-term impact.
14. Are you excited about the future of machine learning? Frightened? Why? How might these technologies create social change and spawn new business opportunities?

7. DATA ASSET IN ACTION: TECHNOLOGY AND THE RISE OF WALMART

LEARNING OBJECTIVES

1. Understand how Walmart has leveraged information technology to become the world's largest retailer.
2. Be aware of the challenges that face Walmart in the years ahead.

Walmart demonstrates how a physical product retailer can create and leverage a data asset to achieve world-class supply chain efficiencies targeted primarily at driving down costs.

Walmart isn't just the largest retailer in the world; over the past several years it has popped in and out of the top spot on the *Fortune* 500 list—meaning that the firm has had revenues greater than *any* firm in the United States. Walmart is so big that in three months it sells more than a whole year's worth of sales at number two US retailer, Home Depot.[80]

At that size, it's clear that Walmart's key source of competitive advantage is scale. But firms don't turn into giants overnight. Walmart grew in large part by leveraging information systems to an extent never before seen in the retail industry. Technology tightly coordinates the Walmart value chain from tip to tail, while these systems also deliver a mineable data asset that's unmatched in US retail. To get a sense of the firm's overall efficiencies, at the end of the prior decade a McKinsey study found that Walmart was responsible for some 12 percent of the productivity gains in the *entire* US economy.[81] The firm's capacity as a systems innovator is so respected that many senior Walmart IT executives have been snatched up for top roles at Dell, HP, Amazon, and Microsoft. And lest one think that innovation is the province of only those located in the technology hubs of Silicon Valley, Boston, and Seattle, remember that Walmart is headquartered in Bentonville, Arkansas.

7.1 A Data-Driven Value Chain

inventory turnover ratio

The ratio of a company's annual sales to its inventory.

The Walmart efficiency dance starts with a proprietary system called Retail Link, a system originally developed in 1991 and continually refined ever since. Each time an item is scanned by a Walmart cash register, Retail Link not only records the sale, it also automatically triggers inventory reordering, scheduling, and delivery. This process keeps shelves stocked, while keeping inventories at a minimum. An AMR report ranked Walmart as having the seventh best supply chain in the country.[82] The firm's annual **inventory turnover ratio** of 8.5 means that Walmart sells the equivalent of its entire inventory roughly every six weeks (by comparison, Target's turnover ratio is 6.4, Sears' is 3.4, and the average for US retail is less than 2).[83]

Back-office scanners keep track of inventory as supplier shipments come in. Suppliers are rated based on timeliness of deliveries, and you've got to be quick to work with Walmart. In order to avoid a tractor-trailer traffic jam in store parking lots, deliveries are choreographed to arrive at intervals less than ten minutes apart. When Levi's joined Walmart, the firm had to guarantee it could replenish shelves every two days—no prior retailer had required a shorter-than-five-day window from Levi's.[84]

Walmart has been a catalyst for technology adoption among its suppliers. The firm is currently leading an adoption effort that requires partners to leverage RFID technology to track and coordinate inventories. While the rollout has been slow, a recent P&G trial showed RFID boosted sales nearly 20 percent by ensuring that inventory was on shelves and located where it should be.[85]

Keeping product stocked is one part of the streamlined value chain equation; prompting customers to return often and buy efficiently is another key element. The firm's Scan & Go app lets customers use their smartphones to scan bar codes of items they put in their cart. At checkout time, customers flash a total purchase barcode at a cash register kiosk screen and pay. Customers can keep an on-app shopping list that's checked off with each item scanned, and the app offers a shopping budget feature, too. App-delivered coupons and specials will help entice buyers to stick with Walmart instead of rivals.[86] If Walmart can cut the number of cashiers, labor savings could be significant, too. Walmart spends about $12 million every second on cashier wages across its US stores.[87] As for paying by app, Walmart's ready to play nice with competitors, too. Walmart has partnered with over a dozen firms, including BestBuy, Target, Sears, and 7-Eleven, to plot a new pay-with-your-phone standard called MCX that will also provide a mechanism for offers, coupons, and loyalty programs.[88] The combined footprint of all these retail partners will help fuel the retailer side of the customer-retailer two-sided market necessary to jump start payments.

7.2 Data Mining Prowess

Walmart also mines its mother lode of data to get its product mix right under all sorts of varying environmental conditions, protecting the firm from "a retailer's twin nightmares: too much inventory, or not enough."[89] For example, the firm's data mining efforts informed buyers that customers stock up on certain products in the days leading up to predicted hurricanes. Bumping up prestorm supplies of batteries and bottled water was a no brainer, but the firm also learned that Pop-Tarts sales spike sevenfold before storms hit, and that beer is the top prestorm seller. This insight has led to truckloads full of six packs and toaster pastries streaming into gulf states whenever word of a big storm surfaces.[90]

Data mining also helps the firm tighten operational forecasts, helping to predict things like how many cashiers are needed at a given store at various times of day throughout the year. Data drives the organization, with mined reports forming the basis of weekly sales meetings, as well as executive strategy sessions.

Walmart leverages its huge Hadoop-based data trove to support some of its data mining efforts, sifting through massive amounts of social media—Twitter posts, Facebook updates, and other so-called unstructured data—to gain insights on product offerings, sales leads, pricing, and more. The firm purchased social start-up Kosmix for $300 million to deepen social and big data expertise in the company's @WalmartLabs.[91] Says Kosmix founder Anand Rajaraman (who previously sold a firm to Amazon and was an early investor in Facebook), "The first generation of e-commerce was about bringing the store to the Web. The next generation will be about building integrated experiences that leverage the store, the Web and mobile, with social identity being the glue that binds the experience."[92] The firm continues to hone tech chops and has aggressively established outposts in Silicon Valley. The firm's Global eCommerce unit is a 1,500-person operation headquartered across the street from Google's YouTube offices,[93] and Valley-based @WalmartLabs has grown from a slew of acquisitions, including social ad firm OneRiot, social commerce firm TastyLabs, predictive analytics firm Inkiru, and the cloud start-up OneOps.[94] The Arkansas giant's Valley offices host "hack days" in the best tradition of Facebook and other tech leaders, allowing developers to blue sky new ideas that may eventually be put into practice.

7.3 Sharing Data, Keeping Secrets

While Walmart is demanding of its suppliers, it also shares data with them, too. Data can help firms become more efficient so that Walmart can keep dropping prices, and data can help firms uncover patterns that help suppliers sell more. P&G's Gillette unit, for example, claims to have mined Walmart data to develop promotions that increased sales as much as 19 percent. More than seventeen thousand suppliers are given access to their products' Walmart performance across metrics that include daily sales, shipments, returns, purchase orders, invoices, claims, and forecasts. And these suppliers collectively interrogate Walmart data warehouses to the tune of twenty-one million queries a year.[95]

While Walmart shares sales data with relevant suppliers, the firm otherwise fiercely guards this asset. Many retailers pool their data by sharing it with information brokers like Information Resources and ACNielsen. This sharing allows smaller firms to pool their data to provide more comprehensive insight on market behavior. But Walmart stopped sharing data with these agencies years ago. The firm's scale is so big, the additional data provided by brokers wasn't adding much value, and it no longer made sense to allow competitors access to what was happening in its own huge chunk of retail sales.

Other aspects of the firm's technology remain under wraps, too. Walmart custom builds large portions of its information systems to keep competitors off its trail. As for infrastructure secrets, the Walmart Data Center in McDonald County, Missouri, was considered so off limits that the county assessor was required to sign a nondisclosure statement before being allowed on-site to estimate property value.[96]

7.4 Challenges Abound

But despite success, challenges continue. While Walmart grew dramatically throughout the 1990s, the firm's U.S. business has largely matured. And as a mature business it faces a problem not unlike the example of Microsoft discussed at the end of Chapter 18; Walmart needs to find huge markets or dramatic cost savings in order to boost profits and continue to move its stock price higher.

The firm's aggressiveness and sheer size also increasingly make Walmart a target for criticism. Those low prices come at a price, and the firm has faced accusations of subpar wages and remains a magnet for union activists. Others have identified poor labor conditions at some of the firm's contract manufacturers. Suppliers that compete for Walmart's business are often faced with a catch-22. If they bypass Walmart they miss out on the largest single chunk of world retail sales. But if they sell to

Walmart, the firm may demand prices so aggressively low that suppliers end up cannibalizing their own sales at other retailers. Still more criticism comes from local citizen groups that have accused Walmart of ruining the market for mom-and-pop stores.[97]

While some might see Walmart as invincibly standing at the summit of world retail, it's important to note that other megaretailers have fallen from grace. In the 1920s and 1930s, the A&P grocery chain once controlled 80 percent of US grocery sales, at its peak operating five times the number of stores that Walmart has today. But market conditions changed, and the government stepped in to draft anti-predatory pricing laws when it felt A&P's parent was too aggressive.

For all of Walmart's data brilliance, historical data offers little insight on how to adapt to more radical changes in the retail landscape. The firm's data warehouse wasn't able to foretell the rise of Target and other up-market discounters. Savvy managers recognize that data use is a vital tool, but not the only tool in management's strategic arsenal.

KEY TAKEAWAYS

- Walmart demonstrates how a physical product retailer can create and leverage a data asset to achieve world-class value chain efficiencies.
- Walmart uses data mining in numerous ways, from demand forecasting to predicting the number of cashiers needed at a store at a particular time.
- To help suppliers become more efficient, and as a result lower prices, Walmart shares data with them.
- Despite its success, Walmart is a mature business that needs to find huge markets or dramatic cost savings in order to boost profits and continue to move its stock price higher. The firm's success also makes it a high impact target for criticism and activism. And the firm's data assets could not predict impactful industry trends such as the rise of Target and other upscale discounters.

QUESTIONS AND EXERCISES

1. List the functions performed by Retail Link. What is its benefit to Walmart?
2. Which supplier metrics does Retail Link gather and report? How is this valuable to Walmart and suppliers?
3. Name the technology that Walmart requires partners to use to track and coordinate inventory. Do you know of other uses for this technology?
4. What steps has Walmart taken to protect its data from competitors?
5. List the criticisms leveled at Walmart. Do you think these critiques are valid or not? What can Walmart do to counteract this criticism? Should it take these steps? Why or why not?

ENDNOTES

1. C. Babcock, "Data, Data, Everywhere," *InformationWeek*, January 9, 2006.

2. L. Mearian, "Digital Universe and Its Impact Bigger than We Thought," *Computerworld*, March 18, 2008.

3. Derived by comparing Walmart's 2.5 petabytes (E. Lai, "Teradata Creates Elite Club for Petabyte-Plus Data Warehouse Customers," *Computerworld*, October 18, 2008) to the Library of Congress estimate of 20 TB (D. Gewirtz, "What If Someone Stole the Library of Congress?" *CNN.com/AC360*, May 25, 2009).

4. A. McAfee and E. Brynjolfsson, "Big Data: The Management Revolution" *Harvard Business Review*, October 2012.

5. T. Davenport and J. Harris, *Competing on Analytics: The New Science of Winning* (Boston: Harvard Business School Press, 2007).

6. C. Gayomali, "How Google's Robots Can Learn Like Humans," *FastCompany*, Feb. 11, 2014.

7. A. Lampitt, "The real story of how big data analytics helped Obama win," *InfoWorld*, Feb. 14, 2013.

8. S. Baker, "Math Will Rock Your World," *BusinessWeek*, January 23, 2006, http://www.businessweek.com/magazine/content/06_04/b3968001.htm.

9. J. Soat, "P&G's CIO Puts IT at Users' Service," *InformationWeek*, December 15, 2007.

10. Patrick Rishe, "Dynamic Pricing: The Future of Ticket Pricing in Sports," *Forbes*, January 6, 2012.

11. L. Gomes, "Data Analysis Is Creating New Business Opportunities," *MIT Technology Review*, May 2, 2011.

12. M. Gorman, "San Francisco Giants (and Most of MLB) Adopt Apple's iBeacon for an Enhanced Ballpark Experience," *Engadget*, March 28, 2014.

13. M. Gorman, "San Francisco Giants (and Most of MLB) Adopt Apple's iBeacon for an Enhanced Ballpark Experience," *Engadget*, March 28, 2014.

14. M. Harvey, "Probe into How Google Mix-Up Caused $1 Billion Run on United," *Times Online*, September 12, 2008, http://technology.timesonline.co.uk/tol/news/tech_and_web/article4742147.ece.

15. R. Braddock, "Lessons of Internet Marketing from FreshDirect," *Wall Street Journal*, May 11, 2009.

16. J. Zhang, "Recession Likely to Boost Government Outlays on Health Care," *Wall Street Journal*, February 24, 2009.

17. S. Milligan, "Business Warms to Democratic Leaders," *Boston Globe*, May 28, 2009.

18. R. Appleton, "Less Independent Doctors Could Mean More Medical Mistakes," *InjuryBoard.com*, June 14, 2009; and B. Obama, President's Speech to the American Medical Association, Chicago, IL, June 15, 2009, http://www.whitehouse.gov/the_press_office/Remarks-by-the-President-to-the-Annual-Conference-of-the-American-Medical-Association.

19. J. Halamka, "IT Spending: When Less Is More," *BusinessWeek*, March 2, 2009.

20. C. Boehret, "ResearchKit, Apple's Medical Data Experiment, Explained," *Re/code*, May 20, 2015.

21. R. King, "Intelligence Software for Business," *BusinessWeek* podcast, February 27, 2009.

22. R. King, "Intelligence Software for Business," *BusinessWeek* podcast, February 27, 2009.

23. A. Gefter and T. Simonite, "What the Data Miners Are Digging Up about You," *CNET*, December 1, 2008.

24. E. Dwoskin, "Data Broker Acxiom Moves to Tie Physical World to Online Data," *The Wall Street Journal*, May 14, 2014.

25. A. Greenberg, "Companies That Profit from Your Data," *Forbes*, May 14, 2008.

26. R. Mitchell, "Why You Should Be Worried about Your Privacy on the Web," *Computerworld*, May 11, 2009.

27. R. Swarns, "Senator? Terrorist? A Watch List Stops Kennedy at Airport," *New York Times*, August 20, 2004.

28. A. Greenberg, "Companies That Profit from Your Data," *Forbes*, May 14, 2008.

29. F. Rashid, "Epsilon Data Breach to Cost Billions in Worst-Case Scenario," *eWeek*, May 3, 2011.

30. M. Warman, "Google Warns against Facial Recognition Database," *Telegraph*, May 16, 2011.

31. N. Bilton, "Facebook Changes Privacy Settings to Enable Facial Recognition," *New York Times*, June 7, 2011.

32. A. Gefter and T. Simonite, "What the Data Miners Are Digging Up about You," *CNET*, December 1, 2008.

33. E. Mills, "Report: Social Security Numbers Can Be Predicted," *CNET*, July 6, 2009, http://news.cnet.com/8301-1009_3-10280614-83.html.

34. L. Spencer, "Australian data laws to mirror the UK, Germany: Fieldfisher," *ZDNet*, June 6, 2014.

35. R. King, "Business Intelligence Software's Time Is Now," *BusinessWeek*, March 2, 2009.

36. R. King, "Intelligence Software for Business," *BusinessWeek* podcast, February 27, 2009.

37. D. Rigby and D. Ledingham, "CRM Done Right," *Harvard Business Review*, November 2004; and R. King, "Intelligence Software for Business," *BusinessWeek* podcast, February 27, 2009.

38. H. Havenstein, "HP Nabs Walmart as Data Warehousing Customer," *Computerworld*, August 1, 2007.

39. Key points adapted from T. Davenport and J. Harris, *Competing on Analytics: The New Science of Winning* (Boston: Harvard Business School Press, 2007).

40. R. King, "Getting a Handle on Big Data with Hadoop," *BusinessWeek*, September 7, 2011.

41. A. McAfee and E. Brynjolfsson, "Big Data: The Management Revolution" *Harvard Business Review*, October 2012.

42. R. King, "Getting a Handle on Big Data with Hadoop," *BusinessWeek*, September 7, 2011.

43. IBM Big Data, "What Is Hadoop?" YouTube video, May 22, 2012, http://www.youtube.com/watch?v=RQr0qd8gxW8.

44. T. Groenfeldt, "Morgan Stanley Takes on Big Data with Hadoop," *Forbes*, May 30, 2012.

45. R. Boucher. "How Big Data Is Influencing Big Companies." *Sloan Management Review*, November 25, 2013.

46. N. Heudecker, "Gartner: Hype Cycle for Big Data, 2013," *Gartner*, July 31, 2103

47. J. Bughin, M. Chui, and J. Manyika, "Ten IT- Enabled Business Trends for the Decade Ahead," *McKinsey Quarterly*, May 2013.

48. S. Buhr, "Apple Launches Beats1, A 24/7 Worldwide Radio Station," *TechCrunch*, June 8, 2015.

49. S. Ransbotham, "Analytics in E Major," *Sloan Management Review*, Feb. 24, 2015.

50. S. Ransbotham, "Analytics in E Major," *Sloan Management Review*, Feb. 24, 2015.

51. C. Wilkinson, "How Pandora's Music Genome Could Fail Against the Likes of Apple," *TheStreet.com*, Oct. 7, 2013.

52. Spotify Information accessed on June 22, 2015 at: https://press.spotify.com/no/information/

53. J. Constine, "Inside The Spotify – Echo Nest Skunkworks," *TechCrunch*, Oct. 19, 2014.

54. S. Ransbotham, "Analytics in E Major," *Sloan Management Review*, Feb. 24, 2015.

55. S. Ransbotham, "Analytics in E Major," *Sloan Management Review*, Feb. 24, 2015.

56. T. Ricker, "First Click: Spotify Running is a surprisingly great music discovery tool," *The Verge*, June 1, 2015.

57. A. Conry-Murray, "The Pain of E-discovery," *InformationWeek*, June 1, 2009.

58. S. Lohr, "Reaping Results: Data-Mining Goes Mainstream," *New York Times*, May 20, 2007.

59. R. Mulcahy, "ABC: An Introduction to Business Intelligence," *CIO*, March 6, 2007.

60. V. Heffernan, "Big Moose is Watching You," Medium, Oct. 31, 2014. V. Heffernan, "Big Moose is Watching You," *Medium*, Oct. 31, 2014.

61. C. Wilson and D. Bryan, Talk: "Transitioning from Original Big Data to the New Big Data: L.L.Bean's Journey," at Strata+Hadoop World, Oct. 15-17, 2014, New York, NY.

62. V. Heffernan, "Big Moose is Watching You," Medium, Oct. 31, 2014. V. Heffernan, "Big Moose is Watching You," *Medium*, Oct. 31, 2014.

63. M. Wilson, "Survey: LLBean.com tops in customer satisfaction among online apparel retailers," ChainStorage (citing J.D. Power and Associates 2012 Online Apparel Retailer Satisfaction Report), Nov. 21, 2012. M. Wilson, "Survey: LLBean.com tops in customer satisfaction among online apparel retailers," ChainStorage (citing J.D. Power and Associates 2012 Online Apparel Retailer Satisfaction Report), Nov. 21, 2012. M. Wilson, "Survey: LLBean.com tops in customer satisfaction among online apparel retailers," ChainStorage (citing J.D. Power and Associates 2012 Online Apparel Retailer Satisfaction Report), Nov. 21, 2012.

64. S. Hansell, "How Wall Street Lied to Its Computers," *New York Times*, September 18, 2008.

65. P. Wahba, "Buffeted 'Quants' Are Still in Demand," *Reuters*, December 22, 2008.

66. Sourced from the Spurious Correlations website, http://www.tylervigen.com, accessed June 4, 2014.

67. J. Stromberg, "Why Google Flu Trends Can't Track the Flu (Yet)," *Smithsonian Magazine*, March 13, 2014. Read more: http://www.smithsonianmag.com/science-nature/why-google-flu-trends-cant-track-flu-yet-180950076/#SOJo2ITpGseqKVch.99 Give the gift of Smithsonian magazine for only $12! http://bit.ly/1cGUiGv Follow us: @SmithsonianMag on Twitter

68. B. Helm, "Getting Inside the Customer's Mind," *BusinessWeek*, September 11, 2008.

69. R. Hof, "Meet the Guy Who Helped Google Beat Apple's Siri," *Forbes*, May 1, 2013.

70. Adapted from J. Kahn, "It's Alive," *Wired*, March 2002; O. Port, "Thinking Machines," *BusinessWeek*, August 7, 2000; and L. McKay, "Decisions, Decisions," *CRM Magazine*, May 1, 2004.

71. C. Gayomali, "How Google's Robots Can Learn Like Humans," *FastCompany*, Feb. 11, 2014.

72. B. Wallace-Wells, "Boyhood (on IBM's Watson)," *New York Magazine*, May 20, 2015.

73. S. Podolny, "If an Algorithm Wrote This, How Would You Even Know?" *The New York Times*, March 7, 2015.

74. S. Lohr, "In Case You Wondered, a Real Human Wrote This Column," *The New York Times*, Sept. 10, 2011.

75. S. Podolny, "If an Algorithm Wrote This, How Would You Even Know?" *The New York Times*, March 7, 2015.

76. W. Oremus, "In Artificial Intelligence Breakthrough, Google Computers Teach Themselves To Spot Cats on YouTube," *Slate*, June 27, 2012.

77. T. Simonite, "Google's Brain-Inspired Software Describes What It Sees in Complex Images," *MIT Technology Review*, Nov. 18, 2014.

78. H. Hodson, "Supercomputers make discoveries that scientists can't," *New Scientist*, Aug. 27, 2014.

79. S. Kohli, "Bill Gates joins Elon Musk and Stephen Hawking in saying artificial intelligence is scary," *Quartz*, Jan. 29, 2015.

80. From 2006 through 2009, Walmart has appeared as either number one or number two in the *Fortune* 100 rankings.

81. C. Fishman, "The Walmart You Don't Know," *Fast Company*, December 19, 2007.

82. T. Friscia, K. O'Marah, D. Hofman, and J. Souza, "The AMR Research Supply Chain Top 25 for 2009," *AMR Research*, May 28, 2009, http://www.amrresearch.com/Content/View.aspx?compURI=tcm:7-43469.

83. Twelve-month figures from midyear 2009, via *Forbes* and Reuters.

84. C. Fishman, "The Walmart You Don't Know," *Fast Company*, December 19, 2007.

85. D. Joseph, "Supermarket Strategies: What's New at the Grocer," *BusinessWeek*, June 8, 2009.

86. M. Isaac, "Taking Cues from Silicon Valley, Walmart Brings the Shotgun Approach to E-Commerce," *AllThingsD*, March 27, 2013.

87. D. Dorf, "Walmart's Mobile Self-Checking," *Oracle Corporation Insight-Driven Retailing Blog*, September 11, 2012.

88. R. Kim, "Target, Walmart, and Co.: Why Leave Mobile Payments to Others?" *GigaOM*, August 15, 2012.

89. C. Hays, "What Walmart Knows about Customer Habits," *New York Times*, November 14, 2004.

90. C. Hays, "What Walmart Knows about Customer Habits," *New York Times*, November 14, 2004.

91. R. King, "Getting a Handle on Big Data with Hadoop," *BusinessWeek*, September 7, 2011.

92. C. Nicholson, "Walmart Buys Social Media Firm Kosmix," *New York Times*, April 19, 2011.

93. M. Isaac, "Taking Cues from Silicon Valley, Walmart Brings the Shotgun Approach to E-Commerce," *AllThingsD*, March 27, 2013.

94. D. Harris, "Walmart Keeps Getting Smarter with Inkiru Acquisition," *GigaOM*, June 10, 2013.

95. K. Evans-Correia, "Dillman Replaced as Walmart CIO," *SearchCIO*, April 6, 2006.

96. M. McCoy, "Walmart's Data Center Remains Mystery," *Joplin Globe*, May 28, 2006.

97. C. Fishman, "The Walmart You Don't Know," *Fast Company*, December 19, 2007.

CHAPTER 16
A Manager's Guide to the Internet and Telecommunications

1. INTRODUCTION

There's all sorts of hidden magic happening whenever you connect to the Internet. But what really makes it possible for you to reach servers halfway around the world in just a fraction of a second? Knowing this is not only flat-out fascinating stuff; it's also critically important for today's manager to have at least a working knowledge of how the Internet functions.

That's because the Internet is a platform of possibilities and a business enabler. Understanding how the Internet and networking works can help you brainstorm new products and services and understand roadblocks that might limit turning your ideas into reality. Marketing professionals who know how the Internet reaches consumers have a better understanding of how technologies can be used to find and target customers. Finance firms that rely on trading speed to move billions in the blink of an eye need to master Internet infrastructure to avoid being swept aside by more nimble market movers. And knowing how the Internet works helps all managers understand where their firms are vulnerable. In most industries today, if your network goes down then you might as well shut your doors and go home; it's nearly impossible to get anything done if you can't get online. Managers who know the Net are prepared to take the appropriate steps to secure their firms and keep their organization constantly connected.

2. INTERNET 101: UNDERSTANDING HOW THE INTERNET WORKS

LEARNING OBJECTIVES

1. Describe how the technologies of the Internet combine to answer these questions: What are you looking for? Where is it? And how do we get there?
2. Interpret a URL, understand what hosts and domains are, describe how domain registration works, describe cybersquatting, and give examples of conditions that constitute a valid and invalid domain-related trademark dispute.
3. Describe certain aspects of the Internet infrastructure that are fault-tolerant and support load balancing.
4. Discuss the role of hosts, domains, IP addresses, and the DNS in making the Internet work.

The Internet is a network of networks—millions of them, actually. If the network at your university, your employer, or in your home has Internet access, it connects to an **Internet service provider (ISP)**. Many (but not all) ISPs are big telecommunications companies like Verizon, Comcast, and AT&T. These providers connect to one another, exchanging traffic, and ensuring your messages can get to any other computer that's online and willing to communicate with you.

The Internet has no center and no one owns it. That's a good thing. The Internet was designed to be redundant and fault-tolerant—meaning that if one network, connecting wire, or server stops working, everything else should keep on running. Rising from military research and work at educational

Internet service provider (ISP)

An organization or firm that provides access to the Internet.

institutions dating as far back as the 1960s, the Internet really took off in the 1990s, when graphical Web browsing was invented, and much of the Internet's operating infrastructure was transitioned to be supported by private firms rather than government grants.

FIGURE 16.1

The Internet is a network of networks, and these networks are connected together. In the diagram above, the "state.edu" campus network is connected to other networks of the Internet via two ISPs: Cogent and Verizon.

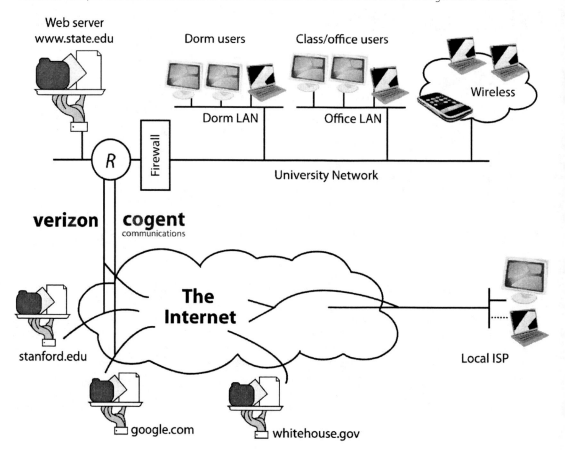

Enough history—let's see how it all works! If you want to communicate with another computer on the Internet, your computer needs to know the answer to three questions: What are you looking for? Where is it? And how do we get there? The computers and software that make up Internet infrastructure can help provide the answers.

2.1 The URL: "What Are You Looking For?"

When you type an address into a Web browser (sometimes called a **URL** for *uniform resource locator*), you're telling your browser what you're looking for. Figure 16.2 describes how to read a typical URL.

URL (uniform resource locator)

Often used interchangeably with "Web address," URLs identify resources on the Internet along with the application protocol need to retrieve it.

FIGURE 16.2   Anatomy of a Web Address

The URL displayed really says, "Use the Web (http://) to find a host server named 'www' in the 'nytimes.com' network, look in the 'tech' directory, and access the 'index.html' file."

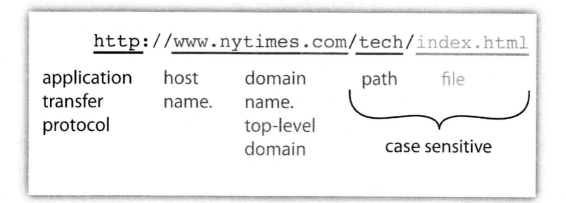

The http:// you see at the start of most Web addresses stands for **hypertext transfer protocol**. A **protocol** is a set of rules for communication—sort of like grammar and vocabulary in a language like English. The http protocol defines how Web browser and Web servers communicate and is designed to be independent from the computer's hardware and operating system. It doesn't matter if messages come from a PC, a Mac, a huge mainframe, or a pocket-sized smartphone; if a device speaks to another using a common protocol, then it will be heard and understood.

The Internet supports lots of different applications, and many of these applications use their own application transfer protocol to communicate with each other. The server that holds your e-mail uses something called *SMTP*, or simple mail transfer protocol, to exchange mail with other e-mail servers throughout the world. **FTP**, or file transfer protocol, is used for—you guessed it—file transfer. FTP is how most Web developers upload the Web pages, graphics, and other files for their Web sites. Even the Web uses different protocols. When you surf to an online bank or when you're ready to enter your payment information at the Web site of an Internet retailer, the http at the beginning of your URL will probably change to https (the "s" is for secure). That means that communications between your browser and server will be encrypted for safe transmission. The beauty of the Internet infrastructure is that any savvy entrepreneur can create a new application that rides on top of the Internet.

Hosts and Domain Names

The next part of the URL in our diagram holds the host and domain name. Think of the domain name as the name of the network you're trying to connect to, and think of the host as the computer you're looking for on that network.

Many domains have lots of different hosts. For example, Yahoo!'s main website is served from the host named "www" (at the address http://www.yahoo.com), but Yahoo! also runs other hosts including those named "finance" (finance.yahoo.com), "sports" (sports.yahoo.com), and "games" (games.yahoo.com).

Host and Domain Names: A Bit More Complex Than That

While it's useful to think of a host as a single computer, popular Web sites often have several computers that work together to share the load for incoming requests. Assigning several computers to a host name offers **load balancing** and **fault tolerance**, helping ensure that all visits to a popular site like http://www.google.com won't overload a single computer, or that Google doesn't go down if one computer fails.

It's also possible for a single computer to have several host names. This might be the case if a firm were hosting several Web sites on a single piece of computing hardware.

Some domains are also further broken down into subdomains—many times to represent smaller networks or subgroups within a larger organization. For example, the address http://www.rhsmith.umd.edu is a University of Maryland address with a host "www" located in the subdomain "rhsmith" for the Robert H. Smith School of Business. International URLs might also include a second-level domain classification scheme. British URLs use

---

hypertext transfer protocol (http)

Application transfer protocol that allows Web browsers and Web servers to communicate with each other.

protocol

Enables communication by defining the format of data and rules for exchange.

file transfer protocol (FTP)

Application transfer protocol that is used to copy files from one computer to another.

load balancing

Distributing a computing or networking workload across multiple systems to avoid congestion and slow performance.

fault tolerance

The ability of a system to continue operation even if a component fails.

this scheme, for example, with the BBC carrying the commercial (.co) designation—http://www.bbc.co.uk—and the University of Oxford carrying the academic (.ac) designation—http://www.ox.ac.uk. You can actually go 127 levels deep in assigning subdomains, but that wouldn't make it easy on those who have to type in a URL that long.

Most Web sites are configured to load a default host, so you can often eliminate the host name if you want to go to the most popular host on a site (the default host is almost always named "www"). Another tip: most browsers will automatically add the "http://" for you, too.

Host and domain names are not case sensitive, so you can use a combination of upper and lower case letters and you'll still get to your destination.

I Want My Own Domain

Web hosting services

A firm that provides hardware and services to run the Web sites of others.

ICANN (Internet Corporation for Assigning Names and Numbers)

Nonprofit organization responsible for managing the Internet's domain and numbering systems.

cybersquatting

Acquiring a domain name that refers to a firm, individual, product, or trademark, with the goal of exploiting it for financial gain. The practice is illegal in many nations, and ICANN has a dispute resolution mechanism that in some circumstances can strip cybersquatters of registered domains.

You can stake your domain name claim in cyberspace by going through a firm called a *domain name registrar*. You don't really buy a domain name; you simply pay a registrar for the right to use that name, with the right renewable over time. While some registrars simply register domain names, others act as **Web hosting services** that are able to run your Web site on their Internet-connected servers for a fee.

Registrars throughout the world are accredited by **ICANN (Internet Corporation for Assigning Names and Numbers)**, a nonprofit governance and standards-setting body. Each registrar may be granted the ability to register domain names in one or more of the Net's generic top-level domains (gTLDs), such as ".com," ".net," or ".org." There are dozens of registrars that can register ".com" domain names, the most popular gTLD.

Some generic top-level domain names, like ".com," have no restrictions on use, while others limit registration. For example, ".edu" is restricted to US-accredited, postsecondary institutions. In a relatively recent development, ICANN has begun to allow organizations to propose and secure new top-level domains (e.g., gTLDs like ".berlin," or ".guru").[1] While for many securing new gTLDs intend to run domain registrars (so shop owners in Berlin can register their names with a ".berlin" suffix), some of the most active firms bidding on new gTLDs are large corporations looking to secure gTLDs for their own trademarks. Google, for example, has applied to secure gTLDs on Google, YouTube, Gmail, Chrome, and Android,[2] and Amazon paid over $4.5 million for ".buy".[3] While unregistered domains ending in .com can be secured for less than $15 a year, the cost to secure a gTLD starts at $185,000.[4] gTLDs are being introduced on a rolling basis, and the European Domain Centre offers a nifty interactive map (at http://blog.europeandomaincentre.com/infographics-launch-dates-for-the-617-new-gtlds/) for those wondering when specific gtlds are (or have been) up for auction.[5]

There are also separate agencies that handle over 250 different two-character country code top-level domains, or ccTLDs (e.g., ".uk" for the United Kingdom, ".ca" for Canada, and ".jp" for Japan). Servers or organizations generally don't need to be housed within a country to use a country code as part of their domain names, leading to a number of creatively named websites. The URL-shortening site "bit.ly" uses Libya's ".ly" top-level domain; many physicians are partial to Moldova's code (".md"); and the tiny Pacific island nation of Tuvalu might not have a single broadcast television station, but that doesn't stop it from licensing its country code to firms that want a ".tv" domain name.[6] Standards also allow domain names in languages that use non-Latin alphabets such as Arabic, Chinese, and Russian.

Domain name registration is handled on a first-come, first-served basis and all registrars share registration data to ensure that no two firms gain rights to the same name. Start-ups often sport wacky names, partly because so many domains with common words and phrases are already registered to others. While some domain names are held by legitimate businesses, others are registered by investors hoping to resell a name's rights.

Trade in domain names can be lucrative. For example, the "Insure.com" domain was sold to QuinStreet for $16 million.[7] But knowingly registering a domain name to profit from someone else's firm name or trademark is known as **cybersquatting** and that's illegal. The United States has passed the Anticybersquatting Consumer Protection Act (ACPA), and ICANN has the Domain Name Dispute Resolution Policy that can reach across borders. Try to extort money by holding a domain name that's identical to (or in some cases, even similar to) a well-known trademark holder, and you could be stripped of your domain name and even fined.

Courts and dispute resolution authorities will sometimes allow a domain that uses the trademark of another organization if it is perceived to have legitimate, nonexploitive reasons for doing so. For example, the now defunct site Verizonreallysucks.com was registered as a protest against the networking giant and was considered fair use since owners didn't try to extort money from the telecom giant.[8] However, the courts allowed the owner of the PETA trademark (the organization People for the Ethical Treatment of Animals) to claim the domain name peta.org from original registrant, who had been using that domain to host a site called "People Eating Tasty Animals."[9] Amazon's application to obtain the ".amazon" gTLD was rejected by ICANN. Several South American countries objected, claiming the word amazon was one of the region's important geographic names.[10]

Trying to predict how authorities will rule can be difficult. The musician Sting's name was thought to be too generic to deserve the rights to Sting.com, but Madonna was able to take back her domain name (for the record, Sting now owns Sting.com).[11] Apple executive Jonathan Ive was denied the right to reclaim domain names incorporating his own name, but that had been registered by another party and without his consent. The publicity-shy design guru wasn't considered enough of a public figure to warrant protection.[12] And sometimes disputing parties can come to an agreement outside of court or ICANN's dispute resolution mechanisms. When Canadian teenager Michael Rowe registered a site for his part-time Web design business, a firm south of the border took notice of his domain name—Mikerowesoft.com. The two parties eventually settled in a deal that swapped the domain for an Xbox and a trip to the Microsoft Research Tech Fest.[13] The issue of cybersquatting has caused many to be critical of new gTLDs, worrying that more suffixes will prompt organizations to spend big to secure scores of domain names simply to stop them being abused. To help mitigate some cybersquatting on the new gTLDs, ICANN requires operators of new gTLDs to offer a thirty-day "sunrise period" during which trademark holders could register trademark names in a new gTLD before they are offered for public sale.[14]

Path Name and File Name

Look to the right of the top-level domain and you might see a slash followed by either a path name, a file name, or both. If a Web address has a path and file name, the path maps to a folder location where the file is stored on the server; the file is the name of the file you're looking for.

Most Web pages end in ".html," indicating they are in **hypertext markup language**. While http helps browsers and servers communicate, html is the language used to create and format (render) Web pages. A file, however, doesn't need to be .html; Web servers can deliver just about any type of file: Acrobat documents (.pdf), PowerPoint documents (.ppt or .pptx), Word docs (.doc or .docx), JPEG graphic images (.jpg), and—as we'll see in Chapter 17—even malware programs that attack your PC. At some Web addresses, the file displays content for every visitor, and at others (like amazon.com), a file will contain programs that run on the Web server to generate custom content just for you.

You don't always type a path or file name as part of a Web address, but there's always a file lurking behind the scenes. A Web address without a file name will load content from a default page. For example, when you visit "google.com," Google automatically pulls up a page called "index.html," a file that contains the Web page that displays the Google logo, the text entry field, the "Google Search" button, and so on. You might not see it, but it's there.

Butterfingers, beware! Path and file names are case sensitive—amazon.com/books is considered to be different from amazon.com/BOOKS. Mistype your capital letters after the domain name and you might get a 404 error (the very unfriendly Web server error code that means the document was not found).

hypertext markup language (HTML)

Language used to compose Web pages.

2.2   IP Addresses and the Domain Name System: "Where Is It? And How Do We Get There?"

The IP Address

If you want to communicate, then you need to have a way for people to find and reach you. Houses and businesses have street addresses, and telephones have phone numbers. Every device connected to the Internet has an identifying address, too—it's called an *IP (Internet protocol) address*.

A device gets its **IP address** from whichever organization is currently connecting it to the Internet. Connect using a laptop at your university and your school will assign the laptop's IP address. Connect at a hotel, and the hotel's Internet service provider lends your laptop an IP address. Laptops and other end-user machines might get a different IP address each time they connect, but the IP addresses of servers rarely change. It's OK if you use different IP addresses during different online sessions because services like e-mail and Facebook identify you by your username and password. The IP address simply tells the computers that you're communicating with where they can find you right now. IP addresses can also be used to identify a user's physical location, to tailor search results, and to customize advertising. See Chapter 18 to learn more.

The original and still widely used format for IP addresses is known as IPv4. Under IPv4, IP addresses are expressed as a string of four numbers between 0 and 255, separated by three periods. Want

IP address

A value used to identify a device that is connected to the Internet. IP addresses are usually expressed as four numbers (from 0 to 255), separated by periods.

to know which IP address your smartphone or computer is using? Simply Google the phrase "what is my ip."

The Internet Is Full—We've Run Out of IP Addresses

If you do the math, four combinations of 0 to 255 gives you a little over four billion possible IP addresses. Four billion sounds like a lot, but the number of devices connecting to the Internet is exploding! Internet access is now baked into smartphones, tablets, televisions, DVD players, video game consoles, utility meters, thermostats, appliances, picture frames, and more. Another problem is a big chunk of existing addresses weren't allocated efficiently, and these can't be easily reclaimed from the corporations, universities, and other organizations that initially received them. All of this means that we've run out of IP addresses. In February 2011 the last batches were made available to regional Internet registries, and the last IPv4 addresses were predicted to be handed out by the summer of 2015. Some firms are buying IP addresses from firms with excess capacity. Microsoft alone has spent millions buying addresses from firms that include Xerox, Eli Lilly, and the bankrupt firm Nortel.[15]

There are some schemes to help delay the impact of this IP address drought. For example, a technique known as **NAT (network address translation)** uses a gateway that allows multiple devices to share a single IP address. But NAT slows down Internet access and is complex, cumbersome, and expensive to administer.[16]

The only long-term solution is to shift to a new IP scheme. Fortunately, one was developed more than a decade ago. IPv6 increases the possible address space from the 2^{32} (4,294,967,296) addresses used in the current system (called IPv4) to a new theoretical limit of 2^{128} addresses, which is a really big number—bigger than thirty-four with thirty-seven zeros after it. That's enough for every gram of matter on the earth to have its own IPv6 address.[17]

But not all the news is good. Unfortunately, IPv6 isn't backward compatible with IPv4, and the transition to the new standard has been painfully slow (for a look at the current rate of IPv6 adoption, see the country by country figures at http://www.stateoftheinternet.com/trends-visualizations-ipv6-adoption-ipv4-exhaustion-global-heat-map-network-country-growth-data.html). This gives us the equivalent of many islands of IPv6 in a sea of IPv4, with translation between the two schemes happening when these networks come together. Others consider it the equivalent of two Internets with a translation bridge between IPv4 and IPv6 (and that bridge introduces a delay).[18] While most modern hardware and operating systems providers now support IPv6, converting a network to IPv6 currently involves a lot of cost with little short-term benefit.[19] Upgrading may take years.[20]

Some organizations have stepped up to try to hasten the transition. Facebook, Google, Microsoft, Yahoo!, and some of the Internet's largest networks have made most of its services IPv6 accessible, the US government has mandated IPv6 support for most agencies, China has spurred conversion within its borders, and Comcast and Verizon have major IPv6 rollouts under way. While the transition will be slow, when wide scale deployment does arrive, IPv6 will offer other benefits, including potentially improving the speed, reliability, and security of the Internet.

The DNS: The Internet's Phonebook

You can actually type an IP address of a website into a Web browser and that page will show up. But that doesn't help users much because four sets of numbers are really hard to remember.

This is where the **domain name service (DNS)** comes in. The domain name service is a distributed database that looks up the host and domain names that you enter and returns the actual IP address for the computer that you want to communicate with. It's like a big, hierarchical set of phone books capable of finding Web servers, e-mail servers, and more. These "phone books" are called *nameservers*—and when they work together to create the DNS, they can get you anywhere you need to go online.

NAT (network address translation)

A technique often used to conserve IP addresses by maps devices on a private network to single Internet-connected device that acts on their behalf.

---

domain name service (DNS)

Internet directory service that allows devices and services to be named and discoverable. The DNS, for example, helps your browser locate the appropriate computers when entering an address like http://finance.google.com.

FIGURE 16.3

When your computer needs to find the IP address for a host or domain name, it sends a message to a DNS resolver, which looks up the IP address starting at the root nameserver. Once the lookup has taken place, that IP address can be saved in a holding space called a cache, to speed future lookups.

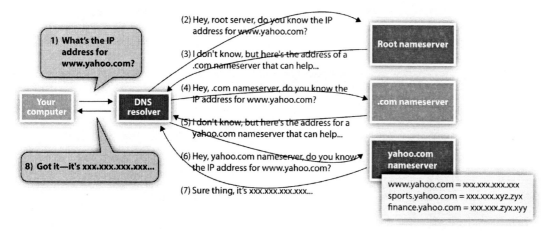

To get a sense of how the DNS works, let's imagine that you type www.yahoo.com into a Web browser. Your computer doesn't know where to find that address, but when your computer connected to the network, it learned where to find a service on the network called a DNS resolver. The DNS resolver can look up host/domain name combinations to find the matching IP address using the "phone book" that is the DNS. The resolver doesn't know everything, but it does know where to start a lookup that will eventually give you the address you're looking for. If this is the first time anyone on that network has tried to find "www.yahoo.com," the resolver will contact one of thirteen identical root nameservers. The root acts as a lookup starting place. It doesn't have one big list, but it can point you to a nameserver for the next level, which would be one of the ".com" nameservers in our example. The ".com" nameserver can then find one of the yahoo.com nameservers. The yahoo.com nameserver can respond to the resolver with the IP address for www.yahoo.com, and the resolver passes that information back to your computer. Once your computer knows Yahoo!'s IP address, it's then ready to communicate directly with www.yahoo.com. The yahoo.com nameserver includes IP addresses for all Yahoo!'s public sites: www.yahoo.com, games.yahoo.com, sports.yahoo.com, finance.yahoo.com, and so on.

The system also remembers what it's done so the next time you need the IP address of a host you've already looked up, your computer can pull this out of a storage space called a **cache**, avoiding all those nameserver visits. Caches are periodically cleared and refreshed to ensure that data referenced via the DNS stays accurate.

Distributing IP address lookups this way makes sense. It avoids having one huge, hard-to-maintain, and ever-changing list. Firms add and remove hosts on their own networks just by updating entries in their nameserver. And it allows host IP addresses to change easily, too. Moving your Web server off-site to a hosting provider? Just update your nameserver with the new IP address at the hosting provider, and the world will invisibly find that new IP address on the new network by using the same old, familiar host/domain name combination. The DNS is also fault-tolerant—meaning that if one nameserver goes down, the rest of the service can function. There are exact copies at each level, and the system is smart enough to move on to another nameserver if its first choice isn't responding.

cache

A temporary storage space used to speed computing tasks.

But What If the DNS Gets Hacked?

A hacked DNS would be a disaster! Think about it. If bad guys could change which websites load when you type in a host and domain name, they could redirect you to impostor Web sites that look like a bank or e-commerce retailer but are really set up to harvest passwords and credit card data.

This exact scenario played out when the DNS of NET Virtua, a Brazilian Internet service provider, was hacked via a technique called *DNS cache poisoning*. Cache poisoning exploits a hole in DNS software, redirecting users to sites they didn't request. The Brazilian DNS hack redirected NET Virtua users wishing to visit the Brazilian bank Bradesco to fraudulent websites that attempted to steal passwords and install malware. The hack impacted about 1 percent of the bank's customers before the attack was discovered.[21]

The exploit showed the importance of paying attention to security updates. A few months earlier, a group that *Wired* magazine referred to as "A Secret Geek A-Team"[22] had developed a software update that would have prevented the DNS poisoning exploit used against NET Virtua, but administrators at the Brazilian Internet service provider failed to update their software so the hackers got in. An additional upgrade to a DNS system, known as DNSSEC (domain name service security extensions), promises to further limit the likelihood of cache poisoning, but it may take years for the new standards to be rolled out everywhere.[23]

KEY TAKEAWAYS

- The Internet is a network of networks. Internet service providers connect with one another to share traffic, enabling any Internet-connected device to communicate with any other.
- URLs may list the application protocol, host name, domain name, path name, and file name, in that order. Path and file names are case sensitive.
- A domain name represents an organization. Hosts are public services offered by that organization. Hosts are often thought of as a single computer, although many computers can operate under a single host name and many hosts can also be run off a single computer.
- You don't buy a domain name but can register it, paying for a renewable right to use that domain name. Domains need to be registered within a generic top-level domain such as ".com" or ".org" or within a two-character country code top-level domain such as ".uk," ".ly," or ".md." ICANN (Internet Corporation for Assigned Names and Numbers) has allowed the expansion of gTLDs to new names and even trademarks.
- Registering a domain that uses someone else's trademark in an attempt to extract financial gain is considered cybersquatting. The United States and other nations have anticybersquatting laws, and ICANN has a dispute resolution system that can overturn domain name claims if a registrant is considered to be cybersquatting.
- Every device connected to the Internet has an IP address. These addresses are assigned by the organization that connects the user to the Internet. An IP address may be assigned temporarily, for use only during that online session.
- We're running out of IP addresses. The current scheme (IPv4) is being replaced by IPv6, a scheme that will give us many more addresses and additional feature benefits but is not backward compatible with the IPv4 standard. Transitioning to IPv6 will be costly, take time, and introduce delay when traffic transfers between IPv4 and IPv6 networks.
- The domain name system is a distributed, fault-tolerant system that uses nameservers to map host/domain name combinations to IP addresses.

QUESTIONS AND EXERCISES

1. Find the Web page for your school's information systems department. What is the URL that gets you to this page? Label the host name, domain name, path, and file for this URL. Are there additional subdomains? If so, indicate them, as well.
2. Go to a registrar and see if someone has registered your first or last name as a domain name. If so, what's hosted at that domain? If not, would you consider registering your name as a domain name? Why or why not?
3. Investigate cases of domain name disputes. Examine a case that you find especially interesting. Who were the parties involved? How was the issue resolved? Do you agree with the decision?
4. Describe how the DNS is fault-tolerant and promotes load balancing. Give examples of other types of information systems that might need to be fault-tolerant and offer load balancing. Why?
5. Research DNS poisoning online. List a case, other than the one mentioned in this chapter, where DNS poisoning took place. Which network was poisoned, who were the victims, and how did hackers exploit the poisoned system? Could this exploit have been stopped? How? Whose responsibility is it to stop these kinds of attacks?
6. Why is the switch from IPv4 to IPv6 so difficult? What key principles, discussed in prior chapters, are slowing migration to the new standard?
7. Test to see if networks that you frequently use (home, school, work, mobile) are ready for IPv6 by visiting http://test-ipv6.com/ (or a similar site). Search online to see if your service provider has posted details outlining their IPv6 transition strategy and be prepared to share your results with the class. Do you use other products not tested by the website mentioned above (e.g., network-enabled video games or other software)? Search online to see if your favorite products and services are IPv6 ready.

3.   GETTING WHERE YOU'RE GOING

LEARNING OBJECTIVES

1. Understand the layers that make up the Internet—application protocol, transmission control protocol, and Internet protocol—and describe why each is important.
2. Discuss the benefits of Internet architecture in general and TCP/IP in particular.
3. Name applications that should use TCP and others that might use UDP.
4. Understand what a router does and the role these devices play in networking.
5. Conduct a traceroute and discuss the output, demonstrating how Internet interconnections work in getting messages from point to point.
6. Understand why mastery of Internet infrastructure is critical to modern finance and be able to discuss the risks in automated trading systems.
7. Describe VoIP, and contrast circuit versus packet switching, along with organizational benefits and limitations of each.

3.1   TCP/IP: The Internet's Secret Sauce

OK, we know how to read a Web address, we know that every device connected to the Net needs an IP address, and we know that the DNS can look at a Web address and find the IP address of the machine that you want to communicate with. But how does a Web page, an e-mail, or an app download actually get from a remote computer to your device?

For our next part of the Internet journey, we'll learn about two additional protocols: TCP and IP. These protocols are often written as TCP/IP and pronounced by reading all five letters in a row, "T-C-P-I-P" (sometimes they're also referred to as the *Internet protocol suite*). TCP and IP are built into any device that a user would use to connect to the Internet—from handhelds to desktops to supercomputers—and together TCP/IP make Internet working happen.

FIGURE 16.4 TCP/IP in Action

In this example, a server on the left sends a Web page to the user on the right. The application (the Web server) passes the contents of the page to TCP (which is built into the server's operating system). TCP slices the Web page into packets. Then IP takes over, forwarding packets from router to router across the Internet until it arrives at the user's PC. Packets sometimes take different routes, and occasionally arrive out of order. TCP running on the receiving system on the right checks that all packets have arrived, requests that damaged or lost packets be resent, puts them in the right order, and sends a perfect, exact copy of the Web page to your browser.

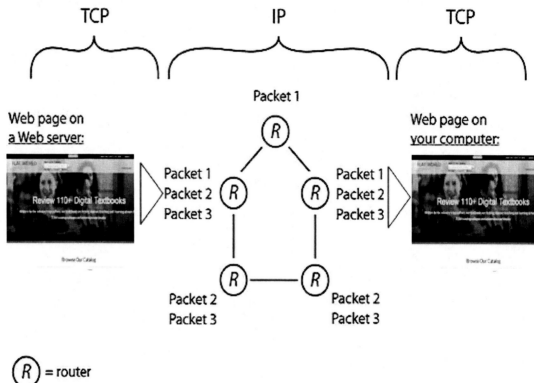

 = router

TCP (transmission control protocol)

Works at both ends of most Internet communication to ensure a perfect copy of a message is sent.

packet (or datagram)

A unit of data forwarded by a network. All Internet transmissions—URLs, Web pages, e-mails—are divided into one or more packets.

IP (Internet protocol)

Routing protocol that is in charge of forwarding packets on the Internet.

router

A computing device that connects networks and exchanges data between them.

TCP and IP operate below http and the other application transfer protocols mentioned earlier. **TCP (transmission control protocol)** works its magic at the start and endpoint of the trip—on both your computer and on the destination computer you're communicating with. Let's say a Web server wants to send you a large Web page. The Web server application hands the Web page it wants to send to its own version of TCP. TCP then slices up the Web page into smaller chunks of data called **packets (or datagrams)**. The packets are like little envelopes containing part of the entire transmission—they're labeled with a destination address (where it's going) and a source address (where it came from). Now we'll leave TCP for a second, because TCP on the Web server then hands those packets off to the second half of our dynamic duo, IP.

It's the job of **IP (Internet protocol)** to route the packets to their final destination, and those packets might have to travel over several networks to get to where they're going. The relay work is done via special computers called **routers**, and these routers speak to each other and to other computers using IP (since routers are connected to the Internet, they have IP addresses, too. Some are even named). Every computer on the Internet is connected to a router, and all routers are connected to at least one (and usually more than one) other router, linking up the networks that make up the Internet.

Routers don't have perfect, end-to-end information on all points in the Internet, but they do talk to each other all the time, so a router has a pretty good idea of where to send a packet to get it closer to where it needs to end up. This chatter between the routers also keeps the Internet decentralized and fault-tolerant. Even if one path out of a router goes down (a networking cable gets cut, a router breaks, the power to a router goes out), as long as there's another connection out of that router, then your packet will get forwarded. Networks fail, so good, fault-tolerant network design involves having alternate paths into and out of a network.

Once packets are received by the destination computer (your computer in our example), that machine's version of TCP kicks in. TCP checks that it has all the packets, makes sure that no packets were damaged or corrupted, requests replacement packets (if needed), and then puts the packets in the correct order, passing a perfect copy of your transmission to the program you're communicating with (an e-mail server, Web server, etc.).

This progression—application at the source to TCP at the source (slice up the data being sent), to IP (for forwarding among routers), to TCP at the destination (put the transmission back together and make sure it's perfect), to application at the destination—takes place in both directions, starting at the server for messages coming to you, and starting on your computer when you're sending messages to another computer.

UDP: TCP's Faster, Less Reliable Sibling

TCP is a perfectionist and that's what you want for Web transmissions, e-mail, and application downloads. But sometimes we're willing to sacrifice perfection for speed. You'd make this sacrifice for streaming media applications like Windows Media Player, Real Player, Internet voice chat, and video conferencing. Having to wait to make sure each packet is perfectly sent would otherwise lead to awkward pauses that interrupt real-time listening. It'd be better to just grab the packets as they come and play them, even if they have minor errors. Packets are small enough that if one packet doesn't arrive, you can ignore it and move on to the next without too much quality disruption. A protocol called **UDP (user datagram protocol)** does exactly this, working as a TCP stand-in when you've got the need for speed, and are willing to sacrifice quality. If you've ever watched a Web video or had a Web-based phone call and the quality got sketchy, it's probably because there were packet problems, but UDP kept on chugging, making the "get it fast" instead of "get it perfect" trade-off.

UDP (user datagram protocol)

Protocol that operates instead of TCP in applications where delivery speed is important and quality can be sacrificed.

VoIP: When Phone Calls Are Just Another Internet Application

The increasing speed and reliability of the Internet means that applications such as Internet phone calls (referred to as *VoIP*, or **voice over Internet protocol**) are becoming more reliable. That doesn't just mean that Skype becomes a more viable alternative for consumer landline and mobile phone calls; it's also good news for many businesses, governments, and nonprofits.

Many large organizations maintain two networks—one for data and another for *POTS* (plain old telephone service). Maintaining two networks is expensive, and while conventional phone calls are usually of a higher quality than their Internet counterparts, POTS equipment is also inefficient. Old phone systems use a technology called *circuit switching*. A "circuit" is a dedicated connection between two entities. When you have a POTS phone call, a circuit is open, dedicating a specific amount of capacity between you and the party on the other end. You're using that "circuit" regardless of whether you're talking. Pause between words or put someone on hold, and the circuit is still in use. Anyone who has ever tried to make a phone call at a busy time (say, early morning on Mother's Day or at midnight on New Year's Eve) and received an "all circuits are busy" recording has experienced congestion on an inefficient circuit-switched phone network.

But unlike circuit-switched counterparts, Internet networks are packet-switched networks, which can be more efficient. Since we can slice conversations up into packets, we can squeeze them into smaller spaces. If there are pauses in a conversation or someone's on hold, applications don't hold up the network. And that creates an opportunity to use the network's available capacity for other users. The trade-off is one that swaps circuit switching's quality of service (QoS) with packet switching's efficiency and cost savings. Try to have a VoIP call when there's too much traffic on a portion of the network and your call quality will drop. But packet switching quality is getting much better. Networking standards are now offering special features, such as "packet prioritization," that can allow voice packets to gain delivery priority over packets for applications like e-mail, where a slight delay is OK.

When voice is digitized, "telephone service" simply becomes another application that sits on top of the Internet, like the Web, e-mail, or FTP. VoIP calls between remote offices can save long distance charges. And when the phone system becomes a computer application, you can do a lot more. Well-implemented VoIP systems allow users' browsers access to their voice mail inbox, one-click video conferencing and call forwarding, point-and-click conference call setup, and other features, but you'll still have a phone number, just like with POTS.

voice over Internet protocol (VoIP)

Transmission technologies that enable voice communications (phone calls) to take place over the Internet as well as private packet-switched networks.

What Connects the Routers and Computers?

Routers are connected together, either via cables or wirelessly. A cable connecting a computer in a home or office is probably copper (likely what's usually called an Ethernet cable), with transmissions sent through the copper via electricity. Long-haul cables, those that carry lots of data over long distances, are usually fiber-optic lines—glass lined cables that transmit light (light is faster and travels farther distances than electricity, but fiber-optic networking equipment is more expensive than the copper-electricity kind). Wireless transmission can happen via Wi-Fi (for shorter distances), or cell phone tower or satellite over longer distances. But the beauty of the Internet protocol suite (TCP/IP) is that it doesn't matter what the actual transmission media are. As long as your routing equipment can connect any two networks, and as long as that equipment "speaks" IP, then you can be part of the Internet.

In reality, your messages likely transfer via lots of different transmission media to get to their final destination. If you use a laptop connected via Wi-Fi, then that wireless connection finds a base station, usually within about three hundred feet. That base station is probably connected to a local area network (LAN) via a copper cable. And your firm or college may connect to fast, long-haul portions of the Internet via fiber-optic cables provided by that firm's Internet service provider (ISP).

Most big organizations have multiple ISPs for redundancy, providing multiple paths in and out of a network. This is so that if a network connection provided by one firm goes down, say an errant backhoe cuts a cable, other connections can route around the problem (see Figure 16.1).

peering

When separate ISPs link their networks to swap traffic on the Internet.

In the United States (and in most deregulated telecommunications markets), ISPs come in all sizes, from smaller regional players to sprawling international firms. When different ISPs connect their networking equipment together to share traffic, it's called **peering**. Peering usually takes place at neutral sites called *Internet exchange points* (IXPs), although some firms also have private peering points. Carriers usually don't charge one another for peering, although if traffic exchange is lopsided (e.g., Netflix sending lots of video inbound to Comcast's network), then the ISP left carrying more inbound content may seek payment for a faster, private-peering direct connection to its network (such relationships are often referred to as *paid peering*).[24] Instead, "the money is made" in the ISP business by charging the end-points in a network—the customer organizations and end users that an ISP connects to the Internet. Competition among carriers helps keep prices down, quality high, and innovation moving forward.

colocation facility

Sometimes called a "colo," or carrier hotel; provides a place where the gear from multiple firms can come together and where the peering of Internet traffic can take place. Equipment connecting in colos could be high-speed lines from ISPs, telecom lines from large private data centers, or even servers hosted in a colo to be closer to high-speed Internet connections.

Finance Has a Need for Speed

When many folks think of Wall Street trading, they think of the open outcry pit at the New York Stock Exchange (NYSE). But human traders are just too slow for many of the most active trading firms. Over half of all US stock trades and a quarter of worldwide currency trades now happen via programs that make trading decisions without any human intervention.[25] There are many names for this automated, data-driven frontier of finance—algorithmic trading, black-box trading, or high-frequency trading. And while firms specializing in automated, high-frequency trading represent only about 2 percent of the trading firms operating in the United States, they account for about three quarters of all US equity trading volume.[26]

Programmers lie at the heart of modern finance. "A geek who writes code—those guys are now the valuable guys" says the former head of markets systems at Fidelity Investments, and that rare breed of top programmer can make "tens of millions of dollars" developing these systems.[27] Such systems leverage data mining and other model-building techniques to crunch massive volumes of data and discover exploitable market patterns. Models are then run against real-time data and executed the instant a trading opportunity is detected. (For more details on how data is gathered and models are built, see Chapter 15)

Winning with these systems means being quick—very quick. Suffer delay (what techies call *latency*) and you may have missed your opportunity to pounce on a signal or market imperfection. To cut latency, many trading firms are moving their servers out of their own data centers and into **colocation facility**. These facilities act as storage places where a firm's servers get superfast connections as close to the action as possible. And by renting space in a "*colo*," a firm gets someone else to manage the electrical and cooling issues, often providing more robust power backup and lower energy costs than a firm might get on its own.

Equinix, a major publicly traded IXP and colocation firm with facilities worldwide, has added a growing number of high-frequency trading firms to a roster of customers that includes e-commerce, Internet, software, and telecom companies. In northern New Jersey alone (the location of many of the servers where "Wall Street" trading takes place), Equinix hosts some eighteen exchanges and trading platforms as well as the NYSE Secure Financial Transaction Infrastructure (SFTI) access node.

Less than a decade ago, eighty milliseconds was acceptably low latency, but now trading firms are pushing below one millisecond into microseconds.[28] So it's pretty clear that understanding how the Internet works, and how to best exploit it, is of fundamental and strategic importance to those in finance. But also recognize that this kind of automated trading comes with risks. Systems that run on their own can move many billions in the blink of an eye, and the actions of one system may cascade, triggering actions by others.

The spring 2010 "Flash Crash" resulted in a nearly 1,000-point freefall in the Dow Jones Industrial Index, its biggest intraday drop ever. Those black boxes can be mysterious—months after the May 6 event, experts were still parsing through trading records, trying to unearth how the flash crash happened.[29] The 2014 publication of the book *Flash Boys* raised additional questions about high-frequency trading (HFT) when author Michael Lewis accused certain HFT trading firms of creating a system that allowed a small and privileged group of traders to get an advance peek at trading orders of other investors. Lewis says this allows them to buy shares ahead of buyers and then sell them to these buyers at a higher price, making a tiny arbitrage premium on billions of transactions.[30] As of this writing, the accusations in Lewis's book have not played out in court, but the FBI and New York State Attorney General have begun to investigate possibly unfair practices in HFT.[31] Regulators and lawmakers recognize they now need to understand technology, telecommunications, and its broader impact on society so that they can create platforms that fuel growth without putting the economy at risk, while managers need to understand the inner workings of telecommunications to ensure their firms are positioned for opportunity and not taken advantage of.

Watching the Packet Path via Traceroute

Want to see how packets bounce from router to router as they travel around the Internet? Check out a tool called *traceroute*. Traceroute repeatedly sends a cluster of three packets starting at the first router connected to a computer, then the next, and so on, building out the path that packets take to their destination.

Traceroute is built into all major desktop operating systems (Windows, Macs, Linux), and several websites will run traceroute between locations (traceroute.org and visualroute.visualware.com are great places to explore).

The message below shows a traceroute performed between Irish firm VistaTEC and Boston College. At first, it looks like a bunch of gibberish, but if we look closely, we can decipher what's going on.

FIGURE 16.5

```
Traceroute to www.bc.edu (136.167.2.220), 30 hops max, 38 byte packets
 1  vlan120.switch.deg.vistatec.ie (85.159.16.65)  0.758 ms  1.141 ms  2.189 ms
 2  ge0-1.router.deg.vistatec.ie (85.159.16.25)  4.109 ms  0.561 ms  0.485 ms
 3  xe-0-1-0-119.dub20.ip4.tinet.net (77.67.66.213)  0.698 ms  0.734 ms  0.691 ms
 4  xe-10-1-0.lon11.ip4.tinet.net (89.149.186.197)  11.290 ms  11.335 ms  11.300 ms
 5  te7-6.mpd02.lon01.atlas.cogentco.com (130.117.15.49)  11.496 ms  11.197 ms  11.454 ms
 6  te0-2-0-1.mpd21.jfk02.atlas.cogentco.com (66.28.4.189)  85.687 ms  85.627 ms  85.685 ms
 7  te2-2.mpd01.bos01.atlas.cogentco.com (154.54.6.1)  233.730 ms  91.406 ms  91.368 ms
 8  te4-2.ccr01.orh01.atlas.cogentco.com (66.28.4.222)  92.498 ms  92.615 ms  92.457 ms
 9  38.104.218.10 (38.104.218.10)  94.491 ms  94.458 ms  94.253 ms
10  136.167.9.226 (136.167.9.226)  94.816 ms  94.475 ms  94.586 ms
```

The table above shows ten hops, starting at a domain in vistatec.ie and ending in 136.167.9.226 (the table doesn't say this, but all IP addresses starting with 136.167 are Boston College addresses). The three groups of numbers at the end of three lines shows the time (in milliseconds) of three packets sent out to test that hop of our journey. These numbers might be interesting for network administrators trying to diagnose speed issues, but we'll ignore them and focus on how packets get from point to point.

At the start of each line is the name of the computer or router that is relaying packets for that leg of the journey. Sometimes routers are named, and sometimes they're just IP addresses. When routers are named, we can tell what network a packet is on by looking at the domain name. By looking at the router names to the left of each line in the traceroute above, we see that the first two hops are within the vistatec.ie network. Hop 3 shows the first router outside the vistatec.ie network. It's at a domain named tinet.net, so this must be the name of VistaTEC's Internet service provider since it's the first connection outside the vistatec.ie network.

Sometimes routers names suggest their locations (oftentimes they use the same three character abbreviations you'd see in airports). Look closely at the hosts in hops 3 through 7. The subdomains dub20, lon11, lon01, jfk02, and bos01 suggest the packets are going from Dublin, then east to London, then west to New York City (John F. Kennedy International Airport), then north to Boston. That's a long way to travel in a fraction of a second!

Hop 4 is at tinet.net, but hop 5 is at cogentco.com (look them up online and you'll find out that cogentco.com, like tinet.net, is also an ISP). That suggests that between those hops peering is taking place and traffic is handed off from carrier to carrier.

Hop 8 is still cogentco.com, but it's not clear who the unnamed router in hop 9, 38.104.218.10, belongs to. We can use the Internet to sleuth that out, too. Search the Internet for the phrase "IP address lookup" and you'll find a bunch of tools to track down the organization that "owns" an IP address. Using the tool at whatismyip.com, I found that this number is registered to PSI Net, which is now part of cogentco.com.

Routing paths, ISPs, and peering all revealed via traceroute. You've just performed a sort of network "CAT scan" and looked into the veins and arteries that make up a portion of the Internet. Pretty cool!

If you try out traceroute on your own, be aware that not all routers and networks are traceroute friendly. It's possible that as your trace hits some hops along the way (particularly at the start or end of your journey), three "*" characters will show up at the end of each line instead of the numbers indicating packet speed. This indicates that traceroute has timed out on that hop. Some networks block traceroute because hackers have used the tool to probe a network to figure out how to attack an organization. Most of the time, though, the hops between the source and destination of the traceroute (the steps involving all the ISPs and their routers) are visible.

Traceroute can be a neat way to explore how the Internet works and reinforce the topics we've just learned. Search for traceroute tools online or browse the Internet for details on how to use the traceroute command built into your computer.

There's Another Internet?

If you're a student at a large research university, there's a good chance that your school is part of Internet2. Internet2 is a research network created by a consortium of research, academic, industry, and government firms. These organizations have collectively set up a high-performance network running at speeds of up to one hundred gigabits per second to support and experiment with demanding applications. Examples include high-quality video conferencing; high-reliability, high-bandwidth imaging for the medical field; and applications that share huge data sets among researchers.

If your university is an Internet2 member and you're communicating with another computer that's part of the Internet2 consortium, then your organization's routers are smart enough to route traffic through the superfast Internet2 backbone. If that's the case, you're likely already using Internet2 without even knowing it!

KEY TAKEAWAYS

- TCP/IP, or the Internet protocol suite, helps get perfect copies of Internet transmissions from one location to another. TCP works on the ends of transmission, breaking up transmissions up into manageable packets at the start and putting them back together while checking quality at the end. IP works in the middle, routing packets to their destination.
- Routers are special computing devices that forward packets from one location to the next. Routers are typically connected with more than one outbound path, so in case one path becomes unavailable, an alternate path can be used.
- UDP is a replacement for TCP, used when it makes sense to sacrifice packet quality for delivery speed. It's often used for media streaming.
- TCP/IP doesn't care about the transition media. This allows networks of different types—copper, fiber, and wireless—to connect to and participate in the Internet.
- The ability to swap in new applications, protocols, and media files gives the network tremendous flexibility.
- Decentralization, fault tolerance, and redundancy help keep the network open and reliable.
- VoIP allows voice and phone systems to become an application traveling over the Internet. This is allowing many firms to save money on phone calls and through the elimination of old, inefficient circuit-switched networks. As Internet applications, VoIP phone systems can also have additional features that circuit-switched networks lack. The primary limitation of many VoIP systems is quality of service.
- Many firms in the finance industry have developed automated trading models that analyze data and execute trades without human intervention. Speeds substantially less than one second may be vital to capitalizing on market opportunities, so firms are increasingly moving equipment into collocation facilities that provide high-speed connectivity to other trading systems.
- The Internet is a network of networks, and these networks swap traffic by peering—that is, connecting their networks together. Most peering between commercial networks (e.g., between firms like AT&T and Verizon) is done without exchanging fees. However, some ISPs are demanding payment (paid peering) for access to faster, private peering points.

QUESTIONS AND EXERCISES

1. How can the Internet consist of networks of such physically different transmission media—cable, fiber, and wireless?

2. What is the difference between TCP and UDP? Why would you use one over the other?

3. Would you recommend a VoIP phone system to your firm or University? Why or why not? What are the advantages? What are the disadvantages? Can you think of possible concerns or benefits not mentioned in this section? Research these concerns online and share your finding with your instructor.

4. What are the risks in the kinds of automated trading systems described in this section? Conduct research and find an example of where these systems have caused problems for firms and/or the broader market. What can be done to prevent such problems? Whose responsibility is this?

5. Search the Internet for a traceroute tool, or look online to figure out how to use the traceroute command built into your PC. Run three or more traceroutes to different firms at different locations around the world. List the number of ISPs that show up in the trace. Circle the areas where peering occurs. Do some of the "hops" time out with "*" values returned? If so, why do you think that happened?

6. Find out if your school or employer is an Internet2 member. If it is, run traceroutes to schools that are and are not members of Internet2. What differences do you see in the results?

4. LAST MILE: FASTER SPEED, BROADER ACCESS

LEARNING OBJECTIVES

1. **Understand the last-mile problem and be able to discuss the pros and cons of various broad-band technologies, including DSL, cable, fiber, and various wireless offerings.**
2. **Describe 3G and 4G systems, listing major technologies and their backers.**
3. **Understand the issue of Net neutrality and put forth arguments supporting or criticizing the concept.**

The **Internet backbone** is made of fiber-optic lines that carry data traffic over long distances. Those lines are pretty speedy. In fact, several backbone providers, including AT&T and Verizon, have rolled out infrastructure with 100 Gbps (gigabits per second) transmission speeds (that's enough to transmit a two-hour high-definition [HD] movie in about eight seconds) with speeds headed higher world-wide.[32] But when considering overall network speed, remember **Amdahl's Law**: a system's speed is determined by its slowest component.[33] More often than not, the bottleneck isn't the backbone but the so-called **last mile**, or the connections that customers use to get online.

High-speed last-mile technologies are often referred to as *broadband Internet access* (or just **broadband**). What qualifies as broadband varies. In 2009, the Federal Communications Commission (FCC) redefined broadband as having a minimum speed of 768 Kbps (roughly fourteen times the speed of those old 56 Kbps modems). By 2015 the FCC had proposed a new definition where download speeds would run at a minimum of 25 mbps and upload speeds of three mbps.[34] Other agencies worldwide may have different definitions. But one thing is clear: a new generation of bandwidth-demanding services requires more capacity. As we increasingly consume Internet services like HD streaming, real-time gaming, video conferencing, and music downloads, we are in fact becoming a bunch of voracious, bit-craving gluttons.

With the pivotal role the United States has played in the creation of the Internet, and in pioneering software, hardware, and telecommunications industries, you might expect the United States to lead the world in last-mile broadband access. Not even close. A recent study ranked the United States thirty-first in download speeds[35] while others have ranked the United States far behind in speed, availability, and price.[36]

Sounds grim, but help is on the way. A range of technologies and firms are upgrading infrastructure and developing new systems that will increase capacity not just in the United States but also worldwide. Here's an overview of some of the major technologies that can be used to speed the Internet's last mile.

Internet backbone

High-speed data lines provided by many firms all across the world that interconnect and collectively form the core of the Internet.

Amdahl's Law

A system's speed is determined by its slowest component.

last mile

Technologies that connect end users to the Internet. The last-mile problem refers to the fact that these connections are usually the slowest part of the network.

broadband

Broadly refers to high-speed Internet connections and is often applied to "last-mile" technologies.

bandwidth

Network transmission speeds, typically expressed in some form of bits per second (bps).

Understanding Bandwidth

When folks talk about **bandwidth**, they're referring to data transmission speeds. Bandwidth is often expressed in bits per second, or bps. Prefix letters associated with multiples of bps are the same as the prefixes we mentioned in Chapter 5 when discussing storage capacity in bytes: Kbps = thousand bits (or kilobits) per second, Mbps = million bits (or megabits) per second, Gbps = billion bits (or gigabits) per second (or terabit), and Tbps = trillion bits (or terabits) per second.

Remember, there are eight bits in a byte, and one byte is a single character. One megabyte is roughly equivalent to one digital book, forty-five seconds of music, or twenty seconds of medium-quality video.[37] But you can't just divide the amount of bytes by eight to estimate how many bits you'll need to transfer. When a file or other transmission is sliced into packets (usually of no more than about 1,500 bytes), there's some overhead added. Those packets "wrap" data chunks in an envelope surrounded by source and destination addressing and other important information.

Here are some rough demand requirements for streaming media. For streaming audio like Pandora, you'd need at least 150 Kbps for acceptable regular quality, and at least 300 Kbps for high quality.[38] For streaming video (via Netflix), at a minimum you'd need 1.5 Mbps, but 3.0 Mbps will ensure decent video and audio. For what Netflix calls HD streaming, you'll need a minimum of 5 Mbps, but would likely want 8 Mbps or more to ensure the highest quality video and audio.[39]

4.1 Cable Broadband

coaxial cable

Insulated copper cable commonly used by cable television providers.

Roughly 90 percent of US homes are serviced by a cable provider, each capable of using a thick copper wire to offer broadband access. That wire (called a **coaxial cable** or *coax*) has shielding that reduces electrical interference, allowing cable signals to travel longer distances without degrading and with less chance of interference than conventional telephone equipment.

One potential weakness of cable technology lies in the fact that most residential providers use a system that requires customers to share bandwidth with neighbors. If the guy next door is a BitTorrent-using bandwidth hog, your traffic could suffer.[40]

Cable is fast and it's getting faster. Many cable firms are rolling out a new technology called DOCSIS 3.1 that can support multigigabit download speeds.[41] Cable firms are also creating so-called *fiber-copper hybrids* that run higher-speed fiber-optic lines into neighborhoods, then use lower-cost, but still relatively high-speed, copper infrastructure over short distances to homes.[42] Those are fast networks, but they are also very expensive to build, since cable firms are laying entirely new lines into neighborhoods instead of leveraging the infrastructure that they've already got in place.

4.2 DSL: Phone Company Copper

digital subscriber line (DSL)

Broadband technology that uses the wires of a local telephone network.

Digital subscriber line (DSL) technology uses the copper wire the phone company has already run into most homes. Even as customers worldwide are dropping their landline phone numbers, the wires used to provide this infrastructure can still be used for broadband.

DSL speeds vary depending on the technology deployed. Worldwide speeds may range from 7 Mbps to as much as 100 Mbps or more (albeit over very short distances).[43] The Achilles heel of the technology lies in the fact that DSL uses standard copper telephone wiring. These lines lack the shielding used by cable, so signals begin to degrade the further you are from the connecting equipment in telephone company offices. Speeds drop off significantly at less than two miles from a central office or DSL hub. If you go four miles out, the technology becomes unusable. Some DSL providers are also using a hybrid fiber-copper system, but as with cable's copper hybrids, this is expensive to build.

The superspeedy DSL implementations that are popular in Europe and Asia work because foreign cities are densely populated and so many high-value customers can be accessed over short distances. In South Korea, for example, half the population lives in apartments, and most of those customers live in and around Seoul. This density also impacts costs—since so many people live in apartments, foreign carriers run fewer lines to reach customers, digging up less ground or stringing wires across fewer telephone poles. Their US counterparts by contrast need to reach a customer base sprawled across the suburbs, so US firms have much higher infrastructure costs. [44]

There's another company with copper, electricity-carrying cables coming into your home—the electrical utility. BPL, or broadband over power line, technology has been available for years. However, there are few deployments because it is considered to be pricier and less practical than alternatives.[45]

4.3   Fiber: A Light-Filled Glass Pipe to Your Doorstep

Fiber to the home (FTTH) is the fastest last-mile technology around. It also works over long distances. Verizon's FiOS technology boasts 50 Mbps download speeds but has tested network upgrades that increase speeds by over six times that.[46] The problem with fiber is that unlike cable or DSL copper, fiber to the home networks weren't already in place. That means firms had to build their own fiber networks from scratch.

The cost of this build out can be enormous. Verizon, for example, has spent over $23 billion on its FTTH infrastructure, allowing the firm to offer some of the fastest home broadband services anywhere. Google has also brought 1 Gbps high-speed fiber to the home in several US communities, including both Kansas City, Kansas, and Kansas City, Missouri; Provo, Utah; and Austin, Texas. Google initially deemed its effort an experiment, claiming it was more interested in learning how developers and users take advantage of ultrahigh-speed fiber to the home (e.g., what kinds of apps are created and used, how do usage and time spent online change), rather than becoming a nationwide ISP itself. However, Google has engaged dozens of additional US communities in exploring further rollout of fast and cheap fiber.[47] Google Fiber appears to be favorable to consumers with its competitive pricing: in communities where Google is present, rivals have dropped prices and increased speeds.[48]

fiber to the home (FTTH)

Broadband service provided via light-transmitting fiber-optic cables.

4.4   Wireless

Mobile wireless service from cell phone access providers is delivered via cell towers. While these providers don't need to build a residential wired infrastructure, they still need to secure space for cell towers, build the towers, connect the towers to a backbone network, and license the **wireless spectrum** (or airwave frequency space) for transmission. As T-Mobile's CEO describes it, "Spectrum is the invisible wireless airwaves that transport information through the ether and into that device into your hand. There's only so much of it" and most mobile firms have exclusive access to the spectrum that they license.[49] This leads to high-stakes regional bidding wars whenever governments put new spectrum up for license. Firms that acquire spectrum rights can gain tremendous market advantages. High-stakes auctions can also inflate operating costs, which eventually are passed down to consumers in the form of higher rates. Perhaps unsurprisingly, T-Mobile has lobbied the US government to set aside more spectrum for smaller carriers, arguing it's in the public interest to offer more carrier competition and keep costs low.

wireless spectrum

Frequencies used for wireless communication. Most mobile cell phone services have to license spectrum. Some technologies (such as Wi-Fi) use unlicensed public spectrum.

We need more bandwidth for mobile devices, too. AT&T now finds that the top 3 percent of its mobile network users gulp up 40 percent of the network's capacity, and network strain will only increase as more people adopt smartphones. These users are streaming Major League Baseball games, exploring the planet with Google Earth, watching YouTube and Netflix, streaming music on Spotify, and more. Get a bunch of smartphone users in a crowded space, like in a college football stadium on game day, and the result is a network-choking data traffic jam. AT&T estimates that it's not uncommon for 80 percent of game-day iPhone users to take out their phones and surf the Web for stats, snap and upload photos, and more. But cell towers often can't handle the load.[50] If you've ever lost coverage in a crowd, you've witnessed mobile network congestion firsthand. Trying to have enough capacity to avoid congestion traffic jams will cost some serious coin. In the midst of customer complaints, AT&T committed to spending $18 billion on network upgrades to address its wireless capacity problem.[51]

TABLE 16.1   Average Demand Usage by Function

Usage	Demand
Voice Calls	4 MB/hr.
iPhone Browsing	40–60 MB/hr.
Net Radio	60 MB/hr.
YouTube	200–400 MB/hr.
Conventional mobile phones use an estimated 100 MB/month, iPhones 560 MB/month, and iPads almost 1 GB/month.	

Source: Based on information from R. Farzad, "The Truth about Bandwidth," BusinessWeek, February 3, 2010.

We're well into the transition from third generation (*3G*) to fourth generation (*4G*) wireless networks. The 3G systems offer access speeds usually less than 2 Mbps (often a lot less).[52] While variants of 3G wireless might employ an alphabet soup of technologies—EV-DO (evolution data optimized), UMTS (universal mobile telecommunications systems), and HSDPA (high-speed downlink packet link access) among them—3G standards can be narrowed down to two camps: those based on the dominant worldwide standard called *GSM* (global system for mobile communications) and the runner-up standards based on *CDMA* (code division multiple access). Most of Europe and a good chunk of the rest of the world use GSM. In the United States, AT&T and T-Mobile use GSM-based 3G. Verizon Wireless and Sprint use the CDMA 3G standard. Typically, handsets designed for one network can't be used on networks supporting the other standard. CDMA has an additional limitation in not being able to use voice and data at the same time.

But 3G is being replaced by high-bandwidth 4G (fourth-generation) mobile networks. The winner in 4G technologies is LTE (long-term evolution). In the United States, the only firm to bet on a rival technology was Sprint, with WiMAX, a technology the firm has since abandoned.[53] Bandwidth for the service rivals what we'd consider fast cable a few years back. US average download speeds above 40 Mbps and upload speeds near 20 Mbps are now common.[54]

4.5 Satellite Wireless

Wireless systems provided by earth-bound base stations like cell phone towers are referred to as *terrestrial wireless*, but it is possible to provide telecommunications services via satellite. Early services struggled due to a number of problems. For example, the first residential satellite services were only used for downloads, which still needed a modem or some other connection to send any messages from the computer to the Internet. Many early systems also required large antennas and were quite expensive. Finally, some services were based on satellites in geosynchronous earth orbit (GEO). GEO satellites circle the earth in a fixed, or stationary, orbit above a given spot on the globe, but to do so they must be positioned at a distance that is roughly equivalent to the planet's circumference. That means signals travel the equivalent of an around-the-world trip to reach the satellite and then the same distance to get to the user. The "last mile" became the last 44,000 miles at best. And if you used a service that also provided satellite upload as well as download, double that to about 88,000 miles. All that distance means higher latency (more delay).[55]

A firm named O3b Networks thinks it might have solved the challenges that plagued early pioneers. O3b has an impressive list of big-name backers that include HSBC bank, cable magnate John Malone, European aerospace firm SES, and Google.

The name O3b stands for the "Other 3 Billion," of the world's population who lack broadband Internet access, and the firm has already begun to to provide "fiber-quality" wireless service to underserved portions of the developing world, as well as others needing connectivity outside traditional cell networks, such as cruise ships and the US Navy.[56] These "middle earth orbit" satellites will circle closer to the earth to reduce latency (only about 5,000 miles up, less than one-fourth the distance of GEO systems). To maintain the lower orbit, O3b's satellites orbit faster than the planet spins, but with plans to launch as many as twenty satellites, the system will constantly blanket regions served. If one satellite circles to the other side of the globe, another one will circle around to take its place, ensuring there's always an O3b "bird" overhead.

Internet penetration in sub-Saharan Africa lags significantly than the rest of the world, and data rates in the few places served can cost as much as one hundred times the rates of comparable systems in nations with high Internet penetration.[57] O3b hopes to change that equation and significantly lower access rates. O3b customers will be local telecommunication firms, not end users. The plan is for local firms to buy O3b's services wholesale and then resell it to customers alongside rivals who can do the same thing, collectively providing more consumer access, higher quality, and lower prices through competition. O3b is a big, bold, and admittedly risky plan, but if it works, its impact could be tremendous.

4.6 Wi-Fi and Other Hotspots

Many users access the Internet via **Wi-Fi** (which stands for *wireless fidelity*). Computer and mobile devices have Wi-Fi antennas built into their chipsets, but to connect to the Internet, a device needs to be within range of a *base station* or *hotspot*. The base station range is usually around three hundred feet (you might get a longer range outdoors and with special equipment; and less range indoors when signals need to pass through solid objects like walls, ceilings, and floors). Wi-Fi base stations used in the home are usually bought by end users, then connected to a cable, DSL, or fiber provider. Many Wi-Fi equipped mobile devices also offer an opportunity to act as a personal hotspot. These devices connect to the Internet over the traditional cell network, but will allow nearby devices (e.g. laptops and tablets) to use mobile Internet access by connecting device-to-device via either Wi-Fi (without needing a base station) or **Bluetooth** (a local wireless technology meant primarily as a replacement for things like printer and speaker cabling, usually requiring devices to be 30 feet or less from each other).

And now a sort of mobile phone hotspot is being used to overcome limitations in those services, as well. Mobile providers can also be susceptible to poor coverage indoors. That's because the spectrum used by most mobile phone firms doesn't travel well through solid objects. Cell coverage is also often limited in the United States because of a lack of towers, which is a result of the *NIMBY problem* (not in my backyard). People don't want an eighty-foot to four-hundred-foot unsightly tower clouding their local landscape, even if it will give their neighborhood better cell phone coverage.[58] To overcome reception and availability problems, mobile telecom services firms have begun offering femtocells. These devices are usually smaller than a box of cereal and can sell for $150 or less (some are free with specific service contracts). Plug a femtocell into a high-speed Internet connection like an in-home cable or fiber service and you can get "five-bar" coverage in a roughly 5,000-square-foot footprint.[59] That can be a great solution for someone who has an in-home, high-speed Internet connection, but wants to get phone and mobile data service indoors, too.

4.7 Net Neutrality: What's Fair?

Across the world, battle lines are being drawn regarding the topic of Net neutrality. Net neutrality is the principle that all Internet traffic should be treated equally and ISPs should not discriminate; slow down access; or charge differentially by user, content, site, platform, application, type of attached equipment, or modes of communication.[60] Sometimes access providers have wanted to offer varying (some say "discriminatory") coverage, depending on the service used and bandwidth consumed.

On one side of the debate are Internet service firms, with Google being one of the strongest Net neutrality supporters. In an advocacy paper, Google stated, "Just as telephone companies are not permitted to tell consumers who they can call or what they can say, broadband carriers should not be allowed to use their market power to control activity online."[61] Google and other Internet content providers worry that without strong net neutrality rules, ISPs may block content or favor their own offerings above rivals. AT&T has previously blocked Apple FaceTime and Google Hangouts, while Verizon and AT&T have blocked Google Wallet.[62] Comcast, the nation's largest cable provider, owns NBCUniversal and has a streaming service that can be considered a competitor to Netflix. Should Comcast, which operates as the only cable company in many of the communities it services, be allowed to use this power as an advantage over competitors? Many Internet firms also worry that if network providers move away from flat-rate pricing toward usage-based (or metered) schemes, this may limit innovation. Metered billing may limit the use of everything from iTunes to Netflix. After all, if you have to pay for per-bit bandwidth consumption and for the download service, then it's as if you're paying twice. Another concern is that if paid peering is the norm, big players like Netflix are likely the only ones with the scale to be able to afford to pay the broadband gatekeepers. If start-ups need to raise capital for "pay to play" on an infrastructure based on government-funded research (that's what the Net is, after all), could this smother the plans of would-be entrepreneurs?

In a scathing critique of US policy in *The Verge*, author Nilay Patel writes, "In the UK, where incumbent provider BT is required to allow competitors to use its wired broadband network, home internet service prices are as low as £2.50 a month, or just over $4. In South Korea, where wireless giants SK Telecom and LG Uplus are locked in a fierce technology battle, customers have access to the fastest mobile networks in the world—up to 300 Mbps, compared to a theoretical max of 80 Mbps on Verizon [in the US]" that's actually more like 15 or 20 Mbps in the real world. As for wireless, in "Germany…T-Mobile customers pay just $1.18 per Mbps of speed. In the US…mostly incompatible wireless networks lock customers in with expensive handsets they can't take elsewhere, allowing AT&T and Verizon to charge around $4 per Mbps each and Sprint to clock in at an insane $7.50." Patel boils the problem down to "four simple ideas: the internet is a utility, there is zero meaningful competition to provide that utility to Americans, all internet providers should be treated equally, and the FCC is doing a miserably ineffective job."[63]

Wi-Fi

A term used to brand wireless local-area networking devices. Devices typically connect to an antenna-equipped base station or hotspot, which is then connected to the Internet. Wi-Fi devices use standards known as IEEE 802.11, and various versions of this standard (e.g., b, g, n) may operate in different frequency bands and have access ranges.

Bluetooth

A standard for short-range (around 30 feet or less) wireless connectivity, typically meant to eliminate cabling used for things like speakers, printers, cameras, and other devices.

The counterargument is that if firms are restricted from charging more for their investment in infrastructure and services, then they'll have little incentive to continue to make the kinds of multibillion-dollar investments that innovations like 4G and fiber networks require, and that these innovations are precisely what is required to power the innovations provided by the next generation of entrepreneurs. Telecom industry executives have railed against Google, Netflix, and others, calling them free riders who earn huge profits by piggybacking off ISP networks, all while funneling no profits back to the firms that provide the infrastructure. One Verizon vice president said, "The network builders are spending a fortune constructing and maintaining the networks that Google intends to ride on with nothing but cheap servers.... It is enjoying a free lunch that should, by any rational account, be the lunch of the facilities providers."[64] AT&T's previous CEO has suggested that Google, Netflix, and other services firms should pay for "preferred access" to the firm's customers.

ISPs also lament the relentlessly increasingly bandwidth demands placed on their networks. YouTube streams as much data in three months as the world's radio, cable, and broadcast television channels combined stream in one year,[65] and Netflix sucks up more than twice the home broadband capacity of YouTube, accounting for over one-third of all US downstream traffic during prime-time hours.[66] Should ISPs be required to support the strain of this kind of bandwidth hog? And what if this one application clogs network use for other traffic, such as e-mail or Web surfing? Similarly, shouldn't firms have the right to prioritize some services to better serve customers? Some network providers argue that services like video chat and streaming audio should get priority over, say, e-mail, which can afford slight delay without major impact. In that case, there's a pretty good argument that providers should be able to discriminate against services. But improving efficiency and throttling usage are two different things.

Internet service firms say they create demand for broadband business, broadband firms say Google and allies are ungrateful parasites that aren't sharing the wealth. The battle lines on the Net neutrality frontier continue to be drawn, and the eventual outcome will impact consumers, investors, and will likely influence the continued expansion and innovation of the Internet. While net neutrality laws vary worldwide, and they continue to evolve in the United States, a 400 page plus 2015 FCC rules update contained many provisions that firms such as Google, Netflix, and many consumer advocacy groups favor. These include prohibiting wired and wireless broadband providers from blocking or throttling (slowing down) content, and prohibiting special paid agreements that allow certain content firms to gain a prioritized fast-lane service. Some exceptions remain in place, for example, coffee shops and airlines can still block certain services, such as Netflix streaming. The FCC has suggested certain specialized services can receive priority, such as health monitoring, Internet telephony, and power monitoring systems. Despite the size of the newest rules document, look for continued evolution, and relentless lobbying, for years to come.[67]

4.8 Summing Up

Hopefully, this chapter helped reveal the mysteries of the Internet. It's interesting to know how "the cloud" works but it can also be vital. As we've seen, the executive office in financial services firms considers mastery of the Internet infrastructure to be critically important to their competitive advantage. Media firms find the Internet both threatening and empowering. The advancement of last-mile technologies and issues of Net neutrality will expose threats and create opportunity. And a manager who knows how the Internet works will be in a better position to make decisions about how to keep the firm and its customers safe and secure, and be better prepared to brainstorm ideas for winning in a world where access is faster and cheaper, and firms, rivals, partners, and customers are more connected.

KEY TAKEAWAYS

- The slowest part of the Internet is typically the last mile, not the backbone. While several technologies can offer broadband service over the last mile, the United States continues to rank below many other nations in terms of access speed, availability, and price.

- Cable firms and phone companies can leverage existing wiring for cable broadband and DSL service, respectively. Cable services are often criticized for shared bandwidth. DSL's primary limitation is that it only works within a short distance of telephone office equipment.

- Fiber to the home can be very fast but very expensive to build.

- An explosion of high-bandwidth mobile applications has strained wireless networks. The transition from 3G to 4G is increasing bandwidth and capacity, but usage continues to skyrocket as smartphone and tablet users stream increasing amounts of video and audio.

- Femtocells are a technology that can improve wireless service by providing a personal mobile phone hotspot that can plug into in-home broadband access.

- The two major 3G standards (the more popular GSM and the less widely adopted CDMA) are being replaced by a single, dominant, higher-capacity 4G standard (LTE).

- Satellite systems show promise in providing high-speed access to underserved parts of the world, but few satellite broadband providers have been successful so far.

- Net neutrality is the principle that all Internet traffic should be treated equally. Google, Netflix, and other firms say it is vital to maintain the openness of the Internet. Telecommunications firms say they should be able to limit access to services that overtax their networks, and some have suggested charging content providers for providing access to their customers.

QUESTIONS AND EXERCISES

1. Research online for the latest country rankings for broadband service. Where does the United States currently rank? Why?

2. Which broadband providers can service your home? Which would you choose? Why?

3. Research the status of Google Fiber. Report updated findings to your class. Why do you suppose Google is becoming an ISP? What other Internet access experiments has the firm been involved in?

4. Show your understanding of the economics and competitive forces of the telecom industry. Discuss why Verizon chose to go with fiber. Do you think this was a wise decision or not? Why? Feel free to do additional research to back up your argument.

5. Why have other nations enjoyed faster broadband speeds, greater availability, and lower prices?

6. The iPhone (and to a lesser extent, other smartphones) have been called both a blessing and a curse for AT&T. Why do you suppose this is so?

7. Investigate the status of mobile wireless offerings available in your area. Which firm would you choose? Why? Which factors are most important in your decision?

8. Have you ever lost communication access—wirelessly or via wired connection? What caused the loss or outage?

9. What factors shape the profitability of the mobile wireless provider industry? How do these economics compare with the cable and wire line industry? Who are the major players and which would you invest in? Why?

10. Last-mile providers often advertise very fast speeds, but users rarely see speeds as high as advertised rates. Search online to find a network speed test and try it from your home, office, mobile device, or dorm. How fast is the network? If you're able to test from home, what bandwidth rates does your ISP advertise? Does this differ from what you experienced? What could account for this discrepancy?

11. What's the difference between LEO satellite systems and the type of system used by O3b? What are the pros and cons of these efforts? Conduct some additional research. What is the status of O3b and other satellite broadband efforts?

12. What advantages could broadband offer to underserved areas of the world? Is Internet access important for economic development? Why or why not?

13. Does your carrier offer a femtocell? Would you use one? Why or why not?

14. Be prepared to debate the issue of Net neutrality in class. Prepare positions both supporting and opposing Net neutrality. Which do you support and why?

15. Investigate the current status of Net neutrality regulations in your nation and report your findings to your instructor. Do you agree with the stance currently taken by your government? Why or why not?

ENDNOTES

1. K. Nielsen, "Your Top 5 Questions about the New gTLD Domain Extensions, Answered," *SearchEngineLand*, February 12, 2013.

2. C. Sherman, "Google Wants Love & Amazon Seeking Joy in New Top Level Domain Names," *SearchEngineLand*, June 13, 2012.

3. J. Del Rey, "Amazon Beats Google With $4.6 Million Bid for ".Buy" Domain," *Re/code*, Sept. 18, 2014.

4. R. Boudreaux, "ICANN's gTLD Program and What It Means to Your Business," *TechRepublic*, January 24, 2012.

5. *The European Centre Blog*, "New Top Level Domains," http://blog.europeandomaincentre.com/infographics-launch-dates-for-the-617-new-gtlds.

6. K. Maney, "Tuvalu's Sinking, but Its Domain Is on Solid Ground," *USA Today*, April 27, 2004.

7. B. Bosker, "The 11 Most Expensive Domain Names Ever," *The Huffington Post*, March 10, 2010.

8. D. Streitfeld, "Web Site Feuding Enters Constitutional Domain," *The Washington Post*, September 11, 2000.

9. D. McCullagh, "Ethical Treatment of PETA Domain," *Wired*, August 25, 2001.

10. M. McGee, "Amazon Loses Bid for .Amazon Domain," *MarketingLand*, May 20, 2014.

11. R. Konrad and E. Hansen, "Madonna.com Embroiled in Domain Ownership Spat," *CNET*, August 21, 2000.

12. D. Morson, "Apple VP Ive Loses Domain Name Bid," *MacWorld*, May 12, 2009.

13. M. Kotadia, "MikeRoweSoft Settles for an Xbox," *CNET*, January 26, 2004.

14. L. Mirani, "An Anti-Obama Dentist Just Bought Up the Best New Democrat Domain Names," *Quartz*, May 23, 2014.

15. R. McMillan, "Coming This Summer: U.S. Will Run Out of Internet Addresses," *The Wall Street Journal*, May 13, 2015.

16. S. Shankland, "Google Tries to Break IPv6 Logjam by Own Example," *CNET*, March 27, 2009.

17. R. McMillan, "Coming This Summer: U.S. Will Run Out of Internet Addresses," *The Wall Street Journal*, May 13, 2015.

18. M. Peckham, "World IPv6 Launch: Only the Biggest Change to the Internet Since Inception," *Time*, June 6, 2012.

19. S. Shankland, "Google Tries to Break IPv6 Logjam by Own Example," *CNET*, March 27, 2009.

20. B. Arnoldy, "IP Address Shortage to Limit Internet Access," *USA Today*, August 3, 2007.

21. D. Godin, "Cache-Poisoning Attack Snares Top Brazilian Bank," *The Register*, April 22, 2009.

22. J. Davis, "Secret Geek A-Team Hacks Back, Defends Worldwide Web," *Wired*, Nov. 24, 2008.

23. J. Hutchinson, "ICANN, Verisign Place Last Puzzle Pieces in DNSSEC Saga," *NetworkWorld*, May 2, 2010.

24. J. Brodkin, "Netflix Is Paying Comcast for Direct Connection to Network," *ArsTechnica*, February 23, 2014.

25. H. Timmons, "A London Hedge Fund That Opts for Engineers, Not M.B.A.'s," *New York Times*, August 18, 2006.

26. R. Iati, "The Real Story of Trading Software Espionage," *Advanced Trading*, July 10, 2009.

27. A. Berenson, "Arrest over Software Illuminates Wall St. Secret," *New York Times*, August 23, 2009.

28. I. Schmerken, "High-Frequency Trading Shops Play the Colocation Game," *Advanced Trading*, October 5, 2009.

29. E. Daimler and G. Davis, "'Flash Crash' Proves Diversity Needed in Market Mechanisms," *Pittsburgh Post-Gazette*, May 29, 2010; H. Moore, "'Flash Crash' Anniversary Leaves Unanswered Questions," *Marketplace Radio*, May 5, 2011.

30. S. Pearlstein, "'Flash Boys': Michael Lewis Does It Again," *Washington Post*, April 12, 2014.

31. S. Pathe, "What's the Big Deal about Michael Lewis & High-Frequency Trading?" *PBS News Hour*, April 2, 2014.

32. T. Spangler, "Cisco Clarifies 100-Gig AT&T Backbone Claim," *Multichannel News*, March 9, 2010; Zacks.com, "AT&T Tests 100 Gb Ethernet in Move toward Faster Internet," *SeekingAlpha*, March 10, 2010.

33. G. Gilder, *Telecosm: How Infinite Bandwidth Will Revolutionize Our World* (New York: Free Press, 2000).

34. M. Orcutt, "You Might Not Have Broadband Anymore," *Technology Review*, Feb. 5, 2015.

35. D. Kerr, "US Download Speeds Sluggish Compared with Other Countries," *CNET*, November 26, 2013.

36. E. Wyatt, "US Lagging in High-Speed Internet Service," *Boston Globe*, December 30, 2013.

37. R. Farzad, "The Truth about Bandwidth," *BusinessWeek*, February 3, 2010.

38. Pandora, "Frequently Asked Questions," http://blog.pandora.com/faq.

39. LG Knowledge Base, "Bandwidth Needed for Instant Streaming," http://lgknowledgebase.com/kb/index.php?View=entry&EntryID=6241.

40. R. Thompson, "DSL Internet vs. Cable Internet," *High Speed Internet Access Guide*, March 23, 2010.

41. J. Brodkin, "Why Comcast and Other Cable Giants Aren't Selling You Gigabit Internet," *CNET*, December 1, 2013.

42. S. Hansell, "The Broadband Gap: Why Is Theirs Faster?" *New York Times*, March 10, 2009.

43. T. Wolverton, "DSL Speeds Could Soon Get a Boost with New Technologies," *San Jose Mercury News*, April 15, 2013.

44. S. Hansell, "The Broadband Gap: Why Is Theirs Faster?" *New York Times*, March 10, 2009.

45. R. King, "Telecom Companies Scramble for Funding," *BusinessWeek*, August 3, 2009.

46. S. Higginbotham, "Verizon Tests 10 Gbps to the Home. Yeah, You'll Have to Share," *GigaOM*, December 17, 2009.

47. C. Welch, "Google Will Explore Bringing Fiber to 34 New Cities Including Portland and Atlanta," *The Verge*, February 19, 2014.

48. M. Reardon, "Google's Fiber Effect: Fuel for a Broadband Explosion," *CNET*, April 30, 2014.

49. I. Fried, "T-Mobile CEO John Legere Wants You to Give a Shit About Spectrum," *Re/code*, June 11, 2015.

50. R. Farzad, "AT&T's iPhone Mess," *BusinessWeek*, February 3, 2010.

51. C. Edwards and O. Kharif, "Sprint's Bold Play on a 4G Network," *BusinessWeek*, March 30, 2010.

52. K. German, "On Call: Welcome to 4G," *CNET*, March 9, 2010.

53. A. Vaupel, "They Grow Up Fast: Sprint Will Shut Down 4G Technology from 2008," *Kansas City Business Journal*, April 9, 2014.

54. L. La, "4G LTE showdown: How fast is your carrier?" *CNet*, Aug. 5, 2014.

55. G. Ou, "Why Satellite Service Is So Slow," *ZDNet*, February 23, 2008.

56. C. Henry, "O3b Sees Contract Surge, Targets New Markets," *Via Satellite*, June 19, 2015.

57. G. Lamb, "O3b Networks: A Far-Out Plan to Deliver the Web," *Christian Science Monitor*, September 24, 2008.

58. G. Dechter and O. Kharif, "How Craig McCaw Built a 4G Network on the Cheap," *BusinessWeek*, May 24, 2010.

59. C. Mims, "A Personal Cell Phone Tower," *Technology Review*, April 7, 2010.

60. K. Hoban, "Why Wasn't There a Huge Outcry against The FCC's Proposed Rules against Net Neutrality?" *Forbes*, May 5, 2014.

61. Google, "A Guide to Net Neutrality for Google Users," 2008, http://www.docstoc.com/docs/1064274/A-Guide-to-Net-Neutrality-for-Google-Users.

62. N. Patel, "The Internet Is F*cked (But We Can Fix It)," *The Verge*, February 25, 2014.

63. N. Patel, "The Internet Is F*cked (But We Can Fix It)," *The Verge*, February 25, 2014.

64. A. Mohammed, "Verizon Executive Calls for End to Google's 'Free Lunch,'" *Washington Post*, February 7, 2006.

65. B. Swanson, "The Coming Exaflood," *Wall Street Journal*, January 20, 2007.

66. T. Spangler, "Netflix Remains King of Bandwidth Usage, While YouTube Declines," *Variety*, May 14, 2014.

67. A. Schatz, "What Net Neutrality Rules Mean for Consumers," *Re/code*, March 12, 2015.

CHAPTER 17

Information Security: Barbarians at the Gateway (and Just About Everywhere Else)

---

1. INTRODUCTION

In late 2013, the Target logo was plastered across media reports throughout the United States, depicted as a bulls-eye that lured cyber criminals. In the days prior to Thanksgiving, a perfect time to take advantage of what would soon be a peak retail shopping season, hackers managed to install malware in Target's security and payments system. This code was designed to steal every credit card used in the company's 1,797 US stores. The bad guys' data snarfing malware went operational on November 27. The hack shouldn't have been as damaging as it eventually became. Target had previously paid roughly $1.6 million for software from the security firm FireEye to detect breaches in real time, and the software worked. A FireEye notification went off shortly after unauthorized software began collecting data inside Target's network, but Target ignored the warning. Another alert went up within the week and Target's team ignored that warning as well. At this point, the malware hadn't begun transmitting the captured data out of Target's network, so had Target heeded the warnings, the firm could have prevented the data theft. Even worse, the firm's security software has an option to automatically delete malware as it's detected but Target's security team had turned that function off. As a result, hackers operating out of Odessa and Moscow vacuumed up records on roughly one-third of US consumers for more than two weeks. Target's investigation didn't start until federal law enforcement contacted the firm in mid-December to report suspicious activities on cards used in its stores.[1]

The malware used to breach Target was described by one security expert as "absolutely unsophisticated and uninteresting." The code was likely snuck into Target's system using the security credentials of one of Target's partners, a heating and ventilation firm. While the area where credit card transactions are processed is supposed to be walled off from other areas of the Target network (e.g., the air conditioning guys should never be able to touch systems that read credit cards) hackers found holes and eventually nestled their code in a sweet spot for grabbing customer data, disguising the code with the label "BladeLogic" the name of a legitimate data center management product.[2]

The damage Target suffered should lead to sleepless nights among managers in any organization that accepts sensitive customer data. The Target hack was one of the largest in US history. Reports say 40 million cards used at Target were stolen and additional personal information on 70 million customers was exposed. The firm's CEO was booted within months. And Target isn't alone in having been caught with their guard down. Neiman Marcus Group, the crafts chain Michael's, and several other merchants were also hacked at about the same time.[3] According to one study, only 5 percent of retailers discover breaches through their own monitoring. Analysts estimate the cost of the Target breach will run into the billions: ninety lawsuits had been filed within ninety days of the attack's public disclosure; on top of that, Target's holiday quarter profits fell 46 percent from the prior year; and the retailer reported its biggest ever decline in transactions.[4]

FIGURE 17.1

Target breach by the numbers.

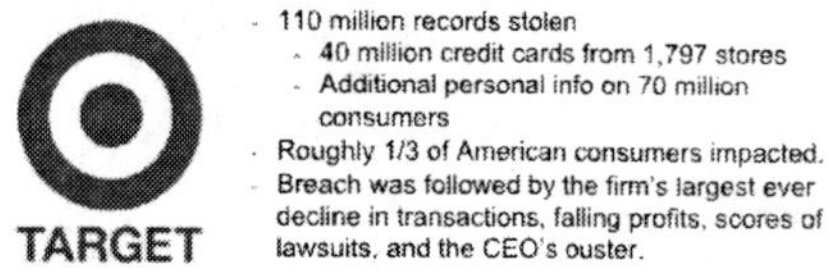

- 110 million records stolen
  - 40 million credit cards from 1,797 stores
  - Additional personal info on 70 million consumers
- Roughly 1/3 of American consumers impacted.
- Breach was followed by the firm's largest ever decline in transactions, falling profits, scores of lawsuits, and the CEO's ouster.

The massive impact of the Target breach should make it clear that security must be a top organizational priority. Attacks are on the rise. Five of the top ten breaches in terms of records stolen occurred in 2013[5] and the total number of records compromised was more than double the previous highest year, just two years earlier.[6] Health insurer Anthem and the US Government Office of Personnel Management are among the organizations that have since suffered high-profile and deeply damaging hacks that have released personal information on tens of millions of people.[7] The 2014 hack on Sony Entertainment associated with the release of the movie *The Interview* is estimated to have done upwards of $100 million in damage, dramatically hurt the firm's reputation in the industry, and resulted in the resignation of at least one high-profile executive.[8] While the examples and scenarios presented here are shocking, the good news is that the vast majority of security breaches can be prevented. Let's be clear from the start: no text can provide an approach that will guarantee that you'll be 100 percent secure. And that's not the goal of this chapter. The issues raised in this brief introduction can, however, help make you aware of vulnerabilities; improve your critical thinking regarding current and future security issues; and help you consider whether a firm has technologies, training, policies, and procedures in place to assess risks, lessen the likelihood of damage, and respond in the event of a breach. A constant vigilance regarding security needs to be part of your individual skill set and a key component in your organization's culture. An awareness of the threats and approaches discussed in this chapter should help reduce your chance of becoming a victim.

As we examine security issues, we'll first need to understand what's happening, who's doing it, and what their motivation is. We'll then examine how these breaches are happening with a focus on technologies and procedures. Finally, we'll sum up with what can be done to minimize the risks of being victimized and quell potential damage of a breach for both the individual and the organization.

KEY TAKEAWAYS

- Information security is everyone's business and needs to be made a top organizational priority.
- Firms suffering a security breach can experience direct financial loss, exposed proprietary information, fines, legal payouts, court costs, damaged reputations, plummeting stock prices, and more.
- Information security isn't just a technology problem; a host of personnel, operational, and procedural factors can create and amplify a firm's vulnerability.

QUESTIONS AND EXERCISES

1. The 2013 data breach at Target Corporation was one of the largest in US history. Were you impacted by this breach (or any other)? How did you find out about the breach? Did you take action as a result? Research and report the estimated costs associated with this breach. Has the theft resulted in additional security issues for the individuals who had their data stolen?

2. What factors were responsible for the Target breach? Who should have been responsible for the breach? How do you think the firm could have prevented this attack, and what should it do in the future to heighten security and win back customer trust?

3. As individuals or in groups assigned by your instructor, search online for recent reports on information security breaches. Come to class prepared to discuss a breach you've researched, its potential impact, and how it might have been avoided. What should the key takeaways be for managers studying your example?

4. Think of firms that you've done business with online. Search to see if these firms have experienced security breaches in the past. What have you found out? Does this change your attitude about dealing with the firm? Why or why not?

2. WHY IS THIS HAPPENING? WHO IS DOING IT? AND WHAT'S THEIR MOTIVATION?

LEARNING OBJECTIVES

1. **Understand the source and motivation of those initiating information security attacks.**
2. **Relate examples of various infiltrations in a way that helps raise organizational awareness of threats.**

Thieves, vandals, and other bad guys have always existed, but the environment has changed. Today, nearly every organization is online, making any Internet-connected network a potential entry point for the growing worldwide community of computer criminals, state-sponsored infiltrators, corporate spies, and other malfeasants. Software and hardware solutions are also more complex than ever. Different vendors, each with their own potential weaknesses, provide technology components that may be compromised by misuse, misconfiguration, or mismanagement. With the rise of "big data," corporations have become data packrats, hoarding information in hopes of turning bits into bucks by licensing databases, targeting advertisements, or cross-selling products. And flatter organizations also mean that lower-level employees may be able to use technology to reach deep into corporate assets—amplifying threats from operator error, a renegade employee, or one compromised by external forces.

There are a lot of bad guys out there, and motivations vary widely, including the following:

- Account theft and illegal funds transfer
- Stealing personal or financial data
- Compromising computing assets for use in other crimes
- Extortion
- Intellectual property theft
- Espionage
- Cyberwarfare
- Terrorism
- Pranksters
- Protest hacking (hacktivism)
- Revenge (disgruntled employees)

Intel's security division estimates that cybercrime and cyber espionage cost the US economy roughly $100 billion per year and the annual global impact is nearly $300 billion.[9] Nearly all of this is done "without drawing a gun or passing a note to a teller."[10] While some steal cash for their own use, others resell their hacking take to others. There is a thriving cybercrime underworld market in which **data harvesters** sell to **cash-out fraudsters**: criminals who might purchase data from the harvesters in order to buy (then resell) goods using stolen credit cards or create false accounts via identity theft. These collection and resale operations are efficient and sophisticated. Law enforcement has taken down sites like DarkMarket and ShadowCrew, in which card thieves and hacking tool peddlers received eBay-style seller ratings vouching for the "quality" of their wares.[11] Some of the cards stolen during the Target breach were found on a cybercrime supermarket called Rescator.[12]

Hackers might also infiltrate computer systems to enlist hardware for subsequent illegal acts. A cybercrook might deliberately hop through several systems to make his path difficult to follow, slowing cross-border legal pursuit or even thwarting prosecution if launched from nations without extradition agreements.

data harvesters

Cybercriminals who infiltrate systems and collect data for illegal resale.

cash-out fraudsters

Criminals that purchase assets from data harvesters to be used for illegal financial gain. Actions may include using stolen credit card numbers to purchase goods, creating fake accounts via identity fraud, and more.

In fact, your computer may be up for rent by cyber thieves right now. **Botnets** of zombie computers (networks of infiltrated and compromised machines controlled by a central command) are used for all sorts of nefarious activity. This includes sending spam from thousands of difficult-to-shut-down accounts, launching tough-to-track click fraud efforts or staging what's known as **distributed denial of service (DDoS)** attacks (effectively shutting down websites by overwhelming them with a crushing load of seemingly legitimate requests sent simultaneously by thousands of machines). Botnets have been discovered that are capable of sending out 100 billion spam messages a day,[13] and botnets as large as 10 million zombies have been identified. Such systems theoretically control more computing power than the world's fastest supercomputers.[14]

Extortionists might leverage botnets or hacked data to demand payment to avoid retribution. Three eastern European gangsters used a botnet and threatened DDoS to extort $4 million from UK sports bookmakers,[15] while an extortion plot against the state of Virginia threatened to reveal names, Social Security numbers, and prescription information stolen from a medical records database.[16] Competition has also lowered the price to inflict such pain. *BusinessWeek* reports that the cost of renting out ten thousand machines, which at the time was enough to cripple a site like Twitter, had tumbled to just $200 a day.[17]

Corporate espionage might be performed by insiders, rivals, or even foreign governments. Gary Min, a scientist working for DuPont, was busted when he tried to sell information valued at some $400 million, including R&D documents and secret data on proprietary products.[18] Spies also breached the $300 billion US Joint Strike Fighter project, siphoning off terabytes of data on navigation and other electronics systems.[19] Hackers infiltrated security firm RSA, stealing data keys used in the firm's commercial authentication devices. The hackers then apparently leveraged the heist to enter the systems of RSA customers, US Defense contractors L-3, Lockheed Martin, and Northrop Grumman.[20] Google has identified China as the nation of origin for a series of hacks targeting the Google accounts of diplomats and activists.[21] The US government has indicted Chinese military officials, even printing up "Most Wanted" posters, claiming those named were behind terabytes of theft from organizations including Alcoa, US Steel, the US Steelworkers Union, electricity and nuclear energy firm Westinghouse, Allegheny Technologies Inc., and SolarWorld.[22] US federal authorities blamed the embarrassing hacking and exposure of internal documents and e-mail from Sony Entertainment on operatives for the government of North Korea, angry about the release of the Kim Jong-un ridiculing comedy "The Interview," while researchers suggested the Sony hack was actually perpetrated by insiders.[23] And the government of Tunisia even attempted a whole-scale hacking of local users' Facebook accounts during protests that eventually led to the ouster of the regime. The so-called man-in-the-middle style attack intercepted Facebook traffic at the state-affiliated ISP as it traveled between Tunisian Web surfers and Facebook's servers, enabling the government to steal passwords and delete posts and photos that criticized the regime (Facebook has since made these efforts more difficult to perpetrate).[24]

FIGURE 17.2

FBI posted images of indicted Chinese military officials charged with cyber espionage against the United States.

Source: FBI.gov website, accessed May 26, 2013, http://www.fbi.gov/news/news_blog/five-chinese-military-hackers-charged-with-cyber-espionage-against-u.s

Cyberwarfare has also become a legitimate threat, with several attacks demonstrating how devastating technology disruptions by terrorists or a foreign power might be (see sidebar on Stuxnet). Brazil has seen hacks that cut off power to millions, and the *60 Minutes* news program showed a demonstration by "white hat" hackers that could compromise a key component in an oil refinery, force it to overheat, and cause an explosion. Taking out key components of the vulnerable US power grid may be particularly devastating, as the equipment is expensive, much of it is no longer made in the United States, and some components may take three to four months to replace.[25]

Stuxnet: A New Era of Cyberwarfare

Stuxnet may be the most notorious known act of cyberwarfare effort to date (one expert called it "the most sophisticated worm ever created").[26] Suspected to have been launched by either US or Israeli intelligence (or both), Stuxnet infiltrated Iranian nuclear facilities and reprogramed the industrial control software operating hundreds of uranium-enriching centrifuges. The worm made the devices spin so fast that the centrifuges effectively destroyed themselves, in the process setting back any Iranian nuclear ambitions. The attack was so sophisticated that it even altered equipment readings to report normal activity so that operators didn't even know something was wrong until it was too late.

Some might fear Stuxnet in the wild—what happens if the code spread to systems operated by peaceful nations or systems controlling critical infrastructure that could threaten lives if infected? In Stuxnet's case the worm appears to have been designed to target very specific systems. If it got onto a nontarget machine, it would become inert. Propagation was also limited, with each copy designed to infect only three additional machines. And the virus was also designed to self-destruct at a future date.[27] Despite these precautions, other malicious code that appears to have a common heritage with Stuxnet has been spotted on systems outside of Iran.[28]

Stuxnet showed that with computers at the heart of so many systems, it's now possible to destroy critical infrastructure without firing a shot.[29] While few want to see Iran get the bomb, what does the rise of cyberwarfare mean for future combat and for citizen vulnerability, and what might this mean for businesses whose products, services, or organizations may become targets?

Other threats come from malicious pranksters (sometimes called *griefers* or *trolls*), like the group that posted seizure-inducing images on websites frequented by epilepsy sufferers.[30] Others are **hacktivists**, targeting firms, websites, or even users as a protest measure. Twitter was once brought down and Facebook and LiveJournal were hobbled as Russian-sympathizing hacktivists targeted the social networking and blog accounts of the Georgian blogger known as Cyxymu. The silencing of millions of accounts was simply collateral damage in a massive DDoS attack meant to mute this single critic of the Russian government.[31]

And as power and responsibility is concentrated in the hands of a few revenge-seeking employees can do great damage. The San Francisco city government lost control of a large portion of its own computer network over a ten-day period when a single disgruntled employee refused to divulge critical passwords.[32]

hacktivists

A protester seeking to make a political point by leveraging technology tools, often through system infiltration, defacement, or damage.

Is Your Government Spying on You?

While sinister and invasive government espionage tools have long been a plot vehicle in Hollywood films, the extent of government surveillance came under scrutiny when a former CIA employee and NSA contractor, Edward Snowden, gathered over 1.7 million digital documents from US, British, and Australian agencies and began leaking them to the press.

FIGURE 17.3
Edward Snowden.

Source: Wikipedia, http://commons.wikimedia.org/wiki/File:Edward_Snowden-2.jpg

The Snowden disclosures revealed that several US government agencies, including the NSA and FBI, had data-monitoring efforts far more pervasive than many realized. These included mechanisms for the "direct access to audio, video, photographs, e-mails, documents and connection logs" at nine major US Internet companies, including Google, Facebook, Yahoo, Microsoft, and Apple,[33] and *unlimited* access to phone records from Verizon's US customers.[34] Another tool, XKeyscore, has been described as allowing the collection of data on "nearly everything a user does on the Internet" and enabling "analysts to search with no prior authorization through vast databases containing emails, online chats and the browsing histories of millions of individuals."[35] A program tapping undersea cables has allowed US and British intelligence authorities to sift through some 21 million GB of data each day.[36] The British intelligence agency GCHQ, using a system code-named "Optic Nerve," allegedly collected Web cam images "from millions of Yahoo users, regardless of whether they were suspected of illegal activity," and up to 11 percent of secretly collected images were thought to have been sexually explicit.[37] Snowden also revealed monitoring programs targeting US allies, including one that eavesdropped on the private phone conversations of German chancellor Angela Merkel.[38]

Whether Snowden was a whistle-blower or traitor is hotly debated. After the revelations, Snowden fled to Russia via Hong Kong (where he had previously been living during the document disclosure), and the Putin government has granted him temporary asylum. The US government has charged Snowden with espionage and revoked his passport, but during this time, Snowden has spoken via remote link at the South by Southwest conference, he's appeared via video conference at a TED event, and has been elected Rector of the University of Glasgow. Regardless of whether you feel that Edward Snowden is a hero, a villain, or something in between, the Snowden case underscores the sensitivity of data collection and the peril that governments and organizations face when technology without adequate safeguards is used along the frontier where privacy and national security meet.

The US government contends that hundreds of terrorists have been captured using techniques revealed by Snowden, implying that this surveillance makes the world more secure.[39] The US government claims that safeguards are in place to prevent widespread abuse. For example, under US law, the NSA is required to obtain a warrant from the Foreign Intelligence Surveillance Court (or FISA) when specifically targeting surveillance in the United States.[40] However, no such warrants are required for intercepting communication between US-based persons and "foreign targets,"[41] and FISA has rejected only eleven of the more than 33,900 requests (less than 0.03 percent) made through 2012.[42] Even if such surveillance programs are well intentioned, risks include having the data fall into the hands of foreign spies, rogue employees, criminals, or unscrupulous government employees. US technology firms have also complained that the actions of surveillance agencies have put them at a disadvantage, with customers looking for alternatives free of the tarnished perception of having (complicity or unwittingly) provided private information to authorities.[43] European firms, in particular, have noticed an uptick in business, and one estimate pins projected collective losses to US firms at $35 billion through 2016.[44]

The bad guys are legion and the good guys often seem outmatched and underresourced. Law enforcement agencies dealing with computer crime are increasingly outnumbered, outskilled, and underfunded. Many agencies are staffed with technically weak personnel who were trained in a prior era's crime fighting techniques. Governments can rarely match the pay scale and stock bonuses offered by private industry. Organized crime networks now have their own R&D labs and are engaged in sophisticated development efforts to piece together methods to thwart current security measures.

"Hacker": Good or Bad?

The terms **hacker** and **hack** are widely used, but their meaning is often based on context. When referring to security issues, the media often refers to hackers as bad guys who try to break into (hack) computer systems. Some geezer geeks object to this use, as the term *hack* in computer circles originally referred to a clever (often technical) solution and the term *hacker* referred to a particularly skilled programmer. Expect to see the terms used both positively and negatively.

You might also encounter the terms **white hat hackers** and **black hat hackers**. The white hats are the good guys who probe for weaknesses, but don't exploit them. Instead, they share their knowledge in hopes that the holes they've found will be plugged and security will be improved. Many firms hire consultants to conduct "white hat" hacking expeditions on their own assets as part of their auditing and security process. "Black hats" are the bad guys. Some call them "crackers." There's even a well-known series of hacker conventions known as the Black Hat conference.

hacker

A term that, depending on the context, may be applied to either 1) someone who breaks into computer systems, or 2) to a particularly clever programmer.

hack

A term that may, depending on the context, refer to either 1) breaking into a computer system, or 2) a particularly clever solution.

white hat hackers

Someone who uncovers computer weaknesses without exploiting them. The goal of the white hat hacker is to improve system security.

black hat hackers

A computer criminal.

KEY TAKEAWAYS

- Computer security threats have moved beyond the curious teen with a PC and are now sourced from a number of motivations, including theft, leveraging compromised computing assets, extortion, espionage, warfare, terrorism, national security, pranks, protest, and revenge.
- Threats can come from both within the firm as well as from the outside.
- Cybercriminals operate in an increasingly sophisticated ecosystem where data harvesters and tool peddlers leverage sophisticated online markets to sell to cash-out fraudsters and other crooks.
- Technical and legal complexity make pursuit and prosecution difficult.
- Government surveillance efforts can put citizens and corporations at risk if poorly executed and ineffectively managed.
- Many law enforcement agencies are underfunded, underresourced, and underskilled to deal with the growing hacker threat.

QUESTIONS AND EXERCISES

1. What is a botnet? What sorts of exploits would use a botnet? Why would a botnet be useful to cybercriminals?

2. Why are threats to the power grid potentially so concerning? What are the implications of power-grid failure and of property damage? Who might execute these kinds of attacks? What are the implications for firms and governments planning for the possibility of cyberwarfare and cyberterror?

3. Scan the trade press for examples of hacking that apply to the various motivations mentioned in this chapter. What happened to the hacker? Were they caught? What penalties do they face?

4. Why do cybercriminals execute attacks across national borders? What are the implications for pursuit, prosecution, and law enforcement?

5. Why do law enforcement agencies struggle to cope with computer crime?

6. A single rogue employee effectively held the city of San Francisco's network hostage for ten days. What processes or controls might the city have created that could have prevented this kind of situation from taking place?

7. Research recent revelations on the extent of government data surveillance. What concerns do government surveillance raise for the computer security of individuals and corporations? Do you believe that there are adequate safeguards to prevent abuse? As a citizen and manager, what changes (if any) would you lobby for and why?

8. The Geneva Conventions are a set of international treaties that in part set standards for protecting citizens in and around a war zone. Should we have similar rules that set the limits of cyberwarfare? Would such limits even be effective? Why or why not?

9. What does the rise of cyberwarfare suggest for businesses and organizations? What sorts of contingencies should firms consider and possibly prepare for? How might considerations also impact a firm's partners, customers, and suppliers?

3. WHERE ARE VULNERABILITIES? UNDERSTANDING THE WEAKNESSES

LEARNING OBJECTIVES

1. Recognize the potential entry points for security compromise.
2. Understand infiltration techniques such as social engineering, phishing, malware, website compromises (such as SQL injection), and more.
3. Identify various methods and techniques to thwart infiltration.

FIGURE 17.4

This diagram shows only some of the potential weaknesses that can compromise the security of an organization's information systems. Every physical or network "touch point" is a potential vulnerability. Understanding where weaknesses may exist is a vital step toward improved security.

Users/Administrators
- Bad apple
- Social engineering
- Phishing
- Weak or easily compromised passwords
- Careless or uninformed user (insecure "sharing" settings, no encryption, software updates turned off, poor configuration)

Physical Threats
- Dumpster diving
- Eavesdropping (key loggers, cameras, mics, devices mailed or left on premises)
- Destruction of property (terror, disaster)

Network
- Sniffers, compromised relays, and equipment
- DNS redirects
- Weak user authentication/ open hotspots

Client Software
- OS holes
- Application weaknesses
- Languages in applications
- Applets in applications

Computing Hardware
- Removable media (USB, DVD, etc.) insert malware or steal data
- PC/device theft
- Physical access (break into room)

Server Software
- OS holes
- Application weaknesses
- Languages in applications
- Applets in applications
- Applications poorly coded (allow for SQL injection, cross-site scripting)
- Unfederated systems (entering one system allows access to others)

Modern information systems have lots of interrelated components and if one of these components fails, there might be a way in to the goodies. This creates a large attack surface for potential infiltration and compromise, as well as one that is simply vulnerable to unintentional damage and disruption.

3.1 User and Administrator Threats

Bad Apples

While some of the more sensational exploits involve criminal gangs, research firm Gartner estimates that 70 percent of loss-causing security incidents involve insiders.[45] Rogue employees can steal secrets, install malware, or hold a firm hostage. Check processing firm Fidelity National Information Services was betrayed when one of its database administrators lifted personal records on 2.3 million of the firm's customers and illegally sold them to direct marketers.

And it's not just firm employees. Many firms hire temporary staffers, contract employees, or outsource key components of their infrastructure (Edward Snowden was an NSA contractor). Other firms have been compromised by members of their cleaning or security staff. A contract employee working at Sentry Insurance stole information on 110,000 of the firm's clients.[46] Verizon claims that 85 percent of "insider" data theft cases were carried out "while in the office and right under the noses of their co-workers."[47]

Social Engineering

As P. T. Barnum is reported to have said, "There's a sucker born every minute." Con games that trick employees into revealing information or performing other tasks that compromise a firm are known as *social engineering* in security circles. In some ways, crooks have never had easier access to background information that might be used to craft a scam. It's likely that a directory of a firm's employees, their titles, and other personal details is online right now via social networks like LinkedIn and Facebook. With just a few moments of searching, a skilled con artist can piece together a convincing and compelling story.

A Sampling of Methods Employed in Social Engineering

- Impersonating senior management, a current or new end user needing help with access to systems, investigators, or staff (fake uniforms, badges)
- Identifying a key individual by name or title as a supposed friend or acquaintance
- Making claims with confidence and authority ("Of course I belong at this White House dinner.")
- Baiting someone to add, deny, or clarify information that can help an attacker
- Using harassment, guilt, or intimidation
- Using an attractive individual to charm others into gaining information, favors, or access
- Setting off a series of false alarms that cause the victim to disable alarm systems
- Answering bogus surveys (e.g., "Win a free trip to Hawaii—just answer three questions about your network.")

Data aggregator ChoicePoint sold private information to criminals who posed as legitimate clients, compromising the names, addresses, and Social Security numbers of some 145,000 individuals. In this breach, not a single computer was compromised. Employees were simply duped into turning data over to crooks. Gaffes like that can be painful. ChoicePoint paid $15 million in a settlement with the Federal Trade Commission, suffered customer loss, and ended up abandoning once lucrative businesses.[48]

Phishing

Phishing

A con executed using technology, typically targeted at acquiring sensitive information or tricking someone into installing malicious software.

Phishing refers to cons executed through technology. The goal of phishing is to leverage the reputation of a trusted firm or friend to trick the victim into performing an action or revealing information. The cons are crafty. Many have masqueraded as a security alert from a bank or e-commerce site ("Our website has been compromised, click to log in and reset your password."), a message from an employer, or even a notice from the government ("Click here to update needed information to receive your tax refund transfer."). Sophisticated con artists will lift logos, mimic standard layouts, and copy official language from legitimate websites or prior e-mails. Gartner estimates that these sorts phishing attacks cost consumers upward of $3.2 billion a year.[49]

Other phishing attempts might dupe a user into unwittingly downloading dangerous software (malware) that can do things like record passwords and keystrokes, copy vital data from your RAM or hard drive, provide hackers with deeper access to your corporate network, or enlist your PC as part of a botnet. One attempt masqueraded as a message from a Facebook friend, inviting the recipient to view a video. Victims clicking the link were then told they need to install an updated version of the Adobe Flash plug-in to view the clip. The plug in was really a malware program that gave phishers control of the infected user's computer.[50] Other attempts have populated P2P networks (peer-to-peer file distribution systems such as BitTorrent) with malware-installing files masquerading as video games or other software, movies, songs, and pornography.

So-called spear phishing attacks specifically target a given organization or group of users. In one incident, employees of a medical center received e-mails purportedly from the center itself, indicating that the recipient was being laid off and offering a link to job counseling resources. The link really offered a software payload that recorded and forwarded any keystrokes on the victim's PC.[51] And with this type of phishing, the more you know about a user, the more convincing it is to con them. Phishers using pilfered résumé information from Monster.com crafted targeted and personalized e-mails. The request, seemingly from the job site, advised users to download the "Monster Job Seeker Tool"; this "tool" installed malware that encrypted files on the victim's PC, leaving a ransom note demanding payment to liberate a victim's hard disk.[52]

spoofed

Term used in security to refer to forging or disguising the origin or identity. E-mail transmissions and packets that have been altered to seem as if they came from another source are referred to as being "spoofed."

Don't Take the Bait: Recognizing the "Phish Hooks"

Web browser developers, e-mail providers, search engines, and other firms are actively working to curtail phishing attempts. Many firms create blacklists that block access to harmful websites and increasingly robust tools screen for common phishing tactics. But it's still important to have your guard up. Some exploits may be so new that they haven't made it into screening systems (so-called zero-day exploits).

Never click on a link or download a suspicious, unexpected enclosure without verifying the authenticity of the sender. If something looks suspicious, don't implicitly trust the "from" link in an e-mail. It's possible that the e-mail address has been **spoofed** (faked) or that it was sent via a colleague's compromised account. If unsure, contact the sender or your security staff.

Also know how to read the complete URL to look for tricks. Some firms misspell Web address names (http://wwwyourbank.com—note the missing period), set up subdomains to trick the eye (http://yourbank.com.sneakysite.com—which is hosted at sneakysite.com even though a quick glance looks like yourbank.com), or hijack brands by registering a legitimate firm's name via foreign top-level domains (http://yourbank.cn).

A legitimate URL might also appear in a phishing message, but an HTML coding trick might make something that looks like http://yourbank.com/login actually link to http://sneakysite.com. Hovering your cursor over the URL or an image connected to a link should reveal the actual URL as a tool tip (just don't click it, or you'll go to that site).

FIGURE 17.5

This e-mail message looks like it's from Bank of America. However, hovering the cursor above the "Continue to Log In" button reveals the URL without clicking through to the site. Note how the actual URL associated with the link is not associated with Bank of America.

Online Banking Alert

Need additional up to the minute account information?
Sign In »

Dear Bank Of America Customer:

Following a recent upgrade of our Online Security Parameters, it was discovered that your online banking details cannot be confirmed with the ones we have on our servers. Thus, a RESTRICTION has been placed on your Bank Of America Online Account.

To lift this restriction, you need to login into your account and complete our verification process. You must reconfirm your credit card details and your billing information as well. All restricted accounts have their billing information unconfirmed, meaning that you may no longer send money from your account until you have reconfirm your billing information on file .

Please click the button below to begin the verification process. Once this is done, you can continue using your online banking access without any future disappointment.

(Failure to verify account details may lead to account disconnection)

Continue to Log In

(It's All About Your   http://www.brassrestaurantandbrewery.com/
brass/id412/5d1/latestupdate.html

Thank you for banking with us.

FIGURE 17.6

This image is from a phishing scheme masquerading as an eBay message. The real destination is a compromised .org domain unassociated with eBay, but the phishers have created a directory at this domain named "signin.ebay.com" in hopes that users will focus on that part of the URL and not recognize they're really headed to a non-eBay site.

Social Media: A Rising Security Threat

Social media tools are a potential gold mine for crooks seeking to pull off phishing scams. Malware can send messages that seem to come from trusted "friends." Messages such as status updates and tweets are short, and with limited background information, there are fewer contexts to question a post's validity. Many users leverage bit.ly or other URL-shortening services that don't reveal the website they link to in their URL, making it easier to hide a malicious link. While the most popular URL-shortening services maintain a blacklist, early victims are threatened by **zero-day exploits**. Criminals have also been using a variety of techniques to spread malware across sites or otherwise make them difficult to track and catch.

The technical openness of many social media efforts can also create problems if schemes aren't implemented properly. For example, Mark Zuckerberg's Facebook page fell victim to hackers who used a hole in a Facebook API that allowed unauthorized status update posts to public Facebook fan pages.[53] APIs can allow firms to share services, collaborate, and enable mash-ups, but if code is poorly implemented it can also be an open back door where the bad guys can sneak in.

Some botnets have even used Twitter to communicate by sending out coded tweets to instruct compromised machines.[54] Social media can also be a megaphone for loose lips, enabling a careless user to broadcast proprietary information to the public domain. For example, a congressional delegation to Iraq was supposed to have been secret. But Rep. Peter Hoekstra tweeted his final arrival into Baghdad for all to see, apparently unable to contain his excitement at receiving BlackBerry service in Iraq. Hoekstra tweeted, "Just landed in Baghdad. I believe it may be first time I've had bb service in Iraq. 11th trip here." You'd think he would have known better. At the time, Hoekstra was a ranking member of the House Intelligence Committee!

FIGURE 17.7

A member of the House Intelligence Committee uses Twitter and reveals his locale on a secret trip.

Passwords

Many valuable assets are kept secure via just one thin layer of protection—the password. And if you're like most users, your password system is a mess.[55] With so many destinations asking for passwords, chances are you're using the same password (or easily guessed variants) in a way that means getting just one "key" would open many "doors." The typical Web user has 6.5 passwords, each of which is used at four sites, on average.[56] Some sites force users to change passwords regularly, but this often results in insecure compromises. Users make only minor tweaks (e.g., appending the month or year); they write passwords down (in an unlocked drawer or Post-it note attached to the monitor); or they save passwords in personal e-mail accounts or on unencrypted hard drives.

The challenge questions offered by many sites to automate password distribution and reset are often pitifully insecure. What's your mother's maiden name? What elementary school did you attend? Where were you born? All are pretty easy to guess. One IEEE study found acquaintances could correctly answer colleagues' secret questions 28 percent of the time, and those who did not know the person still guessed right at a rate of 17 percent. Plus, within three to six months, 16 percent of study participants forgot answers to *their own* security questions.[57] In many cases, answers to these questions can be easily uncovered online. Chances are, if you've got an account at a site like Ancestry.com or Facebook, then some of your secret answers have already been exposed—by you! A Tennessee teen hacked into Sarah Palin's personal Yahoo! account (gov.palin@yahoo.com) in part by correctly guessing where she met her husband. A similar attack hit staffers at Twitter, resulting in the theft of hundreds of internal documents, including strategy memos, e-mails, and financial forecasts, many of which ended up embarrassingly posted online.[58]

Related to the password problem are issues with system setup and configuration. Many vendors sell software with a common default password. For example, for years, leading database products came with the default account and password combination "scott/tiger." Any firm not changing default accounts and passwords risks having an open door. Other firms are left vulnerable if users set systems for open access—say turning on file sharing permission for their PC. Programmers, take note: well-designed products come with secure default settings, require users to reset passwords at setup, and also offer strong warnings when security settings are made weaker. But unfortunately, there are a lot of legacy products out there, and not all vendors have the insight to design for out-of-the-box security.

Building a Better Password

There's no simple answer for the password problem. **Biometrics** are often thought of as a solution. While fingerprint readers have begun to appear on many mainstream mobile devices, technologies that widely replace conventionally typed passwords with biometrics are still rarely used, and PCs that include such technologies are often viewed as novelties. Biometrics are not a panacea. Apple and Samsung[59] are among the high-profile firms that have needed to correct flaws in the biometric systems built into their products.

Other approaches leverage technology that distributes single use passwords. These might arrive via external devices like an electronic wallet card, key chain fob, or cell phone. Enter a username and receive a phone message with a temporary password. Even if a system was compromised by keystroke capture malware, the password is only good for one session. Lost device? A central command can disable it. This may be a good solution for situations that demand a high level of security, and Wells Fargo and PayPal are among the firms offering these types of services as an option. However, for most consumer applications, slowing down users with a two-factor or **multi-factor authentication** system would be an impractical mandate. Also, as with other technologies, some systems have had weaknesses that were penetrated. Hackers have previously figured out how to bypass the two-factor authentication used by Google,[60] and a failure to upgrade one of J.P. Morgan's servers allowed hackers to make off with contact information on millions of depositors.[61]

We're seeing many of these schemes come together to improve credit card security and electronic payments under systems such as Apple Pay and Android Pay. These schemes encrypt credit cards on a mobile device rather than store them at retailers. A scheme called tokenization sends one-time use representations of a credit card over the Internet. While these tokens will buy your stuff, if stolen then can't be reused by bad guys. Fingerprint readers add biometrics to multi-factor authentication at the point of purchase. Devices themselves also have a unique identifier so transactions can only happen from authorized devices. And banks must provide an additional verification step when cards are initially scanned in (added verification is critical. During Apple Pay's rollout, many banks initially approved cards without added customer verification, allowing Apple Pay to be a convenient avenue for fraud card).[62]

FIGURE 17.8

Efforts such as Apple Pay dramatically improve security for credit card transactions by leveraging multi-factor authentication, single-use tokenization, encryption, and biometrics.

Source: https://www.apple.com/pr/products/apple-pay/apple-pay.html.

While you await technical fixes, you can at least work to be part of the solution rather than part of the problem. It's unlikely you've got the memory or discipline to create separate unique passwords for all of your sites, but at least make it a priority to create separate, hard-to-guess passwords for each of your highest priority accounts (e.g., e-mail, financial websites, corporate network, and PC). Remember, the integrity of a password shared across websites isn't just up to you. That hot start-up Web service may not have the security resources or experience to protect your special code, and if that website's account is hacked, your username and password are now in the hands of hackers that can try out those "keys" across the Web's most popular destinations. Software programs such as 1Password or LastPass can help create a secure directory of all your passwords, and it's possible to have these synced across several desktop and mobile devices. Just be sure that if you use this, you never lose your master password, or you've effectively given up the key that holds all of your other keys.

Biometrics

Technologies that measure and analyze human body characteristics for identification or authentication. These might include fingerprint readers, retina scanners, voice and face recognition, and more.

multi-factor authentication

When identity is proven by presenting more than one item for proof of credentials. Multiple factors often include a password and some other identifier such as a unique code sent via e-mail or mobile phone text, a biometric reading (e.g. fingerprint or iris scan), a swipe or tap card, or other form if identification.

Websites are increasingly demanding more "secure" passwords, requiring users to create passwords at least eight characters in length and that include at least one number and other nonalphabet character. Beware of using seemingly clever techniques to disguise common words. Many commonly available brute-force password cracking tools run through dictionary guesses of common words or phrases, substituting symbols or numbers for common characters (e.g., "@" for "a," "+" for "t"). For stronger security, experts often advise basing passwords on a phrase, where each letter makes up a letter in an acronym. For example, the phrase "My first Cadillac was a real lemon so I bought a Toyota" becomes "M1stCwarlslbaT."[63] Be careful to choose an original phrase that's known only by you and that's easy for you to remember. Studies have shown that acronym-based passwords using song lyrics, common quotes, or movie lines are still susceptible to dictionary-style hacks that build passwords from pop-culture references (in one test, two of 144 participants made password phrases from an acronym of the Oscar Meyer wiener jingle).[64] Finding that balance between something tough for others to guess yet easy for you to remember will require some thought—but it will make you more secure. Do it now!

3.2 Technology Threats (Client and Server Software, Hardware, and Networking)

Malware

Any accessible computing device is a potential target for infiltration by malware. *Malware* (for malicious software) seeks to compromise a computing system without permission. Client PCs and a firm's servers are primary targets, but as computing has spread, malware now threatens nearly any connected system running software, including mobile phones, embedded devices, ATMs, point-of-sale equipment, and a firm's networking equipment.

Some hackers will try to sneak malware onto a system via techniques like phishing. In another high-profile hacking example, infected USB drives were purposely left lying around government offices. Those seemingly abandoned office supplies really contained code that attempted to infiltrate government PCs when inserted by unwitting employees.

Machines are constantly under attack. Microsoft's Internet Safety Enforcement Team claims that the mean time to infection for an unprotected PC is less than five minutes.[65] Oftentimes malware attempts to compromise weaknesses in software—either bugs, poor design, or poor configuration.

Years ago, most attacks centered on weaknesses in the operating system, but now malware exploits have expanded to other targets, including browsers, plug-ins, and scripting languages used by software. *BusinessWeek* reports that Adobe has replaced Microsoft as the primary means by which hackers try to infect or take control of PCs. Even trusted websites have become a conduit to deliver malware payloads. More than a dozen sites, including those of the *New York Times*, *USA Today*, and *Nature*, were compromised when seemingly honest advertising clients switched on fake ads that exploit Adobe software.[66] Some attacks were delivered through Flash animations that direct computers to sites that scan PCs, installing malware payloads through whatever vulnerabilities are discovered. Others circulated via e-mail through PDF triggered payloads deployed when a file was loaded via Acrobat Reader. Adobe is a particularly tempting target, as Flash and Acrobat Reader are now installed on nearly every PC, including Mac and Linux machines.

Malware goes by many names. Here are a few of the more common terms you're likely to encounter.[67]

Methods of infection are as follows:

- *Viruses.* Programs that infect other software or files. They require an executable (a running program) to spread, attaching to other executables. Viruses can spread via operating systems, programs, or the boot sector or auto-run feature of media such as DVDs or USB drives. Some applications have executable languages (macros) that can also host viruses that run and spread when a file is open.

- *Worms.* Programs that take advantage of security vulnerability to automatically spread, but unlike viruses, worms do not require an executable. Some worms scan for and install themselves on vulnerable systems with stunning speed (in an extreme example, the SQL Slammer worm infected 90 percent of vulnerable software worldwide within just ten minutes).[68]

- *Trojans.* Exploits that, like the mythical Trojan horse, try to sneak in by masquerading as something they're not. The payload is released when the user is duped into downloading and installing the malware cargo, oftentimes via phishing exploits.

While the terms above cover methods for infection, the terms below address the goal of the malware:

- *Botnets or zombie networks.* Hordes of surreptitiously infected computers linked and controlled remotely by a central command. Botnets are used in crimes where controlling many difficult-to-identify PCs is useful, such as when perpetrating click fraud, sending spam, executing "dictionary" password cracking attempts, or launching denial-of-service attacks. Yahoo! advertisements once inadvertently distributed botnet software that may have enlisted and infected as many as 2 million computers to mine bitcoins (a brute-force guessing technique that effectively gives users access to new units of the cryptocurrency).[70] Other botnets have been used to try and decipher **CAPTCHAs** (those scrambled character images meant to thwart things like automated account setup or ticket buying).

- *Malicious adware.* Programs installed without full user consent or knowledge that later serve unwanted advertisements.

- *Spyware.* Software that surreptitiously monitors user actions, network traffic, or scans for files.

- *Keylogger.* Type of spyware that records user keystrokes. Keyloggers can be either software based or hardware based, such as a recording "dongle" that is plugged in between a keyboard and a PC.

- *Screen capture.* Variant of the keylogger approach. This category of software records the pixels that appear on a user's screen for later playback in hopes of identifying proprietary information.

- *Card Skimmer.* A software program that secretly captures data from a swipe card's magnetic strip.

- *RAM scraping or storage scanning software.* Malicious code that scans computing memory (RAM, hard drives, or other storage) for sensitive data, often looking for patterns such as credit card or Social Security numbers.

- *Ransomware.* Malware that encrypts a user's files (perhaps threatening to delete them), with demands that a user pay to regain control of their data and/or device.

- *Blended threats.* Attacks combining multiple malware or hacking exploits.

The Virus in Your Pocket

Most mobile phones are really pocket computers, so it's not surprising that these devices have become malware targets. And there are a lot of pathways to exploit. Malware might infiltrate a smartphone via e-mail, Internet surfing, MMS attachments, or even Bluetooth. The "commwarrior" mobile virus spread to at least eight countries, propagating from a combination of MMS messages and Bluetooth.[71]

Most smartphones have layers of security to block the spread of malware, so hackers typically hunt for the weakest victims. Easy marks include "jail-broken" iPhones, devices with warranty-voiding modifications in which security restrictions are overridden to allow phones to be used off network, and for the installation of unsanctioned applications. Estimates suggest some 10 percent of iPhones are jail-broken, and early viruses exploiting the compromised devices ranged from a "Rick roll" that replaced the home screen image with a photo of 1980s crooner Rick Astley[72] to the more nefarious Ikee.B, which scanned text messages and hunted out banking codes, forwarding the nabbed data to a server in Lithuania.[73]

The upside? Those smart devices are sometimes crime fighters themselves. Scores of theft victims have used Apple's "Find My iPhone" service to lead cops directly to thieves' doorstep.[74]

CAPTCHAs

An acronym for Completely Automated Public Turing Test to Tell Computers and Humans Apart. CAPTCHAs are those scrambled character images that many sites require to submit some sort of entry (account setup, ticket buying) and are meant to be a *Turing Test*—a test to distinguish if a task is being performed by a computer or a human.[69]

FIGURE 17.9

A "jail-broken" iPhone gets "Rick rolled" by malware.

Compromising Poorly Designed Software

Some exploits directly target poorly designed and programmed websites. Consider the SQL injection technique. It zeros in on a sloppy programming practice where software developers don't validate user input.

It works like this. Imagine that you visit a website and are asked to enter your user ID in a field on a Web page (say your user ID is smith). A website may be programmed to take the data you enter from the Web page's user ID field (smith), then add it to a database command (creating the equivalent of a command that says "find the account for 'smith'"). The database then executes that command.

But websites that don't verify user entries and instead just blindly pass along entered data are vulnerable to attack. Hackers with just a rudimentary knowledge of SQL could type actual code fragments into the user ID field, appending this code to statements executed by the site (see sidebar for a more detailed description). Such modified instructions could instruct the website's database software to drop (delete) tables, insert additional data, return all records in a database, or even redirect users to another website that will scan clients for weaknesses, then launch further attacks. Security expert Ben Schneier noted a particularly ghastly SQL injection vulnerability in the publicly facing database for the Oklahoma Department of Corrections, where "anyone with basic SQL knowledge could have registered anyone he wanted as a sex offender."[75]

Not trusting user input is a cardinal rule of programming, and most well-trained programmers know to validate user input. But there's a lot of sloppy code out there, which hackers are all too eager to exploit. An IBM study claimed that over half a million SQL injection attack attempts are identified each day.[76] The bad guys are clearly probing for weaknesses. Some vulnerable systems started life as quickly developed proofs of concepts, and programmers never went back to add the needed code to validate input and block these exploits. Other websites may have been designed by poorly trained developers who have moved on to other projects, by staff that have since left the firm, or where development was outsourced to another firm. As such, many firms don't even know if they suffer from this vulnerability.

SQL injection and other application weaknesses are particularly problematic because there's not a commercial software patch or easily deployed piece of security software that can protect a firm. Instead, firms have to meticulously examine the integrity of their websites to see if they are vulnerable.[77]

How SQL Injection Works

For those who want to get into some of the geekier details of a SQL injection attack, consider a website that executes the code below to verify that an entered user ID is in a database table of usernames. The code executed by the website might look something like this:

"SELECT * FROM users WHERE userName = '" + userID + "';"

The statement above tells the database to SELECT (find and return) all columns (that's what the "*" means) from a table named users where the database's userName field equals the text you just entered in the userID field. If the website's visitor entered smith, that text is added to the statement above, and it's executed as:

"SELECT * FROM users WHERE userName = 'smith';"

No problem. But now imagine a hacker gets sneaky and instead of just typing smith, into the website's userID field, they also add some *additional* SQL code like this:

smith'; DROP TABLE users; DELETE * FROM users WHERE 't' = 't

If the programming statement above is entered into the user ID, the website adds this code to its own programming to create a statement that is executed as:

SELECT * FROM users WHERE userName = 'smith'; DELETE * FROM users WHERE 't' = 't';

The semicolons separate SQL statements. That second statement says delete all data in the users table for records where 't' = 't' (this last part, 't' = 't,' is always true, so all records will be deleted). Yikes! In this case, someone entering the kind of code you'd learn in the first chapter of *SQL for Dummies* could annihilate a site's entire user ID file using one of the site's own Web pages as the attack vehicle.[78]

Related programming exploits go by names such as cross-site scripting attacks and HTTP header injection. We'll spare you the technical details, but what this means for both the manager and the programmer is that all systems must be designed and tested with security in mind. This includes testing new applications, existing and legacy applications, partner offerings, and SaaS (software as a service) applications—everything. Visa and MasterCard are among the firms requiring partners to rigorously apply testing standards. Firms that aren't testing their applications will find they're locked out of business; if caught with unacceptable breaches, such firms may be forced to pay big fines and absorb any costs associated with their weak practices.[79]

3.3   Push-Button Hacking

Not only are the list of technical vulnerabilities well known, hackers have created tools to make it easy for the criminally inclined to automate attacks. Chapter 18 outlines how websites can interrogate a system to find out more about the software and hardware used by visitors. Hacking toolkits can do the same thing. While you won't find this sort of software for sale on Amazon, a casual surfing of the online underworld (not recommended or advocated) will surface scores of tools that probe systems for the latest vulnerabilities then launch appropriate attacks. In one example, a $700 toolkit (MPack v. 86) was used to infiltrate a host of Italian websites, launching Trojans that infested 15,000 users in just a six-day period.[80] As an industry executive in *BusinessWeek* has stated, "The barrier of entry is becoming so low that literally anyone can carry out these attacks."[81]

Network Threats

The network itself may also be a source of compromise. The retailer TJX (parent of Marshalls, HomeGoods, and T. J. Maxx stores) was hacked when a Wi-Fi access point was left open and undetected. A hacker just drove up and performed the digital equivalent of crawling through an open window. The crooks stole at least 45.7 million credit and debit card numbers and pilfered driver's licenses and other private information from an additional 450,000 customers,[82] a breach that eventually inflicted over $1.35 billion in damages on the retailer.[83] Problems like this are made more challenging since wireless access points are so inexpensive and easy to install. For less than $100, a user (well intentioned or not) could plug in to an access point that could provide entry for anyone. If a firm doesn't regularly monitor its premises, its network, and its network traffic, it may fall victim.

Other troubling exploits have targeted the very underpinning of the Internet itself. This is the case with so-called DNS cache poisoning. The DNS, or domain name service, is a collection of software that maps an Internet address, such as (http://www.bc.edu), to an IP address, such as 136.167.2.220. 220 (see Chapter 16 for more detail). DNS cache poisoning exploits can redirect this mapping and the consequences are huge. Imagine thinking that you're visiting your bank's website, but instead your network's DNS server has been poisoned so that you really visit a carefully crafted replica that hackers use to steal your log-in credentials and drain your bank account. A DNS cache poisoning attack launched against one of China's largest ISPs redirected users to sites that launched malware exploits, targeting weaknesses in RealPlayer, Adobe Flash, and Microsoft's ActiveX technology, commonly used in browsers.[84]

Physical Threats

A firm doesn't just have to watch out for insiders or compromised software and hardware; a host of other physical threats can grease the skids to fraud, theft, and damage. Most large firms have disaster-recovery plans in place. These often include provisions to backup systems and data to off-site locales, to protect operations and provide a fall back in the case of disaster. Such plans increasingly take into account the potential impact of physical security threats such as terrorism, or vandalism, as well.

Anything valuable that reaches the trash in a recoverable state is also a potential security breach. Hackers and spies sometimes practice **dumpster diving**, sifting through trash in an effort to uncover valuable data or insights that can be stolen or used to launch a security attack. This might include hunting for discarded passwords written on Post-it notes, recovering unshredded printed user account listings, scanning e-mails or program printouts for system clues, recovering tape backups, resurrecting files from discarded hard drives, and more.

Other compromises might take place via **shoulder surfing**, simply looking over someone's shoulder to glean a password or see other proprietary information that might be displayed on a worker's screen.

Firms might also fall victim to various forms of eavesdropping, such as efforts to listen into or record conversations, transmissions, or keystrokes. A device hidden inside a package might sit inside a mailroom or a worker's physical inbox, scanning for open wireless connections, or recording and forwarding conversations.[85] Other forms of eavesdropping can be accomplished via compromised wireless or other network connections, malware keylogger or screen capture programs, as well as hardware devices such as replacement keyboards with keyloggers embedded inside, microphones to capture the slightly unique and identifiable sound of each key being pressed, programs that turn on built-in microphone or cameras that are now standard on many PCs, or even James Bond-style devices using Van Eck techniques that attempt to read monitors from afar by detecting their electromagnetic emissions.

dumpster diving

Combing through trash to identify valuable assets.

shoulder surfing

Gaining compromising information through observation (as in looking over someone's shoulder).

encryption

Scrambling data using a code or formula, known as a cipher, such that it is hidden from those who do not have the unlocking key.

key

Code that unlocks encryption.

brute-force attack

An attack that exhausts all possible password combinations in order to break into an account. The larger and more complicated a password or key, the longer a brute-force attack will take.

The Encryption Prescription

During a routine physical transfer of backup media, Bank of America lost tapes containing the private information—including Social Security and credit card numbers—of hundreds of thousands of customers.[86] This was potentially devastating fodder for identity thieves. But who cares if someone steals your files if they still can't read the data? That's the goal of encryption!

Encryption scrambles data, making it essentially unreadable to any program that doesn't have the descrambling password, known as a **key**. Simply put, the larger the key, the more difficult it is for a brute-force attack to exhaust all available combinations and crack the code. When well implemented, encryption can be the equivalent of a rock solid vault. To date, the largest known **brute-force attacks**, demonstration hacks launched by grids of simultaneous code-cracking computers working in unison, haven't come close to breaking the type of encryption used to scramble transmissions that most browsers use when communicating with banks and shopping sites. The problem occurs when data is nabbed before encryption or after decrypting, or in rare cases, if the encrypting key itself is compromised.

Extremely sensitive data—trade secrets, passwords, credit card numbers, and employee and customer information—should be encrypted before being sent or stored.[87] Deploying encryption dramatically lowers the potential damage from lost or stolen laptops, or from hardware recovered from dumpster diving. It is vital for any laptops carrying sensitive information.

Encryption is also employed in virtual private network (VPN) technology, which scrambles data passed across a network. Public wireless connections pose significant security threats—they may be set up by hackers that pose as service providers, while really launching attacks on or monitoring the transmissions of unwitting users. The use of VPN software can make any passed-through packets unreadable. Contact your firm or school to find out how to set up VPN software.

In the Bank of America example above, the bank was burned. It couldn't verify that the lost tapes were encrypted, so it had to notify customers and incur the cost associated with assuming data had been breached.[88]

Encryption is not without its downsides. Key management is a potentially costly procedural challenge for most firms. If your keys aren't secure, it's the equivalent of leaving the keys to a safe out in public. Encryption also requires additional processing to scramble and descramble data—drawing more power and slowing computing tasks. Moore's Law will speed things along, but it also puts more computing power in the hands of attackers. With hacking threats on the rise, expect to see laws and compliance requirements that mandate encrypted data, standardize encryption regimes, and simplify management.

How Do Websites Encrypt Transmissions?

Most Web sites that deal with financial transactions (e.g., banks, online stores) secure transmissions using a method called **public key encryption**. The system works with two keys—a public key and a private key. The public key can "lock" or encrypt data, but it can't unlock it: that can only be performed by the private key. So a Web site that wants you to transmit secure information will send you a public key—you use this to lock the data, and no one that intercepts that transmission can break in unless they've got the private key. If the Web site does its job, it will keep the private key out of reach of all potentially prying eyes.

Wondering if a Web site's transmissions are encrypted? Look at the Web address. If it begins with "https" instead of "http," it should be secure. Also, look for the padlock icon in the corner of your Web browser to be closed (locked). Finally, you can double click the padlock to bring up a verification of the Web site's identity (verified by a trusted third party firm, known as a **certificate authority**). If this matches your URL and indicates the firm you're doing business with, then you can be pretty sure verified encryption is being used by the firm that you intend to do business with.

FIGURE 17.10

In this screenshot, a Firefox browser is visiting Bank of America. The padlock icon was clicked to bring up digital certificate information. Note how the Web site's name matches the URL. The verifying certificate authority is the firm VeriSign.

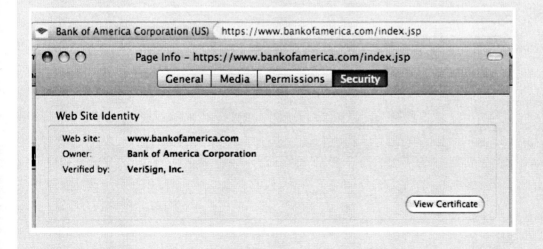

public key encryption

A two key system used for securing electronic transmissions. One key distributed publicly is used to encrypt (lock) data, but it cannot unlock data. Unlocking can only be performed with the private key. The private key also cannot be reverse engineered from the public key. By distributing public keys, but keeping the private key, Internet services can ensure transmissions to their site are secure.

certificate authority

A trusted third party that provides authentication services in public key encryption schemes.

Heartbleed: What Happens When Nearly Everyone Uses Buggy Software?

Open-source software can be a huge benefit to firms, allowing them to use free, reliable software instead of having to develop code on their own or pay expensive commercial license fees. Many of the websites and services that you visit are built on open-source components like the Linux operating system, Apache Web server, and MySQL database. But a vulnerability in widely used software can create a problem for anyone using this code, and while the "openness" of open-source software allows geeks worldwide to search for potential weaknesses, sometimes a hole gets through and inadvertently creates a massive vulnerability.

This is exactly what happened with the Heartbleed bug, a vulnerability in the OpenSSL security software used by about two-thirds of websites and which is embedded into all sorts of Internet-connected products. Heartbleed exploited a bug in a common function that allowed servers to "handshake" or verify they exist and are open for communication. But instead of a program sending the equivalent of a message that instructs a website to *"say 'Hi' to tell me you're there,"* the bug allowed malicious code to instruct in this way: *"say 'Hi' and send me a massive chunk of your memory to tell me you're there."* Why is this bad? That massive chunk of memory could contain usernames, passwords, or even the digital certificate that would allow another server to impersonate a legitimate website. The geek comic site XKCD offered a short, six-panel graphic explanation that gives a good sense of what's happening with Heartbleed (see http://xkcd.com/1354).

As of this writing, few security incidents have been directly attributed to Heartbleed. In one example, authorities bagged a nineteen-year-old who used the flaw to steal hundreds of tax IDs from a Canadian government system. But the full extent of the exploit is hard to know—crooks don't announce "I'm stealing your stuff" and tracing data theft back to a given vulnerability can be difficult. The bug had existed for two years before it was discovered and widely disclosed,[89] so widespread theft is possible. The good news? Publicity and fast-acting open-source advocates helped quickly patch software and eliminate the flaw. All of the top 1,000 most popular websites, and all but fifty-three of the top 10,000 sites, were patched within days of Heartbleed becoming public.[90] However, one of the problems is that OpenSSL is also baked into many hardware products, such as cable modems, routers, and so-called embedded devices (see Chapter 5). Since software in these devices is built into a shipping physical product, it often cannot be upgraded like a server, PC, or phone. As security expert Bruce Schneier points out, "fixing the vulnerability [in many hardware systems] involves a trash can, a credit card, and a trip to the computer store."[91] The Heartbleed bug underscores that managers and technologists need to think about possible software vulnerabilities in all of their smart devices and devise plans for their upgrade or replacement.

KEY TAKEAWAYS

- An organization's information assets are vulnerable to attack from several points of weakness, including users and administrators, its hardware and software, its networking systems, and various physical threats.
- Social engineering attempts to trick or con individuals into providing information, while phishing techniques are cons conducted through technology.
- While dangerous, a number of tools and techniques can be used to identify phishing scams, limiting their likelihood of success.
- Social media sites may assist hackers in crafting phishing or social engineering threats, provide information to password crackers, and act as conduits for unwanted dissemination of proprietary information.
- Most users employ inefficient and insecure password systems; however, techniques were offered to improve one's individual password regime.
- Viruses, worms, and Trojans are types of infecting malware. Other types of malware might spy on users, enlist the use of computing assets for committing crimes, steal assets, destroy property, serve unwanted ads, and more.
- Examples of attacks and scams launched through advertising on legitimate Web pages highlight the need for end-user caution, as well as for firms to ensure the integrity of their participating online partners.
- SQL injection and related techniques show the perils of poor programming. Software developers must design for security from the start—considering potential security weaknesses, and methods that improve end-user security (e.g., in areas such as installation and configuration).
- Encryption can render a firm's data assets unreadable, even if copied or stolen. While potentially complex to administer and resource intensive, encryption is a critical tool for securing an organization's electronic assets.

QUESTIONS AND EXERCISES

1. Consider your own personal password regime and correct any weaknesses. Share any additional password management tips and techniques with your class.

2. Why is it a bad idea to use variants of existing passwords when registering for new websites?

3. Relate an example of social engineering that you've experienced or heard of. How might the victim have avoided being compromised?

4. Have you ever seen phishing exploits? Have you fallen for one? Why did you take the bait, or what alerted you to the scam? How can you identify phishing scams?

5. Have you or has anyone you know fallen victim to malware? Relate the experience—how do you suppose it happened? What damage was done? What, if anything, could be done to recover from the situation?

6. Why are social media sites such a threat to information security? Give various potential scenarios where social media use might create personal or organizational security compromises.

7. Some users regularly update their passwords by adding a number (say month or year) to their code. Why is this bad practice?

8. What kind of features should a programmer build into systems in order to design for security? Think about the products that you use. Are there products that you feel did a good job of ensuring security during setup? Are there products you use that have demonstrated bad security design? How?

9. Why are SQL injection attacks more difficult to address than the latest virus threat?

10. How should individuals and firms leverage encryption?

11. Investigate how you might use a VPN if traveling with your laptop. Be prepared to share your findings with your class and your instructor.

12. Why was the Heartbleed bug so concerning? What sorts of products and services were impacted by the bug? Do some research online. Did you use any products or services that were vulnerable because of Heartbleed? How did you find out about Heartbleed? What are you doing to ensure that you are aware of similar security threats in the future?

---

4. TAKING ACTION

LEARNING OBJECTIVES

1. **Identify critical steps to improve your individual and organizational information security.**
2. **Be a tips, tricks, and techniques advocate, helping make your friends, family, colleagues, and organization more secure.**
3. **Recognize the major information security issues that organizations face, as well as the resources, methods, and approaches that can help make firms more secure.**

4.1 Taking Action as a User

The weakest link in security is often a careless user, so don't make yourself an easy mark. Once you get a sense of threats, you understand the kinds of precautions you need to take. Security considerations then become more common sense than high tech. Here's a brief list of major issues to consider:

- *Surf smart.* Think before you click—question links, enclosures, download requests, and the integrity of websites that you visit. Avoid suspicious e-mail attachments and Internet downloads. Be on guard for phishing and other attempts to con you into letting in malware. Verify anything that looks suspicious before acting. Avoid using public machines (libraries, coffee shops) when accessing sites that contain your financial data or other confidential information.

- *Stay vigilant.* Social engineering con artists and rogue insiders are out there. An appropriate level of questioning applies not only to computer use, but also to personal interactions, be it in person, on the phone, or electronically.

- *Stay updated.* Turn on software update features for your operating system and any application you use (browsers, applications, plug-ins, and applets), and manually check for updates when needed. Malware toolkits specifically scan for older, vulnerable systems, so working with updated programs that address prior concerns lowers your vulnerable attack surface.

- *Stay armed.* Install a full suite of security software. Many vendors offer a combination of products that provide antivirus software that blocks infection, personal firewalls that repel unwanted intrusion, malware scanners that seek out bad code that might already be nesting on your PC, antiphishing software that identifies if you're visiting questionable websites, and more. Such tools are increasingly being built into operating systems, browsers, and are deployed at the ISP or service provider (e-mail firm, social network) level. But every consumer should make it a priority to understand the state of the art for personal protection. In the way that you regularly balance your investment portfolio to account for economic shifts, or take your car in for an oil change to keep it in top running condition, make it a priority to periodically scan the major trade press or end-user computing sites for reviews and commentary on the latest tools and techniques for protecting yourself (and your firm).

- *Be settings smart.* Don't turn on risky settings like unrestricted folder sharing that may act as an invitation for hackers to drop off malware payloads. Secure home networks with password protection and a firewall. Encrypt hard drives—especially on laptops or other devices that might be lost or stolen. Register mobile devices for location identification or remote wiping. Don't click the "Remember me" or "Save password" settings on public machines, or any device that might be shared or accessed by others. Similarly, if your machine might be used by others, turn off browser settings that auto-fill fields with prior entries—otherwise you make it easy for someone to use that machine to track your entries and impersonate you. And when using public hotspots, be sure to turn on your VPN software to encrypt transmission and hide from network eavesdroppers.

- *Be password savvy.* Change the default password on any new products that you install. Update your passwords regularly. Using guidelines outlined earlier, choose passwords that are tough to guess but easy for you (and only you) to remember. Generate your passwords so that you're not using the same access codes for your most secure sites. Never save passwords in nonsecured files, e-mail, or written down in easily accessed locations. Consider a secure password management tool such as 1Password or LastPass and be sure to use the software and manage the master password effectively.

- *Be disposal smart.* Shred personal documents. Wipe hard drives with an industrial strength software tool before recycling, donating, or throwing away—remember in many cases "deleted" files can still be recovered. Destroy media such as CDs and DVDs that may contain sensitive information. Erase USB drives when they are no longer needed.

- *Back up.* The most likely threat to your data doesn't come from hackers; it comes from hardware failure.[92] Yet most users still don't regularly back up their systems. This is another do-it-now priority. Cheap, plug-in hard drives work with most modern operating systems to provide continual backups, allowing for quick rollback to earlier versions if you've accidentally ruined some vital work. And services like Carbonite or Mozy provide regular backup over the Internet for a monthly fee that's likely less than what you spent on your last lunch (a fire, theft, or similar event could also result in the loss of any backups stored on-site, but Internet backup services can provide off-site storage and access if disaster strikes).

- *Check with your administrator.* All organizations that help you connect to the Internet—your ISP, firm, or school—should have security pages. Many provide free security software tools. Use them as resources. Remember—it's in their interest to keep you safe, too!

4.2 Taking Action as an Organization

Frameworks, Standards, and Compliance

Developing organizational security is a daunting task. You're in an arms race with adversaries that are tenacious and constantly on the lookout for new exploits. Fortunately, no firm is starting from scratch—others have gone before you and many have worked together to create published best practices.

There are several frameworks, but perhaps the best known of these efforts comes from the International Organization for Standards (ISO), and is broadly referred to as ISO27k or the ISO 27000 series. According to ISO.org, this evolving set of standards provides "a model for establishing, implementing, operating, monitoring, reviewing, maintaining, and improving an Information Security Management System."

Firms may also face compliance requirements—legal or professionally binding steps that must be taken. Failure to do so could result in fine, sanction, and other punitive measures. At the federal level, examples include HIPAA (the Health Insurance Portability and Accountability Act), which regulates health data; the Gramm-Leach-Bliley Act, which regulates financial data; and the Children's Online Privacy Protection Act, which regulates data collection on minors. US government agencies must also comply with FISMA (the Federal Information Security Management Act), and there are several initiatives at the other government levels. Some level of state data breach laws had been passed in most US states, while multinationals face a growing number of statues throughout the world. Your legal team and trade associations can help you understand your domestic and international obligations. Fortunately, there are often frameworks and guidelines to assist in compliance. For example, the ISO standards include subsets targeted at the telecommunications and health care industries, and major credit card firms have created the PCI (payment card industry) standards. And there are skilled consulting professionals who can help bring firms up to speed in these areas and help expand their organizational radar as new issues develop.

Here is a word of warning on frameworks and standards: compliance does not equal security. Outsourcing portions of security efforts without a complete, organizational commitment to being secure can also be dangerous. Some organizations simply approach compliance as a necessary evil, a sort of checklist that can reduce the likelihood of a lawsuit or other punitive measure.[93] While you want to make sure you're doing everything in your power not to get sued, this isn't the goal. The goal is taking all appropriate measures to ensure that your firm is secure for your customers, employees, shareholders, and others. Frameworks help shape your thinking and expose things you should do, but security doesn't stop there—this is a constant, evolving process that needs to pervade the organization from the CEO suite and board, down to front line workers and potentially out to customers and partners. And be aware of the security issues associated with any mergers and acquisitions. Bringing in new firms, employees, technologies, and procedures means reassessing the security environment for all players involved.

The Heartland Breach: Compliance ≠ Security

Credit card processor Heartland, at the time of the attack that would become one of the largest security breaches in history, was the nation's fifth largest payments processor. Its business was responsible for handling the transfer of funds and information between retailers and cardholders' financial institutions. That means infiltrating Heartland was like breaking into Fort Knox.

It's been estimated that as many as 100 million cards issued by more than 650 financial services companies may have been compromised during the Heartland breach. Said the firm's CEO, this was "the worst thing that can happen to a payments company and it happened to us."[94] Wall Street noticed. The firm's stock tanked—within a month, its market capitalization had plummeted over 75 percent, dropping over half a billion dollars in value.[95]

The Heartland case provides a cautionary warning against thinking that security ends with compliance. Heartland had in fact passed multiple audits, including one conducted the month before the infiltration began. Still, at least thirteen pieces of malware were uncovered on the firm's servers. Compliance does not equal security. Heartland was complaint, but a firm can be compliant and not be secure. Compliance is not the goal, security is.

Since the breach, the firm's executives have championed industry efforts to expand security practices, including encrypting card information at the point it is swiped and keeping it secure through settlement. Such "cradle-to-grave" encryption can help create an environment where even compromised networking equipment or intercepting relay systems wouldn't be able to grab codes.[96] Recognize that security is a continual process, it is never done, and firms need to pursue security with tenacity and commitment.

Education, Audit, and Enforcement

Security is as much about people, process, and policy, as it is about technology.

From a people perspective, the security function requires multiple levels of expertise. Operations employees are involved in the day-to-day monitoring of existing systems. A group's R&D function is involved in understanding emerging threats and reviewing, selecting, and implementing updated security techniques. A team must also work on broader governance issues. These efforts should include representatives from specialized security and broader technology and infrastructure functions. It should also include representatives from general counsel, audit, public relations, and human resources. What this means is that even if you're a nontechnical staffer, you may be brought in to help a firm deal with security issues.

Processes and policies will include education and awareness—this is also everyone's business. As the Vice President of Product Development at security firm Symantec puts it, "We do products really well, but the next step is education. We can't keep the Internet safe with antivirus software alone."[97] Companies should approach information security as a part of their "collective corporate responsibility…regardless of whether regulation requires them to do so."[98]

For a lesson in how important education is, look no further than the former head of the CIA and US Director of Intelligence, John Deutch. Deutch engaged in shockingly loose behavior with digital secrets, including keeping a daily journal of classified information—some 1,000+ pages—on memory cards he'd transport in his shirt pocket. He also downloaded and stored Pentagon information, including details of covert operations, at home on computers that his family used for routine Internet access.[99]

Employees need to know a firm's policies, be regularly trained, and understand that they will face strict penalties if they fail to meet their obligations. Policies without eyes (audit) and teeth (enforcement) won't be taken seriously. Audits include real-time monitoring of usage (e.g., who's accessing what, from where, how, and why; sound the alarm if an anomaly is detected), announced audits, and surprise spot checks. This function might also stage white hat demonstration attacks—attempts to hunt for and expose weaknesses, hopefully before hackers find them. Frameworks offer guidelines on auditing, but a recent survey found most organizations don't document enforcement procedures in their information security policies, that more than one-third do not audit or monitor user compliance with security policies, and that only 48 percent annually measure and review the effectiveness of security policies.[100]

A firm's technology development and deployment processes must also integrate with the security team to ensure that from the start, applications, databases, and other systems are implemented with security in mind. The team will have specialized skills and monitor the latest threats and are able to advise on precautions necessary to be sure systems aren't compromised during installation, development, testing, and deployment.

What Needs to Be Protected and How Much Is Enough?

A worldwide study by PricewaterhouseCoopers and *Chief Security Officer* magazine revealed that most firms don't even know what they need to protect. Only 33 percent of executives responded that their organizations kept accurate inventory of the locations and jurisdictions where data was stored, and only 24 percent kept inventory of all third parties using their customer data.[101] What this means is that most firms don't even have an accurate read on where their valuables are kept, let alone how to protect them.

So information security should start with an inventory-style auditing and risk assessment. Technologies map back to specific business risks. What do we need to protect? What are we afraid might happen? And how do we protect it? Security is an economic problem, involving attack likelihood, costs, and prevention benefits. These are complex trade-offs that must consider losses from theft or resources, systems damage, data loss, disclosure of proprietary information, recovery, downtime, stock price declines, legal fees, government and compliance penalties, and intangibles such as damaged firm reputation, loss of customer and partner confidence, industry damage, promotion of adversary, and encouragement of future attacks.

While many firms skimp on security, firms also don't want to misspend, targeting exploits that aren't likely, while underinvesting in easily prevented methods to thwart common infiltration techniques. Hacker conventions like DefCon can show some really wild exploits. But it's up to the firm to assess how vulnerable it is to these various risks. The local donut shop has far different needs than a military installation, law enforcement agency, financial institution, or firm housing other high-value electronic assets. A skilled risk assessment team will consider these vulnerabilities and what sort of countermeasure investments should take place.

Economic decisions usually drive hacker behavior, too. While in some cases attacks are based on vendetta or personal reasons, in most cases exploit economics largely boils down to:

$$\text{Adversary ROI} = \text{Asset value to adversary} - \text{Adversary cost.}$$

An adversary's costs include not only the resources, knowledge, and technology required for the exploit, but also the risk of getting caught. Make things tough to get at, and lobbying for legislation that imposes severe penalties on crooks can help raise adversary costs and lower your likelihood of becoming a victim.

Technology's Role

Technical solutions often involve industrial strength variants of the previously discussed issues individuals can employ, so your awareness is already high. Additionally, an organization's approach will often leverage multiple layers of protection and incorporate a wide variety of protective measures.

Patch. Firms must be especially vigilant to pay attention to security bulletins and install software updates that plug existing holes, (often referred to as *patches*). Firms that don't plug known problems will be vulnerable to trivial and automated attacks. Unfortunately, many firms aren't updating all components of their systems with consistent attention. With operating systems automating security update installations, hackers have moved on to application targets. But a major study recently found that organizations took at least twice as long to patch application vulnerabilities as they take to patch operating system holes.[102] And remember, software isn't limited to conventional PCs and servers. Embedded systems abound, and connected, yet unpatched devices are vulnerable. Malware has infected everything from unprotected ATM machines[103] to restaurant point-of-sale systems[104] to fighter plane navigation systems.[105]

As an example of unpatched vulnerabilities, consider the DNS cache poisoning exploit described earlier in this chapter. The discovery of this weakness was one of the biggest security stories the year it was discovered, and security experts saw this as a major threat. Teams of programmers worldwide raced to provide fixes for the most widely used versions of DNS software. Yet several months after patches were available, roughly one-quarter of all DNS servers were still unpatched and exposed.[106]

To be fair, not all firms delay patches out of negligence. Some organizations have legitimate concerns about testing whether the patch will break their system or whether the new technology contains a change that will cause problems down the road.[107] And there have been cases where patches themselves have caused problems. Finally, many software updates require that systems be taken down. Firms may have uptime requirements that make immediate patching difficult. But ultimately, unpatched systems are an open door for infiltration.

Lock down hardware. Firms range widely in the security regimes used to govern purchase through disposal system use. While some large firms such as Kraft are allowing employees to select their own hardware (Mac or PC, desktop or notebook, iPhone or BlackBerry),[108] others issue standard systems that prevent all unapproved software installation and force file saving to hardened, backed-up, scanned, and monitored servers. Firms in especially sensitive industries such as financial services may regularly reimage the hard drive of end-user PCs, completely replacing all the bits on a user's hard drive with a pristine, current version—effectively wiping out malware that might have previously sneaked onto a user's PC. Other lock-down methods might disable the boot capability of removable media (a common method for spreading viruses via inserted discs or USBs), prevent Wi-Fi use or require VPN encryption before allowing any network transmissions, and more. The cloud helps here, too. (See Chapter 14) Employers can also require workers to run all of their corporate applications inside a remote desktop where the actual executing hardware and software is elsewhere (likely hosted as a virtual machine session on the organization's servers), and the user is simply served an image of what is executing remotely. This seals the virtual PC off in a way that can be thoroughly monitored, updated, backed up, and locked down by the firm.

In the case of Kraft, executives worried that the firm's previously restrictive technology policies prevented employees from staying in step with trends. Employees opting into the system must sign an agreement promising they'll follow mandated security procedures. Still, financial services firms, law offices, health care providers, and others may need to maintain stricter control, for legal and industry compliance reasons.

Lock down the network. Network monitoring is a critical part of security, and a host of technical tools can help.

Firms employ **firewalls** to examine traffic as it enters and leaves the network, potentially blocking certain types of access, while permitting approved communication. **Intrusion detection systems** specifically look for unauthorized behavior, sounding the alarm and potentially taking action if something seems amiss. Some firms deploy **honeypots**—bogus offerings meant to distract attackers. If attackers take honeypot bait, firms may gain an opportunity to recognize the hacker's exploits, identify the IP address of intrusion, and take action to block further attacks and alert authorities.

firewalls

A system that acts as a control for network traffic, blocking unauthorized traffic while permitting acceptable use.

Intrusion detection systems

A system that monitors network use for potential hacking attempts. Such a system may take preventative action to block, isolate, or identify attempted infiltration, and raise further alarms to warn security personnel.

honeypots

A seemingly tempting, but bogus target meant to draw hacking attempts. By monitoring infiltration attempts against a honeypot, organizations may gain insight into the identity of hackers and their techniques, and they can share this with partners and law enforcement.

blacklists

Programs that deny the entry or exit of specific IP addresses, products, Internet domains, and other communication restrictions.

whitelists

Highly restrictive programs that permit communication only with approved entities and/or in an approved manner.

Many firms also deploy **blacklists**—denying the entry or exit of specific IP addresses, products, Internet domains, and other communication restrictions. While blacklists block known bad guys, **whitelists** are even more restrictive—permitting communication only with approved entities or in an approved manner.

These technologies can be applied to network technology, specific applications, screening for certain kinds of apps, malware signatures, and hunting for anomalous patterns. The latter is important, as recent malware has become polymorphic, meaning different versions are created and deployed in a way that their signature, a sort of electronic fingerprint often used to recognize malicious code, is slightly altered. This also helps with zero-day exploits, and in situations where whitelisted websites themselves become compromised.

Many technical solutions, ranging from network monitoring and response to e-mail screening, are migrating to "the cloud." This can be a good thing—if network monitoring software immediately shares news of a certain type of attack, defenses might be pushed out to all clients of a firm (the more users, the "smarter" the system can potentially become—again we see the power of network effects in action).

Lock down partners. Insist partner firms are compliant, and audit them to ensure this is the case. This includes technology providers and contract firms, as well as value chain participants such as suppliers and distributors. Anyone who touches your network is a potential point of weakness. Many firms will build security expectations and commitments into performance guarantees known as service level agreements (SLAs).

Lock down systems. Audit for SQL injection and other application exploits. The security team must constantly scan exploits and then probe its systems to see if it's susceptible, advising and enforcing action if problems are uncovered. This kind of auditing should occur with all of a firm's partners.

Access controls can also compartmentalize data access on a need-to-know basis. Such tools can not only enforce access privileges, they can help create and monitor audit trails to help verify that systems are not being accessed by the unauthorized, or in suspicious ways.

Audit trails are used for deterring, identifying, and investigating these cases. Recording, monitoring, and auditing access allows firms to hunt for patterns of abuse. Logs can detail who, when, and from where assets are accessed. Giveaways of nefarious activity may include access from unfamiliar IP addresses, from nonstandard times, accesses that occur at higher than usual volumes, and so on. Automated alerts can put an account on hold or call in a response team for further observation of the anomaly.

Single-sign-on tools can help firms offer employees one very strong password that works across applications, is changed frequently (or managed via hardware cards or mobile phone log-in), and can be altered by password management staff.

Multiple administrators should jointly control key systems. Major configuration changes might require approval of multiple staffers, as well as the automatic notification of concerned personnel. And firms should employ a recovery mechanism to regain control in the event that key administrators are incapacitated or uncooperative. This balances security needs with an ability to respond in the event of a crisis. Such a system was not in place in the earlier described case of the rogue IT staffer who held the city of San Francisco's networks hostage by refusing to give up vital passwords.

Have failure and recovery plans. While firms work to prevent infiltration attempts, they should also have provisions in place that plan for the worst. If a compromise has taken place, what needs to be done? Do stolen assets need to be devalued (e.g., accounts terminated, new accounts issued)? What should be done to notify customers and partners, educate them, and advise them through any necessary responses? Who should work with law enforcement and with the media? Do off-site backups or redundant systems need to be activated? Can systems be reliably restored without risking further damage?

Best practices are beginning to emerge. While postevent triage is beyond the scope of our introduction, the good news is that firms are now sharing data on breaches. Given the potential negative consequences of a breach, organizations once rarely admitted they'd been compromised. But now many are obligated to do so. And the broad awareness of infiltration both reduces organizational stigma in coming forward, and allows firms and technology providers to share knowledge on the techniques used by cybercrooks.

Information security is a complex, continually changing, and vitally important domain. The exploits covered in this chapter seem daunting, and new exploits constantly emerge. But your thinking on key issues should now be broader. Hopefully you've now embedded security thinking in your managerial DNA, and you are better prepared to be a savvy system user and a proactive participant working for your firm's security. Stay safe!

KEY TAKEAWAYS

- End users can engage in several steps to improve the information security of themselves and their organizations. These include surfing smart, staying vigilant, updating software and products, using a comprehensive security suite, managing settings and passwords responsibly, backing up, properly disposing of sensitive assets, and seeking education.

- Frameworks such as ISO27k can provide a road map to help organizations plan and implement an effective security regime.

- Many organizations are bound by security compliance commitments and will face fines and retribution if they fail to meet these commitments.

- The use of frameworks and being compliant is not equal to security. Security is a continued process that must be constantly addressed and deeply ingrained in an organization's culture.

- Security is about trade-offs—economic and intangible. Firms need to understand their assets and risks in order to best allocate resources and address needs.

- Information security is not simply a technical fix. Education, audit, and enforcement regarding firm policies are critical. The security team is broadly skilled and constantly working to identify and incorporate new technologies and methods into their organizations. Involvement and commitment is essential from the boardroom to frontline workers, and out to customers and partners.

QUESTIONS AND EXERCISES

1. Visit the security page for your ISP, school, or employer. What techniques do they advocate that we've discussed here? Are there any additional techniques mentioned and discussed? What additional provisions do they offer (tools, services) to help keep you informed and secure?

2. What sorts of security regimes are in use at your university, and at firms you've worked or interned for? If you don't have experience with this, ask a friend or relative for their professional experiences. Do you consider these measures to be too restrictive, too lax, or about right?

3. While we've discussed the risks in having security that is too lax, what risk does a firm run if its security mechanisms are especially strict? What might a firm give up? What are the consequences of strict end-user security provisions?

4. What risks does a firm face by leaving software unpatched? What risks does it face if it deploys patches as soon as they emerge? How should a firm reconcile these risks?

5. What methods do firms use to ensure the integrity of their software, their hardware, their networks, and their partners?

6. An organization's password management system represents "the keys to the city." Describe personnel issues that a firm should be concerned with regarding password administration. How might it address these concerns?

ENDNOTES

1. M. Riley, B. Elgin, D. Lawrence, and C. Matlack, "Missed Alarms and 40 Million Stolen Credit Card Numbers: How Target Blew It," *BusinessWeek*, March 13, 2014.

2. M. Riley, B. Elgin, D. Lawrence, and C. Matlack, "Missed Alarms and 40 Million Stolen Credit Card Numbers: How Target Blew It," *BusinessWeek*, March 13, 2014.

3. "Why the Target Data Hack is Just the Beginning," *Bloomberg View*, January 16, 2014.

4. M. Riley, B. Elgin, D. Lawrence, and C. Matlack, "Missed Alarms and 40 Million Stolen Credit Card Numbers: How Target Blew It," *BusinessWeek*, March 13, 2014.

5. M. Riley, B. Elgin, D. Lawrence, and C. Matlack, "Missed Alarms and 40 Million Stolen Credit Card Numbers: How Target Blew It," *BusinessWeek*, March 13, 2014.

6. J. Hawes, "2013 an Epic Year for Data Breaches with over 800 Million Records Lost," *NakedSecurity*, February 19, 2014.

7. A. Shalal and M. Spetalnick, "Data hacked from U.S. government dates back to 1985: U.S. official," *Reuters*, June 5, 2015.

8. L. Richwine, "Cyber attack could cost Sony studio as much as $100 million," *Reuters*, Dec. 9, 2014.

9. P. Paganini, "2013—The Impact of Cybercrime," *Infosec Institute*, November 1, 2013.

10. S. Kroft, "Cyberwar: Sabotaging the System," *60 Minutes*, November 8, 2009.

11. R. Singel, "Underground Crime Economy Health, Security Group Finds," *Wired*, November 24, 2008.

12. M. Schwartz, "Cybercrime Black Markets Grow Up," *InformationWeek*, March 26, 2014.

13. K. J. Higgins, "SecureWorks Unveils Research on Spamming Botnets," *DarkReading*, April 9, 2008.

14. B. Krebs, "Storm Worm Dwarfs World's Top Supercomputer," *Washington Post*, August 31, 2007.

15. Trend Micro, "Web Threats Whitepaper," March 2008.

16. S. Kroft, "Cyberwar: Sabotaging the System," *60 Minutes*, November 8, 2009.

17. J. Schectman, "Computer Hacking Made Easy," *BusinessWeek*, August 13, 2009.

18. J. Vijayan, "Software Consultant Who Stole Data on 110,000 People Gets Five-Year Sentence," *Computerworld*, July 10, 2007.

19. S. Gorman, A. Cole, and Y. Dreazen. "Computer Spies Breach Fighter-Jet Project," *Wall Street Journal*, April 21, 2009.

20. E. Mills, "China Linked to New Breaches Tied to RSA," *CNET*, June 6, 2011.

21. P. Eckert, "Analysis: Can Naming, Shaming Curb Cyber Attacks from China?" *Reuters*, June 3, 2011.

22. S. Ackerman and J. Kaiman, "Chinese Military Officials Charged with Stealing U.S. Data as Tensions Escalate," *Guardian*, May 20, 2014.

23. R. Faughnder and S. Hamedy, "Sony insider -- not North Korea -- likely involved in hack, experts say," *The Los Angeles Times*, Dec. 30, 2014.

24. A. Madrigal, "The Inside Story of How Facebook Responded to Tunisian Hacks," *Atlantic*, January 24, 2011.

25. S. Kroft, "Cyberwar: Sabotaging the System," *60 Minutes*, November 8, 2009.

26. N. Firth, "Computer Super-Virus 'Targeted Iranian Nuclear Power Station' but Who Made It?" *Daily Mail*, September 24, 2010.

27. M. Gross, "A Declaration of Cyber-War," *Vanity Fair*, April 2011.

28. K. Zetter, "Son of Stuxnet Found in the Wild on Systems in Europe," *Wired*, October 18, 2011.

29. T. Butterworth, "The War against Iran Has Already Started," *Forbes*, September 21, 2010.

30. M. Schwartz, "The Trolls among Us," *New York Times*, August 3, 2008.

31. J. Schectman, "Computer Hacking Made Easy," *BusinessWeek*, August 13, 2009.

32. J. Vijayan, "After Verdict, Debate Rages in Terry Childs Case," *Computerworld*, April 28, 2010.

33. Domestic Surveillance Directorate website, "Surveillance Techniques: How Your Data Becomes Our Data," accessed April 14, 2014, http://nsa.gov1.info/surveillance.

34. G. Greenwald, "NSA Collecting Phone Records of Millions of Verizon Customers Daily," *Guardian*, June 5, 2013.

35. G. Greenwald, "XKeyscore: NSA Tool Collects 'Nearly Everything a User Does on the Internet'," *Guardian*, July 31, 2013.

36. O. Khazan, "The Creepy, Long-Standing Practice of Undersea Cable Tapping," *Atlantic*, July 16, 2013.

37. N. Perlroth and V. Goel, "British Spies Said to Intercept Yahoo Webcam Images," *New York Times*, February 27, 2014.

38. P. Lewis and P. Otterman, "Angela Merkel Denied Access to Her NSA File," *Guardian*, April 10, 2014.

39. G. Greenwald, "XKeyscore: NSA Tool Collects 'Nearly Everything a User Does on the Internet'," *Guardian*, July 31, 2013.

40. N. Totenberg, "Why the FISA Court Is Not What It Used to Be," *NPR*, June 18, 2013.

41. G. Greenwald, "XKeyscore: NSA Tool Collects 'Nearly Everything a User Does on the Internet'," *Guardian*, July 31, 2013.

42. E. Perez, "Secret Court's Oversight Gets Scrutiny," *Wall Street Journal*, June 9, 2013.

43. C. Cain Miler, "Revelations of N.S.A. Spying Cost U.S. Tech Companies," *New York Times*, March 21, 2014.

44. R. Cowan, "Exclusive: U.S. tech industry appeals to Obama to keep hands off encryption," *Reuters*, June 9, 2015.

45. J. Mardesich, "Ensuring the Security of Stored Data," CIO Strategy Center, 2009.

46. J. Vijayan, "Software Consultant Who Stole Data on 110,000 People Gets Five-Year Sentence," *Computerworld*, July 10, 2007.

47. A. Hesseldahl, "It's Official: 2013 Was the Busiest Year Yet for Cyber Criminals," *Re/code*, April 21, 2014.

48. G. Anthes, "The Grill: Security Guru Ira Winkler Takes the Hot Seat," *Computerworld*, July 28, 2008.

49. L. Avivah, "Phishing Attacks Escalate, Morph, and Cause Considerable Damage," *Gartner*, December 12, 2007.

50. B. Krebs, "'Koobface' Worm Resurfaces on Facebook, MySpace," *Washington Post*, March 2, 2009.

51. C. Garretson, "Spam That Delivers a Pink Slip," *NetworkWorld*, November 1, 2006.

52. T. Wilson, "Trojan on Monster.com Steals Personal Data," *Forbes*, August 20, 2007.

53. G. Cluley, "Mark Zuckerberg Fan Page Hacked on Facebook: What Really Happened?" *NakedSecurity*, January 27, 2011.

54. UnsafeBits, "Botnets Go Public by Tweeting on Twitter," *Technology Review*, August 17, 2009.

55. F. Manjoo, "Fix Your Terrible, Insecure Passwords in Five Minutes," *Slate*, November 12, 2009.

56. N. Summers, "Building a Better Password," *Newsweek*, October 19, 2009.

57. R. Lemos, "Are Your 'Secret Questions' Too Easily Answered?" *Technology Review*, May 18, 2009.

58. N. Summers, "Building a Better Password," *Newsweek*, October 19, 2009.

59. J. Zorabedian, "Samsung Galaxy S5 Fingerprint Reader Hacked—It's the iPhone 5s All over Again!" *NakedSecurity*, April 17, 2014.

60. B. Cha, "Too Embarrassed to Ask: What Is Two-Factor Authentication and Why Do I Need It?" *Re/code*, May 21, 2015.

61. M. Moon, "JPMorgan Chase was hacked due to two-factor authentication blunder," *Engadget*, Dec. 23, 2014.

62. J. Heggestuen, "Apple Pay is ringing in a new era of payment security," *Business Insider*, June 3, 2015.

63. F. Manjoo, "Fix Your Terrible, Insecure Passwords in Five Minutes," *Slate*, November 12, 2009.

64. N. Summers, "Building a Better Password," *Newsweek*, October 19, 2009.

65. J. Markoff, "A Robot Network Seeks to Enlist Your Computer," *New York Times*, October 20, 2008.

66. A. Ricadela, "Can Adobe Beat Back the Hackers?" *BusinessWeek*, November 19, 2009.

67. Portions adapted from G. Perera, "Your Guide to Understanding Malware," *LaptopLogic.com*, May 17, 2009.

68. M. Broersma, "Slammer—the First 'Warhol' Worm?" *CNET*, February 3, 2003.

70. J. Wakefield, "Yahoo Malware Enslaves PCs to Bitcoin Mining," *BBC News*, January 8, 2014.

69. J. Charney, "Commwarrior Cell Phone Virus Marches On," *CNET*, June 5, 2005.

72. S. Steade, "It's Shameless How They Flirt," *Good Morning Silicon Valley*, November 9, 2009.

73. R. Lemos, "Nasty iPhone Worm Hints at the Future," *Technology Review*, November 29, 2009.

74. J. Murrell, "The iWitness News Roundup: Crime-fighting iPhone," *Good Morning Silicon Valley*, August 31, 2009.

75. B. Schneier, "Oklahoma Data Leak," *Schneier on Security*, April 18, 2008.

76. A. Wittmann, "The Fastest-Growing Security Threat," *InformationWeek*, November 9, 2009.

77. While some tools exist to automate testing, this is by no means as easy a fix as installing a commercial software patch or virus protection software.

78. B. Schneier, "Oklahoma Data Leak," *Schneier on Security*, April 18, 2008.

79. "Information Security: Why Cybercriminals Are Smiling," *Knowledge@Wharton*, August 19, 2009.

80. "Web Threats Whitepaper," *Trend Micro*, March 2008.

81. J. Schectman, "Computer Hacking Made Easy," *BusinessWeek*, August 13, 2009.

82. J. Vijayvan, "TJX Data Breach: At 45.6M Card Numbers, It's the Biggest Ever," *Computerworld*, March 29, 2007.

83. J. Gacinga, "Will Target's Information Security Breach Play Out Like that of the TJX Companies?" *The Motley Fool*, December 26, 2013.

84. J. London, "China Netcom Falls Prey to DNS Cache Poisoning," *Computerworld*, August 22, 2008.

85. J. Robertson, "Hackers Mull Physical Attacks on a Networked World," *San Francisco Chronicle*, August 8, 2008.

86. J. Mardesich, "Ensuring the Security of Stored Data," CIO Strategy Center, 2009.

87. J. Mardesich, "Ensuring the Security of Stored Data," CIO Strategy Center, 2009.

88. J. Mardesich, "Ensuring the Security of Stored Data," CIO Strategy Center, 2009.

89. K. Zetter, "Has the NSA Been Using the Heartbleed Bug as an Internet Peephole?" *Wired*, April 10, 2014.

90. A. Hesseldahl, "The Hearbleed Bug Is Mostly Fixed, but Not Entirely," *Re/code*, April 18, 2014.

91. S. Berinato, "Heartbleed, the Branding of a Bug, and the Internet of Things," *Harvard Business Review Blog*, April 14, 2014.

92. C. Taylor, "The Tech Catastrophe You're Ignoring," *Fortune*, October 26, 2009.

93. M. Davis, "What Will It Take?" *InformationWeek*, November 23, 2009.

94. R. King, "Lessons from the Data Breach at Heartland," *BusinessWeek*, July 6, 2009.

95. T. Claburn, "Payment Card Industry Gets Encryption Religion," *InformationWeek*, November 13, 2009.

96. T. Claburn, "Payment Card Industry Gets Encryption Religion," *InformationWeek*, November 13, 2009; R. King, "Lessons from the Data Breach at Heartland," *BusinessWeek*, July 6, 2009.

97. D. Goldman, "Cybercrime: A Secret Underground Economy," *CNNMoney*, September 17, 2009.

98. Knowledge@Wharton, "Information Security: Why Cybercriminals Are Smiling," August 19, 2009.

99. N. Lewis, "Investigation of Ex-Chief of the C.I.A. Is Broadened," *New York Times*, September 17, 2000.

100. A. Matwyshyn, *Harboring Data: Information Security, Law, and the Corporation* (Palo Alto, CA: Stanford University Press, 2009).

101. A. Matwyshyn, *Harboring Data: Information Security, Law, and the Corporation* (Palo Alto, CA: Stanford University Press, 2009).

102. S. Wildstrom, "Massive Study of Net Vulnerabilities: They're Not Where You Think They Are," *BusinessWeek*, September 14, 2009.

103. P. Lilly, "Hackers Targeting Windows XP-Based ATM Machines," *Maximum PC*, June 4, 2009.

104. R. McMillan, "Restaurants Sue Vendors after Point-of-Sale Hack," *CIO*, December 1, 2009.

105. C. Matyszczyk, "French Planes Grounded by Windows Worm," *CNET*, February 8, 2009.

106. IBM, *X-Force Threat Report: 2008 Year in Review*, January 2009.

107. For example, the DNS security patch mentioned was incompatible with the firewall software deployed at some firms.

108. N. Wingfield, "It's a Free Country…So Why Can't I Pick the Technology I Use in the Office?" *Wall Street Journal*, November 15, 2009.

CHAPTER 18

Google in Three Parts: Search, Online Advertising, and an Alphabet of Opportunity

---

1. INTRODUCTION

LEARNING OBJECTIVES

1. Understand the extent of Google's rapid rise and its size and influence when compared with others in the media industry.
2. Recognize the shift away from traditional advertising media to Internet advertising.
3. Gain insight into the uniqueness and appeal of Google's corporate culture.

It's hard to match Google for societal impact. The firm has "revolutionized access to knowledge, invigorated democratic forces, boosted productivity and spawned innovation on a scale unrecognized since the dawn of civilization."[1] However, from a revenue perspective, Google is pretty much a one-trick pony.[2] Now as tricks go, this one's pretty exquisite. Google's "trick" is matchmaking—pairing Internet surfers with advertisers and taking a cut along the way. This cut is substantial, as some[3] 90 percent of the firm's $66 billion in 2014 revenue came from advertising. As *Wired*'s Steve Levy puts it, Google's matchmaking capabilities may represent "the most successful business idea in history."[4] Google has already grown to earn more annual advertising dollars than any US media company. No television network, no magazine group, no newspaper chain brings in more ad revenue than Google. And none is more profitable. Google's stated mission is "to organize the world's information and make it universally accessible and useful," advertising drives profits and lets the firm offer most of its services for free.

Those free services have propelled Google into a wide-ranging, multifront war that includes mobile, browsers, cloud infrastructure, e-mail, office apps, social media, maps, e-commerce, payments, and more. While the firm's performance in each space varies, the success of its ad business provides a massive cash hoard, which allows the firm to fuel experimentation, constantly innovate, tolerate failure, acquire aggressively, and patiently build new markets. Google is by no means done. Android now tops the smartphone market share, and Google intends to extend the platform to PC, TV, car, home automation, and accessories such as Google Glass smart watches, virtual reality, more. The firm also relentlessly pursues "moonshot" projects (i.e., wildly ambitious and risky multiyear research efforts). The current list includes driverless cars, smart contact lenses, and world-wrapping satellite and balloon-delivered wireless networks. Google bought eleven robotics firms in a single year for…well, the firm isn't saying.[5] And that's just a fraction of the roughly 180 acquisitions that Google has made overall,[6] which is more than Apple, Microsoft, Amazon, Facebook, and Yahoo!, combined.[7] A *Time* magazine cover story on Google's Calico health and aging research initiative was titled "Can Google Solve Death?"[8] Google's activities are so broad that CEO Page has acknowledged it may be time for a new motto.[9]

Just a few months after that statement, Page announced a reorganization under a holding company named Alphabet (same stock symbol), which will treat Google's core consumer businesses (search, mail, and YouTube) as separate from other efforts, such as Nest home automation, Calico longevity initiatives, the self-driving cars and other 'moonshots' of Google X, and more (details were announced at the alphabetic website http://abc.xyz). While long-time Googler Sundar Pichai is head of what most think of as the 'Google' part of Alphabet, apologies if accounts in this book and chapter continue to refer to the new firm under the legacy name and leadership titles. While a risk-taker, it's important to recognize that Google isn't always a winner. Many of Google's once-hyped efforts are no more. The abandoned e-mail replacement tool Google Wave, the defunct social network Google Buzz, and the firm's flubbed acquisition of Motorola for $12.5 billion (sold for $2.91 billion two years later) are just some of Google's more high-profile busts.[10] Nobody bats 1.000, but ad profits give Google (now Alphabet) the financial stamina to keep coming to the plate and swinging for the fences.

That profit graph keeps moving up and to the right. As more people spend more time online, advertisers are shifting spending away from old channels to the Internet, and Google is swallowing the lion's share of this funds transfer.[11] Add to that Google's lucrative ad network that serves ads to apps and Web sites ranging from small-time bloggers to the *New York Times*, plus Google ad-serving properties like YouTube, Gmail, Google Finance, and Google Maps, and the firm controls about a third of *all* online advertising dollars. Facebook, Bing, Yahoo!, AOL, Twitter—add up all their advertising revenue and combined they're *less than half of* Google's. Add in China's giants Baidu (#3 worldwide), Alibaba (#4), and Tencent (#9) and you're still not even close to Google's total.[12] Google has one of the world's strongest brands[13] (its name is a verb—*just Google it*). It is regularly voted among the best firms to work for in America (topping *Fortune*'s list six times). While rivals continue to innovate (see the box "Search: Google Rules, but It Ain't Over" in Section 10), Google continues to dominate the search market.

FIGURE 18.1 U.S. Advertising Spending Percentages (by Media)

Over the past several years, online advertising represents the only advertising category that is consistently trending with positive share growth.

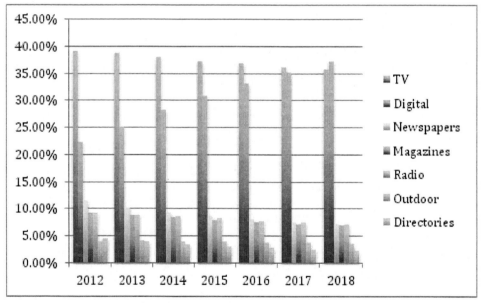

Source: Data retrieved via eMarketer.com June 2014, 2014-2018 are estimates.

market capitalization (market cap)

The value of a firm calculated by multiplying its share price by the number of shares.

Wall Street has rewarded this success. The firm's **market capitalization (market cap)**, the value of the firm calculated by multiplying its share price by the number of shares, makes Google the most valuable media company on the planet. The firm's founding duo, Sergey Brin and Larry Page, are billionaires, regularly appearing near the top of the *Forbes* 400 list of wealthiest Americans. Within five years of going public, Google's market cap was greater than that of News Corp (which includes all of the Fox Networks, and the *Wall Street Journal*), Disney (including ABC, ESPN, theme parks, and Pixar), Time Warner (*Fortune, Time, Sports Illustrated*, CNN, and Warner Bros.), Viacom (MTV, VH1, and Nickelodeon), CBS, and the *New York Times*—combined! Just six years after its IPO, Google had become one of the twenty most profitable firms in the United States and was the youngest firm on the list—by far. Not bad for a business started by two twenty-something computer science graduate students.

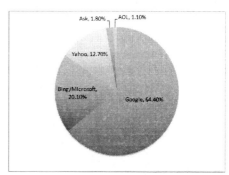

FIGURE 18.2 US Search Market Share (Volume of Searches, March 2015)

Source: Adapted from comScore, "comScore Releases March 2015 US Desktop Search Engine Rankings."

Genius Geeks and Plum Perks

Brin and Page have built a talent magnet. At the Googleplex, the firm's Mountain View, California, headquarters, geeks are lavished with perks that include on-site laundry, massage, carwash, bicycle repair, free haircuts, state of the art gyms, and **Wi-Fi** equipped shuttles that ferry employees around Silicon Valley and the San Francisco Bay area. The Googleplex is also pretty green. The facility gets 30 percent of its energy from solar cells, representing the largest corporate installation of its kind.[14]

The firm's quirky tech-centric culture is evident everywhere. A T-Rex skeleton looms near the volleyball court. Hanging from the lobby ceiling is a replica of SpaceShipOne, the first commercial space vehicle. And visitors to the bathroom will find "testing on the toilet," coding problems or other brainteasers to keep gray matter humming while seated on one of the firm's $800 remote-controlled Japanese commodes. Staff also enjoy an A-list lecture series attracting luminaries ranging from celebrities to heads of state.

And of course there's the food—all of it free. The firm's founders felt that no employee should be more than 100 feet away from nourishment, and a tour around Google offices will find espresso bars, snack nooks, and fully stocked beverage refrigerators galore. There are eleven gourmet cafeterias on-site, the most famous being "Charlie's Place," first run by the former executive chef for the Grateful Dead.

Chairman and former CEO Eric Schmidt said the goal of all this is "to strip away everything that gets in our employees' way."[15] And the perks, culture, and sense of mission have allowed the firm to assemble one of the most impressive rosters of technical talent anywhere. The Googleplex is like a well-fed Manhattan project, and employee ranks have included a gaggle of geniuses that helped invent critical technologies such as the Macintosh user interface, the Python programming language, the XML standard, and even the protocols that underlie the Internet itself.

Engineers find Google a particularly attractive place to work, in part due to a corporate policy of offering "20 percent time," the ability to work the equivalent of one day a week on new projects that interest them. It's a policy that has fueled innovation. Roughly half of Google products got their start in 20 percent time.[16]

Wi-Fi

A term used to brand wireless local-area networking devices. Devices typically connect to an antenna-equipped base station or hotspot, which is then connected to the Internet. Wi-Fi devices use standards known as IEEE 802.11, and various versions of this standard (e.g., b, g, n) may operate in different frequency bands and have access ranges.

1.1 Why Study Google?

Google is without a doubt one of the most influential and impactful firms of the modern era. You'd be hard-pressed to find an organization in any country where Google operates that isn't impacted by the firm's reach, be it in workforce empowerment (search, apps, software, devices); promotion (organic search and paid ads); or infrastructure (cloud). Studying Google gives us a platform for understanding online promotion and advertising, as well as a living case on how quickly technology-fueled market disruptions can happen, and how deeply these disruptions penetrate various industries. The chapter will allow us to study technical issues such as distributed computing, customer profiling, and more. We'll study the chapter within the context of learning the technologies and business issues across the online ad landscape, including search, display, and mobile. We'll also apply strategic thinking to understand current competition and illuminate the landscape for the battles ahead. The transition to the Alphabet corporate structure will be one watched for years—is this a viable model for large firms to break out and nurture new initiatives that create growth through genuine disruptive innovation? You can consider this chapter as consisting of three extended sections. The first part (Section 15.2

"Understanding Search") covers Google Search, the firm's core product and introduces how search works. The second part (Section 15.3 "Understanding the Increase in Online Ad Spending" through Section 15.9 "Search Engines, Ad Networks, and Fraud") covers how the firm makes most of its money—advertising. By reading this section you'll get a solid introduction to various types of online advertising, how customer profiling works, and issues of online privacy and fraud. The last section (Section 15.10 "The Battle Unfolds") covers the firm's evolving strategy, its competition with disparate rivals, and the opportunities and challenges the firm faces going forward.

KEY TAKEAWAYS

- Online advertising represents the only advertising category that, over the last several years, has been consistently trending with positive growth.
- Google dominates Internet search volume and controls the lion's share of the Internet search advertising business and online advertising dollars. The firm also earns more total advertising revenue than any other firm, online or off.
- Google's market cap makes it the most valuable media company in the world; it has been rated as having one of the world's strongest brands, and it ranks among the most profitable firms in the United States.

QUESTIONS AND EXERCISES

1. List the reasons why Google has been considered a particularly attractive firm to work for. Are all of these associated with perks?
2. Market capitalization and market share change frequently. Investigate Google's current market cap and compare it with other media companies. Do patterns suggested in this case continue to hold? Why or why not?
3. Google has been dominant in the US for years. Research online to find out if Google's dominance spreads to international markets, as well. Give examples of markets where Google's share is as strong or stronger than in the US. Give examples where Google isn't a leader. Why do you think Google struggles in these global markets?
4. What other businesses is Google investing in? Is Google a credible innovator in these areas? Do you think innovation across such a broad portfolio is a wise business decision? Why or why not?
5. Make a list of firms that currently compete with Google and that will likely see Google as a significant competitor in the future. Which firms and job titles will require a substantial understanding of how Google operates and competes?

2. UNDERSTANDING SEARCH

LEARNING OBJECTIVES

1. **Understand the mechanics of search, including how Google indexes the Web and ranks its organic search results.**
2. **Examine the infrastructure that powers Google and how its scale and complexity offer key sources of competitive advantages.**

Before diving into how the firm makes money, let's first understand how Google's core service, search, works.

Perform a search (or **query**) on Google or another search engine, and the results you'll see are referred to by industry professionals as **organic or natural search**. Search engines use different algorithms for determining the order of organic search results, but at Google the method is called **PageRank** (a bit of a play on words, it ranks Web pages, and was initially developed by Google cofounder Larry Page). Google does not accept money for placement of links in organic search results. Instead, PageRank results are a kind of popularity contest. Web pages that have more pages *linking to them* are ranked higher (while organic search results can't be bought, firms do pay for preferred placement in some Google products, including Google Shopping, Hotels, and Flight Search).[17]

FIGURE 18.3

The query for "Toyota Prius" triggers organic search results, flanked top and right by advertisements.

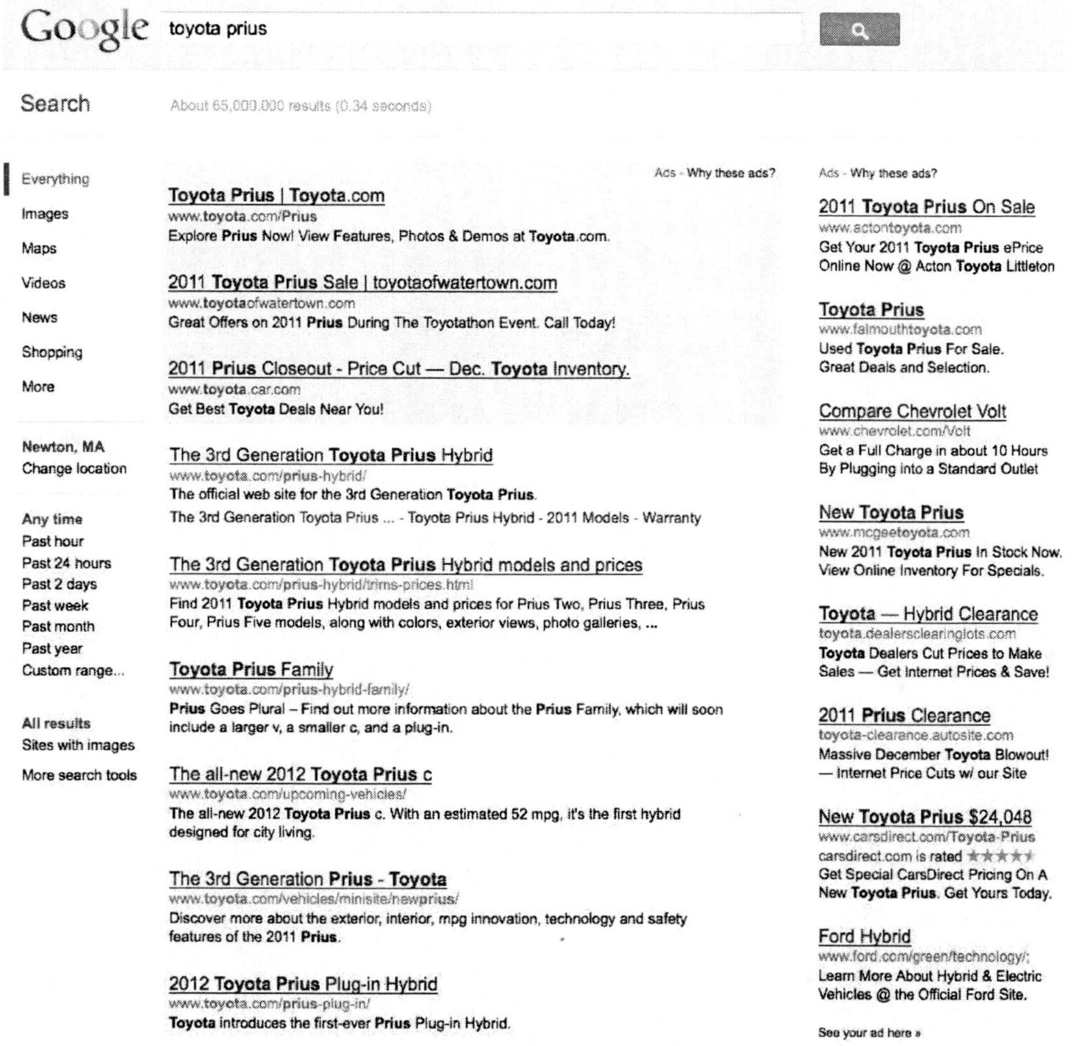

The process of improving a page's organic search results is often referred to as **search engine optimization (SEO)**. SEO has become a critical function for many marketing organizations since if a firm's pages aren't near the top of search results, customers may never discover its site.

Google is a bit vague about the specifics of precisely how PageRank has been refined, in part because many have tried to game the system. In addition to in-bound links, Google's organic search results also consider some two hundred other signals, and the firm's search quality team is relentlessly analyzing user behavior for clues on how to tweak the system to improve accuracy.[18] The less scrupulous have tried creating a series of bogus websites, all linking back to the pages they're trying to promote (this is called **link fraud**, and Google actively works to uncover and shut down such efforts—see the "Link Fraudsters" sidebar).

---

query

Search.

organic or natural search

Search engine results returned and ranked according to relevance.

PageRank

Algorithm developed by Google cofounder Larry Page to rank Web sites.

search engine optimization (SEO)

The process of improving a page's organic search rankings.

link fraud

Also called "spamdexing" or "link farming." The process of creating a series of bogus Web sites, all linking back to the pages one is trying to promote.

Link Fraudsters, Be Prepared to Experience Google's "Death Penalty"

JCPenney is a big retailer, for sure, but not necessarily the first firm to come to mind when you think of most retail categories. So the *New York Times* suspected that something fishy was up when the retailer's site came out tops for dozens of Google searches, including the phrases "skinny jeans," "dresses," "bedding," "area rugs," "home decor," "comforter sets," "furniture," and "table cloths." The phrase "Samsonite carry-on luggage" even placed Penney ahead of Samsonite's own site!

The *Times* reported that "someone paid to have thousands of links placed on hundreds of sites scattered around the Web, all of which lead directly to JCPenney.com." And there was little question it was blatant link fraud. Phrases related to dresses and linking back to the retailer were coming from such nondress sites as nuclear.engineeringaddict.com, casino-focus.com, and bulgariapropertyportal.com. One SEO expert called the effort the most ambitious link farming attempt he'd ever seen.

Link fraud undercuts the credibility of Google's core search product, so when the search giant discovers a firm engaged in link farming they drop the hammer. In this case Google both manually demoted Penney rankings and launched tweaks to its ranking algorithm. Within two hours JCPenney organic results plummeted, in some cases from first to seventy-first (the *Times* calls this the organic search equivalent of the "death penalty"). Getting a top spot in Google search results is a big deal. On average, 34 percent of clicks go to the top result, about twice the percentage that goes to number two. Google's punishment was administered despite the fact that Penney was also a large online ad customer, at times paying Google some $2.5 million a month for ads.[19]

JCPenney isn't the first firm busted. When Google discovered so-called black hat SEO was being used to push BMW up in organic search rankings, Google made certain BMW sites virtually unfindable in its organic search results. JCPenney claims that they were the victim of rogue behavior by an SEO consultant (who was promptly fired) and that the retailer was otherwise unaware of the unethical behavior. But it is surprising that the retailer's internal team didn't see their unbelievably successful organic search results as a red flag that something was amiss, and this case highlights the types of things managers need to watch for in the digital age. Penney outsourced SEO, and the fraud uncovered in this story underscores the critical importance of vetting and regularly auditing the performance of partners throughout a firm's supply chain.[20]

While Google doesn't divulge specifics on the weighting of inbound links from a given website, we do know that links from some websites carry more weight than others. For example, links from websites that Google deems "influential" have greater weight in PageRank calculations than links from run-of-the-mill sites. For searches performed on mobile devices, Web pages that meet Google's criteria for being "mobile friendly" will be ranked higher than those that don't have an option for mobile devices (Google does offer testing tools to see if your pages are compliant).[21] Additionally, different users may not see identical organic search results. Google defaults to a mix of rankings that includes individual user behavior and, for those users searching while logged into Google accounts, social connections (although displaying generic results remains an option).[22]

spiders, Web crawlers, software robots

Software that traverses available Web sites in an attempt to perform a given task. Search engines use spiders to discover documents for indexing and retrieval.

cache

Pronounced "cash," and refers to a temporary storage space used to speed computing tasks.

dark Web

Internet content that can't be indexed by Google and other search engines.

Spiders and Bots and Crawlers—Oh My!

When performing a search via Google or another search engine, you're not actually searching the Web. What really happens is that you're searching something that amounts to a *copy* of the Web that major search engines make by storing and indexing the text of online documents on their own computers. Google's index considers over one trillion URLs.[23] Google starts to retrieve results as soon as you begin to type, and a line above each Google query shows you just how fast a search takes, and how many pages were considered.

To create these massive indexes, search firms use software to crawl the Web and uncover as much information as they can find. This software is referred to by several different names—**spiders, Web crawlers, software robots**—but they all pretty much work the same way. The spiders ask each public computer network for a list of its public Web sites (for more on this see DNS in Chapter 16). Then the spiders go through this list ("crawling" a site), following every available link until all pages are uncovered.

Google will crawl frequently updated sites, like those run by news organizations, as often as several times an hour. Rarely updated, less popular sites might only be reindexed every few days. The method used to crawl the Web also means that if a Web site isn't the first page on a public server, or isn't linked to from another public page, then it'll never be found.[24] In addition, each search engine also offers a page where you can submit your Web site for indexing.

While search engines show you what they've found on their *copy* of the Web's contents that Google has *cache* on its own servers, clicking a search result will direct you to the actual Web site, not the copy. Sometimes you'll click a result only to find that the Web site doesn't match what the search engine found. This is rare, but it happens if a Web site was updated before your search engine had a chance to reindex the changes.

But what if you want the content on your Web site to remain off limits to search engine indexing and caching? Organizations have created a set of standards to stop the spider crawl, and all commercial search engines have agreed to respect these standards. One way is to put a line of *HTML code* invisibly embedded in a Web page that tells all software robots to stop indexing a page, stop following links on the page, or stop offering old page archives in a cache. Users don't see this code, but commercial Web crawlers do. For those familiar with HTML code (the language used to describe a Web site), the command to stop Web crawlers from indexing a page, following links, and listing archives of cached pages looks like this:

⟨META NAME="ROBOTS" CONTENT="NOINDEX, NOFOLLOW, NOARCHIVE"⟩

There are other techniques to keep the spiders out, too. Web site administrators can add a special file (called robots.txt) that provides similar instructions on how indexing software should treat the Web site. And a lot of content lies inside the "**dark Web**," either behind corporate firewalls or inaccessible to those without a user account—think of private Facebook updates no one can see unless they're your friend—all of that is out of Google's reach.

What's It Take to Run This Thing?

Sergey Brin and Larry Page started Google with just four scavenged computers.[25] But in a decade, the infrastructure used to power the search sovereign has ballooned to the point where it is now the largest of its kind in the world.[26] Google doesn't disclose the number of servers it uses, but by some estimates, it runs over 1.4 million servers in over a dozen so-called **server farms** worldwide.[27] Google has been known to spend over $2 billion a quarter on data centers.[28] Building massive server farms to index the ever-growing Web is now the cost of admission for any firm wanting to compete in the search market. This is clearly no longer a game for two graduate students working out of a garage.

Tour a Google Data Center

At this video link, watch a tour of a Google data center. Or visit http://www.google.com/about/datacenters/inside/streetview to explore one of Google's data centers using the firm's Street View technology.

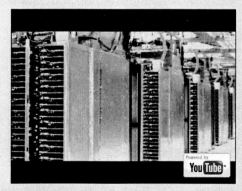

View the video online at: //www.youtube.com/embed/avP5d16wEp0?rel=0

The size of this investment not only creates a barrier to entry, it influences industry profitability, with market-leader Google enjoying huge economies of scale. Firms may spend the same amount to build server farms, but if Google has roughly two-thirds of this market while Microsoft's search draws just a fraction of this traffic, which do you think enjoys the better return on investment?

server farms

A massive network of computer servers running software to coordinate their collective use. Server farms provide the infrastructure backbone to SaaS and hardware cloud efforts, as well as many large-scale Internet services.

fault-tolerant

Capable of continuing operation even if a component fails.

colos (colocation facilities)

Warehouse-sized facilities where telecommunication firms and other corporations bring their fiber optic cables and networking equipment together so that they can exchange networking traffic. These are the interconnection points that help make the Internet function as a network of networks.

The hardware components that power Google aren't particularly special, but they are custom built to contain just what Google needs and eliminate everything it doesn't (e.g., no graphic cards, since servers aren't attached to monitors, or enclosures, since all servers are rack-mounted). In most cases the firm uses the kind of Intel or AMD processors, low-end hard drives, and RAM chips that you'd find in a desktop PC. These components are housed in racks, slotted like very tight shelving. Each server is about 3.5 inches thick yet contains processors, RAM memory, and hard drives.[29] Google buys so many components for its custom-built servers that it, not a PC manufacturer, is Intel's fifth largest customer.[30]

In some cases, Google mounts racks of these servers inside standard-sized shipping containers, each with as many as 1,160 servers per box.[31] A given data center may have dozens of these server-filled containers all linked together. Redundancy is the name of the game. Google assumes individual components will regularly fail, but no single failure should interrupt the firm's operations (making the setup what geeks call **fault-tolerant**). If something breaks, a technician can easily swap it out with a replacement.

Each server farm layout has also been carefully designed with an emphasis on lowering power consumption and cooling requirements. Instead of using big uninterrupted power supply (UPS) systems common in most data centers, Google put smaller battery backups next to each server. These cost less; are more efficient, because they leak about 15 percent less energy than big units; and don't have heavy cooling costs. Employees usually wear shorts inside the data center since the "cool isle" in the front of machines is around 80 °F. The hot aisles venting out the back and cooled via constantly circulating, heat-absorbing water coils can get up to 120 °F. That's hotter than most corporate data centers, but Google learned that its systems could take the heat. These practices allow Google to set the bar high for energy efficiency. The standard used to measure data center efficiency is PUE—power usage effectiveness. 1.0 is a perfect score—it means all the power a facility draws is put to use. Everyone loses power. 2.0 (meaning half the power drawn is wasted) is considered a "reasonable number." Google's PUE is 1.2—astonishingly high. Saving energy helps the firm meet its green goals—the firm is formally committed to being carbon neutral and offsetting its fossil fuel energy needs—but the data centers also help meet other "green" goals: massive cash savings. The firm's infrastructure chief claims that the savings through the firm's ultraefficient data center designs are vital to keeping costs low enough to keep services like Gmail free.[32] Google also uses artificial intelligence to monitor data center performance. If it finds that one of its predicted outcomes doesn't match a current finding (e.g., the temperature is higher than what formulas suggest), this acts as a sort of data center equivalent of a car's "check engine light." AI will then suggest a course of action, like clean an air filtering heat exchanger or check other systems.[33]

The firm's custom software (much of it built upon open source products) allows all this equipment to operate as the world's largest grid computer. Web search is a task particularly well suited for the massively parallel architecture used by Google and its rivals. For an analogy of how this works, imagine that working alone (the human equivalent of a single-server effort), you need to try to find a particular phrase in a hundred-page document. That'd take a while. Next, imagine that you can distribute the task across five thousand people, giving each of them a separate sentence to scan (that's the human equivalent of a multiserver grid). The speed difference between a single searching entity and a search involving many entities simultaneously focused on a subset of the same task gives you a sense of how search firms use massive numbers of servers and the divide-and-conquer approach of grid computing to quickly find the needles you're searching for within the Web's haystack. (For more on grid computing, see Chapter 5 and for more on the server farms employed by cloud computing providers, see Chapter 14)

All this server farm tech helps Google index over 20 billion Web pages a day and serve up results from over 3 billion daily search queries, in most cases with answers coming before you're even done typing.[34] But not all Google-served data comes to you straight from Google's own server farms. The firm also scatters racks of servers in scores of spots all over the world so that it can quickly get you copies of high-value rich media content, like trending YouTube videos. These racks of Google content are tucked away, sometimes within data centers run by big telecom firms like Comcast or AT&T, or kept inside **colos (colocation facilities)**, big warehouse-like facilities where several telecom companies come together to exchange traffic.[35]

FIGURE 18.4

The Google Search Appliance is a hardware product that firms can purchase in order to run Google search technology within the privacy and security of an organization's firewall.

Google will even sell you a bit of its technology so that you can run your own little Google in-house without sharing documents with the rest of the world. Google's line of search appliances are rack-mounted servers that can index documents within the servers on a corporation's own network, even managing user password and security access on a per-document basis. Selling hardware isn't a large business for Google, and other vendors offer similar solutions, but search appliances can be vital tools for law firms, investment banks, and other document-rich organizations.

KEY TAKEAWAYS

- Ranked search results are often referred to as organic or natural search results. PageRank is Google's algorithm for ranking search results. PageRank orders organic search results based largely on the number of websites linking to them, and the "weight" of each page as measured by its "influence."
- Search engine optimization (SEO) is the process of improving a website's organic search ranking. The scope and influence of search has made SEO an increasingly vital marketing function.
- Users don't really search the Web; they search an archived copy stored on a search firm's computers. A firm creates these copies by crawling and indexing discoverable documents.
- Google operates from a massive network of server farms containing hundreds of thousands of servers built from standard, off-the-shelf parts. The cost of the operation is a significant barrier to entry for competitors. Google's share of search suggests the firm realizes economies of scale over rivals required to make similar investments while delivering fewer results (and hence ads).
- Website owners can hide pages from popular search engine Web crawlers using a number of methods, including HTML tags, a no-index file, or ensuring that websites aren't linked to other pages and haven't been submitted to websites for indexing.

QUESTIONS AND EXERCISES

1. How do search engines discover pages on the Internet? What kind of capital commitment is necessary to go about doing this? How does this impact competitive dynamics in the industry?
2. How does Google rank search results? Investigate and list some methods that an organization might use to improve its rank in Google's organic search results. Are there techniques Google might not approve of? What risk does a firm run if Google or another search firm determines that it has used unscrupulous SEO techniques to try to unfairly influence ranking algorithms?
3. Sometimes websites returned by major search engines don't contain the words or phrases that initially brought you to the site. Why might this happen?
4. What's a cache? What other products or services have a cache?
5. What can be done if you want the content on your website to remain off limits to search engine indexing and caching?
6. What is a "search appliance"? Why might an organization choose such a product?
7. Become a better searcher: Look at the advanced options for your favorite search engine. Are there options you hadn't used previously? Be prepared to share what you learn during class discussion.
8. Google offers several tools useful to managers trying to gain insight on the public use of search. One of these is Google Trends. Visit Google Trends. Explore the tool as if you were comparing a firm with its competitors. What sorts of useful insights can you uncover? How might businesses use these tools?
9. Some websites are accused of being "content farms," offering low-quality content designed to attract searchers that include popular query terms and using this content to generate ad revenue. Demand Media, which went public at $1.5 billion, and Associated Content, which Yahoo! purchased for $100 million, have been accused of being content farms. Investigate the claims and visit these sites. Do you find the content useful? Do you think these sites are or are not content farms? Research how Google changed its ranking algorithm to penalize content farms. What has been the impact on these sites? Would you put a site like BuzzFeed in the same category as content farms? Why or why not? Make a list of categories of firms and individuals that would likely be impacted by such moves. What does this tell you about Google's influence?
10. Consider Google's influence on society, understanding, education, and perception. When Google delivers the majority of search results and most users default first to Google's products, do you feel that gives a single firm too much power? Do you think governments have a role in regulating a firm with this amount of influence? Why or why not?

3. UNDERSTANDING THE INCREASE IN ONLINE AD SPENDING

LEARNING OBJECTIVES

1. Understand how media consumption habits are shifting.
2. Be able to explain the factors behind the growth and appeal of online advertising.

For several years, Internet advertising has been the only major media ad category to show significant growth. There are three factors driving online ad growth trends: (1) increased user time online, (2) improved measurement and accountability, and (3) targeting.

Americans (and citizens in many other nations) spend more time on mobile devices than they do watching TV.[36] Even senior citizens spend more time online than they do listening to reading magazines, newspapers, or listening to the radio.[37] So advertisers are simply following the market. Online channels also provide advertisers with a way to reach consumers at work—something that was previously much more difficult to do.

impressions

Each time an add is shown to a user.

Many advertisers have also been frustrated by how difficult it's been to gauge the effectiveness of traditional ad channels such as TV, print, and radio. This frustration is reflected in the old industry saying, "I know that half of my advertising is working—I just don't know which half." Well, with the Internet, now you know. While measurement technologies aren't perfect, advertisers can now count ad **impressions** (the number of times an ad is shown on a Web site), whether a user clicks on an ad, and the product purchases or other website activity that comes from those clicks.[38] And as we'll see, many online ad payment schemes are directly linked to ad performance.

Various technologies and techniques also make it easier for firms to target users based on how likely a person is to respond to an ad. In theory a firm can use targeting to spend marketing dollars only on those users deemed to be its best prospects. Let's look at a few of these approaches in action.

KEY TAKEAWAYS

- Three key reasons for the increase in online ad growth are: (1) increasing user time online, (2) improved measurement and accountability, and (3) targeting.
- Digital media is decreasing time spent through traditional media consumption channels (e.g., radio, TV, newspapers), potentially lowering the audience reach of these old channels and making them less attractive for advertisers.
- Measurement techniques allow advertisers to track the performance of their ads—indicating things such as how often an ad is displayed, how often an ad is clicked, where an ad was displayed when it was clicked, and more. Measurement metrics can be linked to payment schemes, improving return on investment (ROI) and accountability compared to many types of conventional advertising.
- Advertising ROI can be improved through targeting. Targeting allows a firm to serve ads to specific categories of users, so firms can send ads to groups it is most interested in reaching, and those that are most likely to respond to an effort.

QUESTIONS AND EXERCISES

1. How does your media time differ from your parents'? Does it differ among your older or younger siblings, or other relatives? Which media are you spending more time with? Less time with?
2. Put yourself in the role of a traditional media firm that is seeing its market decline. What might you do to address decline concerns? Have these techniques been attempted by other firms? Do you think they've worked well? Why or why not?
3. Put yourself in the role of an advertiser for a product or service that you're interested in. Is the Internet an attractive channel for you? How might you use the Internet to reach customers you are most interested in? Where might you run ads? Who might you target? Who might you avoid? How might the approach you use differ from traditional campaigns you'd run in print, TV, or radio? How might the size (money spent, attempted audience reach) and timing (length of time run, time between campaigns) of ad campaigns online differ from offline campaigns?
4. List ways in which you or someone you know has been targeted in an Internet ad campaign. Was it successful? How do you feel about targeting?

4. SEARCH ADVERTISING

LEARNING OBJECTIVES

1. **Understand Google's search advertising revenue model.**
2. **Know the factors that determine the display and ranking of advertisements appearing on Google's search results pages.**
3. **Be able to describe the uses and technologies behind geotargeting.**

The practice of running and optimizing search engine ad campaigns is referred to as **search engine marketing (SEM)**.[39] SEM is a hot topic in an increasingly influential field, so it's worth spending some time learning how search advertising works on the Internet's largest search engine.

Over two-thirds of Google's revenues come from ads served on its own sites, and the vast majority of this revenue comes from search engine ads.[40] During Google's early years, the firm actually resisted making money through ads. In fact, while at Stanford, Brin and Page even coauthored a paper titled "The Evils of Advertising."[41] But when Yahoo! and others balked at buying Google's search technology (offered for as little as $500,000), Google needed to explore additional revenue streams. It wasn't until two years after incorporation that Google ran ads alongside organic search results. That first ad, one for "Live Mail Order Lobsters," appeared just minutes after the firm posted a link reading "See Your Ad Here."[42]

Google regularly experiments with incorporating video and image ads into search (you'll see images, for example, in paid-product search results), but for the most part, the ads you'll see to the right (and sometimes top) of Google's organic search results are text ads. These ads are **keyword advertising**, meaning they're targeted based on the words in a user's search query. Advertisers bid on the keywords and phrases that they'd like to use to trigger the display of their ad. Linking ads to search was a brilliant move, since the user's search term indicates an overt interest in a given topic. Want to sell hotel stays in Tahiti? Link your ads to the search term "Tahiti Vacation." Google ads show up when many users have some sort of *purchasing intent*. This makes Google search ads far more effective than standard display ads like those on Facebook (see Chapter 11). Google's ability to tie advertising to purchasing intent (or to some other action that advertisers are willing to pay for) is the main reason the firm's ads are so valuable.

Not only are search ads highly targeted, advertisers only pay for results. Text ads appearing on Google search pages are billed on a **pay-per-click (PPC)** basis, meaning that advertisers don't spend a penny unless someone actually clicks on their ad. Note that the term pay-per-click is sometimes used interchangeably with the term cost-per-click (CPC).

If an advertiser wants to display an ad on Google search, they can set up a Google AdWords advertising account in minutes, specifying just a single ad, or multiple ad campaigns that trigger different ads for different keywords. Advertisers also specify what they're willing to pay each time an ad is clicked, how much their overall ad budget is, and they can control additional parameters, such as the timing and duration of an ad campaign.

search engine marketing (SEM)

The practice of designing, running and optimizing search engine ad campaigns.

keyword advertising

Advertisements that are targeted based on a user's query.

pay-per-click (PPC)

A concept where advertisers don't pay unless someone clicks on their ad.

quality score

A measurement of ad performance (CTR) and ad relevance, and landing page experience. Ads that are seen as relevant and that consumers respond to have higher quality scores. The firm uses quality score multiplied by the maximum CPC to determine an ad's display ranking.

click-through rate (CTR)

The number of users who clicked an ad divided by the number of times the ad was delivered (the impressions). The CTR measures the percentage of people who clicked on an ad to arrive at a destination-site.

landing page

The Web page displayed when a user clicks on an advertisement.

dynamic search ads

Ads generated automatically based on the content of a Web site. Dynamic ads are particularly useful for firms with rapidly updating inventory or firms struggling to keep up with new search terms that may be relevant to their product line.

If no one clicks on an ad, Google doesn't make money, advertisers don't attract customers, and searchers aren't seeing ads they're interested in. So in order to create a winning scenario for everyone, Google has developed a precise ad ranking formula that rewards top performing ads by considering three metrics: the maximum CPC that an advertiser is willing to pay (sometimes referred to as an ad's *bid value*), the advertisement's **quality score**—a broad measure of ad performance, and the expected impact of extensions (e.g., added info like a phone number, address, store rating) and ad formats (in some cases images or video may be expected to perform higher). Create high-quality ads and your advertisements might appear ahead of competition, even if your competitors bid more than you. But if ads perform poorly they'll fall in rankings or even drop from display consideration.

Below is the rough formula used by Google to determine the rank order of sponsored links appearing on search results pages.

Ad Rank = f(Maximum CPC, Quality Score, expected impact of extensions and formats)

Google is deliberately vague about precisely how quality score is calculated, and the firm's metrics are regularly tweaked, but factors that determine an ad's quality score have included an ad's **click-through rate (CTR)**, or the number of users who clicked an ad divided by the number of times the ad was delivered (the impressions). The CTR measures the percentage of people who clicked on an ad to arrive at a destination-site. Factors that have also appeared in the quality score weighting include things like the overall history of click performance for the keywords linked to the ad, the relevance of an ad's text to the user's query, and Google's automated assessment of the user experience on the **landing page**—the Web page displayed when a user clicks on the ad. Ads that don't get many clicks, ad descriptions that have nothing to do with query terms, and ads that direct users to generic pages that load slowly or aren't strongly related to the keywords and descriptions used in an ad will all lower an ad's chance of being displayed. In general, the more relevant your ad, and the better the experience of the consumer who clicks that ad, the higher your quality score, and the higher your quality score, the better your ad's position and the less you'll have to pay per click.[43]

Google provides tools that firms can use to identify popular words and phrases for selecting keywords to associate with an ad, and for assessing ad quality score. And Google also offers **dynamic search ads**, where the firm will automatically generate ads based on your website. This is useful if you have a constantly changing and updating inventory or are having difficulty tracking the ever-evolving search terms that may be relevant to users looking for products and services that your site offers.

When an ad is clicked, advertisers don't actually pay their maximum CPC; Google discounts ads to the minimum necessary to maintain an ad's position on the page. So if you bid one dollar per click, but your overall ad rank is so good that you could have beat the ad ranked below yours even if you bid just ninety cents, then you'll pay just ninety cents if the ad is clicked. Discounting was a brilliant move. No one wants to get caught excessively overbidding rivals, so discounting helps reduce the possibility of this so-called bidder's remorse. And with this risk minimized, the system actually encouraged higher bids![44]

Ad ranking and cost-per-click calculations take place as part of an automated auction that occurs *every time* a user conducts a search. Advertisers get a running total of ad performance statistics so that they can monitor the return on their investment and tweak promotional efforts for better results. And this whole system is automated for self-service—all it takes is a credit card, an ad idea, and you're ready to go.

4.1   How Much Do Advertisers Pay per Click?

Google rakes in billions on what amounts to pocket change earned one click at a time. Most clicks bring in between thirty cents and one dollar. However, costs can vary widely depending on industry and current competition. Since rates are based on auctions, top rates reflect what the market is willing to bear. As an example, law firms, which bring in big bucks from legal fees, decisions, and settlement payments, often justify higher customer acquisition costs. Bids for certain legal phrases, such as those referring to structured settlements (a term often referring to payment terms of a legal settlement), or mesothelioma (a type of cancer-associated asbestos and the subject of several big money lawsuits) have been known to go for hundreds of dollars.[45] And firms that see results will keep spending. Los Angeles–based Chase Law Group has said that it brings in roughly 60 percent of its clients through Internet advertising.[46] Top Google advertisers among larger, consumer firms include Amazon, Quicken Loans, State Farm, Home Depot, Apple, Sears, Expedia, Capital One, Walmart, JCPenney, BestBuy, and eBay.[47]

4.2   IP Addresses and Geotargeting

Geotargeting occurs when computer systems identify a user's physical location (sometimes called the *geolocation*) for the purpose of delivering tailored ads or other content. On Google AdWords, for example, advertisers can specify that their ads only appear for Web surfers located in a particular country, state, metropolitan region, or a given distance around a precise locale. They can even draw a custom ad-targeting region on a map and tell Google to only show ads to users detected inside that space.

Ads in Google Search (as well as in Maps and many other offerings) can be geotargeted based on **IP address**. Every device connected to the Internet has a unique IP address assigned by the organization connecting the device to the network. Normally you don't see your IP address. It's likely a set of four numbers, from 0 to 255, separated by periods (e.g., 136.167.2.220), but this standard (known as IPv4) is gradually being replaced by the IPv6 standard, which offers far more potential addresses. IP addresses are used in targeting because the range of IP addresses "owned" by major organizations and Internet service providers (ISPs) is public knowledge. In many cases it's possible to make an accurate guess as to where a computer, laptop, or mobile phone is located simply by cross-referencing a device's current IP address with this public list.

For example, it's known that all devices connected to the Boston College network contain IP addresses starting with the numbers 136.167. If a search engine detects a query coming from an IP address that begins with those two numbers, it can be fairly certain that the person using that device is in the greater Boston area.

FIGURE 18.5

In this geotargeting example, the same search term is used at roughly the same time on separate computers located in Silicon Valley area (Figure 18.5) and Boston (Figure 18.6). Note how geotargeting impacts the search results and that the Boston-based search includes a geotargeted ad that does not show up in the Palo Alto search.

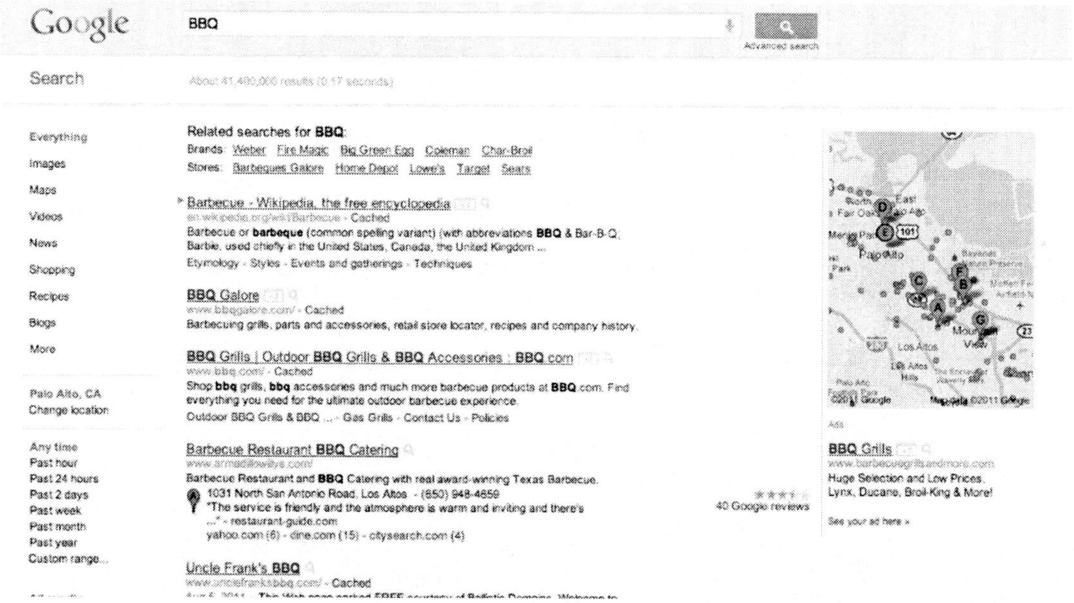

geotargeting

Identifying a user's physical location (sometimes called geolocation) for the purpose of delivering tailored ads or other content.

IP address

A value used to identify a device that is connected to the Internet. IP addresses are usually expressed as four numbers (from 0 to 255), separated by periods.

FIGURE 18.6

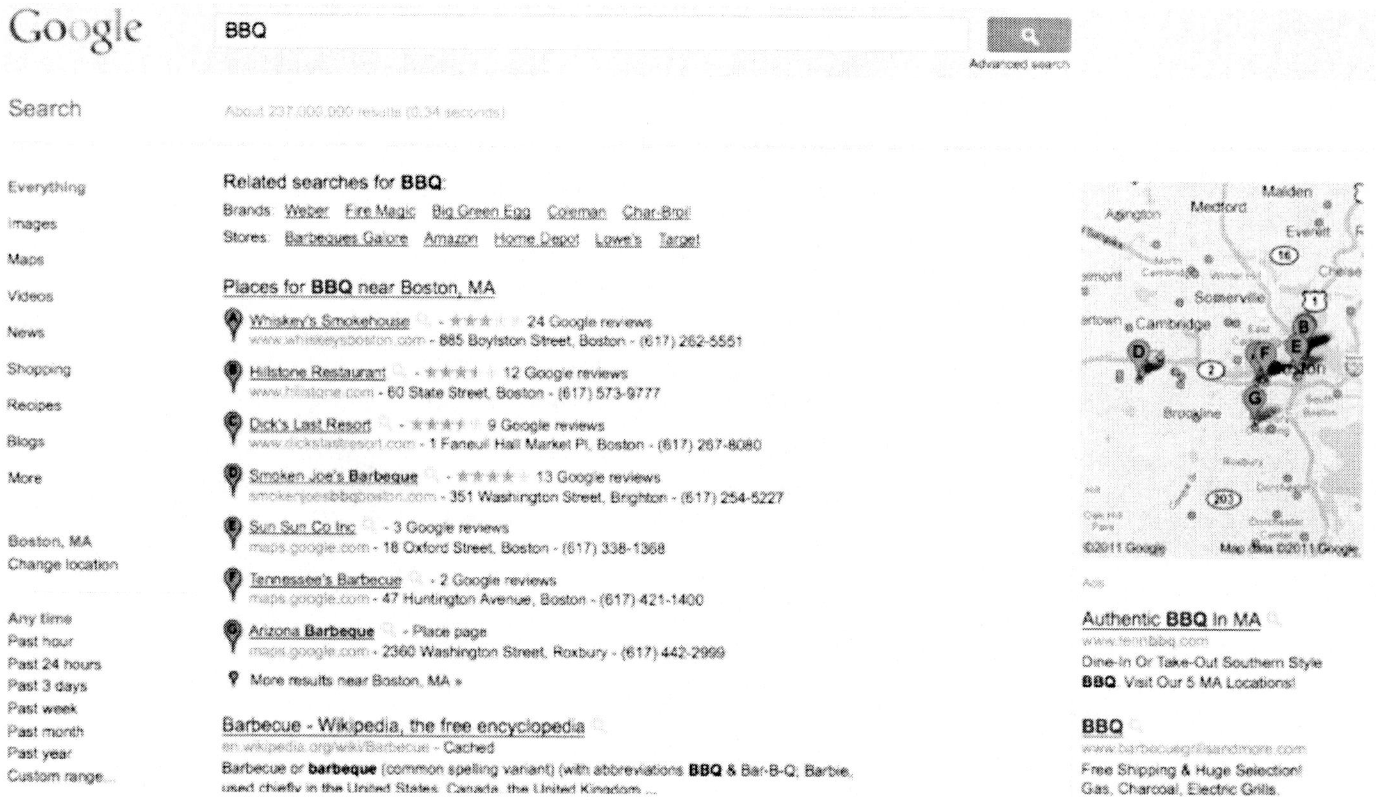

IP addresses will change depending on how and where you connect to the Internet. Connect your laptop to a hotel's Wi-Fi when visiting a new city, and you're likely to see ads specific to that location. That's because your Internet service provider has changed, and the firm serving your ads has detected that you are using an IP address known to be associated with your new location.

Geotargeting via IP address is fairly accurate, but it's not perfect. For example, some Internet service providers may provide imprecise or inaccurate information on the location of their networks. Others might be so vague that it's difficult to make a best guess at the geography behind a set of numbers (values assigned by a multinational corporation with many locations, for example). And there are other ways locations are hidden, such as when Internet users connect to **proxy servers**, third-party computers that pass traffic to and from a specific address without revealing the address of the connected users.

proxy servers

A third-party computer that passes traffic to and from a specific address without revealing the address of the connected user.

What's My IP Address?

While every operating system has a control panel or command that you can use to find your current IP address, there are also several websites that will quickly return this value (and a best guess at your current location). One such site is WhatIsMyIPaddress.com. Visit this or a similar site with a desktop, laptop, and mobile phone. Do the results differ and are they accurate? Why?

Geotargeting Evolves Beyond the IP Address

There are several other methods of geotargeting. Firms like Skyhook Wireless/ TruePosition, Apple, and Google can identify a location based on mapping **Wi-Fi** hotspots and nearby cell towers. Many mobile devices come equipped with **global positioning system (GPS)** chips (identifying location via the GPS satellite network). And if a user provides location values such as a home address or zip code to a Web site, then that value might be stored and used again to make a future guess at a user's location.

Many firms build and maintain accurate location databases by regularly collecting location information from smartphones and using this data to refine maps. Phones submit data anonymously; however, this process can be controversial.

Mobile Apps and the Challenge for Google Search

US mobile users spend roughly three hours each day on smartphones and tablets. While most online desktop time happens via the Web browser, on mobile, mobile users spend an estimated 86 percent of their time in apps and only 14 percent on the Web. This shift concerns Google. When you search for restaurant reviews in Google's search engine, it can serve you ads and continue to build your user profile. But if you search via Yelp's app on an iPhone, Google can't see you at all. Yelp is thought to have earned about $120 million in ad revenue from its mobile app in 2014, up over by 136 percent from the prior year. The growing list of context-specific apps that siphon users away from Google's Web search include Kayak and TripAdvisor for travel, Shazam for music, and even Amazon for shopping. And Apple's Siri is delivering results directly from its partners, making it the search broker, not Google. This fragmenting of mobile is having an impact on Google's share of mobile advertising.[48]

App owners are becoming even more useful advertisers with the rise of so-called **deep linking**. Deep linking allows an advertisement to launch an app and call up requested information, say, clicking a Pinterest link for a vintage handbag and jumping immediately to bag vendor's page within the Etsy app. And, of course, this app-to-app advertising cuts out Google even further.

In 2012, Google had an 82.8 percent share of mobile searches, but research firm eMarketer estimates that when you consider the long tail of app-based searches that are occurring, Google's share was around 65.7 percent in 2014. The app-based niche searches like those mentioned previously have grown from 5.4 percent of mobile search to 22.9 percent in just two years.[49] Even though Google's percentage of mobile search ad revenue is declining, the firm's mobile search ad revenue is still going up. That's because the search ad pie is getting bigger as more users conduct more searches online. But the trends underscore how mobile is different (for more on the challenges of mobile see Chapter 11). Google has offered additional features to give users a reason to stick with its search and map products. Examples include a new hotel format offers the ability to see high-quality photos, hotel ratings and book a hotel right from within a Google listing. A new car format allows a panoramic scroll through the car, the ability to "build and price" a car, and find a dealer. A mortgage format allows for side-by-side comparisons.[50] And a new restaurant format can directly summon a food delivery service via deep link.[51]

Making Google more relevant, especially on mobile, makes sense, but the new functionality comes with risks. Google's move into travel booking is upsetting some of the firm's biggest customers. Priceline spends over $1.5 billion advertising with Google each year. Expedia spends over $1 billion. Just these two firms account for about a 5 percent chunk of Google revenue. If Google can create increased ad revenue directly from hotels, airlines, and other travel providers, this might help make up the difference, but that's a serious bit of channel pressure and market shift that would need to happen. More troubling are potential legal issues. Priceline and Expedia are also members of FairSearch.org, a group that accuses Google of using its dominance in search and other products to favor its own services above those of rivals.[52]

Wi-Fi

A term used to brand wireless local-area networking devices. Devices typically connect to an antenna-equipped base station or hotspot, which is then connected to the Internet. Wi-Fi devices use standards known as IEEE 802.11, and various versions of this standard (e.g., b, g, n) may operate in different frequency bands and have access ranges.

global positioning system (GPS)

A network of satellites and supporting technologies used to identify a device's physical location.

deep linking

A link that takes a user to a specific webpage (rather than the home page), or which launches an app and brings up a unique location rather than just launching the app. As an example, a deep link from Pinterest might take a user directly to the Etsy web page or app listing featuring the vendor of that item, rather than generically opening Etsy.com or the Etsy app.

KEY TAKEAWAYS

- More than two-thirds of Google's revenues come from ads served on its own sites, and the vast majority of this revenue comes from search engine ads.
- Search ads on Google are both more effective (in terms of click-through rate) and more sought after by advertisers, because they are often associated with a user's purchasing intent.
- Advertisers choose and bid on the keywords and phrases that they'd like to use to trigger the display of their ad.
- Advertisers pay for cost-per-click advertising only if an ad is clicked on. Google makes no money on CPC ads that are displayed but not clicked.
- Google determines ad rank by multiplying CPC by Quality Score. Ads with low ranks might not display at all.
- Advertisers usually don't pay their maximum CPC. Instead, Google discounts ads to just one cent more than the minimum necessary to maintain an ad's position on the page—a practice that encourages higher bids.
- Geotargeting occurs when computer systems identify a user's physical location (sometimes called geolocation) for the purpose of delivering tailored ads or other content.
- Google uses IP addresses to target ads.
- Geotargeting can also be enabled by the satellite-based global positioning system (GPS) or based on estimating location from cell phone towers or Wi-Fi hotspots.
- The rise of apps as an alternative to search is a threat to Google and has shrunk the firm's percentage of mobile search. Deep linking allows websites and apps to link directly with content in other sites and apps, bypassing Google altogether. However, its revenues continue to rise as more users conduct more searches online.
- Google offers web and app deep-linking, and new ad formats give the ability to do more in search and maps (e.g. compare and book hotel rooms, car shop). However, offering these services may alienate advertisers, some which spend $1 billion or more with Google. It also adds to concerns that Google uses its dominance in search and other categories to favor its products and services over those of rivals.

QUESTIONS AND EXERCISES

1. Which firm invented pay-per-click advertising? Why does Google dominate today and not this firm?

2. How are ads sold via Google search superior to conventional advertising media such as TV, radio, billboard, print, and yellow pages? Consider factors like the available inventory of space to run ads, the cost to run ads, the cost to acquire new advertisers, and the appeal among advertisers.

3. Are there certain kinds of advertising campaigns and goals where search advertising wouldn't be a good fit? Give examples and explain why.

4. Can a firm buy a top ad ranking? Why or why not?

5. List the four factors that determine an ad's quality score.

6. How much do firms typically pay for a single click?

7. Sites like SpyFu.com and KeywordSpy.com provide a list of the keywords with the highest cost per click. Visit the Top Lists page at SpyFu, KeywordSpy, or a comparable site, to find estimates of the current highest paying cost per click. Which keywords pay the most? Why do you think firms are willing to spend so much?

8. What is bidder's remorse? How does Google's ad discounting impact this phenomenon?

9. Visit WhatIsMyIPaddress.com (or a similar website that displays a device's IP address) using a desktop, laptop, and mobile phone (work with a classmate or friend if you don't have access to one of these devices). How do results differ? Why? Are they accurate? What factors go into determining the accuracy of IP-based geolocation?

10. List and briefly describe other methods of geotargeting besides IP address, and indicate the situations and devices where these methods would be more and less effective.

11. The field of search engine marketing (SEM) is relatively new and rising in importance. And since the field is so new and constantly changing, there are plenty of opportunities for young, knowledgeable professionals. Which organizations, professional certification, and other resources are available to SEM professionals? Spend some time searching for these resources online and be prepared to share your findings with your class.

12. How do you, your friends, or your family members search on mobile devices? How has search changed over time? Are there certain product categories that you used to go to Google for, but where you'll now rely on an app? How do you suppose this impacts Google's revenue? If you were Google, how might you combat challenges as search shifts from a single search engine to niche apps?

13. What is Google doing to combat users migrating to other apps and services for their search? What are the risks in this approach?

5. AD NETWORKS—DISTRIBUTION BEYOND SEARCH

LEARNING OBJECTIVES

1. **Understand ad networks, and how ads are distributed and served based on website content.**
2. **Recognize how ad networks provide advertiser reach and support niche content providers.**
3. **Be aware of content adjacency problems and their implications.**
4. **Know the strategic factors behind ad network appeal and success.**

Google runs ads not just in search, but also across a host of Google-owned sites like Gmail, Google News, and Blogger. It will even tailor ads for its map products and for mobile devices. But about over 20 percent of Google's revenues come from running ads on websites and apps that the firm doesn't even own.

Next time you're surfing online, look around the different websites that you visit and see how many sport boxes labeled "Ads by Google." Those websites are participating in Google's **ad network**, which means they're running ads for Google in exchange for a cut of the take. Participants range from small-time bloggers to some of the world's most highly trafficked sites. Google lines up the advertisers, provides the targeting technology, serves the ads, and handles advertiser payment collection. To participate, content providers just sign up online, put a bit of Google-supplied HTML code on their pages, and wait for Google to send them cash (websites typically get about seventy cents for every AdSense dollar that Google collects).[53]

Google originally developed AdSense to target ads based on keywords automatically detected inside the content of a website. A blog post on your favorite sports team, for example, might be accompanied by ads from ticket sellers or sports memorabilia vendors. Ads can also be targeted based on

ad network

An effort that links advertisers to Web sites and other content providers (e.g., app firms, games) that are willing to host advertisements, typically in exchange for payment.

other criteria, such as the profile of the user visiting a web page. And Google will also serve ads to be displayed inside apps, as well. AdSense and similar online ad networks provide advertisers with access to the long tail of niche websites by offering both increased opportunities for ad exposure as well as more-refined targeting opportunities.

FIGURE 18.7

The images show advertising embedded around a story on the *New York Times* website. The page runs several ads provided by different ad networks. For example, the WebEx banner ad above the article's headline was served by the AOL Advertising network. The "Ads by Google" box appeared at the end of the article. Note how the Google ads are related to the content of the *Times* article.

Some 65 percent of the top 200 ad-supported websites use AdSense for at least a portion of their ad revenue.[54] Google's AdSense program forks over more than $7 billion a year to more than 2 million publishers. There are now quite a few AdSense millionaires.[55] Running ads on your website is by no means a guaranteed path to profits. The Internet graveyard is full of firms that thought they'd be able to sustain their businesses on ads alone. But for many websites, ad networks can be like oxygen, sustaining them with revenue opportunities they'd never be able to achieve on their own.

AdSense content publishers ranging from the history buff behind HistoryOrb.com to the green-thumbed, silver-haired schoolteacher heading MooseysCountryGarden.com have quit their day jobs and now live off of their AdSense-fueled businesses. Handyman column writer Tim Carter saw his first-year AdSense income leap to more than $350,000.[56] AdSense even provided early revenue for the multimillion-dollar *TechCrunch* media empire (now owned by AOL, which itself is owned by Verizon).

FIGURE 18.8

Tim Carter's Ask the Builder website runs ads from Google and other ad networks. Note different ad formats surrounding the content. Video ads are also integrated into many of the site's video tutorials.

Beware the Content Adjacency Problem

Contextual advertising based on keywords is lucrative, but like all technology solutions it has its limitations. Vendors sometimes suffer from **content adjacency problems** when ads appear alongside text they'd prefer to avoid. In one particularly embarrassing example, a *New York Post* article detailed a gruesome murder where hacked up body parts were stowed in suitcases. The online version of the article included contextual advertising and was accompanied by…luggage ads.[57]

To combat embarrassment, ad networks provide opportunities for both advertisers and content providers to screen out potentially undesirable pairings based on factors like vendor, website, and category. Advertisers can also use **negative keywords**, which tell networks to avoid showing ads when specific words appear (e.g., setting negative keywords to "murder" or "killer" could have spared luggage advertisers from the embarrassing problem mentioned above). Ad networks also refine ad-placement software based on feedback from prior incidents (for more about content adjacency problems, see Chapter 11).

Contextual advertising

Advertising based on a Web site's content.

content adjacency problems

A situation where ads appear alongside text the advertiser would like to avoid.

negative keywords

Keywords that prevent an ad from showing up when specific terms are present.

Google bundles its third-party AdSense partners in with its own content properties (e.g., YouTube, Google Finance, Blogger, Gmail), calling this big pool of distribution for your ads the Google Display Network. And Google is by no means the only company to run an ad network; nor was it the first to come up with the idea. Rivals include Yahoo! and AOL's Advertising.com. Advertisers also aren't limited to choosing just one ad network. In fact, many websites will serve ads from several ad networks (as well as exclusive space sold by their own sales force), oftentimes mixing several different offerings on the same page.

5.1   Ad Networks and Competitive Advantage

While advertisers can use multiple ad networks, there are several key strategic factors driving the industry. For Google, its ad network is a distribution play. The ability to reach more potential customers across more websites attracts more advertisers to Google. And content providers (the websites that distribute these ads) want there to be as many advertisers as possible in the ad networks that they join, since this should increase the price of advertising, the number of ads served, and the accuracy of user targeting. If advertisers attract content providers, which in turn attract more advertisers, then we've just described network effects! It also doesn't hurt that Google's search ad business is a great way to gain exposure for its other ad offerings, as well. More participants bringing in more revenue also help the firm benefit from scale economies—offering a better return on investment from its ad technology and infrastructure. All this has worked to help Google build an ad network that serves nearly four times the ads of its nearest rival.[58] No wonder Google's been on such a tear—the firm's loaded with assets for competitive advantage!

KEY TAKEAWAYS

- Google also serves ads through non-Google partner sites that join its ad network. These partners distribute ads for Google in exchange for a percentage of the take.
- AdSense ads are targeted based on keywords that Google detects inside the content of a website.
- AdSense and similar online ad networks provide advertisers with access to the long tail of niche websites.
- Ad networks handle advertiser recruitment, ad serving, and revenue collection, opening up revenue earning possibilities to even the smallest publishers.

QUESTIONS AND EXERCISES

1. On a percentage basis, how important is AdSense to Google's revenues?
2. Why do ad networks appeal to advertisers? Why do they appeal to content providers? What functions are assumed by the firm overseeing the ad network?
3. What factors determine the appeal of an ad network to advertisers and content providers? Which of these factors are potentially sources of competitive advantage?
4. Do dominant ad networks enjoy strong network effects? Are there also strong network effects that drive consumers to search? Why or why not?
5. How difficult is it for a website to join an ad network? What does this imply about ad network switching costs? Does it have to exclusively choose one network over another? Does ad network membership prevent a firm from selling its own online advertising, too?
6. What is the content adjacency problem? Why does it occur? What classifications of websites might be particularly susceptible to the content adjacency problem? What can advertisers do to minimize the likelihood that a content adjacency problem will occur?

6.   MORE AD FORMATS AND PAYMENT SCHEMES

LEARNING OBJECTIVES

1. Know the different formats and media types that Web ads can be displayed in.
2. Know the different ways ads are sold.
3. Know that games can be an ad channel under the correct conditions.

Online ads aren't just about text ads paid for on a cost-per-click (CPC) basis. Ads running through the Google Display Network, or on most competitor networks can be displayed in several formats and media types, and can be billed in different ways. The specific ad formats supported depend on the ad network but can include the following: **display (or image) ads** (such as horizontally oriented banners, smaller rectangular buttons, and vertically oriented "skyscraper" ads); **rich media ads** (which can include animation or video and sometimes encourage user engagement or interaction); and **interstitials** (ads that run before a user arrives at his or her intended destination in a website or app). There are also various formats for other forms of digital advertising, as such video and in-app ads. The industry trade group, the **Internet Advertising Bureau (IAB),** sets common standards for display ads so that a single creative (the design and content of the advertisement) can run unmodified across multiple ad networks and websites.[59]

And there are lots of other ways ads are sold besides cost-per-click. Most graphical display ads are sold according to the number of times the ad appears (the number of **impressions**). Ad rates are quoted in **CPM**, meaning cost per thousand impressions (the M representing the roman numeral for one thousand). Display ads sold on a CPM basis are often used as part of branding campaigns targeted more at creating awareness than generating click-throughs. Such techniques often work best for promoting products like soft drinks, toothpaste, or movies.

Cost-per-action (CPA) ads pay whenever a a user responds to an ad by performing a specified activity such as signing up for a service, requesting material, or making a purchase. **Affiliate programs** are a form of cost-per-action, where vendors share a percentage of revenue with websites that direct purchasing customers to their online storefronts. Amazon runs the world's largest affiliate program, and referring sites can earn 4 percent to 15 percent of sales generated from these click-throughs. Purists might not consider affiliate programs as advertising (rather than text or banner ads, Amazon's affiliates offer links and product descriptions that point back to Amazon's website), but these programs can be important tools in a firm's promotional arsenal.

And rather than buying targeted ads, a firm might sometimes opt to become an exclusive advertiser on a site. For example, a firm can purchase all ads served on a site's main page; it could secure exclusive access to a region of the page (such as the topmost banner ad); or it may pay to sponsor a particular portion or activity on a website (say a parenting forum, or a "click-to-print" button). Such deals can be billed based on a flat rate, CPM, CPC, or any combination of metrics.

display (or image) ads

Graphical advertising (as opposed to text ads).

rich media ads

Online ads that include animation, audio, or video.

interstitials

Ads that run before a user arrives at his or her intended destination in a website or app.

Internet Advertising Bureau (IAB),

A nonprofit industry trade group for the interactive advertising industry. The IAB evaluates and recommends interactive advertising standards and practices and also conducts research, education, and legislative lobbying.

impression

Each time an advertisement is displayed.

CPM

Cost per thousand impressions (the M representing the roman numeral for one thousand).

Cost-per-action (CPA)

A method of charging for advertising whenever a user responds to an ad by performing a specified activity such as signing up for a service, requesting material, or making a purchase.

Affiliate programs

A cost-per-action program, where program sponsors (e.g., Amazon, iTunes) pay referring Web sites a percentage of revenue earned from the referral.

KEY TAKEAWAYS

- Web ad formats include, but are not limited to, the following: *display* (or *image*) *ads* (such as horizontally oriented *banners*, smaller rectangular *buttons*, and vertically oriented *skyscraper ads*), *rich media ads* (which can include animation or video), and *interstitials* (ads that run before a user arrives at a website's contents).
- In addition to cost-per-click, ads can be sold based on the number of times the ad appears (impressions); whenever a user performs a specified action such as signing up for a service, requesting material, or making a purchase (cost-per-action); or on an exclusive basis which may be billed at a flat rate.
- CPM (cost per thousand impressions) ads are often best suited for brand or awareness campaigns that aren't looking to solicit a click-through or other action but rather are more focused on conveying a message to an audience.

QUESTIONS AND EXERCISES

1. What is the IAB and why is it necessary?
2. What are the major ad format categories?
3. What's an interstitial? What's a rich media ad? Have you seen these? Do you think they are effective? Why or why not?
4. List four major methods for billing online advertising.
5. Which method is used to bill most graphical advertising? What's the term used for this method and what does it stand for?
6. How many impressions are recorded if a single user is served the same ad one thousand times? How many if one thousand users are served the same ad once?
7. Imagine the two scenarios below. Decide which type of campaign would be best for each: text-based CPC advertising or image ads paid for on a CPM basis. Explain your reasoning.
   a. Netflix is looking to attract new customers by driving traffic to its website in hopes that this will increase subscriptions.
   b. A movie studio would like to promote the upcoming theatrical release of a new major motion picture.
8. Which firm runs the world's largest affiliate program? Why is this form of advertising particularly advantageous to the firm (think about the ROI for this sort of effort)?

7. CUSTOMER PROFILING AND BEHAVIORAL TARGETING

LEARNING OBJECTIVES

1. **Be familiar with various tracking technologies and how they are used for customer profiling and ad targeting.**
2. **Understand why customer profiling is both valuable and controversial.**
3. **Recognize steps that organizations can take to help ease consumer and governmental concerns.**

cookies

A line of identifying text, assigned and retrieved by a given Web server and stored by your browser.

Advertisers are willing to pay more for ads that have a greater chance of reaching their target audience, and online firms have a number of targeting tools at their disposal. Much of this targeting occurs whenever you visit a website, where a behind-the-scenes software dialogue takes place between Web browser and Web server that can reveal a number of pieces of information, including IP address, the type of browser used, the computer type, its operating system, and unique identifiers, called **cookies**.

And remember, *any* server that serves you content can leverage these profiling technologies. You might be profiled not just by the website that you're visiting (e.g., nytimes.com), but also by any ad networks that serve ads on that site (e.g., Google, AOL, Yahoo/Bing).

IP addresses are leveraged extensively in customer profiling. An IP address not only helps with geolocation, it can also indicate a browser's employer or university, which can be further matched with information such as firm size or industry. IBM has used IP targeting to tailor its college recruiting banner ads to specific schools, for example, "There Is Life After Boston College, Click Here to See Why."

That campaign garnered click-through rates ranging from 5 to 30 percent[60] compared to average rates that are currently well below 1 percent for untargeted banner ads. DoubleClick once even served a banner that included a personal message for an executive at then-client Modem Media. The ad, reading "Congratulations on the twins, John Nardone," was served across hundreds of sites, but was only visible from computers that accessed the Internet from the Modem Media corporate network.[61]

The ability to identify a surfer's computer, browser, or operating system can also be used to target tech ads. For example, Google might pitch its Chrome browser to users detected running Internet Explorer, Firefox, or Safari; while Apple could target Mac ads just to Windows users.

But perhaps the greatest degree of personalization and targeting comes from cookies. Visit a website for the first time, and in most cases, a dialogue between server and browser takes place that goes something like this:

Server: *Have I seen you before?*

Browser: *No.*

Server: *Then take this unique string of numbers and letters (called a cookie). I'll use it to recognize you from now on.*

The cookie is just a line of identifying text assigned and retrieved by a given Web server and stored on your computer by your browser. Upon accepting this cookie your browser has been tagged, like an animal. As you surf around the firm's website, that cookie can be used to build a profile associated with your activities. If you're on a portal like Yahoo! you might type in your zip code, enter stocks that you'd like to track, and identify the sports teams you'd like to see scores for. The next time you return to the website, your browser responds to the server's "*Have I seen you before?*" question with the equivalent of "*Yes, you know me,*" and it presents the cookie that the site gave you earlier. The site can then match this cookie against your browsing profile, showing you the weather, stock quotes, sports scores, and other info that it thinks you're interested in.

Google and others provide a service called **remarketing** (also called **retargeting**), where site operators can tag users according to which page they visit on their site. They can then use this info to serve up tailored ads and special offers to that user as they browse the Web. Visited a scuba suit page on an e-commerce site? That same website can target you with special promotions, custom ads, or even dynamically generated ads when searching Google or visiting any site in the Google Display Network.[62]

Cookies are used for lots of purposes. Retail websites like Amazon use cookies to pay attention to what you've shopped for and bought, tailoring websites to display products that the firm suspects you'll be most interested in. Sites also use cookies to keep track of what you put in an online "shopping cart," so if you quit browsing before making a purchase, these items will reappear the next time you visit. And many websites also use cookies as part of a "remember me" feature, storing user IDs and passwords. Beware this last one! If you check the "remember me" box on a public Web browser, the next person who uses that browser is potentially using *your* cookie, and can log in as you!

An organization can't read cookies that it did not give you. So businessweek.com can't tell if you've also got cookies from forbes.com. But you can see all of the cookies in your browser. Take a look and you'll almost certainly see cookies from dozens of websites that you've never visited before. These are **third-party cookies** (sometimes called *tracking cookies*), and they are usually served by ad networks or other customer profiling firms.

By serving and tracking cookies in ads shown across partner sites, ad networks can build detailed browsing profiles that include sites visited, specific pages viewed, duration of visit, and the types of ads you've seen and responded to. And that surfing might give an advertising network a better guess at demographics like gender, age, marital status, and more. Visit a new parent site and expect to see diaper ads in the future, even when you're surfing for news or sports scores!

FIGURE 18.9

The Preferences setting in most Web browsers allows you to see its cookies. This browser has received cookies from several ad networks, media sites, and the University of Minnesota Carlson School of Management.

---

remarketing

Lets a Web site show custom, targeted ads to a user when visiting other sites if that user has already visited a given page on the advertiser's site. This technique allows firms to "reintroduce" products to users or target them with special messages or promotions.

retargeting

Also known as *remarketing*, a form of online targeted advertising where ads are personalized for consumers based on previous Internet activity that did not result in a sale or conversion. Surf the Web and see ads for products you've looked at on other sties? This is likely a result of retargeting.

third-party cookies

Sometimes called "tracking cookies" and are served by ad networks or other customer profiling firms. Tracking cookies are used to identify users and record behavior across multiple Web sites.

But What If I Don't Want a Cookie!

If all of this creeps you out, remember that you're in control. The most popular Web browsers allow you to block all cookies, block just third-party cookies, purge your cookie file, or even ask for your approval before accepting a cookie. Of course, if you block cookies, you block any benefits that come along with them, and some website features may require cookies to work properly. Also note that while deleting a cookie breaks a link between your browser and that website, if you supply identifying information in the future (say by logging into an old profile), the site might be able to assign your old profile data to the new cookie.

While the Internet offers targeting technologies that go way beyond traditional television, print, and radio offerings, none of these techniques is perfect. Since users are regularly assigned different IP addresses as they connect and disconnect from various physical and Wi-Fi networks, IP targeting can't reliably identify individual users. Cookies also have their weaknesses. They're assigned by browsers and associated with a given user's account on that computer. That means that if several people use the same browser on the same computer without logging on to that machine as separate users, then all their Web surfing activity may be mixed into the same cookie profile. (One solution is to create different log-in accounts on that computer. Your PC will then keep separate cookies for each account.) Some users might also use different browsers on the same machine or use different computers. Unless a firm has a way to match up these different cookies assigned across browsers (say by linking cookies on separate machines to a single log-in used at multiple locations), then a site may be working with multiple, incomplete profiles.

Big Data Analytics: Even for the Little Guy

In order to help arm firms with the insight needed for SEO, SEM, improved website design, and effective online marketing and promotion, Google offers a suite of tracking and analysis tools via a service it calls Google Analytics. The base service is offered free to websites of all sizes, with premium offerings and support available for a fee.

Using Analytics, a content provider can collect statistics on their website or app's traffic, traffic sources (search engine, website, app, geographic origin, or even e-mail or .pdf link), user behavior on site (new/returning visitor stats, pages visited, etc.), sales and advertising success, social media analysis, and more. Analytics typically involve harvesting data that browsers and servers produce on their own, along with data from pages and apps that a firm will tag in advance and data from tracking cookies used to identify users. Google Analytics has more than an 80 percent market share.[63]

Sample Screens from Google Analytics Reports

Source: Google.

Apps, Mobile Browsing, and Default Settings: The Shifting Landscape of Profiling Technology

Mobile apps don't use cookies, as they're a Web-based technology. The technologies for providing a cookie-like feature in mobile apps continue to be developed. Google offers an in-app tracking scheme called Advertising ID; Apple's is called IDFA (Identifier for Advertisers). These technologies are critical for tracking things like ad impression views and click-throughs, but the two schemes behave differently and standards for both schemes have changed in just the past year.

Apple's Safari browser also disables third-party cookies by default. This is a big deal because while Android holds a much larger market share than iOS, Apple users browse way more than anyone else, and Safari holds more than 50 percent share of mobile browser usage.[64] Microsoft has also disabled cookies as the default option for Internet Explorer.[65] When these settings are in effect, traditional cookie-based user profiling by ad networks simply isn't possible.

Apple has also shut down another way mobile users were being tracked using the MAC (media access control) address. The MAC address is a permanent and unique identifier baked into every network-connected device (think of it as an unchanging IP address). All desktop, laptop, tablets, and smartphones have a MAC address. Many retailers were using MAC addresses on Wi-Fi enabled phones to surreptitiously track store foot traffic.[66] In iOS8, Apple began randomizing the MAC number when these sorts of "Wi-Fi probe" requests were made, making it impossible to rely on any reported MAC number as a unique identifier for a repeat visitor. Apple is promoting a new location-based tracking system called iBeacon, which uses Bluetooth and (unlike MAC address snooping) can be turned off by users who wish to stay anonymous.

Taken collectively, these developments show that tracking technologies remain in flux, what works on the desktop doesn't necessarily work on mobile, and that default settings may be changed over time in ways that make life difficult for Google and other firms that rely on digital ad revenue. One analyst suggests that about half of all digital advertising spending leverages third-party cookies, and the shifts previously mentioned put these dollars in jeopardy.[67] Anyone with a stake in the digital advertising world—that is, advertisers, content operators, ad networks, even employees, investors, and regulators—will need to continually monitor the shifting landscape. It's not an understatement to say that billions in revenues are at stake.

KEY TAKEAWAYS

- The communication between Web browser and Web server can identify IP address, the type of browser used, the computer type, its operating system, time and date of access, and duration of Web page visit, and can read and assign unique identifiers, called cookies—all of which can be used in customer profiling and ad targeting.
- An IP address not only helps with geolocation; it can also be matched against other databases to identify the organization providing the user with Internet access (such as a firm or university), that organization's industry, size, and related statistics.
- A cookie is a unique line of identifying text, assigned and retrieved by a given Web server and stored on a computer by the browser, that can be used to build a profile associated with your Web activities.
- The most popular Web browsers allow you to block all cookies, block just third-party cookies, purge your cookie file, or even ask for your approval before accepting a cookie.
- Retargeting, or remarketing, allows advertisers to serve targeted ads to consumers who may have viewed a product page but did not buy that product. Google and other ad networks support retargeting.
- Cookies are a web-based technology, so they don't work in apps. Firms like Google and Apple have app-based tracking technology to help monetize ads (tracking click and impressions), but these technologies differ across platforms.
- Apple and Microsoft have also limited the use of cookies in their browser and mobile products. Apple has also shut off the ability of third parties to reach the MAC address, a unique number that many used to track mobile users. All these developments suggest that the future of profiling and ad technology is in flux, and managers who have a stake in this game will need to pay attention to future developments.

QUESTIONS AND EXERCISES

1. Give examples of how the ability to identify a surfer's computer, browser, or operating system can be used to target tech ads.
2. Describe how IBM targeted ad delivery for its college recruiting efforts. What technologies were used? What was the impact on click-through rates?
3. What is a cookie? How are cookies used? Is a cookie a computer program? Which firms can read the cookies in your Web browser?
4. Does a cookie accurately identify a user? Why or why not?
5. What is the danger of checking the "remember me" box when logging in to a website using a public computer?
6. What's a third-party cookie? What kinds of firms might use these? How are they used?
7. How can users restrict cookie use on their Web browsers? What is the downside of blocking cookies? Check your desktop and mobile devices. What is your current setting for cookie tracking?
8. As firms like Microsoft and Apple block tracking technologies or set defaults for higher levels of user privacy, how might this impact the future of the ad-based Internet?
9. What is remarketing? Have you ever seen an ad that you suspect was part of a remarketing effort? If so, describe what you experienced. Do you think remarketing is effective? Why or why not?
10. Work with a faculty member and join the Google Online Marketing Challenge (held in the spring of every year—see http://www.google.com/onlinechallenge). Google offers ad credits for student teams to develop and run online ad campaigns for real clients and offers prizes for winning teams. Some of the experiences earned in the Google Challenge can translate to other ad networks as well, and firsthand client experience has helped many students secure jobs, internships, and even start their own businesses.

8. PROFILING AND PRIVACY

LEARNING OBJECTIVES

1. Understand the privacy concerns that arise as a result of using third-party or tracking cookies to build user profiles.
2. Be aware of the negative consequences that could result from the misuse of third-party or tracking cookies.
3. Know the steps Google has taken to demonstrate its sensitivity to privacy issues.
4. Know the kinds of user information that Google stores, and the steps Google takes to protect the privacy of that information.

While AdSense has been wildly successful, contextual advertising has its limits. For example, what kind of useful targeting can firms really do based on the text of a news item on North Korean nuclear testing?[68] For more accurate targeting, Google offers what it calls "interest-based ads," which is based on a third-party cookie that tracks browsing activity across Google properties and AdSense partner sites. AdSense builds a profile, identifying users within dozens of broad categories and over six hundred subcategories.[69] Of course, there's a financial incentive to do this too. Ads deemed more interesting should garner more clicks, meaning more potential customer leads for advertisers, more revenue for websites that run AdSense, and more money for Google.

Click-throughs and online purchases are great, but online ads influence offline sales, too. Deloitte Consulting estimates that in 2014, some 28 percent of sales in stores, or $970 billion, was influenced by mobile devices. That's more than three times the overall online sales figure of roughly $300 billion that year.[70] If Google can prove its ads drive in-store sales, it can make the case for greater online ad spending. In a scheme similar to Facebook's, Google is partnering with Axciom, a firm that collect information on customer e-mail addresses. If the Google cookie can be matched to a user's e-mail address, then we can identify that a user has seen an ad. If that user walks into a store, buys something, and the vendor can match their e-mail address to that purchase (perhaps they gave it to receive e-mail coupons, a loyalty card, or they've previously bought online), then a trail from "Saw the ad" to "bought the product" can be drawn. To avoid a total user creep-out, the user-tracking is collected and reported in aggregate and anonymously, and that in this system, no identifying information on users is stored or reported. It's also far from a completely representative system. On Android phones Google's partners can connect just 15 to 20 percent of mobile ads to a customer account, and far fewer for harder-to-track iPhones, but for some retailers, that's enough of a sample to demonstrate ROI on ad spending. Home Depot's VP of Online Marketing says the data "confirmed our commitment" to search ads on smartphones.[71] Target execs claim that one-third of Target's mobile-search ads led to a user visiting one of its stores during the 2014 holiday season.[72]

While targeting can benefit Web surfers, users will resist if they feel that they are being mistreated, exploited, or put at risk. Negative backlash might also result in a change in legislation. The US Federal Trade Commission has already called for more transparency and user control in online advertising and for requesting user consent (**opt-in**) when collecting sensitive data.[73] Mishandled user privacy could curtail targeting opportunities, limiting growth across the online advertising field. And with less ad support, many of the Internet's free services could suffer.

opt-in

Program (typically a marketing effort) that requires customer consent. This program is contrasted with opt-out programs, which enroll all customers by default.

FIGURE 18.10

Here's an example of one user's interests, as tracked by Google's "Interest-based Ads" and displayed in the firm's "Ad Preferences Manager."

Your interests   Below you can edit the interests that Google has associated with your cookie:

Category

Arts & Humanities - Books & Literature	Remove
Business - Advertising & Marketing	Remove
Business - Small Business	Remove
Computers & Electronics - Consumer Electronics	Remove
Finance & Insurance - Investing	Remove
Internet - Search Engine Optimization & Marketing	Remove
Internet - Web Services - Affiliate Programs	Remove
Lifestyles	Remove
News & Current Events - Business News	Remove
Society - Social Science - Psychology	Remove

(Add interests)   Google does not associate sensitive interest categories with your ads preferences

Opt out   Opt out if you prefer ads not to be based on the interest categories above.

(Opt out)

When you opt out, Google disables this cookie and no longer associates interest categories with your browser.

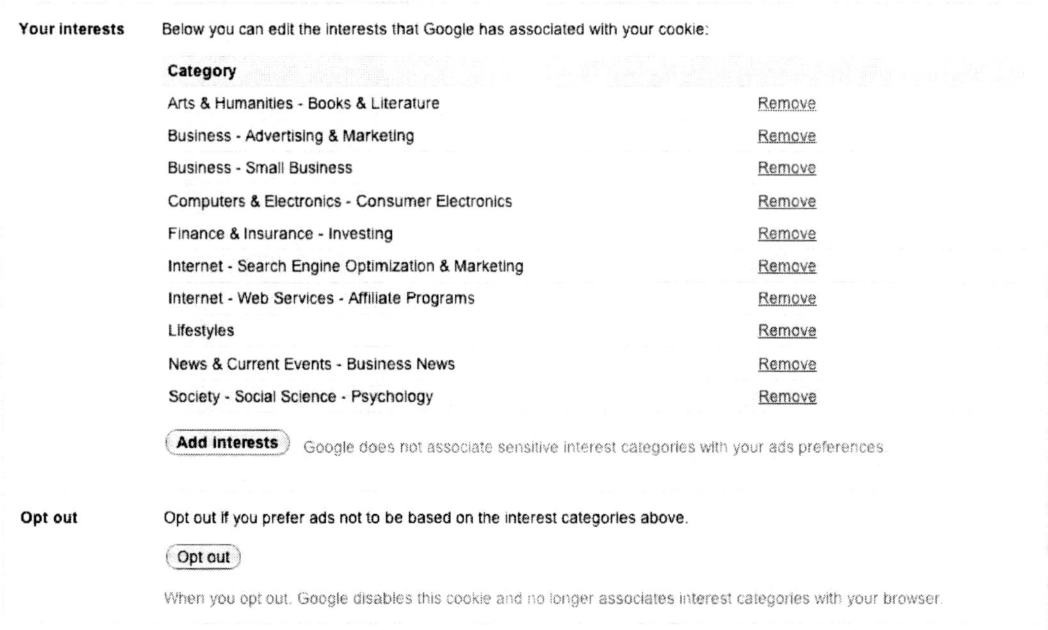

Google's roll-out of interest-based ads shows the firm's sensitivity to these issues. The firm has also placed significant control in the hands of users, with options at program launch that were notably more robust than those of its competitors.[74] Each interest-based ad is accompanied by an "Ads by Google" link that will bring users to a page describing Google advertising and which provides access to the company's "Ads Preferences Manager." This tool allows surfers to see any of the hundreds of potential categorizations that Google has assigned to that browser's tracking cookie. Users can remove categorizations, and even add interests if they want to improve ad targeting. Some topics are too sensitive to track, and the technology avoids profiling race, religion, sexual orientation, health, political or trade union affiliation, and certain financial categories.[75]

Google also allows users to install a cookie that opts them out of interest-based tracking. And since browser cookies can expire or be deleted, the firm has gone a step further, offering a browser **plug-in** that will remain permanent, even if a user's **opt-out** cookie is purged.

plug-in

A small computer program that extends the feature set or capabilities of another application.

opt-out

Programs that enroll all customers by default, but that allow consumers to discontinue participation if they want to.

Google, Privacy Advocates, and the Law

Google's moves are meant to demonstrate transparency in its ad targeting technology, and the firm's policies may help raise the collective privacy bar for the industry. While privacy advocates have praised Google's efforts to put more control in the hands of users, many continue to voice concern over what they see as the increasing amount of information that the firm houses.[76] For an avid user, Google could conceivably be holding e-mail (Gmail), photos (Picasa), social media activity (Google+), a Web surfing profile (AdSense and DoubleClick), location (Google Maps), appointments (Google Calendar), music and other media (Google Play), files stored in the cloud (Google Drive), transcripts of phone messages (Google Voice), work files (Google Docs), and more.

Google insists that reports portraying it as a data-hoarding Big Brother are inaccurate. Data is not sold to third parties. Any targeting is fully disclosed, with users empowered to opt out at all levels.[77] Google has introduced several tools, including Google Dashboard and Google Ad Preferences Manager, that allow users to see information Google stores about them, clear their browsing history, and selectively delete collected data.[78] But critics counter that corporate intentions and data use policies (articulated in a website's Terms of Service) can change over time, and that a firm's good behavior today is no guarantee of good behavior in the future.[79] Google has modified its policy several times in the past, including changes that now allow the firm to link search history to ad targeting. It has also unified its privacy policy in a way that allows for greater profiling, sharing, and tailored services across Google offerings.[80]

Google does enjoy a lot of user goodwill, and it is widely recognized for its unofficial motto "Don't Be Evil." However, some worry that even though Google might not be evil, it could still make a mistake, and that despite its best intentions, a security breach or employee error could leave data dangerously or embarrassingly exposed.

Gaffes have repeatedly occurred. A system flaw inadvertently shared some Google Docs with contacts who were never granted access to them.[81] When the firm introduced its now-scuttled Google Buzz social networking service, many users were horrified that their most frequently used Gmail contacts were automatically added to Buzz, allowing others to see who you're communicating with. As one report explained, "Suddenly, journalists' clandestine contacts were exposed, secret affairs became dramatically less secret, and stalkers obtained a new tool to harass their victims. Oops."[82] Google admitted that some of its "Street View" cars, while driving through neighborhoods and taking photos for Google maps, had inadvertently collected personal data, including e-mails and passwords.[83] Google scrambled to plug a hole that could potentially allow hackers to access the contacts, calendars, and photos on Android phones connecting to the Internet over open Wi-Fi networks.[84] A rogue employee was fired for violating the firm's strict guidelines and procedures on information access.[85] In addition, the firm has been accused of bypassing privacy settings in Apple's Safari Web browser in order to better track users.[86]

Privacy advocates also worry that the amount of data stored by Google serves as one-stop shopping for litigators and government investigators—a concern that gained even more attention following the disclosure of the US government's Prism surveillance program.[87] The counterargument points to the fact that Google has continually reflected an aggressive defense of data privacy in court cases. Following Prism disclosures, Google asked the US Foreign Intelligence Surveillance Court to rescind a gag order barring the firm from revealing government information requests.[88] When Viacom sued Google over copyright violations in YouTube, the search giant successfully fought the original subpoena, which had requested user-identifying information.[89] Google has also resisted Justice Department subpoenas for search queries, while rivals have complied.[90] Google has also claimed that it has been targeted by some foreign governments that are deliberately hacking or interfering with the firm's services in order to quash some information sharing and to uncover dissident activity.[91]

Google is increasingly finding itself in precedent-setting cases where the law is vague. Google's Street View, for example, has been the target of legal action in the United States, Canada, Japan, Greece, and the United Kingdom. Varying legal environments create a challenge to the global rollout of any data-driven initiative.[92] European courts have ruled that EU citizens have the so-called right to be forgotten and can demand that search engines remove links to information deemed "inadequate, irrelevant or no longer relevant, or excessive in relation to the purposes for which they were processed."[93] Does this sound vague? Enforcement of this ruling may be challenging for Google.[94] And rivals are ready to cast Google as a voracious data tracker. Apple has begun to play up the firm's contrast with Google, claiming "You are not our product."[95]

Ad targeting brings to a head issues of opportunity, privacy, security, risk, and legislation. Google is now taking a more active public relations and lobbying role to prevent misperceptions and to be sure its positions are understood. While the field continues to evolve, Google's experience will lay the groundwork for the future of personalized technology and provide a case study for other firms that need to strike the right balance between utility and privacy. Despite differences, it seems clear to Google, its advocates, and its detractors that with great power comes great responsibility.

KEY TAKEAWAYS

- Possible consequences resulting from the misuse of customer tracking and profiling technologies include user resistance and legislation. Mishandled user privacy could curtail targeting opportunities and limit growth in online advertising. With less ad support, many of the Internet's free services could suffer.

- Google has taken several steps to protect user privacy. The firm offers several tools that enable users not only to see information that Google collects but also to delete, pause, or modify data collection and profiling terms.

- Google's "Ads Preferences Manager" allows surfers to see, remove, and add to any of the categorizations that Google has assigned to that browser's tracking cookie. The technology also avoids targeting certain sensitive topics. The firm's Privacy Dashboard provides additional access to and user control over Google's profiling and data collection.

- Google allows users to install a cookie or plug-in that opts them out of interest-based tracking.

- Google has begun to partner with third-party firms to tie together its data on consumer ad viewership to in-store visits. While not perfect, the data has shown that many users who view online ads go on to make in store purchases. Google's data is reported in aggregate, and not on any individual user.

- Some privacy advocates have voiced concern over what they see as the increasing amount of information that Google and other firms collect. Apple is among the firms that have contrasted their approach to products, privacy, and business models with Google's ad-driven, profiling methods.

- Even the best-intentioned and most competent firms can have a security breach that compromises stored information. Google has suffered privacy breaches from product flaws and poorly planned feature rollouts, as well as deliberate hacks and attacks. The firm has also changed policies regarding data collection and privacy as its services have evolved. Such issues may lead to further investigation, legislation, and regulation.

QUESTIONS AND EXERCISES

1. Gmail uses contextual advertising. The service will scan the contents of e-mail messages and display ads off to the side. Test the "creep out" factor in Gmail—create an account (if you don't already have one), and send messages to yourself with controversial terms in them. Which ones showed ads? Which ones didn't?

2. Google has never built user profiles based on Gmail messages. Ads are served based on a real-time scanning of keywords. Is this enough to make you comfortable with Google's protection of your own privacy? Why or why not?

3. List the negative consequences that could result from the misuse of tracking cookies.

4. What steps does Google take to protect the privacy of user information? What steps has Google taken to give users control over the user data that the firm collects and the ads the users wish to see?

5. Which topics does "Ads Preferences Manager" avoid in its targeting system?

6. Visit Google's Ad Preferences page. Is Google tracking your interests? Do you think the list of interests is accurate? Browse the categories under the "Ad Interest" button. Would you add any of these categories to your profile? Why or why not? What do you gain or lose by taking advantage of Google's "Opt Out" option? Visit rival ad networks. Do you have a similar degree of control? More or less?

7. Visit Google Dashboard. What information is Google collecting about you? Does any of this surprise you? How do you suppose the firm uses this to benefit you? After seeing this information, did you make any changes to the settings in the privacy center? Why or why not?

8. List the types of information that Google might store for an individual. Do you feel that Google is a fair and reliable steward for this information? Are there Google services or other online efforts that you won't use due to privacy concerns? Why?

9. What do you think of the Google-Acxiom partnership to show online ad influence for offline purchasing. Does this concern you? Why or why not?

10. Google's "interest-based advertising" was launched as an opt-out effort. What are the pros and cons for Google, users, advertisers, and AdSense partner sites if Google were to switch to an opt-in system? How would these various constituencies be impacted if the government mandated that users explicitly opt in to third-party cookies and other behavior-tracking techniques?

11. What is Google's unofficial motto?

12. What is "Street View"? Where and on what grounds is it being challenged?

13. Cite two court cases where Google has mounted a vigorous defense of data privacy.

14. *Wired News* quoted a representative of privacy watchdog group, The Center for Digital Democracy, who offered a criticism of online advertising. The representative suggested that online firms were trying to learn "everything about individuals and manipulate their weaknesses" and that the federal government should "investigate the role [that online ads] played in convincing people to take out mortgages they should not have."[96] Do you think online advertising played a significant role in the mortgage crisis? What role do advertisers, ad networks, and content providers have in online advertising oversight? Should this responsibility be any different from oversight in traditional media (television, print, radio)? What guidelines would you suggest?

15. Even well-intentioned firms can compromise user privacy. How have Google's missteps compromised user privacy? As a manager, what steps would you take in developing and deploying information systems that might prevent these kinds of problems from occurring?

16. Research the EU's "right to be forgotten" ruling and the current status as it pertains to Google. Why is the ruling so challenging to Google? How does it burden Google? Does this harm other civil liberties like free speech? Why or why not? Advocate in favor of or against the ruling.

17. Research how Apple has contrasted its approach to privacy against those of Google and other rivals that rely on ad-driven business models. Does this contrast influence your decision to choose Apple or Google products? Why or why not?

18. The issue of civil liberties versus national security may be one of the most defining tensions of modern times. Research the U.S. government's Foreign Intelligence Surveillance Act (FISA) and related legislation or programs. What role do tech companies play in this effort? What are the arguments made for and against these programs? Are US firms put at risk by perceived or actual government efforts in this area? How so? If you were leading Google or another well-known US Internet firm, how would you address the tension? Be prepared to discuss and debate issues in class.

9. SEARCH ENGINES, AD NETWORKS, AND FRAUD

LEARNING OBJECTIVES

1. Be able to identify various types of online fraud, as well as the techniques and technologies used to perpetrate these crimes.
2. Understand how firms can detect, prevent, and prosecute fraudsters.

There's a lot of money to be made online, and this has drawn the attention of criminals and the nefarious. Online fraudsters may attempt to steal from advertisers, harm rivals, or otherwise dishonestly game the system. But bad guys beware—such attempts violate terms-of-service agreements and may lead to prosecution and jail time.

Studying ad-related fraud helps marketers, managers, and technologists understand potential vulnerabilities, as well as the methods used to combat them. This process also builds tech-centric critical thinking, valuation, and risk assessment skills.

Some of the more common types of fraud that are attempted in online advertising include the following:

- *Enriching* **click fraud**—when site operators generate bogus ad clicks to earn CPC income.
- *Enriching impression fraud*—when site operators generate false page views (and hence ad impressions) in order to boost their site's CPM earnings.
- *Depleting click fraud*—clicking a rival's ads to exhaust their CPC advertising budget.
- *Depleting impression fraud*—generating bogus impressions to exhaust a rival's CPM ad budget.
- *Rank-based impression fraud*—on sites where ad rank is based on click performance, fraudsters repeatedly search keywords linked to rival ads or access pages where rival ads appear. The goal is to generate impressions without clicks. This process lowers the performance rank (quality score) of a rival's ads, possibly dropping ads from rank results, and allowing fraudsters to subsequently bid less for the advertising slots previously occupied by rivals.
- *Disbarring fraud*—attempting to frame a rival by generating bogus clicks or impressions that appear to be associated with the rival, in hopes that this rival will be banned from an ad network or punished in search engine listings.
- *Link fraud (also known as spamdexing or link farming)*—creating a series of bogus websites, all linking back to a page, in hopes of increasing that page's results in organic search.
- *Keyword stuffing*—packing a website with unrelated keywords (sometimes hidden in fonts that are the same color as a website's background) in hopes of either luring users who wouldn't normally visit a website, or attracting higher-value contextual ads.
- *Social influence fraud* – generating fake followers, likes, +1s, retweets, shares, or YouTube views.

Disturbing stuff, but firms are after the bad guys and they've put their best geeks on the case. Widespread fraud would tank advertiser ROI and crater the online advertising market, so Google and rivals are diligently working to uncover and prosecute the crooks.

9.1 Busting the Bad Guys

On the surface, enriching click fraud seems the easiest to exploit. Just set up a website, run CPC ads on the page, and click like crazy. Each click should ring the ad network cash register, and a portion of those funds will be passed on to the perpetrating site owner—*ka ching*! But remember, each visitor is identified by an IP address, so lots of clicks from a single IP make the bad guys easy to spot.

So organized crime tried to raise the bar, running so-called **click farms** to spread fraud across dozens of IP addresses. *The Times of India* uncovered one such effort where Indian housewives were receiving up to twenty-five cents for each ad click made on fraudster-run websites.[97] But an unusually large number of clicks detected as coming from Indian IP addresses foiled these schemes as well.

---

click fraud

Generating bogus clicks, either for financial gain (enriching fraud), or to attack rivals by draining their online ad budget (depleting fraud).

click farms

A network of users and computers engaged in coordinated click fraud. Since the different computers leverage different IP addresses, click farms can be more difficult to detect.

Fraudsters then moved on to use **botnets or zombie networks**—hordes of surreptitiously infiltrated computers, linked and controlled by rogue software.[98] To create botnets, hackers exploit security holes, spread viruses, or use so-called phishing techniques to trick users into installing software that will lie dormant, awaiting commands from a central location. The controlling machine then sends out tasks for each bot (or zombie), instructing them to visit websites and click on ads in a way that mimics real traffic. The ZeroAccess botnet is said to have infected over 9 million PCs worldwide that were used in click fraud schemes, among other scams.[99]

botnets or zombie networks

Hordes of surreptitiously infiltrated computers, linked and controlled remotely. This technique is used to perpetrate click fraud, as well as a variety of other computer security crimes.

FIGURE 18.11   Spread of the ZeroAccess Botnet

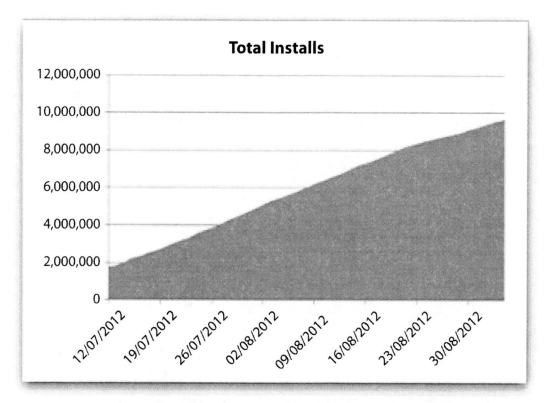

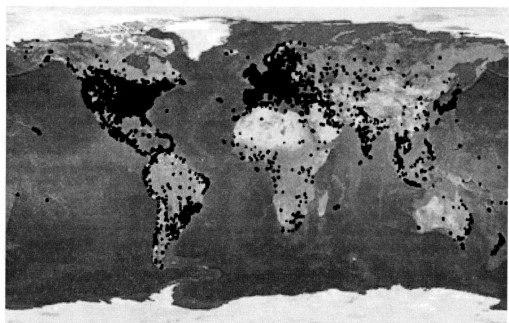

Source: Sophos, http://nakedsecurity.sophos.com/2012/09/19/zeroaccess-botnet-uncovered.

Scary, but this is where scale, expertise, and experience come in. The more activity an ad network can monitor, the greater the chance that it can uncover patterns that are anomalous. Higher click-through rates than comparable sites? Caught. Too many visits to a new or obscure site? Caught. Clicks that don't fit standard surfing patterns for geography, time, and day? Caught.

Sometimes the goal isn't theft, but sabotage. Google's Ad Traffic Quality Team backtracked through unusual patterns to uncover a protest effort targeted at Japanese credit card firms. Ad clicks were eventually traced to an incendiary blogger who incited readers to search for the Japanese word *kiyashinku* (meaning cashing credit, or credit cards), and to click the credit card firm ads that show up, depleting firm search marketing budgets. Sneaky, but uncovered and shut down, without harm to the advertisers.[100]

Social influence fraud is used for many things: ego stroking (my follower count is bigger than yours), attempts at creating social proof (e.g., with so many followers this must be legitimate), attempts at making a post seem popular in hopes it will be highlighted and promoted to others (e.g., trending, among "top tweets"), and trying to influence search results (since Google and Bing take social media into account when computing organic rankings). Among the well-known accused of social influence fraud: Pepsi, Coca-Cola, Mercedes-Benz, and Louis Vuitton, 50 Cent, Paris Hilton, Mitt Romey,[101] and even the US State Department.[102] A New Republic piece on "farms" for creating fake social influence included a photograph of one Philippines-based boss of bogusness pictured lounging on hundreds of brick-like stacks of SIM cards used by his extensive staff to create the perception that social accounts are the work of individual users on separate phones.[103]

Search firm and ad network software can use data patterns and other signals to ferret out most other types of fraud, too, including rank-based impression fraud, spamdexing, keyword stuffing, and social influence fraud. While many have tried to up the stakes with increasingly sophisticated attacks, large ad networks have worked to match them, increasing their anomaly detection capabilities across all types of fraud.[104] Here we see another scale and data-based advantage for Google. Since the firm serves more search results and advertisements than its rivals do, it has vastly more information on online activity. And if it knows more about what's happening online than any other firm, it's likely to be first to shut down anyone who tries to take advantage of the system. The tech behind fraud busting is impressive. Tech Google developed in house, called PowerDrill, has been described as "a freak computer system" capable of processing a half trillion cells of data in less than five seconds.[105] The system looks for fraud patterns and also spits out graphical representations for human inspection. A sort of **Turing test** emerges from the data. If what turns up doesn't follow patterns you'd expect from human–for example, if clicks look too evenly distributed or concentrated in certain places (e.g., uniformly around the edges of some ads instead of being distributed like most other ads), then that's a give-away.

Turing test

A test of artificial intelligence that, if passed, would mean a computer is indistinguishable from a human being. Originally proposed by renown computer scientist Alan Turing.

Click Fraud: How Bad Is It?

The rise in ad fraud botnets has come about because other security is getting stronger. Despite repeated high-profile data breaches, banks are tougher to hack, and credit cards are becoming more secure. AdAge claims ad fraud is "the most lucrative endeavor a cybercriminal can undertake today," and, says one expert interviewed, "We're at a point now where malware is being used principally for ad fraud."[106] Accounts on the actual rate of click fraud vary widely. A study by the Association of National Advertisers and the anti-fraud consultancy, White Ops, pegs ad fraud loses for 2015 at an estimated $6.3 billion.[107] Some third-party firms contend that nearly one in five clicks is fraudulent.[108] But Google adamantly disputes these headline-grabbing numbers, claiming that many such reports are based on logs that reflect false data from conditions that Google doesn't charge for (e.g., double counting a double click, or adding up repeated use of the browser back button in a way that looks like multiple clicks have occurred). The firm also offers monitoring, analytics, and reporting tools that can uncover this kind of misperceived discrepancy.

Google contends that all invalid clicks (mistakes and fraud) represent less than 10 percent of all clicks, that the vast majority of these clicks are filtered out, and that Google doesn't charge advertisers for clicks flagged as mistakes or suspicious.[109] In fact, Google says their screening bar is so high and so accurate that less than 0.02 percent of clicks are reactively classified as invalid and credited back to advertisers.[110]

So who's right? While it's impossible to identify the intention behind every click, the market ultimately pays for performance. And advertisers are continuing to flock to CPC ad networks (and to Google in particular). While that doesn't mean that firms can stop being vigilant, it does suggest that for most firms, Google seems to have the problem under control.

KEY TAKEAWAYS

- Fraud can undermine the revenue model behind search engines, ad networks, and the ad-based Internet. It also threatens honest competition among rivals that advertise online.
- There are many forms of online fraud, including enriching fraud (meant to line the pockets of the perpetrators), depleting fraud (meant to waste the ad budgets of rivals), disbarring fraud (meant to frame the innocent as fraudsters), and methods to lower rival ad rank performance, or gain search engine ranking algorithms.
- While fraudsters have devised ingenious ways to exploit the system (including click farms and botnets), IP addresses and detailed usage pattern monitoring increasingly reveal bogus activity.
- Fraud rates are widely disputed. However, it is clear that if widespread fraud were allowed to occur, advertisers would see lower ROI from online ad efforts, and Internet business models would suffer. The continued strength of the online advertising market suggests that while fraud may be impossible to stop completely, most fraud is under control.

QUESTIONS AND EXERCISES

1. Why is it difficult for an unscrupulous individual to pull off enriching click fraud simply by setting up a website, running ad network ads, and clicking?
2. Why did hackers develop botnets? What advantage do they offer the criminals? How are they detected? Why do larger ad networks have an advantage in click fraud detection?
3. How can you prevent botnet software from inhabiting your computers? Are you reasonably confident that your computer is free from a botnet infection? Why or why not?
4. What are spamdexing and keyword stuffing? What risks does a legitimate business run if it engages in these practices, and if they are discovered by search engines? What would this mean for the career of the manager who thought he could game the system?
5. Which types of fraud can be attempted against search advertising? Which are perpetrated over its ad network?
6. What are the consequences if click fraud were allowed to continue? Does this ultimately help or hurt firms that run ad networks? Why?

10.   THE BATTLE UNFOLDS

LEARNING OBJECTIVES

1. **Understand the challenges of maintaining growth as a business and industry mature.**
2. **Recognize how technology is a catalyst, causing the businesses of many firms in a variety of industries to converge and compete, and that as a result of this, Google is active on multiple competitive fronts.**
3. **Critically evaluate the risks and challenges of businesses that Google, Microsoft, and other firms are entering.**
4. **Appreciate the magnitude of this impending competition, and recognize the competitive forces that will help distinguish winners from losers.**

Google has been growing like gangbusters, but the firm's twin engines of revenue growth—ads served on search and through its ad networks—will inevitably mature. And it will likely be difficult for Google to find new growth markets that are as lucrative as these. Emerging advertising outlets such as social networks and mobile have lower click-through rates than conventional advertising,[111] and Google has struggled to develop a presence in social media—trends suggesting that Google will have to work harder for less money. Google's reorganization as a holding firm named Alphabet with a Google subsidiary breaks many of the new, smaller, riskier but potentially growth-oriented efforts into separate businesses. Says co-founder Page, the firm chose the name alpha-bet as a bet on the financial term alpha, which refers to 'investment return above benchmark.'[112] An additional way to think of this is that Google is hoping to be the first (alpha) big player to double-down (bet) on risky but promising new markets.[113]

To understand what can happen when maturity hits, look at Microsoft. The house that Gates built is more profitable than Google (roughly $22 billion versus about $14.5 billion in 2014) and continues to dominate the incredibly lucrative markets served by Windows and Office. But these markets haven't grown much for over a decade. In industrialized nations, most Windows and Office purchases come not from growth, but when existing users upgrade or buy new machines. And without substantial year-on-year growth, the stock price doesn't move.

FIGURE 18.12 A Comparison of Stock Price Change—Google (GOOG) versus Microsoft (MSFT)[114]

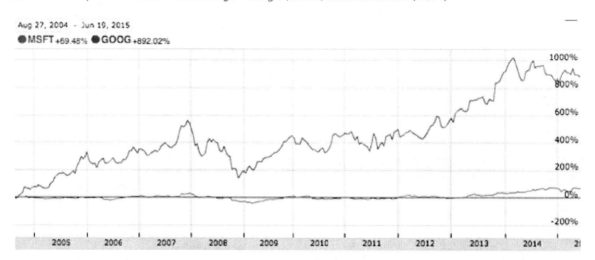

For big firms like Microsoft and Google, pushing stock price north requires not just new markets, but billion-dollar ones. Adding even $100 million in new revenues doesn't do much for firms bringing in nearly $87 billion and $66 billion a year, respectively. That's why you see Microsoft swinging for the fences, investing in the uncertain but potentially gargantuan markets of video games, mobile phone software, cloud computing (see Chapter 14) music, video, virtual and augmented reality, and of course, search and everything else that fuels online ad revenue. Finding new billion-dollar markets is wonderful, but rare. Apple seems to have done it with the iPhone and iPad. But trying to unseat a dominant leader possessing strategic resources can be ferociously expensive, with unclear prospects for success. Microsoft's Bing group lost over $2 billion over just nine months, winning almost no share from Google despite the lavish spend.[115]

semantic Web

Sites that wrap data in invisible tags that can be recognized by search engines, analysis tools, and other services to make it easier for computer programs to accurately categorize, compare, and present this information.

Search: Google Rules, but It Ain't Over

PageRank is by no means the last word in search, and offerings from Google and its rivals continue to evolve. Google supplements PageRank results with news, photos, video, and other categories. Yahoo! is continually refining its search algorithms and presentation. And Microsoft's third entry into the search market, the "decision engine" Bing, sports nifty tweaks for specific kinds of queries. Restaurant searches in Bing are bundled with ratings stars, product searches show up with reviews and price comparisons, and airline flight searches not only list flight schedules and fares, but also a projection on whether those fares are likely to go up or down. Apple's Siri service delivers search results from Bing, not Google, offering a potentially key new channel for pumping up Bing search volume. Apple is also aggressively cutting deals with category players like Yelp and the Weather Channel, and iOS has empowered app firms to integrate Siri into their own offerings, as well, all of which further cut Google out of new emerging channels for search.

Alternative tools like the Wolfram Alpha "knowledge engine" move beyond Web page rankings and instead aggregate data for comparison, formatting findings in tables and graphs. Web sites are also starting to wrap data in invisible tags that can be recognized by search engines, analysis tools, and other services. If a search engine can tell that a number on a restaurant's Web site is, for example, either a street address, an average entrée price, or the seating capacity, it will be much easier for computer programs to accurately categorize, compare, and present this information. This is what geeks are talking about when they refer to the **semantic Web**. Google has begun to draw from several resources on the Web to build its own semantic Web classifications. If you search for "Taj Mahal" on the Web, it presents a summary of the famous Indian landmark, but it also asks if you'd like to see results regarding the Grammy Award-winning musician or the New Jersey casino that also share that same name.[116]

And with the Google Now app, the firm is trying to deliver results to you before you even ask for them. Google Now will send you personalized information throughout the day—calendar reminders, weather updates. But it will also take a guess at what you might be interested in—reviews of nearby restaurants if it's lunchtime, train timetables if you're at a station, flight info if you're at an airport. Land in a new city? Google will send hotel and rental car info based on confirmation messages sent to Gmail. Users have to give Google permission to access data from other services, but one can immediately see how on-demand information could be served up not only via phone but also via other products, like Google Glass or Android TV. If imitation is the sincerest form of flatter, then Apple's Siri has been giving Google some complements. The latest version of the iOS (and its integrated voice assistant) mimics many of the predictive features of Google Now.[117] Looks like users are the winners as constant, deep-pocketed competition creates an imperative for lightning innovation.

FIGURE 18.13   Google Goggles returns search results by photographing objects. It can even translate foreign-language text.

Source: Google.

And who says you need to use words to conduct a search? Google voice search challenges Siri in Android devices and in Google apps. Google Goggles uses the camera in your mobile phone to "enter" search criteria. Snap a picture of a landmark, book, or piece of artwork, for example, and Google will use that image to retrieve search results. The product can even return translations of foreign text. All signs point to more innovation, more competition, and an increasingly more useful Internet!

Both Google and Microsoft are on a collision course. But there's also an impressive roster of additional firms circling this space, each with the potential to be competitors, collaborators, merger partners, or all of the above. While wounded and shrinking, Yahoo! is still a powerhouse, ranking ahead of Google in some overall traffic statistics. Google's competition with Apple in the mobile phone business prompted Google's then CEO Eric Schmidt to resign from Apple's board of directors. Google's three-quarters-of-a-billion-dollar purchase of the leading mobile advertiser AdMob was quickly followed by Apple snapping up number two mobile ad firm Quattro Wireless for $275 million. Now Google and Apple seem to compete in most markets, with each offering web-based office suites, consumer cloud storage, music systems, TV devices, wearables, home automation software, auto platforms, and more. Add in Amazon, Facebook, eBay, Twitter, Salesforce.com, Netflix, the video game industry, telecom and mobile carriers, cable firms, and the major media companies, and the next few years have the makings of a big, brutal fight.

10.1   Strategic Issues

As outlined earlier, Google enjoys major scale advantages in search, and network effects in advertising. The firm's dominance helps grow a data asset that can be used in service improvement, all while its expertise in core markets continues to grow over time. Google's competitive position outside of its core markets is much less clear.

Within Google's ad network, there are *switching costs* for advertisers and for content providers. Google partners have set up accounts and are familiar with the firm's tools and analytics. Content providers would also need to modify websites to replace Google-served ads with those from rivals. But choosing Google doesn't cut out the competition. Many advertisers and content providers participate in multiple ad networks, making it easier to shift business from one firm to another. This likely means that Google will have to keep advertisers by offering superior value rather than relying on lock-in. Facebook's ad network may pose an especially worrisome threat, as some suggest that Facebook's profiles contain more accurate demographics than Google collects.[118]

Another vulnerability may exist with search consumers. While Google's brand is strong, switching costs for search users are incredibly low. Move from Google.com to Bing.com and you actually save two letters of typing!

Still, there are no signs that Google's search leadership is in jeopardy. So far users have been creatures of habit; no rival has offered technology compelling enough to woo away the Googling masses. Defeating Google with some sort of technical advantage will be difficult since Web-based innovation can often be quickly imitated. Google now rolls out over 550 tweaks to its search algorithm annually, with many features mimicking or outdoing innovations from rivals.[119]

After a multi-year run where Google paid the Mozilla Foundation hundreds of millions of dollars to be featured as the default browser in Firefox, Google has been bumped in favor of Yahoo.[120] Google has shown that if it can't buy its way into a distribution channel, it can create one. The firm's Web browser, Chrome, has beaten out Internet Explorer to become the number one product used by Web surfers worldwide.[121]

How Big Is Too Big?

Microsoft's dominance has incurred the wrath of regulators in the United States and Europe. The firm spent roughly half of its existence as a corporation battling various antitrust allegations in the United States and billions in settlement fees.[122] European antitrust officials have taken action against Redmond's bundling Windows Media Player and Internet Explorer with Windows, forcing the firm to offer alternatives alongside its own products and incurring additional fines.[123] Is Google in for a similar or even worse fate?

Being big isn't enough to violate US antitrust laws. Harvard Law School Professor Andrew Gavil says, "You've got to be big, and you have to be bad. You have to be both."[124] While Google has many critics, the firm also has a history of being a relentless supporter of open computing standards. And as mentioned earlier, there's no forcing users to stick with Google—the firm must continue to win this market on its own merits.

That said, a big firm is a big target for attracting serious scrutiny in the United States and abroad. For example, Google was forced to abandon a search advertising partnership with Yahoo! after the Department of Justice indicated its intention to block the agreement (Yahoo! and Microsoft have since inked a deal to share search technology and ad sales). Among the more serious questions: Does Google have an unfair advantage, favoring its own properties, like Maps, YouTube, Google+, and Zagat over rivals? Results from these properties are integrated with Google search, and the toolbar that appears across the top of most Google websites also provides preferred access to Google rather than rival properties. The firm's regulatory outlook seems to differ by region. In the United States, after a nearly two-year probe, one of the biggest investigations in history (generating over 9 million pages in testimony), the Federal Trade Commission (FTC) has essentially said "no," at least for now. The FTC voted unanimously to close its antitrust investigation without bringing charges. The ruling concluded that Google's practices improved search for the benefit of users and that "any negative impact on actual or perceived competitors was incidental to that purpose."[125] Google does face some minor concessions from the FTC's work. Firms like Yelp can opt out of having their results scraped by Google and incorporated into search results. Google will stop offering contractual restrictions preventing ad customers from advertising on competing search platforms. And Google must allow firms (including rivals) to license some of its key mobile patents when offered fair compensation.

The situation in Europe looks decidedly different. The European Union has accused Google of violating antitrust laws, displaying Google-provided results such as shopping, travel, and insurance, over rival products. Google's share of the search market in Europe is actually even larger than in the United States, averaging around 90 percent in most countries.[126] The European Union is also investigating Google's Android business, including tactics requiring hardware firms to comply with the exclusive pre-installation or bundling of Google's apps and services, and restricting modifications or forks of the Android operating system. Fines have the potential to top $6.5 billion.[127] And as concerns in Europe and elsewhere heat up, there's no guarantee that continued Google dominance might once again cause the Department of Justice to consider whether Google's size and practices disadvantage others. Increased antitrust scrutiny is a downside that comes along with the advantages of market-dominating scale.

10.2 More Ads, More Places, More Formats

Google has been a champion of increased Internet access. But altruism aside, more net access also means a greater likelihood of ad revenue.

low latency
Low delay.

Google's effort to catalyze Internet use worldwide comes through on multiple fronts. In the United States, Google has supported (with varying degrees of success) efforts to offer free Wi-Fi. Google announced it would offer high-speed, fiber-optic net access to homes in select US cities, with Kansas City, Kansas; Kansas City, Missouri; Provo, Utah; and Austin, Texas chosen for the first roll-outs.[128] The experimental network offers competitively priced Internet access of up to 1 GB per second—that's a speed some one hundred times faster than many Americans have access to today. The networks are meant to be open to other service providers and Google hopes to learn and share insights on how to build high-speed networks more efficiently. Google will also be watching to see how access to ultrahigh-speed networks impacts user behavior and fuels innovation. Broadband competition from Google seems to be helping even those consumers who don't choose it, with many competitors matching Google on increased speeds and lower prices.[129] Globally, Google is also a major backer (along with Liberty Global and HSBC) of the O3b satellite network. O3b stands for "the other three billion" of the world's population who currently lack Internet access. O3b has begun launching multiple satellites circling the globe, blanketing underserved regions with **low latency** (low delay), high-speed Internet access.[130] Google's experimental Project Loon hopes to bring the Internet to even more underserved, by blanketing regions with twelve-mile-high balloons that act as floating Internet relay points.[131] If balloons aren't enough, maybe solar-powered drones beaming Internet access while orbiting continuously at heights that put them above clouds and inclement weather might do the trick. Google's purchase of Titan Aerospace is reportedly targeted at exactly that prospect.[132] And the firm is experimenting with delivering Internet throughout South Africa via unused or "white" space in the nation's television broadcast spectrum. With Moore's Law dropping computing costs as world income levels rise, Google hopes to empower the currently disenfranchised masses to start surfing. Good for global economies, good for living standards, and good for Google.

For US consumers, Google can also be your wireless provider. Project Fi offers low-cost mobile data plans with unlimited talk, text, and international data roaming with no added fee in 120 countries worldwide, access to hot spots, and a usage-based pricing model where customers receive a refund for the unused data portion of their bill.[133] Google isn't building its own network Instead it's becoming an **MVNO** (Mobile Virtual Network Operator), licensing capacity from T-Mobile and Sprint at a discount for resale under its own brand and plans.[134] Google has said "we don't intend to be a carrier at scale" but instead will use the network for experimental services and pricing models, influencing telecom firms by example. Initial users will need a Google Nexus 6 phone.[135] Efforts like this mean that for some users, Google will be one of the most vertically integrated tech firms the world has seen, offering OS, services, software, hardware, stores, broadband, and mobile.

Google has also successfully lobbied the US.government to force wireless telecom carriers to be more open, dismantling what are known in the industry as **walled gardens**. Before Google's lobbying efforts, mobile carriers could act as gatekeepers, screening out hardware providers and software services from their networks. Today, paying customers of carriers that operate in the United States have access to a choice of hardware and less restrictive access to websites and services.

Android Everywhere

Another way Google can lower the cost of surfing is by giving away an operating system and other software. That's the thinking behind the firm's Android offering, which started on smartphones and has now extended way beyond your pocket. With Android, Google provides hardware firms with a Linux-based operating system, supporting tools, standards, and an application marketplace akin to Apple's App Store. Android itself isn't ad-supported—there aren't Google ads embedded in the OS. But the hope is that if manufacturers don't have to write their own software, the cost of various devices will go down. And cheaper devices mean that more users will have access to the Internet.

For mobile and tablet users this, of course, means more ads. Android is now the world's most popular mobile operating system by a long shot—an 80 percent share of the smartphone OS market according to one survey.[136] Google already controls 97 percent of fast-growing paid search on mobile devices.[137] One analyst estimated that Android brings in $10 per handset in search advertising,[138] helping Google deliver that rare, new billion-dollar growth opportunity sought by large, maturing firms.

Android has the largest market share in the tablet OS market.[139] Android Wear is targeted at watches and other wearables. At the launch of Android Auto, some forty car makers signed up to sell vehicles integrating with the OS. After stutter steps with earlier TV initiatives, Android TV (which can be embedded into TVs or sold via a separate box) will bring apps to your living room with a particular emphasis on game play. Android apps are also on Google's Chromebook, the lightweight laptop that moves much of the hard drive to the cloud—that is Google's cloud, which further strengthens the switching costs that bind Android users to Big G. So do you think Chromebooks are still a niche? They've consistently been the best-selling laptops on Amazon, outpacing Macs and Windows. NPD estimates they took 21 percent of notebook sales in 2013.[140] Google's $3.2 billion purchase of Nest, bringing Nest-founder and former Apple iPod Chief Tony Fadell into the Google family, has offered a glimpse of how Android could run your life. For example, when your Android car approaches your empty home, Android could automatically turn on the heat or A/C.[141] Google has even taken a very Android swipe at Facebook's Oculus VR purchase when it gave out foldable Google Cardboard to developers at the Google I/O conference. Fold it into VR goggles, strap in your Android phone with the included Velcro, look through the embedded lenses to skew the view, and you'll see Larry and Sergey give a cheeky poke to Zuckerberg's $2 billion baby.[142] The expansion of apps, hardware, and other offerings in the Android ecosystem strengthens *network effects* through ever-increasing *complementary benefits*. Taken in concert, the free OS looks like a clear money maker.

Android isn't without challenges. Since Google doesn't control hardware sales, Android is a fragmented platform, where only a small fraction of devices upgrade to the latest OS offerings. This hurts Android developers since there are more devices to code and test for (see "Is This Good for Innovation?" in Chapter 8). It also complicates things for consumers, who may see different user experiences

MVNO

MVNO – Mobile Virtual Network Operator. A wireless telecommunications services provider that doesn't own its own infrastructure. Instead, MVNOs pay a reduced price to license capacity from other providers and repackage the service under their own brand.

walled gardens

A closed network or single set of services controlled by one dominant firm. Term is often applied to mobile carriers that act as gatekeepers, screening out hardware providers and software services from their networks.

across devices.[143] Amazon uses Android in its various Kindle Fire offerings (i.e., phone, tablet) and TV but has altered the OS so much that many Android apps don't run on these platforms. Amazon also diverts customers to its own app store rather than Google Play.[144] Google has had similar "forking" squabbles with Samsung and others,[145] and a firm named Cyanogen has raised money from a series of well-known investors, plus Twitter, to build an open source, "Google-free" version of Android.[146]

In Case of Emergency, Wear Glass

Google Glass, the firm's wearable headset technology with a tiny screen in the upper right-hand corner, has endured lots of ridicule. Some cite the unfashionable dork factor, calling the product a "Segway for your face."[147] Others lament creepy "Glassholes" (a term even Google used in a dos and don'ts doc).[148] Several establishments and governments have sought to ban or limit the device's use (e.g., in casinos, movie theaters, gyms, and bars) since the device has a video camera.[149] Some have questioned Glass's future as a consumer device, especially after the firm cancelled its Glass Explorer sales program. However, transfer of the unit from Google's experimental Project X group to the division where Nest lives may help.[150]

While Google Glass doesn't have a killer app yet, it looks like it's got a few life-saving ones. Boston's Beth Israel Deaconess is the first US hospital to employ Google Glass for everyday medical care. The hospital has posted unique, patient-specific QR codes on patient room doorways, with each code linked to a patient's medical records. Doctors look up and scan the QR code with Glass before entering the room, providing access on the device's display. Early tests have expanded to the entire emergency department, with doctors donning Glass at the start of their shifts. In one example of impact, a patient with a brain bleed told an ER doctor that he was allergic to blood pressure medications but wasn't sure which ones. The doctor was able to access the patient's records on Glass, speeding the administration of life-saving treatment.

FIGURE 18.14

A doctor at Boston's Beth Israel uses Glass to verify patient info prior to a visit.

Glass in the medical community has made a successful breakout. Surgeons at the Indiana University Health Methodist Hospital in Indianapolis have used Glass during an operation to remove an abdominal tumor. "Voice commands enabled the doctors to call up the patient's MRI scans and keep the images in their field of vision for easy reference, without having to put down a scalpel."[151] At the University of California Irvine Medical Center, Glass-wearing residents stream live videos to experienced mentors so they can share their field of view. That facility announced it would be the first in the country to hand out Google Glass to all incoming residents.[152] A Cambridge, Massachusetts, firm named Twiage is developing Glass apps for EMTs so they could use voice commands to snap photos of patient injuries, dictate notes, and send them along to the nearest ER. The firm's cofounder states this is "the holy grail of hospital IT." Researchers in the UK are testing Glass for patients with Parkinson's, using the device's motion sensors to track symptoms and motor movements and providing reminders for taking medication.[153] Firefighters are also using Google Glass to map and provide video feeds of the insides of burning buildings.[154] A growing list of firms has also found different uses: streaming repair information to technicians, guiding soldiers, providing heads-up service reports in the hospitality industry, and more. Maybe Glass isn't ready for the fashion-forward hipster crowd, but it's starting to look like it offers a real and measurable impact across several industries.[155]

10.3 YouTube

It's tough to imagine any peer-produced video site displacing YouTube. Users go to YouTube because there's more content, while amateur content providers go there seeking more users (classic two-sided network effects). This critical advantage was the main reason why Google paid $1.65 billion for what was then just a twenty-month-old start-up. In terms of query volume alone, YouTube, not Bing or

Yahoo!, is the Internet's second largest search engine. But mobile video competition is heating up. Facebook now serves as many streams as YouTube,[156] Twitter's Periscope offers real-time video streaming, and Twitter's Vine and Facebook-owned Instagram battle to be the preferred platform for snippets of socially shared video. While the mobile upstarts attack at the low end of the Internet video market with shorter, mostly webcam-made videos, YouTube is looking to move a portion of its content beyond online amateur hour. The site now "rents" hundreds of TV shows and movies at prices ranging from $.99 to $3.99. It's also been offering seed grants of several million dollars to producers of original content for YouTube.[157] YouTube even poached a senior Netflix executive to help grow the premium content business.[158]

YouTube's popularity comes at a price. Even with falling bandwidth and storage costs, at three hundred hours of video uploaded to YouTube every minute, the cost to store and serve this content would, for most firms, seem cripplingly large.[159] The good news is that YouTube brought in an estimated $4 billion in revenue in 2014. While still not profitable, that's enough to put YouTube at "roughly break even" after adding infrastructure and content costs.[160] YouTube head Susan Wojcicki has been busy on multiple fronts. A deal with the NFL, a YouTube-branded music streaming service, and improved targeting integration with the rest of Google might collectively act to further boost YouTube's appeal and bring in more revenue.[161]

The YouTube Millionaires

AdSense has helped content providers worldwide earn a living off the printed word. Now it's YouTube's turn. The *Wall Street Journal* profiled several YouTube millionaires who bring in a seven-figure check in a given year. The list is eclectic and includes the Swedish Felix Kjellberg (a.k.a., PewDiePie"), a twenty-something goofball who plays and is a commenter for video games. His 35 million-plus subscribers bring in an estimated $7.5 million in ad revenue a year.[162] Michelle Phan, another twenty-something, parlayed a college YouTube assignment into an online following for her makeup tutorials (now, north of 7.7 million YouTube subscribers[163]) and impressed YouTube so much that they offered her a $1 million grant to create twenty hours of content.[164] Phan has used YouTube fame to build Ipsy, a beauty sampling service that now has 100 employees as $120 million a year in sales, putting it roughly on par with venture-backed Birchbox.[165]

FIGURE 18.15

Video game commenter Felix Kjellberg (a.k.a., PewDiePie) and makeup vlogger (video blogger) Michelle Phan are entrepreneurs who have leveraged YouTube fame into multimillion dollar careers.

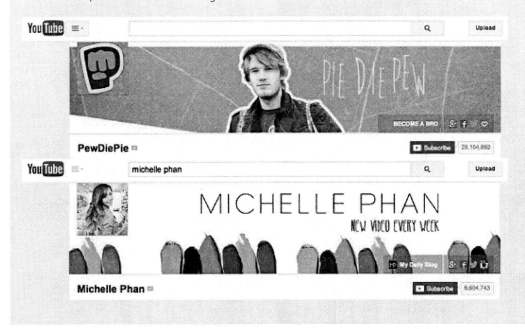

10.4   Android Pay

Android Pay is another example of how the search giant is looking to deliver value through mobile devices. The service allows phones to replace much of the "stuff" inside your wallet. It can be used to pay for goods, store gift cards, collect and redeem coupons and special offers, and manage loyalty programs.[166] Android Pay represents yet another try at payments, coming after a prior effort, Google Wallet, had struggled for four years, and after the firm's online effort, Google Checkout, was shuttered.[167] Like Apple Pay (and Google Wallet before it), Android Pay will leverage **NFC** (near field communication), a payment technology finally making its way into retailer point-of-sale systems. Android Pay and Apple Pay both use a process called tokenization that essentially sends temporary, one-time-use codes for payment, and which credit card companies map to actual cards behind the scenes. Even if tokens are stolen, thieves can't use it for anything. This should prevent damage from major credit card hacks that have occurred at Home Depot and Target.[168] Google will also support fingerprint scanning on phones to make payment one-tap, with 700,000 retailers supporting the system at roll-out, including many of those already on board with Apple.

Google should be able to leverage Android Pay in many ways that dovetail with advertising offerings. The new system will work on websites, too, removing the need for data entry in online ordering.[169] This may be a boon to efforts to bake a "Buy" button into Google ads. Tap from your mobile and it's yours, no data entry required.[170] Integration between ads, loyalty programs, and coupons might also create new products for Google. Android Pay will even automatically prompt you to use a loyalty card or gift card if you have one.[171] One challenge Google faces: unlike Apple, it doesn't own most hardware, so it'll need partners to introduce Android Pay-compatible handsets, and it'll need consumers to buy these. And remember, payments are a two-sided market, with consumer handsets and retailer point-of-sale terminals both necessary for in-store transactions to work. While 700,000 storefronts at launch is a good start, the vast majority of storefronts will need to be on Android Pay for you to be willing to leave your plastic and cash at home.

10.5   Google and Social

Google's success in social media has been mixed. Its two biggest successes—YouTube and Blogger—were both acquired from other firms. Internally-developed Orkut had for years ranked as the top social network in Brazil but is unheard of throughout most of the rest of the world; and Google-hatched Buzz and Wave were both dismal failures. Google+ hasn't captured anywhere near the user loyalty of Facebook, Twitter, Snapchat, Instagram, or other services, and many have wondered if the service's days are numbered.[172] However, to Google's credit, the service has spawned several successful products and updates that have been given stand-alone status outside their initially tight tie-in with Google+. Among them, Hangouts is a video chat service that can support groups, and enables screen sharing and group document editing. Photos, which evolved from Picasa into Google+, has since been broken out into an incredibly robust product, offering unlimited storage and incredibly robust tools that leverage Google artificial intelligence for photo editing, auto-select of best picture (who's smiling and has eyes open), gallery creation and more.[173] Gaining more social sharing via Google's platform could eventually help the firm serve more ads; grow additional revenue lines; and gain additional data and insight that can be used to help in search, content recommendations, and ad targeting. However, as the firm has learned, competing in winner-take-most markets where network effects dominate is tough, even when you bring deep pockets and a stable of existing, successful products to the battle. While its own social networking efforts have yet to take off, Google has incorporated timeliness into search, striking a partnership to surface tweets in organic results.[174]

What's Google Up To?

With all this innovation, it's tough to stay current with Google's cutting edge product portfolio. But the company does offer "beta" releases of some projects and invites the public to try out and comment on its many experiments. To see a current list of many of the firm's offerings, check out http://www.google.com/about/products.

Experimentation and innovation are deeply ingrained in Google's tech-centric culture, and this can produce both hits and misses. While Google introduces scores of products each year,[175] it has also cancelled several along the way, including Jaiku (which couldn't beat Twitter); Google Video (which was superseded by the YouTube acquisition); the aforementioned social flops Wave and Buzz; the payments-offering Checkout; and a bunch more you've likely not heard of, like Dodgeball, Notebook, Catalog Search, and Mashup Editor.[176] But the firm's relentless commitment to developing new products and services, coupled with wildly profitable core businesses, allows Google to survive the flops and push the edge of what's possible. The firm's secretive lab, Google X, is the home of Google's driverless car project, the Project Loon balloon initiative, and Google Glass. The group is working on all sorts of other gee-whiz offerings, including space elevators, smart contact lenses, and refrigerators that can order your groceries when they run low.[177]

Google X has several bold projects cooking, including self-driving cars, now navigating the streets of the firm's home in Mountain View, California and beyond.

View the video online at: http://www.youtube.com/embed/uCezlCQNgJU?rel=0

10.6   Apps, Cloud, and the Post-Hard-Drive World

Google's "apps" are mostly Web-based software-as-a-service offerings. Apps include an Office-style suite that sports a word processor, presentation tool, and spreadsheet, all served through a browser. While initially clunky, the products are constantly being refined. The spreadsheet product, for example, had been seeing new releases every two weeks, with features such as graphing and pivot tables inching it closer in capabilities to desktop alternatives.[178] And new browser standards, such as HTML 5, make it even easier for what lives in the browser to mimic what you're currently using on your desktop, even allowing apps to be used offline when Internet access isn't available. That'll be critical as long as Internet access is less reliable than your hard drive, but online collaboration is where these products can really excel (no pun intended). Most Google apps allow not only group viewing, but also collaborative editing, common storage, and version control. And it seems Google isn't stopping at Office files, video, and photos—Google's cloud will hold your music and other media, too. Google's Play service allows you to upload thousands of the tracks that you already own to what some have called a sort of "locker in the sky." Users can stream the tracks over the Internet, sync frequently played songs and albums for offline play, and even share tracks with friends via Google+ (friends usually get one full listen for free).[179] And Google Drive offers several gigabytes of free cloud-based storage that can be shared and synced across computers. Photos are the ultimate keepsake, and by offering unlimited storage for the new Google Photos, Larry and Sergei have bolted your memories tightly onto their firm.

Unknown is how much money Google will make off all of this. Consumers and small businesses have free access to these products, with usage for up to fifty users funded by in-app ads. But is there much of a market serving ads to people working on spreadsheets? Enterprises can gain additional, ad-free licenses for a fee. While users have been reluctant to give up Microsoft Office, many have individually migrated to Google's Web-based e-mail and calendar tools. Google's enterprise apps group will now do the same thing for organizations, acting as a sort of outsourcer by running e-mail, calendar, and other services for a firm and all while handling upgrades, spam screening, virus protection, backup, and other administrative burdens. Virgin America, Jaguar, National Geographic, Genentech, and scores of school districts and universities are among the Google partners that have signed on to make the firm's app offerings available to thousands. Google Play doesn't just hold your music; it's also an iTunes-like marketplace where you can buy all sorts of media: movies, TV shows, books, and apps. Google Drive is free (the first 15 GB is shared between Drive, and Gmail), but if you want more, you'll have to pay.

And of course, Microsoft won't let Google take this market without a fight. Microsoft has experimented with offering simplified, free, ad-supported, Web-based, online options for Word, Excel, PowerPoint, and OneNote; Office 365 offers more robust online tools, ad free, for a low monthly subscription cost; and Microsoft can also migrate an organization's applications like e-mail and calendaring off corporate computers and onto Microsoft's server farms. Apple continues to build billion-dollar data centers and has introduced iWork Cloud, browser versions of its word processor, spreadsheet functionality, and presentation apps that have leapfrogged Google with products that are nearly as feature rich as desktop offerings. Amazon is also offering free, unlimited photo storage for Prime members. As the cloud becomes the new hard drive, don't look for anyone to yield ground soon.

Google's Global Reach, Censorship, and Other Challenges

Google has repeatedly and publicly with the government of China, a nation that many consider to be the world's most potentially lucrative market (already tops worldwide in sales of Apple's iPhone[180]). For four years at the request of the Chinese government, Google had censored results returned from the firm's google.cn domain (e.g., an image search on the term "Tiananmen" showed kite flying on google.cn, but protesters confronting tanks on google.com). However, when reports surfaced of Chinese involvement in hacking attempts against Google and at least twenty other US companies and human rights dissidents, the firm began routing google.cn traffic outside the country. The days that followed saw access to a variety of Google services blocked within China, restricted by what many call the government's "Great Firewall of China." Even Gmail is blocked in China.[181]

Speaking for Google, the firm's deputy counsel Nicole Wong states, "We are fundamentally guided by the belief that more information for our users is ultimately better." But even outside of China, Google continues to be challenged by its interest in providing unfettered access to information on one hand, and the radically divergent laws, regulations, and cultural expectations of host nations on the other. Google has been prompted to block access to its services at some point in at least twenty-five of one hundred countries the firm operates in.

The kind of restriction varies widely. French, German, and Polish law requires Google to prohibit access to Nazi content. A Spanish law mandating that online news aggregators to pay compensation to Internet publishers for the use of even headlines (media firms couldn't waive their right to the fee) effectively shut down Google News in Spain.[182] French regulators are claiming that French law applying to Google shouldn't just be applied to Google's .fr (French) domains, but should also be reflected across all Google properties, giving French law a global reach, with hefty fines if Google doesn't comply.[183] Turkish law requires Google to block access to material critical of the nation's founder. Access in Thailand is similarly blocked from content mocking that nation's king. In India, Google has been prompted to edit forums or remove comments flagged by the government as violating restrictions against speech that threatens public order or is otherwise considered indecent or immoral. At the extreme end of the spectrum, Vietnam, Saudi Arabia, and Iran have aggressively moved to restrict access to wide swaths of Internet content.

Google usually waits for governments to notify it that offensive content must be blocked. This moves the firm from actively to reactively censoring access. Still, this doesn't isolate the company from legal issues. Italian courts went after YouTube executives after a video showing local teenagers tormenting an autistic child remained online long enough to garner thousands of views.

In the United States, Google's organic results often reveal content that would widely be viewed as offensive. In the most extreme cases, the firm has run ads alongside these results with the text, "Offensive Search Results: We're disturbed about these results as well. Please read our note here."

Other Internet providers have come under similar scrutiny, and technology managers will continue to confront similar ethically charged issues as they consider whether to operate in new markets. But Google's dominant position puts it at the center of censorship concerns. The threat is ultimately that the world's chief information gateway might also become "the Web's main muzzle."

One needs to consider all of Google's offerings to get a sense of what Google has the potential to achieve. It's possible that increasing numbers of users worldwide will adopt light, cheap netbooks and other devices powered by free Google software (Android, Google's Chrome browser, Google TV, and Chrome OS). Productivity apps, e-mail, calendaring, and collaboration tools will all exist in the cloud, accessible through any browser, with files stored on Google's servers in a way that minimizes hard drive needs. Google will entertain you, help you find the information you need, help you shop, handle payment, and more. And the firms you engage online may increasingly turn to Google to replace their existing hardware and software infrastructure with corporate computing platforms like Google Apps Engine (see Chapter 14). All of this would be based on open standards, but switching costs, scale, and increasing returns from expertise across these efforts could yield enormous advantages.

Studying Google allowed us to learn about search and the infrastructure that powers this critical technology. We've studied the business of ads, covering search advertising, ad networks, and ad targeting in a way that blends strategic and technology issues. And we've covered the ethical, legal, growth, and competitive challenges that Google and its rivals face. Studying Google (or Alphabet, if you're inclined to use the 'new' name) in this context should not only help you understand what's happening today, it should also help you develop critical thinking skills for assessing the opportunities and threats that will emerge across industries as technologies continue to evolve.

KEY TAKEAWAYS

- For over a decade, Google's search business has been growing rapidly, but that business is maturing.

- Slower growth will put pressure on the firm's stock price, so a firm Google's size will need to pursue very large, risky, new markets—markets that are also attractive to well-financed rivals, smaller partners, and entrepreneurs.

- Rivals continue to innovate in search. However, those who choose to compete with Google using technology should recognize that it is often easy for a firm to mimic the innovations of a pioneer with a substitute offering, and Google has additional strategic resources, such as brand, scale, and network effects, that will make it a challenge to displace.

- European and U.S. regulators have investigated Google for antitrust violations and, at least initially, have reached different results, demonstrating the challenges dominant firms face as they grow globally.

- Google is investing heavily in methods that promote wider Internet access. These include offering free software to device manufacturers and several telecommunications and lobbying initiatives meant to lower the cost of getting online. The firm hopes that more users spending more time online will allow it to generate more revenue through ads and perhaps other services.

- Google Glass has struggled to achieve consumer acceptance, but several applications have demonstrated broad impact across various industries, improving productivity, lowering costs, speeding delivery time, and potentially even saving lives.

- Android Pay uses NFC communications to allow mobile phones to make credit and debit card payments, manage loyalty programs, redeem coupons, and more. The service leverages tokenization to mask actual credit card numbers, potentially making it more secure to use than conventional credit cards. In order to receive broad adoption, Android Pay will need a critical mas of users with compatible handsets and retailers with hardware capable of taking these kinds of payments.

- Google continues to struggle in social networking and Google+ significantly lags behind Facebook and Twitter in user engagement and overall users, despite Google's attempts to integrate the service into its core offerings. Some efforts that have been part of Google+, such as Hangouts and Photos have been allowed to operate as stand-alone products.

- YouTube demonstrates how a firm can create a large and vastly influential business in a short period of time but also that businesses that host and serve large files of end-user content can be costly. Like AdSense, YouTube channels have become a launching pad for content entrepreneurs.

- Google, Microsoft, and smaller rivals are also migrating applications to the Web, allowing Office-style software to execute within a browser, with portions of this computing experience and storage happening off a user's computer, "in the cloud" of the Internet. Revenue models for this business are uncertain.

- With scale and influence comes increased governmental scrutiny. Google has increasingly become a target of antitrust regulators. The extent of this threat is unclear. Google's extreme influence is clear. However, the firm's software is based on open standards; competitors have a choice in ad networks, search engines, and other services; switching costs are relatively low; users and advertisers aren't locked into exclusive contracts for the firm's key products and services; and there is little evidence of deliberate, predatory pricing or other "red-flag" activity that usually brings government regulation.

QUESTIONS AND EXERCISES

1. Perform identical queries on both Google and rival search engines (Bing, Yahoo!, Blekko, and DuckDuckGo are all possibilities). Try different categories (research for school projects, health, business, sports, entertainment, local information). Which sites do you think give you the better results? Why? Would any of these results cause you to switch to one search engine versus the other?

2. Investigate new services that attempt to extend the possibilities for leveraging online content. Visit Wolfram Alpha and any other such efforts that intrigue you. Assume the role of a manager and use these engines to uncover useful information. Assume your role as a student and see if these tools provide valuable information for this or other classes. Are you likely to use these tools in the future? Why or why not? Under what circumstances are they useful and when do they fall short?

3. Assume the role of an industry analyst: Consider the variety of firms mentioned in this section that may become competitors or partners. Create a chart listing your thoughts on which firms are likely to collaborate and work together and which firms are likely to compete. What are the advantages or risks in these collaborations for the partners involved? Do you think any of these firms are "acquisition bait?" Defend your predictions and be prepared to discuss them with your class.

4. Assume the role of an IT manager: To the extent that you can, evaluate online application offerings by Google, Microsoft, Apple, and rivals. In your opinion, are these efforts ready for prime time? Why or why not? Would you recommend that a firm choose these applications? Are there particular firms or users that would find these alternatives particularly appealing? Would you ever completely replace desktop offerings with online ones? Why or why not?

5. Does it make sense for organizations to move their e-mail and calendaring services off their own machines and pay Google, Microsoft, or someone else to run them? Why or why not? Has your university "Gone Google"? What factors influenced this decision?

6. What are Chrome, the Chrome OS, and Android? Are these software products successful in their respective categories? Investigate the state of the market for products that leverage any of these software offerings. Would you say that they are successful? Why or why not? What do you think the outlook is for Chrome, the Chrome OS, and Android? As an IT manager, would you recommend products based on this software? As an investor, do you think it continues to make sense for Google to develop these efforts? Why or why not?

7. Apple's CEO Tim Cook calls Android a "toxic hellstew" of security vulnerabilities and fragmentation running on so many kinds of devices that it fails to offer the latest features to users. Reach out to friends or visit stores to compare Android and Apple devices and conduct research online. Do you think Cook's claims are valid? Which platform do you favor, Android, iOS, or another? Why?

8. Do research on Google Glass. Come to class with powerful, interesting, or fun examples of Glass use. Advocate for industries that should be using Glass and how the product could deliver value. What challenges does Glass present to IT managers, users, legislators, and to society in general?

9. What will it take for Android Pay to be successful? What challenges must the effort overcome? Research the current state of Android Pay's competitors. What competing efforts exist? Which firms are best positioned to dominate this market? How large could this market become?

10. Google's unofficial motto is "Don't be evil." But sometimes it's challenging for managers to tell what path is "most right" or "least wrong." Google operates in countries that require the firm to screen and censor results. Short term, this is clearly a limitation on freedom of speech. But long term, access to the Internet could catalyze economic development and spread information in a way that leads to more democratization. Investigate and consider both of these arguments and be prepared to argue the case either for limiting work in speech-limiting countries or working within them as a potential agent of change. What other pressures is a publicly traded firm under to choose one path or the other? Which path would you choose and why?

11. Investigate Google+. Are you a Google+ user? Why or why not? What will it take for Google+ to attract users and usage? Compared with rivals, how has the service performed? What advantages does Google have that it can leverage with Google+? What competitive advantages do rivals have over Google?

12. Investigate how Google TV has performed on the market. Why does Google offer a TV product? How might the firm make money from this effort? What obstacles does the firm have to overcome in order for Google TV to grow?

13. Google innovation seems to be so far ahead that our legal regimes can't keep up. What legal issues are raised by driverless cars? Have any laws been changed to address this technology? Google Glass also raises potential privacy concerns. What are the main issues with Glass, and have laws or policies changed regarding the technology? Be prepared to discuss these issues in class.

ENDNOTES

1. J. Polonetsky and O. Tene, "The Right Response to the 'Right to Delete'" *Re/code*, May 21, 2014.

2. C. Li, "Why Google's One-Trick Pony Struggles to Learn New Tricks," *Harvard Business Publishing*, May 2009.

3. Unattributed, "Google's advertising revenue from 2001 to 2014 (in billion U.S. dollars)," *Statista*. Accessed June 18, 2015 - http://www.statista.com/statistics/266249/advertising-revenue-of-google/

4. S. Levy, "The Secrets of Googlenomics," *Wired*, June 2009.

5. S. Henn, "With Google's Robot-Buying Binge, a Hat Tip to the Future," *NPR News*, March 17, 2014.

6. J. D'Onfro, "Meet the man responsible for Google's billion-dollar acquisitions," *Business Insider*, May 2, 2015.

7. V. Stunt, "Why Google Is Buying a Seemingly Crazy Collection of Companies," *CBC News*, February 19, 2014.

8. H. McCracken and L. Grossman, "Google vs. Death," *Time*, September 30, 2013.

9. R. Waters, "FT interview with Google co-founder and CEO Larry Page," *The Financial Times*, Oct. 31, 2014.

10. J. Paczkowski, "Buy High, Sell Low: Google's Losing Bet on Motorola," *Re/code*, January 29, 2014.

11. J. Pontin, "But Who's Counting?" *Technology Review*, March/April 2009.

12. T. Peterson, "Baidu and Alibaba Best Yahoo and Twitter for Digital Ad Revenue," *AdAge*, Dec. 15, 2014.

13. P. May, "Breathing Down Apple's Neck," *San Jose Mercury News*, May 22, 2013.

14. D. Weldon, "Google's Power Play," *EnergyDigital*, August 30, 2007.

15. L. Wolgemuth, "Forget the Recession, I Want a Better Chair," *U.S. News and World Report*, April 28, 2008.

16. B. Casnocha, "Success on the Side," *The American: The Journal of the American Enterprise Institute*, April 24, 2009.

17. G. Duncan, "Pay Your Way to the Top of Search Results with Google Shopping," *Digital Trends*, June 1, 2012.

18. S. Levy, "Inside the Box," *Wired*, March 2010.

19. D. Segal, "The Dirty Little Secrets of Search," *New York Times*, February 12, 2011.

20. D. Segal, "The Dirty Little Secrets of Search," *New York Times*, February 12, 2011.

21. M. Bergen, "Google to Investors: Don't Worry, We've Got Mobile Figured Out," *Re/code*, April 23, 2015.

22. D. Sullivan, "Google's Results Get More Personal with 'Search Plus Your World,'" *Search Engine Land*, January 10, 2012.

23. A. Wright, "Exploring a 'Deep Web' That Google Can't Grasp," *New York Times*, February 23, 2009.

24. Most Web sites do have a link where you can submit a Web site for indexing, and doing so can help promote the discovery of your content.

25. M. Liedtke, "Google Reigns as World's Most Powerful 10-Year-Old," *Associated Press*, September 5, 2008.

26. David F. Carr, "How Google Works," *Baseline*, July 6, 2006.

27. R. Katz, "Tech Titans Building Boom," *IEEE Spectrum* 46, no. 2 (February 1, 2009).

28. S. Ovide, "Google, Amazon and Microsoft's Costly Spending War," *Wall Street Journal*, April 28, 2014.

29. S. Levy, "Google Throws Open Doors to Its Top-Secret Data Center," *Wired*, October 2012.

30. C. Metz, "Google's Top Five Data Center Secrets (That Are Still Secret)," *Wired*, October 18, 2012.

31. S. Shankland, "Google Unlocks Once-Secret Server," *CNET*, April 1, 2009.

32. S. Levy, "Google Throws Open Doors to Its Top-Secret Data Center," *Wired*, October 2012.

33. C. Metz, "Google Uses Artificial Brains to Teach Its Data Centers How to Behave," *Wired*, May 28, 2014.

34. S. Levy, "Google Throws Open Doors to Its Top-Secret Data Center," *Wired*, October 2012.

35. C. Metz, "Super-Secret Google Builds Servers in the Dark," *Wired*, March 15, 2012.

36. D. Smith, "For The First Time Ever, Americans Spend More Time Using Mobile Devices Than TV, *Business Insider*, Nov. 19, 2014.

37. A. Nanji, "How Baby Boomers Use the Web, Social Networks, and Mobile," *Marketing Profs*, July 18, 2013.

38. For a more detailed overview of the limitations in online ad measurement, see L. Rao, "Guess Which Brand Is Now Worth $100 Billion?" *TechCrunch*, April 30, 2009.

39. S. Elliott, "More Agencies Investing in Marketing with a Click," *New York Times*, March 14, 2006.

40. Google, "Google Announces Fourth Quarter and Fiscal Year 2008 Results," press release, January 22, 2009.

41. D. Vise, "Google's Decade," *Technology Review*, September 12, 2008.

42. S. Levy, "The Secrets of Googlenomics," *Wired*, June 2009.

43. "Check and Understand Quality Score," Google, accessed June 30, 2014, https://support.google.com/adwords/answer/2454010?hl=en.

44. S. Levy, "The Secrets of Googlenomics," *Wired*, June 2009.

45. SpyFu, "Keywords with the Highest Cost-Per-Click (CPC)," accessed June 30, 2014.

46. C. Mann, "How Click Fraud Could Swallow the Internet," *Wired*, January 2006.

47. SpyFu, "Domains that Spend the Most on Adwords," accessed June 30, 2014.

48. M. Bergen, "Google's Mobile Search Strategy: Bake In and Take Out," Re/code, May 9, 2015.

49. Unattributed, "US Mobile Ad Dollars Shift to Search Apps," *eMarketer*, June 5, 2014.

50. G. Marvin, "Google AdWords Announces New Tools & Formats As Mobile Search Surpasses Desktop," *SearchEngineLand*, May 5, 2015.

51. M. Bergen, "Google's Mobile Search Strategy: Bake In and Take Out," *Re/code*, May 9, 2015.

52. R. Winkler and C. Karmin, "Google Checks In to the Hotel Business," *The Wall Street Journal*, April 8, 2014.

53. "AdSense Revenue Share," Google, accessed June 30, 2014.

54. Google AdSense, "10 Years of AdSense," http://www.youtube.com/watch?v=8K8YIA7--dk (accessed June 18, 2013).

55. M. Garber, "'Ads by Google': A Billion Dollar Brainstorm Turns 10," *Atlantic*, June 18, 2013.

56. R. Rothenberg, "The Internet Runs on Ad Billions," *BusinessWeek*, April 10, 2008.

57. A. Overholt, "Search for Tomorrow," *Fast Company*, December 19, 2007.

58. A. Kantrowitz, "Inside Google's Secret War Against Ad Fraud," *AdAge*, May 18, 2015.

59. See Interactive Advertising Bureau Ad Unit Guidelines for details at http://www.iab.net/iab_products_and_industry_services/1421/1443/1452.

60. M. Moss, "These Web Sites Know Who You Are," *ZDNet UK*, October 13, 1999.

61. M. Moss, "These Web Sites Know Who You Are," *ZDNet UK*, October 13, 1999.

62. J. Slegg, "Google AdWords Dynamic Remarketing Launches for Merchants," *Search Engine Watch*, June 25, 2013.

63. R. Emerson, "Google Biz Chief: Over 10M Websites Now Using Google Analytics," *TechCrunch*, April 12, 2012.

64. S. Kovach, "Apple's Safari Is Crushing Google in Mobile Browser Market Share," *Business Insider*, November 8, 2013.

65. E. Griffith, "What Will Ad-Tech Look Like without Cookies?" *PandoDaily*, December 15, 2012.

66. E. Griffith, "Apple's Privacy Moves Underscore Its Distaste for the Advertising World," *Fortune*, June 12, 2014.

67. J. Greene, "Kicking Third-Party Cookies to the Curb: The Fallout for the Digital Ad Industry," *MarketingLand*, April 15, 2013.

68. R. Singel, "Online Behavioral Targeting Targeted by Feds, Critics," *Wired News*, June 3, 2009.

69. R. Hof, "Behavioral Targeting: Google Pulls Out the Stops," *BusinessWeek*, March 11, 2009.

70. A. Barr, "Google Says New Store Data Help Mobile Ads," *The Wall Street Journal*, May 21, 2015.

71. A. Barr, "Google Says New Store Data Help Mobile Ads," *The Wall Street Journal*, May 21, 2015.

72. G. Sterling, "Store Visits And Offline Spending Data Will Drive Massive Mobile Ad Growth," *Marketing Land*, May 22, 2015.

73. R. Singel, "Online Behavioral Targeting Targeted by Feds, Critics," *Wired News*, June 3, 2009.

74. S. Hansell, "A Guide to Google's New Privacy Controls," *New York Times*, March 12, 2009.

75. R. Mitchell, "What Google Knows about You," *Computerworld*, May 11, 2009.

76. M. Helft, "BITS; Google Lets Users See a Bit of Selves," *New York Times*, November 9, 2009.

77. R. Mitchell, "What Google Knows about You," *Computerworld*, May 11, 2009.

78. "Policies and Principles," Google, http://www.google.com/policies/privacy (accessed June 11, 2012).

79. R. Mitchell, "What Google Knows about You," *Computerworld*, May 11, 2009.

80. C. Boulton, "Google Privacy Policy Changes are Live: Here Are Your Options," *eWeek*, March 1, 2012.

81. J. Kincaid, "Google Privacy Blunder Shares Your Docs without Permission," *TechCrunch*, March 7, 2009.

82. A. Gold, "Keep Your Buzz to Yourself: Google Misjudged Its Users' Right to Privacy," *The Harvard Crimson*, February 22, 2010.

83. A. Oreskovic, "Google Admits to Broader Collection of Personal Data," *Washington Post*, October 23, 2010.

84. D. Goldman, "Major Security Flaw Found in Android Phones," *CNN*, May 18, 2011.

85. T. Kranzit, "Google Fired Engineer for Privacy Breach," *CNET*, September 14, 2010.

86. D. Basulto, "Google, Safari, and Our Final Privacy Wake-Up Call," *Washington Post*, February 22, 2012.

87. D. Rushe, "Facebook and Google Insist They Did Not Know of Prism Surveillance Program," *Guardian*, June 7, 2013.

88. C. Timberg and C. Kang, "Google Challenges U.S. Gag Order, Citing First Amendment," *Washington Post*, June 18, 2013.

89. R. Mitchell, "What Google Knows about You," *Computerworld*, May 11, 2009.

90. A. Broache, "Judge: Google Must Give Feds Limited Access to Records," *CNET*, March 17, 2006.

91. D. Rushe, "Google Accuses China of Interfering with Gmail E-mail System," *Guardian*, March 20, 2011.

92. L. Sumagaysay, "Not Everyone Likes the (Google Street) View," *Good Morning Silicon Valley*, May 20, 2009.

93. E. Weise, "Europeans Flock to be Forgotten," *USA Today*, June 30, 2014.

94. J. Polonetsky and O. Tene, "The Right Response to the 'Right to Delete,'" *Re/code*, May 21, 2014.

95. D. Smith, "Tim Cook explains why Apple Pay doesn't collect your data: 'You are not our product'" *Business Insider*, Feb. 11, 2015.

96. R. Singel, "Online Behavioral Targeting Targeted by Feds, Critics," *Wired News*, June 3, 2009.

97. N. Vidyasagar, "India's Secret Army of Online Ad 'Clickers,'" *Times of India*, May 3, 2004.

98. C. Mann, "How Click Fraud Could Swallow the Internet," *Wired*, January 2006.

99. S. Ragan, "Millions of Home Networks Infected by ZeroAccess Botnet," *SecurityWeek*, October 31, 2012.

100. M. Jakobsson and Z. Ramzan, *Crimeware: Understanding New Attacks and Defenses* (Cupertino, CA: Symantec Press, 2008).

101. D. Clark, "The Bot Bubble," *The New Republic*, April 20, 2015.

102. S. Gates, "State Department Facebook: DOS Spent $630,000 On 'Likes' For Social Media Pages, Report Indicates," *The Huffington Post*, July 3, 2013.

103. D. Clark, "The Bot Bubble," *The New Republic*, April 20, 2015.

104. M. Jakobsson and Z. Ramzan, *Crimeware: Understanding New Attacks and Defenses* (Cupertino, CA: Symantec Press, 2008).

105. A. Kantrowitz, "Inside Google's Secret War Against Ad Fraud," *AdAge*, May 18, 2015.

106. A. Kantrowitz, "Inside Google's Secret War Against Ad Fraud," *AdAge*, May 18, 2015.

107. A. Kantrowitz, "Inside Google's Secret War Against Ad Fraud," *AdAge*, May 18, 2015.

108. S. Hamner, "Pay-per-Click Advertisers Combat Costly Fraud," *New York Times*, May 12, 2009.

109. M. Lafsky, "Google and Click Fraud: Behind the Numbers," *New York Times*, February 27, 2008.

110. M. Jakobsson and Z. Ramzan, *Crimeware: Understanding New Attacks and Defenses* (Cupertino, CA: Symantec Press, 2008).

111. D. Chaffey, "Are You Using Google's New Search Analytics?" *ClickThrough*, May 29, 2015.

112. L. Page, "Google Announces Plans for New Operating Structure," *Google Press Release*, Aug. 10, 2015.

113. It is hoped the savvy reader will forgive the author for using Google to refer to businesses now technically housed outside of the Google subdivision but inside Alphabet. Owners of the stock can still consider it to be all the same firm they've continued to own, all organized under the same symbol.

114. Created using data from Google Finance.

115. D. Goldman, "Microsoft Profits Soars 31% on Strong Office and Kinect Sales," *CNNMoney*, April 28, 2011.

116. D. Pogue, "Going Beyond Search, Into Fetch," *New York Times*, May 23, 2012.

117. R. Miller, "Apple takes on Google Now with iOS 9's proactive assistance," *The Verge*, June 8, 2015.

118. A. Barr, "Google Says New Store Data Help Mobile Ads," *The Wall Street Journal*, May 21, 2015.

119. S. Levy, "Inside the Box," *Wired*, March 2010.

120. S. Shankland, "Firefox dumps Google for search, signs on with Yahoo," *CNet*, Feb. 2, 2015.

121. D. Ionescu, "Google Chrome Overtakes Internet Explorer," *PCWorld*, May 21, 2012.

122. S. Chan, "Long Antitrust Saga Ends for Microsoft," *Seattle Times*, May 12, 2011.

123. J. Kanter, "European Regulators Fine Microsoft, then Promise to Do Better," *New York Times*, March 6, 2013.

124. S. Lohr and M. Helft, "New Mood in Antitrust May Target Google," *New York Times*, May 18, 2009.

125. C. Cain-Miller and N. Wingfield, "Google Pushes Hard Behind the Scenes to Convince Regulators," *New York Times*, January 3, 2013.

126. M. Scott, "European Regulators Lay Out Demands and Fines in Google Antitrust Case," *The New York Times*, June 19, 2015.

127. M. Bergen, "EU Officially Strikes at Google on Shopping Service, Android," *Re/code*, April 15, 2015.

128. S. Gustin, "'Silicon Slopes': Google Fiber Planned for Provo, Utah," *Time*, April 18, 2013.

129. J. Davidson, "Google Fiber has Internet providers scrambling to improve their service," *Fortune*, April 14, 2015.

130. A. Vance, "Space Internet Has Already Reached Earth," *Bloomberg*, June 17, 2015.

131. K. Fitchard, "Project Loon: Google's Biggest Obstacle Isn't Technology, It's Politics," *GigaOM*, June 21, 2013.

132. B. Womack, "Google Acquires Drone Maker Titan Aerospace to Spread Web," *Bloomberg*, April 15, 2014.

133. K. Fitchard, "Google's Project Fi is going to make us rethink our mobile phone bills," *Fortune*, April 22, 2015.

134. T. Wolverton, "Google to offer wireless service to go with phones and software," *SiliconBeat*, March 2, 2015.

135. C. Welch, "Price comparison: Google's Project Fi versus Verizon, AT&T, Sprint, and T-Mobile," *The Verge*, April 22, 2015.

136. N. Lomas, "Android Still Growing Market Share by Winning First Time Smartphone Users," *TechCrunch*, May 6, 2014.

137. "Google Manages 97 Percent of Paid Mobile Search, 40 Pct of Google Maps Usage Is Mobile," *Mobile Marketing Watch*, March 14, 2011.

138. G. Sterling, "Google Will Make $10 Per Android User in 2012: Report," *SearchEngineLand*, February 9, 2011.

139. C. Page, "Apple's iPad loses Grip on Tablet Market as Android Hits 62 Percent Share," *Inquirer*, March 3, 2014.

140. G. Keizer, "Chromebooks' Success Punches Microsoft in the Gut," *Computerworld*, December 27, 2013.

141. Associated Press, "Google I/O: Android TV, Smart Cars, Wearables, and More," *CBS News*, June 25, 2014.

142. F. Lardinois, "The Story behind Google's Cardboard Project," *TechCrunch*, June 26, 2014.

143. B. Stone, "Google's Sundar Pichai Is the Most Powerful Man in Mobile," *BusinessWeek*, June 24, 2014.

144. D. Bohn, "Amazon Fire TV Hands-on: Prime Comes to Your Living Room," *The Verge*, April 2, 2014; and A. Levy, "Why Samsung Is Rooting for Amazon's Fire Phone...and Google Hopes It Fails," *The Motley Fool*, June 25, 2014.

145. B. Stone, "Google's Sundar Pichai Is the Most Powerful Man in Mobile," *BusinessWeek*, June 24, 2014.

146. M. Helft, "Meet Cyanogen, The Startup That Wants To Steal Android From Google," *Forbes*, April 13, 2015.

147. P. Pachal and B. Womack, "A Segway on Your Face: Can Google Glass be Popular?" *Bloomberg TV*, May 14, 2013.

148. D. Gross, "Google: How Not to be a 'Glasshole,'" *CNN*, February 24, 2014.

149. S. McLean and A. Bevitt, "Google Glass into Europe— A Small Step or a Giant Leap?" *Lexology*, June 27, 2014.

150. R. McCormick, "Nest's Tony Fadell says Google has 'no sacred cows' as it rethinks Glass," *The Verge*, May 19, 2015.

151. C. Borchers, "Google Glass Embraced at Beth Israel Deaconess," *Boston Globe*, April 9, 2014.

152. D. Kerr, "Google Glass Handed Out to Medical Students at UC Irvine," *CNET*, May 14, 2014.

153. B. Bailey, "Some More Potential Glass Users: Soldiers, New Moms and HVAC Repairmen," *SiliconBeat*, April 9, 2014.

154. D. Gross, "Google: How Not to be a 'Glasshole,'" *CNN*, February 24, 2014.

155. M. McGee, "Google Glass Turns 2: Here Are 60 Brands & Businesses Using It," *MarketingLand*, April 4, 2014.

156. N. Carlson, "It's official: Google blew it with YouTube, and Facebook has caught up," *Business Insider*, June 3, 2015.

157. M. Learmonth, "YouTube's Premium-Content Strategy Starts to Take Shape," *AdAge*, March 14, 2011.

158. D. Chmielewski, "YouTube Counting on Former Netflix Exec to Help It Turn a Profit," *Los Angeles Times*, May 31, 2011.

159. YouTube Statistics Page, Accessed January 20, 2015 - https://www.youtube.com/yt/press/statistics.html

160. R. Winkler, "YouTube: 1 Billion Viewers, No Profit," *The Wall Street Journal*, Feb. 25, 2015.

161. R. Winkler, "YouTube: 1 Billion Viewers, No Profit," *The Wall Street Journal*, Feb. 25, 2015.

162. E. Ingham, "A Decade On, YouTube Has 1 Billion Viewers, 1 Million Advertisers, And Millionaire Artists," *Forbes*, April 6, 2015.

163. M. Shields, "Bethany Mota Overtakes Michelle Phan as YouTube's Top Beauty Producer," *CMO Today*, June 9, 2015.

164. M. Phan, "YouTube Makeup Guru Michelle Phan on Becoming a Beauty Superstar: 'My Only Goal Was to Help My Family,'" *Glamour*, September 2013.

165. G. Weiss, "How Ipsy, Michelle Phan's million-member sampling service, is giving Birchbox a run for its money," *Fortune*, March 31, 2015.

166. A. Barr and R. Sidel, "Google Misses Out on Apple's Slice of Mobile Transactions," *The Wall Street Journal*, June 5, 2015.

167. S. Lacy, "Google Closes Down Checking, Pushing Thousands of Merchants into Braintree's Arms," *PandoDaily*, May 20, 2013.

168. C. McGarry, "How Google took a page from Apple to secure Android Pay," *MacWorld*, May 29, 2015.

169. C. Metz, "Google Mimics Apple with Android Pay," *Wired*, May 28, 2015.

170. L. Gannes, "Google Confirms 'Buy Button' Is Coming," *Re/code*, May 27, 2015.

171. S. Hollister, "Android Pay vs. Google Wallet: What's the Difference?" *Gizmodo*, May 29, 2015.

172. D. Pierce, "Google+, as we knew it, is dead, but Google is still a social network," *Wired*, March 2, 2015.

173. D. Pierce, "Google+, as we knew it, is dead, but Google is still a social network," *Wired*, March 2, 2015.

174. S. Frier, "Twitter Reaches Deal to Show Tweets in Google Search Results," *BusinessWeek*, Feb. 5, 2015.

175. M. Shiels, "Google Unveils 'Smarter Search,'" *BBC News*, May 13, 2009.

176. R. Needleman, "Google Killing Jaiku, Dodgeball, Notebook, Other Projects," *CNET*, January 14, 2009.

177. C. C. Miller and N. Bolton, "Google's Lab of Wildest Dreams," *New York Times*, November 13, 2011.

178. D. Girouard, "Google Inc. Presentation" (Bank of America and Merrill Lynch 2009 Technology Conference, New York, June 4, 2009).

179. D. Murph, "Google Music Beta Walkthrough: What It Is and How It Works (Video)," *Engadget*, May 11, 2011.

180. S. Tibken, "China passes US to become Apple's biggest iPhone market," *CNet*, April 27, 2015.

181. P. Carsten, "After Gmail blocked in China, Microsoft's Outlook hacked, says GreatFire," *Reuters*, Jan. 19, 2015.

182. D. Post, "Google News to move "out of Spain"," *The Washington Post*, Dec. 11, 2014.

183. C. Mathews, "France orders Google to delete even more stuff from search results," *Fortune*, June 12, 2015.

Index